The Berkeley manuscripts. The lives of the Berkeleys, lords of the honour, castle and manor of Berkeley, in the county of Gloucester, from 1066 to 1618;

John Smyth

Nabu Public Domain Reprints:

You are holding a reproduction of an original work published before 1923 that is in the public domain in the United States of America, and possibly other countries. You may freely copy and distribute this work as no entity (individual or corporate) has a copyright on the body of the work. This book may contain prior copyright references, and library stamps (as most of these works were scanned from library copies). These have been scanned and retained as part of the historical artifact.

This book may have occasional imperfections such as missing or blurred pages, poor pictures, errant marks, etc. that were either part of the original artifact, or were introduced by the scanning process. We believe this work is culturally important, and despite the imperfections, have elected to bring it back into print as part of our continuing commitment to the preservation of printed works worldwide. We appreciate your understanding of the imperfections in the preservation process, and hope you enjoy this valuable book.

THE BERKELEY MANUSCRIPTS

Lives of the Berkeleys

THE BERKELEY MANUSCRIPTS

The Lives of the Berkeleys

LORDS OF THE
HONOUR, CASTLE AND MANOR OF BERKELEY

In the County of Gloucester

FROM 1066 TO 1618

WITH A DESCRIPTION OF THE

HUNDRED OF BERKELEY AND OF ITS INHABITANTS

BY JOHN SMYTH, OF NIBLEY

VOL. II

EDITED BY SIR JOHN MACLEAN, F.S.A., ETC.

FOR THE BRISTOL AND GLOUCESTERSHIRE ARCHÆOLOGICAL SOCIETY

GLOUCESTER: PRINTED BY JOHN BELLOWS
FOR THE SUBSCRIBERS
MDCCCLXXXIII

PREFACE TO VOLUME II

The second volume of the series of the Berkeley Manuscripts will be found to be not less valuable than the first, indeed it is of more comprehensive and wider interest. James Lord Berkeley, in the 2nd Henry vj., married Isabel eldest daughter of Thomas Mowbray 1st Duke of Norfolk of that house, his second daughter Margaret having become the wife of Sir Robert Howard Knt. Upon her marriage Isabel brought to her husband several manors in Warwickshire, and upon the failure of issue of John Mowbray the fourth Duke of Norfolk and Earl of Nottingham and Marshall (17th Edw. IV.) the heirs of the aforesaid Isabel and Margaret inherited the vast estates of the Mowbray family in divers counties, the said Isabel bringing, Smyth says, "the greatest masse of land to this family of any lady that was before her." These lands consisted of many manors in each of the several counties of York, Lincoln, Essex, Buckingham, Bedford, Warwick, Huntingdon, Salop, Leicester, Derby, Hertford, Cambridge, Sussex, Middlesex, and Surrey, together with divers manors in the Marches of Wales, and several Hundreds and Baronies both in England and Ireland. The acquisition of which of necessity very largely increased the topographical range of this work.

This great alliance, however, through the jealousy and inordinate ambition of William Lord Berkeley, the eldest son and successor of the Lord James by the marriage above mentioned, very nearly brought ruin upon this ancient and noble house. We know of no parallel in ancient or modern history to the lavish and extravagant alienations of this lord.

In 1483 the King conferred upon Sir John Howard, son of Sir Robert by Margaret the younger Mowbray co-heir, the Dukedom of Norfolk and the Earldom of Nottingham and Marshalship of England,

at

at the fame time creating his fon Thomas Earl of Surrey, both of whom were flain at Bofworth fighting for the White Rofe, and were thereupon attainted. The honour granted to his coufin fired the anger and ambition of Lord Berkeley, and determined him to obtain, at whatever coft, a fimilar rank, or if not fo high, at leaft the next in degree. This depended upon the King's favour, to obtain which he was prepared to make any facrifice, however great. For fubftantial confiderations, one of which was that the King fhould difcharge him and James, Maurice and Thomas, his brothers, of £34,000, payable by them and James their late father to the Earl of Shrewfbury and Margaret his wife and John late Vifcount Lifle their fon, he had received from Edward IV. the rank of Vifcount Berkeley, and was made a Privy Counfellor, but, in the words of Smyth, "having in his ambitious opinion too much land and too little honour," in 1483 he induced Richard III. to create him Earl of Nottingham. "This Earledom fatisfying not, for to climb higher" he agreed to convey to the King thirty-five manors, to hold to the faid King and the heirs of his body, but fortunately in default of fuch iffue the remainder was limited to himfelf and his heirs. "Howbeit," Smyth fays, "this profufe fcattering at a clap hurt him not; for this eftate tayle in the king determined the 22nd Auguft following by the kings death at Bofworth field." "Soe prudent," Smyth fays, "was this Earles cariage between thofe adverfe princes (Richard III and the Earl of Richmond) ayding the one wth men and the other with money, neither of both with his perfon, That hee preferved the favor of both, at leaft loft neither of them," and Henry vij foon afterwards created him Earl Marfhal and Great Marfhal of England, and it would feem plain that he was indebted to the good offices of Sir William Stanley the Lord Chamberlain in obtaining thefe honours, for at this time he granted to the faid Sir William his purparty in fome twenty manors, two caftles, and divers lands in Shropfhire and the Marches of Wales. Still grafping at higher honours, and without the inducement as in the firft inftance of the fubftantial releafe of a bond due by his family for a large fum of money, in 1487 he "affayleth" (fayth Smyth) the king for the Marquifate of Berkeley, and covenanted to convey by good affurance to himfelf and the

heirs

heirs of his body the Caftle and Manor of Berkeley and divers other manors, and, in default of fuch iffue, remainder to the faid king and the heirs male of his body, and in default of fuch iffue remainder to his own right heirs. Whereupon in the following year he was created Marquis Berkeley to him and his heirs male, a limitation apparently not of much value, for he had not, and was not likely to have, iffue. But this was not all, for, for their good offices with the king, he eftated the Earl of Derby and other courtiers in all other his lands except a few manors which he fettled upon his wife for the term of her life as dower, with remainder to the king under the fame limitations as above. Maurice, his brother and heir apparent, who is believed to have juftly remonftrated with the Marquis, perhaps with fome natural intemperance, at the wanton and recklefs manner in which, to gratify a felfifh, overweening, perfonal ambition, he was bringing ruin upon an ancient and honourable houfe, had given him great offence, fo that upon his death no lands whatever devolved upon his heirs. Nor in his will does the Marquis name his brother Maurice, or either of Maurice's three fons, or the four fons of his younger brother Thomas, nor did he leave fufficient perfonalty for the payment of his debts, which neverthelefs Maurice, for the credit of the family, took upon himfelf to difcharge. Through the obliging courtefy of the Rev. R. H. O'fflaherty, vicar of Capel, Surrey, I am enabled to lay before the reader the text of this extraordinary teftament, received fince the volume has been made up, or it would have been introduced into the body of the work.

Teſt'm dñi Will'i Marchionis Barkeley & Comitis Notingh'm

In dei nom'i Amen the vth day of the mointh of ffebruary the yere of ou^r Lord God M'cccclxxxxi. And the vijth yere of the Reigne of King Henry the viith I Willyam Markes of Berkeley erle marchall and Notingham and grete marchall of Englond being of goode and hole mynde Loving and preyfing be vnto my Savio^r make and ordeyne this my pñt teftament and Laft will jn mañ and fo'me enfuying that is to fey furft and principally I bequeith and recomend my foule to allmighty God my feid Maker and Savio^r And to the bleffid virgyn ou^r Lady feint Mary and to all the holy company of hevin And my body to be buried in the church of ffrires Auguftin in London And I bequeith to the mother church of ou^r Lady of

Worceftyr

Worceſtyr Cˢ Itm I bequeith to the Vicar of the piſſh church of Barkeley for my tithes negligently forgoton and wᵗdrawn In diſcharge of my ſoule xlˢ Itm I will that myn executours Vndrewreten do by veſtimentis and ornamentis to the valure of xx marc' to be occupied in the ſeid fryre Auguſtines at the auter of Seint Rooke as longe at [ſic] they endure. Alſo I will that my ſeid executoˢs ordeyn ij freres ppetually to ſing in the White freres in ffleteſtrete In the ſubbarbes of Londōn at the auter of Seint Gaſcon there to pray for my ſoule my Lord my fathers ſoule my moders ſoule my wifę ſoule And the ſoules of my ſonne ſyr Thomas Barkeley for euyrmore Alſo I will that my ſeid executours ordeyne an other ffryre ppetually to ſing in the grey ffryres at Glouceſtyr foreuyrmore to pray for my ſoule and the ſoules aforeſeid Itm I bequeith to the bilding of the ſeid Grey ffrires xxˡⁱ Alſo I will that my ſeid executours purcheſe Londes and tenements to the value of x marc' yerely ou' all charges And therwᵗ make and founde A ppetuall chauntry at the aulter of our Lady of Pite in Epworth in the Counte of Lincoln to pray for the ſoules aforeſeid foreuymore Itm I will that my ſeid executoˢs purcheſſe Londes and tenements to the yerely value of xxij marc' And therwᵗ to founde and ordeyne ij ppetuall preeſtę at Longbrigge oōn of them dayly to ſing in the chapell of the Trinite there And that other dayly to ſing in the chapell of the church of Berkeley Where as my ſeid lord my fader and my ſeid ſonne lieth buryed to pray for the ſoules aforeſeid for euyrmore Or elſe I will that the xxij marc' of Rent in fframpton be diſpoſed to the pforming of the ſame Alſo I will that my ſeid executoˢs ſpend and diſpoſe in bilding of an houſe at Longbrigge aforeſeid for ij p̄eſtys to Inhabit [ſic] to dwell in C marc' of money Alſo I will that my ſeid executoˢs do by veſtimentis and ornaments to the ſeid chapell of Longbrigge to the value of xl marc' Alſo I will that my ſeid executoˢs do purcheſſe a p̄don from the court of Rome as Large as it may be had at Longbrig aforeſeid from evenſong to evenſong in the feſt of the Trinite for the playne Remiſſion to them that wilbe confeſſid and contrite And ther then to ſey iij patˈnoſters and iij Aves for my ſoules [ſic] and the ſoules aforeſeid Itm I bequeith to John Wyting xlⁱⁱ to be payd wᵗin x yere after my deceſę Itm to Richard Butteler xˡⁱ Itm I bequeith to John Skyll xx marc' to be paid in x yeres next after my deceſe Itm I bequeith to Margarete Babbam xˡⁱ Itm to Eliſebeth Kelton Cˢ Itm to Symonet Stoute v marc' Itm to Elianore Gough x marc' Itm to Margery Brugh v marc' Itm I bequeith to Eliſabeth Berkeley xx marc' Itm [ſic] to be paid to hir wᵗin x yere after my deceſe Itm I bequeith to Margery Berkeley x marc' Itm to Agnes Mounceney v marc' Itm I bequeith to Richard Berkeley xlˢ Itm to humfrey Stauerton xlˢ Itē I bequeith to Richard Style xxvjˢ viijᵈ Itm I bequeith to Thomas Herne xxvjˢ viijᵈ Item to ſyr Willyam
ffayreway

ffayreway xl^s Itm to ffrere John Wikes xx^s Itm to Robert Alinſon thelder xl^s Itm to Robert Alynſon the yonger xx^s Itm to Nicholas Mody xl^s All theſe to be payd to the pſones aboveſeid w^{t}in x yeres after my deceeſe Itm I will that my ſeid executours after my deceeſe ſatisfie & Recompenſe all treſpaſis and wrongꝭ by me doon and not recompenſed afore my deceeſe in diſcharge of my ſoule ſuche as ſhalbe ſhewid and prouided [sic] before them w^{t}in x yeris next after my deceeſe And that to be proclaimed in euerie place where I have had moſt reſort unto in tymes paſt to thentent my detts and the ſeid wrongis may be truely content and ſatisfied after euery true and reſonable mannes deſire Alſo I will that all my aray plate ſtuffe of houſehold and of the chapell after my deceeſe be deuided in ij partes that is to ſay the oon halfe therof to my welebeloved wiff Anne to hir owne vſe w^{t}out any Lett fraude or delay And the other halfe therof to be diſpoſid and diſtributed in pformyng and fulfillyng of this my Laſt will and teſtament And I will that myn executours have take and pceyne all the iſſues pfits and revenues comyng and growing of my Lordſhippis and Maners of Wing Segrave in Penne And Marlow in the counte of Berks for the terme of xv yeris next after my deceeſe And after that if it fortune me to dye w^{t}out iſſue of my body Then I will that the ſeid Lordſhippis and Maners Remayne to Thomas Erle of Derby And to the heires males of his body Lawfully begoton according to endentures betwene me and the ſeid Erle therof made And for Lake of ſuch iſſue I will that the ſeid Lordſhippis and Maners Remayne to Anne my wyfe for terme of hir Lyfe and after hir deceeſe the Remaynder therof to John [sic] Berkley and to his heires males of hyr [sic] body Lawfully begoton And for Lacke of ſuch iſſue the Remayndre therof to my Right heyres foreuyrmore Alſo I will that myn executōs have take and pceyne all the iſſue pfites and revenues of the maners of Seleby and Mountſorell and of the hundreth of Goſcote w^t thapp^{r}tenncs in the Counte of Leyceſt^r now being in feoffees Handes from the tyme of my deceeſe vnto the tyme that my debts and Legacies be content and payd and this my Laſt Will Truely executed and pformed Alſo I will that if Eliſabeth Ducheſſe of Norff^r deceeſe before that my detts and legacies be paid and my Will pformed Than my ſeid executours have take and perceyne all the iſſues profites and revenues of the Maners of Thurleſton in the counte of Warwik the man of Seh^{a}me in the Counte of Leiceſter the maners of Alcambury Weſton in the Count of huntingd the Maners of Bretby Lynton, Cotton Repingdon Reſtlaſton and Aſſheburne in the Counte of Derby And of the Maners of ffuntyndon and Thorney w^t thapp^{r}tennces in the Counte of Suſſex from the deceeſe of the ſeid Ducheſſe unto the tyme that my ſeid dettis and Legacies be paid and content And this my Laſt Will truely executyd and pformed And alſo I will that the ſame Dame Anne my Wyfe after my will pformed

have

have the feid Maners of Thurlafton Segrave Alcumbury Wefton Bretby Lynton Cotton Repingdon Roftelafton and Affhebōrne wᵗ thapp'tenncis for terme of his Lyfe Alfo I will that if I the feid Markes dye w'out iffue of my body cōmyng Than after my feid Will pformed I will that the feid Anne my wyfe have the feid maner of Seleby for terme of hir lyfe Itm I will and bequeath to my feid wyfe all my tenementis in London and in Chelchehith in the Counte of Midd'x to have to hir that is to fey the tenementis in London to hir in fee fimple and at Chelchithe for terme of his [fic] Lyfe The Remayndre therof to John Wytyng abovefeid in fee fimple And that my feid Wyffe fhall paye for the tenementis in London to the fryrers Auguftines cc. marc' for ij freres there ppetually to fing and pray for the foules aforefeid for eᵛmore Alfo I will that fir Thomas ffitȝ Willyam Knyght Roberd Rede feriaunt of the Lawe and Garter King of Armes be truely content and paid of ther fees for terme of ther lyfe acording to the Grauntis to them made And I bequeath to Thomas frere Late Priorᵉ of the White ffryres in fleteftrete and to his felowe for to fing for my foule xx marc' Alfo I bequeith to the feid ffreres euery yere x marc' in to the tyme the fundation be made Itm I bequeith to Watkyn taylorᵉ xxˢ And of this my p̄nt teftament and Laft Will endentid I mak and ordeyne myn executoᶜˢ that is to fey my feid wyfe the Reuerent fader in God Edmunde Biffhope of Rocheftr maiftᵗ Richard ffitȝ James and Richard Withir And I make and ordeyne Ouerfeers of the fame my Laft Will The mooft famous and criften prince and my mooft finguler goode and gracious Lord King Henry the vijᵗʰ Thomas Erle of Derby aforefeid and John Whiting And I bequeith to euerich of my feyd executoᶜˢ for ther Laboᵉˢ in that ptic̃ to be had xxˡⁱ And fo eu'rey of myn oᵛfeers xˡⁱ in money In witteneffe wherof to this my p̄nt teftament and laft will I haue fette my feale of myn Armes The day and yere abouefeid Item I bequeith to Thomas Armerer xxvjˢ viijᵈ Itm to Thomas Creyford xxˢ to Thomas Ticle Cooke xxˢ to John Goodyf xlˢ to John Doland xxˢ Probatum fuit fupráfcriptum teftamentū coram etc' apud Lamhith feptio die menfis Aprilis Anno dni Millimo ccccᵒ nona-gefimo fecundo juramento Edwardí Konyngifby et Dñe Anne Relicte eiufdem Ac approbat' etc' Et comiffa fuit adminiftratio omniū bonorum etc' dictē dñe Anne de bene etc' Ac de pleno Inuentario etc' cit' feftū Penthecoft Alijs executorᵉ refutam etc'

Maurice Berkeley was as extraordinary a man as his brother, but of a totally different character. The former was intenfely felfifh, unforgiving, and greedy of perfonal rank, rafh and unprincipled in feeking it, and regardlefs of the honour of his family or of his own; the latter was

prudent,

prudent, cautious, laborious, and perfevering, not in the purfuit of his own advantage but for the benefit of his fucceffors, in the endeavour to raife again the grand ftructure of his ancient houfe from the ruin into which it had been caft down by his brother's folly. Seeing himfelf and his heirs, in all human probability, for ever deprived by his brother's act, within a period of lefs than feven years, of the inheritance of every of his anceftral manors, and efpecially of the poffeffion of Berkeley Caftle by the tenure of which the Barony was at that time confidered to be held, he did not, as many would have done, fet himfelf down and fubmit to the inevitable. He at once commenced a careful examination of his brother the Marquis's deeds of fales, and finding therein many flaws of title, with great legal acumen and patient perfeverance, beginning with the King himfelf, he fucceeded in recovering in the fhort fpace of another feven years, out of broken and controverted titles, upwards of fifty manors befides other lands and poffeffions, of which he died feized, and the whole defcended to his fon Maurice, his able affiftant in his legal ftruggles; for, throughout, he acted as his own lawyer in all the courts. Smyth gives a pathetic account of him as "with a milk-white head in his irkfome old age of 70 years, in winter terms and frofty feafons, with a buckram bagg ftuffed with law cafes, in early mornings and late evenings walking with his eldeft fon between the four Inns of Court and Weftminfter Hall, following his law fuits in his own old perfon, not for himfelf, but for his pofterity, to regaine part of thofe poffeffions wich a vaft brother had profufely confumed."

As an evidence that the Barony of Berkeley was at this date deemed to be held by tenure, Maurice Berkeley, though he ftill claimed to be Lord Berkeley, and the title was generally conceded to him, it was rudely rejected by Sir Robert Poyntz, whom Henry vij had appointed as Steward of the Manor and Hundred of Berkeley. That it was confidered a Barony by tenure is alfo fhewn by the fact that Maurice Berkeley was never fummoned to Parliament, and that when his fon Maurice, in the 14 Henry viij (1522) had fummons by reafon that the Caftle and Manor of Berkeley was then vefted in the Crown he had not

the

the precedency of his anceftors but was affigned the loweft place as the youngeft baron. Moreover this Barony, if a new creation fhould have become extinct on the death of Maurice Lord Berkeley in 1523, s.p , and his fon Thomas would not have had any claim whatever to fummons, neverthelefs in the very next Parliament, viz , that fummoned to meet at Weftminfter 9 Aug 21 Henry viij, Thomas Berkeley was fummoned under the ftyle of "Thomas Berkeley de Berkeley Chevalier," (though Smyth does not appear to have noted this fummons,) and was given precifely the fame precedence as that affigned to his fon Henry after he, on the death of Edw. vj, fucceeded to the Caftle and honour of Berkeley We fhall abftain from entering further into the vexed queftion of the Baronial tenure of Berkeley. It will fuffice to refer the reader to Smyth's difquifition thereon (Vol II. p 50,) and to mention that the claims of William Fitzharding Berkeley in 1829, and that of his brother Admiral Sir Maurice Frederick Fitzharding Berkeley, G C.B , in 1838, to be fummoned to Parliament as being feized of the Caftle and honour of Berkeley, were rejected by the Houfe of Lords, the former in 1831 being created Baron Segrave, the former titles having become extinct, and ten years later, the latter Baron Fitzharding in 1841.

This Volume, like the former, will be found to contain many particulars of great intereft illuftrative of the manners and cuftoms, which are now extinct and forgotten, of the period which it covers, and vivid pictures of the habits and ufages of the great baronial families.

The third Volume of the feries, containing the "Hiftory of the Hundred of Berkeley," will be fent to prefs immediately. Its contents will be no lefs valuable and ufeful than thofe of its predeceffors. Though thefe to fome extent will be of a more local character, there will be much of wide general intereft relating to the tenures of lands and manorial cuftoms, to fay nothing of the valuable pedigrees with which the Volume abounds.

J. M

The Life of Thomas the Fourth

The life of Thomas lord Berkeley the fourth of that name ſtiled in writings, Thomas de Berkelee chivaler, And Thomas dñs de Berkele miles. And Thomas de Berkeley dñs de Berkeley. And dñs Thomas dñs de Berkeley. And dñs Thomas de Berkeley dñs de Berkeley. And Thomas Berkeley miles dñs de Berkeley. And dñs Thomas Berkeley miles dñs de Berkeley. And dñs Thomas dñs de Berkeley et de inſula. And in ffrench le honorable ſeignior mounſieur Thomas de Berkeley ſūr de Berkeley And treſhoñ et noble ſeignior mounſieur Thomas &c: And nobilis vir Thomas Berkeley dñs de Berkeley.

And may bee called Thomas the magnificent.
Contemporary with Edward the third, Richard the ſecond Henry the 4th and Henry the fifth, from . 1368 . till . 1417.

The life of this lord I deliver to his poſterity under theſe fifteene titles . vizt

1.—His birth and courſe of youth . fol : [448]
2.—His huſbandries and hoſpitality . fol : [452]
3.—His forraigne imployments . fol : [454]
4.—His recreations and delights . fol : [459]
5.—His purchaſes and ſales . fol : [460]
6.—His lawe ſuites . fol : [464]
7.—His almes and devotions . fol : [466]
8.—His rewards to ſervants . fol : [468]
9.—His miſcellaines . fol : [471]
10.—His wife . fol : [476]
11.—His iſſue . fol : [477]
12.—His ſeales of Armes . fol : [483]
13.—His death and place of buriall . fol : [484]
14.—The lands whereof hee died ſeized . fol : [485]
15.—The Application and uſe of his life . fol : [486]

His

448 His birth and course of youth.

Escæt. in turre London. 42. E. 3. post mortem Mauric: de Berkeley.

The birth of this lord was at Berkeley Castle in the vigill of the Epiphany the fifth of January called the twelvth Eve in the 26th of Edward the third. Anno. 1352. And now at the death of his father aged fifteen years five months and three days.

carta in castro de Berkeley.

The longe sicknes of the last lord Maurice (occationed by his bloud spilt in the battle of Poytiers twelve years before) and the minority of this Thomas his heire, may seem to have quickned the treaty of this Thomas his mariage, to prevent thereby the wardship of his body by a speedy mariage of his son, if his own growing sicknes so constrained. whereupon at Berkeley on wednesday next after the feast of the holy Trinity in the 41th of Edward the third (a year before hee dyed) It was agreed betweene him on the one part And Gerrard Warren lord de Lisle of ye other part, That Thomas de Berkelee his eldest son should marry Margaret daughter of the said Gerrard: And that with her hee should pay to the lord Maurice one thousand and one hundred markes,[1] whereof 400^{li} at the mariage, And 700^{li} at fower days in three years following, And that after the mariage solemnized the lord Maurice should allow them two hundred marks by the yeare for their maintenance, And one hundred marks presently: And that the said Margaret by reason of her tender age (then about seaven) should for fower years remaine with her father, And this Thomas de Berkeley with his father.

original: 50: E. 3. rot. 40. in scčio

claus: 47 E. 3. m. 28. dorso.

fin. 24. E. 3. m. 5.

And it will bee to the illustration of divers passages following, to declare in this place That this Gerrardus Warren dñs de Insula usually called Warrinus de Insula, by Margaret his wife one of the heirs of Sr William Pipard had issue only one son called Gerrard who shortly after dyed without issue, And that the said Margaret now to bee maryed to this Thomas de Berkeley was the daughter of the said Gerrard de Insula son of Warren de Insula and of Alice Tyes his wife daughter and heire of Henry lord Tyes and of Margaret his wife son of Henry lord Tyes who died the first of king Edward the second. Two antient Baronies now to bee grafted into the third of Berkeley.

But

---

[1] Query: pounds as after stated? [ED.]

But the ficknes of the lord Maurice Berkeley increafing, notwithftanding the former agreement of fower years ftay: they were by | his requeft maryed at the faid lord Lifle his houfe at Wengrave in Buckinghamfhire in November next following And being himfelf unable to travell to his fons marriage, fent with his fon to attend him three of his houfhold knights. Sr Richard de Acton, Sr John Tracy and Sr Nicholas de Berkeley, and 23. of his houfhold Efquiers (all named in his houfhold Accompt;) **The** knights were futed in their liveries of fine cloth of ray furred with miniver, And the Efquires in their liveries of courfer ray and lefs coftly furre: And the young bridegroom himfelf was in fcarlet and fattin and a filver girdle **And** the lord Maurice himfelfe that kept home, infirmed in body, in honor notwithftanding of the mariage, made himfelf a fute de panno deaurato, which I thinke I may Englifh, cloth of gold; **And** at the day of the folemnization of the marriage, Sr Richard de Acton gave the minftrels fourty fhillings: Out of this houfhold Accompt I can pick no more of this mariage.

449

Comp: garderob: 41. E. 3. in caftro de Berkeley.

The bridegroome and his knights returne to Berkeley. The lord Maurice dies the 8th of June following. The lands of Thomas his fon (now lord) becomes the kings in ward for two parts, hee then of the age of fifteen years and upwards as aforefaid, the firft wardfhip that ever had happened in the line of Berkeley; **To** his father in lawe Warren de Infula, the king the firft of October following grants the cuftody of two parts of the young lords lands till full age for the rent of 400.^li by the yeare.

Rot. fin. 42. E. m. 9.

The infants mother the lady Elizabeth bringeth her writ of dower which to her is affigned in Cowley, Upton St Leonards and Awre, as before hath been touched, and as after more fully is declared.

Rec: in fcaccio: 16. R. 2. Rot. 21. et 42. E. 3. ibm.

The guardian having hufbanded his fon in lawes eftate to the advancment thereof without detriment, The ward, this lord, attaineth to full age the fifth of January in the 47th of Edward the third Anno. 1373. fueth his livery for his lands difcended unto him in the Counties of Somerfet, Glouc: Wilts, Effex and the City of Briftoll, And accordingly enters upon the Eftate difcended unto him from his father: of new ftocketh his demefnes, And falleth upon the old courfes of father and grandfathers hufbandries, that in this place need no repetition; And forthwith paffeth to the warrs of ffrance as after followeth in his forraigne imployments, being knighted at this time.

claus: 48. E. 3. m. 30.

Rot. franc: 48. E. 3 m: 8.

At the time of this lords marriage and for eight or ten years after this lords wife had a brother living called Gerrard after his fathers name maryed | to Anne

450

daughter

daughter of Mounſieur Michael de la Pole, but dying without iſſue about the begining of Richard the ſecond, the wholl lands of the two baronies of Liſle and Tyes diſcended upon this lords wife and this lord her huſband, which fell the more entirely through the death of her mother who died in 49th of the ſame kinge.

claus: 47. E. 3.
m. 28. dorſo.

The lord Thomas bringeth his wife the lady Margaret to Berkeley about the fifth of Richard the ſecond, whom her ſaid father accompanyeth; And in fewe months declareth his affection ſoe entirely to him, her, and the place, That the thirtieth of November in the fifth of Richard the ſecond in a french deed Indented between them, they publiſh their mutuall agreements That hee the lord Liſle ſhall at his pleaſure come, goe and dwell in his Caſtle at Berkeley at all hours, ſhall have free hunting in all his ſon in lawes chaces, parks, warrens, and in his free fiſhings, And that in all voyages of warre they two travell togeather, And his ſaid ſon in lawe bee unto him an unſeparable companion, And that hee and the iſſues that hee ſhall beget upon the body of his daughter, will always uſe and beare the Armes of him the ſaid lord Liſle, when time, after his death ſhall come.

comp. de Slim-
bridge 6. R. 2.

carta in caſtro
de Berkeley.

And accordingly the Armes of the ſaid lord Liſle and Tyes were by this lord Thomas ſet up quartered in divers places within his Caſtle of Berkeley, whereof thoſe in the windows in the great Chamber and at the head of the hall ſtayres before the Chapple doore do there yet remaine. Anno. 1624.

comp: Recept. in
caſtro de Berkeley.

And to fit the cloſer to the humor of the good old lord, this witty ſon in lawe maketh his daughter a Joynture of all the lands of his inheritance which were then held by the lady Elizabeth his mother, and the lady Katharine his grandfathers widow, in dower or Joynture from either of their huſbands; which two ladies left their lands and lives, the one in the ninth the other in the thirteenth of the ſaid king Richard, as is before expreſſed, the better thereby to catch that great eſtate of his father in lawes, which now comes tumbling upon him.

cartæ in caſtro
de Berkeley.

ffor the good old lord de Inſula the 28th of June next after theſe ſweet and ſociable agreements, in the ſixth of Richard the ſecond, | dyeth: And by offices the ſame year found and returned his ſaid daughter is found to bee his ſole daughter and heire, and to inherit theſe manors & lands, which then and ſhortly after by the death of Jone and Margaret two wives who held part of them in dower and Joynture, fell all in hand to this lord. viz!

Eſcaet. 6. R. 2.
no 41.
451
fin. 6. R. 2. m: 6.
fin: 15. R. 2. pars.
1. m: 6.
claus: 18. R. 2.
m. 17.
cart: 6. H. 4.
m: 1.

The manor of Wengrave in the County of Bucks.
The manor of Kiſlingbury   }
The manor of Stowe   }   In the County of Northton

The

The manor of Chilton foliot The manor of Nethercote The manor of Draycote The manor of Horewell	In the County of Wiltefs.
The manor of Kinge The manor of Hordwell The manor of Colcot The manor of Ordeston The manor of Buden The manor of Collicote	In the County of Berks
The manor of Shirborne The manor of Noke The manor of Fretwell	In the County of Oxon.
The manor of Aylwerton The manor of Trewarnake The manor Penfans	In the County of Cornwall
The manor of Charleton The manor of Tetcote The manor of Clonton The manor of Norbony The manor of Langdon	In the County of Devon

And divers Advowfons of Churches, and many faire farmes, lands and Tenements in ffullam, ffavelore, Uplamborne, Leverton, Bockhampton and other places, As the faid offices and many deeds Accompts and the great Chartulary in the Caftle of Berkeley do fhewe: fhee then of the age of. 22. years, whereby the poffeffions of the two baronies of Lifle and Tyes came to the Berkeleyan family, which by this mariage doubled the eftate thereof.

452 cartæ et compi in caftro de Berkeley.

His husbandries and hospitality.

All thofe years of Edward the thirds raigne, after this lord Thomas came to full age, and untill the 8th of Richard the fecond or neere thereabouts, hee purfued the prefidents of his Anceftors hufbandries as hath been faid; Then began the times to alter, and hee with them (much occationed by the infurrection of Wat Tyler and generally of all the Comons in the land,) And then inftead of manureing his demefnes in each manor with his own fervants, oxen, kine, fheep, fwine, poultry and the like, under the overfight of the Reeves of the manors, who were (as ftill they are) each year chofen at the halimot Court of the manor holden about Michaelmas, and

Comp: divers manors.

Stow et How in vitæ. R. 2. et mult. al:

and were bound to the fame and collection of the lords rents without fallary, by the tenure of their Copihold meffuages and lands for which the Reeve was yearly chofen,) This lord began to joyft and tack in other mens cattle into his pafture grounds by the week, month and quarter; And to fell his meadow grounds by the acre; And fo between wind and water (as it were) continued part in tillage, and part let out and joyfted as aforefaid for the reft of that kings raigne 𝕬𝖓𝖉 after, in the time of Henry the fourth let out by the year ftill more and more by the acre as hee found chapmen and price to his likeing: And fo left his eftate in the fifth of Henry the fifth when hee dyed, 𝕭𝖚𝖙 in the next age that fucceeded, his nephewe and heire male the lord James who fucceeded in thefe manors, (as did all other great lords of manors almoft throughout the wholl kingdome,) in the times of Henry the fixth and Edward the fourth and after, yea to this prefent day, hee and they let out their manor houfes and demefne lands, fometimes at racked improved rents according to the eftimate of the time, And fometimes at fmaller rents, taking a fyne or incombe | of their tenants as they agreed, which is the generall courfe and hufbandry for farr the moft part, to this very day. And (to conclude with the voucher of my felfe,) it is that courfe whereunto after much toyling and turmoylinge with the plough, fervants and hufbandry, I am now fallen into, Hopinge that the litle remainder of my life, fhall thereby have more profit, and Country quiet, then the foure and irkfomenes of toile and hind fervants would hitherto permit mee to taft of: And let me conclude in him that is the true period of all I write or fay, And without whom I had neither written nor brought to birth any thing that is herein fpoken, as being my principale movens and the caufa caufans fine qua non, George now lord Berkeley, And the rather becaufe henceforth I meddle no more in thefe relations with this title of Hufbandry: when hee fhall attaine to one and twenty years, enjoy his lady, and they a family anfwerable to their births and dignities, and fettled themfelves to live at Berkeley Caftle, or elce where in the County of Gloucefter, as all his noble and worthy Anceftors hitherto have done, (his degenerating grandfather in part excepted,) hee will have no better courfe then to advance his demefne lands to an improved rent payable quarterly, (as that Country fafhon is,) And rather to fupply his proviffions for wheat, oates, & Straw, by the Tithes of fome appropriate parfonage not farr from his abode, or by refervacōn upon fuch leafes monthly or quarterly to be brought in, than to keep much tillage in his own hands, (the natures of hind fervants, bayleys of hufbandryes and other incidents confidered;) And no more (at moft) of other grounds, then may fupply his proviffions of beefe and muttons: But for the plough, none gaineth thereby but hee that layeth his eye or hand daily upon it; And as Clownes get it,

Clowns

Clowns againe spend it: Contrary arguments (for the state of that Country) are drawn, but out of the region of S.ᵗ Thomas Moores Vtopia.

As for the days works which his Copihold tenants at each season of the year according to the nature of husbandry, did to him in each of his manors, in helping to dress, till and manure his demesne lands, after a proportionable rate for a yard land, half yard land, and farrundell, they also were turned into money and made as pcell of the old Copihold rents, In which condition they continue to this day now undistinguishable; As also were his rent hens, eggs, and mast money.

Comp. de Slimbridge et Hurst in castro de Berkeley 9. R. 2. et divers: alij.

And (to the praise of this lords husbandry) for soe much as hee kept in hand, none was more profitably husbanded by any of his Ancestors | servants, which soe frugally was accompted for, As in the time of Henry the fifth (when his estate was at the highest, and hee in old age) they accompted not only for the broken wooll, but for the taggs and locks arisinge at the belting[1] of his sheep in the folds.

454 comp: de Slimbridge et Hurst 2. 3. et 4. H. 5. in castro predict.

ffor the provission of his own table, this lord had yearly divers oxen fatted at Simondsfall cum avenis in garbis with oates in the straw, which manner of feeding I have not formerly observed in the dayes of any of his Ancestors, neither do I well conceive the reason thereof: Hee having so rich and sweet feeding grounds for grass and hay in places more neare unto his castle where his abode then was; And henceforth I bid (in effect) farwell to this harmlesse trade and title of Husbandry which hath on its side above all trades, better warranty, a fairer name, a more virgin fame and all seniority.

comp:deSimondsall temp. R. 2. in castrode Berkeley.

His forren imploymentg.

In the 48.ᵗʰ year of the raigne of Edward the third in the 22.ᵗʰ of his age hee went to the warres in ffrance in comitiva Edmundi de mortuo mari Comitis Marchie, At what time went also with him many of the principall gentlemen his neighbours.

franc: 48. E. 3. m. 8.

And being returned from those warrs, this lord and Hugh Earle Stafford are authorized to array all men at Armes in the County of Gloucester between sixteen and threescore, And to erect Becons (beknes) to give tokens by fire from these hills, of the enemies landings &c.

franc: 49. E. 3. m. 8.

In the first and second years of Richard the second, this lord was imployed both by sea and land in the warrs that then were hott both against ffrance and Spaine.

Rot. franc. 2. R. 2. m. 18. Comp. de Ham. 1. 2. R. 2.

In

[1] To *belt* is to shear the buttocks and tails of the sheep.

Rot. franc. 4. R. 2. m: 14. 15. et 16.

In the 4th of Richard the second, this lord was sent into Brittaine against the French with a regiment of men at Armes and Archers, whom his third brother Sr John Berkeley accompanies: And upon the 30th of March the king commands all his officers to provide lodging, victualls, and carriage, for them and their Armes: And for the good succefs of this Army | (over which the Earle of Buckingham the kings unckle, after Duke of Gloucester, went generall,) were publicke prayers commanded to bee made, for that (faith the record) the French making shew of peace under colour of treaties, with great subtilty had deceived the king.

claus: 8. R. 2. dorso. pat: 8. R. 2. pt 2. in dorso:

In July in the 8th year of his raigne, this lord went with the king against the Scots, after hee had all the former part of that year been travelled in mustering and Arming of souldiers, to withstand the invasion of the ffrench, intending a destruction of the kingdome, as the records are.

comp: de Slim-bridge 9. R. 2. How: et at: froisard:

In the 9th year of Richard the second, this lord Thomas with a great troup of his servants and tenants went with the king into Scotland, who, faith the histories of those times, ledd an Army, than which there hath not been seene a fairer, stronger or greater, which harroweth over that Country, And foe returned.

comp: de Slim-bridge et al: 10. R. 2. in castr de Berkeley. How: et at.

The next year the king cometh to Berkeley Castle, whom this lord royally entertained, As by the Accompts of the Reeves of his manors in that hundred may bee collected, from whence hee drew a great part of his provissions what time the wholl kingdome was in preparation to withstand the invasion of the French, then ready to have invaded the land; if wind had served for his transportation between the first of August and the last of November.

Rot. franc: 16. R. 2. m: 10. bis.

In the 16th year of the kings raigne, this lord went beyond seas into ffrance and other Countryes, And upon his departure in September had the kings licence to take ship at Dover, Orwell, or Leistoft, as hee should choose with fifteen servants and so many horses and their Armes, and with one thousand markes in money in exchange for his and their expences beyond seas: This was no martiall expedition, but occasioned as it may seeme upon greefe conceived by the death of his wife, or to avoid the danger of Court stormes, which then began to bluster with an hollow wind.

Hollinges: fo: 498. 504. 505. et at.

Whilst King Richard the second in the last of his raigne was in Ireland revenginge the murder of Roger Mortimer Earle of March and Ulster, comitted by

the

the Irish, Henry Duke of Lancaster returneth from his banishment into England, (whom this lord Thomas too much favoured,) And shortly after his arrivall cometh to Berkeley, in the church whereof and in the Castle of Berkeley upon the sunday after S! James's day was held that famous assembly betweene the Duke and Edmond of Langly Duke of Yorke the kings unckle, Earle also of Cambridge, This lord Thomas and many other the great peeres of the Land, which shortly after cost kinge | Richard his Crowne, which was set upon the head of the said Duke of Lancaster: In which assembly how the affections and Counsell of this lord Thomas swayed, his present imployments declared, for within a fewe days after, hee made himselfe a spetiall witnes at fflint Castle of king Richards promise to renounce the Crowne; And on Michaelmas day following testified the same in the Tower of London before king Richard, who then there subscribed the same to bee true: And the morrow after when by the three estates of the land assembled in parliament, A Bishop, An Abbot, an Earle, a Baron, a Judge, and a knight, were out of that representative body chosen, to take, publish and pronounce the kings actuall resignacōn of his Crown and kingdome, and accordingly to depose him, This lord Thomas was the **Baron** in that waighty and dangerous imployment, having till that time inseparably accompanyed the Duke of Lancaster in pursuit of King Richard since his departure from Berkeley. Anno. 1399. 23. R. 2.
456

Walsingham. fo: 359.

The 31th of July in the third year of Henry the fourth the king sends to this lord to meet him at Hereford, the 27th of August next, thence to goe with him against his malitious enemies Owen Glendourdy whom with his complices hee purposeth utterly to overthrow. claus: 3. H. 4. pars 2. in dorso.

In July in the 4th year of Henry the fourth, the king ordained this lord one of the guardians for safe keeping the Marches of Wales against the incursions of Owen Glendourdy and other rebells: And commanded the Sherifes of six Counties to bee attendant to him as need should require. Rot. voiag. a. 1. ad. 11. H. 4. m. 13. 14.
pat. 5. H. 4. ps. 1. m. 8.

The 22th of March in the fifth year of his raigne, the kinge made this lord Thomas Admirall of his fleet of ships from the mouth of Thames west and southward, with power also over his subjects in the Counties of Devon, Cornwall, Somerset, and Dorset, who are to bee attendant on his directions: And himselfe to bee at Sandwich by the ninth of Aprill following. **And** a litle before was hee chosen and sworn one of the kings privy Counsell in open parliament, where I conceive also hee was chosen Admirall. claus: 5. H. 4. ps. 1. m. 1. eodē pars. 2.

Rot. parliam. 5. H. 4. m. 12.

And

carta in castro de Berkeley.	**And** by Indenture dated the first of May in this fifth of Henry ye fourth It was agreed between the king and this lord, That for safe guard of the Realme hee should for one quarter of the year have with him upon the sea, 300 men of Armes
457	whereof five to bee Bañets himselfe	accompted, eleaven knights, 285. Esquires, which should bee of his own retinue : And to have further in his voyage . 600 . Archers, and seaven shipps seaven barges and seaven ballingers double manned with mariners ; And with these to bee at Southampton the 12th of that month : And the king to have the fourth part of all gaine got at sea from the enemies, And this lord and his company the other three parts. **But** if any great cheiftaine was taken, hee to remaine to the king, yet to bee recompensed reasonably for him ; And further that this lord should continue on the sea with his company till Michaelmas, if the king gives him a monthes warning before the three months bee out ; Howbeit hee
claus : 5. H. 4 pars. 1. m: 29. eodē : dorso. m. 4. 5. 6. et. 7.	kept the sea till December following, And the 24th of that month the king comands him to goe to Plymouth where hee then was with some of his shipps, to Burdeaux for some service there to bee attempted : And for the better furnishing of this voyage, sold his manor of great Wenden in Essex.
comp. rec: 5. H. 4. in castro de Berk. Rot. voiag. a. 1. ad 11. H. 4. m : 18. 19 in arce London.	**In** the same 5th year of Henry the fourth upon the tumults raised by Owen Glendour and his partakers in Wales, this lord was sent thither with a great power for the appeasing thereof, which for that time hee did, wherein hee spent the later part of the yeare; what time the king made him keeper of his Castle of Brecknock, And then also gave him a Comission to take up six barges in the Counties of Bristoll, Somerset and Glouc., and so many mariners as should suffice for them to goe to sea with them at the kings wages, with all diligence, which hee did.
Walsingh : Hollingsh:fol:531. How, fol. 333	**The** ffrench were enemies to the English, And the more to endamage the king of England in the 6th of his raigne came with a Navy of one hundred and forty tall shipps to ayd Owen Glendour then also in Arms against the king, and his most dangerous enemy : These, this lord and Henry Pay a Captaine under him, valliantly set upon neere Millford haven, where they intended to have landed, And after longe fight burned fifteen of their shipps, and tooke 14. others stuffed with men, munition, and victualls, And soe returned with honor and profit.
Walsingham	**And** at another time this lord and Pay, and Thomas Swynburne (one of his domestick knights) tooke fourteene other French shipps as they sailed towards Wales to the souccor of the said Owen Glendour, wherein the Seneschall of ffrance and divers Captaines of note were taken prisoners.

And

And in the sixth year the 28th of October the king writes to his Collectors of the Tenth of the Clergy granted at the last parliament in the province | of Canterbury in the Arch deaconryes of Exon, Totton, and Barnstable, declaring that whereas the lord Berkeley his Admirall hath lent him one thousand pounds towards his warres by sea, That they do repay him out of the first moneys of the subsidy of those Counties of Devon, Cornwall, and Dorset, And for default thereof out of the said Tenth of the Clergy, And it should bee allowed them upon their accompt.

claus. 6. H. 4. m: 23.
458

And the 15th of July in the said 6th year, the king authorizeth this lord alone to muster and Arme all the able men in the Counties of Glouc., Bristoll, and Somerset, to withstand the in-cursions of the Welsh. And willeth him if need should so require whilst hee should bee in his service in the North, That then hee make Willm Beauchamp lord of Abergavenny his Leivtenant in South Wales to execute his directions.

Pat: 6. H. 4. m. 15. in dorso.

And in the 7th year of Henry the fourth, hee was the generall commander and Ingeneer in the Timber works used in the Welsh warrs, for the seige and debellation of the Castle of Lampadervar in Wales, held by the kings enemies.

Rot. voiag. a. 1. ad. 11. H. 4. m. 9. et. 28.

In March in the third of Henry the fifth this lord was required with his son in lawe the Earle of Warwicke to muster and trayne men in the Counties of Glouc: Somerset and Bristoll; And in June following by a second cōmand, to defend with them the borders of Wales, and to resist the welsh, wherein that somer was spent.

pat: 3: H. 5. pars. 1. dorso.
eodē pars. 2. dorso.

Of this lord, Michaell Drayton in his description of the battle of Agencourt fought against the wholl power of the ffrench in the year. 1415. in two stanzaes hath thus:

> Berkeley and Burnell two brave English lords,
> fflesht with ffrench bloud and in their valors pride,
> Above their Armed heads, brandishing their swords
> As they tryumphing through the Army ride,
> Finding what prizes fortune her affords
> To every Soldier, and most wistly eyde
> A gallant prisoner by his Arminge, see,
> Of the great Bourbon family to bee. |
> And from the soldier they this prisoner take,
> Of which the ffrench lord seemeth wondrous faine,

Lewis Duke of Bourbon taken prisoner by a mean soldier and after stab'd by him.

459

Thereby

Thereby his safety more secure to make,
Which when the soldier finds his hopes in vaine,
Soe rich a booty forced to forsake,
To put himself and prisoner out of paine
Hee on the sodaine stabs him, and doth sweare
Would th'have his ransome, they should take it there.

His recreations and delights.

comp. temp. R. 2. manor de Slimbridge, Ham, Cowley et divers. al. in castro de Berkeley.
Comp. de Hurst 6. R. 2. in castro p'dict.

Of all his Ancestors this lord was the most magnificent stately and sumptuous, and more given to the sports of the field, (if more may bee,) then any of his forefathers; As may be collected, from his yearly charges in keeping of hounds and gray hounds for the chace of the hare, deere, fox, and badger, which hee not only did at his own mansion houses, but at most of his granges and farm houses: where at Hurst those hounds of that place in the 6th of Richard the second eate him eighteen quarters of Barley and Oates. And of his several kinds of hawks for the feild and river. Hee also would to the threshing of the cock, pucke with hens, blindfold, and the like; Hee also kept his severall stables of great horses at Berkeley and Wotton, And at Berkeley hee kept great store of tame Pheasants, As by the wheat allowed for their feeding and wages of their keeper appeareth.

comp. 12. R. 2. in cast.p'dict. de Slimbridge et al:

comp: de Berkeley 12. 13. R. 2. et al. ibm.

Hee had also at Berkeley his barge house at the Castle bridge foote, and his barge for his delight and recreations, aswell upon the haven as the river of Seavern, in which were his sea furnitures in a sumptuous manner.

comp. de Berkeley 9 et. 10. R. 2. ibm.

Hee much inlarged the ditch of Berkeley Castle, by taking a part of the Church yard, which hee recompenced with an yearly rent of . 6^s 8^d to the prishioners for amends, out of three tenements in Berkeley, and for the buying and maintaining of a litle sans bell, whereby the garden that was formerly in that place was destroyed; And this hee did with better successe then Maurice the first that committed the like act. |

460
cartæ. 12. H. 4. in castro de Berkeley.

Hee also inlarged divers of his parks, As Newparke, Over, and others, increasing therewith his games of deere; And by buying in the freeholds of Robert Hurd and others made the Worthy, (called the Worthy or Castle park,) first a parke; In the further end whereof, called the Twichen, next Newport, was the Capitall messuage or Scite of the manor of Alkington, where the Courts of that manor were ever kept, still discernable by the mott that compassed that house; In the floore or

pavement

pavement whereof are ſtill, (though divers of late years have been cut down and ſold,) many faire great Elmes growing.

His purchaſes and ſales of lands.

The care which this lord Thomas had to inlarge his eſtate, (notwithſtanding his coſtly delights and pleaſures,) ſeemes litle inferior to the carefulleſt of his Anceſtors; which addeth the more honor to his memory, in that hee had noe iſſue male of his body to inherit him, as after appeareth.

In the 49ᵗʰ of Edward the third, (aſſoone as hee had ſued livery,) hee purchaſed divers meſſuages lands and Tenements in Slimbridge priſh of Ralph Wallies, which at this day are the greateſt part of the manor of Sages.

clauſ: 49: E: 3: pars: 2: Eſcaet: 5: H: 5: poſt mort. Tho: dni: Berkeley.

In the 4ᵗʰ of Richard the ſecond, this lord purchaſed of one Sʳ John Roch one knights fee and one acre of land in Cricklade in Wiltſhire, & the Advowſon of that Church. Whereupon take this note, That an entire knights ffee conſiſteth of fower hides of land, one hide of fower yard land, one yard land of fower farrundells. And one farrundell of ten acres; A proportion throughout this barony, in all the old grants made by this lords fower firſt Anceſtors, of lands by them enfeoffed in the hundred of Berkeley and elcewhere; As in my regiſter booke of the lord Berkeleys tenures by knights ſervice I have touched; which booke if God grant health I intend hereafter to reviewe.

Cartæ in caſtro de Berk.

In the ſeaventeenth of Richard the ſecond, this lord purchaſed of Walter lord fitz wauter the Advowſon of Saint Andrews church by Baynards Caſtle in London.

magn: chart: fol. 239. in caſtro de Berkel.

In the 18ᵗʰ of that king, hee purchaſed one fayre to bee holden at his Towne of Berkeley, in the vigill and day of the invention of the holy croſſe, called hollirood day, in May, with all liberties and free cuſtoms to ſuch a faire appertaininge, dated the 16ᵗʰ of ffebruary; which ſoe continueth to this day. Anno. 1624. And ſeems to have been wanting thitherunto: And the reaſon in part may ſeeme to have been becauſe in times ſo ſtirring as former ages had been, the lords of that Burrowe Towne would not draw ſuch concourſe of people to their Caſtle gates, wherunder ſo great danger and ſo eaſy a ſurprize might by their oppoſites have been practized.

461 Rot. cart. 18. 19. R. 2. m: 13.

In the 22ᵗʰ of Richard the ſecond hee purchaſed of Sʳ Thomas Arthur knight divers meſſuages and Tenements in Weſton in Gordano in the County of Somerſet, inlarging thereby his antient manor of Portbury.

carta in caſtro de Berkeley.

The

carta in caſtro de Berkeley.	**The** ſame year hee purchaſed of Thomas Norton, an antient meſſuage called Whelpſplace, and divers other lands in Wraxell in the ſaid County whereby hee further inlarged his ſaid manor of Portbury.
cartæ in caſtro de Berkeley.	**The** ſame year hee purchaſed of Almaricus de Sancto Amando, the manors of Southcerny and Cerniwike in the County of Glouc^r
cart: 2. H. 4. pſ. 2. m: 1. pat: 1. H. 5. pars. 1. m: 11.	**The** 24th of Auguſt in the ſecond of Henry the fourth hee purchaſed of the king free warren in his manors of Walton, Weſton Portſhead and Charelton in the County of Somerſet, which alſo in the firſt of Henry the fifth were by that king confirmed unto him: As alſo then was the grant of free warren made to his Anceſtor Maurice the ſecond in the 8th of Edward the firſt, As in his life is expreſſed.
carta in caſtro de Berkeley. See before fol. [324]	**In** the 12th of Henry the fourth hee purchaſed divers lands and tenements at Wixtowe near the woods end of Hill; and two groves there called cat grove and hanginge grove, for the inlarging of Newparke, part whereof his grandfather the lord Thomas the third, before in the 33th of Edward the third, got in.
fin. in banco Term Michis. 12. H. 4.	**The** ſame year hee purchaſed of Robert Stanſhawe and Iſable his wife a meſſuage and ſixteen acres of land in Bradley near Wotton under edge.
carta in caſtro de Berkeley.	**In** the 13th of Henry the fourth hee purchaſed the manor of Wike in Wiltſhire of Sr William Eſturmy knight.
carta in caſtr. de Berk: finis. 13. H. 4. in banco.	**The** ſame year hee purchaſed a meſſuage and divers lands in Horton and Yate of Robert Stanſhawe and Iſable his wife aforeſaid.	
462 carta in caſtro de Berk: clauſ: 13. H. 4. m. 17. et. 18. dorſo.	**The** ſame year hee purchaſed the Advowſon of the Church of Porteſhead in Gordon, and goreacre, of Reginald Hall in the County of Som^t now the inheritance of the mayor and Cominalty of Briſtoll; And alſo at the ſame time the Advowſon of Walton in the ſaid County.
finis in banc: 13. H. 4. moſt antiently called acholt. See fol.	**In** the ſame year hee purchaſed the Advowſon or foundaçõn of the Abby of Kingſwood, otherwiſe called the Abby of Myryford by Wotton under edge, of the Ciſtertian order, of Richard Chedder and Elizabeth his wife, daughter and heir of Robert Cantelo, ſon of Robert and Maud his wife, ſiſter and heir of Sr Nicholas Berkeley

Berkeley lord of Durſley; (In which Nicholas failed that antient Saxon name of Berkeley of Durſley,) as formerly hath been ſaid in the life of Robert the firſt.

In the 14th year of the ſaid king hee purchaſed of John More and Margery his wife, daughter and heire of Reginald Walleis, a meſſuage and carucate of land, and divers other lands, wood, and cheife rents, in Wike, Berkeley, Hame, and Alkington.

carta in caſtro de Berkeley.

In the firſt year of Henry the fifth this lord purchaſed of Julian Baniſter the moytie of the manor of Nethercote in Wiltſhire for her life, And the fee thereof of Trevilines and Alet.

carta in caſtro de Berk: magn: chart: fo. 229.

The ſame year hee purchaſed divers fair lands and tenements in Eſtpike in the Tything of Tetcote in Devonſhire.

carta in caſtro de Berk:

The ſame year hee obtained a confirmation from the king of free warren throughout all Berkeley herneſſe, and in Portbury in the County of Somerſet.

fin: 1 H. 5. ps. 2. m. 10.

In the ſecond of Henry the fifth hee purchaſed of John Ap-Adam and Margaret his wife, the manor and lordſhipp of Sherncote in Wiltſhire.

carta in caſtro de Berk. magn: chart. fo. 399.

In the third of Henry the fifth hee purchaſed by fine the manor of Tykenham in the County of Somerſet, of Sr Thomas fitz Nicholl knight, a diſcendant from the lord Robert the firſt, as formerly I have written in his life.

finis in banco. 3. H. 5.

And to eaſe my pen, If this family caſt an eye into the ſeverall Inquiſitions found after the death of this lord in the fifth of Henry the fifth, and into the Inquiſition in the 17th of Henry the 6th And into a quæ plura the ſecond year after, all found after the death of Richard Beauchamp Earle of Warwicke who had married this lords only daughter and heire, they ſhall find nigh ſowerſcore other purchaſes made by this lord of houſes and lands in the City of Glouc: Berkeley, Wotton, Awre, Arlingham, and other places in the County of Gloucester; And in Portbury, Bedminſter and other places in the County of Somerſet; And in Chicklade and other places in the County of Wilts; none of wch are formerly mentioned; (of all which the ſaid lord made a feoffment to Walter Poole on midſomer day before hee dyed, not declaring to what uſe;) And if this family will looke further into a heap of little deeds themſelves remaining in Berkeley Caſtle, and into certaine rolls or abſtracts of many other deeds in Berkeley Caſtle alſo, (whoſe originalls are periſhed,) they ſhall find above five hundred other ſmall purchaſes more, by this lord

Eſcaet. 5. H. 5. poſt mort. dcti Thom: **463**

Eſchaet: 17. 18. H. 6. in arce London.

Carta in caſtro de Berkeley

lord and by his father and grandfather, (some of lesse then an acre,) of free hold lands that lay intermingled with their demesnes and the Copiholds of their tenants, none of which are formerly quoted by mee; which gave this lord, (as they did them,) the means to inclose the Worthy or Castle parke, and to make a parke of it, as this lord first did, And to reduce many other faire inclosures into severalty; And no one endeavour was greater with this lord and them, those two precedent Ancestors, then to buy out as many of such freeholds as would bee sold, the maine obstacles to their inclosures improvements and converc̃ons, and to the beauty and inriching of their barony.

But insteed of this title of purchases, I shall in the lives of those lords that follow, have sales of manors, without rebuyings; And insteed of husbandry I shall have swarmes of law suites without gaine or recoverings, And the like a cleane contrary way, as after followeth.

claus: 5. H. 4.
pars. 1. dorso:
m. 4. 5. 6.

And for the sales of this lord Thomas, hee sold only, (for ought I find,) the manor of great Wenden in Essex, in the fifth of king Henry the 4th to Willm Loveny; which was done to furnish himself to sea, then made lord Admirall, the king wanting money to set out his fleet, which this lord in part thus supplyed; And the rather because hee was cast into that office by the appointment of the parliament, as already is touched. |

His suites in lawe.

464

Trim. 16. R. 2.
rot. 21 in scc̃io
cum rem̃ thesaur̃.
Baronia

In the 16th year of Richard the second, hee was questioned in the Exchequer for a Releefe for those manors and lands which the lady Katharine his grandfathers second wife held of his inheritance in the Counties of Gloucester and Somerset, (there named,) estimated to a third part of his lordshipp of Berkeley, shee dead then seaven years past; And which were holden of the king in Capite by five knights fees, saith the record; In avoydance of which demand, hee pleadeth that no releefe was due, for that hee was in ward to king Edward the third after the death of his father, aswell for the reverc̃on of those manors and lands held by the said Katharine, as for his other manors and lands discended upon him in possession. whereof the said king by his then Escheator was answered the profits; As of the Castle and Town of Berkeley with the members thereof, as Hame, Alkington, Appleridge, Hinton, Slimbridge, with the Advowson thereof, Cowley, Upton St Leonards, and two parts of the hundred of Berkeley; **And** further set out That to the lady Elizabeth his mother, was then assigned for her dower after his fathers death, the manors

of

of Cowley, Upton St Leonards, and Awre, as the third part of two parts of his fathers lands: And further averreth that Warren de Infula (his wives father,) had the profits of the said two parts of his fathers lands, by the kings grant made to him the first of October in the 42th of Edward the third, during his minority; And from his fathers death till that grant, the kinge himself by his said Escheator was answered the profits, as in his Accompt appeareth: which longe proces was continued upon the roll, till the 11th of Henry the fourth, And then was this lord overruled to pay . 6^li 15^s for a releefe for those manors, which the said lady Katharine held in dower, as the tenth part of the barony of Berkeley. Baronia

The same year arose another Exchequer buisines more full of trouble, about the hospitall of St Katharines in this lords manor of Bedminster, whereof his Ancestor Robert the second was founder as in his life appears; wherein the maine question was, whether the said hospitall, and the Chantry founded in the Chapple there were one and the same or not; which was by Jury found soe to bee, And so avoided the charge | of the record; which tooke begininge from an injurious Inquisic̄on found before the Escheator of that County of Somerset. 16. R. 2.

465

In the ninth of Richard the second, the said Lady Katharine his grandfathers second wife being then dead, this lord sued livery for such lands as shee held for her life of his inheritance in the Counties of Gloucester and Somerset, And for twenty shillings hath his homage respited. fin: 9. R. 2. m. 4.

In the 13th of Richard the second, the lady Elizabeth his mother dying, this lord entred upon the lands which shee held in Joynture and dower, As the manors of Cowley, Upton St Leonards and Awre, with Etlowe and Blakeney and the hundred of Blediflowe, and one messuage and yard land in Saintly, And the manor of Hurst, and twenty and two marks rent in fframpton, And—12^li 12^s rent in Came; And upon great Wenden in Essex, and upon two parts of the manor of Portbury, And three messuages and two yard land and one dove house in Porteshned, Criston and Uphill, with the Advowson of Brene, And ten pounds rent out of the lands of the lord Zuch in Bridgwater, And upon the Isle of Stepholmes, in the County of Somerset; And a messuage and threescore acres and ten shillings rent in Chicklade in Wiltshire. claus: 13. R. 2. pars. 1. m: 26.

In the 11th of Henry the fourth, this lord Thomas brought his Assize of novell disseisin against Willm Test and two others of Frampton upon Seaverne for Rec: exemp: in castro de Berk:

six

D VOL. II

six hundred acres of land in Slimbridge, wherein upon a Tryall before Judge Hulls at Gloucester Assizes hee recovered his seisin, and five pounds for damages: This was of Slimbridge Warth, which his heir male the lord James in the fifteenth of Henry the Sixth exemplified, when further suite was about that warth. |

vide fol:

His Almes and devotions.

Bulla papal: sub sigillo plumbeo in castro de Berkeley.

Pope Vrban the sixth in the second year of his popedome, the 9th of July in the fourth of Richard the second. Anno: 1380, by his Episcopall bull gave leave to this lord Thomas and to the lady Margaret his wife to chuse for their confessor such a fit and discreet priest as they pleased, to heare their confessions, give them absolution of their sins, and to enjoyne them wholsome penance, unles it bee in those cases, wherein the Apostolike sea is first to bee consulted with: Assuring all men that infringe this his holines grant, that they incurre the indignation of Allmighty God and of the blessed Apostles Peter and Paul.

And the same day and year by his other bull, granted to this lord Thomas and Margaret his wife to have a portable altar, whereat either by their own priest or any other they might say masse and other divine service in their own presence.

And the same day and year by his third bull granted that the Confessor which either of them the lord Thomas and Margaret should choose, should have from the Apostolike authority by vertue thereof, full power to give them full remission of all their sins, for which they were contrite in hart and which they had confessed with their mouthes once only in the instant of their deaths, they then persisting in sincerity of faith, and in the unity of the holy Roman Church, and in the obediance and devotion of his holines or of his successors canonically entringe into that chaire: yet soe that what their confessor should enjoyne them, bee by them performed if they live, or by their heir if they dye; And soe that for this grace obtained they bee not made more prone, (which God forbid,) to unlawfull things, which, if upon confidence of this remission of their sins, they doe the rather comit, That then as to those sins the foresaid remission shall not extend.

And hereupon I may by a pardonable digression say, That at this time the Schisme in the papacy continued, Clement the seaventh was now also pope and held his see at Avignion in France; And was, (as many histories in those and these times report,) generally acknowledged for lawfull pope by the ffrench, Spaniards and English; Howbeit it | seemeth the perticuler affection of this lord and his wife went after Vrban, or els graces were of him obtained at an easier price than of Clement.

Of

Of which Vrban it is thus written, That he was the 204th Bishop of Rome, chosen pope in the year—1378. A Neopolitan, Arch-bishop of Bari and no Cardinall, created pope at the pursuite of the Romans, hee being absent: That hee was a cunninge, seditious, and revengefull man, not seeking the peace of Christendome, as his duty required, but striving to revenge the injuries which his Cardinalls and Jone Queen of Cicely had done unto him; which was the cause of the 26th schifme: And haveing caused five Cardinalls to bee drowned hee dyed, having held his See eleaven years six months and five days, And that hee celebrated the third Jubile.

It seems this lord Thomas relyed much on this grace from pope Vrban, for I find not any one act of devotion which hee performed to any monastery Chantry or order of religion, nor ought else which was done for his wives soule after her death, As by all their Ancestors had been accustomed for their predecessors, untill I come to this lords will made the second of ffebruary in the year. 1415. in the third year of Henry the 5th which was one year fower months and eleaven days before hee dyed. And thereby hee gave to the mother church of Worcester fourty shillings, To the church of Berkeley fourty shillings and one greene pair of vestments with all their furniture; And to the Church of Wotton five pound, And to the Church of Slimbridge fourty shillings, And to the Church of Cowley fourty shillings, And to the Church where his body should bee buried his best pair of vestments with all their furniture, and twenty pound in money, and one gilt crosse with all the relikes inclosed in the same, with all his best gilt cruetts, And also one white paire of vestments with all their furniture, And also the best pair of his black Vestments, and his best missale with a good Chalice; And to the Chapple within Berkeley Castle one pair of satten vestments, one missale, two Chalices and one pair of cruets; And to the sisters of Mary Magdalens hospitall by Bristoll, one psalter with a glosse, and the legends of Saints in English, one paire of vestments one Chalice and five pound in money. And to the Church of Kingswood his best collar of the kings livery, his paire of gilt vestments wrought with white Angells; And to the Church of Portbury one pair of vestmts, | one psalter, one porter, and fourty shillings. And to every of his houshold chaplens ten markes to pray for his soule one year after his death; And all his goods whatsoever not by his will disposed hee appointed should by his Executors bee distributed for the health of his soule and of the soule of the lady Margaret his wife; And to a knight to goe to the holy land when any goinge should bee, one hundred pound, which sum was heretofore devised by his Ancestors, saith the will.

vlt. voluntas in cur. prerogat. Cantuar.

468

His rewards to servants.

<small>magn: chart. fo. 217. in castro de Berkel:</small>

This lord Thomas in the 7ᵗʰ of king Richard the second gave to Walter Dyar for his life, an Anuity of fourty shillings by the year out of Charelton in Wiltshire in recompence of his service.

<small>carta in castro de Berkeley.</small>

In the 13ᵗʰ of the said [King] hee gave to Thomas Rig, all his lands and Tenements in Chicklade for his life, in recompence of his service.

<small>carta in castro pʳᵈict.</small>

In the twentieth of the said king hee granted to Willm Cauleigh one of his Esquires, for his life, in recompence for his service, a messuage mill and lands in Woodford, and a messuage in Church lane in Berkeley.

<small>carta in castro de Berkeley:</small>

In the 21ᵗʰ of the said kinge hee gave to John Banbury his manor of Upton Sᵗ Leonards by Glouc: for his life, in recompence of his service, whereof the old rent then was ten markes.

<small>carta in castro pʳᵈict.</small>

The same year hee gave to John Harsfeild a messuage and divers lands and Tenements in Bradley and Wike Dangerfeild for his life in recompence of his service.

<small>469
carta in castr: pʳᵈict.</small>

In the 22ᵗʰ of the said king, hee gave to John Dyar for his own life, and of his wife and daughter, a messuage in Berkeley and divers lands in Hame and Alkington.

<small>carta in castro de Berkeley.</small>

The same year hee gave to John Copiner for his life in recompence of his service, divers lands and Tenements in Dursley.

<small>carta in castro de Berkeley.</small>

In the first year of king Henry the fourth, this lord gave to John Winter and to Elizabeth his wife in recompence of his service, divers houses in Berkeley, and divers lands in Hame and in Came, And in the tenth of the said king did the like for Alice his second wife.

<small>carta in castro de Berkeley.</small>

The same first year of Henry the fourth hee gave to Thomas Browne and Isable his wife, a messuage and yard land in Clapton in Hame for their lives in recompence of his service: And in the tenth of the said king did the like for Mawd his second wife. And the 13ᵗʰ yeare rewarded him as bountifully and made him keeper of Whitcliffe park.

<small>carta in castro de Berkeley.</small>

The same first year of Henry the fourth, hee gave to Phillip Waterton and Cicely his wife for their lives in recompence of their services, all the lands and tenements

ments within the lordship of Berkeley which late were of Robert Poyntz. And in the first year of king Henry the fifth, gave to them and the heirs which hee should beget on her body, eight severall Tenements and divers lands in Berkeley, Hame, Hinton and Alkington, Rendringe unto him and his heires the rents and services of old due and accustomed; which entayle yet continueth, And whereof I shall speak after in the issue of Thomas Berkeley son of the said James the first of that name.

In the same first of Henry the fourth, this lord gave to Robert Herblinge and Alice his wife for their lives in recompence of his service, five houses in Wotton, and divers lands in his manor of Wotton Forren. *carta in castro de Berkeley.*

In the third of the same king hee gave to John Chinham for his life and Jone his wife, in recompence of his service, a messuage and divers lands, in Chepinge lane in Wotton. *carta in castro de Berkeley.*

In the 11th of Henry the fourth hee gave to Willm More and Edith his wife, in recompence of his service, two houses and six shops in Glouc: for their lives. *carta in castr. prdict. 470*

About the same time hee gave his litle manor of Wike neere Rodlyes weare by Arlingham, to Richard Ecton and Alice his wife for their lives without rent, who longe enjoyed the same. *Comp: ballivi de Wotton libtat. 12. et. 14. H. 6.*

And about the same time hee gave Bayes place in Horwood to Nicholas Alderly for his life. *comp. prdict.*

In the first year of Henry the fifth, this lord gave to Robert Shottesbroke one of his Esquires in recompence of his service, for his life fourteen pounds by the year out of his manor of Ordeston in Barkshire. *magn: charta. fo: 279.*

In the second year of the same kinge, hee gave to Nicholas Alderly for his life in recompence of his service, all his lands in Horton & Yate called Bayes. *carta in castro de Berkeley.*

In the same year hee gave to Phillip Chamberlen for his life in recompence of his service, a messuage in Wotton, and divers lands in Wotton fforren. *carta in castro de Berkeley.*

In the 5th year of the said king (three months before his death) hee gave to John Plomer and Jone his wife for their lives in recompence of her service, a house in Wotton, with liberty to buy and sell tollfree within the said Burrow. *carta in castro de Berkeley.*

By his will hee gave to Robert Knollis Citizen of London, his Inne called Berkeleys Inne at Baynards Castle in London.

In cur: prerogat. Cant.

To every gentleman in his house by his said will hee gave—100ˢ.

To every yeoman and groome, (valettus et garcio) in his house by his said will, hee gave forty shillings.

To every of his fower Executors (being fower of his servants) hee gave twenty pounds.

What more I have not observed. |

471 His miscellanies or various passages not aptly to bee reduced under the former titles.

fo: [401]
Bale in cent. 7. n° 18.
Hollingshed

Of the learned labours of John Trevisa vicar of Berkeley Chaplen to this lord, as also to his father and grandfather, I have formerly written; who concludinge one other of his translations of Bartholomeus de proprietatibus rerum, which hee dedicated to this lord Thomas, in the end thereof hath thus: Endles grace, blisse and thankinge to our lord God alweldinge, these translations ended at Berkeley the sixth day of February the year of our lord 1398. the year of king Richard the second after the conquest of England the 22ᵗʰ The year of my lords age Sʳ Thomas lord of Berkeley that made mee to make this translation, the 47ᵗʰ

Trevisa. man ēm. Geor. dno Berk:

Reg: Wigorn.

This Trevisa dyed the 13ᵗʰ year of king Henry the fourth, whom John Bone-John succeeded in that vicarage, whom this lord made one of his Executors; And proved a false preist to the heir male of his said lord as after I shall touch.

pat. 11: R. 2. ps. 1. m: 16.

In the 11ᵗʰ of Richard the second, this lord and his cozen Sʳ John Berkeley of Beverston with others, were indited before the Justices of the forrest of Dean, for unlawfull killing of some of the kings deere there, for which they now obtained their pardons.

Amongst the wills of the dead, I find that in the 8ᵗʰ year of king Richard the second, one Margery Legat of Wotton widowe gave to this lord for a legacy, a brasse morter and an Iron pestle; And to the lady Margaret his wife a ringe of fine gold, And to Elizabeth their daughter an other gold ringe, And to the lady Katharine de Berkeley an other gold ringe, making this lord Supervisor of her said will.

When

When in the tenth of Richard the second, the kings purveior came to purvey in the manor of Wotton, hee gave him secretly—3ˢ 4ᵈ and his man. 4ᵈ to speak a good word to his master, (saith the Accompt,) And for their freindship bestowed more on them in wine—12ᵈ |

comp. de Wotton 10. R. 2. in castr̃ de Berkeley.

In the Twentieth of Richard the second, Ivo fitz Waryn knight made this lord his Atturney to govern for him his manor of fframpton upon Seaverne.

472 carta in castro de Berkeley.

In the third of Henry the fourth the king awarded his spetiall Comission to this lord Thomas to punish divers mallefactors in the County of Glouc.

pat. 3 : H. 4. pars. 2. dorso :

In the fourth of that king this lord bought of Henry Talbot 24 Scottish prisoners, taken by him upon the land by the seaside, in way of warre, as the kings enemies.

comp. recept. in castro de Berkeley.

In the sixth of Henry the fourth this lord obtained of the kinge to have a market each Wednesday and three fairs each year in his wives manor of Pensans in Cornwall.

cart: 6. et. 7. H. 4. m. 1.

In the eleaventh of Henry the fourth the king writes to this lord Thomas, That whereas hee had by his tres patents in the 8ᵗʰ of his raign granted for ten years, liberty to the Marchants of Jenoa with their carracks to bring into England any their wares and there to sell them, And to carry out into fflanders and other parts cloth and wooll from England paying the customs due and doinge noe damage; That hee is given to understand That divers of this lords men and servants in a shipp of his sailing towards Burdeaux, have violently set upon one of the carraks called the Sᵗ Mary and Sᵗ Bridget loaden with wines and other marchandize to the valewe of Ten thousand pounds, as shee was sailing towards London. And have carryed that shipp to Millford haven, and taken away their wines and other marchandize, And therefore requires this lord either presently to cause restitution to bee made, or himself to come and answer the same before his privy Counsell forthwith. **The** sequell whereof was, That the servants of this lord, Sᵗ John Greyndore and others of Bristoll did the wronge, who made restitution for part, but went away with a great part of the rest of the Jenoa goods.

claus : 11. H. 4. m. 34. et in dorso. m : 21.

In the 8ᵗʰ of Henry the fourth, this lord was one of those lords, who by his seal of Armes in parliament that year confirmed the Crown to | that king and entayled the succession upon his issue, to the utter abolition of the house of Yorke.

Rot. parliam. 8. H. 4. pat: 8. H. 4. pˢ. 1. m. 4.
473

When

When for the good service of the husband this lord rewarded both husband and wife with an estate for their lives in such lands as hee bestowed upon them, as almost still hee did; hee ever restrained by a provisoe in his deed, the second marriage of the wife, without his consent, if shee survived her husband; which out of a double respect was a prudent course in him.

<small>Pat: 49. E. 3. p^s. 1. in dorso.</small>

The tenth of October in the 49th of Edward the third, a Comission was awarded to this lord to enquire of divers conventicles in the County of Glouc: tending to the disturbance of the government and peace of the Realme, requiring him as hee loved the king and his hon^r and would avoid his greevous indignation, that hee would carefully looke into and punish the same.

<small>Pat. 51. E. 3. dorso.</small>

And in the one and fiftieth of that king was a comission awarded to this lord and others to muster and Arme all able men in the said County to withstand the intended invasion of the ffrench.

<small>Pat: 5. R. 2. pars. 1. in dorso. Pat: 6. R. 2: pars. 2. m: 13.</small>

In the fifth of Richard the second were three severall Comissions directed to this lord and others to represse those mischeevous persons, who in hostile manner had taken and put to death the Arch-bishop of Canterbury, lord Chancellor, and others, without any fault by them committed; In which service this lord was imployed into divers other Countyes.

<small>Rot. fin: 6. R. 2. m: 15.</small>

In the sixth year of the said king, hee granted to this lord Thomas the custody of the manor of Lye neer Deerhurst which was the land of John son of W^{ilm} de Rodborrowe and then in the kings hands.

<small>fin: 8. R. 2. m. 16.</small>

The 16th of December and 19th of January in the 8th of Richard the second, the king comitted to this lord the government of the wholl County of Glouc. in a more ample and different manner then I have elswhere observed: At this time the wholl kingdome seemes in Armes to withstand the French and Scotts.

<small>claus: 12. R. 2. m: 16.</small>

The 13th of ffebruary in the 12th of Richard the second, this lord was commanded to proclaime the keeping of the kings peace at Wittenden and other places adjoyning according to the Statute of Northton, for | not doing whereof, proces went out against him for that omission and contempt: But upon his oath taken in Chancery That hee received not the Comission nor heard thereof, the proces by the kings command doth cease: Howbeit this foe awaked him That within one month after

hee

hee sent divers both preists and laymen to the comon Goale of Gloucester; As their supplicavits for their bayles, body for body, do declare.

In the 16th of Richard the second, one Ruyale and Otho late Clark of the peace certified falsly into the Chancery a record concerning this lord Thomas and the king, supposed to bee before Judge Caffey and his fellow Justices of the peace; for which unjust fact, (in times so dangerous,) this lord complaines; And upon hearing thereof Ruyale is fined one hundred markes, and Otho five markes, which either of them doe pay; And soe obtaine their pardons, the one this year the other in the eighteenth. *fin. 16. R. 2. m. 3. pat: 18. R. 2. pars. 1. m: 26.*

This lord Thomas was one of those that were on Michaelmas day sent to Richard the second then in the Tower of London from the parliament then in being to mind him of his promise made to the Arch-bishop of Canterbury and the Earl of Northumberland for renouncing the Crowne, which hee now did, and subscribed it, and gave therein his oath also. *Rot. parliament. 1. H. 4. n? 10.*

And after at the same parliament, this lord was the only procurator for the Barons to declare to king Richard his deprivation by parliament; And how none of the great estates of the Realme nor Comons would for time forwards beare him faith, or doe to him obeisance as to their kinge. *Rot. predict. n? 59.*

And in the name of Richard the second, did renounce from him his kingdome to that parliament; whereupon king Henry the fourth did claime it by title from king Henry the third, And soe by that parliament was chosen kinge. *Rot. predict. n? 74.*

And was one of those spetiall lords in that parliament who gave advice and consent That Richard the king should bee safely kept, and in secret place where noe concourse should bee to him, nor any of his frends or acquaintance admitted to him, And to bee continually guarded by sure and sufficient persons. *Rot. prædict. n? 74.*

And in the first of Henry the fourth the king directed his Comission | to this lord to muster Arme and trayne all able men within the County of Glouc: The like the king did in the fourth year of his raigne. *Pat. 1. H. 4. pars. 5. dorso.* **475** *Pat. 4. H. 4. ps. 2. dorso.*

And in the third of that kings raigne this lord was one of those eleaven lords chosen out of the wholl state to secure the payment of forty thousand nobles, being the *franc: 3. H. 4. m: 7.*

E VOL. II

the mariage portion of Blanch the kings daughter, maryed to Lewis Earle palatine and of the Rene, and Duke of Bavaria, son of Rupert king of the Romaines, allways Augustus.

<small>Rot. parl: 5. H. 4. m: 12.</small>

At the parliament holden the fifth of Henry the fourth, It is recited That for the good government of the Realme and remedy of many complaints, greevances and mischeifes, shewed to the king in that parliament, The king at the reverence of God, and at the great instance and spetiall request to him oftentimes made in this parliament by the Comons of his Realme, Hath for the ease and comfort of all his Realme ordained six Bishops, one Duke, two Earles, fower Barons, and eight others

<small>claus: 5. H. 4. pars. 1. m: 2. pat. 5. H. 4: pars. 1. m: 18.</small>

to bee of his grand and continuall Counsell: The first of all the fower Barons is this lord: which being concluded upon in parliament by both houses, was to him a singular honor, and an assured testimony to his posterity, That this their Ancestor was an able and wise man, being at this time about the age of fifty yeares. And now also was this lord chosen Admirall by this parliament as before is written.

<small>pat: 7. H. 4. pars. 1. m: 1.
pat. 11. H. 4 pars. 2. m: 13.</small>

And in the 7th of Henry the fourth was this lord spetially imployed in the Counties of Glouc̃ and Hereford to borrowe moneys for the king and to give securities for repayment; And in the 11th of Henry the 4th was imployed in the like borrowinge of money in the Counties of Warrwicke, Worcester, Gloucester, and Bristoll, to bee repaid out of ye fifteenth granted unto the kinge at the last parliament then before.

<small>Rot. parliament. in eisdem annis.</small>

I find this lord present in person at most parliaments holden beetween his full age and death: And at the parliaments holden in the first, fourth, sixth, seaventh, ninth, eleaventh, and thirteenth of Henry the fourth, was a tryer of the petitions; And soe in the first, second, third and fourth of Henry the fifth.

Manifold others were the imployments of this lord Thomas Aswell in Comissions of severall natures, as in the extraordinary affaires of State, Church and Comon wealth, besides his constant travell in the ordinary Comissions of the peace,

476 from full age till death; some of | which extraordinaries in divers Counties and corporate Cities the records hereunder vouched will guide such of his posterity unto as desire to bee satisfied in the particularityes of that kind, none of which are formerly mentioned. vizt Rot parliament. 5. E. 3. / 2. R. 2. pars. 1. in dorso / 3. R. 2. pars. 2. in dorso. / claus: 8. R. 2. m. 14. / pat: 8. R. 2. pars. 2. in dorso: et eodẽ bis dorso. / pat. 9. R. 2. pars. 1. in dorso ter. / et eodẽ postea. / pat. 21. R. 2. pars. 3. m. 23.

m. 23. dorſo. / pat. 22. R. 2. pars. 3. m. 9. in dorſo / pat. 1. H. 4. pars. 7. dors / Rot. parliament. 2. H. 4. / pat. 2. H. 4. pars 3. m. 7. dorſo / pat. 3. H. 4. pars. 2. in dorſo ter : / claus. 5. H. 4. pars. 1. m. 4. dorſo : / Rot. parliament. 7. H. 4. pars. 2 : m : 15. et al / pat. 7. H. 4. pars. 2. m. 33. / pat. 8. H. 4. pars. 1. dorſo / pat. 13. H. 4. pars. 2. in dorſo : / pat. 1. H. 5. pars 1. dorſo. / pat. 22. R. 2. pars. 3. m : 9. dorſo. Beſides divers others which with a dry foot I paſſed by.

His wife.

Whoſe daughter the lady Margaret wife to this lord was, And when, where and at what age maryed, what portion in money & land ſhee brought to her huſband, when firſt ſhee came to Berkeley with other circumſtances, is before in the firſt title of this lords life declared.   fol : [448, 451]

The courſe of her life went with her huſbands in often removes from one of their houſes to another, which then, (contrary to the proverbe that the rolling ſtone gathers noe moſſe,) was held the greater honor. **As** at Berkeley, Wotton, Portbury, London, Syde and at ffulham, and ſome other houſes of her inheritance. **It** ſeemes ſhee was a very mild and devout lady but nothing active in her family.

In the prime of her age ſhee brought her huſband a daughter called Elizabeth of whom much hereafter is to bee ſpoken; And for any thinge I have obſerved, never conceived more, before or after, yet lived ſhee and her huſband in a moſt ſweet and contented ſociety; | **Herein** much reſe[m]blinge the lady Elizabeth Spenſer,   477 maryed to Geo: lord Hunſdon, (of whom after,) who having brought her huſband not longe after mariage, Elizabeth, (mother of the now lord George Berkeley,) held it ſufficient honor and frutefullnes to have been the mother of a child ſoe peerleſſe.

This lady Margaret died at Wotton under edge, the twentieth of March about   Newl: ped. in caſt: the fifteenth year of Richard the ſecond, then about thirty years of age; having   de Berkeley. been maryed at ſeaven; And lyeth buried in the pariſh Church of Wotton under a   Eſcaet. poſt mort. faire Tombe by the ſide of her huſband, whither her bones were tranſlated as after   Gerard Warren followeth : The greefe of whoſe death ſoe faſtened upon the affections of her lord   d͠ni Liſle. 6. R. 2. and huſband, That hee never after affected mariage, although hee was at her death   Rot. franc: 16. R. but thirty eight years of age, and of an able conſtitution, and then without iſſue male   2. m : 10. bis. to uphold his name and barony : whereat I have not only muſed, but at the cauſe why, in ſewe monthes after her death, hee betooke himſelfe to a forraigne pilgrimage As in the title of his forraigne imployments is already written.

His

His issue.

Escaet. 5. H. 5. post mort. Tho: dni Berkel:

Magn: chart. fol: 240. in castro de Berkeley.

Elizabeth was this lords onely daughter and heir of the age of twenty six and upwards, at the time of his death. In September in the 16th of Richard the second this lord entred into covenants wth Thomas Beauchamp Earle of Warrwike concerning a mariage to bee had between Richard his son and heir, and his said daughter shee then under the age of seaven yeares, That their mariage should bee assoone as conveniently it may; That her Joynture should bee three hundred markes by the year, after the death of the said Earle and of Margaret his wife; That hee the said lord Berkeley would grant the manors of Kislingbury Draycote and certaine others to the said Richard and Elizabeth for their lives, and fower | hundred markes more to them by the yeare of those lands which were the inheritance of Margaret late wife of him the said lord Thomas; To hold to them after his death; And that hee would pay fower hundred pound in money for the mariage portion of his said daughter; for performance of which agreements, either of them became bound to other in two thousand pounds.

Escaet. 17. H. 6. post mort. Rici Beauchamp. vlt. voluntas Rici Beauchamp. 18. H. 6. in prerog: Cant:

liber Gloveri als Somerset Herald. vetus manuscript. et divers: al.

The said Elizabeth by her husband, (who after his fathers death was Earle of Warwike, and Regent of France,) had issue onely three daughters, Margaret, Ellenor, and Elizabeth; And dyed the 28th day of December in the first of Henry the sixth, then about the age of one and thirty years, and lyeth buried at the said monastery of Kingswood, whereof shee was hereditary foundres, by her fathers purchase of the patronage as afore is mentioned, with this Epitaph upon a goodly Tombe of marble nowe demolished set up by her husbands Executors according to the direction of his will. Hic jacet dna Elizabetha nuper comitissa et prima vxor Rici de bello campo nuper Comitis Warwici ac filia et hæres Thomæ nuper dni de Berkeley et de Lisle. Quod quidem dominium de Lisle idem Thomas tenet per legem Angliæ post mortem Margaretæ nuper vxoris suæ, matris predictæ Elizabethæ: qui qudem Ricus et Elizabetha habuerunt exitum inter se Margaretam Elianoram et Elizabetham, quæ vero Elizabetha comitissa obiit vicesimo octavo die Decembris Anno domini. 1422. Cuius animæ propicietur deus Amen.

And her husband, afterwards marying, (and haveing other issue wherewith I meddle not,) dyed the last of Aprill. 1439. in the 17th of Henry the sixth; Between whom and their said three daughters and their issues, and James the heire male of this lord Thomas were the greatest sutes in lawe and of longest continuance that were in those times or since, As after will bee declared.

The said Margaret was the second wife of John Talbot the first Earle of Shroesbury of that name, by whom shee had issue John Talbot created viscount Lisle, And dyed the 14th of June in the 7th of Edward the fourth, And lyeth buried in Jhesus Chapple | in St Paules Church in London, with this Epitaph; Here before the image of Jhesu lyeth the worll and right noble lady Margaret Countes of Shrewsbury, late wife of the true and victorious knight and redoubtable warriour John Talbot Earle of Shrewesbury, which worshipfull man dyed in Gwyen for the right of this land: Shee was the first daughter and one of the heires of the right famous renowned knight Richard Beauchamp late Earle of Warwike, (which dyed in Roan,) and of dame Elizabeth his wife, the which Elizabeth was daughter and heire to Thomas late lord Berkeley on his side, and on her mothers side lady Lisle and Tyes, which Countes passed from this world the 14th of June . 1468 . on whose soule Jhesu have mercy, Amen. *Survey of London 479*

The said John Talbot viscount Lisle by Jone his wife, one of the two daughters and coheires of Sr Thomas Chedder, had issue Thomas Talbot viscount Lisle, who maryed Margaret daughter of Willm Harbert Earle of Penbroke, and was slayne by Willm lord Berkeley the 20th of March in the Tenth year of Edward the fourth, without issue; Elizabeth, and Margaret; which Margaret was maryed to Sr George Veer knight and dyed without issue in the 14th of Edward ye fourth. *Escaet. 21. H. 6. post mort: Tho: Chedder. Escaet: 7. E. 4. post mort. Johæ vxoris Johis Talbot. pat. roll: 15. E. 4. pars. 1. m. 5.*

The said Elizabeth sister and heire of Thomas Talbot viscount Lisle, was maryed to Sr Edward Gray, who in the fifteenth of Edward the fourth was created lord Lisle, in right of his wife; shee dyed in the third of Henry the seaventh, And hee fower years after, leaving issue by her John, Margaret, Anne, and Elizabeth. *Rot. cart. 15. E. 4. in vlt. dat. 14. marcij. Inq. sub sigillo in Castro de Berkeley.*

The said Sr John Gray son of Sr Edward was viscount Lisle; And by Myriell his wife daughter of Thomas Howard Earle of Surrey, lord Treasorer of England, had issue Elizabeth onely, born after his death the twentieth of March in the twentieth of Henry the seaventh; And after being very younge was maryed to Henry Courtney Earle of Devon, And dyed without issue about the ninth of Henry the 8th And the said Myriell was after marryed to Sr Thomas Knevet. *Escaet. 20. 21. H. 7. post mort. Johis Gray vic: lisle in div's Com: pat: 18. H. 7. pars. 2. Carta in castro de Berkeley.*

Margaret the eldest sister was maryed to Edward Stafford Earle of Wiltshire, And dyed without issue. **Anne** the second sister was maryed to John Willoughby of Wollaton, And dyed without issue; | **Elizabeth** the third and youngest sister of John Gray viscount Lisle, was first maried to Edmond Dudley, who was beheadded *480*

in

in the firſt of Henry the eighth, And after to Arthur Plantagenet baſe ſon to Edward the fourth; ſhee dyed the 33th of Henry the 8th leaving iſſue John Dudley, who by ſeverall patents was created viſcount Liſle Earle of Warwike, and Duke of Northumberland.

The ſaid John Dudley, ſon of the ſaid Elizabeth and Edmond, was duke of Northumberland; And by Anne his wife daughter of Sr Edward Guilford left iſſue, (of whom only I need to write,) Ambroſe, Robert, Katharine and Mary; And was beheaded in Anno. 1553. in the firſt year of Queen Mary for treaſon: Of whom ſee more in the life of Henry lord Berkeley the firſt of that name.

Ambroſe Dudley was in the 4th year of the raigne of Queene Elizabeth created Earle of Warwike, and maryed for his third wife Anne daughter of Francis Ruſſell Earle of Bedford, (of whom I need to write onely,) And dyed in the 32th of Elizabeth without iſſue by any wife; As alſo did the ſaid Anne in the firſt of king James.

Robert Dudley was created Earle of Leiceſter in the 6th of Elizabeth, and marryed Lettice daughter of Sr Francis Knolles, And dyed in the thirtieth of Elizabeth without lawfull iſſue; And Lettice is yet livinge. 1628. The Tombe of whoſe only ſon, interred at Warwicke, hath thus; **Here** reſteth the body of the noble Impe Robert of Dudley, Baron of Denbigh, ſon of Robert Earle of Leiceſter, nephewe and heire unto Ambroſe Earle of Warwicke, brethren, both ſons of the mighty prince John late Duke of Northumberland, that was Cozen and heire to Sr John Gray viſcount Liſle, cozen and heire to Sr Thomas Talbot viſcount Liſle, nephewe and heire to the lady Margaret Counteſs of Shrewſbury eldeſt daughter and co-heire of the noble Earle of Warwicke Sr Richard Beauchamp, here interred, a child of great parentage, but of greater hope and towardlineſs, taken from this tranſitory unto everlaſting life in his tender age, at Wanſteed in Eſſex on ſunday the 19th of July. 1584. the 26th year of the happy raigne of the moſt vertuous and godly princeſſe Elizabeth And in this place layd up amongſt his noble Anceſtors. |

And about the tombe of Ambroſe Earle of Warwicke, elder brother of the ſaid Robert Earle of Leiceſter, is thus. **Edmond** Dudley Eſqr, one of the privy counſell to king Henry the ſeaventh, maryed Elizabeth ſiſter and ſole heire of John Gray viſcount Liſle, diſcended as heir of the eldeſt daughter and co-heire of Richard Beauchamp Earle of Warwike, and Elizabeth his wife, daughter and heir of the lord

lord Berkeley and heir of the said lord Lisle and Tyes, And had John Duke of Northumberland &c.

Katharine was maried to Henry Hastings Earle of Huntington by whom shee had no issue.

Mary was maried to Sr Henry Sidney president of Wales, And had Sr Phillip Sidney knight, and Sr Robert and others.

Sir Phillip Sidney had issue Elizabeth, and dyed in the 28.th yeare of Queene Elizabeth in the low Country warrs; And the said Elizabeth his daughter and heir was maryed to Roger Manors Earle of Rutland and dyed without issue.

Sir Robert Sidney, brother of Sr Phillip, was created lord Sidney, viscount Lisle, and Earle of Leicester; And by Barbara his wife daughter and heire of John Gamage Esqr had Willm Sidney knight, who dyed unmaryed in. Anno. 1612. in the tenth of king James: Robert Sidney after his father Earle of Leicester, and others, Anno. 1627. of whom much is to bee written in the life of Henry lord Berkeley the first of that name. *See fol: [775]*

2. **Ellenor** the second daughter of Elizabeth Countesse of Warrwike sole daughter of this lord Thomas, was first maryed to Thomas lord Roos of Hamelake, And after to Edmond Beaufort Duke of Somerset, by both whom shee had issue; And dyed alsoe in the 7.th of Edward the fourth. By her first husband she had issue Thomas lord Roos, and Margaret marryed to Thomas A-Burrough of whom is issue; The said Thomas lord Roos dyed in the life of his mother, leaving issue Edmond and Ellenor; Edmond was an Ideot, and dyed without issue; And Ellenor his sister & heir was maryed to Sr Robert Manors, who had issue between them Geo: Manors lord Roos, who had issue Thomas Manors created Earle of Rutland in the 17.th of Henry the 8.th to him and the heires males of his body, And dyed in the 35.th of Henry the eighth, leaving issue Henry Manors lord Roos Earle of Rutland, who dyed in the fifth of Elizabeth, leaving issue Edwd | lord Roos and Earle of Rutland, and John Manors: Edward dyed in the 29.th of Elizabeth, haveing issue onely Elizabeth maryed to Willm Cicell nowe Earle of Exeter, son of Thomas late Earle of Exeter: which Willm and Elizabeth had issue Willm lord Roos who deceased in Anno. 1618. without issue, who maried the daughter of Sr Thomas Lake, whereon arose that famous Starchamber sute, heard by king James then sitting in Court.

John

John Manors, brother and heire male of the said Edward, was after his death Earle of Rutland, And by Elizabeth his wife daughter of ffrancis Charelton had issue Roger Manors Earle of Rutland, who maryed Elizabeth daughter of S:r Phillip Sidney aforesaid ; And John dyed in . Anno . 1587. But of the said Roger Manors Earle of Rutland and of the said Elizabeth his wife is noe issue, as aforesaid.

The foresaid Ellenor by Edmond Beaufort Duke of Somerset her second husband, (slaine at S:t Albans . 1455,) had issue Henry Beaufort Duke of Somerset eldest son ; beheaded in Anno . 1463 . father to Charles lord Harbert, of whom are the Earles of Worcester : And Edmond duke of Somset, second son, who dyed without issue ; Ellenor whose second husband was S:r Robert Spenser knight, (of whose issue in this place I will only write,) and fower other daughters, called Margaret, Elizabeth, Jone, and Anne, of whom is much honourable issue.

Inquis. in Canc. 21 H. 8. in Com. Oxon.

The said Ellenor and S:r Robert Spenser had issue, Margaret maryed to Thomas Carey Esq:r And Katharine maryed to Henry the fifth Earle of Northumberland, of whom is discended the Earle that now is . 1624.

The said Thomas Carey and Margaret had issue John Carey and W:m; which W:m maryed Mary second daughter and co-heire of Thomas Bullein Earle of Wiltshire and Ormond, and of Elizabeth his wife daughter of Thomas Howard Duke of Norfolk ; and had issue Henry Carey and Katharine maryed to S:r Francis Knolles, of whom is issue.

The said Henry Carey, (created lord Hunsdon,) by Anne his wife daughter of S:r Thomas Morgan knight, had issue George Carey lord Hunsdon, Henry Carey, John, William, Edmond, Robert, Katharine marryed to Charles lord Howard, Earle of Nottingham and Admirall, Philadelph. and Margaret.

The said George Carey lord Hunsdon by Elizabeth his wife second | daughter of S:r John Spenser knight, had issue Elizabeth maried to S:r Thomas Berkeley knight, father of George now lord Berkeley, and of Theophila wife of S:r Robert Coke knight Anno . 1624 . the noble dedicatees of these collections ; of whom more is hereafter written in the life of Henry lord Berkeley the first of that name.

3. **The** foresaid Elizabeth third daughter of Elizabeth Countesse of Warwicke, sole daughter of this Thomas lord Berkeley, was maryed to George Nevill lord Latimer,

Latimer, a younger son of Ralph Nevill Earle of Westmorland by his second wife; which George dyed in the ninth of Edward the fourth; And the said Elizabeth his wife the Twentieth of Edward the fourth; And had issue Henry Nevill lord Latimer, who dyed also in the ninth of Edward the fourth. And was father of Richard Nevill lord Latimer who dyed in the twentieth of Henry the 7th. And was father of John Nevill lord Latimer, and Willm, (from which Willm is issue male at this day;) The said John Nevill lord Latimer dyed in the 34th of Henry the 8th leaving issue John Nevill lord Latimer, who dyed in the 19th of Elizabeth, leaving issue fower daughters and co-heires. vizt Katharine maryed to Henry Earle of Northumberland, Dorothy maryed to Sr Thomas Cicell late Earle of Exeter, Lucy marryed to Sr William Cornwallis, And Elizabeth maryed to Sr John Danvers knight, And after to Sr Edmond Carey aforesaid. Of whose multiplyed posterityes flourishing at this day, to write in particular would enoble some pages in this place; which I here omit, As onely pointing at the honorable posterity of this lord Thomas, now livinge Anno. 1628. which the labours of most heralds do performe.

Latimer. id est Interpreter.

His Seales of Armes.

1. The Seales of Armes which this lord used were different: At first when hee attained full age, hee sealed with the Cheveron and ten crosses, about two Inches diameter, without supporters or crest, circumscribed sigillum Thomæ de Berkelee. |

2. In the middle part of his life, hee sealed with the Cheveron and ten crosses supported by two mairmaides without crest, sircumscribed sigillum Thomæ dni de Berkeley, in bredth as aforesaid.

3. In the later part of his life hee sealed with the Cheveron and ten crosses cornerwise, with the mairmaides for supporters, and the helmet for crest, The circumscription and bredth as last aforesaid. See the representations.

His death and place of buriall.

Upon the 13th of July in the fifth year of that victorious king Henry the fifth Anno . 1417 . the glaſſe of this lord Thomas runneth out, at Wotton Vnder edge, hee then of the age of 64. yeares ſix monthes and eight days, whereof hee had ſate lord . 49 . yeares one month and . 5 . dayes ; And lived a widdower the laſt twenty ſix years thereof or neer thereabouts ; And lyeth buryed in the pariſh Church of Wotton vnder edge with the tranſlated bones of the lady Margaret his wife reſting by him, under a faire Tombe there.

Marginalia: Newl: ped. in caſtro de Berkeley. Eſcaet. poſt mort. Tho: dni Berkeley 5. H. 5. et bis ſub magno ſigillo in caſtro de Berkeley

> Nos quos certus amor primis conjunxit ab annis
> Iunxit idem tumulus, junxit idemque polus.
> In youth our parents joyn'd our hands, our ſelves our harts,
> This Tombe our bodyes hath, th'heavens our better parts.

To his onely daughter the Countes of Warwicke by his will, this lord gave his beſt pair of morninge mattens, and one boll and twenty pound in it. **And** to his nephewe and heire male James Berkeley hee gave his beſt bed, and his great boll of Jett, And twenty compleat Armors and twenty lances, which will was proved the tenth day after his death. |

Marginalia: Vlt. volunt. in Cur. prerog : Cant. anno 5. H. 5.

485 His lands whereof hee dyed ſeized.

Betweene the ſaid Elizabeth this lords onely child, and James Berkeley his brothers ſon, were all this lords lands divided ; **To** Elizabeth diſcended all the mannors and lands which came by the lady Margaret her mother, before mentioned in the life of this lord ; And alſo all the manors and lands whereof this lord her father died ſeized in ffee ſimple or in ffee tayle generall, whether of his own purchaſe, or which came to him by diſcent, in the Countyes of Gloucester, Somerſet, Buckingham, Wilts, Northton, Devon, Cornwall, Oxon, and Berks ; and in the Cities of London and Briſtoll, and ſome other places, which were about thirty manors, beſides Advowſons of Churches, Abbathies, Chantryes, hundreds, knights fees, and many lands, tenements, fiſhings, and liberties, not being parcell of any manors ; As by divers Inquiſitions found after his death in moſt of the ſaid Counties appeareth ; ſhee then of the age of twenty ſix yeares and upwards.

Marginalia: Eſcaet : 5. H. 5. poſt mort. Thomæ dni : Berkeley. Inquis: ſub magno ſigillo in caſtro de Berkeley :

And to the ſaid James, (then of the age of twenty three years and upwards,) diſcended the Caſtle and Barony of Berkeley ; And the manors of Berkeley, Hame, Appleridge, Alkington, Hinton, Slimbridge, Came, Cowley, Wotton-Burrow, Wotton fforren,

Marginalia: Eſcaet : 5. H. 5. poſt mort. Tho : dni Berkeley :

fforren, Simondfall, and Vpton S.t Leonards, and the hundred of Berkeley in the county of Glouc: by force of the fine leavyed in the said 23.th of Edward the third, to the heires males, and by the assurances as is before declared; **And** the manor of Portbury and Porteshned, and the hundred of Portbury in the County of Somerset, by force of the like fine leavyed to the heires males, by the said lord Thomas in the 26.th of the same kinge: And also the manor of Hurst and two and twenty markes rent in fframpton upon Seaverne, by force of a conveyance thereof made in the sixteenth of Edward the third, As formerly in his life and of Maurice his son is declared. dated 26. Septem.r apud Beverston.

The same James had alsoe at this time of his unckles death, or shortly thereupon, from his own father and mother and younger brother, the manors of Ragelon, Talgarth, Tore, Edishall, Straddewy, and divers others in Wales, Daglingworth in the County of Gloucester, And also by other mixt means | the manors of Sages, litle Marshfeild, and Arlingham, in the said County of Gloucester, as after followeth in his life. 486

Soe that an honorable and opulent revenue still remained to the male line for support of the honor thereof, notwithstanding the great and rich possessions caryed from it by the said Elizabeth cozen germane of the said James.

The application and use of his life.

1. **This** lord Thomas to the smart of his double posterity (nephewe and daughter, line masculine and femynine) greatly erred, either by too longe a deliberacon or by an inconstancy in his resolution, as a man seeming over-combated in himself, betweene name and nature, whether to leave his barony lands and name to his heire male his brothers son, or to the frute of his own body, his onely daughter the Countes of Warwicke, then wife to the first Earle of the land: The ill effect wherof, the lives of the two next lords at large bewailes: whereby it might have been reproached and fully said to him, as the prophet Elijah said to the children of Israell before Ahab their kinge, **Howe** longe halt ye ebetween two opinions, If the lord bee God follow him, But if Baall bee hee then followe him. **The** counsell of Isaiah the prophet to king Ezekiah was good, because sent from God, put thine house in order for thou shalt dye and not live, which this lord Thomas neglecting, hee hath thereby damnifyed his posterity more then one hundred thousand pounds, And insteed of setlinge a perpetuity of good to his posterity, which a constant Testament would have done, By | omission thereof hee cast both his heires male and female on their knees, as the sequell alonge the lives that follow will make too manifest.

The use.

Rot. parliam. 23. H. 6.

1. Kings. chap. 18. vers: 21.

2: Kings. ch. 20. vers. 1.
38. Isaiah. vers. 1. 2. 3.

487

2. The

2. The fairest mold that this lords posterity can cast this error in, is to say, That this their Ancestor beinge a deep wise man, (as the double uses hee made of both the opposite houses of Yorke and Lancaster in advancement of his own ends, if nothing els there were, declares,) Hee would on the one side serve himselfe with the Court favour of his son in lawe, one of the most powerfull and best favored subjects of his time, loaden with honors and offices of state, And on the other side, simul et semel, in the same seasons make harvest of the person of his said nephewe and heire male, by a double sale of his mariage, first to Sr John St John, and after to Sr Humphry Stafford, not sticking in those agreements to declare his said nephewe to bee heir to all his inheritance intailed. And yet turning to the other shoulder declares to others about him his purpose to bee, That his daughter should inherit the wholl lumpe of his lands, as in the next life is deposed: Not more certainly declareing by any overt act, who should bee his heire, or lord Berkeley after him, then Queene Elizabeth did her successor, to keep thereby all competitors and parties in hope, fear, and love, and soe make use of all: But this altum sapere with this lord almost marred all.

3. And againe, That by not declareing his heire, both parties had care, if not to serve yet not to discontent him; And againe prevented envy and practice in the one of them towards the other, and preserved his own reputation and authority with both, And kept all dependance of servants and others upon himselfe.

4. Againe let this lords posterity take into consideracōn how this their Ancestor counselled and aided the fall and deposition, (I will not say death,) of king Richard the second his Soveraigne lord, for the love hee bare to Henry the fourth, and the advancement of his own ends; And how that disloyalty and doublenes seemes to bee punished by the searcher of all secrets, aswell in his bereaft of issue male of his body, As in the blouddy and irksome controversies of more then fower generations, that fell into his family through his waveringe and ill settlement of his estate, and other judgments of God. |

A short Corollary.

To summe up all that hitherto from Hardinge hath been said: It is to bee acknowledged that this antient family of the lords of Berkeley was in the dayes of this lord Thomas, and in him, (who in statelynes and magnificence peramounted all his Ancestors,) in the highest exaltation that it had before reached unto, and inriched with the amplest possessions for support of the honor thereof, with a likely

outwardnefs

outwardnefs foe to have continued, which alfo this lords opinion of himfelf feems to bee futable unto : who after the manner of Princes in his ľres and writings would joyne the pronoune plurall to his name in the fingular number, And write, nos Thomas Berkeley dñs de Berkeley, Wee Thomas Berkeley lord of Berkeley ; And daī. in manerio noftro de Portbury, Dated in our manor of Portbury ; And the like, which none of his Anceftors had foe prompoufly before ufed to doe. not, ego.
not, meo.

And it is an eminent enfigne of the greatnes and pious merits of this family, That one no more travelled than my felfe, fhould have feen above one hundred churches and oratories in the Counties of Gloucefter and Somerfet, and in the Cities of Gloucefter, Briftoll, and Bath, (befides as many more in other Counties and places, as mine acquaintances have faithfully related to mee,) having their coates of Armes and Efchucheons, yea fome their pictures, fet up in their windows and walls, in and before this lords dayes, and their croffes formees, in their true bearings, to bee as the fimbriæ, edges or philacteries in the fkirts and borders of many of them, not yet in thefe devaftating times, demolifhed.

And my old age, (now in my great climaterique year of 63,) would think the knowledge rare for any Antiquary now living in this Kingdome, to fhew mee any other race of the Englifh Nobility foe to have continued unattainted for twenty fucceffive generations in a male line, And to have foe eminently excelled in Armes and Almes, as this Berkeleyan family hitherto had done : But now cleaves this noble houfe in funder, rending her poffeffions into fundry parts, by the | default of this overwife lord Thomas, And lyes preffed under blouddy brauls and lawe futes of . 192 . years agitation, between the faid heire male, and heire generall, two cozen germans and their iffues, before they came to peace ; And as old S.r Thomas Harris a ferjeant at lawe in the time of king James once merrily faid to a Sollicitor of the then lord Berkeleys, had with their longe walkings beaten fmooth the pavements betweene Temple barre, and Weftminfter hall, To leave a memoriall whereof, invited my effayes to thefe collections. 489

And henceforth in the lives that follow, it is a kind of misfortune to my labors, That with the life of this lord Thomas ended all that regularity which for many ages had been obferved in th'eftate and houfhold affaires of thefe lords, in the Accompts of their Receivors, keepers of the wardrobe, Steward of houfhold, Clark of the kitchen, Reeves & Bayleys of manors and hundreds, and the like accomptants, which were by their Auditors with fingular care and exactnes, yearly caft up,

and

and preserved ingrossed in parchment, As the marginalls hitherto have witnessed, which henceforth are neglected: And, vbi nullus est ordo, ibi est confusio; All for want of order, is found out of order, and come to wast; And it is a true observation in all great families, That where noe government or order is observed, there consumption followes, if not of all, yet of too great a part of that great mans estate.

490 blank

The Life of James the First   491

The Life of James lord Berkeley son of James, called James the first, stiled in writings Jacobus de Berkeley chivaleir. And Jacobus de Berkeley dñs de Berkeley, **And** Jacobus Berkeley de Berkeley miles **And** Jacobus dñs de Berkeley miles. **And** Jacobus de Berkeley dñs de Berkeley miles. And Jacobus de Berkeley miles dñs de Berkeley. **And** nobilis vir dominus Jacobus Berkeley miles dominus de Berkeley.   Anno. 6. H. 6.

And was tritavus to George now lord Berkeley, the sixth lineall discendent from this lord James.

And may bee called James the Just.

Contemporary with Henry the fifth, Henry the sixth and Edward the fourth from . 1417 . till . 1463.

Whose troubled life I present to his posterity under these thirteen titles . viz:

1.—**His** birth and education . fol : [492]
2.—**His** sutes in lawe . fol : [493, 512]
3.—**A** discourse of the barony of Berkeley and of the precedency thereof . fol : [502]
4.—**His** rewards to servants . fol : [535]
5.—**His** miscellaniæ or various passages . fol : [536]
6.—**His** wives . fol : [538]
7.—**His** issue . fol : [541]
8.—**Berkeley** of Worcestershire . fol : [546]
9.—**Berkeley** of Herefordshire . fol : [545]
10.—**His** seales of Armes . fol : [553]
11.—**His** death and place of buriall . fol : [554]
12.—**His** lands whereof hee dyed seized . fol : [555]
13.—**The** application and use of his life . fol : [556]

His

His birth and education.

492

This lord James son and heire of that Sr. James Berkeley whom formerly I have diftinguifhed by the name of James the welfhman, was born at Ragelan in Monmouthfhire, where his father then dwelt upon his wifes inheritance, under whom hee was fomwhat too indulgently brought up till the death of his father, when fhortly after upon the remariage of his mother to Wiłłm Thomas a gentleman of that nation, his unckle the lord Thomas the fourth of that name, (whofe life is laft related,) then a widdower, and without iffue male, and not intending, (as the fequell declared,) to marry againe, fent for this James and his younger brother Maurice, about the 8th year of king Henry the fourth; where with him at Berkeley Caftle, and at Wotton and other his removeing houfes, this James and his brother Maurice continued, being generally reputed as heires males and inheritable to the barony of Berkeley by virtue of their great grandfathers entaile; And the 19th of Aprill in the eleaventh yeare of the faid king Henry the fourth It was by Articles mutually fealed between the faid lord Thomas, and Sr John St. John knight, agreed, That the faid lords two nephews and heires male James and Maurice, (the one then fixteene years of age, and the other fourteen,) fhould marry the two daughters of the faid Sr. John St. John, wherein they are declared to bee the heires males of their faid unckle, and inheritable to all the lands intayled, if their faid unckle fhould dye without iffue male of his body; And each of them gave to the other fecurity of . 600li. penalty to performe the agreements; Which agreement (if it tooke effect) was foone diffolved by the death of this James's wife; for the faid Thomas by like articles fower years and three monthes after, bearing date the 25th of July in the fecond year of king Henry the 5th agreeth with Sr. Humphry Stafford knight, for a mariage to bee had between his faid nephewe James, and the daughter of the faid Sr Humphry; whofe portion was agreed to bee fix hundred markes; And herein alfo his faid uncle declares this James to bee his heir male to the inheritance intail'd. And this mariage alfo tooke effect, as under the title of the wives of | this lord James more largely doth appeare: But whether the faid lord Thomas really intended, as his agreements purported, that his faid nephews fhould foe inherite him, I determine not, becaufe proofe by oath was made after his death to the contrary.

carta in caftro de Berk: (first occurrence)

carta in caftro de Berk: (second occurrence)

493

His suites in lawe.

This lord James at the deceafe of his faid unckle the lord Thomas was neer about twenty three years old, and at the houfe of the faid Sr Humphry Stafford in Dorfetfhire, whofe daughter not longe before hee had maryed according to the forefaid later articles, whofe chriftian name, (neither of the daughter of Sr John St John,) I could never find in any writing or record. **The** Earle of Warwicke and the lady Elizabeth his wife were either at Wotton or at Berkeley Caftle at the f.^d lords death, whereby they had the advantage to enter upon the faid manor houfe and Caftle, and to poffeffe themfelves of all the evidences of the faid lord Thomas, whereof forthwith they caufed abftracts in many longe rolls of paper of each manor to bee made of all fuch deeds as they tooke not away, moft of which rolls at this time are in the faid Caftle, regained by Willm lord Berkeley fon of this lord James in the tenth year of king Edward the fourth; when having flaine the lord Thomas vifcount Lifle great grandchild of the faid Countes Elizabeth, hee forthwith enforced and plundred the faid manor houfe of Wotton, whereof much is after written in the life of the faid lord Willm **And** to the faid Earle and his wife, as to the more noble and potent party, did all the Executors and greateft fervants of the family of the faid lord Thomas prefent their fervices and adhere.

And the provident Earle to make the poffeffion of the faid Caftle and of the entayled manors, (which hee then alfo got,) the more legall and faire unto him, or at leaft foe to feeme, Hee the 21.th of July, (the 8.th day after the lord Thomas's death,) obtained of king Henry the fifth a grant of the cuftody of all the faid lords lands and Caftle, as longe as they fhould bee in the kings hands, under fuch a valew as fhould bee mentioned in the offices to bee found, by the manucaption of Thomas Berkeley Clarke become the Earles Receivor; which rent the 12.th of June in the next year was remitted to the Earle; And by force of the faid grant in the fame year and in the two next, the faid Earle received the rents, and kept Courts in all the faid manors entayled to the heires males, as the rolls thereof in the names of himfelf and of the lady Elizabeth his wife, without any relation to the kings grant, doe fhewe: whereby it appeareth that the Earle and his wife pretended right to the Barony of Berkeley and to all the manors and lands thereto belonging; which alfoe the anfwer of the lady Margaret their eldeft daughter and co-heire made in Chancery, (mentioned at large in the life of this lords fon,) fheweth to bee true.

494.
pat. 6. H. 5. m: 29.

Court rolls. 5. 6. 7: H. 5. in caftr. de Berk:

Refpon : in Canc: 6. E. 4.

This lord James on the other part, the fifteenth of July, (which was the fecond day after his unckles death whereby their pofting on both fides appeareth,) fueth

out

out of Chancery a writ of diem clit extremum directed to the Escheator of the County of Glouc, to enquire of what manors and lands and of what estate his said unckle dyed seized, and who was inheritable thereunto, (I speak not of other the like writs into fowerteen other Counties sued out by the said Earle,) whereupon twelve of the most worshipfull gentlemen and of the best liveliode within the County of Glouc, (they are the words of an old record,) were impanelled at Glouc the munday before Michaelmas day then next following, And sworne to present according to the tenure of the said writ; what time through the opposition then arising upon the evidence, the jury was adjourned to a further day: But the Earle having, (as it seemeth,) tasted the purpose of the Jury to find against him, procureth the 22th of October following, a second writ out of the said Court, in the nature of a supersedeas, to countermaund the former; This lord James laboreth to have the Jury proceed, and an Inquisition to bee found, And obtaineth a third writ out of the said Court commanding the Escheator to appear in that Court in person; when all the Judges of both benches are sent for by the lord Chancellor, by whose advice an other writ dated the fifth of Novemr. is awarded, whereby the former countermandment is recalled, and the Escheator commanded to proceed upon his first writ of diem clit extrem; And soe the Jury at length give up their verdit, And found this lord James heire male to his said unckle Thomas, And that hee was to inherite the said Castle of Berkeley and the twelve manors of Berkeley, Hame, Appleridge, Alkington, Hinton, Hurst, Wotton, Simondsfall, Came, Cowley, Slimbridge, and Upton St. Leonards, with Advowsons of the Churches of Wotton and Slimbridge and the hundred of Berkeley, and twenty two marks | rent in Frampton upon Seaverne in the County of Glouc., by vertue of the said fine leavyed by the lord Thomas the third in the 23^d year of king Edward the third, and by other affurances by him made, as formerly in his life hath been declared; And that the same were holden of the king in capite by two knights fees and an half; But to all other manors and lands of the said lord Thomas, (Portbury in Somersetshire excepted,) they find the said Elizabeth wife to the said Earle of Warwicke to bee heire. Accordingly shee and her husband, the fifteenth of December following, sue their livery for the same manors and lands, And for five markes paid to the king have their homage respited; And in the fifth of Henry the sixth the said Earle paid his Releefe according, setting over the Releefe of the intayled lands upon this lord James, in perticular names, accordingly to the said Inqusicon; And likewise the lord James the first of the same December for the said Castle and manors intailed doth his fealty; And for ten markes paid into the Hanaper hath his homage respited.

And because this family is now rent asunder, And this Inquisition after the death of the last lord Thomas, the very wedge, (as it were,) that cleaveth it between the two brothers children, the heir male and the heir generall, I will here present this family with the words of an old writing of that time, which age and bad keeping have made almost illegible, in these words. It'm after deces of Thomas late lord Berkeley, unckle to James that now claymeth, upon a diem clausit extremū take before one Robert Glōt, Eschetor of the Shire of Glouc., which was a suffitient learned man, & a sadde, And in his precept to the Shreve of the said County which returned twelve the worthiest Squires of the said shire at Glouc., And the having grete deliberacōn of divers dayes by the space of nyne weeks, And both parties and their Counsells being present, That is to say, Richard Earle of Warr̄ and Elizabeth his wife daughter to the said Thomas, and her counsell on the one party, and the said James and his counsell on that other pty, And all matters shewed to them at that time, as is now, They found the Taill of the said James of the said lordshipp and manors, and would not in noe wise allowe the matteirs on the said Erle is perte; whereby it appereth evidently, That though that were an enquest of office, yet sin it was don openly and by gode Courts of lawe, And the perties being in travers thereof having knowledge and being thereat, and hadden their resonable challenges to the polles by the which all such persons were avoyded and put out by the discretion of the said Escheter, And by the which it was founden, | that the said James had right according to his evidence shewed to them, notwithstanding the great might of the said Earle And that hee and his wife that time were in possession in the Castle of Berkeley, And in all the wholl lordship, having in ward all the evidences thereof with them; upon which office the said James had livery of record.

duo veter: manuscr: in castro de Berkeley.

496

It'm after the said livery was awarded to the said James upon the said office, the said Richard Earle and Elizabeth his wife kept the said Castle lordship and manors with strength divers years, unto the time of our Soveraigne lord king Harry the fifth father to our soveraigne lord that nowe is, upon a remonstrance of the right of this lord James, being greatly displeased with the said Earle, cōmaunded him to voyd the possession thereof; And then after decese of our said Soveraigne lord, the said Richard Earle entred agen in the said manors of Wotton and others, And laid about the said Castle of Berkeley grete multitude of people in maner of warre; In which time were many persons hurt and maymed, and some slayne, for which cause, by mediation and labor of the worshipfull in God Phillip late Bishop of Wircestr̄, the said parties were put in ordinance of the said Bishop and S.r John Iuyn Justice, which to pese the matter for a tyme, ordained to the said Earle the manors of Wotton, Cowley,

Cowley, and Simondfall, for the terme of his life by expres words in writing, not fpecifying as by the courtefy of England as it appeareth ; And to the faid James all the remnant comprifed within his fine, to him and to his heires males of his body according to his title: Thus the two old writings of that time.

This lord James laboureth alfo to fue his livery and to pay his Barons releefe, and to have thefe his lands, (according to the ceremony of the lawe,) out of the kings hands, which through the favor of the time, and the overgreatnefs of the Earle, (not fattisfied with the Inquificon,) hee could not procure.

The ninth of June following in the fixth year of king Henry the fifth, Lionell Sebroke late Steward of [the] houfhold to the faid lord Thomas, is by procurement of the faid Earle brought before the Mayor of Southton, and there depofeth That the faid lord his late mafter, in Chriftmas time in the fourth of that king, (the laft before his death,) | beinge in his withdrawing chamber in his manor of Wotton, fhewed to him, (amongft many other writings,) one old deed of entaill of the caftle and lordfhipp of Berkeley with all the members thereof, made in the time of Robert fitz Harding, which hee then faw and read over; upon his reading whereof his faid lord very haftely fnatched the fame from him, fayinge hee well remembred the contents of that writing.

<small>497
An untrue oath certainly.</small>

<small>cartæ in caftro. de Berkeley.
comp. de Slimbr:
4. H. 5. pro. rec:
in caftro de Berkeley.</small>

And about the fame time John Bone-John vicar of Berkeley, (fucceffor to learned Trevifa,) and one of the faid Lord Thomas Executors, and till his death his Receiver, before the Mayor of Briftoll made oath That the faid lord Thomas about the time of his paffage towards the parts of Britayne, to conduct from thence the Queene of England into England, or about the time that hee was created lord Admirall by king Henry the fourth, enfeoffed him and others of the Caftle lordfhip and hundred of Berkeley and of all his lands within the County of Glouc., and of the manor and hundred of Portbury and of the third part of the manor of Portifhned, and of the manors of Walton and Bedminftre, with the hundreds of Bedminftre and Hareclive, To hold to them in fee without any Condicon, And that the Deed was executed by livery and feifin, & by Atturneament of the Tenants, And that Courts accordingly were holden in the feoffees names.

<small>ch̃res: 6. H. 5. pars. 1.</small>

Thefe and others the like made the Earle foe confident of his right to the wholl Barony, That the fifteenth of June in the fixth of Henry the fifth, hee procured of the king a confirmation of the firft charters of King John of the manor and barony of Berkeley and of all Berkeley herneffe.

ffrom

ffrom the time that this lord James did his fealty in the Exchequer, and was thereby and by the refpiting of his homage accepted the kings tenant in cheife for his Barony, hee for two years togeather continued the poffeffion of his faid Caftle of Berkeley and of moft of his faid entailed manors: After which time the faid Earle, incouraged afwell by the former Affidavits and other of like kind, as by the affiftance of all the greateft fervants to his late father in lawe, (as after I fhall touch,) came with great force and befeiged the faid Caftle, wherein the faid James then was: Howbeit upon the refort thither of Phillip Morgan then Bifhop of Worcefter, (in whofe dioces it then was,) and of divers others of great worfhip, they ceafed that great ryot, and caufed the faid Earle to leave the Seige and to depart: Thus faith that record.

vetus manufcr: in caftro de Berkeley.

498 bill. in Canc. 6. E. 4.

And yet in that mean time, the firft of Aprill in the feaventh of Henry the fifth, this Earle of Warwicke had a privy feal from the Cuftos of England, not to bee fued or impleaded by this lord James or any other.

Rot. franc. 7. H. 5. m: 11.

This lord not finding in himfelfe fufficient ftrength to wraftle wth foe potent an adverfary, And confidering that all the old and principall fervants of his unckle had turned their intelligences againft him, And that hee was deprived of his antient evidences, wifely winneth with his purfe the affiftance of Humphry Duke of Gloucefter the kings brother; And privately at London the firft of November in the 8th of Henry the fifth, (about one year after the faid Seige,) becometh bound to Tyrrell and Sherington, (men whom the Duke much trufted,) in ten thoufand markes, to pay them one thoufand markes within one year and an half after hee fhould have fued livery of his Caftle and lordfhip of Berkeley and have the quiet poffeffion thereof, (from whence it feems the faid Earle had lately ejected him,) And to grant to the faid Duke the revercōn in ffee Simple of all his lands in Wales and elfe where to the valewe of four hundred markes by the year, which were the inheritance of his mother; favinge only to himfelfe an eftate therein for his own life after the fame fhould bee recovered: But if by means of the faid Duke hee the faid James could not get livery of his faid Caftle and lordfhipp of Berkeley out of the kings hands, Then the faid bond of ten thoufand markes to bee void.

carta in caftro de Berkeley.

By this clofe compact this lord James who before was as a weak hopp, havinge now got a ftrong pole faftly to wind about, grew up and bore the fruite of his own defires; And within few months after in Michaelmas Terme in the ninth of the faid king, upon a petition to the king feconded by the Said Duke of Glouc., had licence

Rec. in fcaccio cum rem. thes. 9. H. 5. term Mich. rot. 1. lib: reliors. 9. H. 5. cm rem thefaur̄.

licence to sue his livery of the said Castle and lordshipp of Berkeley, And payeth, as the Releefe of a Baron and peere of the Realme, one hundred markes according to the Statute of magna charta for his inheritance soe intailed, and found by Inquisicõn | fower years past as aforesaid; which saith this record are holden per servicium vnius baroniæ integræ, by the service of an intire barony, And for better proofe of the tenure soe to bee, voucheth that excellent record in the same office in the fourth of Edward the third, formerly mentioned in the life of his great grandfather, Thomas lord Berkeley the third of that name. And herewith also agreeth the Escheators Accompt of this County in the second year of Henry the sixth.

margin: 499 Baronia.
Comp. Escaet: 2. H. 6. in baga de pertic: in sc*c̃io cum rem: thes:

And then also the second of September is this lord first brought into the Comission of the peace in this County of Glouc., and first of all other therein named. And the king the twentieth of the next month sent his writ to this lord to bee at the parliament the first of December following, as hee then did to other peeres of the Realme: And being in the said somons of parliament named the last of all other Barons, it may bee conjectured That his writ was sealed and sent by it self after hee had paid his Releefe in the Terme before, for in other somons of parliament hee is named. with the first, or first of all. And by his being in the said Comission of the peace the said second of September the same ninth yeare named the first Comissioner of all the fowerteen therein, And this being seaven weeks before the somons of parliament, And hee placed before the Judges, It may give assurance That hee was taken for a Baron from his unckles death, though not called to the parliament till after.

margin: pat: 9 H. 5. ps. 1.
Rot. parliam. 9. H. 5. in dorso.
claus: 9. H. 5. dorso.
pat. roll. 9. H. 5. pars. 1. in dorso.
pat: 10. H. 5. dorso.

And now at whitsontide this yeare did the Tenants of the manor of Cowley, and such others as had stood out or were drawn against this lord, (now become their landlord,) Atturne and recognize their tenures and services, and pay to him their rents; And this was the influence of the foresaid private Articles with the Duke of Gloucester, at this time protector of the Realme, That in this sort soe changed the season of the times and the benefit of the lawes in them; And as a further addition of honor to that private bargaine, (as it may seeme,) this lord James was also about this time knighted, for the 17th of November in the first year of Henry the sixth, I find the Bishop of London, Chancellor of the dutchy of Normandy, to deliver up that seale to the young king at Windsor in the presence of the said duke of Glouc., Richard Earle of Warwicke, and this lord James, by the name of Jacobus de Berkeley chivaler, when, no doubt | they were met at Court about their arbitrement; for the tenth of September before, the said Earle of Warrwicke and this lord

margin: Rot. recogn. tenen. manerij de Cowley. 9. H. 5.
claus: 1. H. 6. m: 19 in dorso.
500

lord James, (by the name of Jacobus dñs Berkeley without miles or chivaler,) had claus: 1. H. 6. m.
mutually entred into feverall recognizances of ten thoufand markes the peece each 12. in dorfo.
to other to ftand to the arbitrement of Phillip Bifhop of Worcefter, Judge Iuyn and
others, concerning all articles wanting any declaration, contained in two Indentures
late made betweene the faid Earle and lord Berkeley; Provided allways that the
Arbitrators meddle not with any fecurity of any manors in the faid Indentures
contained, or of the manors of Wotton, Portbury, Cerney, and Cernecote; And
alfo doe ftand to their award for all futes and debates touching their fervants heretofore moved or depending, (excepting thofe that arofe between their fervants at
Hamerfmyth by London, and of the blows then given, which they have fubmitted
to the Duke of Gloucefter;) Soe that the award bee made before Chriftmas day
next.

Many were the bickerings of the faide Earle and lord James and of their
fervants wherefoever they met: And oftener were the inrodes incurfions and depredations which each of them made upon each others tenants, as after will more
perticularly appeare.

As for the Indentures mentioned in the Condicon of the faid recognizances, I
could never have the hap to receive that light which their perufall would have
given, to the ground of the troubles which fell out upon the faid Earles death.

Upon the faid referance nothing feemes to have been done, for that the Twen- claus: 1. H. 6. m.
tieth of May following they entred into new recognizances of ten thoufand markes 2. in dorfo.
apeece either to other, to performe the award of the bifhops of London and Worcefter and of three others, or of any three of them, or of any other three fit perfons,
by the faid Earle and lord Berkeley to bee named, Soe that the award bee made
before midfomer day next.

Nothing being done upon that fecond reference, A third was to the fame claus: 2. H. 6. m:
parties, for performance whereof the faid Earle and lord Berkeley became bound 18. in dorfo.
mutually each to other in the fum of ten thoufand | pounds apeece, Soe that the
award were made before all Sts day then next, whereupon though noe award was 501
made, yet upon another reference, an award was in part made the 24th of November ex vetufto codice
in the third year of king Henry the fixth compofing part of the differences between manufcr: c̄mWillo
the faid Earle of Warrwicke et reverendum dominum Jacobum dominum de Berke- Oldifworth Ar: de
ley, by the faid Phillip Bifhop of Worcefter and John Iuyn, through the great and medio templo. fo.
unwearied 265.

unwearied labor of the lord Henry Bishop of Winchester, wherein also the said Arbitrators promised their further award before Michaelmas day next after, which was performed on the sixth of October in the fourth year of king Henry the sixth, by the said Phillip Morgan bishop of Worcester and John Iuyn cheife Justice of the kings bench, whereby the manors of Wotton, Simondsall, and Cowley, and divers lands, tenements, and rents in fframpton upon Seavern, Cromall, Acton, Kingscote, Michelhampton in the County of Glouc., and the hundreds of Hareclive and Portbury and the manor of Porteshned, Limeridge wood, Weston in Gordan, and certaine lands in Uphill and Criston in the County of Somerset, were awarded to the said Earle for his life, And the manors of Came, Hinton, and Slimbridge, and all lands tenements and hereditaments in those manors in the County of Gloucester, were (amongst others) awarded to the said Lord James and the heires males of his body.

carta in castro de Berkeley.

And thus was peace setled for the Joynt lives of the said Earle and this lord James, which held for thirteen yeares, till the Earle dyed, both of them then newly marryed to their second wives, as in fit places shall bee delivered: what the Earle gained I know not, but this peace I am assured cost the lord James soe deere, having no personall estate from any of his Ancestors, and none of the portion of his first wife, that hee became much indebted; a continuall borrower, and often of small sums, and some of those upon pawnes, yea of Church vestments and Altar-goods; And recovered not himself in estate, (through the worser troubles that fell upon him after the death of the said Earle,) whilst hee lived, Soe that he lived and dyed in a farr meaner port and condition than any of his Ancestors from the dayes of Harding the Dane. |

Of the Barony of Berkeley and of the precedency thereof.

502

Havinge now the advantage of a place most proper for that purpose, I will deliver mine opinion of the place and precedency of George now lord Berkeley amongst his fellow Barons, in the assembly of parliament or other honorable meetings; which is the discharge of the promises I made in the life of Robert the first, when I treated of the first grant of this Barony of Berkeley made to the said Robert and his heirs, makeing the question to bee, (as made it is,) whether the lord George shall take his precedency from the said Robert the first, made a Baron by king Henry the second in the first of his raigne, Or from the death of the said lord Thomas the fourth that dyed in the fifth year of King Henry the fifth, Anno. 1417, leavinge issue Elizabeth his onely daughter and heire, maryed to Richard Beauchamp

Earle

Earle of Warwicke, as often formerly hath been declared; Or from the call by writ of king Henry the eighth in the fourteenth year of his raigne, made to Maurice the sixth, As after followeth in his life. fol: [634]

In the life of the said lord Robert the first, I have mentioned three sorts of Baron, 1st by tenure. 2d by writ, and 3d by patent or creation; And how the said lord George is a Baron by tenure, And not called originally by writ nor by any patent creation, which is a truth past all question upon the records hitherto mentioned in the life of each lord untill the death of the said lord Thomas the fourth. And that this lord James tooke not his place of precedency from the time of his unckles death, neither was called anew by any writ, but that hee was, upon the inherency of the dignity to the honor and splendor of the Castle and manor of Berkeley, setled at this his first parliament in the ninth of king Henry the fifth, within a few weekes after his livery sued, (what time the said Elizabeth was livinge,) upon the cushion of his old Ancestors, is also as certaine. fol: [37]

It will bee denyed at the first chop, That at the parliament in the 9th | yeare of Henry the fifth when this lord James was first called thereto, That the said Elizabeth was then livinge; And urged will this family bee to prove it; for soe (as I have heard) more then twenty years past was this lord Abergavenny put to doe, when hee vouched this president in proofe of his assertion, before Robert Deverox Earle of Essex then Earle Marshall. 503

First therefore to prove her death is her Epitaph before mentioned, which declareth That shee dyed the 28th of December in the first year of Henry the sixth. Anno. 1422. as are the collections of Heralds in their traditionary bookes, and divers old manuscripts; which is much confirmed by the will of her husband, proved in the prerogative Court of Canterbury seaventeen years after. And there is one Court roll amongst the evidences of the lord George Berkeley, holden in the ninth year of Henry the fifth after the somons of the said parliament, stiled Curia Rĩci de bello campo et Elizabethæ vxoris ejus &c: And at a reference to Judges in serjeants Inne hall, in the times of controversy between Henry lord Berkeley and Robert Sidney now Earle of Leicester, in October Anno quinto Jacobi Regis, his Counsell, (himself then present,) shewed forth an Accompt of a manor proving her livinge in the first of Henry the sixth, And no doubt but with his lordship and Sr. ffulke Grevill lord of Warwicke Castle are many others of like kind. fol: [478]

Rot. Curiæ in castr. de Berkeley.

Amongst

Amongst the prefentations in Trinity Terme in the 4th of Henry the fixth in the Exchequer, it doth appear that the Sheriffs of Gloucefter and other Counties had in Michmas Terme in the firft and fecond of Henry the fixth returned her dead: And thefe kind of Records and the writs of Hillary Terme in the firft of Henry the fixth, in divers Counties where fhee had lands of inheritance, (formerly mentioned,) do make the time of her death certaine after that parliament of the ninth of Henry the fifth was ended.

<small>Trim: 4: H: 6. rot. 2. ex parte rem. thefaur: inter prefentacoes et dies dat:</small>

I have alfo faid in the life of the lord Robert the firft, That a Baron by tenure is hee that holdeth any honor Caftle or manor as the head of his barony in capite per baroniam which is grand Serjeanty: Now if the Caftle honor or manor foe holden in Baronage, (as moft affuredly this of Berkeley is,) bee alyened without the kings licence or confent it is forfeited to the kinge; | And fuch dignity or eftate is no longer to continue and bee borne, but to bee refumed and extinguifhed in the Crown from whence it was derived, As in ye cafe of Willm de Brufe in the time of Edward the firft, who aliened part of his barony of Brember without licence.

<small>fol: [37]</small>

<small>504
Coke: 2: part: 80. b.</small>

And it is a generall received orthodox opinion amongft all heralds and Antiquaries, That till the time of king Richard the firft or of king John his brother and heire, each man to whom the Crown gave lands to hold by knights fervice in Capite, was thereby made a Baron and peere of the Realme, & had voice in parliament; And that all thofe mentioned in the red booke in the Exchequer, (formerly vouched by mee,) whereof this Robert the fon of Harding was one, to have accordingly certifyed their tenures to king Henry the fecond, father of the faid king Richard and king John, about the 14th of his raigne, where the Barons of that time: But after Barons had a more fpetiall creation by patent, and laftly by writ.

But to draw a little nearer to the point I aime at; If the alyenation bee by licence, it is either made for continuance of his barony honor and lands, in his own name bloud and iffue male, (as this of Thomas the third in the fourteenth of Edward the third was,) or els the fame alienation is made for money or other recompence, or otherwife to a meer ftranger; And hereof enfueth this fecond conclufion or affertion. vizt: That if fuch alienacon bee made for the continuance of the barony in his name and bloud or iffue male, (as many befides the faid lord Thomas Berkeley have in all ages made the like,) Then have fuch iffues male togeather with the Barony bee it Caftle manor or honor foe holden, held alfoe and lawfully enjoye'd the name ftile, title, and dignity of a Baron with their Anceftors place of precedency;

And

And thereof the heires generall or next heires female have been utterly excluded and debarred. And for the proofe of this conclusion or assertion manifold presidents may bee produced, whereof some have happened almost in every age for. 300. years space, namely soe longe in effect as there have beene observacõns thereof; of which kinds take these ten here ensuing. viz!

1. It appeares by Inquisition after the death of Willm de fferrarijs lord of Groby in Leicestershire, That Margaret lady of Groby gave to William fferrars her second son and to the heirs of his body the manor of Groby &c, by vertue whereof the said Willm fferrars and his heires were ever after Barons of Groby.

2. Robert Walleron Baron of Killpeck dyed in the first of Edward the first without heires of his body, And Robert Walleron son of William brother of the said Robert was his next heire; yet notwithstanding the said Robert dying gave to Allen Plogenet son of Alice his sister the Castle lordship and manor of Killpecke with appurtenants, To hold to the said Allen and the heires of his body, as appeareth by the said inquisicõn; by vertue of which entaile, the said Allen was Baron of Killpecke and somoned amongst other barons to the parliaments, And dyed in the 27.th of Edward the first.

3. It appeareth by divers Inquisitions in the time of Edward the third, That John Handlowe in right of Mawd his wife, was seazed of the manor of Holgate, Acton Burnell, and others, for terme of her life, The remainder to Nicholas Handlowe als Burnell son of the said Mawd and John, by a fyne in the kings Court leavyed, And that John Lovell was next heire of the said Mawd, and her first born son by her first husband; And afterwards the said Nicholas was somoned amongst other lords to parliament by reason of the fyne aforesaid, And not the said John Lovell who was next heire to Mawd.

4. Thomas de Beauchamp th'elder Earle of Warwicke, by a fyne leavyed in the 18.th of Edward the third, entailed the Castle and manor of Warwicke with other possessions to himself for terme of his life, The remainder thereof to Guy his eldest son and to the heires males of his body; And for want of such heires males, The remainder to Thomas Beauchamp brother of the said Guy and to the heires males of his body &c: Afterwards the said Guy dyed without heires males of his body, leaving two daughters and heires livinge: Afterwards the said Earle dyed, And the said Thomas the son entred into the Castle and manor aforesaid with the other possessions,

possessions, And was Earle of Warwicke by reason of the Entayle aforesaid, notwithstanding that Katharine daughter | of Guy and next heire to Thomas th'elder the Conuzor,[1] was living thirty yeares after his death: And this later Thomas was father of our Richard Beauchamp, and the man that articled the mariage with Thomas lord Berkeley the fourth, as before in his life is declared.

5. **Richard** Earle of Arundle, by a fine leavyed in the first of Edw.d the third, entailed the Castle, Town and manor of Arundle with other lands, to himself and his heires males begotten on the body of Ellenor his wife; by vertue of which entaile John lord Maltravers was Earle of Arundle after the death of Thomas the Earle, who dyed without issue in the third of Henry the fifth; Although the sisters of the said Earle Thomas possessed divers manors and honors, of the which the said Thomas dyed seized in ffee simple.

6. **John** de Vere Earle of Oxford seized in his demesne as of ffee taile to him and his heires males of his body issuinge, of the honor and County of Oxford, with divers other lands, dyed in the 18th of Henry the 8th without heires males of his body, And his three sisters were his next heires generall; But John de Vere his next heire male was Earle of Oxford by reason of the said entaile, And none of the three sisters obtained the dignity.

7. **William** lord Paget of Beaudesert was seized in his demesne as of ffee of the Baronies of Langden and Hawood, and of and in the manors of Beaudesert Langden &c: And being soe seized, by fine in the fifth of Queen Mary, entailed the baronies and manors aforesaid to him and the heires males of his body issuing, And afterwards in the fifth year of Queen Elizabeth dyed, leaving Henry his son next heire male; which Henry entred into the said baronies and lands, and dyed thereof seized in the 11th of Elizabeth, leaving Elizabeth his only daughter and heire; After whose death Thomas Paget brother and heire male of the said Henry entred into the Baronies and manors aforesaid, and was somoned to the parliament by vertue of the said fine.

8. **Robert** lord Ogle entred into the Barony of Bothall and Ogle wth divers other manors and lands in the County of Northumberland, by | conveyance, which was to himself for terme of his life, the remainder to the heires males of his body begotten; And hee tooke to his first wife Dorothy Withrington, by whom hee had issue Robert Ogle his eldest son, and Margaret his daughter maryed to Gregory Ogle

---

[1] Conuzor—from Fr. *Connoisant*, knowing or understanding: as, "if the son be conusant and agree to the feoffment, &c."—*Co. Litt.*, 159.—[ED.]

Ogle of Chippington; And the said Robert the father, after the death of the said Dorothy his wife, tooke to his second wife Jone Ratcliffe, by whom hee had issue Cutbert his second son, and after dyed: After whose death Robert the son was lord Ogle, from whom the same discended to Cutbert, being brother of the half bloud, by vertue of the said entaile, and not to the said Margery nor unto her heires being of the wholl bloud unto the said Robert the son.

9. **Thomas** de la Ware dyed seized in his demesne as of ffee taile to himself and to the heires of his body issuing, by reason of a fine leavyed in the time of his Ancestors, of the Barony de la Ware, with divers other lands in divers Counties, and dyed in the fifth of Henry the sixth without heires of his body; And Reginald West knight of the half bloud, was nephew and heire by reason of the Entaile aforesaid, and was somoned to the parliament by the name of Reginald lord de la Ware knight, Although John Griffith was heire generall of the aforesaid Thomas de la Ware being of the wholl bloud, as appeareth by the genealogy ensuing. viz: John de la Ware son of Roger had issue John de la Ware, and Katharine maryed to Nicholas Latimer; The said John son of John had Roger de la Ware, who by Elizabeth his wife daughter of Adam lord Wells had issue John de la Ware, who dyed without issue, and Thomas de la Ware who also dyed without issue; The said Roger de la Ware, by Elizabeth his second wife daughter of the lord Mowbray, had issue Jone maryed to S: Thomas West knight, who had issue S: Reginald West, lord de la Ware by the said Entaile: The said Katharine, wife of Nicholas Latimer, had issue Katharine maryed to [Thomas[1]] Griffith who had issue John Griffith heire generall to the lord de la Ware.

10. **And** quid obstat, what lets, That I may not paralell the foresaid Thomas lord Berkeley and this lord James his nephewe with these former presidents, And made their case thus.

Thomas lord Berkeley, grandfather of the said Thomas, was seized in his demesne as of ffee of the Castle manor and barony of Berkeley &c: And by him a fyne was leavyed in the kings Court by licence in the 23th of Edward the third of the said Castle manor &c: To him for terme of his life, The Remainder to Maurice his son and to the heires males of his body coming, with other Remainders over; The which Maurice had issue Thomas lord Berkeley and James Berkeley, knight; which James dyed in the life of his brother leaving this James his son and heire livinge. Afterwards the said Thomas lord Berkeley dyed in the fifth of Henry the fifth,

Banks' Baronage. Vol. II. p. 161.—[ED.]

fifth, leaving Elizabeth his onely daughter and heir maryed to Richard Beauchamp Earle of Warwicke: After whose death James his nephewe on his brothers side entred into the said Castle, manor, lands and remainder aforesaid, by vertue of the said entaile, And was somoned to the parliament as Baron of Berkeley in the ninth yeare of Henry the fifth assoone as his livery was sued, Although Elizabeth was then living, and dyed not till the first of Henry the sixth as before is declared.

And if all these noble families mentioned in these foresaid nine presidents have had their places of precedence according to the places of their Ancestors, (whereto more may bee added,) why not then this lord James, And consequently the lord George Berkeley that now is, as his heire male, Anno. 1620. And that this lord James so tooke his place in that parliament in the nynth of Henry the fifth, and in the somons of parliaments in the. 4th 7th 10th 11th 12th 13th 15th 18th 20th 23th 25th 27th 28th 29th and 38th yeares of Henry the sixth, And in the first and second of Edward the fourth, appeareth by the Rolls of somons thereof, in all which hee was placed the first Baron of all. And if noe just order were therein observed, yet it seemes strange that it should still so fall out by chance: But if order of place were observed, then certainly it was for his true place of precedence, and not for the honor of his age, (then under forty,) nor for any office of state, for hee had none. **And** as the fathers place stood in these rolls of somons to parliament, soe was his son the lord Willm ranked after him all the residue of Edward the fourth his time, till hee was created viscount Berkeley: Neither is any thing (for ought I know) to the contrary, save whilst Thomas de la Ware Clark was lord de la Ware in the times of [Rich. II., Hen. IV., Hen. V.,] and of Henry the sixth, who for the honor of his preisthood was ranked before others.

Rot: claus: in ijsdem annis in turre in dorso eodem

claus: 9. E. 4. dorso.

509   **And** if question should arise hereafter between the said lord George Berkeley and the lord de la Ware, (both at this time in their minorities,) for precedency of place, As I have heard it is likely to doe, in that the lord Berkeley thinketh his Ancestor was unevenly in the time of Queene Elizabeth placed next above his grandfather: mee thinks the place and honor of precedence should belonge of right to the said lord Berkeley, whether wee consider their places from their first Ancestors, or whether but from the discents of their Ancestors severall Entailes; Sith this of the lord Berkeley was cast upon his Ancestor this lord James in the fifth of Henry the fifth; And that of his upon Sr Reignold West but in the fifth of Henry the sixth, ten years after; and hee also but of the halfe bloud, as is before declared; And the fine of the Lord Berkeley in the xxiiith of Edward the third to

the

the heires males was, (as I take it,) before the entayle that advanced the said Sir Reignold West to the Barony of de la Ware.

And somewhat the better to informe the younger yeares of the lord George Berkeley, I will comend to his consideration the case of the late lord de la Ware, and the resolution it received, not unfit for this place and question, mentioned by Sr. Edward Coke in the 11th part of his reports, which was thus.

Thomas lord de la Ware, in the third of Edward the sixth, being in some displeasure with Willm West his nephewe and heire, who was father to Thomas late lord de la Ware, procured an act of parliament by the which the said Willm West was during his naturall life cleerly disabled to claime demand or have any manner of right, title, or interest, by discent, remainder or otherwise, in or to the manors lands Tenements or hereditaments, title or dignity of Thomas lord de la Ware his uncle. Afterwards the said Thomas de la Ware dyed, and the said Willm West was in the time of Queene Mary attaynted of treason by verdit, And afterwards pardoned by Queene Mary, And afterwards by parliament in the time of Queene Elizabeth restored; And after in the eighth yeare of her raigne was created lord de la Ware by patent, and had place in parliament according to his creation by patent, for that by the said act of parliament in the third of Edward the sixth hee was excluded to challenge the former antient Barony, And after hee dyed: whether the now lord de la Ware should take his place according to the antient barony by writ, or according to his fathers creation by patent, was the question: The opinion of her Maties Atturney generall and Sollicitor was, That the acceptance of the new creation by the said Willm West, could not extinguish the antient dignity in him at the time of his creation; but the dignity was at that time by the act of parliament in the third of Edward the sixth in abeyance, suspense, or consideracōn of law, and hee thereby utterly disabled to have the same duringe his life only. Soe as other acceptance could not extinguish that dignity which hee then had, nor could not exclude his heire, who was disabled by the said Act of the third of Edward the sixth to claime the antient Barony: wch opinion of theirs was seen and allowed by the resolution of the cheife Justice of England and lord cheife Baron, and soe signifyed to the lord Keeper.

Coke. 11. part. fo: 1. sur. de la wares case.

But note by the reasons made for the said resolution; That if the said Willm West had been Baron and intituled or in possession of the antient dignity when hee accepted the said creation, the lawe perchance might have been otherwise, but that

remaineth

Coke. reports ps. 7 fol:

remaineth as yet unresolved: Neverthelefs the rule is Eodem modo quo quid conftituitur, diffolvitur; But by a grant which is but a matter of fact, a man cannot transfer his title of honor. Whereupon at the faid parliament in the 39th of Elizabeth the lord de la Ware in his parliament robes, was by the lord Zouch, fupplying the place of the lord Willoughby within age at that time, And Henry lord Berkeley alfo in his robes, brought into the houfe, and placed in his place next after the lord Berkeley, (faid the booke,) but therein is the queftion. Thus Sr Edward Coke.

Coke. ps. 11. fo. 1. privil: of parliamt fol: 30.

And further That in all the aforementioned fommons to parliaments, the lord de la Ware is almoft the laft in place in thofe Rolls: And alfo I have obferved, That from the firft fomons of parliaments that is of record in rotul: claufaȝ in the Tower, vizt from the 49th of Henry the third to the forefaid fifth of Henry the fifth, the writs directed to the lord Berkeleys are almoft allways entred in thofe Rolls before | the writs to the lord de la Ware, whereof I have obferved the moft parliamentary yeares.

fol: [654]

And for calling Maurice the fixth to the dignity of lord Berkeley, conferred upon him by Henry the eighth before mentioned, the fame was but perfonall; at what time the barony of Berkeley, by reafon of the entaile of Willm lord Berkeley in the third of Henry the feaventh made to that kinge, and the heires males of his body, as followeth in the next life, was in abeyance fufpence or confideration of the lawe, as before is refolved in the cafe of the lord de la Ware; Neither was the faid Maurice, nor Maurice his father brother and heire of the faid William, either Barons in effe or in poffeffion of the antient dignity, when that honor was by king Henry the 8th conferred upon him: Neither could the acceptance or continuance of the dignity by Thomas his brother, or by Thomas fon of the faid Thomas, bee any barre or hindrance to his fon Henry, when through want of iffue male of the body of king Henry the feaventh, the faid Henry entred upon his Anceftors dignity Barony honor and manor of Berkeley in the firft year of Queene Mary, both as right heire to the faid lord Willm the Conuzor, (the laft remainder man in the faid fyne,) And alfo by difcent of the antient dignity from the firft lord, which could not bee extinguifhed; And whereto the faid lord Henry feemes the rather remitted by his minority, being at the death of King Edward the fixth but nineteen years old, as after followeth in his life: And foe I conclude That the now lord George, notwithftanding all objections to the contrary, ought to have his honor and precedency from the firft year of Henry the fecond, And before the lord de la Ware: And now I returne to the former troublefome title of this lords fuites in lawe.

fee after fol: [727]

Of

Of this lords lawe suites.

The said Richard Earle of Warwicke dyeth the thirtieth of Aprill in the 17th of king Henry the sixth, Anno. 1439. And the 6th day of September following, an Inquisition after his death is taken at Gloucester, finding that hee dyed seized as Tenant by the curtesy of England after the death of Elizabeth his wife, (amongst other lands,) of the manors of Hinton, Came, Cowley, Wotton, and Symondsall, with the Advowson of the Church of Wotton, And that the revercõn thereof in ffee taile belonged to Margaret, Ellenor and Elizabeth his daughters, as heires to the said Elizabeth his late wife, by force of an entaile made in the time of kinge Henry the third, by Maurice then lord Berkeley, to himself and Isable his wife and to the heires of theire two bodies, the remainder to the right heires of the said Maurice; And accordingly the said Inquisition deduceth down the discent of that entaile to the said Countes Elizabeth and her three daughters, Avoiding the fine to the heires males in the 23th of Edward the third, (often before mentioned,) by a remitter in Maurice son of the lord Thomas the Conuzor.

Escaet: 18. H. 6. in turre.
Rec: sub magno sigillo.
fin: 17. H. 6. m: 4.
fin: 19. H. 6. m. 11.

And further finding, That as Tenant by the curtesy of England the said Earle Richard likewise dyed seized of the manor of Slimbridge with the Advowson thereof, the revercõn in ffee taile after his decease to his said three daughters belonginge, by force of a guift in franke mariage made by Roger Berkeley lord of Dursley, longe after the coronation of king Richard the first, to Maurice Berkeley and Alice his wife daughter of the said Roger; And in like manner deduceth down the discent in taile to the said three coheires, And avoyd thereby the fine to the heirs males by a Remitter in Maurice aforesaid.

Against this Inquisition or office and these old rusty Entailes therein found, (which begat more trobles and expence then is credible,) it may seem this lord James had roughly resisted; for the second of July before, the greatnefs of his adversaries had caused him to bee committed to the Tower, from whence the 14th of that month hee was brot before the king into the Chancery, and there entred into a recognizance of one thousand pounds to appear againe there personally, tres Miches after, and foe from day to day till hee should bee dismissed, and further to abide the order of that Court: Whereupon I gather hee was then released out of the Tower, for the 28th of September following hee was somoned to the parliament which began the 12th of November, where hee was one of the tryers of petitions: A like course whereunto they tooke by turning him out of the Comission of the peace, and subsedy, and all other Comissions that resented any command lustre or authority

claus. roll. 17. H. 6. m: 5.
eodẽ. m: 5. in dorso.

Rot. parliam. 18. H. 6.
claus: 18. H. 6. dorso.
franc: 30. H. 6. m: 6. 12. et ult.

I VOL. II

authority in his Country, when in the 29th and 30th yeares of this king they oppreffed him and his fons, as after followeth ; At what time his adverfaries had the greateft authorities and offices of honor and power the Crowne could give, And indeed were themfelves the upholders of the kings regality and Crowne.

Vafcon: 31. H. 6. m. 2. 5. 7.

Two years after, viz! the fecond of November in the 19th of kinge Henry the fixth, was alfo another Inquifition after the faid Earles death, by vertue of a quæ plura, found at Cirencefter, which intituled the faid three coheires partly as heires in fee Simple, and partly as heires in generall taile, to a great quantity of land within every of the aforefaid manors, and of the other manors of this lord James, more then was comprehended in the former Inquifition of the 17th of king Henry the fixth ; which apparently declareth how all the deeds and evidence of the lord Berkeley had been under the canvafing and moft narrow view of the faid Earle and his Counfell, which Inquifitions not only remaine in the Tower of London, but their tranfcripts alfo in the Exchequer, and in the bags of the Efcheators Accompts there to this day : whereto I may add the two offices found in one yeare in the fame County of the like quality in the 7th of king Edward the fourth, the one after the death of the faid lady Margaret, the other after the death of her fifter the lady Ellenor.

Efcaet. 19. H. 6. poft mort. Riĉi Beauchamp.

A like Office was alfo, the forefaid 17th of king Henry the fixth, found after the faid Earles death, in the County of Somerfet ; whereby his faid daughters and coheires were intituled to the manor of Portbury and other lands there : Howbeit the faid lord James had, the 18th of July before, obtained the cuftody of them from the king from the death of the faid Earle till the feaft of all Saints after, according to the Statute of the eighth of king Henry the fixth.

Efcaet. 17. H. 6. in turre. Orig: in fcaĉio. 17. H. 6. Rot. 23. Portbury fines. 17. H. 6. m. 3.

514

Upon returne of which Inquifitions, (which paft all queftion were very indirectly carryed,) this lord James found himfelf much wronged ; but being overpreffed with the greatnefs of the three Co-heires and theire powerfull hufbands, and with the extraordinary favour which they had with that weake kinge, and efpetially with Queene Margaret who ruled and over ruled all affairs, could not avoid them: yet for three years or thereabouts after the returne of thofe Inquifitions hee kept the poffeffion of the manors of Cowley, Wotton, and Symondsfall, (as always hee did of Came and Hinton,) but thereupon fprunge up fuch contentions, fuites, quarrelings, bloudfheds and other mifcheifes, as are irkfome in theire very remembrance, continuing five or fix years togeather. A fmall taft whereof, take[n] out of a Starchamber

Hillar: 18. H. 6. rot. 2. in fcaĉio cum rem. regis.

fub figillo in caftro de Berkeley.

chamber order made on Satturday the 12th of September in the 23th of king Henry the sixth, then sitting at Westminster, the kings Counsell, the Chancellor, Treasorer, privy seale, the Duke of Suffolk, and the cheife Justice; where, the parties themselves all appearinge, It was agreed That all distresses taken between them and their tenants should bee delivered by a writ of replegiare, And not to be eloyned[1] into forren shires; And that both the said parties should thenceforth bee of peaceable bearing for themselves their tenants and servants, not attempting any thinge to the breach of the peace; And thereupon the said James had licence to depart into his Country, with this comaundment, That hee should againe appeare in Hillary Terme following in his own person; for which and for observing of this order hee became bound in two thousand pounds, And the Earle of Shroesbury husband to the said Margaret in the like sum, by his Counsell: And hee that searcheth into the books of that Courts orders from the times of these first offices till the end of that kings raigne, shall find matter of riot, force, violence, and fraud, enough to blot more paper then I intend in the wholl life of this lord: And shall also find Willm this lords eldest son, the 11th of May in the 24th of Henry the sixth, comanded under the great seale of England upon his allegiance to appeare forthwith before the kings Counsell to answere his misdemeanors in these buisinesses.

bria regis : 24. H. 6. pars. 1. in turre.

Of these stirrings take also a litle further tast out of the Court of Common pleas in the 18th of king Henry the sixth, which shews how David Wodburne with divers others of his fellow servants, by direction of their master John Talbot viscount Lisle, (son and heire of the said Margaret,) cominge to Wotton, served this lord James with a subpena for his appearance in the Chancery: Insteed of obeying the proces, this lord James not only beat the parties, but will hee nill hee, inforced the said David to eat the subpena, wax and parchment; for which severall actions were forthwith brought against this lord James and his men, by the said lord Lisle and his man David.

Mich : term. 18. H. 6. rot. 126. 421. et 567.
515
Trin : and Easter termes : 18. H. 6. rot. 279. et. 180.

Of these stirrings also in these times, take a further tast out of the Court of Chancery, wherein William lord Berkeley shewes, That after the said Earle of Warwicks death, this lord sent fower of his servants and tooke a quiet possession of the manors of Wotton, Simondsall and Cowley, which hee continued by three years and more, untill the said Margaret Countess of Shroesbury by great subtilty and might entred againe upon him, whereupon was made great dispoile, robbery, murder, and many other inconveniences and heynous mischeifes, to the importable hurt

Billa dni Berkeley in Cancellar.

---

[1] Eloine, (from the Fr. *Esloigner*) signifies to remove—to send a great way off.—[ED.]

hurt of the said lord James and the lady his wife, and in effect to their utter destruction and of their children: Thus the bill.

fran: 18. H. 6.
m: 9.
Mich: pasch: Trin.
38. H. 6. in scᵃčio
Mich: 3. E. 4. rot.
51. in sc čio:
Pasch: 4. E. 4. rot.
9. in scᵃčio c̄m
rem̄. thes:

And the same year, the said three Coheires and theire husbands arraigned an Assize of novell disseizin against this lord and the lady Isable his wife, and Wiłłm Berkeley knight their son and heire, for the foresaid manors of Came, Slimbridge and Hinton.

And contrarily this lord James arraigned his Assize of novell disseisin also against the said three Co-heires and theire husbands for the said manors of Wotton under edge and Cowley.

claus: 19. H. 6.
m: 20. in dorso.

These suites and many others, the 18ᵗʰ of ffebruary in this 19ᵗʰ yeare, brought a reference to Hody cheife Justice of the kings bench, Newton cheife Justice of the Comon-pleas, and ffray cheife Baron, arbitrators indifferently chosen by all the said parties to decide the controversies that were amongst them, for any the lands that were Thomas late lord Berkeleys in the Counties of Gloucester and Somerset, Soe that their award were made before midsomer day then next; And to stand to their award each party became bound to other in severall recognizances of 5000 markes the peece. |

516
eodem in dorso
m. 6.

And when noe end was by that day made by the said Arbitrators, All the said parties renewed their reference to them againe in like maner as before And each became bound to other in the like sums the 12ᵗʰ of July after, soe yᵗ theire award were made before Octabis Michis then following: Neither came any end from this reference, But the 24ᵗʰ of October following John lord Talbot husband of the said lady Margaret obtained from the king a protection from all suites for a year then followinge.

Rot. franc: 20.
H. 6. m. 24.

Rot. parliament.
20. H. 6. m. 11.

Whereby (as it seemes) this lord James finding himself bound up from the comon liberty of a subject and peere, tooke such exception, That the lord Talbot in January following petitioned to the parliament then in being, to have from the parliament a protection allowed to him, and a stay of all suites, duringe his absence in France in the kings service, which hee obtained for a yeare; But with this provisoe That if either hee or Margaret his wife, Edmond Earle of Dorset or the lady Allienor his wife, or Geo: Nevill lord Latimer and Elizabeth his wife, or any of them,

them, or any in their names or by their commandment, enter into any lands or Tenements whereof James lord of Berkeley, and Wiłłm Berkeley knight fon of the faid James, or either of them are feized or were feized the firſt day of this prefent parliament, Then in that cafe the protection fpecifyed in the faid petition to bee difallowable in any action fued upon the lands or Tenements upon which entry is thus made: Provided alfo, That if the faid three Coheires or their hufbands or any of them or theire heires, fue any action againſt this lord James or Wiłłm his fon or their heires, or againſt any of the faid lands or Tenements of the which the faid lord James or Wiłłm is or was feized the firſt day of this prefent parliament, within the faid yeare, Then the faid protection to bee void and of no force in lawe.

The 19th of ffebruary in the faid twentieth yeare of king Henry the fixth, near about the time of the former ſtirrings in parliament, A like new reference was by all the faid parties to Fortefcue cheife Juſtice of the kings bench, and to Newton and ffray aforefaid, Soe that their award was made before palmfunday then followinge; And like recognizances of 5000 marks each party gave to other to perform the fame. | claus: 20. H. 6. in dorfo: m: 14.

In which times the faid John lord Talbot was by L'res patents dated the twentieth of May in the Twentieth of king Henry the fixth created Earle of Shroefbury; And fower years after was loaden with new honors in England, France, and Ireland; And Edmond Earle of Dorfet was created Marques Dorfet in the 21th of Henry the fixth, And Duke of Somerfet in the 26th of Henry the fixth; And was great grandchild of king Edward the third: And John Talbot fon of the faid Earle of Shroefbury by the faid lady Margaret his fecond wife, was made lord Lifle, by reafon of the tenure of the manor of Kingſton Lifle in the County of Berks.

cart. ab anno. 1. vfque 21. H. 6. m: 11. 20 n° 14. **517** pat: 8. E. 4. pars. 1. m: 1. pat. 24. H. 6. pars. 2. m: 16. et 26. H. 6. pars. 1. m: 6. Camden in Ireland 76. D. et. 80. C. cart: 21. 22. 23. et 24. H. 6. m. 26. n°. 46 et membr. 44. cart. ab anno. 25 vfque 27. H. 6: n°. 9. m. 7. carta in caſtro de Berkeley. petitio in Canc. 15. E. 4. pars. 1. pro Wenlocke.

After all thefe quarrellings and outrages from the 17th to the 26th of Henry the fixth, between the faid three Co-heires and their hufbands of the one part, And this lord James on the other part, the fifth of Aprill that year An award was made between them at Cirencefter by the lord Ferrars, lord Beauchamp, Judge Fortefcue, Judge Yelverton and others Arbitrators; wherein they recite the former award made by the Biſhop of Worcefter and Judge Iuyn in the fourth of Henry the fixth; And now award to the faid three co-heires the manors of Wotton, Simondfall and Cowley in fee fimple: And all the other lands and Tenements which in the 4th of Henry the fixth were by the then Arbitrators awarded to the faid Earle of Warwicke,

wicke, except the twenty two marks rent in fframpton upon Seavern and ten pound rent in Slimbridge, (now called Sages manor;) And to the said James and the heires males of his body they awarded the manors of Came, Hinton, Slimbridge, Hurst, Portbury, and all the other lands then in controversy in those places; And that each party should make to other such further assurance thereof as the s.d two Judges, ffortescue and Yelverton, should devise.

<small>carta in castro de Berkeley.</small>

The said Judges fifteen months after, in July in the 27th yeare of Henry the sixth, did for further assurance mutually to bee made each party to other, further award; That all the said parties should labour instantly to the parliament then in being, That an act might bee had for ratifying their former award; But if the same could not bee procured, Then either party to make to other such security and discontinuances, for to take away all entryes by either party, as they the said Arbitrators hereafter should further devise.

Against this award this lord James much opposed, neither would by any meanes at any time bee drawn to give assent thereto during his life, much less to labor for the parliaments ratification thereof, as was by the Arbitrators directed.

On the other part as great violence was used to enforce him to the performance of that award as law or greatness could cast upon him; which storms to avoid, hee was enforced to keep home and to man his Castle with some strength, for his defence and preservacon: And his sons being also imbroiled in many troubles, kept close with their father: And the good lady Isable his wife was by meere necessity inforced to travell to London, And to become the sole Sollicitor of her husbands law causes; from whence let us hear what that vertuous lady did and howe her husbands causes proceeded, by a lre of her own hand remaining in Berkeley Castle in these words.

To my right worshipfull and reverend lord and husband bee this lre delivered.

Right worshipfull and reverend lord and husband, I commend mee to you with all my whole hart, desyring alwayes to heare of your good wellfare, the which God maintayne and increase ever to your worship. And it please you to heare how I fare, S.r Squall and Squall; Thomas Roger and Jacket have asked surety of peace of mee, for their intent was to bringe mee into the Tower, But I trust in God to morrow That I shall goe in bayle unto the next Terme, and soe to goe home And then

then to come againe; And Sur I truſt to God and you will not treat with them, but keep your own in the moſt manlyeſt wiſe, yee ſhall have the land for ones and end: Bee well ware of Venables of Alderley, of Thom Mull and your falſe Counſell; keep well your place, The Earle of Shroeſbury lyeth right nye you, and ſhapeth all the wyles that hee can to diſtruſſe you and yours, for hee will not meddle with you openly noe manner of wiſe, but it bee with great falſdome that hee can bring about to beguile you, or els that hee cauſed that yee have ſo fewe peopull about you, then will hee ſet on you, for hee ſaith hee will never come to the king againe | till hee have done you an ill turne; Sur your matter ſpeedeth and doth right well, ſave my daughter coſteth great good; At the reverence of God ſend money or els I muſt lay my horſe to pledge and come home on my feet: keep well all about you till I come home, and trete not without mee, And then all thinge ſhall bee well with the grace of the Almighty God, who have you in his keeping: written at London the wedneſday next after whitſunday.

519

Your wife the lady of Berkeley

This lord James hereupon borroweth twenty two markes of Mr. Nicholas Pointz, whereof to repay twelve marks on midſomer day following, and the other ten markes on Michaelmas day after followinge; for aſſurance whereof hee pawned to him one guilt maſſe booke, a chalice of Silver weighing eighteen ounces, A cheſipull with ſtolys and fanons of red ſattin, three aubes, three amices, one white Autercloth with croſſes of black ſilk therein, with one valence fringed ſewed thereto, of red cloth of gold, one cloth of red palle to hange aſore an aulter of the ſame, an other cloth of the ſame for a reredote, and two ridles of red tartryn.

carta in caſtro de Berkeley.

Hereby this family ſeeth the true fidelity of mariage in a juſt huſband to a correſpondent wife, who would rather ſeeme to disfurniſh God of the ornaments of his worſhip, then leave her neceſſitous eſtate unſupplyed.

And becauſe this lady directeth her lre to her worſhipfull lord, and wiſheth increaſe to his worſhip, I will by a ſhort digreſſion comend to my reader the great honor and eſtimation of the word Worſhip, ſomewhat before, at, and ſomewhat after thoſe dayes, and how ſublime the acceptation thereof then was.

of the word Worſhip.

1. **In** this time of Henry the ſixth, bills and petitions in Chancery were directed unto my right worſhipfull and gratious my lord of Canterbury, chancellor of England.

pat: 23. H. 6. pars. 2. m : 16.

2. **When**

claus: 8. H. 5. m: 10. in dorso.	2. **When** king Henry the fifth out of France, advertized the Duke his brother Custos of the Realme in his absence, the Arch-Bishops, Bishops and lords of his Counsell, of the peace hee had made with ffrance, and of his mariage with the daughter of France, hee directed his lres, To the worshipfull and right worshipfull.	
520 Rot. parliament. 31. H. 6.	3. The Earle of Devon having been acquited of the treason whereof he was accused, complained at the next parliament in the 31th of Henry the sixth That false accusation did right nigh touch his worship, honesty, and truth.
Rot. indic. 1. H. 4. in turre.	4. **In** the first of Henry the fourth It was adjudged in parliament That for their offences the Dukes of Aumarle and Exeter, the Marques Dorset, and the Earle of Gloucester, should loose their names and the worship thereof.
Rot. parliament. 5. H. 4. m: 16.	5. Henry Percy Earle of Northumberland in excuse of the crime objected, did by his petition pray the kinge to have in remembrance his coming into his worshipfull presence to Yorke, of his own free will.
Rot. parlia: 7. H. 4. pars. 2.	6. In the seaventh of Henry the fourth, Sr Henry Boyton was authorized to treat with the worshipfull prince, Robert the king of Scotland and his Counsell.
Rot. parliament. 27. H. 6. articl: 18.	7. In the twentyseaventh of Henry the sixth, it is ordered in parliament, That Willm Earle of Arundle shall have his place as worshipfully as any of his Ancestors Earles of Arundell.
claus: 4. H. 6. dorso.	8. In the fourth of Henry the sixth the Earle of Huntingdon, touching the payment of his ransom, sweares by the truth of our lady and our worship, and in word of true knight, That &c.
Caxton. fol: 316.	9. I John Trevisa, vicary of Berkeley, at the request of the right worshipfull lord Thomas lord of Berkeley, have translated Polichronicon out of latin into English, &c. Anno: 1357, in the thirtyfirst of Edward the third.
Caxton fol: 317.	10. In the thirty sixth yeare of Edward the third Anno: 1361. came into England the three kings of France, Cipres and Scotland which were worshipfully received.—**These** ten from more then one hundred the like, in these times observed by mee, suffice in this digression.	
521 bill in Canc. 6. E. 4.	**Nowe** what followeth within three monthes after this ladies fre, read out of a bill in Chancery exhibited by Willm lord Berkeley, son of this lord James, against the

the said Margaret Countefs of Shroefbury; wherein hee fets forth, That the fixth of September in the said thirtieth year of Henry ye fixth, The said Countefs and her hufband being then unjuftly feized of the manors of Wotton, Symondfall, Cowley, the warth, newleyes, and Sages lond, by their fubtile and damnable imaginations, labored, intreated and hired one Rice Tewe, being then fervant to the lord James, to deceive and utterly to deftroy him the faid lord James and his fower fons, Willm, James, Maurice, and Thomas, then being in the Caftle of Berkeley with the faid lord James their father: which faid Rice, having the keeping of the keys of the said Caftle, early in a morning let in the lord Lifle, fon to the faid Earle and Countefs, with great numbers of people warlike arrayed, And there tooke the faid lord James and his faid fower fons in their beds, and there kept them in prifon in great dures by the fpace of eleaven weekes, by the commandment of the faid Countefs; they by all that time knowing noe fuerty nor certainty of their lives, but ever awaiting the hour of their cruell death: And there the faid Counteffe compelled and coharted[1] them to enfeale certaine Indentures of Covenants againft all right and confcience, And after enforced them by might to reherfe the matter contained within the faid unlawfull Indentures, to fuch perfons as were affigned by the faid Counteffe, to their great forrow and heavinefs: And the fourth day of November then next following in the faid thirtieth yeare of Henry the fixth, the faid Counteffe made the faid lord James and his faid fower fons to bee brought to the gray fryars at Briftoll, with great multitude of people warlike arrayed, with force, And there brought to them the Maior and Conftable of the Staple, And there by Dures, compelled them to bee bound in divers feverall obligations and recognizances of the Statute of the Staple in twelve thoufand two hundred and fowerfcore pounds to the faid Earle and Counteffe; At which time they did as they were compelled, for foe much as they durft none other doe, for dread to bee murdered by the faid Earle and Counteffe and their fellowfhipp: And after that they were carryed by the faid Earle and Counteffe and their faid riotous fellowfhip unto the faid Caftle of Berkeley, and there kept ftill in ward, unto the time that | the faid Earle and Counteffe, at that time being in foe great favour with the Kinge, purchafed an oier determiner, granted before certaine of the kings Juftices and Comiffioners at Circefter; At which time the faid lord James and his faid fons were brought thither by force, And there by Dures compelled to anfwer to actions of trefpas brought againft them, and to plead fuch pleas before the faid Judges and Comiffioners as the faid Earle and Counteffe and their Counfell advifed and miniftered unto

---

[1] *Coarted*—compelled, forced. "Dyues by dethe was ftrayteley *Coartid* of his lyf to make a fodeyne tranflacion."—*MS. Land*, 416, f. 101. See Bayley, Afhmole's Theat. Chem. Brit. p. 276, Halliwell. [ED.]

unto them: And alfo the faid Earle and Counteffe compelled them there to make and enfeale feverall releafes of all their right and title that they had or might have in the faid manors, and all other actions, and to knowledge them to bee inrolled of record, which they did for fear of their death: Soe the bill.

Anfwer in Canc: 6. E. 4.

Nowe heare what anfwer the faid Counteffe in her own words likewife maketh: **That** Thomas lord Berkeley grandfather to her the faid Countefs was feized of the faid manors of Wotton, Simondfall, and Cowley, (amongft others,) of a generall eftate tailed to him and the heires of his body cominge, and of fuch eftate of the faid manors dyed feized; After whofe deceafe the fame manors difcended to Elizabeth his daughter and heire, who entred, and tooke to hufband Richard Earle of Warwicke, and by him had iffue her the faid Counteffe and her Copertioners; And that after the death of the faid Elizabeth, The faid Earle of Warwick held him in as Tenant by the curtefy of England, And dyed thereof foe feized; After whofe death the Earle of Shroefbury and fhee his wife and her copertioners, as daughters and heires to the faid Elizabeth, into the fame manors entred, and thereof was feized by force of the f^d. Entayle, unto the time that Willm Berkeley by the affent, commandment, agreement, and will of the f^d. lord James his father, (which at that time kept within the Caftle of Berkeley a great number of right riotous, unlawfull, and evill difpofed people, afwell in felonies, as ryots, affrayes, and other mifgovernances, and unruly demeanings amongft the kings leidge people,) and there affembled to them a great multitude of fuch mifgoverned people arrayed in manner of warre, the faid Earle of Shroefbury (late lord and hufband | to the faid Counteffe) then being in Normandy upon the fafeguard of the dutchy of Normandy, ryotoufly came to the faid manor of Wotton, and entred into the fame, And the gates and doores of the faid manor they brake, and all to hewe and cutt the great and principall timber of the roofes and galleryes, and other nefefaryes fawed and cut in two, The walls, vautes, quines of doors and windows they razed and tere a down, The ferments of iron in the windows, hingyngs for doares and windows, gutters and condutes of lead, afwell upon the houfes as under the earth, they brake and beare away; And the faid manor of Wotton in all that they could defaced and deftroyed, infomuch that the reparations thereof coft the faid Earle Counteffe John vifcount Lifle and their fervants then there being, to the valewe of fower thoufand markes, difpoiled, robbed and beare away; And upon the which ryot and robbery the faid Earle of Shroefbury fued an oier and determiner; And at a Seffion holden at Glouc: by force of the faid oyer and determiner, the faid James lord Berkeley, Willm his fon and other were indited; But the faid James, Willm and the other,

allwayes

allwayes intendinge the continuance of their mischeevous rule and governance, continually enforced them and kept them within the said Castle of Berkeley, which is a stronge and mighty place, Soe that the Sherife nor none other officer of the Shire of Glouc., might not in any wise execute any precepts against them: And right oftentimes they issued out of the said Castle, and beat robbed and dispoiled many of the kings leidges of that Country, And when they or any of them had done such a mischeevous deed, they allwayes resorted into the said Castle, and there were received, defended, and kept, and all that they might rob and pill brought into the same: whereupon the people of the said Country came to the said Viscount Lisle, then being one of the Justices of the peace in that County, and in great number full piteously and lamentably complained to the said viscount of the heinous and mischeevous governances aforesaid, beseeching him to put himself in devoire for their remedy releefe and succour in this behalf; And the said viscount, intending to reforme that abhominable misgovernance, bade the people enquire and espye secretly when any of those theeves and robbers or any of their maintainers were about ryot and robbery, and hee would assay to take them, and bringe to an answer after the kings lawes: And on a night the same Willm Berkeley sent twenty of that same mischeevous men to a Tenants house of the said Earle of Shroesburyes called Richard Andrewes, which was a blind man, dwelling from the said Castle ten miles, to rob the said Richard Andrews, whereof the said viscount had warning that such a fellowship were issued out of the said Castle; And hee tooke a company with him and rode into the Country to assay if hee might meet them; And of the Country that had been evill treated before by the same Willm and his felyship followed them, till they had beset the said blind mans house, And as hee went homewards againe, hee fortuned to meet some of the said viscounts serv^{ts}, and told them how it was, And then the said viscounts servants sent the same man to their master to tell him thereof; And they rode straite in all that they could or might thither as the theeves were, to rescue the blind man if they might, And yet ere they came thither, the Theeves had gotten the house and all the people that were therein, and had upturned every place of the house: And for cause they found but litle good in substance, they tooke a brand iron and set it on the fire till it was glowing hott, And then they tooke the blind man and would have set him upon it, for hee would bee a knowe of noe more good, And through that dread that they soe put him in, hee told them where his good was, and limetted them a place under earth in the same house, wherein they had in money coined as the same blind man did swear and avowe before them, two hundred and fowerscore pounds: And even as they were departing out of the said house, the said viscounts servants set upon them, and

with

with right great and fore fight tooke divers of them, amongſt the wᶜʰ, the foreſaid Rice Tewe was one; And the ſaid Rice in ſavation of his life offered to them that had taken him to get them into the ſaid Caſtle, ſoe that they might take the reſidue of the ſaid riotous miſgoverned and endited people; And ſtreight they rode to the ſaid Caſtle, And wⁿ they come to the Caſtle gate Rice called upon the watch, And anon the ſaid watch went to the ſaid lord James who had the keys in his own keeping, And hee them delivered to one Thomas ffleſhewer then being yeoman of his chamber, who came and opened the wicket gate of the Caſtle, And the ſervants of the viſcount Liſle entred to take the ſaid miſgoverned men, And tooke the place without any hurt or miſdoing to any perſon; And faithfully, otherwiſe then thus was never the ſaid Rice hired entreated or deſired by the ſaid Earle Counteſſe nor none other perſon for them, nor had noe keeping of the keys of the ſaid Caſtle: And further ſaith, that after ſhee came into the ſaid Caſtle of Berkeley where ſhee found the ſaid James and his ſaid ſower ſons, they nor none of them neither were impriſoned nor indureſſed nor coarted to make ſeale declare plead nor confeſſe, the Indentures obligations pleas releaſes before reherſed, nor noe parcell thereof; but were ſuffered to bee in the ſaid Caſtle at their large, And had their learned Counſell and all other their frends and ſervants continually repairing and attending upon them at their pleaſures: And then they conſidering amongſt them the great ryots offences and treſpaſſes in breaking diſpoiling and robbing of the ſaid manor of Wotton, and other divers abhominable deeds which they had done to the ſaid Earle Counteſſe, viſcᵗ, and others, whereof of part they were indited, and conſidering alſo the great and huge coſts which they diverſly put the ſaid Earle and Countes too through their miſguiding, and alſo the great punition which they underſtood they had deſerved after the due courſe of the lawe, likely upon them to enſue and fall, by the advice of their ſaid learned Counſell and of their own frends, freely offered to the ſaid Earle and Counteſſe, the ſaid lands and Tenements called the warth, newleyes, and Sagiſtond, To have to them and their heires for evermore, And made thereof as good eſtates as could bee deviſed by the Counſell of both parties, and more liveries accordinge, and one thouſand pounds in money; wherefore ſuretie was made before the Maior and Conſtable of briſtoll aforeſaid, in recompence of the ryot beating down and defaceing the manor of Wotton aforeſaid, and diſpoiling and bearing away their goods aforeſaid: And to the ſaid viſcount, they offered two hundred pounds for the ſtealing and bearing away of his goods there, which drewe in value better then ſeaven hundred markes; for the payment of which ſums they made ſeverall obligations before the ſaid Maior and Conſtable of the Staple of Briſtoll; And over that the ſaid lord James and his ſaid ſons, by the

the advice of their said learned Counsell and frends, offered to the said Earle and Countesse to remit, releafe and extinct to the said Earle and Countesse and her Copertioners and their heires, all such title interest and clayme as they had, might, or pretended to have in the said manors of Wotton, Simondsfall and Cowley, and to make it sure to the said Earle Countesse and her copertioners, as the said Earle and Countesse counsell should devise, And made there oath in forme aforesaid; for the performing wherof the said lord James and his said fower sons bound themselves their heires and executors to the same Earle and Countesse in the sume of ten thousand pounds: And all these things aforesaid were offered by the said lord James and his sons, they having with them their frends and their learned Counsell, without any Dures constraint coartion or quarrell by the said Earle and Countesse, or of any person on theire behalfe, other then is as aforesaid. **Thus** the answere.

Havinge heard the complaint and defence of both parties, who indeed in their own cases are partiall, Take the truth from him that partakes with neither party; Thus,

This lord James and his fower sons with him, are in the night time the sixth of September in the thirtieth of king Henry the sixth, by the falshood of Rice, surprised in their Castle: And forthwith a Comission of Oyer and terminer is sued forth of the Chancery directed to Judge Bingham, Willm Lucy, and others: The first session whereupon, is at Campden in the remotest part of Gloucestershire, five and thirty miles from Berkeley, upon the fourth day of October following, w^n the said three lady Copertners and their husbands put in their declaration against this lord James and his fower sons, Willm, James, Maurice, and Thomas, grounded upon the Statute of the fifth of Richard the second, for forceibly entringe into their manors of Wotton, Simondsfall, and Cowley; And prayed proces of Attachment to bring the Def^{ts} to answer at Cirencester against the ninth of December following.

At this time this lord James and his said fower sons, (being prisoners | in the power of as angry a lady as I have observed in all my readings,) were between the said two Sessions enforced to seale twelve severall deeds, dated on the 8th 12th 20th and 26th days of October; whereof **One** was a leafe for two years to the said three lady Coperceners and their husbands of the Castle of Berkeley; Saving therein habitacõn and housroome for themselves and six servants; **Others** were deeds of Covenants to make sure to the said Coperceners their said three manors, And that neither this lord James nor his sons should sue, implead, vex, greeve, nor trouble, the

527
Bancus reg. 30. H. 6. rot. 40. 41.

the said ladies nor their husbands by the law nor otherwise, nor none of their servants, adherents, nor Counsellers, but should bee their true cozens, faithfull men, and servants; with an obligation of ten thousand pounds to perform the same; **Others** were releases of all their rights and interests in the said three manors of Wotton, Simondsfall, and Cowley, with generall warranties, and of all actions and appeals, made to them and to eighteen of their servants and kinsmen: **One** other deed was in the nature of a bond of seaven hundred markes for payment of two hundred markes to the said viscount Lisle, in recompence and satisfaction of divers trespasses and wrongs done to him by the said Willm Berkeley, in riotously taking away his goods out of the manor house of Wotton, to the valewe of seaven hundred markes: **And** one other was a feoffment of the manor of Sages the Warth and Newleyes to the said lady Margaret and her heires, in part of recompence for horrid great trespasses and wrongs done to her husband by them and their riotous people, in takinge away the value of two thousand pounds of the said Earles goods out of Wotton; And a releese of the said manor and lands accordingly.

carta in castro de de Berkeley.

And, the 4th of November following, were by an Armed band of men carryed to the gray ffryars to Bristoll, whither John Stanley, then Maior, was sent for; And there before him constrained to acknowledge three Statutes, whereof one of ten thousand pounds, defeizanced by an Indenture between the parties, That if this lord James and his said fower sons should performe all feoffments and grants, and should keep all covenants and promises made between the said parties, Then the same to bee void.

carta in castro de Berkeley.

The second Statute was of two thousand pound to the said viscount Lisle. And the third Statute was by the said Willm and James his brother alone, of two hundred pounds absolute without any defeizances; which done, Then were this lord & his sons hurried back to Berk? with the same rout y^t caryed y^m to Bristoll.

528

And on the ninth of December followinge, this lord James and his fower sons were againe carried from Berkeley to Cirencester, the day and place for the second sittinge upon the said Comission, where in their own persons, (not by Atturny,) they plead, not the generall issue, but their title at large as heir male under the said fyne of the 23th yeare of king Edward the third: **Upon** which day also cometh in the barre, replication, reioynder and surreioynder; whereupon issue being joyned A venire facias is the same day awarded to the Sherife to returne a Jury against the next morninge: **The** Jury are returned from many the remote parts of the County, And

And somoned, (as may seeme,) and appeare, And the same morning try the issue; And find the entayle made in the time of Henry the third to Maurice lord Berkeley the second of that name and to Isable his wife and to the heires of their two bodies, according as was laid down in the Inquisicōn of the 18th of king Henry the sixth, after the death of Richard Beauchamp Earle of Warwicke: And assesse damages to one hundred pounds, and costs of sute to twenty pound, which the plts forthwith remit to the said lord James and his sons, two of whom at this time were under eighteen years of age.

Esch: post mort. marchiōn Berkeley. 8 : H. 7.

Judge Bingham lived twenty eight years after these irregular proceedings, yet never could certify this record thus taken, in all his life time: But the same was certified by his widow upon a writ of certiorare to her directed in the fourth of king Henry the seaventh, as the record it self sheweth: whereby may bee gathered that hee held the shuflinge fowle, howsoever the dealing might seeme faire before him.

Esch: in Com. Wilts 20. E. 4. post mort. Bingham. fine roll: 20. E. 4. m: 14.

This lord James is not yet soe freed but another Inquiry upon the like Comission is at Glouc., where this lady and wife following her husbands businesse as Sollicitor, found worse successe, as a petition by her son Willm exhibited to king Edward the fourth in the fourth of his raigne shall declare in his own words. vizt That the Earle of Shroesbury and lord Lisle beinge of Counsell and singular favor with king Henry the sixth, by that support and favor the Countesse his wife came to Glouc., And there caused an Inquiry by her own men, and strangers, upon the oyer and terminer, and there against all right and conscience, his said lady and mother tooke and imprisoned in the Castle of Glouc.; And by the said support and favor her there kept, Soe that by lawfull processe nor | otherwise shee might not bee delivered, till shee was dead in the most piteous wife that ever was lady of her birth, being discended of your high bloud: And further that the night of the said enquiry, the servant of one Lacon murthered his said master, who longe time had been greatly cherished of him, who being for that murther taken and adjudged to death, confessed hee was tempted to murder his master for his untrue dealing in the said enquest: And that the said Countesse stood soe high in that kings favor, yt shee feared nothing to doe, were it never soe unlawfull; And how shee tooke the lord James his father, himselfe, and his brethren, and carryed them to Cicestre, And they were plainly told by the said Countesse, that if they would not in each thing do as they were required, they should plainly dye: whereupon to their great heavinesse they did whatsoever they would, how prejuditiall so ever to their inheritance and contrary to all right and conscience: And setteth out further, how shee the said

Bill in Canc: 4. E. 4.

Shee was great, great grandchild of Tho: Brotherton son to king Ed: ye 1st
529

Countesse

Countesse put the people of the County to fine and ransome at the utterance of their goods, And they that might not bere, shee caused them by the members to bee hanged: And that shee afterwards caused James and Thomas his brethren to goe beyond seas with her husband, where James was slaine, and Thomas taken prisoner and put to fynance to him importable: **And** that afterwards the said Countesse for two years kept the said lord James his father out of his Castle of Berkeley, and all the tenancyes and lordshipps thereto belonging utterly wasted. **Thus** hee:

<small>carta in castro de Berkeley.</small>

The 29th of September following in the 31th of Henry the sixth the said Countesse drew from this lord James and his sons one other Indenture, whereby it was of newe agreed, That if this lord James and his said sons would sue a writ of Attaynt of the said verdict given at Cirencester in an Inquiry between the said parties, And the same Attaint pursue with effect without nonsute or discontynuance, And plead not, nor evidence challenge, nor any other matter, but such as shall bee devised by the said Earle, the lord Lisle, and their Counsell, ne nothing doe ne labor, ne procure to bee done ne labored, but by their said advise, That then the said Earle, nor lord Lisle his son, will take noe benefit ne advantage against the said lord James nor his said sons by way of forfei | ture of the bond of ten thousand pounds dated the 8th of October last which they had of them, but thereof, every of them to be discharged and pardoned.

<small>Rec: 31. H. 6. super extent̃ statut̃.</small>

And the more to quicken this lord James and his said sons, in the short dispatch of this plot, the second of October following (being the third day after) was the said statute of ten thousand pounds, (acknowledged the fourth of November before,) extended upon the lands of the said lord James, by James Clifford then Sherife of the County; whereby all his manors and lands, (perticularly named and valued,) are taken from him, both in this County of Glouc. and also of Somerset: And proces is sued out against all their persons also, whereby now was left to this lord James and his said sons neither lands nor liberty.

<small>pasch: 31. H. 6. in banc: regis. rot. et in salacijs ibm.</small>

Whereupon the attaint goeth forward, And upon a tryall the Jury find, That the former Jury at Cirencester had made a good and lawfull verdict in all that they had said: Howbeit by reason of the death of the said Earle, and lord viscount Lisle, and of James son of this lord James, no Judgment was after entred upon the said verdict: And this Earle is that noble soldier of whom the ffrench made the proverbe, The Talbot comes, And wee called our English Achilles; And was buryed at Whitchurch

<small>Camden in Shropshire pag: 598. E.</small>

Whitchurch with this Epitaph, orate pro anima prænobilis domini D. Joħis Talbot quondam Comitis Salopiæ, marischalli franciæ, qui obijt in bello apud Burdeux. 7. Julij 1453. Anno. 31. H. 6. And was created the first Earle of Shroesbury of his name of Talbot in the one and twentieth of King Henry the sixth; As his eldest son by the said lady Margaret his second wife, was in the 23th of Henry the sixth, viscount Lisle, as hath been said.

<small>Inq: capt. apud Wenlok in Com. Salop. obijt. 20. Julij.</small>

To deliver the exceptions which upon the later tryalls in the time of Queen Elizabeth were by the lord Berkeleys Counsell, (when time and diligence had ripened their knowledge,) taken to the foresaid Inquisition of the 18th of Henry the sixth, after the death of the said Earle of Warwicke; And to the said award of the 27th of Henry the sixth; And to the said action upon the statute of the fifth of Richard the second; And to the said attaint thereupon brought in the 31th of Henry the sixth; And to the foresaid twelve deeds made and acknowledged as aforesaid; would alone require like leaves to this lords life; for these were the principall pillars and suporters of the adversaries title, and the places of retreat to which they ever fled and trusted; wherein I had the honor to Collect ye breviats for Counsell, which now sleep in peace amongst the other evidence of the now lord George at Berkeley Castle; which upon reading hereof, hee may perhaps bee moved to awake and read, when this hand of mine wch thus seemeth to glory in the remembrance of its own labors, is turned into dust.

<small>531</small>

Doubtles the inrodes and spoiles that each party and their followers made each upon others lands and tenants, as the lord Lisle into Berkeley, Hame, Alkington, Hurst, and other manors of this lord James's: And the lord James and his sons into Wotton, Paynesfwike, Whaddon, Moreton, and other manors of the said Earle and Countesse and lord Lisle their son, in the same County, produced the ill effects and destructions of a petty warr: wherein the burrowe Town of Berkeley, for her part, sawe the burning and prostration of many of her antient houses, as her old rent which till that time was—22li by the year and upwards, and by those devastations brought down to eleaven pounds and under, where it sticketh to this day, without recovery of her antient lustre or greatness.

<small>Comp: ministroř temp: H. 5. H. 6. et. E. 4.</small>

These unjust incursions and depredations thus reciprocally retorted each upon other, made both parties fly to the king for pardons, the easier to wind out from the justice of the lawes: Of which sort this lord James for his part, had one the tenth of July in the fifteenth of Henry ye sixth; And an other the third of July in the 24th of

<small>Rot. pdon: 15. H. 6. m: 12. pat. 28. H. 6. ps. 1. m: 10.
Rot pdon. 24. H. 6. m. 41. claus: ibm.</small>

L VOL. II

24th of Henry the sixth; And an other the 22th of November in the 28th of Henry the sixth; And an other the twentieth of July in the 30th of Henry the sixth; And an other the 20th of November in the same thirtieth yeare; And the like at the same time to Willm, James, Maurice, and Thomas the fower sons of this lord; And an other the first of November in the 34th of Henry the sixth; And an other the tenth of January in the 36th of Henry the sixth, and to Jone his wife; And an other the sixth of February in the first of Edward the fourth; And some others. |

Rot. pdon. 30. H. 6. m. 25. et. 32. pat. 30. H. 6. pars. 1. m. 14. Rot. pdon: 36. H. 6. m. 27. Rot. pdon: 36. H. 6. m. 27. Rot. pdon: 1. E. 4. m. 41. et al.

532   And the lady Isable his wife had her pardon also, dated the 29th of May in the thirtieth of Henry the sixth, not longe before shee was murdered at Glouc., as hath been said.

And the said Earle of Shroesbury and Countesse his wife, and lord Lisle their son, had as many pardons or more, which sufficiently shew the ill humors wherewith either party abounded; And besides also the fifteenth of July in the thirtieth of Henry the sixth, the said Earle wrought with the king to take them for their persons, lands, tenements, goods and chattles in his protection, And to free him the said Earle and his sons from all mens actions and sutes espetially duringe their absence in France.

pat: 30. H. 6. pars. 2. m: 15. 22.

In the 27th of Henry the sixth, this lord James, by the putting on of his adversaries, was called into the Exchequer to answer the meane rates of the manors of Slimbridge, Hinton, Came, Cowley, Wotton and Simondsall, from the last of Aprill in the 17th of Henry the sixth, (on which day the Earle of Warwicke dyed,) untill the finding of his office the year after; in which record, the severall titles of the said Earles heires are laid down against the lord James, as in the said office they are found.

Term: Michis. 27. H. 6. rot. 25. in sc^ccio cum rem thesaur.

This lord James in discharge thereof, doth not plead his title as heire male to his uncle by force of his grandfathers entayle, as hee might well have done, though with a longer plea and more charge; but taketh a course more speedy and of less cost, espetially against the king himself, And pleadeth his Maties pardon to him granted the third of July in the 24th of his raigne, as afore is mentioned, And so avoided the charge:

This record, I remember, was at a tryall in the Comon pleas in ye 39th of Queen Elizabeth strongly urged by the Counsell of Anne Countesse of Warwicke, widow,

widow, then demaundant, in a writ of pertition againſt Henry lord Berkeley, tenant for the third part of the ſaid manors of Slimbridge, Came and Hinton, as being, (in their opinion,) unanſwerable; for that this lord James had himſelf therein waved and departed from his own title of heire male, confeſſing thereby as was inferred, the right of the title to bee on the other ſide in the heire generall: whereto, as the allegation of the record was ſodaine, (for it was then unknown to the Counſell of the lord Berkeley,) old Serjeant Harris, of Counſell with the lord Berkeley, gave this ſodaine anſwer; If the lord James had done otherwiſe, hee had done fooliſhly: for who will refuſe the benefit of Gods bleſſings and the kings pardons; And having two ways to diſcharge himſelf, hee tooke the beſt cheap and ſpeedieſt courſe, eſpetially againſt the kinge; which blunt and preſent anſwer ſeemed to ſattisfy the Court.

533

And upon a ſecond putting on of his adverſaries in the ſame Court, of another ſute in the like nature for the meane profits of the manor of Portbury and other lands in the County of Somerſet, whereto an untrue Inquiſicõn had entitled the Coheires, found by them in the 18ᵗʰ of Henry the ſixth, as is afore rehearſed, This lord James out of the ſame reaſons pleaded an other of the kings pardons granted to him the 22ᵗʰ of Novemʳ the ſame yeare.

Michas: 28: H. 6. rot. 23. in ſcᵃc̃io.

The Earle of Shroeſbury being (with his ſon the lord viſcount Liſle) ſlaine in France as is before declared, The time of his widdows mourning for the loſſe of ſuch an huſband and ſon, gave to this lord James and his two ſons Wiłłm and Maurice, left at home with him, ſome reaſonable time of breathing, yet not free from as great ſorrow, for that James his ſecond ſon was ſlaine with the ſaid Earle in France, and Thomas his youngeſt ſon at the ſame time taken priſoner by the French in that overthrowe; which alſo on the part of this lord James and his family was the more redoubled through the unnaturall diſcord that at this time ranckled between the ſaid lord and his eldeſt ſon Sʳ Wiłłm, which alſo ſeemes the more to feſter by the jealouſyes infuſed by a ſtepmother the lady Jone, whom this lord James had not longe before maryed, by beating upon yᵉ weake pulſe of her huſbands old age: which inteſtine diſſention had not a little advanced the affaires of the adverſe parties for divers of yᵉ late years.

Howbeit the twentieth of Auguſt in the 38ᵗʰ of the ſaid king Henry the ſixth, the father and ſon came to an agreement under their ſeverall ſeals of Armes, upon theſe ten capitulations: **firſt** that the ſaid Sʳ William ſhould not henceforth greeve

carta in caſtro de Berkeley.

1.

vex

vex nor trouble the said lord James his father, nor any of his servants Counsellors or tenants of any of his Lo^dps manors in Gloucestershire, by lawe nor otherwise:

2. That hee should not support nor favor noe persons that his said father shall put out of his service: That the said Willm shall keep the peace against his said lord father
3. and his servants duringe his life, but provided that neither his fathers nor his servants should give no occation of provocation to the said Willm or his servants:
4. That the said Willm should bee at large in all matters against Thomas Mill and
5. John Poyntz, except the said James own matters: That the said Willm shall not come into the lordship of Berkeley, (for hee now dwelt at Portbury,) with more persons then ten by day or night duringe the life of this lord his father without his
6. leave: That hee and they so coming shall come peaceably, and send word to his father of their coming half a day before hand, but not to stay at any their comeings
7. above seaven dayes: That the said Willm shall not alyen, nor seoffment make of
8. the manor of Portbury nor of any part thereof: That if the said lord James sue any
9. person by lawe, the said Willm shall bee with him in such sute lawfully: That for the observance of these Covenants the said Willm shall enter into a Statute at Bristoll of one thousand pound to his said father, And then hee will amit and receive him as his son and heire to his favor and good saderhood: And Lastly that
10. none of those seaventeen servants of the said Willm, (mentioned in the schedule to this Indenture annexed,) shall at no time come within the manors of the said lord James in Gloucestershire, but as strangers to baite and goe their way: And the like in effect, both Covenants and Statute from this lord James with his said son Willm, mutatis mutandis, whereby they purged the foure leaven of one the others family: which disagreements between this old lord and his said son seems also to have drawn

carta in castro de Berkeley dat. 15. Maij. 33. H. 6.

ill nourishment from a disobedient lease which this Willm, three years before against his fathers mind, had made of his manor of Portbury to James Earle of Wiltshire and of Ormond for twelve years, contrary to Williams promise as it seemeth; when

carta in castro de Berkeley dat. 5 Maij. 18. H. 6.

his said father in the 18th of that king Henry the sixth, had for his better maintenance, granted the same for his life; To the demisinge or sale whereof, this good old lord was the more averse, because it was the first land his Ancestors had ever purchased in England. |

His rewards to servants.

Noe lord from Harding the Dane had more use for men, and wise men, then this lord James, from his first age of discretion to the houre of his funerall, and consequently more use for bounty to tye such men to his affaires: Howbeit, whether it was his shallow purse, never halfe full, or whether the memory of his liberalityes have perished with time, I have only observed these. vizt

In

In the third of Henry the sixth hee gave to Richard Venables one of his Esquiers, an Anuity of ten marks yearly out of his manor of Hurst for his life; And also let to him the Scite of the said manor called Hurst Farm at sixteen marks rent, which is the old rent to this day. 1624.   *carta in castro de Berkeley.*

In the seaventh of that king, hee and the lady Isable his wife gave to Nicholas Stanshawe, for the life of the said lady, the manor of fflekenhoe in the County of Warwicke, rent free, which this lord held in her right.   *Esch: 11. H. 6. post mort. Johis. Mowbray.*

In the 11th of the said king, hee gave to Elizabeth Ithell for her life, an Anuity of fourty shillings by the year, for the paines shee had taken in nursing of Willm his eldest son, and an house in Berkeley rent free.   *carta in castro de Berkeley. comp: rec: 18. H. 6. in castr: de Berk:*

In the 19th of the said king, hee gave to John Grevill, one of his Esq:, for his life, an Anuity of—4li 6s 8d by the year, out of his manor of Alkington, and two pasture grounds called cowmoor and hurdham in the said manor, of like value.   *carta in castro de Berkeley.*

In the twentieth of that king, hee gave to John Phillip als Morgan, for his life, an Anuity of twenty nobles by the year, whereof three pounds out of his manor of Appleridge, And—3li 6s 8d out of Clapton, And—6s 8d out of Hame.   *carta in castro de Berkeley.*

In the same 20th year, hee gave to John Dunstable for his life, an anuity of fourty shillinges by the year, out of the warth and new leyes in Slimbridge.   *carta in castro de Berk:*

In the same year hee gave to John With for his life, an Anuity of fourty shillings by the year, out of the said warth and new leyes.   *carta in castr: de Berkeley.*

In the 21th of the said king, hee gave to John Biford, for his life, an Anuity of forty shillings by the Yeare, out of the said warth and new leyes.   *carta in castro de Berkeley.*

In the 23th of that king, hee gave to William May for his life, an Anuity of forty shillings by the yeare, out of culver feild in Alkington.   *carta in castro de Berkeley.*

The same yeare hee gave to Gilbert Johnson for his life, an Anuity of forty shillings by the year out of the said feild.   *carta in castro de Berkeley.*

In the 33th of the said king Henry the sixth, hee gave to George Pullen, one of his Esquires, for his life, an Anuity of fourty shillings by the yeare.   *comp. de Portbury: in castro de Berkeley. 36. H. 6.*

In

carta in caſtro de Berkeley.	ℐn the 34th of the ſaid king, hee gave to Sr Walter Deverox for his life, in conſideration of his ſervice, an Anuity of twenty markes by the year out of his manor of Hinton.
Comp:de Berkeley 37. H. 6. in caſtro de Berkeley.	ℐn the 37th of the ſaid king, hee gave to Thomas Holt Steward of his houſe, for his life, an Anuity of fourty ſhillings by the year, out of the new Inne in Berkeley. 𝔗𝔬 know more I have not attained.

His miſcellaniæ or various paſſages not properly reduceable under any the former titles.

This lord James of all his forepaſt Anceſtors from Harding the Dane, and of all his poſterity to George lord Berkeley that now is, in minority, ſtands ſingle in his generations from wearing Armes in any martiall voyage, abrode or at home.

Polichron:fo. 313. Caxton. cap: 248. fo : 335. claus : 1. H. 6. m : 19. in dorſo.	ℐn the 4th of Henry the ſixth, the Duke of Bedford, Regent of ffrance and uncle to the kinge, returned into England; And on whitſunday at Leiceſter dubbed the king knight; And forthwith after, the king dubbed knts many Dukes, Earles, and lords, Amongſt whom, this lord James was one, as thoſe hiſtoryes ſay; After which time hee always aſſumed into his ſtile, the title of knight; Howbeit I have already truly ſhewed him to bee written, Jacobus de Berkeley chivalier, three yeares before this time.
537 carta in caſtro de Berkeley.	ℐn the 7th of Henry the ſixth, this lord James borrowed nine hundred marks of John Merbury of Hereford Eſq; for repayment whereof hee mortgaged to him his manors of Portbury in the County of Somerſet, and of Alkington in the County of Glouc., And beſides gave his Statute acknowledged at Briſtoll for repayment of the ſaid money.
Rot. parl: 11. H.6. m : 17. pat : 12. H. 6. ps. 2. m : 29.	This lord James was at the parliament holden in the 11th of Henry the ſixth, ſworn with other lords not to keep or harbour any ryotous or notorious diſorderly perſons, nor to maintaine the quarrells of others, nor to conceive any diſpleaſure againſt any Judge for doing his office and juſtice &c.
claus : 18. H. 6. dorſo.	The 30th of Auguſt in the 18th of Henry the ſixth, the king ſent to this lord his Comiſſion in the nature of a patent of Leivtenancy, requiring him to make proclamation in the County of Glouc., for the peace of the Country to bee preſerved, And to prevent all conventicles, unlawfully aſſembled, And to carry a watchfull eye to prevent

prevent ryotous congregations and assemblyes; And if such appear to arise, to destroy them forthwith, least greater evill ensue.

In the 34th of king Henry the sixth, this lord James by his conge de lere, gave leave to the sisters and covent of Nuns of St. Magdalens by Bristoll, to choose them another prioresse insteed of Jone Waleis their late prioresse, lately dead: And what more I have to say of presentations and matters of this kind made by this lord or his Ancestors to Abbyes, Nunryes, pryoryes, Chantryes, or the like religious places, of any of their foundations, I doe referr this pious family to the life of their Ancestor the lord Thomas the sixth of that name, where they shall read their losse in honor and profit, by that dismall and black Statute of the dissolution of monasteryes in the 31th of Henry the 8th and of others in his raigne.

carta in castro de Berkeley.

fol: [699]

For the extraordinary Comissions, besides those annuall of the peace, wherein this lord was often imployed in divers Counties, As in raising of money by lones for the king, takinge of musters, Arming of Soldiers, appeasing of tumults and insurrections, and the like, these following records will direct to the principall of those I have observed, none of which are before mentioned; As: pat: 4. H. 6. pars. 2. m. 8. / pat. 6: H. 6. pars. 2. m: 16. / pat. 7. H. 6. pars. 1. dorso. / pat. 8. | H. 6. pars. 2. m. 3. / fin. 12. H: 6. m: 13. / fines. 14. H. 6, m. 20. / pat. 14. H. 6. m. 1. dorso. / pat: 17. H. 6. pars. 1. m. 12. / fines. 18. H. 6. m. 12. 17. / pat: 20 H. 6. pars. 3. m. 22. et. pars. 2. m. 40. in dorso. / fines. 28 H. 6. m. 6. / pat. 1. E. 4. pars. 3. in dorso.

538

His wives.

This lord had three wives (if not fower) a good or ill hap that had not formerly befallen any of his Ancestors from Harding the Dane.

The first was   the daughter of Sr. Humphry Stafford of Dorsetshire, whom by the direction of his uncle the lord Thomas, hee maryed in the third yeare of king Henry the fifth, with the portion of six hundred marks, pursed by his said uncle; Shee dyed very young without issue; Howbeit an old breviat written about the 17th of Henry the 6th hath these words; Itm, Thomas late lord Berkeley aiell[1] to my lady Dorset and her Coperceners, and uncle to James now lord of Berkeley, in his life, tooke the said James for his heire of all the manors comprized within

carta in castro de Berkeley.

vetus manuscr: in castro de Berk:

---

[1] Forefather—"To gyve from youre heires that youre aiels you lefte." *Piers Plowman*, p. 314. See Halliwell.

within the faid fyne, And fold his mariage twyes for a thoufand markes, and another time for one thoufand two hundred markes: whereby it may bee gathered, That this lord James had a former wife to this.

His fecond wife, (if but three,) was Ifable the eldeft daughter of Thomas lord Mowbray, Duke of Norfolke, Earle Marfhall and of Nottingham, (who was banifhed the Realme by king Richard the fecond, in which banifhment hee dyed at Venice the 27th of Decemr. in the firft year of king Henry the fourth,) and of Elizabeth his wife eldeft fifter and one of the Coheires of Thomas fitz Alen Earle of Arundle and Surrey. |

<small>539
comp: rec: de Mowbray 2. H. 6. in caftr. Berk: hillar: fin: 24. H. 6. in fcaccio.</small>

This lady Ifable was firft maryed to Henry fferrars, fon and heire to William fferrars lord of Groby, in the fecond yeare of king Henry the 5th, by whom fhee had iffue Elizabeth, maryed to Sr. Edward Gray lord fferrars and Groby, who had iffue between them Sr. John Gray flaine at ye battle of St. Albons in the 33th of Henry the fixth, whofe widowe the lady Elizabeth was after maryed to king Edward the fourth: And Edward Gray their fecond fon, who in right of Elizabeth his wife fifter and heire of Thomas Talbot vifcount Lifle, was in the firft of Richard the third, created vifcount Lifle, of whofe iffue between them, I have formerly written in the life of Thomas lord Berkeley the fourth of that name.

<small>fol: [479]</small>

<small>finis levat. apud Vfke. 3. H. 6. de manerio de Ragelond.</small>

And fecondly the faid Ifable was maryed to this lord James Berkeley in the fecond year of Henry the fixth, And continued his wife twenty nine yeares ere fhee dyed, By whom fhee had iffue fower fons and three daughters, as after followeth.

<small>Efch: 11. H. 6. poft mort. Johis Mowbray et 31. H. 6. poft mort. dict. Ifable in arce London.</small>

With her this lord James had in mariage the manors of Afpley, Alfpath and fflekenho in the County of Warwicke, And fome other lands in Effex, and in other Counties, which her brother John Duke of Norfolke in the 4th of Henry the fifth conveyed to her, what time fhee was wife to the faid fferrars: Howbeit fhee brought further the greateft maffe of land to this family of any lady that was before her, as after will bee declared in the life of the lord Willm her eldeft fon.

<small>fol: [518]
Efch: in Com: Effex 31. H. 6. poft mort. dict. Ifabellæ.</small>

Shee was a lady of great vertue, entirely lovinge her hufband, and the children fhee had by him; And in their diftreffes the principall ftay and follower of their futes and buifineffes; whereof noe other teftimony needeth then her lre from London to her hufband formerly mentioned, and the manner and means of her death at Gloucer, the fatterday before Micħmas day in the 31th of Henry the fixth, Anno.

Anno. 1452. under the rigorous hand of that mercileſſe lady Margaret Counteſſe of Shroeſbury, as before is touched out of the complaints of her ſon Wiłłm to king Edward the fourth and to his Chancellor againſt the ſaid Margaret; And whoſe bloud, hee and her other ſons after revenged in the death of her grandchild and heir; And lyeth buried in the Chancell of the Church of the ffryars mynoꝝ ałs gray ffryars at Glouc., which place her grandchild the lord Maurice | Berkeley in honor of her memory in the 21ᵗʰ of king Henry the 8ᵗʰ afterwards repaired.

<small>Rot. fin. 31. H. 6. m. vlt.</small>

<small>Newland: pedigr̃.</small>

<small>volunt. Mauricij Berkeley. 15. H. 8. 540</small>

Touching this lady Iſable, Mʳ Mills in his catalogue of honor hath a four fold error; **First** in telling us That ſhee was firſt maryed to this lord James And after to Henry fferrars laſt lord fferrars of Groby; whereas ſhee was firſt the wife of the ſaid Henry and after of this lord James, as formerly is delivered: **Secondly** in ſaying that by this lord James ſhee had iſſue Wiłłm and Maurich: whereas they had iſſue between them ſower ſons and three daughters, as after followeth, but none of them called by yᵉ name of Maurich; neither doth the lord Berkeley that now is, Anno. 1620. or the lord Henry that was when Mills wrote. Anno. 1557. diſcend from any of that name; which I would have made the printers error, but that I find it not in the errata of his booke directed to bee reformed: **Thirdly** by makeing this Iſable younger then her ſiſter Margaret, whereas ſhee was the elder, and maryed longe before her ſiſter; Howbeit its true, That the iſſue of the younger ſiſter was advanced in honor before th' elders, which was the ſole ground not only of Mills conjecture, but of Vincents and ſome other late writers alſo: **Lastly**, in writing, That this Iſables huſband was the laſt lord fferrars of Groby of that ſtock; whereas Henry fferrars her huſband was ſon and heir of Wiłłm lord fferrars, And dyed in the life of his father, as formerly is ſaid.

<small>Catalouge of honor fol: 880.</small>

<small>Vincent fol: 346.</small>

<small>Eſch: 36. H. 6. poſt mort. Edi Gray.
hillar: rec:in ſcᵃc̃io 15. E. 4. rot: 311.
Paſch: 16. E. 4. rot. 410. in banco c̃oi.</small>

<small>fol: [539]</small>

The laſt wife of this lord was Jone ſiſter to John the ſecond Earle of Shroeſbury, whom hee maryed in the end of the 35ᵗʰ year of king Henry the ſixth, and daughter of the often mentioned John Talbot Earle of Shroeſbury ſlaine in France five yeares before: A litle before which mariage, on the 25ᵗʰ of July in the ſaid 35ᵗʰ of Henry the ſixth, it was agreed between John then Earle of Shroeſbury and this lord James, That hee ſhould marry his ſiſter Jone, if ſoe hee the ſaid Earle might get an obligation of one thouſand pounds in which the ſaid lord James ſtood bound to the king, and deliver it to the ſaid lord James on the mariage day or before; And that the ſaid Earle ſhould pay to the ſaid lord James on the marriage day, one hundred marks, and provide his ſiſter her mariage apparell as may bee worſhip to him the ſaid Earle and to the ſaid lord James and to her. And ſhould bee alſo good

<small>carta in caſtro de Berkeley.</small>

M VOL. II

good lord to all the Counsellors, Tenants, and servants of the said lord James that bee to him well willed and true: And shall support him by his Counsell in all sutes that bee taken against | him. And that the said lord James shall make to her an estate of one hundred and twenty pounds by the yeare for her life, And shall bee seized the day of the mariage of all his other lands and Teñts of such estate as y^t the said Jone may bee dowable of them.

541

And to speake as I conceive of this mariage, It was of much pollicy in this old lord James, then in his great climactericall yeare of sixty three: for hereby hee not only gave strength to his own affaires, but hee weakened the power of the adverse party, not only by drawing from the said Margaret her two greatest pillars, her son in lawe and daughter in lawe, with an intelligence of her private purposes and practises past and present, but by opposing their endeavors against her by expresse covenants.

carta in castro de Berkeley.

By this Jone, this lord James had noe issue, but after six yeares and fower months mariage, hee by his death left her his widowe: And within two months after, her son in lawe the lord Willm Berkeley agreed by Indenture to pay her one hundred pounds yearly for her life, in lieu of her dower and of such manors and lands as were by her husband conveyed to her; And about fower years after shee maryed Edmond Hungerford Esqr to whom the said hundred pounds Anuity was many years paid.

carta in castro de Berkeley: et divers: acq: ibm.

His issue.

1. 3. Of Willm who dyed without issue, And of Maurice his brother lord Berkeley also after him, and of his issue I shall after write in their severall turnes, under whom this family saw, as various alterations, as in the life of this lord James had happened.

> Each state is subject unto change,
> Why then to us should this seeme strange,
> Yea, th'eavens and earth must passe away
> And not continue at one stay.

542

2. James who was second son of this lord James and Isable, was, in the | floure of his youth after hee had suffered imprisonment with his father and brethren, and been made a party to all those enforced conveyances as formerly is declared, hurryed into France by the said Earle of Shroesbury and lord Lisle, against his will

petitio Willmi ad Edrm quartum

will, by the procurement of his Counteffe the often mentioned Margaret; where with them hee was flaine the fame year, before hee tafted the fweet or foure of nuptiall fruit, And feems to lye by the body of this lord James his father in the Chapple on the fouth fide of Berkeley Church, differenced in his bearings with a file of three lambeauxes, fables, though of the tranfportation of his body out of France, I have found nothinge.

4. **Thomas** fourth fon of this lord James and Ifable, was alfo both at home and abrode in ffrance, partaker of his brother James double misfortunes, onely hee had the hap to have his life faved in that overthrow wherein the faid Earle and his fon, in the 31th of Henry the fixth, perifhed; but his body was taken prifoner, And (as his brother the lord Wiłłm complained after to king Edward the fourth,) was put to ranfome importable for him to beare; At which time hee was under nyneteen years of age: of whom, and the difcendants from him, I will inlarge my felf, (as I have formerly done in other branches of this noble family continuing to this day. 1634.) And the rather alfo becaufe this Thomas is ftock-father of the Berkeleys, comonly called of Worcefterfhire, and of Herefordfhire, multiplyed into many generations; whofe later difcents have not been foe fully infifted upon by the geneologifts of this family, as feemed due to male branches lately bloffomed from foe noble a ftocke, as this lord James and the lady Ifable his wife.

petitio predict.

Berkeley of Worcefterfhire Berkeley of Herefordfhire

This Thomas in his fathers life time was ftiled Thomas Berkeley Ar fil Jacobi Berkeley dni de Berkeley mił, And after his death, Thomas Berkeley Ar frater dni Wiłłmi Berkeley dni de Berkeley.

cartæ cum Wiłłmo Munday. 2. et. 7. E. 4.

In the 34th of Henry the fixth upon the petition of this Thomas and for fpeedier payment of his finance, the king grants leave for three of his factors to goe with the fhip called the Chriftopher with any lawfull merchandize, and to fell the fame, and returne, and goe againe. And the year before, this Thomas and two of his partners had the like licence to goe with their fhipp called the Trinity of Berkeley, to Burdeaux, and there to unlode, & lode againe, & bring any merchandize into England. | ffor his portion hee had by the feverall conveiances of his father, the manor of litle Marfhfeild and divers lands in Clapton, late the lands of John Edwards, and all other his lands, Tenements and hereditaments in the county of Gloucefter, which the faid lord James held in ffee fimple, whereof fome lay in Berkeley, Durfley, and Hinton: And the 13th of December in the 22th of king Edward the fourth, Wiłłm vifcount Berkeley his brother and Jone his then wife,

Vafcon. 34. H. 6. m. 3.

Vafcon. 33. H. 6. m. 4.

543
carta in caftro de Berkeley.

carta in caftro de Berkeley.

gave

gave to this Thomas his brother, for his laudible service, an Anuity of nineteen pounds p anñ for his life, whereof . 6^{li}. 13^s. 4^d. to bee issuing out of his manor of Wotton, And—12^{li}. 6^s. 8^d. out of his manor of Hame. And also this Thomas had by conveyance from his father in the xiiith of Henry the sixth, then very younge, the manor of Daglingworth, and the moytie of the Manor of Brokenburgh, with the alternate course of presentinge to the chantry of our Lady in Almondesbury, entayled upon him and the heires of his body, with remainders to his elder brothers in tayle.

carta in castro de Berkeley. dat. 4 Nov. 13 H. 6.

Humphry duke of Buckingham, by his patent dated the eighteenth of March in the 32th of Henry the sixth, made this Thomas Berkeley receivor generall of all his lands in the County of Gloucester, Wiltes, and Hampshire, with the fee of five pounds p anñ, And two shillings for his wages for each day hee should travell in his buisiness; which seemes to bee upon his first returne after hee had taken order for his ransome in ffrance.

carta cum Johe Smyth de Midleton.

This Thomas was present with his two elder brothers, Willm & Maurice at the death of the lord viscount Lisle, slayne by them at Nibley greene in the Tenth of king Edward the fourth, as after followeth.

Hee marryed Margaret the daughter and heire of Richard Guy of Minsterworth, heire to Phillip Waterton of Waterton in Wales, an antient family, to whom Thomas lord Berkeley had formerly given divers messuages and lands in Berkeley, Alkington, Hinton, and in the lordship of Berkeley, under the rent of 24^s paid by the heires and assignes of this Thomas Berkeley to this day . 1634. **By** her this Thomas had issue 1 John Berkeley, 2 Thomas, 3 Richard, 4 Edward, 5 Margaret, 6 Isable, and 7 Margery; And dyed the second day of July. Anno. 1484. in the second yeare of king Richard the third, as the brasse about his marble Tomb in the chancell of Berkeley Church doth witness, whereout twenty four years agone, I copied forth this Epitaph; Hic jacet Thomas Berkeley insignis armiger frater illustrissimi domini Willmi Comitis Nottinghamiæ, qui quidem Thomas obijt secundo die Julij, Anno Domini . 1484 . cujus animæ propitietur deus . Amen. |

carta 20. E. 4. in castro de Berk: volunt. Marchion. Berkeley: 7. H. 7. carta in castro de Berkeley 3 H. 8.

John eldest son of the said Thomas Berkeley and Margaret, by Margery his wife had issue John and Thomas, And dyed in the 27th yeare of kinge Henry the 8th And the said John son of John was servant to Anne lady Berkeley widowe, And dyed without issue at Callowdon in the County of Warwicke in the 31th of the said king

carta. 3. H. 8: in castro de Berkeley. Rentall de Berkeley 8. H. 7. in dicto castro.

king Henry the 8th. **And** Thomas, brother and heire of the said John son of John, by Suzan his second wife daughter of Curnocke of Cowley, (for by his first wife hee had noe issue,) had issue two daughters, Jone and Frances, And dyed in the twentieth yeare of Queen Elizabeth at Berkeley, where hee lyeth buryed.

<small>Moyles survey book 35 H. 8. in castro de Berkeley.</small>

The said Jone by Morgan Griffith her first husband, had issue Edward, ffrances, and Blanch maryed to Thomas Barber of Berkeley-heath, by all which is issue. And by Richard Oldland her second husband had issue Thomas and James, neither of whom are yet maryed, And Richard who maryed Jone Richards of Wanefwell, Anno. 1622.

The said ffrances second daughter and coheire of the said Thomas Berkeley, was maryed to John Smith of Middleton in Hinton, (hee yet living, blind. 1622,) by whom shee had issue John Smith, Willm Smith, Henry, Elizabeth, Margaret, Mary, Jone, Edith, and Agnes; The said John by Martha his wife daughter of Robert Cloterbooke hath issue Thomas and Henry.

The said William is not maryed.

The said Henry by Jane his wife, daughter of James Bayly of Swanley, hath issue John, Willm, Henry, Elizabeth, and Mary.

The said Elizabeth was maryed to Phillip Wither of Littleton who had issue Katharine, first maryed to John Atwood of Berkeley by whom shee had no issue, And after maryed to Charles Jay, between whom is issue ffrancis. Anno. 1634. an infant very young.

The said Margaret was first maryed to Thomas Nelme, by whom shee hath issue Thomas: And secondly maried to John Nelme by whom shee hath yet noe issue, 1622.

The said Mary was first maryed to Mathew Skull of Newport, by whom shee had issue, John, Thomas, Henry, and Nicholas; And 2dly to John Noote of Oldbury, by whom shee hath noe issue. |

The said Jone is maryed to John Hurne of Hinton, by whom shee hath issue Sara maryed to Nathaniell Mallet. 1635.

The

The said Edith is marryed to John Clutterbooke, by whom shee hath issue John, maryed to ffortune Lawrence, and Agnes. 1634.

And the said Agnes is maryed to James Hurne lately deceased, by whom shee hath issue John, Mary, and Edith.

<small>carta in castro de Berkeley et cum Robto ffowler de Alderly</small>

Richard third son of the said Thomas Berkeley and Margaret, (to whom his uncle Willm Marques Berkeley by his will in the seaventh of king Henry the seaventh, gave a legacy of forty shillings,) possessed part of his fathers lands in Dursley sower miles from Berkeley, where sometimes hee dwelt, which are now the inheritance of Robert ffowler of Alderley and others; And by Margaret his wife, daughter of Dyer, had issue 1 Richard, 2 Thomas, 3 Edward, 4 William, 5 Humphry, 6 Jone, and 7 Edith, of whom in order as followeth: **Richard** eldest son of the said Rich^d had issue John, who maryed the daughter of Slead, between whom was noe issue; And also the said Richard had another son of the same name of John, who was written John Berkeley of Hereford, and was twice Maior of that city, vizt in the 8th and 24th yeares of Queen Elizabeth; And by Jone his first wife daughter of Havard had issue Thomas, who after dyed without issue; And by Margaret his second wife daughter of Hues had issue, William, Humphry, Oswald, John, Nicholas, Richard, James, Mary marryed to Whittach, Margaret maryed to — Mynors, and Ellenor maryed to — Cosby: **Of** whom, the said Willm the eldest son by Elizabeth daughter of Willm Burghill had issue Willm Berkeley, now living at Killruddon in the county of Limbricke in Ireland, Anno. 1632. **And** the said John Berkeley of Hereford, who (as aforesaid) was twice Maior of that city, hath his portraiture to bee yet seen in the house of Willm Norman a Mercer in Hereford, pictured in an Aldermans gowne, blacke faced with Ermins, sent him, as report there goes, out of Russia by his son then Interpreter between the English and the Russian, with this inscription; Vera effigies Johannis Berkeley geñ bis quondam hujus civitatus Hereford præturam gerentis, prius Anno Eliz. 8º posteà verò eiusdem imperij. 24to Anno. ætatis facta. 65. et Anno dñi. 1585. with | this motto under it servire deo regnare est, with the coat of Armes of this James lord Berkeley differenced by a bordure argent[1]; which house the said Willm Berkeley of Kyllruddon in Ireland sold to the said Willm Norman; And the ground whereupon that house was built was by the said John Berkeley grandfather of the said Willm purchased of John Kinge and others in the first of Queen Mary, as by the deed appeares.

<small>Ex archivis civit. Herefordiæ.</small>

<small>carta cum Willmo Berkeley de Killrud:</small>

Thomas

---

[1] We cannot gain any intelligence of this portrait. [ED.]

Thomas Berkeley the second brother of Richard son of Richard son of Thomas Berkeley, was of Allensmore in the jurisdiction of the deanry of Hereford, And dyed in the 4th and 5th of Phillip and Mary, As by the administration of his goods then comitted to Anne his wife appeares, Of whom I find noe issue ; Neither have I found any issue of **Edward** his next brother.

Registrm civitat Hereff:

Willm Berkeley 4th brother of the said Richard, son of Richard, son of Thomas Berkeley, dwelled in Hereford, And was in the 35th of Henry the 8th Anno Dñi. 1545. Maior of that City ; And by Elizabeth his wife had issue fifteen sons and daughters, viz:t 1 Richard who dyed without issue, 2 Robert who also dyed without issue, 3 Willm who had issue George who dyed in the east Indies leaving a son yet living, 1634. 4 Henry, doctor of the civill law and a master of the Chancery, who dyed without issue, whose originall will dated in May in ye 26th of Eliz: 1584 I have seen, sealed with Berkeleys ten crosses ; 5 Thomas who also dyed without issue ; 6 John Berkeley sometimes a fellow in New Colledge in Oxford, from whence hee went to Ipswich where hee dyed ; 7 Edward Berkeley a mercer in London and a benefactor to that company, whose Escutcheon, (the Berkeleys ten crosses,) is set up in the hall at Mercers chapple in London, and dyed without issue ; 8 Rowland Berkeley, (of whom after,) Leonard Berkeley who dyed without issue, Margaret maryed to Richard Bramwich and six other daughters.

Registrm civitat Hereff. cm maiore ibm.

voluntas Henrici cum Robto Berkeley milte.

The said Rowland Berkeley the 8th son of the said Willm the maior of Hereford, dyed at his manor of Specheley in the County of Worcester the first of June in the ninth year of king James Anno Doñi. 1611 : whose monument is in the chancell of that Church ; Howbeit his funerall was the 18th of the next month solemly solemnized at the | Cathedrall Church in the City of Worcester, where for the most part hee had lived, Chester Herald then present marshallinge the funerall, in presence of Willm and Robert his two eldest sons, his executors : Howbeit I am bold in love to truth, with reverence to the memory of learned Campden, to write ; That in his register booke of certificates of funeralls, fol. 330. remaining in the office of Armes at London, (a place much to bee honored,) is a mistake in the genealogy of this Rowland Berkeley, the rather here soe precisely by mee pursued for rectifying the error therein recorded.[1] This Rowland Berkeley maryed Katharine daughter

547

---

[1] Through the courtesy of STEPHEN TUCKER, Esq., *Somerset Herald*, we are enabled to annex a copy of the Funeral Certificate referred to in the text, but we do not see any discrepancy between it and the Author's statement. In the recorded Pedigree (I. 16, fo. 330) however there are some few slight discrepancies, *e.g.* Rowland Berkeley is shewn to have married a daughter of Heywood, instead Hayward, and Mary, the daughter of Rowland, is stated to have married Wyn, instead of Mynne.

daughter of — Heyward by whom hee had iffue fix fons and nine daughters; whereof Willm the eldeft fon was high Sheriffe of the County of Worcefter in the 14th of Kinge James: And Robert Berkeley fecond fon of the faid Rowland was in the life time of his father, called to the degree of an vtter Barrifter in the Midle Temple, my felf then and fome yeares after of the fame fociety: And in the 12th year of king James was high Sheriffe of the County of Worcefter, two yeares before his eldeft brother; After which office in the minifteriall part of the lawe expired, hee returned to the Midle Temple, where hee foe enabled himfelf for the juditiall part, That in Michalmas Terme in the firft yeare of king Charles, (then by reafon of the plague in London held at Readinge,) hee was called to the Bench amongft the Readers of that houfe, And defigned to read in the Summer following; which done, in Efter Terme in the third year of king Charles, hee was made Serjant at lawe, And the fame Terme one of the faid kings Serjants, And then alfo honored with knighthood by his Maj^{tie} And in Michaelmas Terme in the eighth of that kinge, was made one of the Judges of his Maj^{ties} Court of kings bench: The faid Sr Robert Berkeley maryed Elizabeth one of the daughters and Co-heires of Thomas Coniers Efquier, difcended of the family of the Coniers of Sackborne in the Bifhopricke of Durham, whofe bearing I take to bee, A manch or in a feild Azure; By mariage with his faid wife hee had, (inter alia,) an houfe and lands in Eaft Barnet in the County of Hertford, ten miles from London, whither in vacation times hee often retireth himfelf.

Edward

Rowland Barkeley De Spechley in com Worcefter obijt (1) Die Junij 1611 (8) Jacobi R^{is} Angl: ffr et hibnie et Scotie (44) his bodye buried the 2 June att Spetchely his funerall folemnized July 18. 1611 att the Cathedrall Churche in the citie of Worcefter.

Chefter Herauld prefent, William Barkeley and Robert Barkeley his (2) eldift fonnes Executours.

Ro : Barkeley.

(I 10, 205.)

The Arms exemplified are: Gu. a Chev. betw. ten Croffes ar. differenced by a Crefcent furmounted by a mullet. Creft a bears head Couped ar. muzzled gu.

Extracted from the Record now remaining in the Herald's College, this 21 July, 1883.

STEPHEN TUCKER, *Somerfet Herald.*

Rowland Barkley, only fon of William eldeft fon of this Rowland, born 1613, was knighted at Worcefter, 30 June, 1641, and was nominated by Charles II one of the Knights of the Royal Oak. He married Dorothy daughter of Sir Thomas Cave, Knt., of Stamford.

Robert, fecond fon of the above mentioned Rowland, became one of the King's Serjeants at Law, as ftated in the text, and was knighted 14 April, 1627. [ED.]

Edward, John, Henry, and **Thomas,** the third, fourth, fifth, and sixth sons of 548 the said Rowland Berkeley, have theire names onely here mentioned by mee.

Of the forefaid nine daughters, Dorothy is maryed to Thomas Wild; Katharine is maryed to Willm Worfeild; Elizabeth is maryed to Robt Crosby; Ellenor is maryed to   ffrogmere: Jane is maryed to   Stinton; Jone is maryed to Henry Bright; Mary is maryed to   Mynne of London; Anne is maryed to Thomas More; And Joyce is maryed to   Newton of London, of whom is a numerous pofterity.

Humphry Berkeley fifth brother of the faid Richard fon of Richard fon of Thomas Berkeley, was a profeffed Monke in the monaftery of St Peter in the City of Glouc. at the time of the diffolution thereof; To whom king Henry the 8th the tenth day of February in the 31st of his raigne granted an yearly penfion of eight pounds for his life, which hee received till the 14th year of the raigne of Queen Elizabeth; And is beleeved by many to have outlived all of the like Monkifh penfioners in England.

Irr: in Curia Augmentac:

Of Jone and Edith fifters of the faid Humphry, I can fay nothing, fave that I here conclude with them, the iffue of the faid Richard Berkeley third fon of Thomas Berkeley youngeft fon of this lord James and of the lady Ifable his wife.

Of Edward fourth fon of the faid Thomas Berkeley and Margar^t I can fay nothing, fave that

Margaret, eldeft daughter of the faid Thomas and Marg^t was maryed to   Shipward gent., an honeft and carefull Agent in all the waightieft buifineffes of Maurice lord Berkeley the fixth and laft of that name, efpetially whilft hee lived at Calais, as many of his lres in Berkeley Caftle written to that lord doe plentifully witnes, which declare him to bee, as I here deliver him; who had iffue between them   Shipward father of Maurice, father of Maurice and Willm, which Maurice was of Alvefton, and dyed without iffue about the twentieth year of the raigne of Queen Elizabeth leaving the faid Willm his brother and heire; which Willm had iffue five fons and daughters, vizt 1 Maurice Shipward of the City of Weftmfter, father of divers children; 2 Willm who by Elizabeth the daughter of Anthony Halfe Efq^r is alfo father of divers children, 3 Giles Shipward, 4 Elizabeth, and 5 Ellenor.

diverfa muniment in caftro de Berk:

549

Isable

Isable second daughter of the said Thomas Berkeley and Margaret (to whom her uncle Willm Marques Berkeley in the seaventh of Henry the seaventh gave a legacy of twenty markes,) was in the third yeare of king Henry the 8th maryed to Humphry Lluellin gent. son and heire of Willm lluellin of Pucklechurch gent, between whom was issue John ffluellin, [sic] who by Anne his wife daughter of John Atwood had issue, Willm, and Hugh: which Willm by Cicely his wife daughter and heire of Robert ffrize of Pucklechurch had issue Christopher, Agatha, Ellenor, Anne, and Mary.

The said Christopher by Anne his wife, daughter and heire of John Burnell of Westerly, had issue William, who by Anne his wife daughter of John Brittaine of Bitton hath issue William, John and fower daughters.

The said Agatha was maryed to Willm Organ of Westerly and hath issue John and George.

The said Ellenor was maryed to John Gregory of Wike, who had issue Willm lately dead without issue, and Walter who had a son. And the said Mary was maryed to John Mayo who have issue John Mayo, and a daughter called Elleanor, maryed to Willm Buckle.

The said Hugh ffluellin brother of Willm, son of John, had issue Willm, of whom is issue.

7 **Margery** youngest daughter of the said Thomas Berkeley and Margaret, (to whom her uncle Willm Marques Berkeley by his will in the 7th of Henry the seaventh gave a legacy of five marks,) dyed, as I conceive, wthout issue; And these three daughters Margaret, Isable, and Margery, had, by the conveyances of their father and Mother, divers lands and remainders in tayle limited to them in Berkeley and Dursley &c, Hitherto of the said Thomas and his issue, fourth son of this lord James.

carta in castro de Berkeley et cum Robto ffowler de Alderly.

550   5. **Elizabeth**, eldest daughter of this lord James and Isable his wife, was | in their life times maryed to Thomas Burdet of the County of Warrwicke Esqr. And had two hundred pounds for her mariage portion, And from her husband forty pound Joynture p^r ann; which Joynture land was entayled to them and the heires of their two bodies, as the Deed it self dated on thursday after St Katharines day in

carta in castro de Berkeley.

in the 27th of Henry the fixth doth witneffe, A litle before which time they were maryed: And for any thing I yet underftand fhee dyed without iffue.

6. **Isable,** the fecond daughter of this lord James and Ifable, was maryed to Willm Try of Hardwike in the County of Glouc, Efq. to whom by deed dated the 18th of Auguft in the 16th of king Edward the fourth, Willm lord Berkeley her brother granted an yearly cheife rent, (which the lord George Berkeley receiveth at this day, 1628,) of forty fhillings paid him by the faid Willm Try and his Anceftors out of certaine lands and woodground called Inwoods in Stinchcomb within the parifh of Came; To hold to the faid Wm Try and Ifable his wife in part of payment of three hundred marks, (the like portion to her elder fifters,) untill the fame bee paid, according to the will of James lord Berkeley his late father, as the mariage portion of the faid Ifable.

carta in caftro de Berkeley.
carta cum Willmo Try de Hardwike.

This Willm Try dyed in the 13th yeare of Henry the feaventh, whofe office then found fheweth, That the third of September in the 21th of Edward the fourth hee had enfeoffed her brother Thomas Berkeley and others of his manor of Parkcourt in Hardwike, To the ufe of himfelf and Ifable his wife and of the heirs of their two bodies, And that fhee was now dead: Howbeit fhee was livinge in the fourth of Henry the feaventh, when by the kindnes of her faid huband, her Joynture was further enlarged with his lands in Beoly and Clehungre in Berkeley hundred.

This Willm Try was difcended from Sr Robert Berkeley fecond fon of Maurice lord Berkeley the fecond of that name, as in the title of his iffue is to bee read, from whofe conveyance came the faid lands in Beoly and Clehungre, and the forty fhillings rent charge out of Vley there mentioned, which that family poffeffe to this day, 1620.

Rec: in banco: Term Anno H. 7. 1ot. vetus manufcr. in caftro de Berkeley. vide fol: [177]

The faid Willm and Ifable Berkeley had iffue John Try, who dyed without iffue, and Willm Try, who by Anne his wife, daughter of Thomas | Bainham and widowe of Mr Clifford, had iffue Edward Try, and Thomas Try of Callowdon, a wife and faithfull fervant to this family, of whom much is after written, And dyed in the 16th of Henry the eighth.

551

The faid Edward Try fon of Willm and Anne, by Sibill his wife, had iffue John Try, Arthur, and George, which Arthur and George dyed without iffue; And
Willm

Wiłłm Try of Pucklechurch, who by Cicely his wife daughter of Whitokesmead, had issue Sibill maryed to Henry Denis, and Anne maryed to Roger Kemis of Wickwicke; and the said Edward had also issue Katharine maryed to Hugh Denis of Pucklechurch, of whose issue see after; And the said Edward dyed in the 18th of Henry the 8th.

The said John Try by Elizabeth his wife daughter and coheire of Mr Gurney of Suffolke, had issue John Try, Edward Try that dyed without issue, Anthony Try, Anne, Elizabeth, and Katharine maryed to Mr Serjeant of Stone.

The said John son of John by Margaret his wife daughter of Mr Skipwith had issue, Wiłłm, Henry dead without issue, Thomas, Peregrine, John, Edward, Suzan, Elizabeth, Margaret, and Frances.

The said Wiłłm eldest son of John maryed Mary daughter of Sr Edward Tirrell knt, by whom hee had issue Wiłłm, Henry, Edward, John, Frances, and Mary; And was in a private quarrell slaine at Gloucester, Anno 8. Jacobi.

The said Thomas third son of John maryed Ursula daughter of Mr Foster, by whom hee had issue, Wiłłm, Elizabeth and ffrances.

The said Peregrine, fourth son of John, is yet unmaryed; Anno. 1618.

The said John the fifth son, maryed Elizabeth daughter of John Chambers of Tresham, by whom hee hath issue, Thomas.

The said Edward the sixth son maryed Millicent then attendant on the lady Elizabeth Berkeley widowe; At what time also the said Edward was her gentleman vsher, And have issue, 1628.

Suzan and Elizabeth are yet unmaryed. 1620. Margaret is maryed to M. Drayner of the Inner Temple, And ffrances is dead without issue. |

The said Katharine sister of the said John Try son of Edward was maryed to Hugh Denis of Pucklechurch Esqr by whom shee had issue Henry that dyed without issue, John, Walter not maryed, Anne maryed to Mr Petit and have issue, Cicely not maryed, and Audely maryed to Mr Bryers of Coventry; ffrances maryed to Mr Thomas

Mr Thomas Ligon of Elston, and have issue, Thomas Ligon, Will'm, Richard, John, and Katharine maryed to Mr Jerrat, who have issue; And Jone dead without issue, and Alice first maryed to Mr Brokesby and after to Mr Berry, who also have issue.

John Denis brother and heire of Henry, sons of the said Hugh and Katharine, by Ellen his wife daughter of Thomas Millet of Sowe hath issue henry Denis, who hath maryed Margaret daughter of Sr George Speake and have issue; Will'm Denis not maryed, Cicely maryed to Will'm Guyes son and heire of Sr Will'm, and have issue, And Katharine not yet maryed. Anno. 1624.

7. **Alice** third daughter of this lord James and Isable his wife, was maryed to Richard Arthur of Clapton in Somersetshire near Portbury, and had issue John and Isable; which Isable was first maryed to Mr Stanshawe, And after to Mr Harrison, both whom shee survived, And as I take it, dyed without issue.

carta irr: in Canc: 17. H. 7. et in banco eodē anno, Term Michis rot. 1. See fol:

The said John Arthur son of the said Richard and Alice, by Margaret his wife daughter of John Butler of Badmington, had issue Thomas, and Margaret maryed to Roger Porter in the 22th year of Edward the fourth, of whom after.

The said Thomas Arthur by the daughter of Mr Shipman of Bristoll had issue, whereof many remaine at this day.

The said Margaret maryed to Roger Porter had issue Arthur, who by Alice daughter of John Arnold had issue Thomas Porter of Lanthony by Glouc: knight, Tacy maryed to Edward Oldisworth, Isable maryed to Giles Codrington, and Bridget maryed to Christopher Bainham of Clowerwall.

The said Sr Thomas Porter, by Anne daughter of Richard Denis of | Siston, had issue Arthur Porter knight and others, of whom see after in the issues of Maurice the fifth, third son of this lord James.

553 fol: [625]

The said Tacy maryed to Edward Oldisworth had issue Arnold Oldisworth late Clark of the Hanaper, who by Lucy his wife daughter of ffrancis Barty a fflorentine gentleman of a noble family, had issue Edward maryed to Elizabeth Masters late of Cirencester, by whom hee hath issue Bridget; Michaell Oldisworth Secretary to the Earle of Penbroke lord Chamberlaine, and Elizabeth maryed to Alexander Bainham of Westbury by whom shee hath issue.

The

The said Isable maryed to Giles Codrington had issue ffrancis Codrington of fframpton upon Seaverne, Richard Codrington of Dodington, and Cicely maryed to Willm Ruswell of Dunkerton in Somersetshire.

The said ffrancis Codrington by Mary his wife daughter of Sr Nicholas Poyntz had issue Margaret, first maryed to Edward Bromwich of Frampton upon Seavern, And secondly to John Sydnam; of whom see more in the life of the lord Thomas the fifth.

fol:[683]

The said Richard Codrington brother of ffrancis, by Joyce his wife daughter of John Burlace Esq, hath issue Samuell, who hath maryed Elizabeth daughter of Thomas Stephens of Lippiat Esq: and sister of Edward Stephens of Sodbury, Esq, (farmer also of the impropriate Tythes of Berkeley Rectory,) Richard, Robert, Willm, Giles, Anne, Elizabeth, ffrances, Joyce, and Isable Codrington; Of whom the said Isable is maryed to Samuell eldest son of Christopher Stokes of Stanshawes by Sodbury gent.

And the said Bridget was maryed to Christopher Bainham of Clowerwall, who had issue George Bainham, dead without issue.

His Seales of Armes.

This lord James in his first accesse to his Barony sealed with the Cheveron and ten crosses cornerwise, the two mairemaydes supporters, and the helmet and myter for crest, (the miter not charged,) circum|scribed, sigillum Jacobi domini de Berkeley; And afterwards, upon what grounds I find not, the miter was charged with the crosses also; And the circumscription of that seale was sigillum Jacobi domini de Berkeley militis, in other things agreeing: both of one bredth of two inches and an half diameter, without any reverse or privy seale on the dorse: Behold the resemblances.

The mitre is shewn charged in the seal as "tricked" by the Author. See *fac simile*. [ED.]

His death and place of buriall.

The 22th of October in the third yeare of king Edward the fourth, it was agreed between this lord James and the often before named Margaret Counteſſe of Shroeſbury, That they would thenceforth ceaſe ſuites & the reſidue of their lives live in reſt and peace togeather; And that either of them ſhould enjoy ſuch manors lands and Tenements in ſuch ſort and form as either of them then held and were poſſeſſed of, without interupting one of the other.

carta in caſtro de Berkeley.

At this time was the lord James of the age of .69. years and upwards, and the ſaid Margaret about fifty and two; Neither of whom ſince their ages of diſcretion having till that time enjoyed any three months of freedom from lawe ſuites: And with this peace enters the everlaſting peace of this lord James, an honeſt humble and juſt lord; for within thirty ſix days after, hee dyeth at Berkeley Caſtle in the end of November Anno .1463. where hee had lived all his life time ſince his unckles death; And lyeth buryed under a fair tomb of alablaſter beautifyed with the Eſchucheons of his Armes in ye Chapple on the ſouth ſide of the high Altar in the pariſh church of Berkeley, which Chapple himſelf formerly had built, then entred into | the ſeaventieth yeare of his age, whereof hee had ſit lord forty ſix years fower months and about twelve days.

*Rot. fin. 3. E. 4. m. vlt.
Newl: pedegr: in caſtro de Berkeley. clauſ: 3. E. 4. m. Newland pedegree faith hee dyed. 1462. but falſly. vlt: vol: willi Marchioñ Berkeley. 7. H. 7.*

555

> And now Gods holy angells are attendinge
> To crowne him with thoſe joyes that know noe endinge.

Of whom this teſtimony is juſtly tranſmitted to his poſterity; That amongſt all the generations of his houſe before and after him, none is found to have walked more with God in a vertuous and harmleſſe life, not once obſerved to have ſlipt into diſorder, vice or paſſion; much reſembling the pious part of king Henry the ſixth his life, in whoſe raigne the greater part of this lords life ran out.

And in the uneven parrallell between this lord and the lord Willm his eldeſt ſon, is verifyed, That parents beget the bodyes, not the minds, nor manners of their children; for two more diſſenting from the cradle to the grave are not to bee found in the wholl catalogue of their generations, as by their lives appeareth.

That hee made a will it is apparent by the deed of his daughter Iſables mariage, but to have been proved of record I find not in any place.

Contra

Contra vim mortis non eſt medicamen in hortis;
Noe herbes do growe in any mould
Gainſt ſtroke of death that can bee found:
The graſſe that grows, to-morrow's hay,
And man that's now, aſſoone is clay.

The lands whereof hee dyed seized.

By the death of this lord James diſcended to the lord Willm his eldeſt ſon,

The manor of Berkeley burrowe The manor of Hame The manor of Appleridge The manor of Alkington The manor of Hinton The manor of Hurſt The manor of Slimbridge The manor of Came The manor of Daglingworth The manor of Upton St Leonards The hundred of Berkeley	In the County of Glouc.

The manor of Portbury and Porteſhead, with the hundred of Portbury, in the County of Somerſet.

pat: 5. E. 4. pars. 1. m: 22.

And certaine lands in the County of Hereford, as his pardon for intruſion ſhewes.

All the reſidue of his antient patrimony were othe[r]wiſe ſcattered and entred upon, as his life in part hath declared, And now further follows to bee ſpoken of in the life of the lord William, his eldeſt ſon.

The application and use of his life.

The uſe

1. The power and malice of the adverſaries of this lord James kept him for the moſt part within doors like a priſoner, from youth to age, as his life hath declared: That malice God turnes to the ſafety and preſervation not only of himſelf but of his poſterity alſo; freed thereby from actuall ſidinge with either of the two royall houſes of Yorke and Lancaſter, all this lords time by the eares for the Crown: wherein noe other family of like eminency to this is found that deeply ſuffered not in the alternate fortunes of thoſe two houſes, through the various ſucceſſes of their Armes: Soe the more oppreſſed, the more preſerved; the more
dejected

dejected, the more bleſſed was this lord, and in him, his poſterity: A ſtrong conſideration, raiſing his diſcendants to joyne in Chore with the angell and that multitude of heavenly ſoldiers with him, in that celeſtiall himme of alleluiah recorded by Sᵗ Luke. Glory bee to God on high. &c. who in his bleſſed providence turned the evill of this lords reſtraint, wrought by malice and greatneſs, to the preſervation of himſelf and his poſterity, as farr as humane wiſdome may divine: whereby hee and his in their ſucceſſive generations are invited to double and|treble the remembrance and acknowledgment of that benefit and preſervation: A preſervacōn which the able and active ſons of this lord make more remarkable, not otherwiſe then by this reſtraint to have been reſtrained from diverſly pertaking in unnaturall Armes with either of thoſe two houſes, to the mutuall unſheathing of their ſwords againſt one the other, as the ſequell ſhewes their ſeverall affections would have driven them; And as often and againe happened amongſt brothers and parents in thoſe inteſtine warres, which divided not the kingdome alone and Counties, but Cities alſo and private familyes.

Luke. 2. vers: 13. 14.

557

2. **And** againe let the example of this lord, (Then whom, non illo melior quiſquam, nec amantior æqui, none more juſt in words and deeds in all his generations,) aſſure his poſterity, That howſoever through the power of time they may wrongfully ſuffer for a ſeaſon, as this lord longe did, yet God the juſt rewarder of every man according to his works will in due time give deliverance, as hee did to him; And that godlyneſs of life hath the promiſe both of good things in this life, and of better in the life to come, from the mouth of him that lyeth not: And therefore let this lords poſterity allways inveſt themſelves with a prudent patience, as with an individuall companion, and Counſellor, which ever atcheiveth that fair victory whereat honeſt ends are levelled.

558
559 } blank
560

The Life of William Marques Berkeley

The life of Wiłłm lord Berkeley the firſt of that name, ſtiled in writings, Wiłłm Berkeley knight; And Wiłłm Berkeley of Berkeley knt.; And Wiłłm lord Berkeley; And Wiłłm lord Berkeley viſcount Berkeley; And Wiłłm Earle Marſhall and of Nottingham. And Wiłłm Marques Berkeley; And after the 4th of king Henry the 7th his ſtile was, Wiłłm Marques Berkeley, Earle Marſhall and of Nottingham, great Marſhall of England, viſcount Berkeley, lord of Berkeley, lord of Mowbray, and Segrave, and Baron of Bedford; with theſe and the like words in Indentures and dedications ſet before his ſtile; As, Between the. &c. or, To the right high mighty and noble lord, Wiłłm Marques Berkeley, Earle. &c, as before.

And may bee called Wiłłm the waſt all.

Contemporary, with Edward the fourth, Edward the fifth, Richard the third, and Henry the. 7th from. 1463. till. 1491.

The life of this lord I doe preſent under theſe twelve titles, viz:

1.—His birth and education, fol: 562.
2.—His acceſſe to honor and offices, fol: 563.
3.—His lawe ſuites with the death of the lord Liſle at Nibley greene, fol: 564.
4.—What lands this lord was at one time ſeized of, fol:[586]
5.—His alyenations and ſales of lands, fol: [590]
6.—His Almes and devotions, fol: [597]
7.—His miſcellaneæ or various paſſages, fol:[601]
8.—His wives, fol:[604]
9.—His ſeales of Armes, fol:[613]
10.—His death and place of buriall, fol: [614]
11.—The lands whereof hee dyed ſeized, fol: [614]
12.—The Application and uſe of his life, fol: [617]

His

562 His birth and education.

This lord Wiłłm, eldest son of the lord James and of the lady Isable his wife, was born at Berkeley Castle in the 4th yeare of king Henry the sixth, Anno. 1426, And there bred up with his parents, who then had not any other removinge house.

Repl: Wiłłmi in Canc. 6. E. 4.

Carta in castro de Berkeley.

About the. 13th of his age hee betooke himself to the service of Henry Bishop of Winchester and Cardinall, with whom at that time in the 17th of Henry the sixth, hee went over sea to Calais; And not longe after his returne, before full age, received the order of knighthood; At what time his father gave him the manor of Portbury and all his lands in that County of Somerset for his maintainance; At the death of his father hee was of the age of thirty eight years and unmaryed.

This lord Wiłłm closeth the second septenary number from Harding the Dane; and much differing from his last ancestors as the lord Thomas the first septenary lord did from his six former forefathers.

Philo the Jewe de legis Alleg: lib. 1. Hipocrates. Bodyn de republica lib. 4. cap. 2. see the practize of piety. fol: 418. 410. Censoriū de die natali. cap: 12. Seneca: varro in Gellius, lib. 3. Bucholcer. Jerom: in Amos. 5.

I will not bee superstitiously opinionated of the misteries of numbers, though it bee of longe standing amongst many learned men; neither will I possitively affirm that the number of six is fatall to weomen, and the numbers of seaven and nine to men: **Or,** that those numbers have, (as many have written,) magnam in tota rerum natura potestatem, great power in kingdoms and comon wealths, in families, ages of bodies, sicknefs, health, wealth, losse, &c : **Or,** with Seneca and others, septimus quisque annus, &c, Each seaventh year is remarkable with men as the sixth is with weomen ; **Or,** as divines teach, That in the numbers of seaven there is a misticall perfection which our understanding cannot attaine unto; And that nature her self is observant of this number.

vide fol: [184]

But hee that marketh well the discent of the generations of this perticular family shall find in their septenary numbers extraordinary men and extraordinary changes : The first, a man of men, the very Salomon of his age, as his life hath declared :

The

The relation of this lords life, (taking in what hath been already said of him in the life of his father,) will raise an opinion, That hee was a causelesse re|pudiator of his first wife; An unaturall contender with his own father; A shedder of innocent bloud in the time of peace; An irreconciliable hater of his brother and heire; A disinheriter of his race and family; A consumer of the fower baronies of Berkeley, Mowbray, Segrave and Bedford, and of half the dukedome of Norfolke; A man above measure ambitious; A frequent leader of ungratious multitudes in night sallyes and inrodes upon his adversaries tenants and fautors; And exalted in honor and dignities above all his predecessors; Quod nova testa capit, inveterata sapit, vices grafted in the bones, are like to stick fast in the flesh: But,

> Happy his estate above the fate of Kinges,
> That could but truly know the cause of things.

And,

> Right happy doe I count that man,
> Of things, the reasons give that can.

His accesse to honors and offices.

In November in the third yeare of kinge Edward the fourth, by the death of his father, hee became lord Berkeley as hath been said; And at ye parliament in the sixth of Edward the fourth was rancked the fourth baron in the roll.

Rot. claus: 6. E. 4. in arce londini.

The 21th of Aprill in the 21th yeare of king Edward the fourth, (not the twentieth yeare as Mr Mills saith,) hee was created viscount Berkeley, by the name of fidelis miles noster, to him and the heires males of his body, without fee; Howbeit there is a faire deed under seale in Berkeley Castle dated the tenth of Aprill in the fifteenth yeare of king Edward the fourth, made by Willm viscount and lord Berkeley, which as I reject not, soe I may not approve it.

Catalog: of Honor fo: 883.
cart: de anno 15. E. 4. vsqz 22. m. 6.
carta in castro de Berkeley.

And the 5th of March in the 23th yeare, the same king made him one of his privy Counsell; And for his better attendance thereat, gave him one hundred marks p anñ, out of the subsidyes of London and Bristoll, during life.

pat: 22. 23. E. 4. pars. 2. m. 2. in vñ rotulo.

The 28th of June in the first yeare of king Richard the third, the 6th day after that kings coronation, hee was created Earle of Nottingham to him and the heires males of his body, with the yearly fee of twenty pound out of the Sherifwicks | of Nottingham and Derby.

The 26th of October in the first yeare of King Henry the seaventh, hee was created Earle Marshall at the kings pleasure, with twenty pound fee.

pat: 1. H. 7. ps. 3.

The

cart. 4. H. 7. m. 13.
cart. subsigillo in
cast. de Berkeley.

The 19th of February next after in the same first yeare of Henry the seaventh, hee was created Earle Mareschall and great Mareschall of England, to him and the heires males of his body, with twenty pound ffee; And by reason of a mistake in these lres patents about the said fee of twenty pound, (as I take it,) had a new grant, the 17th of ffebruary in the fifth of Henry the seaventh, of the same dignity.

memor. Sccii.
pasch. 4. H. 7
rot. 6 exparte
rem. regis.

The 28th of January in the 4th of Henry the seaventh, hee was created Marques Berkeley, to him and the heires males of his body, with thirty five pound ffee out of the lesser customs of London.

His lawe suites.

carta in castro de
Berkeley.

Havinge compounded with his motherinlawe the lady Jone, and thereby drawn into his own possession all the mannors and lands which shee was to have held in Joynture and dower, which was one of his first and wisest works after the death of his father, (wherein hee found her kind above the comon condition of stepmothers), as formerly is declared, His next was the procuringe of a pardon and releafe from king Edward the fourth for his intrusion into the Castle of Berkeley and other his lands discended unto him after the death of his father, in the Countyes of Glouc., Somerset, and Hereford, and of all debts, Accompts, fynes, forfeitures, amerciaments, and other demaunds, which had any manner of ways before that time accrewed to the kinge; which bearing date the ninth of March in the fifth of that king, hath a marginall note in the originall record, (vacat quia aliter in anno quarto,) But in that fourth yeare, it is not now to bee found.

pat: 5. E. 4. pars.
1. m : 22.

Rot. fin. 3. E. 4.
in vlt.
565

And though a writ of diem clausit extremū was within ten days after his father James death, sued out by him the fifth of December in the third yeare of king Edward the fourth, directed to the Escheator of | the County of Glouc., yet noe Inquisition was thereupon taken, through the controversies which forthwith upon the lord James death began the stream afresh between this lord Willm and the said Margaret Countesse of Shroesbury, (two mercilesse natures not unevenly encountringe,) which omission drave this lord Willm to the foresaid pardon; which done, and havinge thereby set his estate rectus in curia, hee soone turned himself by a contrary course upon the said widowe, malitious Margaret Countes of Shrewsbury, whose mutuall hatreds each to other, ended not before their breaths: Against whom hee exhibited a petition to king Edward the fourth by the name of his Alder liegelord, Shewing therein, how that hee, (this Ld Willm,) ought by right to have and inherite the manors of Wotton, Symondsall, Cowley, Newleyes and Sagisfond; And

vetus manuscr. in
castro de Berkel:

And how that the late Earle of Shroefbury and the Lord Lifle his fon, (fince dead,) and the faid Margaret his Countes, tooke his father, his brethren, and himfelf by their practice with one Rice their fervant and porter, in their Caftle in the night time, and there imprifoned them in places apart, And conftrained them to feale writings and acknowledge Statutes to fifteen thoufand pounds and more; And alfo tooke and imprifoned the wife of the faid James in Gloucefter Caftle, to which time fhee by Dures of imprifonment there dyed: (then follow divers lines worne out with wet,) And therefore beinge not to bee helped by the ftrictnes of the laws, prayeth that his Judges and other learned of the lond by his authority may call the faid Countes, and heare & determine their interefts and rights; And hee will bee ready to ftand to and abide their order therein; Thus that old writinge.

It may feeme, that the king referred over the confideration of this petition to the lord Chancellor, to whom the faid Counteffe (upon notice) addreffeth herfelf by her counterpetition; And by way of recrimination greevoufly complaineth of the great and manifold wrongs offered to her and her tenants of Wotton, Symondfall, and other lands by this lord Willm, who (faith fhee) without any title or caufe of right, with many riotous people, brake into her manor houfe of Wotton, fawed the great window timber and pofts afunder, razed the walls, iron works and windows, carrying away the barrs and goods of her hufband and felf and her fon to a great value; for fattisfaction whereof Statutes were given which yet in fubftance are unpaid: for which forcible entry an action upon the ftatute of Richard the fecond was brought, and a recovery therein had; but the faid Willm lord Berkeley, neither dreading God, the kinge, | the breach of his lawes, nor the wrongs nor oppreffions of the kings leige people and fubjects, dayly vexeth and troubleth her, in forbidding her rents, woodfales, and other profits of the faid manors, and menaceth her officers, fervants, and tenants, that they dare not imploy themfelves in her fervice; Soe that fhee can neither have her debt of him, nor enjoy her lawfull old inheritance, And therein prayeth releefe: *vetus manufcr: in caftro de Berkeley.* 566

Hereto this lord Willm maketh a kind of remonftrance, fhewing yt his father and mother, himfelf, and his brethren, have fuffered as great injuryes and oppreffions at the hands of the faid Counteffe, as ever did any of their worfhip, or leffe, within the Realme. *vetus manufcr. in caftro de Berk.*

But this lord Willm upon a fecond deliberacon, to draw thefe troubles into a readier way for tryall, exhibiteth his bill of complaint into the Chancery, the fixth yeare of the faid king Edward the fourth; And fheweth, That fhortly after the death *Bill in Canc. 6. E. 4. in turre. exempl.*

death of the lord James his father, the said Counteſſe of her evill diſpoſition damnably imagining and purpoſing the utter deſtruction of him, and his perpetuall diſinheriſon, where hee intended to have ridden from London to have ſeen his livelyhood, and to have communed with ſuch as had eſtate in his ſaid manors and lands afore that time, the ſaid Counteſs havinge knowledge of his intent of departing, intreated and hired one called Chamberlen, being a ſanctuary man at Weſtminſter, to have accompanyed himſelfe ſtrongly and to have murdered him the ſaid Willm by the way; The which act the ſaid Chamberlen enterpriſed and tooke upon him to doe; And after, that the ſaid matter was diſcloſed to a well diſpoſed man called Mr. Thomas Oldbury, And hee perceiving the ſaid great miſcheife and murther like to fall, ſtirred and moved the ſaid Chamberlen to give warning to him the ſaid Willm, And ſoe hee did; And afterwards the ſaid Chamberlen brought certaine ſervants of his the ſaid Williams into a ſecret place to heare a ſervant of the ſaid Counteſſe, which exorted and ſtirred the ſaid Chamberlen to perform and fullfill the intent of all the murder aforeſaid, as it ſhall bee evidently proved; And ſince that time the ſaid Counteſſe hath divers times moved and ſtirred and ſent writings to one Thomas Holt that had the keepinge of his Caſtle of Berkeley, as ſervant to him, That hee ſhould keep the ſaid Caſtle to the behoofe of her the ſaid Counteſſe, And | that hee ſhould keep out of the ſaid Caſtle him the ſaid Willm, to his utter diſheriſon and finall deſtruction; which writing is, and at all times ſhall bee ready to bee ſhewed; And ſoe the ſaid Counteſſe both keepeth away the livelode of him the ſaid Willm, and continually laboreth to have his body and lands in execution, to the utter deſtruction of his perſon, livelode, and goods. Thus the bill.

Anſwer in Canc. 6. E. 4. in turre londinenſi.

To this bill the ſaid Counteſſe anſwereth; **That** where the ſaid Willm lord Berkeley of his ſinfull and ſeditious imagination, intendinge to eſtrange her from the lord Chancellors grace and right wife favor, untruly and damnably accuſeth her of that ſhee ſhould have intreated and hired one Chamberlen a ſanctuary man of Weſtminſter to have murdered him in his going home into his Country, which had been too abhominable for a chriſtian creature to have done, whereof as God knoweth, ſhee was never guilty in deed nor thought; And that ſhee is, and allways ſhall bee ready to prove and declare her ſelf off, as can be thought moſt convenient and behooſefull to bee done; And beſeecheth that there may bee ſuch order and direction ſet and taken in this matter for the punition of the untruth therupon, That the ſaid Willm and other of ſuch damnable diſpoſition may have cauſe of dread to accuſe any of the eſtates of this Realme wrongfully of ſoe great a crime, and according to a Statute in that caſe provided: And as touching the ſanctuary man,

man, that hee should have enterprized that foule deed, It was soe that the said Wiltm Berkeley for such consideracons as moved him, tooke the sanctuary of Westminster, And that sanctuary man perceived a servant of her the said Countess hearing masse in Westminster church, and came to him and told him, That Sr Wiltm Berkeley had taken sanctuary there; And hee asked the said Countess servant whether the said Wiltm Berkeley were through with the said Countess for such bonds as it was said shee had of him; And the said Countesse servant said, nay. Then said Chamberlen, That if shee had any suites against him, for a reward hee would find the way how an officer should meet with him and arrest him; And thereupon there was divers writs of capias vtlagatum directed to severall Sherifes upon divers outlayries pronounced against the said Wiltm, which yet standeth in their forces, and an officer of the kings purveyed to have executed it, if | hee might have been met without the sanctuary, which the sanctuary man enterprized to bring about; And other matter or desire then this was there never any with that sanctuary man by her the said Countesse, nor any of her servants by her commandment: And for the more proof of the same, the said Wiltm Berkeley the 4th yeare of the kings raigne, raised such a foule slanderous fame against the said Countesse of the same matter, which came to the Abbot of Westminster his eare; And the Abbot sent for the said Chamberlen, and called to him his Archdeacon and other persons, and examined the said Chamberlen of his demeaninge in that behalfe; And upon his own confession, for soe much as such a heinous noise of an intended mischiefe was made and had without cause, as hee confessed himself and by his assent, the Abbot decreed him to bee had to an open place in the sanctuary of punishment and reproofe, And made him to bee arayed in papires painted with signes of untroth, sedition, and doublenesse, And was made to goe before the procession in that aray, and afterwards soe set in the stocks, that the people might behold him: **And** whereas the said Wiltm Berkeley complaineth him of that, That the said Countesse should have moved, stirred, and sent writings to one Thomas Holt that had the keeping of the said Castle of Berkeley, That hee should keep the said Castle to the behoofe of her the said Countesse, The same Countesse saith, That shee was seized of the same Castle in her demesne as of ffee till shee was disseised by the foresaid James lord Berkeley, this Wiltm, and his brethren; And afterwards shee wrote and desired the said Thomas Holt to have delivered her the said Castle, or to have kept it to her use, according to her right and title, as lawfull was for her: Thus shee.

To this answer of the Countesse this lord Wiltm replyed, maintaining his bill to bee true; **And** the Countesse rejoyned, maintaining her answer, whereby they
descended

P VOL. II

Eſcaet. 7. E. 4. nº 20.	**569** descended to issue; but before any witnesses were examined on either part, or any further proceeding thereupon had, (for any thing I have found,) the said Counteſſe dyed, the 14th of June next in the ſeaventh yeare of the said king Edward the fourth, Anno. 1468, as formerly in the life of Thomas the fourth her grandfather, is declared: And by her death left to Thomas Talbot viſcount Liſle her grandchild and heir, the manors of Wotton, Symondsfall, the burrowe of Wotton, the moytie of the manor of Erlingham, and divers meſſuages, lands, Tenements, and fiſhings in Erlingham, Cromhall, Alkington, Hurſt, Durſley, Nibley, Sherneclifſe, Kingſcote, and of the ſixth part of the manor of Acton Ilger, and Iron Acton, and of divers lands in Horwood, Morecote, and Glouc., the manor of Wike by Arlingham, Sageſ-place and Sageſlond in Slimbridge, the hundred of Wotton late called the hundred of Berkeley, and the Advowſon of the Church of Wotton in the County of Glouc.;
carta. 15: Nov. 6. E. 4. in caſtro de Berkel:	To all which this lord Wittm pretended title; And which by a petition made the fifteenth of November before the Counteſſe death between herſelfe and the Dutches Eleanor and the lady Elizabeth, her ſiſters, were alotted to her in ſeveralty in lieu of other lands thereby alotted to her other ſiſters; To ſome alſo whereof, (as the manor of Cowley and the manor of Porteſhened allotted to the said Dutcheſſe
Eſcha: in turre lond: 7. E. 4. nº 20. Comp. eſcaetor. 15. E. 4. rot 9. in fcᵃčio. memor: fcᵃčij. Mich. 1. E. 4. rot. 25. ex pte rem: thes. Rot. cur: de Wotton 7. E. 4. in caſtro de Berkeley.	and alſo to Limeridge wood in Portbury allotted to the said Elizabeth,) this lord Wittm alſo pretended title: And alſo by her death diſcended to her ſaid grandchild, the manor of Sages in the pariſh of Slimbridge, and the advowſons of the Chantries of Sᵗ Giles in Hilleſly, and of Sᵗ John baptiſt in Wortly by Wotton, (mentioned in the offices found after the deaths of the said Counteſs and dutches the ſame yeare,) whereto likewiſe this lord Wittm pretended title; The said Viſcount Liſle, then being of the age of nineteen years and upwards and maryed to Margaret daughter of William Herbert Earle of Penbroke, then reſidinge at Wotton.
fine 7. E. 4. in banc. pat. 7. E. 4. pars. 2. m: 3. 5.	And thus in this yeare, (which was of jubile to this lord,) death rid him of three great lady widowes his great adverſaries, the said Counteſs Margaret, Dutches Alienor, and viconteſſe Jone late wife of John viſcount Liſle; And the 26th of October the ſame year were all the manors and lands of the said Counteſs Margaret and viſconteſſe Jone comitted by the king to the said Earle of Penbroke, during the minority of the said Thomas Talbot viſcount Liſle, his ſon in lawe.
pat. dat: 6 Julij 1. E. 4. **570** Mich: rec: 1. E. 4. in fcᵃčio cum rem. regis rot. 25.	What angry charge or motherly command the said Counteſs Margaret left to her ward and grandchild Thomas Viſcount Liſle, for purſute of theſe titles againſt her enemy this lord Wittm, charity forbiddeth mee to conjecture; Sure I am ſhee left in him an high ſpirit, foſtered by malignant attendants mortally hatinge this lord

lord Wi*ll*m, who forthwith fell into the plotts of the said Countesse; And havinge their maine Ayme (as hers was) to get from him this Castle of Berkeley, which hee now kept as his sanctuary and subterfuge from detts utlagaryes Statutes and the like; And which if they had effected, by all probability hee had been ruined; They fell in practise againe with the said Thomas Holt, then also his keeper of Whitcliffe parke, whom they corrupted, and with Maurice King porter of his Castle gates: The method of which trecherous plott and treaty the lres bonds and patents that passed between them and Robert Veell the viscounts Ingineer, which to this day remaine in Berkeley Castle, shall speake themselves in their own language.

cart et muniment in castro de Berkeley.

Maurice Kinge, I grete you well and hartely pray you as you will your one wellsare, and as I may shewe you such true and faithfull good will and kindnefs as of old time hath bene and continued between us, according to our oathes and ensurance, the which I have in mind and ever shall have; and spetially for the great truth and faithfull love that I found in you at the appointment between the lord Berkeley that now is, and us; and by the token that when M.r Thomas had gave up the matter and failed us, That ye and I yede into the Chapple out of the great chamber, And there I found you true, as you ever have bene hyderto; And by the token that wee lay togeder at Micheldene in one bed, and comuned there of such purposes as now is brought to the poynt, which will not faile, soe God bee pleased, wherein I suppose you know my old dealing; wherefore by the tokens afore rehearsed, I heartely pray you for all the lovis that hath been between us, and as you will your own wele, That ye wele geve very faythfull credence unto M.r Robert Vele, which ye know for a worhipfull gentleman and never non haster, but his worship is known nie you, and me: And such assurance my lord and I have taken about the matter, that of my life ye may trust thereto, wherein also I will that ye take the same surete of him, and care that your comunication bee secret between ye, And upon both your comunication y.t ye do agree well togeder what night ye may in hasty time speke with mee, which shall be to your perpetuall weal, And thus I leave you w.th goddis grace.

Thomas Holt to Maurice Kinge.

A chaplein

visc: lisle.

By your sworn brother in the Parke of Whitcliffe in the out house without the logge. Thomas Holt. |

My most trusty and welbeloved frend, I grete ye wele, praying ye hartely That ye will remember the matter that ye and I comoned of last; And for your matter, it is spede, your patent is spede of five markes and Wotton parke, with all that belongeth theirto, and your obligacon also, and all other that ye understand that can prevaile you to grant them; fee by patent, terme of life.

571 The same Holt to the same Kinge.

Nowe take the obligacon and condicon.

Vele to Kinge.   **Nob'int** Vniv̄si p presentes me Robertm Vele teneri et firmiter obligari Mauricio Kinge in centum libris sterlingor̄m legalis monete Anglie, Solvend eidem Mauric̄ Kinge heredibus aut assignat̄ suis in festo purificacōis beate Marie virgiñ proximè futuro post dat̄m p'sentiū, Ad quā quidem solucōem bene et fideliter faciend obligo me heredes et executor̄ meos per presentes, In cujus rei testimoniū huic p'senti scripto sigillum meū apposui, dat̄. 26.º die Januar̄ Anno regni Regis Edwardi quarti, Nono.

The Condition of this obligation is such, That if the Castle of Berkeley bee brought into the hands of Thomas Talbot lord Lisle by the faithfull help guyding and means of the said Maurice Kinge, And thereupon, That yᵉ said Maurice have his sufficient patent delivered him under the seale of Armes of the said lord Lisle, of the park of Wotton with the fees and wages of the keeping of the same of old time due and accustomed; And moreover by the same patent have five marks annuite duringe his life to bee had and received yearly of the lordship and revenues of Wotton; That then this obligation to bee void, or els it doe stand in his full strength and vertue.

Take also the patent.

lord lisle his pat. to Kinge   **Omnibus** xp̄i fidelibus ad quos p'sens scriptm pervenerit, Thomas Talbot vicecomes Lisle, salutem in d̄no; Sciatis me p'fat̄m vic̄ Lisle in fidelitate dilecti mihi Mauricii Kinge plenè confidentem, pro bono et gratuitu servicio suo mihi et hered meis impendend, concessisse eidē Mauricio officium custodis parci mei de Wotton subtus Egge in Cōm Glouc̄, ac ferarū ib̄m existeñ, et ip̄sm custodem eoȝdem ordino et per p̄sentes constituo: Habend et occupand et exercend officiū p̄dict pro termō vite sue, Capiend pro officio p̄dict exercend anuatim feoda et vadia eidē officio de antiquo debita et consueta; Ac | etiam sciatis me p̄fat̄ vic̄ concessisse eidem Mauricio Kinge quendā anualē redditm quinque marcaȝ exeunt de et in ōibus terris et teñtis meis in Wotton sub Egge in Cōm Glouc̄; Habend et percipiend redditm p̄dict añuatim p̄fato Mauricio ad termō vite sue: In cuius rei testimoniū p̄sentibus Sigillm meū apposui, dat̄ 26.º die Januarij Anno regni Regis Edwardi quarti post conquestm Anglie, Nono.

carta cum Willmo Throgmorton baronett.   **This** Robert Vele at this time was owner of Tortworth Charfeild and Huntingford, which last hee held of the visconts said manor of Wotton by knights service; whose well contriving of this plott soe highly pleased the said viscount, That by his

other

other deed under his feale of Armes of the fame date, hee gave to Wiłłm Vele his fecond brother, (or rather to him the faid Robert in his brothers name,) the office of Stewardſhip of his manor of Wotton, and the office of keeperſhip of his chace of Michaelwood, with the yearly fee of—13$^{li}_{..}$ 6$^s_{..}$ 8^d—for exercife thereof, to bee iſſuinge out of his manor of Wotton, payable at the feaſts of Efter and of St Michaell by equall portions: **Which** manor and chafe are adjoyning to the other lands of the faid Roberts.

This plot thus contrived and brought to ripenes was foon after revealed to this lord Wiłłm, And, as I take it, by Maurice Kinge himſelfe, whereby in all probability the ruin of the perfon of this lord W$^m_{..}$ was prevented; And how deeply the blowe had alſo pearced into the pofterity of this family, I take noe comfort to confider.

The vifcount Lifle underſtanding by the flight of Holt and his repair to him how the plot was difcovered, And the former writings under the feales of Armes of himfelf and Robert Vele come to the poſſeſſion of his enemy the lord Wiłłm, hee then begins to unmaſk himſelfe, & openly to act his ill cogitations, whereby may bee read the former purpofes of himfelf and his Counfell; **And** let the frute of the łre of challenge which from Wotton hee writes to this lord Wiłłm tell us the nature of the tree; **Thus,**

William called lord Berkeley, I marveill ye come not forth with all your Carts of gunnes, bowes, with oder ordinance, that ye fet forward to come to my manor of Wotton to bete it down upon my head: | I let you wit, ye ſhall not nede to come foe nye; for I truſt to God to mete you nere home with Engliſh men of my one nation and neighbors, whereas ye by ſuttle craft have blowin about in divers places of England, That I ſhould intend to bring in Welſhmen for to deſtroy and hurt my one nation and Cuntry; I lete the wit, I was never foe difpofed, nere never will bee; And to the proof hereof, I require thee of knighthood and of manhood to appoynt a day to meet me half way, there to try between God and our two hands, all our quarrell and title of right, for to efchew the ſhedding of Chriſtian menns bloud, or els at the fame day bringe the uttermoſt of thy power, and I ſhall mete thee; An anfwere of this by writinge, as ye will abide by, according to the honor and order of knighthood.

Thomas Talbot the Vifcont Lifle.

This łre was fent the nineteenth day of March in the tenth year of king Edward the fourth, Anno: 1469. about feaven weeks after the former plot was contrived;

573

Efcha: poſt mort.
Marg:Com:Salop:
7. E. 4.
rot. fin. 9. E. 4.

contrived; The said viscont then somewhat under the age of twenty two yeares, having sued his livery but the 14th of July before, whose lands then valued 1873: marks twelve shillings and three pence in old rent: And the lady Margaret his wife then priviment ensent with her first child.

This lord Willm receiving this lre at Berkeley Castle, the same day returneth this answer.

Thomas Talbot, otherwise called viscont Lisle, not longe continued in that name but a new found thing brought out of Strange Contryes: I marveill greatly of thy strange and lewd writinge, made I suppose by thy false untrue Counsell that thou hast with thee, Hugh Mull, and Holt: As for Hugh Mull it is not unknown to all the worshipfull men of this Relme, how hee is attaynt of falsenes and rasinge of the kings records; And as for the false mischevous Holt, what his rule hath be to the destruction of the kings lege pepull in my lordship of Berkeley, aswell to the hurt of their bodyes, as the losse of their goods, against Goddys lawe, consciens, and all reason, it is openly known, Soe that every worshipfull man should refuse to have them in his fellowship; And also of his own free will undesired of mee, before worshipfull and sufficient witnes, was sworn on a masse booke, That hee never should bee a | gainst mee in noe matter that I had a doe, and espetially in that untrue title that ye clayme, which ye hold my lyvelode with wronge; **And** where thou requirest mee of knighthood That I should appoynt a day and mete thee in the myd way between my manor of Wotton and my Castle of Berkeley, there to try betwyxt God and our two hands all our quarrell and title of right, for to eschewe the schedding of Christen mens bloud, or els the same day to bring the uttermost of my power, and thou would mete me: **As** for the determining betwixt our two hands of thy untrue clayme, and my title and right of my land and inheritance, thou wottest right well there is noe such determinacon of land in this Relme used, And I ascertaine thee That my livelode, aswell my manor of Wotton as my Castle of Berkeley, be entayled to mee by fine of record in the kings Courts by the advice of all the Judges of this lond in that dayes being; And if it were soe That this matter might bee determined by thy honds and myne, the king our Soveraigne lord and his laws not offended, thou shouldst not so longe desire but I would assoone answere thee, in every poynt that belongeth to a knight: for thou art, God I take to record, in a false quarrell, and I in a true defence and title: **And** where thou desirest and requirest mee of knighthood and of manhood to appoynt a day, And that I should bee there with all the power that I could make, and that thou would mete mee

half

Marginalia:
Inq: post mort Tho: Talbot: 10. E. 4. in Com: Gloucest pat. 9. E. 4. ps. 1. m. 1. fin: 10. E. 4. m: vlt. vetus extent terrar' in castro de Berkeley.

574

half way, I will thou underſtand, I will not bring the tenth part that I can make, And I will appoint a ſhort day to eaſe thy malitious hart and thy falſe Counſell that is with thee: faile not to morrow to be at Niblyes green at eight or nyne of the clock, And I will not faile with Gods might and grace to meete thee at the ſame place, the which ſtandeth in the borders of the livelode that thou keepeſt untruly from me, redy to anſwere thee in all things, That I truſt to God it ſhall be ſhewed on thee and thine to thy great ſhame and diſworſhipp: **And** remember, thy ſelf and thy falſe Counſell have refuſed to abide the rule of the grete lordis of this lond, which by my will ſhould have determyned this matter by thy evidences and mine, And therefore I vouch God to record and all the company of heaven, That this fact and the ſcheddinge of Chriſten mens bloud which ſhall be atwixt us two and our fellowſhipps, if any hap to bee, doth grow of thy quaryll, and not of mee, but in my defence, and in eſchewing of reproche, and onely through thy malitious and miſchevouſe purpoſe | and of thy falſe Counſell, and of thy own ſimple diſcretion; And keepe thy day, And the trouth ſhall be ſhewed by the marcy of God.

575

William lord of Berkeley.

The day and place is kept by both parties, The battle is ſtroke, and the lord viſcount Liſle is ſlaine with ſome others of his fellowſhipp.[1]

At this time both before and after the State was in much combuſtion, for upon the 13th of this March, ſeaven days before this ſkirmiſh, the king declared by his proclamation in all ſhires his victory againſt the rebells in Lincolne Shire and their Captaine Sr. Robert Wells: **And** the 21th of Mar: (the next day after this lord Liſles death,) the king proclaimes his brother the Duke of Clarence and Richard Nevill Earle of Warrwicke, then in Arms in Lancaſhire, to bee Traytors and Rebells, with the reaſons leading him therunto; whereby that trobled time was ſoe farr from takeing notice of this ryot, That the 26th of that month the king ſent his Comiſſion to this lord Willm to find out ſuch rebells as had been againſt him in this County of Glouc: **And** at Eſter in the 11th of his raigne was the battle of Barnet, with the death of the ſaid Richard Nevill Earle of Warrwicke; And the 27th of Aprill proclamations as before of treaſon againſt the wife of Henry the ſixth and prince Edward her ſon; Soe noe time to take notice of theſe Nibley tumults.

Rot. fine: 10. E. 4. m: vlt: teſt: 28. marcij in.10 Com̃. claus: 10. E. 4. dorſo.

pat: 10. E. 4. m: 7. in dorſo. claus: 11. E. 4. m. vlt:

And in the 13th of this kinge was this lord Willm ſpetially imployed wth Anthony Earle Ryvers, for the diſcovery of Traytors and their goods in the Counties of Glouceſter, Worceſter, and others.

pat: 13. E. 4. pars. 2. in dorſo.

Margaret

---

[1] An intereſting account of the great Berkeley Law Suit and of this battle, by Mr. J. H. COOKE, is given in the *Tranſactions of the Briſtol and Glouceſterſhire Archæol. Society*, Vol. III., p. 305.—[ED.]

Margaret the widowe of the said viscount daughter of the Earle of Penbroke, for the death of her husband, bringeth her appeale against this lord, by the name of William Berkeley of Berkeley knight, Maurice Berkeley and Thomas Berkeley his brethren, James Hiet Esqr, John Beley, Richard Hilp, and others; **And** after as many delays used by the defendants as might bee invented, And after a certificat enforced out of the Exchequer, That such a liberty as Barkeley hundred was with return of writs, (the Sherrives of the County in their returnes of the proces favouring the delayes,) The said Margaret, in Ester terme in the 12th year of Edward the fourth, declared against the said Beley, (who only appeared as principall,) That hee of malice prepensed the Twentieth day of March in the Tenth yeare of the said kinge, at Nibley at ten of the clock in the forenoone, feloniously | with the said Sr Willm Berkeley, Maurice and Thomas his brothers, James Hiet, Richard Hilp and others, stroke her said husband with an arrowe on the leaft part of his face to the braine, And after with a dagger thrust him into the leaft side; &c. Beley demands judgment upon the originall writ, because there was (saith hee) never any such man as Richard Hilp, therein named, (an other delay,) **And** to the fact pleadeth not guilty. Shee pursueth the rest of the defendants by proces untill the 6th day of October in the twelvth of the same kinge, when the parliament beginneth at Westminster, whereat upon the joynt petition of this lord W^m and of Ione his wife, and of the said Margaret viscountesse Lisle, it was enacted, That for the appeasing divers and many great variances and other exorbitant causes and quarrells between them moved and of longe time continued, That the said lord Berkeley and his wife and the heires of the said lord should quietly enjoy the manor and burrowe of Wotton Vnderedge, and the manors of Simondsfall and Arlingham, against the said viscountesse, paying to her one hundred pounds yearly at St Peters Church at Gloucester at the fower usuall feasts in the yeare, of equall portions, with a clause of distresse in the said manors, and a nomine penæ of five pound for non payment after fourty dayes; And a re-entry and holding for her life without impeachment of wast for non payment after a yeare and three monthes: Savinge to every other person their estate title and interest in the said manors; And with a provisoe, that this Act should not bee prejuditiall to the said lord Willm and his wife nor to the heires of the said lord, for their right title and interest in and to the said manors.

And the first and 16th of March in the said 11th yeare, for the fyne of fourty shillings, this lord Willm had a confirmacōn of all his old chres of Berkeley and Bedminster granted to his Ancestors by Henry the second, Richard the first, kinge John, and by Edward the third, upon oath made in Chancery that the same were casualy lost, as by the roll and parchment is suggested. **Shortly**

Shortly after peace thus established between this lord Willm and viscontesse Lisle, shee maryed Henry Bodrugan of Bodrugan in Cornwall Esqr, whose acquitances shew the receipt of this hundred pounds many years after: In readinge whereof I have observed, That shee allways wrote her name before her husbands, And hee onely wrote, Bodrugan, without his Christian name; **What** bad and good conditions were in him let the | parliament rolls in the 14th of Edward the fourth, and other records here marginally vouched declare.[1]

Acq: in castro de Berkeley.

Rot. parl: 14. E. 4. m: 1. 20. 26.
577
pat. 14. E. 4. ps. 2. dorso. m. 20. et. at.

ffor further manifestation of the day of battle and manner of the death of the said viscount Lisle, are the writs into ten Counties to enquire after his death, dated the Twentieth day of March in the Tenth of Edward the fourth, And an office in the County of Stafford the same yeare, And another under the great seale in the County of Glouc: (whereof the originall is perished,) at Berkeley Castle; And the kings licence dated at Banbury the sixth of Aprill in the Tenth of Edward the fourth, to Elizabeth and Margaret his sisters and heirs to enter into the manors and lands that were the said visconts their brothers: Before which time, (being but sixteen days after their brothers death,) their sister in lawe the viscountesse seemes to have been delivered of her child, whom (perhaps) sorrow for the untimely death of her husband, (lamenting like a virgin girded in sackcloth for the husband of her youth, as the prophet Ioell hath,) cast into an abortive travell: And the more probable becaufe the same day, perhaps the same hour, of this victory, this lord Willm with his riotous company advanced forwards to Wotton, where shee then was, rifled her house, And thence, (amongst other pillages,) brought away to Berkeley Castle many of the Deeds and evidences of the said Viscounts own undoubted lands, many of which remaine there to this day; Togeather with a peece of Arras, wherein the Armes of the Viscount and of the lady Jone his mother, daughter and coheire of Sr Thomas Chedder, were wrought, which twenty years agone I there also sawe.

post mort. Tho: Talbot
fin: 10. E. 4. m: ult.
pat. 9. E. 4. ps. 1. m. 1.
pat. 10. E. 4. m: 11.
orig: in scaccio eodē anno rot. 16.
orig: 10. E. 4. rot. 11. et. 15. in scaccio.
claus: 10. E. 4. m. 7. in dorso.

Joell chap: 1. verse. 8.

Many steps not yet worn out poynt unto this family how strongly the said viscountesse and other her frends, with the kindred of her husb^d, pursued this lord Willm Maurice and Thomas his brethren for the death of the viscount her husband; insomuch as to acquit Phillip Mead, (whose daughter the said Maurice Berkeley had maryed, as after followeth in the relation of his life,) and of John Shipward, two Marchants of Bristoll, The Maior of that City the second day of May next after,
                                                                                                examined

---

[1] Sir HENRY BODRUGAN was attainted and convicted of treason, 9 Nov., 1487. As he escaped to Foreign Countries the date of his death is not known, but it occurred before 1503. The Viscountess predeceased him. See *History of Trigg Minor*, Vol. I., pp. 553, 555.—[ED.]

Q VOL. II

carta in caſtro de Berkeley.

578
comp: Recept. in caſtro de Berkel:

examined twenty ſeaverall pſons upon oath upon fuſpition conceived againſt them, to have ſent Armed men in manner of warre to the aid of this lord Wiłłm Berkeley, againſt the lord Liſle; All which Examinates acquit them of that ſcandall and imputation, ſaith the ſaid Maiors teſtimoniall, yet extant under the ſeale of that City: Howbeit I have ſeen other notes | and memorialls of a ſtronger dye That aſſure mee That many came both from that City, procured by Maurice and them, and out of the forreſt of Deane, that morning wherein the ſkirmiſh was, to the ayd of this lord Wiłłm: And from Thornbury, (of whence the ſaid Richard Hilp was,) and where the ſaid Maurice Berkeley then dwelt, came both himſelf and all the ſtrength that on ſoe ſhort a ſomons hee could make: 𝔄nd if traditions might bee here allowed, I would aſſure this noble family, That within thirty two yeares laſt, by reaſon of my dwelling at Nibley, and of my often reſort to Wotton and to the villages adjoyning, I have often heard many old men and weomen in thoſe places, as Wiłłm Longe, John Cole, Thomas Phelps, Adrian Jobbins, Thomas Dykes of Woodford, Thomas Roberts of Woodford, Wiłłm Legge of Wike, John Smyth of Nibley, mother Birton, mother Purnell, mother Peeter, and others, many of whoſe parents lived in the time of king Edward the fourth, and moſt of themſelves were born in the time of king Henry the ſeaventh, as their leaſes and copies declared, ſome of them one hundred and ten yeares old, divers an hundred, and none under fourſcore, relate the reports of their parents kinsfolks and neighbours preſent at this ſkirmiſh, ſome with the one lord, and others with the other; and of ſuch as carryed victualls and weapons to ſome of thoſe companies, as this lords party lay cloſe in the utter ſkirts of Michaellwood chace, out of which this lord Berkeley brake, when hee firſt beheld the lord Liſle with his fellowſhip diſcending down that hill from Nibley Church, and after climbed up into trees, (being then boys of twelve and ſixteen yeares,) to ſee the battle: And how the lord Berkeleys number was about one thouſand, and exceeded the other in greatneſs: That the place of 𝔰𝔱𝔞𝔫𝔡 was at fowleſhard, whence this lord Wiłłm ſent upon the lord Liſle the firſt ſhower of his arrowes; That one black Will, (ſoe called) ſhould ſhoot the lord Liſle, as his beaver was up; And that Thomas Longe father of the ſaid Wiłłm was ſervant to one of them who helped to carry the lord Liſle when hee was ſlayne, and of many other perticularyties, (which I purpoſely omit,) not poſſible almoſt by ſuch plaine Country people to be fained: And that a ſpetiall man of the lord Liſles company was then alſo ſlaine, and buryed under the great ſtone tomb which yet remaines in the ſouth ſide of Nibley Church yard; inſomuch as I cannot otherwiſe but deliver

579

them as | truths; And much the rather for the full diſcourſe thereof which old Mr Charles Hiet, (whoſe great grandfather James is one of the Defts in the ſaid appeale,)

appeale,) had with the lord Henry Berkeley at Berkeley Caftle the 25th of September. 1603, which my felf then heard foe perticularly delivered from the relation of his father and grandfather as if the fame had been but yefterday : The faid lord Henry himfelfe feconding moft of what Mr Hiet related, from the reports of divers others made to himfelfe in his youth, fome of whom were then born and of the age of difcretion, as his L^{dpp} then affirmed : But enough of thefe traditions and reports, wherein I have exceeded mine own Inclination becaufe this paffage is of moft remarkablenefs in this family; And the bloud now fpilt was not cleane dryed up till the feaventh year of kinge James, as after in many places of thefe relations appeareth : **And** thus did all the fons joyne in revenge of the innocent bloud of that virtuous and princely lady Ifable their mother, malitioufly fpilt at Gloucefter feaventeen yeares before by Margaret this vifcounts grandmother, and whofe heire and ward hee was : **And** this wound ftroke the deeper for that the blowe thereof fwept away all her iffue male from the earth, And in the fame quarrell where[i]n the bloud of the faid lady Berkeley was fhed, as formerly is written.

fols : [528, 529]

Of this fkirmifh Camden writeth, That Wotton underedge yet remembreth the flaughter of Thomas Talbot vifcount Lifle here flaine in the time of king Edward the fourth in an encounter with the lord Berkeley about poffeffions, fince which time have continued fuites between their pofterities, untill now lately they were finally compounded.

Camden Brit :
in Com. Glouc.
fo : 464.

Upon the death of the faid vifcount Lifle this lord Willm entred alfo into the mannors of Wotton forren, Wotton burrowe, Simondsfall, Arlingham, and Sages, and into the Newleyes and the Warth in Slimbridge, and into divers other lands in Kingfcote, Horwood, Acton, Cromhall, and other Hamletts thereabouts, which had been the inheritance of his father James : **Howbeit** this lords poffeffion was not three yeares peaceable, (though hee had pleafed the Kitchen of the vifcounteffe with one hundred pound anuity, and her bed with a youthfull hufband,) before hee was powerfully fet upon by Sr Edward Grey, his mothers grandchild, as being fecond fon to Elizabeth Lady fferrars daughter of the lady Ifable, this lord Willms mother, as before hath been declared : who by | mariage of Elizabeth eldeft fifter and coheire of the faid Thomas Talbot, as in her right the 14th of March in the fifteenth of king Edward the fourth created lord Lifle, And after created vifcount Lifle by king Richard the third, in the firft yeare of his raigne, what time Margaret her other fifter and fellowe coheire, maryed to Sr George Vere, was dead without iffue.

Efch : 9. 10. E. 4.
origin: 10. E. 4. rot.
11:et. 15. in fc^acio.
origin: 11. E. 4.
rot : 15. in fc^acio
origin : 15. E. 4.
rot. 26. in fc^acio
c̃m rem. thes :
580
cart. 15. E. 4. m.
vlt.
pat. 18. H. 7.
pars. 2.

Between

carta counsell: in castro de Berkeley.

Between these two, this Sr Edward Grey, and this lord Willm, was longe tossed with equall malice and greatnes the title of these manors and lands, like a ball of discord, taken up and banded, with much toyle and expence; untill by the mediation of Thomas Grey Marques Dorset, elder brothers son to the said lord Grey, (frend also and near kinsman to the said Willm,) It was by Indenture dated the 25th of ffeb: in the 21th of Edward the fourth, agreed between this lord Willm, (then viscount Berkeley,) on the one part, And the [said] Edward Grey lord Lisle and Elizabeth his wife on the other parte, That for the setling of those great discords, quarrells and debates, which of longe time had been for the burrowe and manors of Wotton underedge and Simondsall, the advowson of Wotton Church, the rent of assize of—34^s_ 4^d in Nibley and Shernecliffe, the sixth part of the manor of Acton Ilger, Newleyes, the Warth, Sages, Westmancotes land in Arlingham &c, That the same should bee setled to the said viscount Berkeley and to the heires male of his body, with remainder to the said lord Lisle and Elizabeth his wife and to her heires for ever, by fyne or otherwise: **And** that the said viscount Berkeley should grant an Anuity of twenty pound p ann: to them and the heires of the said Elizabeth, going out of the said manors and lands, but to cease upon the death of Margaret Viscont^s Lisle, And then the same to bee one hundred pound p ann: **Or** if the said viscount Berkeley bee discharged of the hundred pounds wch hee now payeth to the said Margaret, Then the said hundred pounds annuity to begin presently: **And** they the said Edward Grey and Elizabeth his wife to bee barred from claiminge any of the said manors, or lands contrary to the purport of this Indenture: Howbeit they fell off from this agreement, but by whose default I find not, and betooke themselves to their former discords; Insomuch as, the ninth of May after, this viscount Berkeley was convented before the kings Counsell for his misdemeanor, and there enforced to enter into a recogni|zance of a thousand pound to appeare againe that time twelve month before the king and his counsell, And in the meane time to doe noe damage to the said Grey lord Lisle, or his servants.

claus: 22. E. 4. in Canc:

581

And the stiffe pursute of the said lord Lisle against this lord Willm Berkeley in nothing more strongly appeareth, then in that hee obtained in the fourth yeare of king Henry the 7th to have the irregular proceedings that were in the thirtieth of Henry the 6th, upon the Statute of the fifth of Richard the second, of forcible entries against this lord Berkeley, his father and three brethren at Cirencester before Judge Bingham, to bee certifyed thirty seaven years after by Margaret Judge Binghams widow and Executrix; And to procure the same to bee exemplifyed under the great seale of England, notwithstanding all resistances of this lord Berkeley

Berkeley

Berkeley to the contrary, then Earle Marshall and Marques Berkeley; A manifestation of eagernes, potency, and prudence.

During the time of these contentions, this viscount Berkeley was not altogeather passive, as warding blowes and returninge none: for with the like weapons of Westminster hall, hee stroke both the lord Lisle, and those that were favored by him.

And not onely himself but his two brethren, Maurice Berkeley and Thomas, assailed John Wenlocke, Nicholas Daunt, John Daunt, John Howell, Clark, and others his espetiall mynions with severall actions of false imprisonment, for that by their means and assistance they were taken and imprisoned from the 23^d of September in the 30th of Henry the sixth untill the 10th day of December following; which actions in both Courts were, after issue Joyned and ready for tryall, stayed by Injunction out of the Chancery obtayned by the said Wenlocke upon his bill exhibited against this lord Berkeley and Maurice his brother, untill the matter of the said actions should bee there first heard; wherein Wenlocke declareth at large the great variances that were between them and the Earle of Shroesbury, whom hee then fearved in ordinary, for the manors of Wotton, and other lands in the County of Glouc^r. And how the same were then ended by the mediation of John lord Beauchamp, Willm lord fferrars, and ffortescue and Yelverton Judges, as by their award (saith hee) under their seales ready to bee shewed may appear: **But** therein hee mistooke, for the false imprisonment was three years after that award, as formerly is declared; yet this false allegation for this time served his turne. | Other some this lord Berkeley by fairer courses took off from the assistance of his said adversary, (for great guifts are litle gods,) Amongst whom Kenelme Digas by deed under his seale of Armes, promiseth, That for the good lordship which the right noble lord Willm Berkeley knight lord Berkeley of his great noblenefs, hath diversly of late time shewed unto him, That hereafter hee will not bee of Counsell against him nor his heires, in his great matter touching the title of the lordship manor and burrowe of Wotton and other manors, of longe time in debate; Soe the words of the deed. Some others there bee of like straine, which I pass by.

At the parliament begun the . 17th of ffebruary in the 17th of king Edward the fourth, it is shewed how Richard the kings second son had been created Duke of Yorke and of Norfolke, Earle Marshall, Warren, and of Nottingham, And that for support thereof, the king hath now maryed him to Anne daughter and heire to

John

Marginalia:
Mich: 15. E. 4. rot. 56: et. 514. in banco c̃oi: Mich. 15. E. 4. rot. 66. coram rege.

petitio in Canc: 15. E. 4. pars. 1.

582 carta. 12 April. 14. E. 4. in castro de Berkeley.

Rot. parliam. 17. E: 4. m. vlt. pat: 17. E. 4 pars. 2. m. 6.

John late Duke of Norfolke, to the great honor of her and of her bloud, shee being but six years old. Now for reasons in this Act laid down, It is enacted, That if shee dye without issue, Then the said Duke of Yorke her husband shall for his life hold the half of fifty nine manors named in this Act, lying in the Counties of Salop, Sussex, Surrey, Middlesex, Leicester, Essex, Lincolne, Norfolke, Yorke, Bedford, and Derby; And the moitie of twenty knights fees in divers places, (named in this Act,) besides divers other chases hundreds and houses, Of which Katharine Dutches of Norfolke holds part for her Joynture: And that whereas Elizabeth late wife to the said Duke of Norfolke holds in Joynture and in dower many manors and other great possessions of the said Dukes her late husbands, Now in regard of the great advancement and honor of her daughter Anne with the said Richard the kings son, shee is content to rest sattisfyed with these manors following, and to depart with the residue to her said son in lawe the Duke of Yorke; viz! Duningworth, Hoseley cum Sutton, Staverton cum Bromeswell, &c. in the County of Suffolk, Dalby Chalcombe, Coldoverton, Segrave, Melton Mowbray. &c. in the County of Leicester; Bosham and others in the County of Sussex, and with others, (all named in this Act,) in the Counties of Norfolke, Cambridge, Warwike, Derby, and Hereford, which shee is to hold for her life without impeachment of wast; And in regard of her kindnes in departing with the residue, her estate in these is hereby confirmed, And after to Richard Duke of Yorke for his life against the heires of the said Anne, if shee dye without issue; with a provisoe that this Act bee not pr[e]juditiall to John lord Howard and Margaret his wife for the manor of Pritwell in Essex, nor to Jone wife to Willm lord Berkeley for the manors of Newsam, Kirkby Malsart, Burton in Londesdale, Brind, Gribthorp, and Thorneton, in the County of Yorke, to her made by Katharine Dutches of Norfolk her mother, nor bee prejuditiall to S!. Humphry Talbot for th'estate hee hath in Callowdon for his life by the grant of John late Duke of Norfolke. Which Act of parliament is after severally exemplifyed by all the said parties.

In these times also this lord Willm winneth even the king himself favorably to partake with him in these sutes; an argument both of an haughty spirit, and of a willfull disposition: for the 28th of May in the 16th of king Edward the fourth, It was agreed by Indenture between the king and him, That hee should convey to Richard Duke of Yorke the kings second son, and to the heirs of his body, all such right title and interest as hee hath or claimeth to have in all such manors and lands as for default of issue of John late Duke of Norfolke should come to him the said lord Berkeley; And for default of issue of the body of the said Duke of Yorke, Then to the

margin notes:
583
pat: 17. E. 4. ps. 2. m: 6.
pat: 18. E. 4. ps. 1. m: 2. et. 16.

carta in castro de Berkeley.

John Duke of Norf: died: 10. Jan: 15. E. 4.

the king himself and the heires males of his body, The remainder to this lord Willm and his heirs: And after security soe made, the king on his part promiseth to bee his good and gratious lord according to his lawes, And to cause to bee delivered up unto him all such Statutes and Obligations wherein the said Willm stands bound to John late Earle of Shroesbury, Margaret his late wife, and to Jn̄o. Talbot late viscount Lisle or any of them, or els to discharge the same: And if in the mean time this lord Berkeley bee arrested for any of them, the king will discharge him thereof: **The** twentyfirst of Aprill in the 21ᵗ of his raigne the king created him viscount Berkeley. **And** for performance of this agreement the said viscount Berkeley the twentieth of ffebruary following enfeoffed the Arch-bishop of Yorke and others, of his Castle and manors of Berkeley, Hame, Appleridge, Alkington, Hinton, Hurst, Slimbridge, Came, and Upton St Leonards; upon condicōn, That if this viscoṭ Berkeley doe performe the said Covenants and agreements made between the king and him, contained in the said Indenture, Then this feoffment to bee void: And soe also that the king at his own charges both require and make such conveyances before that time twelvemonth. |

Anne his daughter and heire died. 16. Jan⁹ 17.E.4.1478. Shee was maryed to Richard second son of. E. 4. duke of York 15. Jan: 1478. 17. E. 4. who was also. 7. feb: 16. E. 4. created duke of Norf: and Earle Warren. cart: 16.E.4.m: 12. pat: 16. E. 4. ps. 2. carta in castro de Berkeley.

Yet did not the king soe rely upon this feoffment, but at the parliament begun the twentieth of January after, (whereat this viscount Berkeley was one of the Tryers of forren petitions,) It was at the kings desire, with consent of this viscount Berkeley, enacted, That in consideracōn that the king should discharge him and James Maurice and Thomas his brothers, of sower and thirty thousand pound payable by them and James their late father to the Earle of Shroesbury and Margaret his wife and to John late viscount Lisle their son, And in consideration of other grants to bee made by the king to the said viscount Berkeley, That all the part and interest which to this viscount Berkeley belonged of all the Castles, honors, lordships, manors, and other hereditaments whatsoever in England, Ireland, Wales, or Calais, which for defalt of issue of Anne late daughter and heire of John Duke of Norfolke late wife of the said Richard Duke of Yorke the kings son, ought to come to this viscount Berkeley and his heirs, should remaine to the said Duke of Yorke and the heires of his body; And for default of such issue to the king and the heires males of his body; And for defalt of such issue to vest in this viscount Berkeley and his heires, as though this Act had never been made: And that all debts owing by this viscount Berkeley James Thomas and Maurice his brethren, to the king or to the said Earle of Shroesbury, Margaret his wife, and viscount Lisle, bee discharged, And henceforth bee void.

584 Rot. parli: 22. E. 4. m: 13.

The nynth of Aprill following dyed the said king Edward the fourth, and within a few months after, the kings two sons, king Edward the fifth and his
brother

brother Richard the said Duke of Yorke, were murthered by their unnaturall unckle and protector Richard Duke of Gloucester called Richard the third; whereby, (they being all the issue male of king Edward the fourth,) these estates in tayle determined, And this viscount Berkeley was againe vested in ffee Simple in all the said manors and lands, as though the said Act of parliament, or former conveyances, had never been.

The lord Berkeleys motives to assent to this Act of parliament seemes to bee three, **first** to bee freed, himself and his brethren, their lands and goods, from that heavy sum of . 34000ˡⁱ. mentioned in the said Act of parliament, noe inferiour course remaining to evacuate | those Statutes in the hands of a potent adversary: **Secondly** to have the kings favor and to bee created Viscount: **And lastly** to receive other benefitiall grants from the king: But what these should bee, I have not found: Onely the fifth of March following, the king made him one of his privy Counsell, And for his attendance thereon granted him the yearly fee of one hundred marks during his life out of the subsedyes of London and Bristoll, as hath been already said: It may bee that the death of the king, which followed within thirty fower days, hindered the residue of those benefitiall grants: But the blouddy tragedy which Richard the third acted upon his two nephews by their murder, returned againe upon this viscount Berkeley all that part of the Duke of Norfolks lands which hee had made away as aforesaid, And the said Statutes also discharged: An ill wind it is (saith the proverb) that bloweth noe man profit.

And if this viscount Berkeley could have contained his ambition and held himself contented in the pitch hee was now mounted unto, hee had soared in height of honor and greatnes of Estate above the heads of all his Ancestors, yea above his great uncle Thomas the fourth, in whom I have noted this family to bee in its highest somers solstice: **ffor** by the death of Anne the sole daughter and heire of John Mowbray Duke of Norfolke, the sixteenth day of January in the seaventeenth year of Edward the fourth, shee then under seaven years of age, (her father ending his dayes the tenth of January in the fourteenth of the said king,) And by the death of yᵉ king himself, and his two sons, To the younger of whom, (if Stowe bee true,) shee was maryed but the day before her death, This Viscount Berkeley, as heire to the lady Isable his mother, great Aunt to the Duke of Norfolke, had now the one entire moitie of all the Dukes estate; As to the lord John Howard, (shortly after by Richard the third made Duke of Norfolke, and his son Thomas, Earle of Surrey the same day,) had the other moytie, as son and heire of the lady Margaret his mother,

mother, sister and fellowe Copartner with the lady Isable: And upon the partitions made thereof, (some of which were after confirmed by Act of parliament,) this lord Berkeley had for his part these manors and lands allotted to him and his heires, as followe. |

    The manor of Donyngton,
    The manor of Twaytes,
    The manor of Thriske,
    The manor of Hovingham,
    The manor of Kirkby Malsart,
    The manor of Thornton,   } In the County of Yorke.
    The manor of Brynd,
    The manor of Gribthorpe,
    The manor of Newsam,
    The manor of Burton in Lonesdale,

586
Rot. parl: 4. H. 7.

    The manor of Eppeworth,
    The manor of Cothorpe,
    The manor of Belton,
    The manor of Westburrowe,   } In the County of Lincolne.
    The manor of Ouston,
    The manor of Haxey,
    The manor of Wrote,

    The manor of Mawvy,
    The manor of Dovercourt,
    The manor of Herwich,   } In the County of Essex.
    The manor of great Chesterford,
    The manor of Denge als Dengy,

    The manor of Segrave in Pen,
    The manor of Marlowe,   } In the County of Buckingham
    The manor of Winge,

    The Castle and manor of Bedford,
    The manor of Scotseild,   } In the County of Bedford
    The manor of Haunce,
    The manor of Bromham,

The manor of Callowdon,
The manor of Thurlaston,
The manor of fflekenhoe,
The manor of Alfpath,   } In the County of Warrwicke.
The manor Mereden,
The manor of Afpele,
The manor of Kington, |

587

The manor of ffenyftanton,
The manor of Hilton,   } In the County of Huntington.
The manor of Auconbury,
The manor of Wefton,

The manor of Stodefdon, in the County of Salop.

The manor of Melton Mowbray,
The manor of Coldoverton,
The manor of Mountforrell,
The manor of Sileby,
The manor Segrave,   } In the County of Leicefter.
The manor of Dalby Chacombe,
The manor of Witherly,
The manor of Twyford,
The hundred of Gofcot,

The manor of Bretby,
The manor of Linton,
The manor of Cotton,   } In the County of Derby.
The manor of Repington,
The manor of Roftlafton,
The manor of Afhborne,

The manor of Wefton Baldocke, in the County of Hartford.

The manor of Hinton,
The manor of Kenet,   } In the County of Cambridge.
The manor of Kentford,

The

The manor of ffuntington,
The manor of Bosham,
The manor of Thorny, } In the County of Suffex.
The manor of Buckfold,
The manor of ffindon,
The manor of Slagham,

The manor of North pedle in the County of Worcefter.
Divers lands and Teñts in Weftminfter in the County of Middlefex.
Divers lands and Ten^{ts} in the Town of Calais.
The manor of Wiffelee in the County of Surrey. |

The fourth part of the manors, of, vizt: 588
  Brighthelmefton,
  Clayton,
  Middleton, } In the faid County of Suffex.
  Mechinge,
  Seford,
  Alington,

The fourth part of the moytie of the manors, of, vizt:
  Cokefeild,
  Hounden,
  Kymer,
  The Chace of Cleers,
  The forreft of Worth, } In the faid County of Suffex.
  The burrowe of Lewis,
  The barony of Lewes,
  Nomanfland,
  Divers rents in Ilford,

The fourth part of the manors of Rigate and Dorkinge, in the faid County of Surrey.
The fourth part of the moytie of the Toll of Guilford and Southwerke, in the faid County of Surrey.
The fourth part of the moytie of the manor of Tiborne als Maribone; in the faid County of Midlefex.

                                                       The

The Castle of Holt,
The l:ship and manor of Bromfeild,   } In Northwales.
The manor of Yale,

The moytie or halfe part of the manors, of, viz:

Pickhill,
Seffewike,
Bedewall,
Iscoyd,
Hewlington,   } In Wales and the Marches of
Cobham,   Wales, to the County of Salop
Heme,   adjoyning.
Wrexham,
Burton,|

589 **And**, Allington,
Estclusam,
Eglesecle,
Ruabon,
Abinbury,
Dymill,
Morton faboy,
Armere,   } In Wales and the Marches of
Osbaston,   Wales, to the County of Salop
Sonford,   adjoyning.
Ofeleston,
The castle of Leons,
The town of Leons,
Almore,
Wolston,
Groffard advowson,

The moytie of the lordships or Seignioryes, of, viz:
Catherlagh, Oldcrosse, and of two
baronies and divers other manors   } In Ireland.
and lands.

And

And which are mentioned in the Acts of Parliament in the fourth, fifth, 7th 17th and. 19th years of king Henry the seaventh and in the severall deeds in the possession of the now lord Berkeley.

<small>carta in castro de Berkeley.</small>

And of his own paternall inheritance, which discended to him after the death of his father the lord James, hee now also had, as hath been already written,

The Castle, Burrough and hundred of Berkeley, The manor of Hame, The manor of Appleridge, The manor of Alkington, The manor of Hinton, The manor of Hurst, The manor of Slimbridge, The manor of Came, The manor of Cowley, The manor of Daglingworth, The manor of Upton St Leonards,	In the County of Gloucester
The manor of Portbury The manor of Porteshead, The hundred of Portbury,	In the County of Somerset.

And divers lands in the County of Hereford.

590

And also this lord Willm now had more in his own possession, which hee entred upon imediately after the death of Thomas Talbot Viscount Lisle, as before is touched,

The burrowe of Wotton, The manor of Wotton fforren, The manor of Simondsall, The manor of Sages, The manor of Arlingham, 22. marks rent in fframpton, Newleys and the warth in Slimbridge, Divers lands and rents in Kingscote, Horwood, Cromhall, and Acton, The Advowson of Wotton Church and of the Chantries of Hillesley, and Wortly,	In the said County of Glouc.

Also

carta in caſtro de Berkeley.

Alſo hee now had by the lady Jone his wife ſix manors in Yorkſhire, and the manor of Pritwell in Eſſex.

Paſch : 1 : R : 3. rot. 2. in ſc^ac̃io. carta in caſtro de Berkeley.

And likewiſe hee now had in fees pentions and Annuities, ſome in ffee and ſome for life, from the king and other great parſonages, by ſeverall patents—478^{li} 6^s 8^d by the year ; And divers other more both lands and fees, which I comforted not myſelfe in ſeeking after.

Soe that if any reſpect or huſbandry towards himſelf, conſcience towards God the giver, care of reputation towards the world, love or regard towards his poſterity, had been in this lord, hee had advanced this family beyond the pitch of the worthieſt of his Anceſtors ; And to his eternall fame in all generations of his houſe paſt and to come, had been highlieſt honored in their memorialls : But to his ever during obloquy and reproach, hee in leſs then ten years following, ſcattered gave and caſt away all the forementioned poſſeſſions, (a thing ſcarce credible to bee written,) not leaving any acre | to poſterity, nor ought els, ſave tears and tongues to complaine, whereof my weeping pen now mournfully begins to write.

591

His alienations and sales of lands.

This viſcount Berkeley beheld his Cozen germaine and fellowe Copartner, John lord Howard, to bee created Duke of Norfolke ; his ambition labored, if not to bee dignified as his equall, yet to ſit in the next throne, for in the moulds that caſt them both, hee found noe difference, nor in the mettall ; Siſters ſons they were, And this viſcount diſcended of the elder ; only the kings favor made the ods ; which hee caſteth about to gaine, And thus compaſſeth :

carta in caſtro de Berkeley.

Having in his ambitious opinion too much land, and too litle honor, hee is upon the 28th of June the ſixth day after the coronation of Richard the third, created Earle of Nottingham, to him and the heires males of his body, with the fee of twenty pound p añ out of the Sherifewicks of Nottingham and Derby: This Earledom ſattisſyeth not : for to climb higher, hee agreeth with that uſurping king the 2th of March following in the ſame year, by Indenture, That when hee ſhould bee required, hee would make to the king and to the heires of his body a good eſtate in his manors of Melton Mowbray, Segrave, Coldoverton, Dalby Chawcombe, Twiford, Witherly, Sileby, Mountforrell, and the hundred of Goſcote, in the county of Leiceſter: And in the manors of Donyngton, Twaytes, Thriſke and Hovingham in the County of Yorke: And in the manors of Harewich, Dovercourt, Mawney,

and

and Chesterford, in the County of Essex; And in the manors of Winge and Segrave in Penne, in the County of Buckingham; And in the manors of Calthrop, Westborrowe, Eppeworth, Belton, Haxey, and Ouston, in the County of Lincoln; And in the Castle and manors of Bedford and Bromham in the County of Bedford: And in the Castle of Holt with the lordship of Bromfeild and yale in Northwales: And in the reverçon of the manors of Kirkby Malsart, Newsam, Thornton, Gripthorp, Brind, and Burton in Lonesdale, in the said County of Yorke, after the decease of Jone his wife; And for default of such issue of the kinge, to remaine to him | the said Earle of Nottingham and his heires for ever. And it was further agreed between them, That the king should grant to the said Earle for his life, when hee should require it, an yearly rent of fower hundred marks out of the great Customs of the City of London; And for performance thereof, for soe much as was by him to bee performed, hee the said Earle of Nottingham became bound to the king in a recognizance of ten thousand pounds; And accordingly by Indenture dated the 23th of October in the second year of the said king, the same manors were by this Earle conveyed to the said king accordingly: And the fifteenth day of the next month, The said king Richard by Indenture under his hand and seale, Aswell for the true and faithfull service that this Earle of Nottingham in manifold wise hath done to his highnes, in the same, did promise and grant to the said Earle, That at all times thenceforth, hee will ayd, comfort, and assist the said Earle, as lawe, right, and conscience will, aswell in and for his inheritance and all titles concerning the same, As of and in all other causes that the said Earle hath to doe; At what time this Earle was not released from a recognizance of one thousand pound, wherein hee stood bound for his personall appearance in the Starr chamber, And to doe noe damage to the said Edward Gray lord Lisle or to his servants: Howbeit this profuse scattering of those thirty five manors at a clap hurt him not; for this estate in tayle in the king determined the 22th of August following, by the kings death at Bosworth feild, And by the death of his wife and of his only child the prince, dead a litle before his father: Soe willing was Gods gracious eye to have made this Earle looke back, and to retire himself into the consideration of himselfe, and to have preserved those possessions which had been from heaven showred upon him: But hee rather chose to bee branded by St. Paull with the livery of infidelity, then to have any care of his family house or kindred, present or to come.

592

claus: rolls. 1. R. 3.
claus: rolls. 2. R. 3.

carta in castro de Berkeley.

ordo in Camera stellaṫ. 9. Maij. 22. E. 4.

2. Tim: 5 : 8.

Henry the seaventh, by the overthrow and death of Richard the usurper, obtaineth the Crown and weareth it; And soe prudent was this Earles cariage

between

between thofe adverfe princes and their adherents, (ayding the one wth men, the other with money, neither of both with his perfon,) That hee preferved the favor of both, at leaft loft neither of them: **And** as a teftimony of this kings good acceptance of his fervice, upon the 26th of October following (fower days before his own coronation,) hee created him Earle Marifchall, To hold during pleafure, with the fee of twenty pound: And the 19th of February following, created him Earle Marifchall and great Marefchall of England, To hold to him and the heires males of his body, with the like fee of twenty pound: **In** which patent of creation, the king gives him | power, afwell in his prefence as in his abfence, to have and bear a ftaff of gold wth a black ringe at both ends, with the kings Armes at the upper end, and his own Armes at the lower end thereof: **And** in the meane between his two patents, the 12th of December, grants him a generall pardon for all offences comitted before the 7th of November then laft.

pat. 1. H. 7. m.
pat. 1. H. 7. m.
pafch: rec: 1. H. 7. rot. 3. in fc^ačio.
593
pat: 1. H. 7. m.

It feemeth fomewhat plaine That a precontract was concluded upon between Sr Will'm Stanley lord Chamberlaine to the king, and this Earle, for furthering him into thefe great offices of honor: for upon the fame 19th of ffebruary, this great Marefchall by his deed of the fame date with his patent of creation, And with his new ftile of Will'm Earle Marfhall and of Nottingham, vifcõnt Berkeley and lord of Berkeley, hee gave to him the faid Sr Will'm Stanley, (by the name of cozen,) and to the heirs of his body, All his part and purpart of his manors of Pickhill, Seffewyke, Bedewall, Ifcoyd, Hewlington, Cobham, Hem, Wrexham, Burton, Alington, Eaftclufan, Eglofecle, Ryabon, Abinbury, Dimill, Morton faboy, Armere, Ofbafton, Sonford, and Ofelefton, And of the Caftle and manor of Dynefbran, and of the Caftle and town of Leons, Bramfeild, Yale, Wrexam, Almore, Wobfton, and Sonford, in Wales and in the marches thereof to the County of Salop adjoyning; And for defalt of fuch iffue of the body of Sr Will'm Stanley To remaine to the faid Earle Marfhall and to his heires: **And** thus for the confideracõn of honor did this Earle Marfhall runne out of two Caftles and twenty eight manors and parts of manors: **And** yet was not his ambitious humor fattisfyed: **And** juftly might Maurice Berkeley his brother and heire apparant, and Maurice his fon and heire, complaine, as they did, That out of a high and pompous mind, hee afpired to bee made a **Marqueſs**; Between whom, great difpleafures now arofe, never after reconciled, upon the occation of thofe and other like affurances, fynes, and recoveryes, (whereof many now enfue,) which this lord Will'm paffed: **ffor** the better to cut off the antient entaile to the heires male, created by his Anceftor the lord Thomas the third, as in his life appeareth, This vaine and pompous Earle did in Miclimas

carta in caftro de Berkeley.

petitio Mauricij in carfto de Berk:

Michmas and Easter Termes in the second of Richard the third, upon severall writs, de recto præcipe in capite suffer recoveryes of the advowson of Slimbridge Church, and of the manor of Portbury, and of the Castle and manors of Berkeley, Hame, Appleridge, Alkington, Hinton, Came, Hurst and Slimbridge, and of divers others: In many of which by his feoffments after these recoveryes executed in August in the first of Henry the seaventh, hee for default of issue of his own body, estated Thomas Marques Dorset in tayle :| which notwithstandinge, within two years after, hee againe altered and estated upon the king, as now followeth.

In banco c̄oi rot: 453: Michis rot: 147. Pasch: et 154.

carta in castro de Berkeley.

594

And having twice made advantage of honor and profit, (but against his purpose or will,) by two contracts with king Edward the fourth, and with king Richard the third, hee assayleth a like chapman, king Henry the seaventh, for a third fortune, (for Marques Berkeley, the Earle Mareschall of England will bee at least :) And thereupon by Indenture dated the 10th day of December in the third year of Henry the seaventh, (by the name of Willm Earle Mareschall and of Nottingham, great Mareschall of England,) hee covenanteth with the king to convey by good assurance the Castle and manor of Berkeley, and the manors of Hame, Appleridge, Hurst, Slimbridge, and Cowley, To the use of himself and the heirs of his body, And for want of such issue, To the said king Henry the seaventh and the heires males of his body, And for want of such issue To the use of his own right heirs : And to convey the manors of Alkington, Came, Hinton, and Portbury, To the use of himselfe and Anne his wife and the heires of his body, And for want of such issue, To the said king and the heires males of his body, And for want of such issue, To the use of his own right heirs as aforesaid : In lieu whereof the king gives him leave to convey twenty five of his other manors, severally named in the said Indenture, to what uses and to whom hee pleaseth, without any fine to bee paid into the Hanaper upon such alienations : And promiseth to confirm unto him all manner of franchises and liberties granted heretofore by him or his progenitors to him the said Earle, or to any of his Ancestors.

Mich: term. 1. Mariæ ex parte rem̄ regis inter scripta et rec: in banco carta in castro de Berkeley.

pat. 1. H. 7. pars. 4.
pat. 3. H. 7. pars. 1.

And according to these covenants are recoveries suffered of the said Castle and manors, And of the manors and Advowsons of Wotton underedge Simondsfall, Arlingham, and others: And severall fines also are by him leavyed of the said Castle and manors at the same times, with renders of like estates; and of many others in seaverall Counties ; As with small labor is (at once) to bee read in the severall Inquisitions found in the . 7th. 8th and 9th. yeares of king Henry the seaventh, after this Marquesse death, remaining of record in the Chancery.

Hillar. 3. H. 7. rot. 354. 360. 357. et. 343.
Hillar : et Trin : terms 3. H. 7. et. 7. H. 7.

Eschaet : in Canc : temp. H. 7.

And

Act of parl: annis 4. 7. 17. et 19. H. 7.	**And** to conclude, hee thus estated upon the king and the heires males of his body for defalt of issue of his own, **His** Castle of Berkeley, twelve manors and three advowsons in the County of Glouc.; **Two** manors in the County of Somerset; **ffower** manors in the County of Warwick; **Eight** manors and one hundred in
595	the County of Leicester; **Six** manors in the | County of Derby; **ffower** manors in the County of Essex; **ffive** manors, a fforrest, a chace, and a barony in the County of Sussex; **Two** manors in the County [of] Surry; **ffower** manors in the County of Huntington; **One** manor in the County of Hartford; **Three** manors in the County of Cambridge; **A** barony, and fower manors in the County of Bedford; **And** others in other Counties, And in Calais, Ireland, and Wales, besides divers advowsons of churches and chapples, And divers hundreds and other regalityes, with a great multitude of knights fees; **Soe** that by increasing in the kings favor, hee proved more profitable to the king then his first covenants comprized in
pat: 4. H. 7. m: 13.	the said Indentures; **And** hereupon the 28th of January in the fourth of his raigne, the king created this Earle Marshall **Marques** Berkeley, to him and the heirs males of his body, with the fee of thirty five pounds pr ann out of the lesser Customs of London.
hillar: 3. H. 7. cart. in castro de Berkeley. cl: roll. 3. H. 7. Bacon in vita H. 7. fo. 236.	**And** besides these foresaid Conveyances to the king and the heirs males of his body, **Hee** further sold and gave divers others to the said Sr. William Stanley lord Chamberlaine, and to others; **And** also in the third of king Henry the seaventh gave to Sr. Reignold Bray knight, (whom Sr. ffrancis Bacon calleth a Counsellor of antient authority with his king,) his manor of Haunce in the County of Bedford, and his manors and lands in Kensington and Marybon als Tiborne in Midlesex, in ffee Simple, which were but rewards for his Court favour.
Inq: post mort. Marchion, Berkeley. 8. H. 7. Com. pleas Mich: 21. H. 7. rot. et 17. H. 7. ibm. His will 7. H. 7. in Cur. prerog. carta. 4. Nov. 3. H. 7 in castro de Berkel: com: pleas: Mich. 17. H. 7. rot.	**And** the 23th of February in the third yeare of Henry the 7th gave for like Court favor to Thomas Stanley Earle of Derby the kings father in law, for defalt of issue of his own body, The manors of Donyngton, Twaites, Thriske, Hovingham, Kirkby Malsart, and Burton in Lonesdale, in the County of Yorke; **And** his manors of Winge, Segrave in Pen, and Marlowe, in the County of Buckingham; **And** the manor of Denge als Dengy in the County of Essex; And the manors of Eppeworth, Belton, Haxey, Owston, and Wrote, in the County of Lincolne; **And** the manors of Alspath and Mereden, in the County of Warrwike; To hold to the said Earle of Derby and the heirs of his body; **Who** had also by like conveyance the manor of Slagham in the County of Sussex, **And** the manor of Wisselee in the County of Surry, which cost him like Court-holywater, as aforesaid.

In

In the same month and year hee severally conveyeth the manors of Hinton and Kenet in the County of Cambridge, to the use of himself for life, The remainder to Richard Willoughby for his life, The remainder to the heirs of the body of him the said Earle, The remainder to the heirs male of the body of the said Richard Willoughby, The remainder to Edward Willoughby Esqr and to the heires males of his body, The remainder to the right heires of him the said Earle; which manor at this time was in the hands of Elizabeth Dutches of Norfolke for her life: Of which manor of Kenet, see after in the life of the lord Henry the first.

And in July following, in the self same manner hee conveyed the manor of Callowdon in the County of Warrwicke, with like remainders to the same parties, which at this time was in lease for life to Sr Humphry Talbot: And for better confirmation of this assurance, did in the 6th of Henry the 7th leavy a fine thereof.

And also the said Earle of Darby, (for default of issue of the body of this said Marques Berkeley,) had also divers other manors and lands, As by the will of the said Marques appeareth.

And to his wife the lady Anne Berkeley and her heires, hee devised by his will all his messuages and lands in London, paying . 200 . marks to the ffryars Augustines; And his house in Chelsey in Middlesex hee by his said will gave to John Whitinge and his heires with a legacy of fourty pounds; And to conclude, what by fines and recoveryes and other conveyances of record, and what by deeds executed by livery and by Atturnement, And what by his last will and Testament, hee soe conveyed and gave away all the forementioned masse of Castles, Baronies, manors, hundreds, Chaces, Parks, knights fees, and other hereditaments in all the said Countyes in England and Wales, and in Ireland and Callais, as that nothing remained to his heire; And made more effectuall those to the king by an Act of parliament in the 7th. of his raigne.

And having in Michaelmas Terme in the seaventh of Henry the 7th by fine and other assurances, setled the manor of great Chesterford in Essex, upon himself and the lady Anne his wife and the heires of his own body, with remainder to the king and the heirs males of his body, As though it was not enough to give the king his land, but hee would build him an house also; Hee, the eleventh of December following, agreeth by severall deeds under seale, with Carpenters Masons and other workmen, forthwith to build him a spatious house upon the same manor; At which time

carta in castro de Berkeley.
licentia regis 8. Feb: 3. H. 7.
596

fols: [806, 807]

carta. 10. Julij. 3. H. 7. in castro de Berkel.
fin. 6. H. 7. in banco.

his will. 7. H. 7. in cur. prerogat:

His Will. 7. H. 7. in Cur. Prerog.
fines in banco. 3. 5. 6. H. 7. cōes. recuper: in banco. 1. 3. 5. H. 7. divers: cartæ in ijsdem annis. Inq: 7. 8. 9. H. 7. in divs: Com. post mort. Marchion. Rot: parl. 17. Oct. 7. H. 7. memor. sc^acij Trin. 9. H. 8. rot primo.

fin. 7. H. 7. in banco.

carta in castro de Berkeley.

time, without a like miraculous bleſſing as was ſent to Abraham and Sara, there was noe hope of iſſue between him and his wife, And himſelf before the finiſhing could not but fall into his grave, as hee did, as after followeth; yet hereby alſo appeares, | the power of an over-rulinge wife, that for her own end could draw her huſbands old age this exceſſive building upon a peece of ground wherin neither of them, upon the matter, had any longer an eſtate then for their own lives.

<small>597</small>

<small>Liber feod. miſtum in ſcćio. temp. H. 3. Rot. ſervičr. in rubeo libro in ſcćio. fol. 232 Rot. claus. 1. R. 2. m. 45 Rot. ſervic. 1. H 4. m. 2. Eſch. 1. H. 4. poſt mort. Thom. Ducis Norf. Bedford. claus 1 H. 5. apud le coronnac. coram Ričo Beauchampe nuper Com. Warw. Fin. 8 R. 2. m. 20 Claus. 7 E. 1. m. 6. 8.</small>

In the vaſt volume of which his ſales, none ſeemes more diſpleaſinge to his poſterity then the ſale of his Caſtle and Barony of Bedford, and of the honourable ſervices whereby he held the ſame; beinge by the tenure thereof, at each kinges coronation, Ellemoſiner or Almoner, havinge for his fee the cloth which the Kinge on his coronation day went upon from his hall or chamber to the church doore where hee was crowned: And after dinner had the ſilver diſh which uſed of cuſtome, as the Almeſdiſh, to ſtand before the Kinge at dinner, and one tun of wine: whereby alſo hee ſold one of his titles of honour, ceaſinge thenceforward to be ſtiled Baron of Bedford: An office of honor which had deſcended from the antient family of Willm. de Bello Campo, who in the 7th of Edward the firſt leaft it to his daughters and Co-heires, the eldeſt of whom was maried to the lord Mowbray; and from them it came to Willm. de Latimer, and John de Mowbray Earle of Nottingham; and from Latimer, by Elizabeth his daughter and heire, to John Nevill of Raby; and upon the partition of Mowbrayes lands, Duke of Norfolke, was allotted to this Marques and his heires, that which to the Dukes of Norfolk appertayned.

His Almes and Devotions.

<small>carta. 3. H. 7. in caſtro de Berkel:</small>

The lands which this lord gave to the prioreſſe of our ladies houſe within Carleton parke ats Wallinge wells, were of ſuch value, That in return thereof the pryoreſſe and her covent granted to accept him and his heirs for ever as one of their founders, And to doe them ſuch honor and in ſuch ſort to pray for them and their good eſtate, as they doe for their founders in each thinge; And to obſerve all ſuch oriſons prayers obſervances obites and other divine ſervices, for his ſoule and of his heires, and of his fader and moder, and for the good eſtate of Dame Anne his wife, as the ſaid prioreſſe and Covent have uſed to doe for their founders; And ſpetially to pray for the ſoule of the lady Jane his late wife, and for the good eſtate of Thomas Stanley Earle of Derby and his heires, and for their ſoules health for ever.

<small>carta. 4. H. 7. in caſtro de Berkeley.</small>

The like liberality this lord extended to the pryor and Chapiter of the Cathedrall Church of Worceſter; In recompence whereof the ſaid pryor and Covent

Covent accepted this lord Marques and the lady Anne his wife into their spirituall society and fraternity; And admitted them to the participation of all the benefits workes and merits wrought by them, aswell in masses hours prayers watches fastings disciplines and hospitalityes; as in Almes and other benefites which hereafter shall bee done or had in their Cathedrall Church; **With** this addition from their speciall grace and bounty, (saith the deed,) That when the deaths of this lord and his wife shall bee intimated to them, there shall bee as much | said and done for their soules as for the brothers and sisters and other benefactors of the said place, and for the soul of John ffynes father of the said lady Anne, and for the soules of the children of the said Marques and of Jane his late wife.

598

And surely this invention of spirituall fraternityes which are appurtenances or annexaries to the orders of ffryars, Nunns, &c. which in these times was grown frequent, was a prudent and profitable late devise; for into it lay people of all sorts, men and weomen, maryed and single, desired to bee inrolled; as thereby enjoying the spirituall prerogatives of pardons indulgences and speedy dispatche out of purgatory.

To the pryor of the fryar Augustines in London this lord gave in hand one hundred pounds in money; **In** lieu whereof and of other benefits and guifts, (saith the deed,) which this Marques intends to give to that place, The said pryor and covent agree to say two masses presently and for ever at the altar of our lady and of St James, where the body of Jane Countes of Nottingham his former wife lyeth buryed, between the said Altars; And to pray for the prosperous estate of the said Marques and of Anne his now wife, and of Edward Willoughby, Richard Willoughby, Anne Beauchampe, Elizabeth Willoughby, and John Whitinge his gentleman usher; with all the issue of the said Marques and Jane; And espetially for the saule of the said Jane and of Katharine her mother, sometime Dutches of Norfolke, and for the soules of James lord Berkeley and of Isable his wife father and mother of the s.^d Marques, and of Thomas Berkeley brother of the said Marques, And after the deaths of the said Marques and Anne Then the said two masses to bee sunge for their souls also; which they the s.^d pryor and Covent doe promise to doe unto the worlds end; And also to say a solemne obite yearly in the said place on St Mathias day in ffebruary for the soules of the said ladyes; And the like then for the said Marques and Anne his wife when they shall die: **And** that this Indenture of agreement shall bee yearly read in their Chapiter house in the feast day of St Michaell, for the better performance thereof, as they shall answer afore God at the dreadfull day of doome. |

carta: 3: Nov: 6.
H. 7. in castro de
Berkeley.

And

599
Will: 5. feb: 1491.
7. H. 7. in cur.
prerog.

And the fifth of february twelvemonth after in the seaventh of the said king Henry the seaventh, This Marques by his will bequeathed his body to bee buryed in the said Church of ffryar Augustines, and gave thereto twenty marks to buy vestments to bee used at the Altar of St Rooke there. And also two hundred marks more for two fryars there perpetually to singe for his soule, And twenty marks for two other fryars to singe in the white ffryars in ffleetstreet at the Altar of St Gasion there, for his own soule, and for the soules of his father and mother, and of his son Sr Thomas Berkeley, for ever: And besides to bee endowed with ten marks yearly; And likewise ordained, That another fryar should singe at the gray fryars at Glouc., in like maner, for the said soules; To the repair whereof hee gave twenty pound in money.

By his said will, this Marques ordained, That his wife and other his Executors should after his death purchase ten marks yearly rent, therewith to found a Chantry at the altar of our lady of pitty at Eppeworth in the County of Lincolne.

To fryar John Wikes hee gave twenty shillings. And appointed that his executors should recompence all trespasses and wrongs by him done, in discharge of his soule, as should bee proved before them within ten yeares after his death; And this to bee proclaimed in every place where hee hath had most resort unto in time past, after every true and reasonable mans desire.

The one half of his array, plate, stuffe of hushold, and of Chapple, hee gave to his wife Anne, And the other half to goe towards the performance of his will.

To Isable Berkeley hee gave twenty markes.

To Margery Berkeley hee gave five marks.

To Richard Berkeley hee gave five marks.

And to twenty other of his servants hee gave the like legacies: And made his wife, the Bishop of Rochester, Judge fitz James, and Mr Wythers, his Executors; To each of whom hee gave twenty pound a peece; And for his overseers made king Henry the seaventh, and the said Earle of Derby, and John Whitinge his gentleman usher, To each of whom hee gave ten pound a peece. |

600

Hee also in his life time gave divers Anuities pentions and fees, whereof these following are the cheifest I observed. vizt

In the Tenth year of Edward the fourth hee granted to his brother Maurice ten markes by the yeare for his life, out of his lordshipp of Nibley, for the great service hee that year did to him at the incounter with the lord Lisle. *carta in castro de Berkeley.*

The same year in consideracōn of service, hee granted an Anuity of fower markes p anñ to John Cassey Esq. out of this manor of Slimbridge, for his life, who was at the skirmish at Nibley green with him. *hillar : in banco 21. E. 4 rot. 352.*

About the same time hee granted an anuity of five pound p anñ to Willm lord Hastings for his life. *Acq : in 15. E. 4.*

The 22th of Edward the 4th hee granted to Thomas his brother, in consideration of his laudable service, an Anuity of nineteen pound p anñ : out of his manors of Wotton and Hame. *carta in castro de Berkeley.*

And about the first of Henry the seaventh granted an Anuity of ten pound p anñ, to the lord Daubeny for his life, out of his manor of Portbury : And also an Anuity of fower pound p anñ, to Ralph Skelton for his life. *comp : recept. in castro de Berk.*

In the third of Henry the . 7th, hee gave an Anuity of ten marks p anñ to Thomas Tiler for his life, who also was his generall Receivour. *carta in castro de Berkeley.*

The same year hee granted to Thomas Sampson for his life, all his land in Calais, rendring the third part of the revenue. *carta in castro de Berkeley.*

About the same time hee granted to Sr. James Blount an Anuity of ten marks for his life out of his manor of Sileby in the County of Leicester ; Some other the like, there were, which I passe by. | *Acq : in castro de Berkeley.*

His miscellaniæ or various passages.

601

By comon intendment those that seek often to the phisition have diseased bodyes ; what constitution this lord was off not onely his life past but the many pardons hee purchased from those kings whose laws hee had transgressed, which now followe, doe declare.

The . 17th of March in the 36th of Henry the sixth, the king pardoned this lord Willm all offences generall. *cart. in castr. de Berk : rot. pdon : 36. H. 6. rot. 30.*

The

cart. in caſtr. de Berk.
rot. pdon: 2. E. 4. m. 32.

The firſt of May in the ſecond of Edward the fourth, the king pardoned him all offences untill the fourth of November then paſt.

Rot. pardon: 10. E. 4. m: 2.

The 25ᵗʰ of May in the 10ᵗʰ of Edward the fourth the king pardoned him all offences till the 25ᵗʰ of December then paſt.

carta in caſtro de Berkeley.
rot. pdon: 12. E. 4. m. 23.

The twentieth of May in the 12ᵗʰ of Edward the fourth, the king pardoned him all treaſons murders rebellions and offences untill the firſt of September before; whereby hee ſtood diſcharged from the viſcount Liſles death, and his utlagaryes thereupon.

carta in caſtro de Berkeley.

The tenth of March in the firſt of Richard the third, the king pardoned him all offences untill the 21ᵗʰ of ffebruary paſt.

carta in caſtro de Berkeley.

The 9ᵗʰ of December in the ſecond of Richard the third, the king eſpetially pardoned him all offences debts recognizances &c, untill the tenth of November before.

Trin: 3. H. 7. cum rem. theſaur:

The fifteenth of ffebruary in the third of Henry the ſeaventh, the king pardoned him all offences and matters whatſoever; which in diſcharge of divers debts demaunded of him by proces out of the Exchequer, hee pleaded in Trinity Terme after: One or two more there are, which I omitted in my notes.

ffor the better diſcharge of his houſhold port, when hee abode at Berkeley Caſtle, which was from the death of his father, untill ſuch time as king Edward the fourth with an augmentation of his ſtile and honor, drew him to his Counſell table, Hee uſed yearly to ſend a ſhipp for wines to Burdeaux in ffrance: And in the year

chres: in Berkeley Caſtle.

1477, being the ſeaventeenth of the ſaid king, upon returne of his ſhipp, hee retained twenty Tunns, for | his own proviſion: the reſidue the maſter of the ſhipp had: Some of which charter parties for furniſhing the ſaid voyages yet remaine in Berkeley Caſtle, eſpetially for the ſetting forth of the ſhipp called the George of Berkeley, whereof the Chre ſheweth this lord to bee owner, and John Pembroke his ſervant to bee maſter.

602

The abidinge of this lord Willm in his fathers life time, was for moſt part at Portbury, Afterwards at Berkeley Caſtle, between which places his uſuall travell was by water, and over at the paſſage called Crokarſpill; The paſſer whereof in the time

time of Henry the fixth, exhibited a petition againſt this lord Wiłłm to Richard Duke of Yorke, (father of king Edward the fourth,) then lord of the manor of Eaſton, whereof one part of the ſaid pill is accompted to bee parcell; complaining that this lord and his ſervants paſſed and would paſſe at their pleaſure without paying anything for their feryage, to the difinheritage of the ſaid Duke and his ſaid Tenants wronge; And prayeth, that at the dukes ſaid manor hee might ſhew his evidence for his difcharge and freedome in paſſage, or els to pay as other men in paſſing over there between the two Countyes of Glouceſt and Somerſet, doe pay. *petitio cum Thoma Morgan Arm:*

The firſt of January in the 21ᵗʰ year of king Edward the fourth, the Duke of Buckingham by his warrant charged all his keepers and officers, That whenſoever and as oft as the right worſhipfull and his right entirely welbeloved cozen the viſcount Berkeley lift to take his pleaſure to hunt within any of his fforreſts, parks or chaces within the Counties of Kent, Surry, and Effex, That every of them ſhould give him due attendance, and to make him as good diſport as they can, as they intend to pleaſe him, from year to year and time to time. *Warrant in caſtro de Berkeley.*

This lord having in the 17ᵗʰ year of Edward the fourth been outlawed at the fute of Richard Seintle of London for non-payment of debt of 9ˡⁱ, Reverſed the ſame by error, for that hee was ſued and outlawed by the name of Wiłłm Berkeley of Berkeley knight, whereas hee was at that time one of the lords and peeres of the realme; And for proofe pleads verbatim his writ of fomons to the parliament the ſame yeare. *Trin: 17. E. 4. rot. 191. in banco.*

And it is not improper here to ſhewe, That this lord dyed indebted to Wiłłm Moore his ſecretary for thirty old nobles which hee lent him, | And for. 70ˢ. wages, for which his brother Maurice was ſued in Chancery ſeaven years after his death, by Wiłłm Gifford Executor to the ſaid Wiłłm Moore, whoſe title and proofe was, That this lord Marques lying ſicke, a litle before his death willed that the ſaid Moore ſhould bee paid thoſe ſums before any others; which the ſaid Maurice did, though hee was neither heire nor Executor, and not having any Aſſets in land or perſonall eſtate from his ſaid brother; whereby appeares a great diſtance between the difpoſition of theſe two brothers; The Marques hatinge Maurice at his death, Maurice lovinge his memory and the repoſe of his ſoule after life ended. *Bill in Canc: 15. E. 4. 603*

In the 33ᵗʰ of Henry the fixth, Edward lord Abergavenny granted to this lord Wiłłm the Stewardſhip of Chepſtowe in Wales for his life, with the fee of twenty marks by the yeare. *carta in caſtro de Berkeley.*

<small>carta in castro de Berkeley.</small>

In the 39th of Henry the sixth, Anne Dutches of Buckingham made this lord Willm master of her games of Deere, and supervisor of all her parks forrests chases and warrens in the County of Gloucester.

<small>carta in castro de Berkeley.</small>

In the 31th of Henry the sixth John Mowbray Duke of Norfolke made this lord Willm Supervisor of his dominions of Gower and Kilvey in Southwales, and his steward of Chepstowe, for his life, with the yearly fee of twenty pound.

<small>carta in castro de Berkeley.</small>

In the first year of king Edward the fourth, the foresaid Anne Dutches of Buckingham made this lord Willm Steward of her lordship and manor of Thornbury, for the life of his father the lord James, taking the fees thereto belonging and accustomed; And at this time was this Willm soe feared of his fathers tenants, or grown soe potent over his old fathers affairs, as none of his Tenants would take any lease or estate from that old lord, but that they would either have this Willm to confirme the same by his deed, or joyne with his father in the grant.

Divers personall differences being between this lord Willm and John Lord Beauchamp, aswell for such of his fathers goods the lord James as came into his hands, as for other causes, they referred themselves in the sixth of king Edward the fourth to the award of the lord Chancellor and of the Bishop of Bath, whereto they promised to stand upon their faiths of Knighthood. |

604
His wives.

Out of what humor I know not, but longer did this lord solace himselfe in a single life then any of his Ancestors from Harding the Dane, neither could any perswasion work him to wivinge in the life of his father: Yet, in a contrary quality, more forward to contract his own son and heire at younger years then any of his Ancestors, as after followeth.

This lord had three wives, who in their simpathies and antipathies stood thus in relation to him: The first hee loved not, nor shee him: The second hee loved entirely both living and dead, and shee him: The third hee loved, and shee overruled him for her own ends, to the advancement of her selfe and her kindred.

<small>Vincent: fol: 631.</small>

His first wife was Elizabeth the daughter of Reginald West, lord de la ware, and of Magaret his wife daughter and heire of Robert Thorly Esq: whom hee maryed in the sixth yeare of king Edward the fourth in the third yeare after his

fathers

fathers death, then about the age of one and forty yeares: **From** her hee was divorced shortly after, before any issue had between them, by the sentence of Carpenter the Bishop of Worcester; which shee held, (and I beleeve,) to bee unjust and partially given in his favor; from which shee appealed to the Court of Rome, and procured thence from pope Paul the second, tres compulsary dated the twentieth of November. 1467. being the seaventh year of the said king, to have all the writings acts sentences dispositions and myniments touching the said divorce to bee sent to Rome, As by the in[s]trument thereof under seale in the Castle of Berkeley may appeare: **her** husband and the partiall Bishop held it wisdome to stop the stream, ere it flowed to Rome, And soe ended that sute.

carta in castro de Berkeley.

Now, for that I have observed some differences in opinion amongst some worthy branches of this family about this lords lawfull or unlawfull putting away of this wife, (admitting it to bee for adultery,) and his mariage with another in her life time; some of them making this unlawfull Act one of the greatest outward causes, (in the eye of man,) of this lords dying issuelesse after soe hopefull a posterity had, and of | the consumption that followed of his patrimony, with other crosses, Gods angry hand seeming streched out against him in a troubled life ever after: I will a litle inlarge my self upon this point, And tell his posterity That his second mariage as I conceive it was adulterous, wherein hee longe lived, and had issue that miscaryed; And that though the adultery were proved, and the sentence of divorce recorded, yet was not hee soe set at liberty that hee might, in her life, marry with another, as hee did.

605

1. **First**, the Act of adultery doth not dissolve the knot, or (as wee speake,) break the bond of mariage; for then it would follow That the party offending could not upon reconciliation bee received againe by the innocent to former society of life, without the solemnizing of mariage anew; which is a thing never heard off, and contrary to the continuall practise of all churches.

2. **Secondly**, the sentence of divorce cannot releeve him neither, for there is noe lawfull sentence in any Court in case of divorce but it ever containeth an express inhibition to either party to marry with another; with intimation in flat termes, That from the time that they or either of them shall goe about an other mariage, Quod extunc prout ex nunc, et ex nunc, prout extunc, (it is the stile of the Court,) That present sentence upon record shall bee utterly void to all purposes, and they in the same case as if it had never been given.

3. **Againe**,

3. **Againe**, if the comitting of Adultery should dissolve mariage, Then both parties are in the same case as they were before they were maryed, free and at liberty; And then may either of them, aswell the guilty as the innocent, marry againe, which is the very gaine the Adulterer or Adulteress propounds to themselves; And soe would the comitting of sin, bee made gainfull or benefitiall to an offender.

Ambr: in. 1. Cor. 7.

4. **Againe**, if adultery dissolve the marriage bond and all, (as with this lords practice it did,) Then not onely every christian is excluded from that charity of receiving his wife againe, (having been faulty,) to conjugall duties, without a new mariage, as hath been said: but which is worse, the innocent party, if hee have knowledge of the body of his wife, having been false that way with another, should in soe doing comitt adultery himself, in as much as hee hath had the | use of her body that is now none of his; I say none of his, because their mariage is utterly dissolved by the act precedent of his wicked wife, if this opinion bee allowed.

Augustine 606

5. **Againe**, if at the pleasure of every lewd man, or light woman, by comitting the sin with another, they might dissolve as many former mariages, and make way to as many new mariages as they list; for being weary of the first, it is but to bee lewd of body and presently the bond is broken, & liberty given to make choice of another; And upon the like wearines, by the like Act, of a third and fourth; It would bring with it a world of troubles and confusions and evill consequences, as the second mariage of this lord Willm in the life of this his former wife might have done, between his issue of his second mariage and his next brother and heire.

Iherom: in Math. 19.

6. **And** againe, if the word of God bee sought to, whether any favor may bee had there, it will appear, That duringe the primitive church even till of late years the Judgment of many great divines and the present practice of the law ecclesiasticall were one and the same, and great reason why: for the authority of the fathers was the ground of the antient Canons, by which the law in this case is ruled: Soe that but for the opinion of some later divines, there need not bee sought any opposition between lawe and divinity in this question, nor that distraction happen, wherein wee see divines to give their hands for licence to that for which law will convent men and censure them too.

7. **And** againe lastly, it seems an unanswerable ground, viz! That one may not in any wise have two wives at once; for by the originall institution there can bee but two in one flesh: But this lords wife, though shee profaned mariage with another,

another, was not thereby become the wife of him with whom shee prophaned, but remained this lords wife still, whose first shee was, and whose only shee can bee soe longe as hee liveth: And the word of God seems to mee plaine in this, The woman is bound to the man soe longe as hee liveth; Soe that if while hee liveth shee becometh another mans shee shall bee holden an Adulteresse; from which very words the vow of mariage seemeth to have been framed, which then was and still is made in the congregation by either party, forsakinge all other keepe thee onely unto her soe longe as you both shall live: And againe, To have and to hold for better for worse till death us do part: **And** these plainly shew, (as I conceive,) That the bond of mariage is not broken but by death, And that though shee should become another mans, yet | shee is not become his wife: **The** places of S.t Mark and S.t Luke seem plaine, That a man having put away his wife cannot marry againe; And for the place of S.t Matthew, where it seems to bee qualified with (unles it bee for adultery,) it is all the shewe that can bee made for these mariages; **The** rules both of divinity and reason are, That when there falleth out any diversity in places, first to expound the lesser number by the greater and not contrary, That is one Evangelist by two, and not two by one: Secondly, to expound the former writer, (which is granted S.t Mathewe was,) by the later that writ after him, as both S.t Marke and S.t Luke did, and not contrary; espetially where both may stand, as here methinks both may; They two interpreting it, It is thus, Hee that putteth away his wife, (which but for Adultery is not lawfull,) and maryeth an other, comitteth adultery himself: **howbeit** because the position, that a man putting away his wife for her adultery may lawfully marry an other, is maintained by the learned writings of soe many late juditious divines, in most of the reformed Churches at this day, And hath soe troubled the pulpit in S.t Maryes in Oxford, which my younger yeares there heard neere forty years agone, I stand an unable man to determine of either opinion, leaving this family to the censure of this fact of this great lord their Ancestor as it self shall affect: **But** mee thinks, That a wife y.t is an Adulteresse doth not cease to bee a wife, unles at least shee bee manifestly divorced, and dispoyled of her mariage ringe.

Rom. 7. 2.

607
Mark. 10. 11.
Luke: 16. 18.
Math: 19. 9.

defence of John Raynalls printed 1610.

I have seen an old writing of this lords time, laying the pedegree of this Elizabeth to bee the daughter of Reginald West lord de la ware, son of Thom̃ West and Jone his wife, daughter of [Roger] lord de la Ware and Alienor his wife, daughter of John lord Mowbray and Elizabeth his wife, daughter and heire of John lord Segrave; which John lord Mowbray and Elizabeth his wife had issue also Thomas created Duke of Norfolke father of Isable maryed to James lord Berkeley mother of this lord Wiłłm; Averring thereby That they were within the forbidden

In castro de Berkeley.

degrees

degrees of mariage, hee in the third, and shee in the fourth, And the divorce to bee thereupon: **Which**, if a cause then and at this day, then more then twenty maryed couples within five miles of Berkeley Castle, (not to spread my knowledge further,) may bee divorced; But to this old writing I wholly subscribe not.

<small>608
Vincents discovery of errors fol: 631.
4. cartæ in castro de Berkeley.
Esch: post mort. Willmi Hastings. pat: 15. E. 4. in arce London.
4. cartæ in castro de Berkeley.</small>

His second wife was Jone, (written also Jane,) who had formerly been maryed to Sr. William Willoughby, and was daughter, (as Mr. Vincent saith,) of | Sr. Thomas Strangwayes and Katharine his wife, daughter of Ralph Nevill Earle of Westmerland and widowe of John Mowbray Duke of Norfolke; which Katharine was thirdly maryed to John Viscount Beamond, and lastly to Sr. John Woodvile; And dyed in the first year of King Richard the third.

<small>pat. roll: 8. E. 4.</small>

This said Jone was maryed to this lord in November Anno 1468. in the 8th year of king Edward the fourth; And for her mariage portion brought the manors of Kirkeby Malsart, Burton in Londesdale, Thornton, Newsame, Brind, and Gribthorp in Spalding moore, in the County of Yorke, And the manor of Donver in Norfolke, for her life, of the inheritance of John Duke of Norfolke, son of the said John; And one hundred marks p ann out of the kings Customs of London.

<small>claus: 8. E. 4. m. 12:

capt. et recognit. 30. Octobris.</small>

The agreement about the mariage of this second wife will best appear out of this lords obligation dated the 18th of October in the 8th of King Edward the fourth, whereby hee became bound to the Arch-bishop of Yorke, Robert Danby cheife Justice of England, and to Richard Pigot Serjeant at lawe, in three thousand pound, with Condicon, That if before Christmas next hee maryed Jone Willoughby daughter of Katharine Dutches of Norfolke and sister of John late Duke of Norfolke, And shall before Candlemas day next following cause himself and her to be enfeoffed of the manor of Hame in the County of Glouc, of the yearly value of one hundred and threescore pounds p ann, To hold to them and to the heires males of his body, with the remainder to his heires, And also shall permit her to take the profits of the said manors of Kirkby Malsart, Burton in Londesdale, Thorneton, Newsam, Brend, and Gripthorp in Spalding moor, in the County of Yorke, and of the manr of Donver in the County of Norfolke, And of one hundred marks yearly rent out of the kings Customs at London, to bee disposed of at her pleasure, for the maintenance of her self and her children, and of her weomen servants, without the interruption of him the said Willm, Then the said bond to bee void.

<small>pat: 8. E. 4. ps. 2. m: 25:
609</small>

Which foresaid hundred marks yearly rent out of the profits of the customs in the Port of London, king Edward the fourth | had by his tres patents dated but the

the 18th of August before, granted to the s'd Jone sister of John late Duke of Norfolke, late wife of S'r Will'm Willoughby Knight, To hold to her and the heires of her body untill the king should provide her of soe much land with like estate; And for the other manors, they were the inheritance of her brother the Duke of Norfolke. *carta in castro de Berkeley.*

Her Joynture from this lord was at severall times made extraordinary great, as the Castle and manor of Berkeley, the manors of Hame, Apleridge, Alkington, Hinton, Hurst, Slimbridge, Wotton, Cowley, Cam, Simondsall, Daglingworth, Portbury, and many others: Nothing thought too much, The greatest too litle, for her. *cart: 8. 12. et. 17. E. 4. in castr. de Berk:*

And to declare his further affection by adding what more hee had to give, hee the 28th of January in the fifteenth of king Edward the fourth, gave all his goods and Chattles to Thomas lord Stanley, Thomas Berkeley Esq'r and others, to dispose off, as their proper goods; And by another deed of the same date declares, That the former is made to them upon this great trust, That hee shall use those goods during his life without their contradiction, And if hee dye before Jone his wife daughter of Katharine Dutches of Norfolke Aunt to our Soveraigne lord king Edward the fourth, Then they by their deed to grant those goods and chattles to the said Jone as her proper goods, within ten days after his death, And not to come at all to his Executors. *Claus. 15. E. 4. m. 6. in dorso:*

This Jone by her first husband had issue Edward Willoughby, Richard, Cicely maryed to Edward lord Dudley, and Anne maryed to S'r John Beauchamp knight son and heir apparent of Richard lord Beauchamp in the Twentieth of king Edward the fourth; To whom this lord Will'm, in advancement of her mariage, gave his manor of Erlingham for their lives. *carta: 6. H. 7. in castro de Berkeley.*
carta. 20. E. 4. in castro de Berkeley.

And by this lord Will'm her second husband, shee had also issue Thomas Berkeley, and Katharine Berkeley.

Thomas was born that year the lord Lisle was slayne at Nibley Green, as formerly hath been said; And on the eighteenth of Aprill in the fifteenth year of king Edward the fourth, at the creation of Edward | his eldest son prince of Wales, and of Richard his second son duke of Yorke, and the said Thomas made knight of the Bath: At what time, though hee was not past the age of five years, yet his father in June following enters into an agreement about his mariage with Mary daughter of Anne Countesse of Penbroke; And besides the portion received in hand, *Stow. in vita: E. 4.*
610
carta: 6. Junij in castro de Berkeley.

hand, tooke of her nine feverall obligations of one hundred pound the peece for the refidue of the mariage portion of the faid Mary: wherein it was alfo agreed, That if fhee dyed before mariage or before carnall knowledge had, And that Willm then Earle of Penbroke had none iffue female within five years after to bee maryed to the faid Sr Thomas Berkeley, Then the faid obligations to bee voyd.

About one year before hee had by the faid Jone the faid daughter called Katharine, to whom her grandmother the dutcheffe her godmother gave name; And to her in the fame fifteenth year of Edward the 4th this lord conveyed his manor of Came in generall tayle, after the deceafe of himfelf and his wife: Howbeit both the faid Sr Thomas and Katharine very fhortly after deceafed to the great forrow of their parents, And lye buryed in the Chapple of Berkeley church wth the body of their grandfather the lord James.

Though the manner of thefe two childrens deaths bee by many old tales diverfly delivered, As that they fhould dye by the biting of a mad dogg; others that they fhould bee drowned in one of the caftle wells; And others that they fhould fall from off the leads over the Caftle wall; (all which by feverall perfons at feverall times I have heard related,) yet I find not otherwife then that they dyed by natures ordinary vifitation, And foe I beleeve.

And not many years after, (without further iffue,) on St Mathias day in ffebruary in the firft year of king Richard the third, dyed the faid Jone, after that her hufbands creation had advanced her to the degree of a Counteffe; And lyeth buryed in the pryory Church of the ffryar Auguftines in London, between the Altars of our lady and St James; for the repofe of whofe foule her hufband ordained two maffes to bee there fung for ever, and a folemne obite yearly to bee there kept on the faid day, as formerly hath been faid.

The third wife of this lord was Anne daughter of Sr John ffynes lord Dacres of the fouth, and of Alice his wife daughter and heire of Henry lord fitz Hugh, whom hee maryed about two years after the death of the faid lady Jone, towards the end of the firft year of king Henry the feaventh, by whom he had noe iffue: This Anne was this lords wife about feaven years, And after his death lived his widowe, and the wife of Sr Thomas Brandon, almoft the like time: And dyed the tenth of September in the .13th of the faid king Henry the feaventh, by whofe death the faid king had a full poffeffion of all the manors and lands conveyed to

him

him by this lord Marques; A great part whereof and of divers other manors shee held for her life in joynture and in dower, As Came, Cowley, Wotton manor, Wotton burrowe, Simondsall, Wotton liberty, Arlingham, Slimbridge, Portbury, Alkington, Hinton, Hame, Newleyes, and the Warth.

<small>divers: comp. in curr. Augm: et in castro de Berk: 18. H. 7. et: al: ann: Comp: 10. H. 7. ibm.</small>

This lady Anne wrought profitably upon the age of her old husband both for the advancement of her self and of her kindred; And, if not the raiser yet certainly a continuer of the storme that blew soe unnaturall a vapour between her husband and Maurice his brother and heire. Upon whom also Henry the seaventh played as handsomely, in getting from her into his hands forthwith after her husbands death, such of those manors as lay nearest to Berkeley Castle, as, Hame, Hinton, Alkington, Hurst, and Slimbridge, as though hee had longed for the present possession thereof; which hee desires forthwith to see, as also those others still held by the Marques widowe, And in preparation against his coming and ten days stay att Berkeley Castle, takes down the hall at Wotton house, And makes therewith the roofe of the great kitchen in Berkeley Castle, adding to the sheets brought from Wotton five fodder of new lead, whereby that prime mansion seat of Wotton became wholly devasted; which for the space of. 280. years had been as a Queen of houses to this noble family; having thereby nothing left her but ruins and those ill witnesses of her perished beauty, declaring thereby that houses as well as men have their ages and destines; In rakeing up of which rubbish, after John Staunton in the seaventh year of king James had pur|chased the fee farm of the Scite place of Henry lord Berkeley, Hee then shewed mee and others many signes in guilded bricks stones and peeces of timber, digged by him out of the depth of the rubbish earth, which witnessed a perished excellency.

<small>claus: 9. H. 7. m. pat. 8. H. 7. m. breve de privat. Sigillo in Canc: 9. H. 7.</small>

<small>comp: rec: 10. H. 7. liber in castro de Berkeley.</small>

<small>612</small>

And now by the king are Sr John Walsh, Sr Robert Poynz and others, placed Stewards Receivors Surveyers baylyes keepers woodwards and porters, over these manors Castle and lands, (called in all accompts henceforth in the kings Courts, by the name of Berkeleis lands;) which after threescore years (shorter by ten then Iheremies Babilonian captivity of the Jewes,) God revisits this family againe with all, upon the death of king Edward the sixth, As after followeth in the life of Henry lord Berkeley.

<small>orig: scācio. 7. H. 7. rot. 28. et. 36. orig: 8. H. 7. in scāciorot.16. et.19. et. 9. H. 7. rot. 42. et. 13. H. 7. rot. 38. et. 21. H. 7. rot. 16.</small>

<small>fol: [727]</small>

Mr Mill in his Catalogue of honor maketh this Anne to bee daughter of Sr Thomas Strangwayes, and the widowe of Sr Willm Willoughby; And T: T: as hee there affirmeth maketh her the Daughter of the lord Beamont and of Katharine Dutches

<small>catalog: of honor fol: 884.</small>

Vincent fo: 53. Dutches of Norfolke his wife: And Vincent affirmeth her to bee the widowe of St Thomas Brandon knight when this lord maryed her; miftakes on all three fides, as formerly appears; fomwhat by my means corrected by Mr Vincent in his difcovery of Yorks errors, printed 1622, out of the notes fomewhat before (for the

Vincent fol: 630. love of truth,) given him by mee, which hee accordingly helped in the later part of that booke. |

613

His seales of Armes.

This lord in the feals hee ufed feems to taft too much of the mother, for in the eighth and tenth of king Edward the fourth and other years, before the difcent of the inheritance of Mowbrayes land was caft upon him and his fellow Co-partner, hee, for his manuall or lre feale ufed the lyon born by Mowbray; And for his greater feale, the Arms of Brotherton and Berkeley in one Efchucheon cornerwife; And for creft the helmet and Bifhops miter; And for fupporters, two unicorns, circumfcribed. S: honorabilis dñi Willi de Berkeley et Wotton. Behold the refemblances in true proportion.

His death and place of buriall.

Efchaet: 7. H. 7. This lord in the fifth year of king Henry the feaventh tooke an houfe within
in Com Suffex the precinct of the fanctuary at Weftminfter for five years at five pound rent, where
Wigorn: Warr: for his more comodious attendance at the Court hee lived till his death, which
Glouc: happened on St Valentines day the 14th of ffebruary. 1491. in the feaventh yeare of the faid king, then of the age of 66. years and three months or thereabouts; whereof hee had fit lord, Vifct, Earle, and Marques, about. 28. years and three monthes; And lyeth buryed in the Church of the Auguftine ffryars in London aforefaid.

His

His lands whereof hee dyed seized.

I have hitherto in the end of each lords life set down what lands each of them left to his heire, whereof I nowe have better means to inform my self then at any time before; The Inquisitions after the death of this lord Marques in the Counties of Gloucester, Warwick, Leicester, Wigorn, Essex, Sussex, Somerset, Eboz, and other Counties, still fairly remaining in the chapple of the Rolls, And those in the County of Glouc: under seale in Berkeley Castle: But when I look into them, I find king Henry the seaventh and many other persons interessed, and already entred into the possession of the great masse thereof, by their severall remainders and conveyances therein found: **But** unto Maurice his brother and heire, Or to his three sons, Maurice Thomas and James, all at mans estate and of apparent hopes, or to the fower sons of Thomas his youngest brother formerly mentioned, I find noe discent, or conveyance of any land at all.

Exemp: Sub magno Sigillo in castro de Berkeley 8 : H : 7.

In forgetting these, I feared this lord had forgot his name, for they were all the males then living, discended from the loynes of his father, | and princely pious mother: And therefore I hoped for better in his last will, for, dies dabit quod dies negabit, what is not of this day may bee of too morrow; But quanta de spe decidi, how farr was I deceived in this great Marques!

615

I found in his will that which was more harsh; To Isable Berkeley daughter of his said brother Thomas, a legacy of twenty markes given her by this lord, to bee paid in ten yeares; And to Margery Berkeley her sister five markes; And to Richard Berkeley their brother, a legacy of forty shillings; And to John Berkeley another brother, a remainder of lesse valewe then the least of all the former legacies: **Many** manors and lands and great legacies given to divers strangers, for life and in ffee simple; but noe more, or other, to any of his brothers, nephewes, or neeces.

Volunt. Marchion: 7. H. 7. in Cur: prerog : Cant.

I feared that at the making of this will sicknes had bereaved this lord of understanding, but the date and composure thereof declared it to bee in the time of health and memory; I called to mind that this lords brethren, Maurice and Thomas, were adventurers of their lives with him and for him and for the honor of their fathers posterity in the skirmish at Nibley green; That Maurice out of brotherly love to him and his honor, upon ye short warning of one night at most, stole from his young wife and tender son, (the hope at that time of both their posterities,) and met him with a fair band of men, M^r. Hilpe, and others, suddainly

raised

raised from Thornbury, where hee then dwelt, early the next morning neer Nibley green; **That** for his sake and in his quarrell, both their lives were soe farr indangered That they stood outlawed for felony, and ranne the hazard of an appeale of murder, strongly prosecuted; **That** Thomas till his death, And Maurice till this lords vast havocking of his patrimony, were as servants under his direction.

carta in castro de Berkeley.

Cicero:

616

And casting mine eye into the distribution of his lands given to charitable uses, and to pray for soules, I saw the soule of Thomas remembred with an Ave Maria, and Pater noster; but the soule of Maurice, malitiously and purposely omitted; ô curvæ in terris animæ et cælestium inanes; This man was born for himself and intended his house and family should | end in himself; A position that the heathen abhorred.

Rot. parl: 17. E. 4. m: 12. n°. 16.

Vincent fol: 48. 49, 50.

Nevizañ silva nupt: lib. 4. fol: 354.

Hee was present at the parliament in the 17th of king Edward the 4th, when George Nevill Duke of Bedford, son and heire of John Nevill Marques Mountague, for want of means to support that estate, was degraded from the degree of Duke Marques Earle and Baron; And the reason by this lord Willm with other his fellow peeres in that parliament then given to bee, for that the law is soe when any wanteth livelode to support the dignity: for it nothing availeth to have honor to discend to the heire of the house, and litle or nothing to maintain that estate or dignity: A learned civilian holdeth, That diminutis divitijs, diminuitur honor, nam dat census honores, census amicitias; And that if a noble mans estate bee decayed, hee shall noe more, (saith hee,) bee accompted noble, because hee cannot maintaine that state and title of honor: **And** thereupon, saith the glosse, Baro non potest dici baro, nisi sit potens ad tenendum equos et arma: And that when fitting means and livelodes are wanting to maintayne those great callings and titles of honor, divers inconveniences cannot but happen in the Country in which such needy nobility shall abide: **And** that learned man concludes, That paria sunt perdere vitam ac perdere dominium, nàm bona temporalia sunt vita hominis, et per divitias decus et honor in familijs conservatur, et propter paupertatem familiæ sordescunt; A like it is (saith hee) for a great man to loose life, and to loose lands; for temporall possessions are the life of man, And by Riches is worshipp and honor preserved in familyes, whereas by poverty they grow contemptible; And therefore this lord leaving nothing to discend upon his brother and heire, hee declared his malice to bee eternall, even in bereaving him of the dignity of a Baron: who neverthelesse is not found to have given any other offence then in contesting against his cutting off the old entaile of the Barony of Berkeley, and in estating the same and a threefold greater masse,

upon

upon ſtrangers, for aire and vain glory; forgetting withall the rule of the divine lawgiver, Doe not to another that which thou wouldeſt not another ſhould doe unto thee; otherwiſe hee would have thought upon his forefathers, And not have expoſed their poſterity to ruine or baſenes, as though hee had deſired that all their honor and antiquity ſhould end in him, and himſelf in his own infamy: Not now remembringe what his own petition to king Edward the fourth had affirmed of his ſaid brother Maurice and himſelf, to bee the ſons of that lady that was diſcended of his high bloud; inſtancing that lineage as an argument for favour from that king, and for better ſpeeding in his ſuites; But God otherwiſe diſpoſeth than this Marques did purpoſe; And how could hee purpoſe good at his end, that did ſoe litle in his life; But his harveſt day is come, let him reape as hee hath ſowed; hee deſerveth noe honorable memoriall in this Catalogue of the generations of his fathers. 617

The application and uſe of his life.

1. FFrom the foule life of this lord may bee drawn many faire inſtructions for his poſterity; firſt to begin with God in our youth, That our elder years may relliſh him the better; The proverbe is wicked, A young Saint, and an old devill; for quod nova teſta capit, inveterata ſapit: All veſſells taſt of their firſt ſeaſonings; Soone crookes the tree that a good cambrill will bee; Quickly pricks the tree that a good thorn will bee; Seldome doth that man end well, that began ill; hee that walketh mad a mile, feldome comes homes wiſe; As in this lord, whoſe ill led life in youth grew worſe in age; A man that from the font to the grave, from his ſwathing bonds to his winding ſheet, walked alwayes byaſwife.[1]

The uſe.

2. Secondly not to dipp the tipp of their finger in bloud leaſt the wholl body bee defiled, as hear wee ſee it: Margaret Counteſs of Shroeſ|bury, lawleſly powring out the bloud of the lady Iſable this lords mother, had the ſame meaſure returned upon the head of her grandchild and heire, the lord viſcount Liſle, by this lord Willm, ſon and heire of that lady Iſable; And the cry of bloud in both ſoe prevailed with God, That againſt hope and likelihood they left noe iſſue to poſterity, as before appears; And it is to bee noted, That howſoever this fact may in honor and reputation ſeeme juſtifiable, yet evill doing is ever attended with ill ſucces; for this family ſeeth That this their Anceſtor who made another childleſs had by the returning hand of heaven his own children ſhortly after taken from the earth, and the bodies of himſelf and his wife, contrary to hope, dryed up in barrennes. 618

3. Thirdly,

---

[1] In a ſloping or ſlippery manner.—[ED.]

3. **Thirdly,** not to daube up our titles with the morter of violence or bloud, as this lord did, which notwithstanding all possible art used in the smoothing, yet never left shaking till it dissolved and fell about the workmans ears : **Yea,** and from the posterityes of all this lords brethren also, for that their pertaking hands were imbrued in the same bason, The staine whereof remained till fower generations did wash it out, As in the life of Henry lord Berkeley appeares.

4. **ffourthly,** That it is not much having That maintaineth a family in a plentifull estate or maketh rich, for none of this lords Ancestors had so much as hee; But a provident saving and a wise husbanding what wee have, which this vast lord neglecting, scarce found sufficient for his later years, and left nothing to posterity save a thriftless president; which if they seriously viewe this example in their own meridian of this unadvised prodigall man, may serve as a reclaymer from inordinate prodigality, And bee a perswader to discreet frugality, the true conserver of state and families.

5. **ffifthly,** not to transgresse that morall duty required by God and nature, our obedience to our parents ; a commandment which this lord for many yeares grossly transgressed, And sped thereafter.

6. **Sixthly,** not to make our malice or displeasure immortall towards any, but least of all to our brethren or Allies ; An offence of this lords | which I pray the heavens may blot out from the remembrance of men, and never bee againe beheld in this family.

7. **Seaventhly,** not to bee too popular or ambitious : for mens titles are but mens breath, a blast of air and wind ; **If** popular titles, the wind of a vulgar pair of bellowes ; **If** of a higher straine, the wind of a guilt pair of bellowes, Soe all but wind. **Swell** all thou canst, thou art but a shadowe ; **Take** the wall of the gods if thou wilt, All thy glory is but vanity ; **And** under thy name, (man,) are comprehended all the vanities and miseries of this world, Quemcunque miserum videris, hominem scias :

Seneca trag:

8. **Eighthly,** sith **goodnes** and **greatnes** are the true ends whereto each man intends, And according to that choice, of being good or great, each man doth frame the practice of his life : Sith this lord by choosing greatnes did nothing benefit himself but hurt his posterity, I wish his present heire may, (by this error of his Ancestor,)

Anceftor,) after that choice, And furely by being Good hee will be great alfo, And better fpeed with God and man.

9. **Againe,** it is not the leaft of wifdoms meditations for this lords pofterity to confider, how this great lord and Anceftor of theirs was befool'd or flattered out of his eftate, or fuffered himfelf foe to bee; And to obferve the miferable fate of princes and great perfonages, to bee eaten up and their pofterities alfo, by flatterers, the cruelleft of all beafts, Beafts that bite fmiling; whereas wife men are never much affected with the applaufes of the rude and unfkilfull vulgar, but hold faft to their own well chofen and well fixed refolutions: Every foole knows what is wont to bee done, But what is beft to bee done is known onely to the wife: The wifer the man, the lefs hee will looke after the vain and popular multitude.

10. **Laftly,** by the death of this Marques children, and his dying iffueles, his pofterity may conceive That hee paid thereby the debt of bloud wch himfelf had fhed; A crying fin, which I pray may never houle in the generations of this family: And take his character from this, That hee was much trufted And received alike honors and favors from thofe four kings, Henry the fixth, Edward the fourth, Richard the third, and Henry the feaventh; as oppofite | and difcording amongft themfelves, as man might bee to man; And yet this lord held unfufpected by each of them: But, whether with this ferpentine prudence hee had columbine fimplicity, I leave his life to declare, and his pofterity to Judge, and thereafter to make their ufe.

The Life of Maurice the Fifth

The Life of Maurice Lord Berkeley the fifth of that name, ſtiled in writings, Maurice Berkeley of Thornbury Eſqr; And Maurice Berkeley, brother and heire of William late Marques Berkeley; And Maurice lord Berkeley, brother and heire of William late Marques Berkeley and Earle of Nottingham; And Maurice lord Berkeley; And Maurice Berkeley, lord Berkeley.

And was Attavus, or as our Anceſtors the Saxons called him fiftha fader, to the now George lord Berkeley; And wee at this day in Engliſh, great-great-great-grandfather, or great grandfathers grandfather.

And may bee called Maurice the Lawier.

Contemporary with king Henry the ſeaventh, from the year 1491 till 1506.

Whoſe life I deliver under theſe Nine titles, viz:

1.—His birth and education, fol: 598.
2.—His Suits in law, fol: 599.
3.—Of the Advowſons of Wotton and Slimbridge Churches. fol: 613, 615.
4.—His wife, fol: 618.
5.—His iſſue, fol: 623.
6.—His ſeales of Armes, fol: 633.
7.—His death and place of buriall, fol: 633.
8.—The lands whereof hee dyed ſeized, fol: 634.
9.—The application and uſe of his life, fol: 636.

His

[1] The numbers of the folios in paſſing from Vol. II. to Vol. III. of the MS. overlap. Vol. II. ends with fo. 620, and Vol. III. begins with 597.—[ED.]

His Birth and Education.

598

Escha: 8 et 9. H. 7. m. 7. Com.

This lord Maurice was the third son of the lord James his father and of the lady Isable his wife, born at Berkeley in the yeare of our lord 1435, in the fourteenth year of king Henry the sixth, if the Inquisitions after the death of his brother Marques Berkeley have his age aright; And now at his age of fifty six years, (by the death of the two elder sons without issue,) becometh in this . 7th of Henry the . 7th heire to his fathers Barony, but without any of that land; who being the first of third seaven, by his industry recovers all, As Maurice the first of the second seaven, by his Rebellion lost all.

The education of this lord Maurice was likewise at Berkeley under his parents, untill the forceing of the Castle by the lord Lisle in the 30th of king Henry the sixth, and the murder of his vertuous mother in the year after, about the 17th of his age; what time himselfe with his father and three brothers were made prisoners, holding their lives at the mercy of those that hated them, as in the two last lives of this lords brother and father, is at large related.

Diversæ cartæ in castro de Berkeley.

In the fifth yeare of king Edward the fourth, about one year and a halfe after his fathers death, this lord Maurice, then in the thirtieth year of his age, maryed and lived with his wife at Thornbury, (where of his own and hers hee had faire lands, and thereby was comonly called Maurice Berkeley of Thornbury,) untill the fifth year after, when hee assisted his elder and younger brothers in the encounter at Nibly green, whereat the lord Lisle by them was slaine; for which fellonious fact, hee was outlawed, and inforced for some time after, (till peace was made and pardon procured,) to withdraw himself and leave Thornbury, as formerly is related; whither after hee returned and for many yeares remained. |

His suits in Lawe.

599

At such time as this lord Maurice beheld all his elder brothers Children dead without issue, And the lady his wife whereby hee had them not more likely to live then unlikely to have more: when after hee saw her dead, and his brother as unlike by reason of age and other defects to beget any other: but more espetially when

afterwards

afterwards hee saw his brother remaryed to another wife, as unlikely by reason of her years to conceive, as hee to become a father, his pulse could not otherwise beat, then with a strong assurance that himself, (at least his son,) should inherite that estate whereof the Earl his elder brother was in those times seized; wherein hee was soe confident, That upon the mariage of Maurice his own son and heir in the second year of king Richard the third, (as at some other times,) hee covenanted under his hand and seale to assure unto his daughter in lawe one hundred marks Joynture by the yeare, out of the manors of Came Slimbridge and others, which should discend to him after the death of his said elder brother; never suspecting that any passion could soe prevaile as to work his disinheritance of the Barony lands of Berkeley: ffaith and Hope can never forsake an honest man, And every noble creature upon earth liveth under hope; So did hee: But this Accompt hee cast without his host, for within less then seaven years hee had nothing that was his Ancestors left unto him, or to his sons, in possession, in reall or personall estate, more then a tongue to complaine of the injustice of a brother; And soe might have stood upon the tune of Jobs naked coming, and naked againe returning; And how that that God that gave had againe taken away what hee had given; And have contented himself with the consideration of fortunes change in this great theatre of the world, and to have acknowledged it to bee but as the personating of a player, or change of garments, on the lesse theatre; And have said, Job: cap. 1. vers: 21.

   That man is not unlike a tenis ball,
  Now tost aloft, now dasht against a wall.

But hee turned another way, and added a wise industry to every ordinary meanes;|
  The date tree mounteth most, when burden presseth down,
  And virtue most doth shine, when fortune most doth frown.

And according to the Nobler parts of his excellent spirit, resolved in this his æconomicall distresse to turn every stone, and to begin with a juditious examination of the validity of his brother Marques Deeds of sales, as his first attempts of rowsing up of fortune; wherein hee found a greater spring of Gods mercy flowing upon those endeavours than at first hee might have hoped for, leaving thereby a more memorable example to his posterity then himself had found in any of his ancestors; which his industry was soe blessed from heaven That hee justly hath the honorable testimony amongst his generations to bee the restorer of his house, and a second father to his family.

When the Inquisitions after his brothers death the Marques were returned into the Chancery, which presented unto him out of all Counties the Alyenations which
              hee

hee had made, hee then perceived himſelf born under the ſame conſtellation with his father and brother, That with them hee muſt enter with ſuites and as unlike as they to end them but with his own days, which proved true; In this only different, they to defend their old inheritance diſcended upon them, hee to regaine part of that, (if hee could,) which his elder brother had profuſedly given away and ſcattered, with the ſuſpention of his Barony.

The firſt of his brothers conveyances which this lord took into conſideration was the fine leavyed in the third year of king Henry the ſeaventh of the manor of Slimbridge with the appurtenances, (amongſt others,) in the County of Glouc.; with a render therein to himſelf and to the heirs of his body, the remainder to the ſaid king and the heirs males of his body, the remainder to the right heirs of him the ſaid Marques: Hee found withall, That in Slimbridge was another litle manor called Sages, which his Anceſtor Thomas the third had in the time of king Edward the third, purchaſed of one John Sage, conſiſting of ſeaven Tenements and 290 acres of Land, of the value of 15ᵗ p ann̄ or thereabouts, lying ſcatteredly diſperſed within the pariſh of Slimbridge: Here hee eſpyed the firſt glimpſe of the dawning of a faire day, for under colour of that fine, (of the manor of Slimbridge cum ptinen̄,) the king, (the | Marques being dead without iſſue,) had entred alſo into the little manor of Sages, And as part of Slimbridge manor tooke the rents and profitts.

carta in caſtro de Berkeley.

601

Whereupon this lord exhibits his petition to the kinge, ſhewing that this Sages manor, (called alſo Sages livelode,) was an antient manor of it ſelf and noe part of the manor of Slimbridge, nor comprehended in any ſpetiall or generall words of the ſaid fyne; And that the king beſides this manor of Sages, had as much in Manors acres and rent as was contained in the fine; All which, after ſurvey taken by Comiſſion, and certificate from the kings Auditor Surveyor and Receivor, (returned into the Excheqer,) being found to bee true, hee was licenced to enter into and hold the ſaid manor of Sages; And this was the harveſt of his firſt labours, and part of the crop of five years paines. The tenth of Aprill following in the 14ᵗʰ yeare of Henry the 7ᵗʰ hee enters and holds his firſt Court for the ſaid manor of Sages, whereat each tenant did atturne and recognize what ſeverally they held; And the twentieth of May following, (mindfull of his ſaid Covenant made upon his daughter Anne her marriage,) demiſed the ſaid manor, (by the name of Maurice lord Berkeley,) to Willm Denis his ſon in lawe for nine years, which was part of her mariage portion.

Rec: in ſcc̄io
Rec: in cur. Aug m̄.

Rec. cur̄ in caſtro de Berkeley.

carta in caſtro de Berkeley.

His

His second onset was againe upon the king, to whom, (whilſt the former for Sages manor was in chaſe,) hee exhibits a ſecond petition, wherein hee layeth down the words of his brothers fines levyed, (with like remainders as aforeſaid,) of the manors of Berkeley, Hame, Apleridge, Cowley, Alkington, Came, Hinton, Wotton, Simondſall, and Arlingham, and of certaine meſſuages, lands Tenements and rents in Slimbridge, Kingſcote, Horwood, Horton, Nibly, Sherncliffe, Erlingham, Iron Acton, and Acton Ilger, in the County of Glouc.; And ſhews, That under colour thereof John Walſh his Maj^ties Receiver had taken from him two and twenty marks of yearly rent in Frampton upon Seavern, which was not compriſed in any of the ſaid fynes, and whereof his brother Marques dyed in ffee, as of a rent in groſs out of the ſ^d manor of Frampton, And was not a rent appertaining to any of the ſaid manors: And for proof, layeth down the firſt creating of that rent by his Anceſtor Thomas the ſecond in the 33th yeare of king Edward the | firſt; And alſo how it appeared by the laſt will of the ſaid Marques That it was not contained in any of the ſaid fines, for that his intent therein was That two Preiſts ſhould after his death bee maintained with the ſame to ſing for his ſoule; And therefore deſired to bee reſtored to the ſaid rent, And to have lres of diſcharge to his Maj^ties officers; which was done in the like courſe of Survey and certificates as of Sages manor; And this was the further crop of his ſecond harveſt.

His third induſtry, (labored alſo whilſt the two former were on foot,) was with Sr Thomas Brandon knight, Aſwell whilſt hee was huſband to Anne the third and laſt wife of his brother Marques, As after her death; between whom upon a ſuite in Chancery at laſt it was agreed, (ſhee being dead,) That the ſaid Sr Thomas ſhould ſuffer this lord Maurice to receive all the rents and profits of the manors and lands that were his ſaid brothers, which the ſaid Sr Thomas had to diſpoſe for the performance of the ſaid Marques will, from Michaelmas before, And to releaſe all his right and intereſt in them, and to deliver up all the evidences concerning them, And to doe his beſt endeavour that others enfeoffed with him ſhould doe the like: And to juſtifie all ſuch ſuites as this lord Maurice ſhould bringe in his name againſt any perſons as adminiſtrator to the ſaid Marques his brother, for any debts covenants or duties due unto him: Hee on the other part covenanting to ſave harmleſſe the ſaid Sr Thomas Brandon from all actions that ſhould bee brought againſt him as Adminiſtrator to the ſaid Marques, And to pay all the Marques debts, or to compound for the ſame: And thus did this lord wiſely winde himſelf into the poſſeſſion of the manors of Winge, Segrave in Pen, and little Marloe in the County of Buckingham; And into the manors of Sileby, and Mountforrell, and the hundred of Goſcote, in the County

Petitio in caſtro de Berkeley.
finis Hillar. 3. H. 7. in banco.
fin. Trin. 3. H. 7. in banco.

finis. 32. & 33. E. 1. in banco.
602
carta in caſtro de Berkeley.
Voluntas marchioñ 1491. 7. H. 7.

carta: 25. Junij 16. H. 7. in caſtro. de Berkeley.
Bill in canc. 15. H. 7.

carta. 16. H. 7. in caſtr. de Berkeley.
Voluntˉ Marchionis Berkeley. 7. H. 7. in cur. prer. Cant.

County of Leicester, and divers others; And also enabled himself to take the benefit of his brothers Covenantors, and the better to dive into his titles and conveyances, none of which the gall of Anne the Marques widow whilst shee lived would permit him to doe.

Whilst these and many other questions raised by this lord Maurice were controverted, the manor of Tetbury in the County of Glouc., and of Maningford Brewes in the County of Wilts, the moitie of the manors of Leigh, Cothorne, and Gate Burton, in the County of Linc., and of Woversthorp in the County of Yorke, discended upon him as being one of the two coheirs of the lord Breouse; | whereby hee was the better enabled both in estate and reputation to pursue the Westminster hall warrs, wherein hee dyed imbroyled, as after followeth.

About this time a declaration or claime was drawn by this lord and his counsell of his title and his fellow copartners to divers other manors and parts of manors, and lands, wherein the discent and title is in these words thus laid down, as in an old hand-writing of that time in the Castle of Berkeley appeares;

1. **Maurice** lord Berkeley is cozen and one of the heires of Thomas sometime duke of Norfolke, Earle Marshall and Warren, lord Mowbray, Segrave, Gower, and Brewes; of the Castle and lordships of Holt, Bromfeild, Yale and Wrexham; That is to wete, The said Maurice is son of Isable, sister of John, fader to John, fader of John late Duke of Norfolke, which third John late Duke of Norfolke had issue Anne, married to Richard the second son of king Edward the fourth.

2. **Item**, That Thomas Earle of Surrey is another Cozen and heire unto the said John third Duke of Norfolke; That is to say, son of John Howard knight last Duke of Norfolke, son of Margaret sister to the said Isable, and sister to the said John fader of John, fader of John; which third John was fader to Anne that was maryed to Richard second son to king Edward the fourth. **And** so the said Maurice now lord Berkeley is cozen and one of the heires to all the said three dukes, And to the said Thomas sometime Earle Marshall and afterwards Duke and fader to the first of the said three Johns Dukes of Norfolke, &c. and comperciner with the said Thomas Howard now earle of Surrey, and inheritable with the same Thomas to the Dukedom of Norff. Earle Marshall and Warren, lord Mowbray, Segrave, Gower, and Breouse.

3. **Item**

3. **Item,** the said Moreys now lord Berkeley is Cozen and one of the heires of Thomas sometimes Earle of Arundle, and of Richard fader of the said Tho⁵: That is to say, son of Isable daughter of Elizabeth, one of the daughters and heires of the said Richard late Earle of Arundle, and sister and one of the heires of the said Thomas.

4. **Item,** Thomas Earle of Surrey is Cozen and another of the heires aswell of the said Richard late Earle of Arundle, as of Thomas late Earle of Arundle; That is, son of John Howard knight late Duke of Norfolke, son of Margaret daughter of the said Elizabeth, and one of the heires of the said Richard late Earle of Arundle, and sister and one of the heires of the said Thomas Earle of Arundle.

5. **Item** Thomas Standley knight Earle of Darby is a Cozen and third heire of the said Richard and Thomas late Earles of Arundle; That is to wete, The s⁴ Thomas Earle of Darby son of his moder daughter of the said Elizabeth late Dutches of Norfolke, daughter of the said Richard late Earle of Arundle, and sister to the said Thomas.

6. **Item,** S⁵ John Wingfeild knight is Cozen and one of the heires of the said Richard and Thomas late Earles of Arundle; That is to wete, the son of John Wingfeild knight, the son of his moder daughter of the said Elizabeth late Dutches of Norfolke, one of the daughters and heires of the said Richard late Earle of Arundle, and sister to the said Thomas.

And then in the said old writinge followeth thus:

Memorandum, that the said Elizabeth late Dutches of Norfolke had two husbands, That is to say, Thomas Earle Marshall, afterwards Duke of Norfolke, by whom they two had issue the said Isable moder of my said lord Berkeley and Margaret grandmother to the said Thomas now Earle of Surrey.

And then thus:

Memorandum, that there was a third daughter of the said Richard Earle of Arundle and sister to Thomas, called Margarett, and maryed to one Lentall, which Margarett is dead without issue: And soe the s⁴ Earle of Surrey, lord Berkeley, the Earle of Darby, and S⁵ John Wingfeild, been heires to the said Elizabeth late Dutches of Norfolke, and inheritable to the moitye of the Arundle lands that bee not entailed to the heires males in the form abovesaid.

Item,

Item, George Nevill knight lord Burgevenny is Cozen and one of the heirs, aswell to the said Richard late Earle of Arundle, as to the said Thomas late Earle of Arundle, and inheritable to the moitye of all the manors and Castles that longed to the said late Earles of Arundle not entailed to the heirs male hooly; Againe, the said Earle of Surrey, lord Stanley, lord Berkeley, and Sr John Wingfeild knight, That is to wete, son of George, son of Elizabeth, daughter of Thomas late Earle of Worcester, son of Jane somtime Lady Burgevenny, the second daughter to the said Richared late Earl of Arundle, and sister and one of the heires to Thomas late

605 Earle of Arun|dle, and the said Jane full sister to the said Elizabeth late Dutches of Norfolke, and one of the heires and compertioners unto the said Thomas late Earle of Arundle: **Thus,** this antient writing, which I have hear laid down in the same words, Aswell for the great Noblenes of the Allience and discent of this industrious lord, whose princely bloud yet streameth in the veynes of the numerous posterities of himself and of Thomas Berkeley his youngest brother, and others discended of their mother, as before in the issue of that Thomas and his sisters, and as after in the issue of this lord Maurice appeareth; As also for avoiding of often repetitions in the titles which this lord pretended to divers great possessions, which now doe follow, not otherwise soe fairely to have been avoided.

Esch: in Com̃
Ebox 8: H. 7. in
Canc.

The Inquisition after the Marques Berkeleys death taken in the County of York the 30th of August in the . 8th year of king Henry the 7th findeth a conveyance by him made the 23th of February in the third year of the said king, of the manors of Donington, Thwaites, Thriske, Hovingham, Kirkeby Malasard, and Burton in Lovisdale, to the use of himself and ye heires of his body, And for default of such issue, To the use of Thomas Stanley Earle of Derby, and the heirs of his body; And for default of such issue, To the use of the right heires of him the said Marques; That the Marques was dead without issue in ffebruary before, And that the said Earle of Derby had entred and taken the proffitts of the said manors, and that this lord Maurice was brother and heire to the said Marques, fifty six years old and upwards. **Other** Inquisitions also in other Counties find the like Conveyances of estateing of the said Earle of Derby, for default of issue of the said Marques, in the manors of Winge, Segrave, and Penne, in the County of Bucks, And in the manor of Denge a̅ts Dengy in the County of Essex, And in the manors of Epworth, Belton, Haxey, Ouston, and Wrote, in the Isle of Exholme in the County of Lincolne, And in the manor of Alspath in Meriden in the County of Warwicke; **Against** which conveyances this lord Maurice raiseth his utmost opposition, and soe strongly pursueth against the said Earle and George lord Strange his

eldest

eldest son, And after their deaths against Thomas Earle of Darby son of the said George, That the 8th of November in the 21th yeare of the said king, (after many References in five former yeares to divers noble and learned Arbitrators, which bare noe fruite,) they came to an agreement; and a finall peace amity and award, (to use the very words of the deed of | Award,) by the mediation and advice of their kinsfolks and friends, and of Sr John Fyneux cheife Justice of the kings bench, and of Sr Thomas Frowicke cheife Justice of the Comon pleas, was made between the said Earle on the one part and this lord Maurice and Maurice Berkeley his son and heire apparant on the other part, whereby this lord Maurice had to him and his heires the lordships and manors of Winge, Segrave, and Penne, in the County of Buckingham, the manor of Denge als Dengy in the County of Essex, and the manors of Hovingham Donington and Twaytes in the County of Yorke. And the said Earle of Derby had to him and his heires the said manors of Belton, Haxey, Ouston, Wrote, Thriske, Kirkeby Malsard, Burton in Lovisdale, and Alspath in Meriden, and all lands in any of them. And recoveryes and other assurances were had and suffered accordingly by either party, each to other.

carta irrot. in banco cōi: in Mich. 21. H. 7.

606

Recov'y. Trin. Terme 21 H. 7. rot. 420. Ebor̃ &c. in banco.

Hanging this suite, which was longe and chargeable, and against as noble and potent adversaries as lived in those days, and upon whom shined the favours of the time, As many indirect and collaterall courses were laboured to barre the titles and claimes of this lord Maurice, by collaterall Warranties and otherwise, as wit, money, law, favour of time and greatnes could worke; whereof, (omitting many which I have observed,) I hear only mention three Deeds which the said Earles procured in Aprill in the 13th of King Henry the 7th, and in August in the 16th of the said king; whereby Isable Harrison widowe, daughter and heire of Alice, one of the daughters of James lord Berkeley and sister of the whole bloud to the said Marques Berkeley and to this lord Maurice, (for so the Deeds lay down her pedegree,) released to the said Thomas Earle of Derby and his heires all her right in all the said manors perticularly, And also in Slagham in the County of Sussex, and in Wisfeld in the County of Surry, And in Segrave in the County of Leicester. And the said Earle, the better to strengthen his title, did in the 20th of king Henry the 7th give 1300 marks to Elizabeth Dutches of Norfolke, to wind himself into possession by buying out her estate for life in some of the said manors, which (as her death declared,) would have fallen into his hands within two yeares after, whereby hee made noe very good markett; yet did this industrious lord Maurice breake through all barrs and obstacles, and prevailed as aforesaid.

2 Cartæ irrot. in com. banco. Mich: Term. 17. H. 7. Carta irrot. 22. H. 7. in Canc:

carta in castro de Berkeley.

Howbeit this peace was not so soundly on each part sawdred, but | that afterwards it leaked at certaine crannells, which were once againe cemented by an order

607

v VOL. II   in

Cancellar̃

in Chancery dated the 22th of February in the 5th year of king Henry the 8th, made between Thomas Howard then Duke of Norfolke, the said Earle of Darby and the lord Maurice this lords son; whereby two chests of Evidence remaining in the Rolls Chapple were perused and sorted touching those manors and lands which were in variance, by friends in trust appointed by each of them: which being done, the lord Chancellor and the Two cheife Justices of the kings bench, and comon pleas, did

Ordo in Cam̃ stell 5. H. 8.

the fourth and 7th days of March after in the starrechamber, deliver such of those evidences to each party as appertained to them; Appointing notwithstanding many still to remaine there in two canvas bags in a chest, which for ought I can find should remaine there to this day. Anno. 1628. which through want of leisure I have

carta in castro de Berkeley.

not searched after, and only talked thereof with the Usher that keeps other huge heaps and chests there also.

And somewhat to sattisfie Curiosity and to enlighten the legall part of this lords life and his sons, I tell his posterity, That this lords titles to the said Manors of Thiske, Hovingham, Burton in Lovisdale, and Kirkeby Malsart, somtime parcell of the lands of Roger le Bigod Earle of Norfolke, And to the manors of Epworth, Ouston and Haxey members of the said manor of Thriske, were derived from the grant of king Edward the second to his brother Thomas de Brotherton and Mary his wife, and to the heires of their bodies; And to the manors of Segrave in Penne in Com̃ Buck: and Twaytes in Com̃ Ebor, and to Doningworth in Com̃ Suff. by an entaile made to John lord Segrave, and Margaret his wife daughter and heire of the said Thomas Brotherton. **And** to the manor of Winge in Com̃ Buck, by an entaile made by Richard Earle of Arundle to Thomas Mowbray duke of Norfolke and Elizabeth his wife, daughter and coheire of the said Richard the Earle: And so to these and other manors layeth the discents as aforesaid; Concluding, That in the partition between the Howards and his brother Marques, these were alotted to his said brother, whose heire hee was.

petitio in Cancell̃ in castro de Berkeley Rec: in sec̃io 8. H. 7. rot. 16. inter originñ cum rem Thesaur̃.
608
Acc̃o in cur̃ augm: 10. et. 11. H. 7. de Berkeleislands.

Now falleth this lord upon an adversary somewhat less potent, but more bitter then any of the former; And by the name of Maurice Berkeley lord Berkeley exhibits his bill in Chancery against Sr Robert Poyntz of Acton knight, then an Esqr of the body to King Henry the 7th and whom that king a little before had made his Steward of the manor and hundred of Berkeley; demaunding thereby to have divers evidences which hee detained from him | touching his manor of Daglingworth in the County of Glouc., entailed upon him from divers of his Aunceftors, and whereof, (as speaks his bill,) hee was peaceably possessed and seized.

Sir

Sir Rob: Poyntz, (fcornfully flighting as it feemes the honor of the plt and his title of lord Berkeley, and perhaps the rather becaufe hee was the kings high Steward of that honor and Barony,) maketh anfwere to the Bill of Maurice Berkeley Squire, And faith, That that manor of Daglingworth is his rightfull inheritance difcended to him from his Anceftors, for which hee hath a Scire facias hanging againft the faid Maurice at the comn law for the recontinuance of his right in the fame, And foe Juftifieth the keeping of whatfoever evidence hee hath.

Refponfit Rec: in fcc̃io. 8. H. 7. rot. 16.

This lord Maurice taketh notice of the defendants flighting of his honor dignity title and ftile of lord, And thereupon in his replication to the faid Anfwere, enlargeth his ftile, and faith, This is the Replication of **Maurice** lord Berkeley brother and heire of William late Marques Berkeley: **And** further faith, **That** after the death of the faid Marques Berkeley his brother, one efpetiall Deed of the faid manor with an obligation of a great fum concerning the right title and fecurity of the fame manor to and for the Anceftors of him the faid lord, and for the fuerty of him the fame lord and his heires in the fame manor, with many other evidences belonging to him the faid lord Berkeley, were (amongft others) in a cheft within the Gray ffryars of London, which cheft afwell for the fuerty of divers evidences pertayninge to the kinge, as for the evidences ptaining to him the faid lord Berkeley, was fealed up by William Maryner then comon preift to the Cardinall Archbifhop of Canterbury, unto the time the faid Sr Robert Poyntz, pretending title without ground or caufe to the faid Manor, by finifter, and corrupt meanes came to the faid cheft, and there with an hott knife loofed the under part of the wax of the fame feale from the fame cheft, and opened the cheft and fearched all the evidences therein at his pleafure; And thereupon took away the faid deed of entaile and obligation, with divers other evidences concerning the faid manor, which were in the keeping of the faid Marques, and put there by him fafely to bee kept to the ufe of him and of his heires, whofe brother and heire hee the faid lord Berkeley now is, And therefore for the faid evidences hath fued a fubpena againft the faid Robert; And that his fuing of his Scire facias is but to colour his wrongfull keeping of the faid evidences from him the faid lord Berkeley. |

Replicatio

The defendant Sr Robert rejoyneth, and in the title of his rejoynder feemeth more to flight the honor and ftile of this lord then before; faying, **This** is the rejoynder of Sr Robert Pointz knight to the replication of Maurice Berkeley, (omitting the word Squire, which formerly in his Anfwere hee had beftowed,) And faith, That after the death of one John Walfh who held the faid houfe in the gray ffryers in London,

609 Rejoynder

London, And before hee the said Sr Robert entred or dealed with the same, an Inventory was made of all such goods as the said Walsh had in that house, and prayfed by the said Maryner, then being preist to the said Cardinall; At which time the said Maryner found three chests there well locked with evidences, which hee then sealed with his own Seale; And after hee the said Sr Robert tooke the house of the Warden of the said ffryers for certaine years, and found there the said three chests locked and sealed with the seale of the said Maryner, (hee skippeth over the opening,) which three chests after that time at the spetiall labour of the said Maurice, and by the comandment of Sr Reginald Bray knight, a Councellor of state, were delivered, sealed with the same Seale of the said Maryner, to Willm Heydon and Thomas Try, with other servants and freinds of the said Maurice; And further that the Scire facias was sued to recontinue the true title of him the said Sr Robert, longe before the said Subpena had against him.

The titles of either of the said parties made to the said Manor of Daglingworth stood thus.

Ralph Bluet, (in whose name the said manor had continued for many discents,) entailed the same upon Ralph his son and Elizabeth his wife, and the heires of the said Ralph the son begotten on the body of the said Elizabeth; who had issue John Bluett, who had issue Elizabeth marryed to Sr James Berkeley, who had issue James lord Berkeley father of the said Marques and of this lord Maurice. That James lord Berkeley afterwards enfeoffed Richard Venables and others of the said manor to certaine uses; and after by fyne the said lord James and Isable his wife granted the same to Nicholas Poyntz and Elizabeth his wife and to the heirs of the said Nicholas, who was father of Sr John Poyntz, father of this Sr Robert; The estate of which Richard Venables | and his fellow feoffees the said Marques Berkeley had from whom the said manor discended to this lord Maurice as to his brother and heire, who entred, and thereby was remitted to the entaile made by Ralph Bluett the father, And soe is seized; And soe also, That the said lord James his father and other parties to the said fine, had nothing in the said manor at the time of the fyne leavyed.

There was also banded with like bitternes one other suite at lawe between this lord and the said Sr Robert Poyntz, for certaine other lands in Daglingworth and Cirencester, whereto Sr Robert made title under a guift in taile made by Ponce Poyntz, son of Nicholas, unto Thomas Poyntz and Alice his wife and to the heirs of of their bodies; And layeth down, That the said Thomas and Alice had issue Robert Poyntz, father of Nicholas before mentioned, who by Elizabeth his wife had issue John, father of the said S:r Robert plt. in the Acc͠on. But this lord carryed the action and said lands against him by like nicety as before.

I have often observed, aswell in the titles and suites which I mention in this lords life, as in divers others which I purposely omit, (becaufe the lands are longe since alyened from this family,) That the pinches & advantages which this lord, and after him his eldest son Maurice, (no way inferior to his father,) took to divers manors lands services and tenures, to help themselves in pleadings and in evidence, were soe witty soe strict and soe nice, standing, (as I may truly say,) oftentimes upon differences without diversities, That I have wondered, reading the straines of Counsell, That they would fasten upon such pinches and extremities, and against adversaries soe potent; And more, how they could bring them to soe gainfull Conclusions, for they ever gained the whole or part; But as they stood in need of land to rebuild their house which their vast Ancestor the Marques had burned down, Soe were they learned made wise by adversity and experience, and excellent Solicitors in their own persons: And such as the Sollicitor is, such commonly is the successe: They knew how to take every advantage, but to give none.

Upon this double suite between this lord and S:r Robert Poyntz, (as the root from whence the bitternes of many after years contentions did spring,) I might in due courfe of Storey fall upon the perticular enumeration of those successive suites, riotts and braules that afterwards | too often burst forth and blustered between their severall posterityes, for five or more discents togeather, and which were scarce perfectly cured when the late lord Henry dyed; Yet was an intermarriage between their grandchildren for that effect spetially; But I am unwilling to take any occation to ravell one thread of that coate which among kindred should bee seamless; Unsavory vapours will fast enough arise, (sith truth of story will not permitt the omission,) and let him that loveth the aiery memory of such contentious passages seek them in their severall places; my pen shall bee noe index therein.

Here also might not unfitly bee taken to consider the ground which might lead the said S:r Robert soe to slight this lord Maurice, as in a kind to untitle and dislord him; And whether this Barony of Berkeley at this time stood soe suspended in the possession of the Crown, by reason of the Marques Berkeleys entaile made to kinge Henry the seaventh and the heirs males of his body, as that this Maurice was really noe Baron nor Peere of this Realme; But time shall bee taken for examination
thereof

thereof in the life of the lord Maurice this lords son, being unwilling to make soe large a digression in the midst of this lords lawsuits, whereto I now againe returne.

After long attendance at Court, many petitions delivered to the king, many freinds raysed not without great expences and greater promises, at the last the lord Maurice obtained the kings direction to have an Act of parliament passed in the 19th yeare of his raigne, to make void two former Acts of the 5th and 7th of the said king Henry the seaventh; whereby this lord obtained the manor of Chesterford with the Advowson thereof in the County of Essex (where his brother was in building at his death, but not for him,) The fourth part of the manors of Brighthemston, Cleiton, Middleton, Meching, Seford, and Alington; And the fourth part of the moitie of the manors of Cokefeild, Hunden, and Kymer; And the fourth part of the moitie of the Chace of Cleres, the Forrest of Worth, the Burrowe of Lewes, the Barony of Lewes, the profits of the Courts of No mans land, and of 36ˢ 2ᵈ, rent in Iford, in the County of Sussex; And of the fourth part of the manors of Reygate and Dorking; And the fourth part of the moitie of the Toll of Guilford and Southwerke, in the County of Surrey: And of the fourth part of the manor of Tyborne als Marybone in the County of Middlesex; to bee restored to him and his heirs, which (amongst many others,) his brother Marques Berkeley had conveyed to the king, as in his life is mentioned. But the said Acts of the 5th and 7th years of the said king to stand in force for all the other manors and lands mentioned in either of them.

All which manors and parts of manors and lands and other profitts in the said Counties of Sussex, Surrey, and Middlesex, this lord Maurice within four months after conveyed to George Nevill lord Burgevenny and his heirs, (retaining the rest,) in which Assurances his two sons Maurice and Thomas Berkeley joyned with their father; And for performance of the Agreements bound themselves in 3000ˡⁱ bond the peece to the said lord Burgevenny.

In May in the same 19th year of king Henry the 7th this lord Maurice exhibited another petition of right to the king, praying to bee restored to the manor of Bosham in the County of Sussex; wherein hee layeth down his title by the grant of king Edward the second in the sixth of his raigne, made to Thomas de Brotherton his brother and to the heirs of his body, drawing down the discent of that estate taile to himself as heir therunto; Shewing, That upon his brothers pertition with Thomas Howard Earle of Surrey, the said manor (amongst others) was allotted to his said Brother and his heires; And also the fine of his said brother leavied

Margin notes:
fol: [654]

Act of Parliam.
19. H. 7.
mem in scēij. Trin Terme. 9. H. 8.
rot. 1. carta in castro de Berkeley.

612
Inq: 9. H. 7. post. mortem Marchioñ Berkeley.
Fin: in banco. 5. H. 7. Michas terme.

cart. 16 Febr. 19. H. 7.
cart. 2 Julii. 19 H. 7.
Pasch 19. H. 7. in banco.
Hill rec. 19. H. 7. rot. 22. in Scēio.

carta in castro de Berkeley.
Plita coram rege in canc: 19. H: 7. in filas: in le petty bag.
carta: 16: Decem: 6. E. 2. m: 14. in arce Londoñ.

leavied of the f.d manor in the fourth year of king Henry the feaventh, with a render to himfelf in taile, the remainder to the king and the heires males of his body, the remainder to his own right heirs; And foe by avoiding the difcontinuance, declareth himfelf to bee in right of law remitted, praying in conclution of his petition That juftice and right thereupon may by the king bee done unto him; whereto, (after his title and truth of his petition found by office pticularly in the faid County the fame yeare,) the king was outed and this lord reftored to his faid man.r of Bofham, which yet remaineth with his pofterity, Anno 1628.

The like petiton of right in the fame 19th year this lord exhibited to the faid king, praying therein to bee reftored to the manor of ffenyftanton in the County of Huntington; wherein hee layeth down his right under a | fyne leavyed of the faid manor (amongft others) in Michmas Terme in the 19th yeare of king Edward the third by John lord Segrave, with a render to himfelf and to Margaret his wife and to the heirs of their bodies; And fo deduceth down the difcent of the eftate taile to himfelf, and making title as formerly is mentioned in the reftitution of Bofham: And after the like courfe holden for finding his title in that County by Office, the hands of the king were removed, and this lord reftored to his manor of ffenyftanton: **Which** two reftitutions being exemplyfyed togeather under one feale in October in the 22th of king Henry the feaventh, are expreffed therein to bee ad requificõem Thome Try, &c, at the requeft of Thomas Try Efq.r one of the Cozens of the faid lord Maurice, **Declaring** thereby the ambition of a Sollicitor to have his name kindred and diligence perpetuated to his mafters pofterity: A modeft pride wherewith the obferver obferveth himfelf to bee in part infected, as hath already appeared in the pedegree of his wife and Children laid down in the life of Robert the firft; **And** this proceeding of this noble lord in this petition of right is to all pofterity made a prefident in the new book of Entries, printed, 1614. unter that title of Petition de droit, from fol: 428 to fol: 434. which I wifh the lord George may read; to value aright the worth of this lord his Anceftor, and to imitate his induftry for his prefident; **And** the faid Thomas Try fhall for the perpetuating of his memory and fervices in thefe times to this noble houfe have this teftimoniall of mine avowing, **That** fince his death this family hath not been ferved with a wifer nor more induftrious fervant and follicitor; **Which** I wifh may alfo incite others to like diligence and fidelity in the generations of this family which are to come.

The 17th of March in the fame 19th year of king Henry the feaventh, this active lord exhibites one other like petition of right to the king, praying therein that

Juftice

ex filac: canc: in petty bag. 19. H.7. carta exempt.
613
finis in thefaur. recept: fcãcio. 19. E. 3.

Plita in Canc: 19. H. 7. Exempt:

liber Intratioñ: imprefs. 1614. fol. 428.

Plita in Canc. 19. H. 7. in filac; in le petty bag: Advocatio de Wott

Juſtice and right may bee done unto him, and to bee reſtored to the Advowſon of the Church of Wotton in the County of Glouc.; And for his title of right thereto layeth down the fine leavyed by his Anceſtor Thomas the third in the 23th year of king Edward the third of the ſaid Advowſon, (amongſt other things,) with a render therein to himſelf for life, the remainder to Maurice his ſon and heire and to the heires males of his body, &c. as in his life is declared: Which eſtate in taile this lord deduceth down to his brother Marques Berkeley and himſelf, and ſheweth how his brother in the third year of his highnes raigne leavyed a fine thereof with a render to himſelf and the heirs of his body, the remainder to his | highnes and to the heirs males of his body, the remainder to his own right heires; And how that upon the ſaid Marques death in the ſeaventh of his raigne without any iſſue, hee the ſaid Maurice was remitted to his old eſtate taile created in the 23th. of king Edward the third; Whereupon after this lords title by Inquiſition and the advice of the Judges of both benches taken and the kinges warrant to Hubart his Atturny generall hee was in June following reſtored to the ſaid Advowſon: Wherein appeareth this lords admirable diligence and wiſdom in effecting a ſuite of ſo longe a courſe in two Termes only: And the more becauſe hee then had the ſame title and right without any difference unto the Caſtle and barony of Berkeley, and to all the manors compriſed in the ſaid fine of the 23th of king Edward the third: And perhaps moſt of all, in that hee by a prudent and quick carriage of his buiſineſs blindfolded the eyes both of the kings Attorney and other his learned Counſell, and the Judges of both Benches and Court of Chancery, from underſtanding either a Recovery ſuffered in the. 2: E. 4. thereof, and of the manors of Wotton, Simondſall, Cowley, and others, or the recoveries his brother Marques ſuffered in the ſecond of king Richard the third, whereby the ſaide entaile was docked; Or the Acts of Parliament in the 5th and 7th years of the ſame king Henry, whereby the Marques aſſurances to him made were made good & confirmed, evidently appearing by their inrollments both in Chancery and Exchequer; And then imediatly alſo obtaining the ſaid Act of reſtitution in the preſent Parliament, whereinto hee caſt theſe manors of Boſham and Fenyſtanton and the ſaid Advowſon of Wotton, repealing the former Acts of the 5th and 7th of king Henry the 7th as hath been ſaid. And this lord thus being ſeiſed of this Advowſon of the Church of Wotton, Hee, according to certaine Covenants which the 16th of March before had been agreed upon between him and Maurice and Thomas his ſons on the one part, And the Abbot and Covent of the Monaſtery of Tuexbury on the other part, For the aſſurance of this Church of Wotton to that Monaſtery before the 13th of July next; Now they imediatly upon this reſtitution aſſigned the ſame accordingly. And noe ſooner

sooner in effect was that Monastery thus seized thereof, but they the same yeare found means to appropriate or incorporate the same to their house, As the composition about the Viccaridge shews: What time 20. marks was thought a competent living for the Vicar, to bee paid in | fruits and not in money as now it is; which at this day Anno. 1628. is more than fourty pounds per ann. And this Advowson was continued in lease at the yearly rent of 33^{li} to that monastery till the dissolution in the 31th of Henry the 8th; And so rested in the Crown till that king by his L^{res} patents dated the 11th day of December in the 38th of his raigne, gave the same, (amongst other possessions of the value of 2200^l p Ann) to Christ Church Colledge in Oxford; And is at this day by the Colledge severally demised to Bedle and Purnell, with soe poore an allowance to the Ministers both of Wotton and of Nibley, (a Chaple thereto,) that it scarcely sufficeth for the bread of those that serve at the Altars. **But** I would not have this family ignorant, That in the third year of Queen Elizabeth the lord Henry Berkeley impleaded the said Colledge for the said Rectory of Wotton Underedge, and in the year following came to an agreement, whereby the Colledge granted to the said lord Henry and his heires, the Advowson and patronage of their Vicaridge of Tetbury in the same County, upon condition that they might quietly hold the said Rectory of Wotton against him and all claiminge from him or under his title or in his name. **In** recompence whereof this lord Henry acknowledgeth That the Colledge hath good title to the said Rectory, for that the same was by his Ancestor the true Patron thereof granted to the Abbot and Covent of Teuxbury, who after by licence from the king with the confirmation of the Bishop of that Diocese incorporated the same, And that king Henry the Eighth, after the dissolution of that Monastery, sufficiently conveyed it to the Colledge, And therefore acknowledgeth himself fully sattisfyed of their right, and promiseth to make them further assurance at any time within two years after; **And** how before, in time of Queen Mary, shortly after his restitution to the manor of Wotton hee presented to this Church one   Knight, who had been his Tutor, who was admitted instituted and inducted, And, (notwithstanding the Colledge suite against him,) continued Incumbent there till the time of the said agreement, and then this church returned to the Colledge as an impropriation againe; In which condition it still remaineth.

In the same 19th year of king Henry the seaventh this restless lord attempts for the Advowson of the Church of Slimbridge; And according by his | deed dated the 16th of January Anno. 19th H. 7. presents Edward Bromfeild, Clarke, to Silvester Bishop of Worcester, to bee by him admitted to the Rectory of the said church

Recovery, et 525. et plita. 20. H. 7. rot. 532.

615

Irrotul in canc:

carta dat. 19. Nov. 4. Eliz: in castro de Berkel:

Annis. 4. & . 5. Ph: & Mar:

Slimbridge Advowson.
616
carta in castro de Berkeley.

church, then void by the death of David Liare late parson there; which to doe the bishop refuseth; whereupon this lord brings his Writt of Quare impedit against the said bishop of Worcester, and against Richard president of Magdalen colledge in Oxford, (who then was also bishop of Hereford,) and the schollers of the said colledge, and Robert Thay the then incumbent of the said church: During the dependancy of which Quare impedit, All the parties by their severall obligations dated the 20th of Aprill. Anno. 20th H. 7th submit their titles to the award of Robert Brudnell and William Grevill, serjents at lawe; who, having heard the Counsell of both sides, and substantially (saith the award) understood their titles, Awarded, that the said president and schollars should hold to them and their successors the patronage presentment and guift of the said Advowson: And that this lord should discontinue his said Writt of Quare impedit, and should make to them such further assurance as their Counsell should devise, but that before such assurance the said president and schollars should pay to this lord Twelve Pounds; which they did. **Whereupon** a discontinuance was had, and a Comon Recovery was suffered of the said advowson, and the same accordingly settled upon the colledge and their successors, where it still remaineth, Anno. 1628. **On** the other part the colledge, (to use their own words,) in acknowledgment of this lords conveyance, and of his singular devotion and ardent affection, and of his manifold benefits which hee had shewed to them, they in recompence thereof, willing to requite soe great courtesies with spirituall suffrages and prayers for his soule, and of his progenitors, doe grant that hee shall dayly and for ever henceforth and his posterity bee made partakers of all their prayers and suffrages, in their collegiate church by them to bee celebrated, without fraud: And that when hee shall die, that in convenient time after notice had, they will hold his obite, with the placebo and dirige, and the masse of requiem, in the morrow after, solemly and with note; ffor performance whereof they bind themselves to this lord and his heirs for ever.

And though in the last forty years I have known, that Tirer, Savage, and others, by obtaining the tres of Henry lord Berkeley to the president and fellows of this colledge grounded upon the guift of this advowson, have been placed Demyes or schollars in that corporation, and soe have con|tinued till they proceeded graduates; yet that this family should have right to such schollerships by any agreement in writing I have not found, though I have heard it affirmed by one or two domestick chaplins in the family of the lord as sometimes were members of that colledge; But the College draweth yearly from that Rectory Ten pounds paid by the incumbent for the time being, which I take to bee spent in a gaudy day in bettering the Colledge

Colledge commons, and therefore with them noe Symony though paid upon an Oblig[a]cōn taken at his presentation. **Howbeit**, notwithstanding the fair countenance cast upon the colledges old title by this award, who claimed by the grant of the said Marques Berkeley then Earle of Nottingham, the colledge relyed not soe confidently thereupon, but that afterwards they procured, (as good cause they had,) severall releases and confirmations from Maurice and Thomas the two eldest sons of this lord Maurice, and from their feoffees and Recoverors, with the like confirmation also from the king himselfe, as desirous to hold fast an Advowson of neare three hundred pounds value by the year.

Other were the restitutions to divers other manors, which this lord obtained upon the defects pretended to bee in his brother Marques Berkeleis conveyances, by reason of old entailes and his own remitters, as appears in the Catalogue of the lands whereof hee dyed seifed, here for brevity by me omitted.

In the Toile of the foresaid prosecutions this lord finding himself, at his first coming to visit Callowdon and other his manors in those parts in the 16th of king Henry the seaventh, not soe honored in his entertainment with the Abbot of the monastery of Combe in Warwickshire as hee conceived to bee his right, being one of their founders heirs; (perhaps but out of the Abbots ignorance of his discent;) exhibits his bill in Chancery, and shews that hee is one of the Cozens and heires of Thomas Mowbray late Duke of Norfolke, Earl Marshall and Warren, lord Mowbray, Segrave, Gower and Brewes, who was in his life time received in that Monastery with procession and other observances as belongeth in such a case for the founder; The right of the foundation of which monastery, (saith this lords bill,) after the decease of the said Duke discended to Thomas Howard Earle of Surrey and to him the said Maurice lord Berkeley as Cozens and heires of the said Duke; **That** is to say, To the said Earle, as son of John, son of Margarett, one of the daughters of the said duke; And to this Lord Maurice, as son of Isable one of the daughters of the said Duke; And for | proofe layeth down That the said John father of the said Earle was slaine at Bosworth field, And was entred in the said Abby with due observances as belongeth; And the said Earle was lately received there with procession and other solemnities as belongeth of right and laudable custome used in this Relme of England, which the Abbot hath neglected towards him being thereto required; And therefore prayeth that hee may bee compelled to enter him as one of the founders, and soe to bee accepted and entreated as of right to him belongeth; Which honor, upon a referance to Wiłłm Grevill and Thomas Marrowe arbitrators, this

Bill in canc: Vetus manuscript in castro de Berkeley.

6x8

carta in castro de Berkeley

div'sæ t̃re in caſtro de Berkeley.	this lord obtained, and accordingly left it to his poſterity, who were in their ſeverall times received as founders, till the diſſoluc̃on of the Monaſtery; as alſo appeareth by this Abbots attendance on the dead body of the lady Iſable this lords wife, and his cenſing and perfuming of her herſe at Binly bridge, in her conveying to London, the place ſhee had appointed for her ſepulture; as after followeth.
carta in caſtro de Berkeley.	**The** 13th of November in the 18th yeare of king Henry the ſeaventh, Thomas Earle of Surry granted to this lord Maurice, by the name of Maurice Berkeley lord Berkeley, and to his heires for ever, one Bucke and one Doe yearly out of his parke called Seggewicke park in Suſſex, with liberty to enter and kill the ſame at pleaſure.
Acqu[i]t̃ in caſtro de Berkeley.	**What** the offences were which this Maurice had committed I find not, but in the 28th yeare of king Henry the ſixth hee paid the Duke of Yorke 11li. by agreement for Injuryes and greeves by him and his two ſervants, Cater and Chriſtopher, done to the ſaid Duke, as the acquittance ſaith, given upon receipt of that money: **But**, being then a batchelor and in the 24th yeare of his age, and living often near to ſome of the Dukes parks, I conceive it was for killing ſome of his Deere.

His Wife.

Volunt̃ Phil Mead probat̃ A°. 1475. A°. 15. E. 4.	**The** wife of this lord Maurice was Iſable daughter of Phillip Mead Eſqr and of Iſable his wife; ſon of Thomas, ſon of Thomas Mead, diſcended of the ancient family of the Meads of Meadſplace in ffeyland in the pariſh of Wraxall near Portbury in the County of Somerſt,	where antiently they had continued; whom this lord married in the thirtieth year of his age, about eighteene months after his fathers death, ſhee then a widowe and mother of three children, who all dyed very young.
619 An antient pedegree wth Wm Denis, Eſqr	
regiſter Roḃti de Ricart cum Maiore de Briſtoll.	**At** the time of this her ſecond marriage, her father was an Alderman of Briſtoll & at divers times Maior there; And for her Dowry, beſides her perſonall eſtate, ſhee brought to this lord her huſband, (then a younger brother,) divers lands in Somerſetſhire, and others in Thornbury in Glouceſterſhre (where this lord then alſo had other lands both of his own purchaſe, and of the guift of his elder brother,) and a leaſe of the ſaid Meads-place for one and twenty years: and was after one of his executors, as his will ſhewes.
carta. 14. E. 4. in caſtro de Berkeley.	
Carta. 20. Octo. 7. E. 4. in caſtro de Berk.	
Carta. 9. Decem. 22: H: 7. in caſtro de Berkeley.	**ffor** her Joynture ſhee had from this lord her huſband all the lands in effect which hee then had; which alſo hee in the later part of his life, (for the longer they lived the more they loved,) much augmented with divers other manors in the Counties of Huntington, Leiceſter, Warwicke, and Glouceſter, and in the Counties

Counties of the Cities of Coventry and Gloucester; of all which shee made the said Thomas Try her receivour generall soone after her husbands death.

This lady Isable had one only brother called Richard Mead, who first marryed Elizabeth   , And after maryed Anne daughter of Thomas Paunsfoot of Hasfeild in Gloucestersh:ᵣᵉ Esqʳ, a family for antiquity inferior to none in that County, (this of Berkeley excepted;) But his issue dying very younge without issue, about the third of king Henry the seaventh, this lady Isable became heire to divers manors and lands in the County of Glouc., And to divers Messuages and tenements in Bedminster, Felond, Ashton, Wraxall, and Midle Tykenham, in the County of Somersett. *carta cum Rogero Kemis de Wickwicke.*

How little cause the Marques Berkeley had to complaine of the obscure parentage of the lady Isable, which he vainly called base: and of the unworthynes of his brothers match with so mean bloud, as hee reproached it, making that a motive to his own vast expences, and of the disinheritance of this lord his brother, least any of her base bloud should inherite after him, may to his further reproof bee returned upon his memory to bee but a fained and unbrotherly quarrell picked on purpose to give colour for his own exorbitances: Like vaine were his exceptions to his said brother and heire, for defending the vertue of his wife and worthines of her parentage. *vetus manuscriptᵐ in castro de Berkel:*

Shee was a virtuous lady and evermore content with better or harder fortunes; | And what goodnes and disposition shee was of in her last widowhood, after this lord her husbands death, may bee conceived out of these few rellicks of her many devotions.

The 29ᵗʰ of May . 1514 . in the 6ᵗʰ of king Henry the 8ᵗʰ, (amongst other liberalities,) shee gave to the Pryor of the fryars heremites of the order of Saint Augustine in London the sum of—72^{li}. 13ˢ. 04ᵈ. towards the repair of their house, grown ruinous with age; for which they bound themselves & their successors in a full chapitre to say on the seaventh of November the exiquies of the aniversaries of her and her husband, to bee sunge with note by all the Covent in the quire of their church: And the morrow after, a Masse of requiem at the high Altar by all the covent, for the souls of the said lady and her husband the lord Maurice, and for the souls of James lord Berkeley and of Isable his wife, father and mother of the said lord Maurice, and of all faithfull deceased: **And** three days in every week for
ever

ever, one prieſt, being a fryar in the houſe, to ſay a maſſe curſarily, with the ſpeciall collects of vnus deus qui charitatis, com̃ ſecreto, et poſt com, ad id pertinen̄; And alſo Inclina cum ſecreto, et poſt com̃, ad id pertinen̄; As in the table afterwards in this deed is ſpecifyed and deſcribed, for the ſoules of her and her huſband and the ſ.ᵈ lord James and Iſable, at the Altar of S.ᵗ James in the ſaid Church under the high crucifix, on Mundayes wedneſdays and frydays, after the ſixt maſſe is ſaid; And in every maſſe ſoe ſaid, after the goſple and before hee goe to the lavertory, the pſalme of De profundis with the prayers accuſtomed; which Maſſe ſhall for ever in the Engliſh tongue bee called Berkeleys maſſe. And likewiſe the maſſe de quinque vulneribus. And further, that for an everlaſting memory, this Indenture in the Vigill of S.ᵗ Michaell ſhall for ever bee read yearly in their Chapitre houſe publickly. And for performance hereof the pryor and covent bind themſelves in their pure conſciences, as they will anſwer at the dreadfull day of Judgment before the ſupream Judge.

Berkeleys maſſe.

And for better ſecurity and performance of all and every thing aforeſaid they further grant, That as often as any failing ſhall bee in any part of the premiſſes by the ſpace of a month, That they will forfeit and pay—20.ˢ—to the maſter and brethren of Burton Lazars, in that their houſe to bee charitably beſtowed for the ſoules aforeſaid, which maſter for that cauſe was made a party to this deed. And, (w.ᶜʰ was more then formerly I have found,) fryar Hugo lovericus, provinciall of this order, doth ratify this Indenture, and binds the ſaid pryor and covent in the bond of holy obedience, and under the puniſhment of rebellion, That they faithfully performe the whole contents of this deed.

621

Two yeares it ſeemes this was in contriving, And in the end were two deeds ſealed by the pryor, both which remaine in Berkeley Caſtle.

carta in caſtro de Berkeley.

She dyed at Coventry in the eighth yeare of king Henry the 8.ᵗʰ then aged 70 years, having overlived her huſband about 9 years; And with him lyeth buryed in the Auguſtine Fryars in London, leaving iſſue three ſons and one daughter, as next followeth. And it is ſome what obſervable, That this lady juſt ſoe long ſurvived her huſband as to make the period of both their ages alike; And then in the ſame place to lay down her bones by his in that 70.ᵗʰ year that bringeth compleatnes to the daies of man; As 10. times, 7. or 7. times, 10. which Moſes in the 90.ᵗʰ Pſalme of Davids bundle makes the common age of all men. And that this lord, as after follows, ſhould over live his brother Marques twice ſeaven years,

Comp: de Feny-ſtanton. 8 H. 8. in caſtro de Berkeley.

Pſalm 90.

years, and one seaven months; As though all their circumferences were closed in that number of seaven; The manner of whose death and funerall pompe, with the conveyance of her body from Coventry to London, take, in the same words as Thomas Try, a speciall officer and servant to this lord, and the said ladies administrator, sent the description thereof to the lord Maurice her son, then at Calais, being the proper hand writing of the said Thomas Try, endorsed thus

> This bill bee delivered to his right worshipfull and speciall good Maister, Sir Maurice Berkeley knight.

Originall in Berkeley Castle.

Pleseth your good mastership, the ordering at thenterement of my lady your mother hereaft' folowith,

1. **First,** when I pceved she bygan to draw from this liff, I caused certen prests to say dyvs oryfons, And also to shewe hir of the passion of crist and of the merits of the same, wherunto shee gave merveluous goodly words, for aft' hir Aneyling she cam to good and pfit remembrance.

2. Itm, aft she was departed I caused David Sawter to bee said continually untill the day of her buryeng, for as sonne as oon company had seid on other company of prests bygan, and so she was wached with prayer continually fro wensday untill monday.

3. Itm, ryngyng dayly with all the bells continually; That is to say, at St Mighells xxxiij. peles, At Tryntye xxxiij. peles, At St Johns xxxiij. peles At Babyl-lake becaufe hit was so nygh hyr lvij peles, And in the mother cherch, the p'orye, xxx. peles, and every pele xij^d.

4. Itm. upon sonnday whan her horse letyr was appeled, and wax and all other things redy, she was set forwards aft' this maner.

5. **First** xxx^{ti} women of her levery in blake gownes and kerechews upon their heds, of oon ele evy kyrchew, which was not surveled nether hemmed bycause they mought be knowen lately cut out of new cloth, and every woman beryng a tapyr of wax of a li. wyght & a half.

6. Itm after theym fowlowed xxxiij crafts with their lights to the nombr of CC. torches.

7. Itm

7. Itm about hir horſeleter was hir owne ſerv.ᵗˢ and other, berynge torches of cleyne wax, to nombr of xxx. in blake gownes.

8 Itm the orders of freerˢ whyt and gray, with their croſſes, next after the lyghts of the crafts.

9. Itm preſts to the nombr of oon C. and more wᶜʰ went with their croſſes next before the herſſe.

10. Item aft' the horſletyr v. gentylwomen morners.

11. Item aft' them Mr Recorder, and I, Mr Bonde, and my cozen Porter, ynſtede of thexecutors and ſupᵣvyſors.

12. Item then Mr Maire, the Mr of Yeld, Aldermans, Shreffs, Chamblyns, and Wardens.

13. **And** ſo ſhe was cōveid to the mother church, the pᵢorye, wher ſhe reſted yn the quere byfore the high altar all that nyght, and had ther a ſolem derege, and the Maire and his bredren went to Sᵗ Mighell, ther as was derege in like mañe; And aft' dereḡ, the Maire and his brethren went in to Sᵗ Mary hall, wher as a drynking was made for theym; fyrſt cakys, comfetts and ale, the ſecund courſe marmelet, Snoket,¹ redd wyne and claret, and the 3rd courſe wafers and Blanch powder wᵗ romney and muſkadele; And I thanke God, noe plate ne ſpones was loſt yet ther was xxᵗⁱ deſyn ſpones.

14. **Upon** Monday ſhe ſate forward aft' maſe wᵗʰ the ſaid lights and crafts, the ſeyd v. morners rydyng in ſedſadells and ther horſes traped with blake, Mr Recorder, and I, Mr Bonde, and Porter rydyng aft' theym, and then Mr Maire, Aldermen, Shreſis, Wardens, and Chambleyns rydyng in lyke order as they were; And at Bynley brygge met my lord the abbot | of Combe wᵗ his mitre, ſenſyng the herſe, and in his company Mr Broune Mr Bowghton and many other, ye may be ſure to the nombre of v. or vi. thoſand pepull: I am of a ſuerty ther was at every ſittyng above xjˣˣ or xijˣˣ meſſeʒ, and the bordes was divˢ times ſet, & Thomas Berkeleis preſt ſay the orderyng of all: wryten at Caloughdon the xvjᵗʰ day of Apʳle.

Yoʳ ſervᵗ Thomas Try.

His

---

¹ Query, Sonket=Sweets.

His issue.

By the said Isable this lord Maurice had issue, Maurice, Thomas, James, and Anne.

1. **Maurice** the eldest son succeedeth his father in the Barony, advancing his house with honor and reputation; And after dyed without lawfull issue, as his life that followeth doe declare.

2. **Thomas** the second son was also lord Berkeley after the death of his said elder brother, whose life in due place also followeth.

3. **James** the third son and youngest, maryed Susan the daughter of Mr. Veill and the widow of William Vele Esqr., and survived her husband: By her hee had issue John Berkeley who dyed at mans estate before marriage, and Mary Berkeley, first marryed to Sr. Thomas Perrot son of Sr. Owen Perrot, who had issue Sr. John Perrot, Elizabeth and Jane.

Sr. John Perrot had issue Sr. Thomas, father of Sr. James Perrot yet living. 1618. And of Penelope maryed to Sr. William Lover[1] knight, And of Lettice first maryed to Rowland Langharne Esq., and after to Walter Vaughan Esqr., And at this day wife to Sr. Arthur Chichester lord Deputy of Ireland; and of Anne Perrot married to John Phillips of Picton Esqr. yet living. 1618.

The said Elizabeth sister of Sr. John Perrot was maryed to Mr. Price Esqr. who had issue Sr. Richard Price of Gogarthan knt., & others yet living. 1618.

The said Jane the other sister of the said Sr. John Perrot was marryed to William Phillips Esqr., who have issue two daughters, the one marryed to George Owen, and the other to Alban Stepneth Esqr.

And secondly the said Mary Berkeley, daughter of this James Berkely, was marryed to Sr. Thomas Jones knight who had issue Sr. Henry Jones, father of Sr. Thomas, father of Sr. Henry Jones that now is, 1618: And Katharine marryed to Mr. Vaughan, who had issue Sr. Walter Vaughan knight that now is; And Ellenor marryed to Mr. Griffith Rice, who had issue Sr. Walter Rice knight that now is, and others, Anno, 1618.

And, as Sr. James Perrot formerly named hath informed mee, all the cheife gentlemen of most eminency in the three shires of Pembroke Carmarthen and Cardigan

---
[1] Sir William Lower of Treventy, Co. Caerm. and St. Winnow and Trelaske, Co. Cornw. (*Hist. of Trigg Minor*, Vol. III. 386.)—[ED.]

Cardigan at this day living, are difcended of this Mary Berkeley, of whofe memory in thofe parts is made moft honorable mention to this day.

<small>Carta dat. 19. H. 7 irrot. in Canc. Rec: in fcacio. 21. H. 7. rot. 16.

Comp: de Mangotsf. 13. H. 8. in caftro de Berkeley.</small>

The faid James Berkeley, for a third brother's portion, had the manor of Hilton in the County of Huntington, to him and the heires males of his body, and twenty pounds p anñ, by the graunt of this lord his brother; And the Conftablefhip and Porterfhip of Berkeley Caftle, and the keeping of the Caftle park, and of Chefelhunger and Redwood, and the gale and profit of other fifhings in Seaverne with the fee of 3^{lb}. from the kinge; and was to Henry the 7th vnus generoforum hoftiariorum camere Regis, one of the gentlemen porters of the king's chamber, which hee enjoyed till the 6th yeare of king Henry the 8th when hee left both it and the world, and his faid wife Sufan to furvive him, which fhee did about fix years; And fome of his offices to his elder brother Thomas.

4. The faid Anne Berkeley only daughter of this lord Maurice was in the time of king Henry the 7th married to Sr Willm Denis of Dirham knight; who had

<small>Denis.</small> iffue between them 1 Sr Walter Denis, 2 Sr Maurice Denis, 3 William Dennis, 4 Ifable, 5 Elleanor, 6 Anne, 7 Margaret, 8 Katharine, 9 Mary, and eight others that dyed young without iffue; Of thefe nine, as followeth,

1. The faid Sr Walter Denis by Margaret his wife daughter of Sr Richd Wefton knight, had iffue four fons and two daughters, Richard, Thomas, Francis, William, Jane and Anne; of whom ffrancis is dead without iffue.

<small>625</small> The faid Richard Denis by Anne his wife daughter of Sr John | St John of Bletfoe, had iffue, Walter, William, Gilbert, Maurice, Anne, ffrances, Katharine, Mabill, Mary, and Margaret; of whom Gilbert Maurice and Mary are dead without iffue, And Willm is yet unmarryed; Of the other fix in order.

The faid Walter fon of Richard by Margaret his wife daughter of Richard
<small>Pigot.</small> Paunsfoot Efq^r had iffue two daughters; Katharine, firft marryed to Mr Lewis Pigot,
<small>Coplefton.</small> of Bedfordfhire, and after to Mr Coplefton, of Devonfhire, yet living Anno. 1618.
<small>Cokeine.</small> And Jane marryed to Mr Cokeine of the faid County of Bedford.

<small>Porter.</small> The faid Anne daughter of Richard Denis was maryed to Sr Thomas Porter knight, of Lanthony by Glouc.; (of whom read before in the iffue of James the firft,) who had iffue Sr Arthur Porter, Ambrofe, Anne, Katharine, ffrances, and Margaret.

The

The said Sr. Arthur Porter, by Anne his wife daughter of Sr. John Danvers, had issue Elizabeth lately maryed to John, son and heire of Sr. James Scuddamore of Homelacy in the County of Hereford. — Scuddamore.

The said Ambrose Porter hath maryed Frances the daughter of George Chancey of Yardlebury of Hartfordshire, by whom as yet hee hath no issue, 1618.

Anne sister of the said Sr. Arthur Porter is maryed to Sr. Gabriel Pyle of Collingborne in Wiltshire, who have issue Francis, William, Thomas and Gabriell, which ffrancis hath lately married the daughter of Sr. Francis Popham. — Pyle.

Katharine, another sister of the said Sr. Arthur Porter, was marryed to Sr. Richard Walsh of Shelsey in the County of Worcester, who have issue Anne, marryed to Sr. Thomas Bromley, mother of four children by him; And Joyce, maryed to Sr. Rowland Cotton, as yet having noe issue, Aº. 1618. — Walsh. Bromley. Cotton.

ffrances, another sister of the said Sr. Arthur Porter, was maryed to Mr. Peter Marten; who have issue Thomas, Edward, Anne, Martha, and Lucy, Anno, 1618. — Marten.

And the said Margaret, the youngest sister of the said Sr. Arthur Porter, was marryed to George Thorpe, of Wanesswell Esquire, by Berkeley, by whom he had noe issue. — Thorpe.

The said ffrances, another daughter of the said Richard Denis, was maryed to John Gwillm, Esqr. who wrote that methodicall book called A Display of Heraldry; And have issue Saint John, John, Margaret, ffrances, and Priscilla. | — Gwillm.

The said Katharine, another daughter of the said Richard Denis was maryed to Willm Chester of Almondsbury in Berkeley hundred, Esqr. who have issue Thomas Chester, who first maryed Anne, daughter of Samuell Bacchus Esqr., by whom hee hath issue Anne; And secondly maryed the daughter of Sr. George Speake knight, And in this present year 1617, as I am writing hereof, high sheriffe of the County of Glouc.; William Chester a batchelor; Katharine Chester maryed to Phillip Langley, of Mangotesfeild, Esqr. who have issue; And Alice Chester married to Mr. Persival of Somersetshire. — Chester.

The said Mabill, another daughter of the said Richard Denis, was maryed to Anthony Dowle of Duntisborne Abbot in the County of Glouc. gent, who have issue Edward, Walter, and others. — Dowle.

And

|Hill.| And the said Margaret, (the last of the daughters of the said Richard Denis,) was first maryed to Maurice Hill of Tockington in the County of Glouc. gent, by whom she had issue Walter Hill; and secondly to one Mr. Spencer.

The said Thomas Denis, brother of the said Richard by Jone his wife daughter of Mr. Paunsfoot, had issue Thomas and Margaret; which Thomas son of Thomas, (yet living in Glouc., Anno, 1618,) by Dorothy his wife daughter of Mr. Compton, hath issue William and divers others.

|Evans.| And the said Margaret was maryed to Willm Evans of Glouc., an Attorney at lawe, who have issue Thomas Evans and Elizabeth.

The said William Denis another brother of the said Richard, by Anne his wife daughter of Mr. Rastle, had issue William Denis only now living Anno. 1618.

|Compton.| The said Jane sister to the said Richard Denis was maryed to Willm Compton of the County of Glouc., who have issue Walter Compton and others.

And the said Anne the last of the sisters of the said Richard Denis was maryed to Simon Codrington Esqr., who is dead without issue.

2. The said Sr. Maurice Denis, second son of the said Anne Berkeley and of Sr. William Denis her husband, dyed without issue; As also did Willm Denis his brother, but longe remarkable in their generations. |

627   3. The said William Denis third son of the said Anne Berkeley, and of Sr. William Denis her husband, dyed also without issue.

|Berkeley. see before in the life of Maurice the third fol: 273. 274. 275.| 4. The said Isable Denis, daughter of the said Anne Berkeley and Sr. William Denis her husband, was maryed to Sr. John Berkeley of Stoke Gifford knight, who hath issue Sr. Richard Berkeley, Mary, and Elizabeth maryed to Henry Ligon, whereof I have formerly written amongst the issues of Maurice the third.

The said Sr. Richard Berkeley, by Elizabeth his first wife daughter of Willm Read of Mitton by Tuexbury Esqr., had issue Henry, Elizabeth, Marye, Katharine, Anne, and Dorothy; And by Eleanor his second wife, daughter of Robert Jermy Esqr. and widowe of Robert Rowe Esqr., son of Sr. Thomas Rowe knight, had noe issue.

The

The said Henry, son of Sr. Richard Berkeley by Mirriell his wife, daughter of Thomas Throgmorton of Cawghton in the County of Warr., Esqr. had issue Richard Berkeley, Elizabeth, and Margaret.

The said Richard Berkeley by Mary his first wife daughter of Robert Rowe aforesaid hath issue, Sr. Maurice Berkeley knight, John, Thomas, Giles, Richard, Robert, Elizabeth, Hellena, Myriell, Katharine, Mary, and Margaret; Of whom I have in part formerly written in the life of the lord Maurice the third. fol. 275. 276.

The said Elizabeth daughter of Sr. Richard Berkeley, formerly mentioned to bee maryed to Sr. Thomas Throkmorton of Tortworth, knight, have issue Sr. William Throkmerton created Baronet, Margaret, Mary, and Elizabeth.

The said Sr. Willm Throkmerton by Cicely his first wife, daughter and Coheire of Thomas Bainham of Clowerwall Esq, hath issue Baynham Throkmerton and many others: As also hee hath by two other wives his maides, maryed since the death of the said Cicely. Throkmerton.

The said Margaret sister of Sr. Willm Throkmton was maryed to Sr. Barnaby Samborne of Somsetshire knight, who have issue. Samborne.

The said Mary, another sister of the said Sr. Willm Throkmton, was first maryed to Sr. Thomas Baskervile knight, by whom shee had issue Hannyball: And after married to Sr. James Scuddamore knight, by whome shee hath issue Sr. John Scuddamore, who by his wife onely daughter of Sr. Arthur Porter hath issue, John. Baskervile.
Scuddamore.

And the said Elizabeth, youngest sister of the said Sr. Willm Throkmton, liveth the widow of Sr. Thomas Dale knight, having noe issue. 1626. Dale.

The said Mary, another Daughter of the said Sr. Richard Berkeley, was maryed to Sr. John Hungerford of Down Amny knight, who have issue, Sr. Anthony Hungerford knight, John, Bridget, Elizabeth, Barbara and others; Of whom is a plentifull posterity with opulent possessions. Hungerford.
628

The said Katharine, another daughter of the said Sr. Richard Berkeley, was first maryed to Sr. Rowland Lee of Longbarrowe in Gloucshire Esqr, by whom shee had issue. And secondly remarried to Thomas Babington Esqr. Lee.
Babington.

The

The said Anne and Dorothy two other daughters of the said Sr Richard Berkeley are dead without issue.

Walsh.
Herbert.
The said Mary, daughter of the said Isable Denis and of Sr John Berkeley her husband, was maryed to Nicholas Walsh of Sodbury Esqr who had issue Henry Walsh, slaine in single combat by Sr Edward Wintour, without issue, and three daughters: And after his death the said Mary was remarried to Sr William Herbert of Swansey.

Ligon.
And the said Elizabeth, sister of the said Mary, one other of the daughters of the said Isable and of Sir John Berkeley, was maryed to Henry Ligon Esqr, who had issue Sr Arnold Ligon knight, Henry Ligon, Mary, & Elizabeth.

The said Sr Arnold Ligon, by Jone his wife the widow of John Baker, had issue Henry, Thomas and Elizabeth.

The said Henry, brother of Sir Arnold, is dead without issue.

Clinton.
Hall.
Longe.
The said Mary, sister of Sir Arnold, was marryed to Samuell Clinton gent. who have issue Samuell, Richard, Elizabeth, Anne, Mary, Margery, and ffrances; whereof Elizabeth was maryed to Mr Hall; Anne marryed to Mr Longe of Ashelworth; the other three daughters not marryed, Anno 1628. The said Samuell maryed the daughter of John Nest of Chasely in the County of Worcester, who have issue: And Richard is dead without issue.

Basset
fol: [144]
And the said Elizabeth the other sister of Sr Arnold, was maryed to Edward Basset of Ewley Esqr of whom read before in the life of Thomas the first; who had issue Willm Basset, Barnaby, Edward, Giles, Elizabeth, Margery, Susan, and Jane.

The said Willm marryed the daughter of Willm Davy, who had issue William Basset now in ward to the king, Anno. 1618.

The said Barnaby Basset by Elizabeth his wife daughter of John Dorney of Ewley, hath issue Willm Basset, Edward, Robert, Elizabeth, Jane, & Hester.

The said Edward Basset maryed the daughter of Mr Danyell of Marleborowe, by whom hee hath issue one Daughter.

The said Giles is not yet maryed; Since executed at Glouc., 1640. for mur-dering of Christopher Willis of Wotton.

629

The said Elizabeth Baffet was first marryed to William Clavile by whom shee had noe issue; And after to Thomas Poyntz by whom shee hath issue Matthewe, Thomas, Joseph, John, Elizabeth, Sara and Martha, Anno. 1624.

Poyntz of Uley.

The said Margaret is married to Samuell Shellam of Woodchester, who have issue five children, Anno. 1624.

Shellam.

The said Susan is married to Michaell Dorney who have issue Thomas and Elizabeth, Anno, 1624.

Dorney.

And the said Jane is married to John Deighton of Glouc., Surgeon, who have issue John and five others, Anno, 1624.

Deighton.

5. The said Ellenor Denis, another daughter of the said Anne Berkeley and of Sr Willm Denis her husband, was maryed to William Ligon of Madresfeild in the county of Worcester, who had issue Richard, Thomas, Ralph, Hugh, ffrances, Margery, Ellenor, Elizabeth, and the lady Gorges, of each of whom in order.

The said Richard Ligon maryed the daughter of Sr John Russell, and have issue Willm Ligon, Henry, ffrances, Penelope, Elizabeth, Elleanor, and one other.

The said Willm by Elizabeth his wife daughter of Mr Horwell, hath issue Sr William Ligon, Richard, Thomas and Elizabeth.

The said Henry and ffrances are dead without issue.

The said Penelope was married to Mr Wallin of Woodfeild in the County of Worcester, who have issue.

Wallin.

And the said Elizabeth Ligon is married to Doctor Miles Smyth lord Bishop of Glouc.: who hath no issue.

And the said Elleanor, (sister of the said Elizabeth,) was first maryed to John Washborne of Wichingford in the county of Worcester, who have issue.

Washborne.

And

And the said   (younger sister of the said Elleanor) was married to

Ligon of Elston. The said Thomas Ligon called of Elston in the county of Glouc., second son of Willm and Elleanor his wife, maryed ffrances daughter of Hugh Denis of Pucklechurch, who have issue Thomas Ligon, ffrancis, William, Richard, John Katharine, and Jone.

630 The said Thomas was Receivour to Henry Lord Berkeley, and is now farmer of Callowdon; And by his wife daughter of Denys Pratt hath issue.

The said ffrancis and William are lately dead without issue. Richard is also unmarried, 1630.

John was attendant on George lord Berkeley in Oxford at the finishing of these collections, a partaker of his first travells, And since dead without issue.

Gerrard. Katharine is married to Mr Gerrard of Stanford in the county of Som!, who have issue six daughters.

And the said Jone youngest daughter of the said Jone was married to

The said Ralph Ligon, third son of the said Willm Ligon and Ellenor Denis, since the beheading of Thomas Howard Duke of Norfolke in ye 13th of Elizabeth, hath lived beyond seas and hath noe issue.

The said Hugh Ligon, 4th son of the said William and Elleanor; hath issue Henry Ligon, Hugh, Ralph, William, and others.

The said ffrancis, fifth son of the said Willm Ligon and Elleanor Denis, maryed Grace daughter of John Bub of Bentham neare Glouc., who have issue Hugh and John.

Russell. The said Margery Ligon, eldest daughter of the said William Ligon and Elleanor Denis, was first marryed to Sr Thomas Russell, by whom shee had issue, Thomas, who hath maryed the widowe of Frances Brace; And secon[d]ly, shee was maryed to Sr Henry Berkeley of Bruton in ye County of Somerset, by whom
Berkeley of shee hath issue Sr Maurice Berkeley and others; of which remarkable line see in
Bruton. fol: 276. the life of the Ld Maurice the third.

The

The said Elizabeth, daughter of the said William Ligon and Ellenor Denis his wife, was maryed to Thomas Foliot of Perton in the County of Worcester, who have issue Sr John ffoliot, Sr Henry ffoliot, Willm, Elleanor, and Constance.

The said Sr John ffoliot by Elizabeth his wife daughter of Doctor John Elmer late bishop of London hath issue Elmer, Thomas, ffrancis and others.

Sr Henry and Willm are not yet maryed.

Elleanor ffoliot is maryed to Sr John Bucke. | Bucke.

Constance is maryed to Mr Baugh.   Baugh.
    631

The said Elleanor Ligon, daughter of the said Willm Ligon and Ellenor Denis, was maryed to Willm Norwood of Leckhampton in the County of Glouc., Esqr son of Henry Norwood; of whose issue, (by falling into a neerer degree,) see after at large in the life of Thomas the fifth son of this lord Maurice.   Norwood.
    fol: 682.

And the fourth daughter of the said Willm Ligon and Ellenor Denis, was married to Sr Edward Gorges of Wraxall in the County of Somerset, who have issue Sr Edward Gorges, Sr Ferdinando Gorges, and others, from whom is a plentifull posterity.   Gorges.

6. **The** said Anne Denis, an other daughter of the said Anne Berkely and of Sr William Denis her husband, was first married to Sr John Ragland, and after to Sr Edward Carne.   Ragland.
    Carne.

By her first husband shee had issue Sr Thomas Ragland, father of Thomas and others: And Margaret married to Mr Carne: and others: Which Margaret had issue Cicely married to Mr Kemys: Barbara marryed to Mr Turvill: And one other married to Mr Basset; and one other married to Mr Griffiths; And one other marryed also to ———.   Kemys.
    Turvill.
    Basset.
    Griffith.

And the said Anne Denis by Sr Edward Carne her second husband had issue Thomas Carne; who married the daughter and coheire of Sr Walter Hungerford, who had issue: And one other married to John Huntley Esqr son of George, son of John (called with the great legge,) who had issue George Huntley of Frocester knight,   Huntley knight, who by Ellenor his wife daughter of S.' William Wintour of Lidney had issue seaven sons and daughters, viz.' William Huntley who married Elizabeth the daughter and heir of M.' Read, both dead without issue: And 2 Edward not married in 1634, And 3 George dead without issue: And 4 Jane marryed to M.' Read of Mytton, who had issue: And 5 Mary married to M.' Giles ffoster, between whom is a numerous posterity: And 6 Elizabeth marryed to M.' Abrahall: And Elleanor Huntley not yet married, Anno, 1634.

Read
Foster
Abrahall

7. **The** said Margaret Denis, an other daughter of the said Anne Berkeley and of S.' William Denis her husband, was in the 20.th of Henry the 8.th marryed to S.' Nicholas Arnold son and heire of John | Arnold, to whom her uncle Thomas lord Berkeley, the ffifth, by his will gave two hundred marks to her marriage; who had issue Rowland Arnold, who by Mary his wife daughter of John Bridges created lord Chandois, had issue Dorothy marryed to S.' Thomas Lucy, who had issue Joyce maryed to S.' William Cooke knight, whom Henry lord Berkeley made one of his executors in trust; who had issue S.' Robert Cooke, William Cooke slaine at the Isle of Ree without issue, Thomas Cooke, Elizabeth married to John Scudamore Esq.' ffrances not married, Mary not maried, Dorothy marryed to another John Scudamore, Anne married to Peter Ball of the Middle Temple Esq.', who have issue William Anno. 1629. And Mildred maryed to John Maxey Esq.', who have issue William, Anno, 1629.

632
Arnold

Lucy
Cooke

Scudamore

Ball
Maxey

The said S.' Robert Cooke, by Dorothy his wife daughter of S.' Miles ffleetwood, are the fruitful parents of many hopefull children, Anno, 1629.

8. **The** said Katharine Denis, another daughter of the said Anne Berkeley and of S.' William Denis her husband, was marryed to S.' Edmond Tame son and heir of S.' Edmond of ffayreford in the County of Glouc.; And secondly to S.' Buckley knight; And thirdly to M.' Ligon; but had no issue by any of them.

Tame

9. **And** the said Mary Denis, the youngest daughter of the said Anne Berkeley and of S.' William Denis her husband, was a professed Nunne at Lacocke, And dyed at Bristoll longe after the dissolution of that monastery.

Thus have I let in a little light in the delineation of this lords issue, branched from his youngest son and onely daughter, James and Anne; That this lords present posterity might behold as in a glasse of Gods own making, how by an immortall
blessing

blessing conferred upon this good and pious lord, (who according to his own ordinance did eat his own bread in the sweat of his own browes,) his divine goodnesse hath multiplyed his posterity in a handfull of years into many thousands, disperfed through the veins of the most illustrious families in most of the countyes of this kingdom: Whereto I shall after add thousands more of like eminency and remarkablenes, when I come to write | of the issues of the lord Thomas this lords second son, and foe successively from him.

633

His seales of Armes.

I have not observed any other seales that this lord Maurice used then a small seale manuell with the ancient coat of Berkeley only, without crest supporters or circumscription: And a little seale with the Lion rampant, the coat of Mowbray: The like whereof Henry lord Berkeley sometimes used, as followeth in his life.

fol: [875]

His death and place of buriall.

September is now come, when within one month after king Henry the seaventh had entred into the 22th yeare of his raigne, Anno. 1506, This lord Maurice then in action strikes saile; And from his warrs of Westminster hall obtaineth that port which the toile of his life, through care for his posterity, would not afford; for his labors found no haven but the grave; then of the age of threescore and ten yeares and odd months, whereof hee had been lord in stile of writings and generall reputation since his brother the Marques death, fourteene yeares and seaven months or neer thereabouts; And is buryed in the Augustines Fryars at London, with some other of his Aunceftors, leaving behind him the testimony, vitæ bene actæ, of a life well lead, and an example of admirable industry to all his posterity. |

origin: in sc^{a}cio. 22. H. 7. rot. 24.

Volunt: Mauricij dni Berkeley 15. H. 8.

The lands whereof he dyed seised.

That no lands were left by the Marques Berkeley upon his death to discend to this lord his brother and heire hath in both theire lives been declared: Now, behold what this lord left to his son and heire; And let his posterity tell their succeeding generations whether this their Anceftor did not foe well husband the last fowerteen

634

years

years of his life as Juftly hee may bee faid to bee the reftorer of his houfe and Barony, And a perfect lawier, to gaine thefe goodly poffeffions for the moft part out of broken and controverted titles, As

claus 22 H 7 m
Originñ in fc̃cio
22. H. 7. rot. 24.

carta in caftro de Berkeley.

Pat. 22 H 7 ps. 3

The burrowe and manor of Tetbury,
The manor of Sages,
Twenty two marks rent in Frampton,
Divers lands in Thornbury,
The manor of Daglingworth,
The manor of Upton St. Leonards,
} In the County of Glouc.

The manor of Winge,
The manor of Segrave in Penne,
} In the County of Buckingham.

The manor of Denge,
The manor of Bridgewicke,
} In the County of Effex.

The manor of Hovingham,
The manor of Donington,
The manor of Twaytes,
The moitie of Winefthorp manor,
} In the County of Yorke.

The manor of Bretby,
The manor of Linton,
The manor of Coton,
The manor of Repingdon,
The manor of Roftlafton,
The manor of Afhburne,
The manor of Howys,
} In the County of Derby.

635

The manor of Melton Mowbray,
The manor of Coldoverton,
The manor of Segrave,
The manor of Witherly, |
The manor of Sileby,
The manor of Mountforrell,
The hundred of Gofcote,
The manor of Dalby Chawcombe,
} In the County of Leicefter.

The

The Advowsons of Coldoverton, Segrave, Howby, Kegworth, Sutton-Bonington, and some others, } In the County of Leicester.

The manor of Thurlaston,
The manor of ffleckenhoe,
The manor of Aspely, } In the County of Warrwicke.

The manor of Callowdon, in the Counties of the Citie of Coventry and Warwick.

The manor of Auconbury,
The manor of Weston,
The manor of ffenystanton,
The manor of Hilton,
The manor of Guyherne & Murrow, } In the County of Huntington.

The manor of Bosham and Buckfold,
The manor of Thorney,
The manor of Funtington,
The manor and Park of Bewbush, } In the County of Suffex.

Fifteen houses and fower gardens in Calais.

A Messuage in Churchstreet in Berkeley purchased by him of Richard James.

The manor of Hinton,
The manor of Kent and Kentford, } In the Counties of Cambridge and Norffolk.

ffower pounds yearly rent out of the manor of Bromley in Surrey.

The manor of Maningford Bruse in the County of Wilts.

ffor which manors and lands soe discending, his son Maurice did the 5th of May next after his fathers death sue his speciall livery, wherein the same are mentioned; but found no offices at all, though hee tooke out writts of Diem Clausit extrem̃. dat:

pat: 22. H. 7. ps. 3.
originĩ : in sc^{a}c̃io 22.
H. 7. rot. 24. exp^{r}te remẽm. Thesaur̃.
Carta exempl : in castro de Berkeley.

dat. 13.th Octo : in the 22th of Henry the 7th to have inquired after his fathers death according to the courſe of the Chancery And theſe manors and lands, thus by this lords wife induſtry gleaned up and brought back into the old barne, is that faire graynary whereon his poſterity in their ſeverall ſucceſſions have ever ſince ſoe fedd and feaſted, upon the invitements of their preſent occaſions, by ſeverall ſales, as ſcarce a fifth part now remaines unſold for the repaſt of future generations, Añ .

Purchaſers. 1628 Upon which alienations alſo ſuch numberles peeces of evidence have to the ſeverall purchaſers been delivered out of their Evidence houſe, as I much miſſe hundreds of them, for the further beautyfying and inlarging of this hiſtory |

636 **The application and uſe of his life.**

The uſe It being an inherent truth, That the love which man naturally oweth to his progenitors is felt in every mans heart as a forcible motive to draw on imitation of their vertues and goodneſs with their poſterity, I cannot but hope from the noble worth and induſtry of this lord, That as his virtue ripened in his two ſons, (both lords,) that next followed, neither was any wayes blaſted in their ſucceeders ; ſoe it will invite the lord George, (lyneally from them,) in his maturity of years, reading this his Anceſtors life, to beare like fruite , not only as a reall acknowledger of his eſtate and dignity, renated (as it were) by this lord Maurice, But to become a true imitator of his induſtry and providence for his own future poſterity Of whom I may truly ſay, hee was a king of worthyes ; And to know, that although our cheifeſt hopes ought to bee fixed in the goodneſſe of God, yet by puting to that account our own endeavors the remedy is made more eaſy, and wee the ſooner maſters of our ends, as lively wee ſee in this lords example

2. **Againe**, from the example of the mean eſtate wherein this Lord Maurice was left by his laſt Anceſtor the Marques, whoſe heire hee was, his poſterity may compound a ſoveraigne treacle againſt worldly pride, unbrotherly contention, inſtabillity of greatnes, and the like · And may alſo apprehend, That all greatnes honor wealth and the like, are but a ſhadow, duſt and wind And may more truly comprehend whence men and honor come, and whither they are to goe.

3 **Againe**, That to the laborious God is propitious, And that neceſſity makes men ſkilfull Artiſts who never meant to have practiced And that where honor and profit are propoſed greater ſpurrs cannot bee ſet to a man that hath ſpirrit, even to perform actions and bring buſineſs about that ſeems beyond power, As this lords poſterity

ſees

fees in the life of this their industrious Ancestor; which I wish may ever lye open before them.

4. Againe, when this noble family shall by way of object reflect itself to see this their Ancester, with a milk white head in his irksome old age of 70. years, in Winter Terms and frosty seasons, with a buckerom bagg stuffed with lawe cases, in early mornings and late evenings walking with his eldest son between the fower Inns of Court and Westm^r. hall, following his law suites in his own old person; not for himself, but for his posterity, to regaine part of those possessions which a vast brother had profusedly consumed; to leave thereby whereon to live honorably like his forefathers: It cannot but stirre up an active care in his posterity to pre | serve and frugally to husband those possessions thus painfully obtained; The end, why this application and use is proposed.

5. Againe, this noble family may observe that this their Ancestor erred in his resolution, holding it better to prove the evill once, then always to fear it; A cause why hee fell sodainly out with the lord Marques his elder brother, whereby hee was the sooner disinherited of his barony: whereas hee should have considered the conclusions of things, rather than their beginings: Of helps wee oft make hindrances. There are many herbs very sweet when they are gently handled, but they loose their favour when they are roughly rub'd: This with this lord fell out too true; But semper sapere vix Iovi conceditur, the wisest are not alwayes wise; Sometimes not to erre is beyond the power of Humanity.

6. Againe, let this lords posterity sweeten their meditations with the remembrance of the blessings which Heaven, from the death of this lord to the present infancy of his great-great-great-grandchild the lord George, hath showred down upon this lords generations, as a visible reward of a life well lead, according to the ordinance of the Almighty, his lawgiver and creator: ffor further use whereof I returne this family to what is written in the end of the title of this lord's issues, which I wish may bee of use to them in their generations to come; And that the supreme hand of divine providence may uphold the honor of this lord in a blessed perpetuity, which hath done this good for his posterity.

7. Againe, the life of this lord tells his posterity, how much those men mistake the nature of God's divine ordinance, who neglecting the reason that God hath given them, do noe otherwise avoid the perills and crosses of this life then as if they
were

were ſtupified in the groſſe opinion of fate or deſtiny, neglecting either to beg counſell at Gods hands, or to exerciſe that wiſdom or foreſight wherewith God hath inriched the mind of man

8. **Againe**, This lords poſterity ſeeth that this their Anceſtor contented not himſelf to ſit ſtill and ſay That God was pleaſed to have it ſoe and ſoe with him, and thereon to reſt; which had been a true but an Idle anſwer, (for who knoweth not that Gods ſecret will is the cauſe of all things,) But to know with all That God giveth ſpirit, courage and invention, when and where it pleaſeth him to give an happy iſſue to our undertakings and deſires, Yet not ſo altogeather to reſt upon our ſelves, that wee will noe longer ſeeme to ſtand in need of God; **ffor** the iſſue of humane wiſdome is commonly unſucceſsfull when it depends upon that proviſſion which it ſelf hath made **And** let this family obſerve withall, That the All-powerfull God diſdained not to inſtruct Samuell to avoid the fury of Saul by the accuſtomed cautious waies of the world, when hee ſent him upon that dangerous ſervice of anoynting David for that kings ſucceſſor in the Crowne And how, though Moſes well knew that hee came out of Egypt under the mighty hand of heaven, And that God guided his underſtanding in all his enterpriſes, yet hee lay not ſtill in the ditch crying for help, but uſing the underſtanding that God had given him, hee left nothing unperformed becoming a wiſe man and a valiant and ſkillfull conductor, as by all his actions and counſells well appeared, And found his ſucceſſe accordingly; as this lord alſo did, And his poſterity after may, uſing the ſame meanes

1 Sam.l cap 16

638

Exodus 13 & 14 chap

9 **Againe**, from this memorable Anceſtor this uſe may bee drawn, That as noe adverſity accompanied with the leaſt or poſſibility of recovering, could ever vanquiſh his endeavor, but would firſt looke over every promiſe, true or falſe, that the preſent time could make him, and accordingly ſucceeded happily in his tryalls And knowing that wiſe men work out their own ends by the medium of mens affections and naturall appetites · Hee ſo perſevered in a wiſe conſtancy, That hee ever went away maſter of his own ends to his great profit and honor; Yet with ſuch a magnanimity of ſpirit, that hee ſcorned to fawn upon or fear the greateſt, as his life hath declared, And as a man of motion ſoe perſonally beſtirred himſelf, That to the example of his poſterity hee brought all his purpoſes to execution. adverſity never leſſening his courage, nor proſperity his circumſpection

639 } blank
640 }

The Life of Maurice the Sixth

The life of Maurice lord Berkeley the sixth of that name, ftiled in Writings, Maurice Berkeley Efq^r, And Maurice Berkeley knight, And Sr Maurice Berkeley of Yate, knight. And Maurice Berkeley knight pro corpore dni regis, for the body of the king; And Maurice lord Berkeley, And Maurice Berkeley lord Berkeley; And Maurice Berkeley knight, Ld Berkeley; And Maurice Berkeley of Berkeley, knight, lord Berkeley.

And was Ab-patruus, great-great-great-uncle, to George now lord Berkeley. And may bee called Maurice the Courtier.

Contemporary, with king Henry the 8th from the year 1506, [fic] till 1523.

The life of this lord is delivered under thefe eight titles, vizt.

1.—His birth and education, fol : 641.
2.—His forreigne imployments, with his law fuites, fol : 644.
3.—His creation of Baron, fol : 654.
4.—His wife, fol : 658.
5.—His feales of Armes, fol : 660.
6.—His death and place of buriall, fol : 660.
7.—The lands whereof hee dyed feized, fol : 663.
8.—The Application and ufe of his life, fol : 665.

His birth and education.

This lord Maurice was born in the feaventh year of king Edward the fourth, Anno. 1467. and his youths education under his father, who for moft part continued at Thornbury, as in his life hath been faid.

In the fecond year of king Richard the third, Anno. 1484, then in the 17th year of his age, hee was by his fathers means marryed to a gentlewoman of his own age

carta in caftro de Berkeley.

642 age and name, as after followeth, But their nuptiall | bed not bleſſing them with iſſue, or giving hope thereof, this lord with his wives liking betook himſelf to travaile and to a martiall life; In which faculty hee became a great ſoldier and commander, as the ſequell of his life declareth

A great part of the later ten years of the raigne of king Henry the 7ᵗʰ hee was his fathers lawbook bearer, extreamly toiled in the paper warrs of Weſtminſter hall, And in ſuch ſort for moſt part continued till the death of his father, two years before that king.

<small>diverſi comp͞i hoſpicij in caſtro de Berkeley.</small> At ſuch time as this lords father dyed, and all his life after, if this lord were in England, hee was either at Yate in Glouceſterſhire, or attendant on the kings perſon, If abroad, yet his wife and ſtanding houſe were uſually reſident at Yate, where alſo ſhee continued during the two years ſhee ſurvived her huſband, As alſo did the lord Thomas his brother and heire, as followeth in his life.

<small>carta in caſtro de Berkeley</small> The 22ᵗʰ of November, Anno. 22 H 7 this lord granted the ſtewardſhip of Boſham with the yearly fee of Ten Pounds, to Edmond Dudley, which is the firſt work I find done by him, ſoe wiſely willing hee was to have a frend about the king

<small>cartæ in caſtro de Berkeley</small>
<small>carta in caſtro de Berkeley.</small> Though upon the death of his father and for one year after, this lords uſuall addition of ſtile was but Maurice Berkeley Eſqʳ, yet in the 23ᵗʰ and laſt of Henry the 7ᵗʰ and in the firſt of Henry the 8ᵗʰ, then fallen into their ſervice, hopes altered his pen, And his ſtile was, Maurice Berkeley ſon and heire of Maurice Berkeley lord Berkeley deceaſed, and cozen and heire of Willm Marques Berkeley Earle Marſhall and of Nottingham, Viſcount Berkeley and Lord Berkeley

In the firſt of Henry the 8ᵗʰ hee was made knight, and as I think of the Bath, at that kings Coronation

<small>Carta dat. 30 Apr 4 H 8</small> In the 4ᵗʰ of that king, hee was ſworn, pro corpore regis, a knight for the body of the king, for that year and not before I find that addition of ſtile

<small>carta in caſtro de Berkeley</small> And in the 7ᵗʰ of king Henry the 8ᵗʰ, hee increaſed his eſtate in the ſcite of the manor of Yate with the parke, by a new leaſe taken of Henry lord Dawbeny for fowerſcore years from the death of the ſurvivor of himſelf and his wife, (having a

leaſe

leafe for their lives before;) where, within two years after, hee began to build a faire houfe, the accompt of which charge in building appeareth in a book kept by George Sheppard his principall Survayor, yet extant; fetching moft of the ftones from hafelbury quarre, and the Timber from Kingfwood forreft. |

lib: in caftro de Berkeley. 9. 10. et. 11. H. 8.

In September in the 6th of Henry the 8th, this lord was by fpeciall appointment one of that princely traine that attended the lady Mary the kings fifter into ffrance, to bee maryed to Lewis the twelvth, fhee then accompted the faireft lady of the world; And returned for England before Xmas following; And on newyears-eve dyed the faid French king after hee had been marryed to the faid lady . 82 . dayes.

643 Annal: of England Stow and others Martin. fol: 365.

In the 6th and 7th years of Henry the 8th, this lord was high Sheriffe for the County of Glouc.; And John Strange his underfherriffe, who alwaies directed his lres To my moft fingular good Mr, Sr Morys Berkeley knight, Sheriffe of the County of Glouc.; And foe did Edward Spenfer keeper of the comon gaole at Glouc.; An argument that hee was not then accepted as a peere of the Realme, As after alfo more fully doth appear: In which year, and after, hee procured many of the Quarter Seffions for the peace to bee holden at Tetbury, for his own eafe and that markett town's advantage, himfelf being lord thereof.

Pat. fub figillo in caftro de Berkl:

divers lræ in caftro de Berkeley.

Comp: de Bitton Manor: 9. H. 8. et al in caftro de Berkeley.

During that time of his Shreevewicke, and for many years before and after, hee was a great houfkeeper under a large expence at his houfe in Yate aforefaid; yet fuch neverthelefse was his providence, as each fatturday hee caft up his houfhold books of accompts, for what was difburfed by his Steward, Clarke of the kitchen, Cator, and for his Stable; And fubfcribed each weeks totall Summe with his own hand, as the books themfelves doe fhew.

Books in Berkeley-Caftle.

Such alfo was the exact methods by him and his houfhold officers obferved, that the perticular expences of each kind of provifion, in each day appeared: **And** when the ordinary allowance was exceeded above the comon fet rate, the margent renders the reafon, by fuch and fuch ftrangers being there, with their number of attendants and their horfes. As the Duke of Buckingham in . 10 . H . 8 . and others, when as I conceive a reconciliation was laboured between them. **Yea,** the good lady this lords wife appears alfo in thofe marginall notes, taking exception to fome perticular Acates that were in redundance, and to other forts that wanted; giving direction to ye Steward for time to come what fhee would have done, which for his better memory hee entred into the margent of his faid houfhold book; As,

Comp: Johis Jochim Señli hofpic: 11. et. 12. H. 8.

Comp: de Bitton 11. H. 8. in caftro de Berkeley.

thus

thus and thus, commanded by my lady   And fuch was this lords liking to his feate at Yate, and his hopes of repoffeffing really the Caftle and Barony of Berkeley with the members thereof, That hee fold himfelf out of the manor of Wing in the County of Buckingham, and fome others in remote Counties, as after appeareth, And with the moneys thereby raifed, bought the manors of Bytton and | Hannam, Mangottsfeild, Aylmington and divers lands in Henbury in the County of Glouc, lying near to his faid houfe at Yate, declaring himfelf thereby to bee a reall Gloucefterfhire man as his forefathers had been, and that himfelf henceforth would bee a forreigner in all other Counties; as more largely fhall bee delivered in an hiftory of thofe and other manors, which I have, in effect, already finifhed, by it felf

pat. dat 9. Nov.r 6 H 8 in caftro de Berk Cartæ in caftro de Berkeley

And fcarce was this lord difcharged of the office of being high Sheriffe, but hee procured from the king a generall pardon of all trefpaffes, forfeitures, &c, made to him, by the names of Maurice Berkeley of Yate knight, als Maurice Berkeley of Stoke Gifford, knight, als Maurice Berkeley late of Tetbury knight, als Maurice Berkeley late of Melton Mowbray knight, als, Maurice Berkeley knight one of the Juftices of peace in the County of Glouc, als Maurice Berkeley late Sheriffe of the County of Glouc, als Maurice Berkeley knight

His forraigne imployments.

Carta in caftro de Berkeley

The king purpofing warrs with france, great preparations were made, and fpetiall Captaines affigned, whereof this lord Maurice was one, between whom and the king, it was by Indenture, fubfcribed with the proper hand of the king, dated the 30th of Aprill in the fourth of his raigne, (wherin hee is ftiled one of the knights for his body,) agreed, That hee fhould do the king fervice of warr in the Army which hee now fendeth under the conduct of Thomas Gray Marques Dorfet his Leivtenant generall into Gafcoigne and Gwyen, for reduceing them under the kings obedience, & to have in his retinue in that fervice, fower hundred and eleaven able men, defenfibly arrayed for the warre, himfelf being one of the number. And to place for his faid retinue, Leivtenants and petty Captaines under him, and to make his own mufters and the like, as by the Indenture appears

Hollingfh Stow Marten, et div'fi alij

In June after, the whole Army took fhipping at Southton, and returned in December following; The fucceffe of which Journey I leave to the relation of the Annalls of thofe times, who all agree That much was not done

In

In July following in the 5th of his raigne, the king in perfon went into ffrance with a powerfull Army, what time hee tooke Tirwine and Turney | and fome other Cities, And returned into England in October following; with whom went and returned this lord, But what charge or comand hee had in that royall Army I have not found.[1]

645

Howbeit, this lord (then in the 46th year of his age,) being required to expreffe his opinion for the ordering of the Army fent into Gafcoigne, I find as followeth, which I the rather here infert, Afwell becaufe the fame is this lords own rough draught and proper hand writing, As for his pofterity to difcerne the difference of military difcipline in thefe times from thofe of the 4th of King Henry the eighth.

Orders to bee obferved for the Army.

Imprimis, to divide the Army into three parts; That is to fay, the Voward, Battle, and Rereward.

Maurice Lord Berkeley Manufcr. in caftro de Berkeley.

Item, to appoint the cheifeft Captaine of the Voward, and what Captaines and number fhall goe with him.

Item, to appoint the Captaine and number of the battle.

Item, to appoint the cheife Captaine of the rereward, and what Captaines and number fhall goe with him.

Item, the high Marfhall for the Army.

Item, the provoft Marfhall.

Item

---

[1] Little mention is made of Maurice Lord Berkeley in the State Papers of Henry viij. He is named in a letter of Cardinal Wolfey, dated 20 Aug., 1523, to be required with Lord Sandes "for affiftance to be gyven unto the Lieutenant (the Duke of Suffolk,") Vol. I. p. 123; and in another letter from Wolfey, dated at Hampton Court, the 30th of the fame month, it is mentioned that, "the Kinges Grace hathe levied a puiffant armye of as tal active and elect perfons, with as expert and good Capitains, as hathe paffed out of this Realme at any tyme this 100 yeres; whiche armye largely furnifhed and pourveyed of Ordenaunces Artillarye and other abilyamentes of werre, and femblably of vitailes in fufficient quantite is commytted unto the governaunce and leding of the Kinges entierly beloved Coufin and Counfaillour the Duke of Suffolk as his Graces Lieutenaunt General of the fame. In whofe company be affigned diverfe Lords and other difcrete and experte Counfaillors and Capitains, as the Lords Mountjoy, Montague, Ferrers, Sandes, Berkeley, &c." (Vol. V. 170.) We do not however fee Lord Berkeley named in the proceedings againft Thèrouenne and Tournay. [ED.]

Item, the Treaforer

Item, the mafter of the ordinance

Item, three Captaines of the pyoneers, whereof one to bee with the voward, Another with the battle, And the third with the rereward

Item, a principall Captaine for the Scowtes

Item, feaven Captaines to have the rule of the watch nightly, whereof one to watch And to have the rule of the ftale[1] in the market, And the fcoute to fend word to the Captaine of the ftale from time to time if the cafe foe require, And hee to advertize the Lievtenant; And the faid Captaine to fend certaine of the ftale to view the watch of the Ringe fower times of the night

Item, before two of the clock in the morning the watch and fcout to bee releived with others.

Item, the Marfhall to goe daily before, and to take and appoint the place where the Campe fhall lye; And every lord and Captaine to fend a furrier | to receive the ground and place for their mafters lodgings.

Item, to appoint one man with three officers under him to have the overfight of the carts and carriages, and to fee them conveyed out of the campe, from the tents unto the outfide of the feild, And foe to march in that order as they fhall bee appointed, not fuffering any carriage to goe ten fcore before the voward, nor ten fcore behind the rereward, And alfo at their coming to the Campe, having difcharged their carriages and fetched their forege, to place them for the fortifying of the campe as they fhall bee appointed by the Marfhall.

Item, one principall man to have the rule and charge of all kind of victualls, and to fee the diftribution thereof, And alfo to receive money for the fame, And hee to have a convenient number under him for the better order and execution of that charge; and to bee Clarke of the Market.

Item, the campe to bee fet every day at a convenient houre

Item, the voward to remaine in order of battle untill all the carriages of the fame bee come where they fhall bee appointed, and the tents almoft fet up, And then they of the voward to goe to their lodgings

Item,

[1] ftall

Item, the battle to remaine in order till the coming of the rereward, and then to goe to their lodgings.

Item, the rereward to remaine in order of battle till all the carriages bee come into the campe, and then they to go to their lodgings.

Item, every day a Captaine with a convenient number to bee appointed to goe for the forrage; And that noe man to goe out of the forrage untill the faid Captaine be ready and in order for their defence.

Item, the faid Captaine to fend out good fqyryors (fic) before his going forth.

Item, that noe man goe to the forrage but fuch as their Captaines will appoint; And they to goe noe further nor tarry longer then the captaine of the foriage fhall appoint them.

Item, every morning when the trumpets fhall give warning, every man to take down their Tents and lade their carts; And the captaine of the voward to bee ready in order of battle before the going forth of any of the carts.

Item, the battle to do the like.

Item, the like order for the rereward.

Item, the voward and rereward to have good fqyriors out in every fide. |

Item, that no man after the campe fet goe forth of the campe without licence of the Lievtenant, the Scouts only excepted.

647

Item, to appoint to the voward a Captaine of Horfmen.

Item, the like for the battle.

Item, the like for the rereward. Thus this lords writing.

Whilst this voyage was in preparation and this lord bent towards the Journey, Hee for his better provifion borrowed one thoufand pound of John Heron Sergeant at lawe; And for the fetling of his eftate and repayment of the faid money in cafe hee fhould dye in that warre, by his Deed tripartite dated the 26th of March in the

third

cartæ cum Edr̃o Deringe milite et baronet. dat 26 m'cij 3 H 8 Subfcrib Morys Berkeley	third year of Henry the 8th, by the name of Maurice Berkeley knight, enfeoffed Sr William Read knight, Richard Brook Sergeant at law, and others, of his manors of Bofham ffuntington and Thorney in the County of Suffex, **And** of his manor of Winge in the County of Bucks, And of his manors of Bretby, Roftlafton, Cotton and Linton in the County of Derby, And of the manor of Wetherly in the County of Liefter, And of the manor of Denge in the County of Effex, and of his manors of Auconbury and Wefton in the County of Huntington; To the ufe of himfelf and his heires and to performe his laft will.
Duæ cartæ cum pdc̃o Edr̃o Deringe mil[i]te et barronetto.	**And** by another Deed of the fame date, It was between all the faid parties and the faid John Heron agreed, And this Maurice did accordingly covenant, That the faid ffeoffees fhould ftand feized, To the ufe of the faid John Heron and his heires untill hee were paid one thoufand pounds wth his charges in levying the fame, which fomme hee hath borrowed of him, And after to the ufe of himfelf and his heires, and to performe his laft will.
Pafch 4 & 5 H 8. rot. 333 in banco	**In** Eafter term in the 4th and 5th of king Henry the 8th then upon his faid voyage into Gafcoigne as hath been faid, hee fuffered com̃on Recoveries of all or moft of his lands, thereby to cut off all old entayles, and to draw a fee fimple to himfelf, the better thereby to difpofe of his eftate in fettling of his affairs by his laft will; Having alfo the year before made divers feoffments of the fame manors the better to perfect the faid Recoveries **All** which hee declared to bee, To the ufe of himfelf
Volunt̃ Sub Sigillo 5 H 8 in caftro de Berk.	and his heires, and to the intent to perform his will, which, firft in the third year, and after in the fifth year of Henry the 8th hee did at large, **And** declareth that the manors of Melton Mowbray, Coldoverton, Sileby, Mountforrell, Segrave, Thurlafton, fflekenhoe, Tetbury, Daglingworth, and Sages, fhould bee To the ufe of Katharine his wife for life in lieu of Joynture and Dower, And the manors of
648 Funtington	Bofham, ffunt|ington, Thorney, Winge, Segrave in Penne, Bretby, Cotton, Roftlafton, Lynton, Repington, Witherly, Auconbury, and Wefton, fhould bee to the ufe of John Heron untill hee were paid the faid thoufand pound borrowed of him, according to Indentures thereof made in the third of king Henry the eighth as before is touched, And then his feoffees to grant thefe Annuities to thefe perfons following for their feverall lives, vizt To James Berkeley Efqr his brother, Twenty pounds p Añ To Thomas Try his Sollicitor Ten pounds p Añ To Margaret
Office 29 H 8 poft mort Thomæ Dñi Berkeley, vith vide in vita Jacobi Dñi. Berkeley,	Shippard. 3li 6s. 8d To Raph Butler 4li To Thomas Berkeley 4li (of whom were the Berkeleys of Berkeley Town,) To Richard Berkeley 4li (of whom are the Berkeleys of Worcefter and Herefordfhires,) To Peter Swift. 6li 13s 4d To George Shippard 4li To

4^{li} To James lluen. [sic] 6^{li} 13^s 4^d: And soe to twelve others for their severall lives out of the manors last mentioned; And after for payment of his debts; And after to his right heires; wherein his providence, (least his will should bee suppreſt,) was such that, with the privity of his said sollicitor, hee left three severall wills, (one and the same,) all ingroſſed in parchment under his hand and seale at Armes in three severall freinds keepings; All which came after togeather, and are now in Berkeley Castle. **And** afterwards in the 12th of king Henry the 8th, hee added a Codicell to the former will, and thereby gave five hundred marks to the said Mary Berkeley his brother James daughter, so that in her marriage shee bee ruled by his executors and by the Pryor of Bath and by the Master of the Gawnts at Briſtoll; And appointed alſo a great portion of money towards the building of the body of the Church and Monaſtery of St Auguſtines, And in making of a Chapple of our bleſſed lady within the same Church, wherein, (ſaith the will,) I intend by Gods grace my body after my deceaſe ſhall lye. And for the reedifying and building of the church and chancell and ſtalls of the ffryars minors in Glouc., whereof (ſaith his will) I am founder, And where dame Iſable Berkeley my grandame lyeth buryed; which work (ſaith the said will) I have now began, and in caſe I dye, Then my executors ſubſtantially to finiſh the ſame: **And** this Lord further declared by his said will, That if any perſon ſhould put out or moleſt his said Cozen Thomas Try out of the manor of Callowdon, which hee hath for Terme of his life by the joynt demiſe of him and his mother in the 5th of Henry the 8th, or ſhall avoyd any leaſe, grant by Copy, or anuity by him made or to bee made, Then his executors to ſell his manor of Bretby from him and his heirs, And with the money ariſeing, to ſattisfy his said Cozen Try, and every of his leſſees and Grantees which ſhall happen to bee expulſed. | **And** by an addition the ſame year to this will and Codicill, hee giveth his leaſe of Yate of 80 yeares after his wives death to his nephew Thomas, (after lord Berkeley,) ſon of his brother Thomas; And to his said wife the one half of all his plate and goods both at Yate and elſewhere, And the other half to the said Thomas his nephew. **And** now at Calais, the 11th of Septr 1523, in the fifteenth of king Henry the eighth, by a further codicill annexed to the former will, appointeth his body to bee buried in Trinity Chapple in St Nicholas Church in Calais; And that his two chaplins Handly and Aſkwith ſhould celebrate and pray twenty years for his ſoule, The firſt ten years in Trinity chapple, and the other ten years in St Auguſtines monaſtery in Briſtoll, And to have ten pounds a peece yearly wages out of his man^r of Boſham. And gave further ſeaven other anuities, (beſides thoſe afore mentioned,) to ſeaven ſervants during their lives. **And** further increaſed his wives joynture with the manor of Tetbury for her life.

Volunt̃. 12. H. 8. in caſtro de Berkel:

See fol: [540]

649

Volunt. Mauric. 15 H. 8. in caſtro de Berkeley.

After

carta cum Edro Deenng milite et Barronett[o]

After whofe death his executors, Sr John ffitz-James cheife baron of the Exchequer and others, (per nõia executoř teftī d'ni Mauricij Berkeley militis d'ni Berkeley,) having difburfed great charges about his funerall, had their difcharge from Thomas Wolfey then Cardinall and Legate, And from William Archbifhop of Canterbury and Legate alfo, by deed under both their feales dated the 12th of February 1523 Anno 15th of Henry the 8th

pat dat 25 Octob 24 H 7 in caftro de Berkeley

mich rec. 24 H 7 rot 1 in fc^ac̃io cum reḿ Thefauř

Henry the 7th in the 24th of his raigne granted to this lord for his life the rangerfhip and cuftody of the forrefts of Kingfwood and ffillwood, and the ftewardfhip of the manor and hundred of Portbury, Upon furrender of which łres patent, (found infufficient,) hee had a new grant the 20th of July in the 3th of King Henry the 8th with the fee of feaven pence halfpeny by the day for Kingfwood and ffillwood, and Ten pound fee for Portbury

Carta dat. 6 Nov 1 H 8 in caftro de Berkeley

In the firft yeare of king Henry the eighth, Sr Adrian Fortifcue knight made this Sr Maurice fteward of his manors of Bradfton and Stinchcomb and of all other his manors and lands in the County of Glouc, for his life, for the fee of twenty fhillings.

carta in caftro de Berkeley

fol: [479]

The fame year Sr Thomas Knevet and Mirriell his wife made this lord Steward of their manors of Paynfwick, Moreton, and Whaddon, in the Coḿ of Glouc, for the life of the faid Mirryell, with the fee of 53^s 4^d Of which Mirryell fee before in the life of Thomas lord Berkeley the fourth

carta in caftro de Berkeley
650

And in the 4th of king Henry the 8th Sr Charles Brandon made this lord fteward of his manors of Paynfwick, Whaddon, Moreton Valence, and | Rengworth, in the county of Glouc, and mafter of his game of Deer, with a few buck and few Doe and 53^s 4^d fee, for his life

Carta 27 m'cij 1515 in caftro de Berkel

In the 6th of king Henry the 8th Adrian, Cardinall and bifhop of Bath and Wells, granted to this lord the keeperfhip of Pucklechurch parke, (not two miles from Yate,) for the terme of his life.

Carta in caftro de Berkeley

In the 12th of king Henry the eighth, Sr Arthur Plantagenet made this lord fteward of his manor of Panefwick and of all other his manors and lordfhips in the County of Glouc, and mafter of his game of Deere there, with the fee of 3^h 6^s 8^d for his life And doubtles this lord Maurice was a very able man, And, befides his military knowledge, better fkilled in the laws and ftatutes of the realme than any

of

of his Anceſtors, his father excepted, whoſe ſollicitor hee was, as in his life hath been ſaid.

In the 7th of king Henry the 8th this lord bought of the king the wardſhip of the body and lands of John ſonne and heire of Richard Berkeley of Stoke Gifford; for which hee paid five hundred marks; And by his will five years after, directed, that at ſixteen years of age hee ſhould marry Iſable Denys his ſiſters daughter; And if ſhee dyed or refuſed, Then to marry Ellenor Denys her ſiſter, And ſo to Margaret another ſiſter: But the marriage held with the ſaid Iſable, as in the lives of the lord Maurice the third and of the lord Maurice the fifth is formerly written, propagateing an eminent poſterity of many thouſands at this day 1627.

pat: dat. 24. Maij 7. H. 8. in caſtro de Berkeley.

Volunt: 12. H. 8 in caſtro de Berkel:

fol: [315]

In the 14th of king Henry the 8th this lord Maurice bought of the king the wardſhip and mariage of Thomas ſon and heir of Sr Owen Perrot, whom by his will hee directed to marry his brother James Berkeleys daught, which after his death tooke an happy effect, ſhee proving as matchleſſe a lady as lived in her days; from whom an army of eminent gentlemen and a fair race of great nobillity at this day living, (1627,) are diſcended, as in the life of the lord Maurice the fifth this lords father hath appeared.

Carta in caſtro de Berkeley.

By the award of Sr Edmond Tame, Sr John ffitz James chiefe baron, and Robert Bowringe, the 24th of ffebruary in the 5th of Henry the 8th That great controverſy which had many years been tumbled with variable ſucceſſe, between this lord and his father And Sr Robert Poyntz, was ended; whereby this lord had to him and his heires the manor of Daglingworth, And the moitie of the moitie of the manor of Brokenburrow, extending into the Townſhipps of Tockington, Almondeſbury and others, ſometime ye lands of John Knull ſon of Rys ap Evan; And the ſaid Sr Robert had to him and his heirs the manor of litle Marſhfeild, and the other moitie of the moitie of Brokenburrow: And they to preſent to the chantry of Al | mondſbury called Brokenburrows Chantry by alternate turnes: And that Iſable mother of this lord, and John Berkeley ſon of Thomas this lords uncle, ſhould ſeverally releaſe, vizt Iſable, all her right in Brokenburrow, and Jno Berkeley all his right in litle Marſhfeild, to Sr Robert Poyntz. And this alſo finiſhed that tryall at lawe which had paſſed againſt this lord, And the writt of Error which hee had brought for the reverſall of the judgment given upon that verdict.

Carta in papir in caſtro de Berk:

651

In banco. Ao 5. H. 8.

In the tenth of king Henry the 8th began this lord Maurice to allow 6li 13s 4d p ann, ex eleemoſyna ſua, out of his almes and bounty, towards the repaire of the church of the Gray ffryars in Glouc.; which liberallity hee continued many years, yea

Comp: manerij de Vpton St Leonards cum Arn: Ligon milte Voluntas Mauricij 12. H. 8.

yea after his death, till the same was finished; Of which place this family were founders, as before is touched in this lords life

<small>fol 648</small>

<small>rec. in sc̃c̃io cum rem̃ thesaur̃ 9. H 8 rot 55.</small>

In the ninth year of king Henry the 8th what time this lord held himself half assured of a restitution, the king, (by this lords own meanes noe doubt,) awarded his comission to this lord and others, to find out what wasts and spoiles of Deere wood and timber were committed upon his lands called Berkeleys lands, within his hundred of Berkeley. Of the carefull execution whereof and returne, small question needs bee made

<small>carto in castro de Berkeley.</small>

The 7th of July in the year 1516, in the 8th year of king Henry the 8th This lord Maurice and eleaven others of the like ranke joined in a devout petition to the popes holines, And obtained graces of having power to chuse each of them a preist to bee their confessor, And hee to bee by this grace enabled to absolve them and give them absolution ab omnibus suis peccatis, criminibus, excessibus et delictis, quibuscunque, de quibus corde contriti et ore confessi fuerint, from all their sins, crimes, excesses, and offences, whereof they should bee contrite in heart and confessed with their mouthes, with many other graces, one whereof was, to enter into any nunnery, et cum monialibus conversari dūmodo ibm non pernoctent, And to converse with the Nunns there, so that they stay not with them all night &c And some other of the graces were de com̄utatione votorum et relaxiac̃one juramentorum, of changing their vowes and releafe of oaths; And de plenaria remissione et absoluc̃one peccatorum, semel in vita et in mortis articulo, of plenary remission and pardon of their sins once in life and in the instant of death, And de ingrediendo monasterio monialium, to have recourse to the Monasteries of Nunns as before, And divers others, All which they obtained from his holines as they had petitioned·
Upon the power and efficacy of which Indulgence, past question this lord greatly relyed.

<small>Liber ordinis garterij, manuscr̃
652</small>

Whereas in the scruteny for Election of new knights of the honorable order of the garter, to supply any one deceased, each knight of that order nameth three princes, three of the baronage, and three knights whereout the king | as soveraigne of the order chooseth as best him pleaseth,[1] This Maurice was in the sixth yeare of king

---

[1] At the foot of the Manuscript is the following note to this passage, in a different hand-writing.—
" 1723 I dont know how it might bee in those days, but now it is only for forms sake they are named but never any choose but whom the Sovereign appoints but is an easy mistake for so did this Prince of Wales when Ld Halifax carried him the Garter from Queen Anne and shewed him all the form of chusing he started and said 'How came I to have it, you have the most votes?' "—[ED]

king Henry the eig[h]th named for one by Thomas Howard the Duke of Norfolk, and by Charles Brandon duke of Suffolk, by the Earle of Worcester, and by S.ʳ Thomas Lovell, but missed the election.

In the 8ᵗʰ year hee was againe in the scruteny named by the said Duke of Suffolk, S.ʳ Thomas Lovell, and S.ʳ Henry Marney, after Lord Marney.

8. H. 8.

In the 10ᵗʰ year hee was againe in the scruteny named by Thomas Gray Marques Dorset, S.ʳ Thomas Lovell, and the lord Poynings.

10. H. 8.

In the 14ᵗʰ year hee was againe in the scruteny named by the Earles of Devon and Worcester, and S.ʳ Thomas Lovell.

14. H. 8.

In the 15ᵗʰ year, (about five months before hee dyed,) this lord was againe in the scruteny named by the Duke of Suffolk, the Earles of Devon and Essex, S.ʳ Thomas Lovell, and S.ʳ Richard Wingfeild, but allwayes missed the Election; All which five times hee was named a knight and not a baron.[1]

In the 7ᵗʰ of king Henry the 8ᵗʰ the king made him Leivtenant of the Castle of Calais, and Captaine over 50 men at Armes, whereof one was to bee Constable of the said Castle; which was of great profit unto him in regard to the fees and allowances belonging to those offices: And what great services hee often did against the French whilst hee was lievtenant the marginall will informe his posterity.

Volunt: 15. H. 8. pred: Mauricij. Pat: 7. H. 8. in castro de Berkeley.

Marten. fol: 396.

And many lres remaine in Berkeley Castle directed to the right reverend and worshipfull S.ʳ Maurice Berkeley knight and Leivtenant of the Castle of Calais: Amongst others, one from Thomas Norton master of Burton S.ᵗ Lazar, wherein after hee had acknowledged that their Mills neere Melton Mowbray were given to that monastery by his noble progenitors fower hundred years agoe and more, hee tells him his officers at Melton are by his direction, as they say, about to set up Mills at Melton, to their great prejudice in their succom̃, which none of his progenitors lords nor ladies have ever attempted: And further, that our holy fathers, popes of Rome, have confirmed all such guifts, with many dangerous words and sentence to them that either hurt, harme, lessen, or minish any possessions of their said house; Trusting, that it is not his mind to bee any of these, whereon it seemes, that that project was laid aside for a time. Which lre also shewes, that at this time this lords wife was with him at Calais. |

Toll.

Many

[1] In the same hand-writing as the last is this note in the margin:—" James Earl of Berkeley was the first of this family that was a Knight of the Garter 1617 [1717?] and Vice Admirall of England, first L.ᵈ of the Bedchamber to King George y.ᵉ first, Commissioner of the Admiralty &c."—[ED.]

653 Many were the petitions of right which this lord Exhibited at feverall times to king Henry the 8th, to have reftitution according to right and the laws of England of the Caftle and Manor of Berkeley, and of the manors of Hame, Appleridge, Alkington, Hinton, Came, Hurft, Wotton, Simondfall, Cowley and Simbridge, in the County of Glouc., and of Wefton befides baldock in the County of Hartford, and of Portbury in the County of Somerfet; And of Kington in the County of Warwick, (which were all that remained in the kings hands of the Marques Berkeleys entayles made to his father king Henry the feaventh,) And divers kinds of propofitions at feverall times were made by him to the king, the better to fweeten his fuites and draw on expedition, wherein at laft hee foe farre prevailed that hee had the kings hand to bee reftored to them   In one whereof hee ufed thefe words, That this lord William his unkle conveyed thofe manors to his maj^{ties} father without any money receiving, but onely from an high and pompous mind to bee exalted to the degree of a Marques, and to bee created Marques Berkeley   Howbeit death prevented this lords defires, caufing all that labor to bee loft, which was never after profecuted by any of his heires, till the hand of heaven returned thefe manors and lands to the lord Henry the firft, upon the death of king Edward the fixth, As after followeth in his life

Between Edward Stafford duke of Buckingham, (who by divers writers is noted to bee a man of an high fpirit, and very ambitious, and a daily plotter of Treafon againft king Henry the eighth, for which at laft hee loft his head in the 13th of that kinge,) and this lord Maurice was much bitternefs, which continued till neare the Dukes death, fome ill relifhes of whofe impofthumed malice are not yet wafhed out of divers papers in Berkeley Caftle, As the Dukes calling this lords wife, falfe chorle and wiche, And him, falfe unnaturall Maurice. And that the leaft that is *then at Yate neere Thornbury* towards him, fhould fet right nought by him at his own doors where hee dwelleth, And that hee fhall be faine to feed piggs, as hee did afore when hee dwelled at Portbury, the which is more meet for him then any other worfhip both for his reafon and his perfon, or for any goodnefs or vertue that is in him, fave falfe covetoufnefs and falfe defire of that hee hath noe right to   And on the other fide, this lord Maurice caufed one of his fervants to tell the duke, that thofe words belonged to the duke and to his Earldome, and that hee fent them back againe to ftop muftard pots with, And that hee loved him not, nor none of his, nor never would,   Of which hatred between thefe two neighbors the country towns in thofe parts had foe open
654 notice, That the Duke coming in his | way towards London to lodge the firft night at Tetbury, ten miles from his houfe at Thornbury, the Baily and burgeffes,
(hopeing

(hopeing belike to pleafe thereby this lord Maurice their landlord,) kept him from their Town, not fuffering him to lodge in any of their Inns or houfes: whereof this lord Maurice was forthwith advertized, then at Calais, by the lre of one of his preifts. Lies in Berkeley caftle.

And it is more then probable, that this lord had a finger in removing the Dukes head from his fhoulders, within two years after thefe unfavoury vents.

In the 14th of king Henry the 8th this lord is celebrated in the Annalls of thofe times to bee one of thofe cheife and valerous Captaines, worthy of all praife, who under the Earle of Surrey, generall of the Army, did fo great fervice againft the french king, in facking of his Towns and Caftles, with the gaine of an incredible booty; And other martiall imploym.ts of this lord, afwell at home againft Perkin Warbeke in the time of Henry the 7th,[1] as againft the Scots and ffrench in the time of Henry the 8th, each fecond year at leaft till hee dyed; Witnes his valour and worth in Martiall affaires. Marten: fol: 396.
Marten. fol: 348.

His creation of Baron.

This is the place promifed in the lives of the lord Robert the firft and of the lord James the firft, and of the lord Maurice the fifth this lords father, to fpeake further and more largely of the Barony of Berkeley, and of this lords new calling by writt to the eftate, ftile, and dignity of a Baron or peere of the Realme, And really to bee lord Berkeley; and of the place of precedence which the lords Berkeleys now have or ought to have in Parliament amongft their peeres, then in the lives of thofe three lords I have done: **The** nominall title of lord Berkeley afwell this lord Maurice himfelf, as his father before him, had frequently ufed in their ftiles, in moft of their own Deeds and Indentures; And foe alfo ufed many great perfons, as the Duke of Norfolk and others in writing to them to call them; And fuch alfo was the ufuall fpeech of fervants in their families at home and abroad: **Howbeit**, neither was this lord Maurice, nor the lord Maurice his father, re verâ and really, a peere of the realme, nor a Baron of Parliament, nor called to | any parliament fince the death of Willm Marques Berkeley in the 7th year of king Henry the 7th till the end of this 14th year of king Henry the 8th. So that for thofe 31 yeares this barony of Berkeley, (as the phrafe of comon law is,) was in Abeiance, fufpence, or confideration of law; for it may not bee faid, That the Marques Berkeley by the grant of the Caftle and manor of Berkeley, which is folio 39.
502

655

but

---

[1] Sir Maurice Berkeley is mentioned by Hall as one of thofe who followed the King to Taunton on this occafion. Chron. p. 485. [ED.]

but a matter in fact, did transferr his title of honor to king Henry the 7.th and foe the king to bee lord Berkeley, Neither, in truth, in all the Marques his grants to that king is any fuch word as Barony, dignity, title, ftile, or honor, found, but only words fitting for transferring the corporeall fubftance of the caftle of Berkeley and of the hundred and manors and fervices thereto belonging. **And** therefore in regard of fuch the kings poffeffion in the Caftle and manor of Berkeley, the name, honor, ftile, and dignity of Ld Berkeley, was fufpended in the Crown, **And** now upon this calling of the faid Maurice by writt, hee became puifne or youngeft baron of all others, loofinge, by acceptance thereof, his Anceftors ancient place of precedency in parliament, as himfelf, upon receipt of his Writt, brought-him to Calais by George Scheppard his kinfman, and fervant, judicioufly conceived Upon whofe returne back into England, three of his deareft and moft intimate wife friends, in their reply, thus wrote unto him

To the lord Berkeley, lieutenant of the Caftle of Calais.

Letter in ye caftle of Berkeley.

In our right hearty manner, wee recomend us to your good L^dfhipp So it is, wee perceive by your fervant George Scheppard, That yee would bee content to know our advice in taking of this honor, which the kings grace by his writt hath lately called you too, S^r, wee all will advife you to take the honor, and howbeit that as yet yee have not the roome in the parliament chamber that the lord Berkeleys have had of old time, yet wee will advife you to take this roome appointed to you at this time, and to make noe labor of the higher roome at this time, for caufes to longe to write And yet divers lords your frends here would have had you labor for the lord Berkeleys roome, howbeit peradventure yee fhall have more convenient time hereafter then now, And for your farther fpede in this matter, wee have caufed your name to bee enterid into the parliament roll, with your writt, and have defired the lord Mountgoie to appier there for you, and to give his voice for you in like manner as in time paffide hath bene ufed one lord to doe in the abfence of another; So that you | ftand now by matter of record in the full eftate and degree of a Baron, wherein wee pray God to fend you good continuance, with as much honor as ever had Baron before you

At London the 6th of May 1523.

Your own affurede
John ffitz James.
Richard Weyfton
William Denys.

1. **Of** whom Sr John ffitz James was lord cheife baron of the Exchequer, and then one of his feoffees, trusted with his estate, and the principall executor in his will.

2. **Sir** Richard Weyston, was of the kings privy Chamber, a discreet valiant and temperate man, as Marten and others call him.

Marten chron. fol: 391.

3. **And** William Denys had maryed his only sister, Anne Berkeley, of the kings privy chamber alsoe; Who all knew That the king at this time had signed with his hand his petition of Right, for his restitution to the barony Castle and manor of Berkeley, and of the other manors formerly named, the true essentialls thereof; And therefore, (if noe other cause were,) their advice was good, that this lord should not bee too earnest at first for the shadowe but to stay a while for the substance, till a more convenient time should invest him in the actuall possession of his said castle and lands, either by that kings restitution, or by the kings death without issue male, then having none, nor likely by his wife to have any; and then the place of precedence would follow of course and by lawe.

fol: [653]

Yet for all this would not this lord take this Stile and Calling upon him, unles withall hee had his Ancestors place in parliament, as another tre written to him by his said kinsman and servant George Schipward the 13th of the said May doth intimate; wherein he tells him, That the lord Cheife Baron and Master Denys have knowledge that yee use not your name within your house according, wherein they think, that if you should soe doe ye doe not well: And also their advice is, that yee shall provide a sadd gentlewoman in the court, to wayte upon my lady, to attend upon her according: meaning according to her new honor of Baronesse; Whereupon this lord at last accepted of the Honor conferred by the said writt, And contented himself with the kings pleasure of being the youngest Baron in place at that Parliament. **And** at this time, many tres congratulating this his new | honor, were written to him, (as also many others were, upon buisines,) which from henceforth were directed, To the right honorable and my espetiall good lord, my lord Berkeley, Lieutenant of Calais; which words of right honorable, neither hee nor his father had received before. **And** amongst others, Thomas Burghull preist, in his tre from London dated the 5th of that May, writes, (inter alia) to him, That where the kings grace hath create you lord Berkeley, this is a good preparative for the hope that his grace will hereafter endue you with the very lordship of Berkeley, your inheritance, which I pray God I may see.

Lies in Berkeley Castle.

657

And

2 E VOL. II

And thus, (for ought I have perceived to the contrary,) stood the place of this lord Maurice in his precedency, but from the end of this 14th yeare of king Henry the 8th And soe also of Thomas his brother and heire, and of Thomas his son and heire, and soe also of Henry his posthumus son and heire, till the 19th of his age, when by the death of king Edward the sixth without issue male the Ancient dignity barony honor castle and manor of Berkeley reverted to the said lord Henry, both as right heire to the lord William Marques Berkeley, the conuzor in the fyne often before mentioned, And also by discent of the ancient dignity from the first creation of the lord Robert the first, in the first year of the raigne of king Henry the second, Anno Dom 1154 which by the former acts or conveyances made to the heirs males of king Henry the seavenths body, could not bee extinguished, As that profound

Coke 11 rep learned Judge Sr Edward Coke hath in the case of the lord De la Ware, (formerly mentioned,) delivered **Neither** could the acceptance of the dignity by this lord Maurice, or the continuance thereof by the two next lords, Thomas and Thomas, bee any barre hindrance or estoppell to the lord Henry, when through want of issue male of the body of king Henry the seaventh, hee entred upon his ancestors honour, and dignity in the first yeare of Queen Mary whereto also hee is the better remitted by reason of his minority and his then wardship to the Crown, as in his life will more

fol [727 et seq] fully appear **Whereupon** I conclude, That the lord George, grandchild and heir of the said lord Henry, notwithstanding any thing to the contrary, hath and of right ought to have, place of precedence and anteriority from the said first year of king Henry the second, Anno. 1154 and consequently before the lords De la Ware, or any other now in the state of a Baron in England, for ought I have found to the contrary neither needs any paynes to bee taken to looke after restitutions in bloud, for none of his Ancestors have at any time been attainted

And besides, this lord, howbeit hee had his proxey, as by the former Lre

658 appeareth, yet never came personally to that parliament, but still kept at Calais, where hee dyed in September followinge, as after appeareth

His wife.

carta in castro de Berkeley **This** lord Maurice married Katharine the daughter of Sr Willm Berkeley of Stoke Gifford, knight in the second year of king Richard the third, then in the 17th year of his own age, and shee not much under, with the good liking of their parents, as hath been partly before touched, As also that shee brought in portion as her dowry Forty marks in hand, and seaven hundred marks more payable by five marks every quarter, for security whereof the said Sr Willm made a lease of his manor of

Kingston

Kingston Seamor in the County of Somerset, for 35 years, and also gave his obligation of one thousand marks; Howbeit, neither party fully performing their covenants, the same was afterwards by another indenture between this lords father and Richard Berkeley son and heire of the said Sr Willm, dated the 17th November in the 17th of Henry the 7th, reconciled and performed without suite, each remitting to other their mutuall breaches.

The Joynture of this lady at the time of her marriage was agreed only to bee one hundred marks by the year, and noe more, in regard of her husbands apparant possibillity to the Barony of Berkeley: his unkle viscount Berkeley and Earle of Nottingham then being without issue, whereby the hope of each parents side, (all parties then standing upon brotherly terms,) seemed assured of possessing one day his said unkles estate; whereof not only the Covenants of this lord Maurice of estating the said Katharine in one hundred markes Joynture out of his said brothers manors of Cam Slimbridge and others, which were to discend upon him after his said unkles death, but also the stile wch this lord therein gave himself of being brother and heire of the said Earle of Nottingham, doe sufficiently declare.

But when her husbands father and himself had raised their estates, her Joynture successively by them was increased also, insomuch as now upon her husbands death, shee had left unto her for her life in leiu of Joynture and dower as hath been said, the Manors of Melton Mowbray, Sileby, Coldoverton, Mountsorrell, and Segrave, in the County of Leicestr; | The manors of Thurlaston and fflekenhoe in the County of Warrwick; The manors of Tetbury, Daglingworth, Sages, and Yate, in the County of Glouc.; And the one half of all her husbands personall estate whatsoever; which intimates to posterity, her vertue and their affections.

In the later two years of her husbands life, this lady Katharine being but lately returned from her husband, then at Calais, came twice from Yate to Berkeley, not 8 miles asunder, what time her brother in lawe Sr Thomas Berkeley had the keeping of the Worthy Parke under king Henry the 8th; In the one of which Journeys of pleasure, shee was attended with 36 Horses, and in the other with forty of her own servants.

And when shee and the said Sr Thomas, (then lord,) a fewe months after her husbands death, parted into two parts such houshold furniture, (according to her husbands will,) as then was at Yate, the said Thomas brought from thence in the behalf

Margin notes:
Obli: dat: 28. Jan. 2. R. 3. in castro de Berkeley
carta in castro de Berkeley.

cartæ: dat 28. Jan: 2. R. 3. in castro de Berkeley.

3. cartæ in castro de Berkeley.
Volunt. dc̃i Mauric̃ in castro de Berkeley.
Inq: pt morĩ Maur̃ 16. H. 8. in div's Com̃
659
Origiñ in sec̃c̃io. 16. H. 8. rot.

Comp: hospicij 14. et. 15. H. 8.
Pat: 6. H. 8. in castro de Berkeley.

Cartæ dat 1 Dec. 15. H. 8. in castro de Berkeley.

behalf of his fon and heire, as part of his half, a truffing bed and tefter of cloth of gold, divers peeces of Arras imbroidered with gold, divers cufhions of gold, embroidered w:th ramping lyons of filver, a fhaving bafon of filver weighing threefcore ounces. Candlefticks with their prickets and fnuffers of filver of thirty ounces, two great flagons of filver, two potts of filver parcell guilt, a filver chafing difh, two great falts of filver with covers double guilt two gobletts of filver with covers parcell guilt, a great goblett of filver double guilt with a hind upon the cover, and three flatt bowles with covers pcell gilt, &c, leaving the like for her, as by the note indented between them appears, which argueth the furniture to bee the more honorable, and fhee a lady of the more ftate, for that the Weft Indies had not at this time fhowred her barrs and Ingots of filver and gold upon Europe

Carta indent in caftro de Berkl

And this Thomas the fon not longe after received from the executors of his father, one chaine of gold with a croffe, containing—324 links and a hook of gold, a gown of ruffet velvet furred with Martens, one rich coat of tinfel, one plagard[1] and foreftocks of cloth of gold rayfed; and a roll of parchment of his fathers pedegree, which I mention for the caufe aforefaid

Acq 26 Apr 25 H 8

It was not her good hap to have any iffue by this lord her hufband, but his hap to have a bafe fon by another woman, whilft hee lived at Calais, whom hee called Humphry Berkeley, but by what woman I could never find, neither would this lord ever mention it, Which Humphry dyed in youth without iffue

And further fuch was this lords difcretion, that hee would never in his lifetime fuffer his bafe fon to fee England, And fuch this ladies wifdom and love to her hufband, as fhee never tooke exception to that dalliance, but lived with great refpect and obfervance towards him. And noe lady more carefull in government over her hufbands family, nor more for his profit, then this good lady to the laft of her hufbands dayes

660 Comp. hofpic temp. H 8 in caftro de Berkeley.

This Joynture thus lovingly from time to time increafed by this lord her hufband, this lady enjoyed not full three years after her hufbands death, before by her death fhee left it to the faid lord Thomas her hufbands brother and heire, and her foule to him that gave it, and her body to bee buried at Yate, fhee then of the age of fifty feaven years, whereof marryed to her hufband forty years and upwards, by whome for any thing I have obferved, fhee never conceived with child.

His

---

[1] *Query?* "Placket," a woman's pocket See *Halliwell*

His Seales of Armes.

This lords ufuall feale was the Armes of Berkeley and Brotherton in one brode efchucheon of two inches and an half diameter, borne cornerwife; The creft was the helmet with a half lyon on the top thereof; The fupporters were, two lyons rampant, fupporting the helmet, circumfcribed figillum Mauricij Berkeley militis.

And for his privy feale, this lord ufed a little Lyon rampant, the old paternall coate of the Mowbrayes: Behold the figures.

His death and place of buriall.

That this lord purpofed his body fhould have been buried in S! Auguftines Monaftery by Briftoll amongft the clufters of his honorable Anceftors, (where for that purpofe hee had built a Chapple,) his three wills made in 3th 5th and 12th of Henry the 8th before | touched doe declare; **But** God difpofed that hee fhould dye in Calais, beyond feas, and bee buryed in Trinity Chapple within the parifh Church of S! Nicholas there, with fuch devotions for the repofe of his foule as formerly is declared out of the Codicill annexed to his laft will made the day before hee dyed; And having perfect memory during a lingring ficknefs, it cãnot otherwife bee conceived but that his confeffor, (who feemes by the popes grace formerly mentioned to have been purpofely provided againft that day of death,) then gave him a plenary remiffion of all his fins, efpetially having that fair advantage of time, to bee Corde contritus et ore confeffus, repentant in heart and his fins acknowledged with his own mouth; **But** I may not prefumptuoufly looke into this fecret cabinet; But doubtles this lord fo much relyed upon the efficacy of this papal grace, That the

prints

Volunt. 3. 5. 12. 15. H. 8 in cur: prerog: et in caftro de Berkeley.
661
fol: [648]

fol: [649]

prints of his Almsdeeds and other works of piety are found to be fewer then of most of his Ancestors.

The lord Sands, (stiled in his will his entirely beloved freind,) was present at his death, to whom hee bequeathed ffive hundred marks to purchase lands to the use of the said Humphry Berkeley his bastard son and his heires, to whose rule and custody hee comitted him **And** this is the first and last base child in all the generations of this ancient family of the Berkeleys, or of their branches, which I have observed in the space of five hundred and fifty years; whose posterity ended in himself, Bastard slipps seldome take deepe rootes

<small>Inq in com Hunting Warr Leic^r Glouc^r Suffex 16 H 8 in Canc</small>

This lord dyed the 12th of September, the feast day of the exaltation of the holy crosse, Anno. 1523. in the fifteenth year of king Henry the 8th the Autumnall equinoctiall day, A day wherein all creatures of the Earth beheld the sun, and hee the suns creator, then of the age of fifty five years or neare thereabouts, whereof hee had been lord in stile and reputation from the death of his father almost seaventeen years; but re vera, really, since his calling to the state of Baron by the writt of Henry the 8th, not halfe one yeare, **Then** whom amongst his generations none more wise and prudent, a soldier, Courtier, and great house keeper, neither any man more loving to his brothers and sisters and their children, which in life and death hee cherished and provided for, as a naturall father.

<small>Inq in Com. Hunt. 16 H 8 662</small>

And for his servants, besides the Anuities before mentioned and many other by mee omitted, and besides those that time hath hidden from my finding, let this Instance of bounty to Thomas Try his follicitor, in his perticuler, speake for many, who out of ffenystanton in the County of Huntington | had an Anuity of Twenty marks p ann for his life

<small>Inq p^rdict</small>

Also a lease of certaine pasture grounds called Sart feild and the hermitage, in Auconbury in the same county, for 31 years at nyne pounds rent, worth at this day —200^{li} p Ann

<small>Inq in com Warr· 16 H 8</small>

Also a lease of the manor of Aspele in Warrwickshire for one and forty years, at Ten pound rent, of a great value

<small>Volunt 15 H 8</small>

Also a lease of the manor of Callowdon in the Countyes of the City of Coventry and Warrwick for his life, at 33^h 8^s 4^d rent, worth—360^{li} at this day.

Also

Also other anuities out of other manors, of ten pound; and—6^{li} 13^s 4^d for being his generall Sup:visor and governour of all his lands in England and Calais, And steward of many of his manors. And some others.

4. cartæ in castro de Berkeley et comp. Rec: 22. H. 7. ibm. et al.

All which, like a provident man, (not knowing whether a new king after this lords death might arise that knew not Joseph,) hee fortified by finding them in the offices after the death of this lord Maurice, which himself follicited: **And** surely hee was a wise diligent and trusty servant, neare forty years, to fower discents in this family; whose reciprocall bounties raysed his estate and reputation to bee of principall authority and in Commission of the peace in the Countie of the Citie of Coventry, and a steward of great power in that Corporation; And a wise Commissioner in many imployments for neere ten years before his death, which happened in the 36th yeare of king Henry the 8th **Of** whose excellent Counsells given by a pen of spirit to this lords brother and heire, I shall after write in his life: **And** shall also after that in the days of his grandchild, againe bring him to the Test, whether hee continued of perfect mettall and faithfull to his end to this family or not; till when I adjourne his further tryall, truth being the soule of this my history: |

Acts. 7. v: 18. Exodus: 1. v. 8.

The lands whereof hee dyed seized. 663

Were it not that I will constantly pursue my former method unto the end of these relations, I would have here omitted this title, having formerly mentioned almost all this lords lands perticulerly out of his Will and other conveyances, before mentioned; But take them as in a table here together.

The manor of Tetbury,
The manor of Sages,
The manor of Daglingworth,
Twenty-two marks rent in fframpton,
Divers messuages and lands in Thornbury,
The 4th part of the manor of Brokenburrow
   with the Advowson of the Chantry there,
Divers lands in Tockington, Hempton, Almondsbury, and Winterbourne,
The manor of Bitton and Hannam, purchased by him of Robert Dormer,
The manor of Mangottesfield purchased by him of Robt Dormer,
} In the County of Glouc:

The

The manor of Aylmington, purchafed by him of Wiłłm Huffy, } In the County of Glouc^r

The manor of Upton St Leonards in the County of the City of Glouc^r

The manor of Hovingham in the County of Yorke

The manor of Bretby,
The manor of Linton,
The manor of Coton,
The manor of Repington,
The manor of Roftlafton,
} In the County of Derby

The manor of Melton Mowbray,
The manor of Coldoverton,
The manor Segrave,
The manor of Witherly,
The manor of Sileby,
The manor of Mountforrell,
The manor of Dalby Chawcomb,
The hundred of Goftcote,
The advowfons of Coldvton, Segrave, Howly Kegworth, and Sutton Bonnyngton,
} In the County of Leicefter

664 The Advowfons of the Abbathies of Croxton, Combe, and Burton Lazers, } In the County of Leicefter.

The manor of Thurlafton,
The manor of fflekenhoe,
The manor of Afpele,
} In the County of Warrwicke

The manor of Callowdon, in the Counties of the Citie of Coventry and Warrwicke

The manor of Auconbury,
The manor of Wefton,
The manor of ffenyftanton,
The manor of Hilton,
The manor of Guiherne and Murrowe,
} In the County of Huntington

The

The manor of Maningford Bruse in the county of Wilts.

The manor of Hinton,
The manor of Kenet and Kentford, } In the counties of Cambridge and Norfolke.

The manors of Bosham and Buckfold,
The manor of Thorney,
The manor of ffuntington,
The manor and Parke of Bewbush, } In the County of Suffex.

ffifteen houses and tofts and 4 gardens in Calais.

A Messuage in Berkeley.

ffower pounds rent out of Bromly in Surrey.

All which, (then of the value of—1207ˡⁱ. 7ˢ. 6ᵈ in old rent,) discended upon the lord Thomas his brother and heire, then ffifty years old and upwards, as by severall Inquisicōns the next year after his death returned into the Chancery appeareth; wherein most of the Recoveries, Fynes, feoffments, and other assurances formerly mentioned, are found.

ffor which the said lord Thomas sued his speciall Livery the same Yeare, notwithstanding the not finding of any Office, or not probate of his age.

The residue, not found in this list but mentioned in the life of his father to have discended upon him, as Winge, Bedford, &c. were either estated upon this lords brothers, or by him sold or exchanged, as hath before in part appeared. |

Comp : Rec : 13. 14. H. 8. in castr de Berk :
Pasch : fines. 18. H. 8. rot. 5. in scᵃcio.
pa : 17. H. 8. cum rem̄ regis in scᵃcio.
Hill : 16. H. 8. rot. 29. in scᵃcio cum rem̄ thesaur̄.
Pat. 10. ffebr : 16. H. 8. ps. 1. in Canc.
Trin. rec. in scᵃcio 23. H. 8. rot. 19.
Claus : 7. H. 8. in cancell.

The application and use of his Life.

665

1. **The** imitable practice of this lord invites his posterity not to deferre the setting of their estates till old age or sicknes; And also to leave behind them a testimony of care and conscience, That neither kinsmen nor servᵗˢ, rewarded for their well deservings, be molested; **And** to consider, as this lord did, That a new king may arise that knew not Joseph. **And** also to provide, as this prudent lord did, That his tenants bee not disquieted in those estates which they have bought and paid for, least the cry of violence or oppression, (however dawbed with the colour

Exod : 1. v. 8.
Acts : 7. v. 18.

of

of the lawes,) drawe from heaven the displeasure of that God, that will reward each one according to their most secret workings and intentions.

2 Againe, this lord, to all elder brothers in the generations of this family that have noe children of their own bodies, becomes a president, That brothers and collaterall kindred should bee to them instead of children, and as dearly cherished, wherein this noble lord equalled the best in his generations.

3. Againe, it was not soe truly said of Ulisses, That having been ten years absent the smoke of his own country Ithaca was sweeter to him then the fire of any other, As it may of this lord Maurice, ffor, though all his fairest possessions did lye in other Counties, where alsoe hee had better seats and sweeter aire, Yet, out of an inbred affection and memory of the place where his father and all his forefathers were born, bred, flourished, and buryed, hee allways aimed his endevors to become a Gloucestershire man, and to bee a stranger in all other counties; As his purchases of Yate, Bitton, Mangottsfeild, Elmyngton, and other lands do manifest, And his father and himself having now been thrice ten yeares out of the possession of Berkeley, hee never ceased to follicite the king for a restitution, at what rate so ever, As being out of the proper spheare where his ancient honor dwelled, but dying in the pursuite thereof, though thrice ten yeares more expired before that Castle with her members reverted, as in the life of the lord Henry will bee delivered, Yet his posterity still held themselves till that time fast unto their County, where they lived with ample honor and command, as by the lives that follow will appeare. And it will bee manifest to him that duely considers of these relations, that the lives of such of this family as have estranged themselves from this County have lesse prospered in their estates, And how the same may bee ve | rified hereafter, let the life of the lord George and his posterity become further wittnesses. My application hereupon is, That sith few or none can in these days bee of remarkable honor and estimation in many counties at once, or where noe former memoriall or footsteps have been of their forefathers, That this Berkeleian family should ever professe themselves natives of this County, as the proper Orbe of their ancientest possessions, and wherein the greater half of the gentry are their kinsmen and allies, But espetially not to spend their days in London, or in the Court, which none of their forefathers have done save the Marques Berkeley who thereby wasted all, And to make a lord Berkeley any other then a Gloucestershire man is to turne him from his ancient honor estimation and Inheritance: If any others otherwise conceive, I hold them Ignorant of the ways and antiquity of this ancient family Liberavi animam meam.

4 Againe,

4. **Againe,** the awe and reverence borne towards this lord, especially with the Clergy, hath in nothing more clearly shined, then that fewe or none of the Abbots Pryors or other heads of those religious monasteries whereof hee was founder by discent from his ancestors, made any leases to their farmors or tenants but that hee was made acquainted therewith and a party to the same, and therein mentioned, That such leases were made by his assent, being their patron; whereof I have in the first ten years of king henry the 8th seen many. A speciall observation of his greatnes and of the respect hee carryed with these monasticall governors; By whom hee was allwaies received into their houses by processions censing and other rights belonging to a founder.

5. **And** Lastly, noe observation can bee more honest and usefull to this family then the president of this prudent lords care and course taken for the true payment of his debts owing at his death; Wherein to the honor and due memoriall of him And of this family in twenty generations, I have not observed, (heaven is my witnes,) that any man or woman have justly complained and gone away unsatisfied, or had cause to say of any of them, Thy dust is my debtor for a penny. |

$\left.\begin{array}{r}667\\668\end{array}\right\}$ blank

The Life of Thomas the Fifth

The life of Thomas Lord Berkeley the fifth of that name, ftiled in Writings after his brothers death, Sir Thomas Berkeley knight lord Berkeley, And Thomas Berkeley knight lord Berkeley Mowbray and Segrave.

And was proavus, or as our Anceftors the Saxons called, fortha-fader; And wee at this day great-great-grandfather, or the grandfathers grandfather to George now lord Berkeley.

And may bee called Thomas the Sheepmafter.

Contemporary with Henry the 8:th from 1523. till 1532.

The Life of this lord, I deliver under thefe eleaven titles, viz:

1. — His birth and manner of education, fol:
2. — His imployment in warre and peace. fol:
3. — His Almes and devotions; fol:
4. — His fale of lands, fol:
5. — His Hufbandries, fol:
6. — His wives, fol: 676.
7. — His iffue, fol: 677.
8. — His feales of Armes, fol: 686.
9. — His death and place of buriall, fol: 687.
10. — His lands whereof hee dyed feized, fol: 691.
11. — The application and ufe of his life, fol: 692.

His Birth and Education.

The Inquificons found after the death of this lords elder brother declare his birth to bee about the 12:th year of king Edward the fourth, Anno. 1472. what time and for many years after, his father lived | at Thornbury, where during his pupillage this lords education was, in that populous market town: And as affaires then ftood with his parents, his inftruction and practice more bowed towards

Inq. 16. H. 8. in div's: Com. poft mort: Maur. de Berkley.

towards a country life, befitting a younger brothers younger fon, then for the Court or greatnes, as the fequell of his life declared. And to render this lord that honorable mention which hee deferves, Hee, for the moſt part of his elder brothers life, both before hee went to dwell at Hovingham in York fhire and after his thence returne to the keeping of Berkeley Caſtle, was a perfect Cotſwold ſheppard, living a kind of graziers life, having his flocks of Sheep fommering in one place and wintering in other places, as hee obſerved the feilds and paſtures to bee found, and could bargaine beſt cheape And the better to bee his own Auditor, hee kept a book of his own hand writing, of all his receipts and payments gaines and loſſes touching thoſe flocks   during which time hee fold his wooll ufually for . 12ˢ 8ᵈ the todd And this kind of huſbandry in theſe his daies of a younger brother became to him foe habituate, That when hee was a baron and a great hous keeper at Yate after the death of his fiſter in lawe his elder brothers wife, hee obſerved the like order of Accompts keeping with his own hand for all his receipts, houſhold Expences, and buildings. knowing what happines that houſholder brings to himfelf and family, that with the morning faith to himfelfe, as the page was appointed to fay to the king of Perfia, Arife Sir, and take order for your affaires

Liber in caſtro de Berkeley Comp. 11. 12. H 8 in caſtr̃ de Berkley.

Comp: 18 19 29 H. 8 in caſtro de Berkeley

And as a further fruite of this lords prudence and frugallity, hee upon the death of his elder brother, fojourned with his wife children and family with his brother in lawe Jnᵒ Arnold at Hynam by Glouc, the fooner to recover his eſtate, furniſh his houfes, and get before hand, at what time a great part of his land was in Joynture to his brothers widowe, and in feoffees hands for payment of his brothers debts and performance of his Will · A confiderable prefident for poſterity, which his fon and grandchild immitated, as in their lives appeares.

In the twentieth year of king Henry the feaventh, then in the 31ᵗʰ year of his age, hee married Alienor the widow of John Ingleby Efq, what time and ſhortly after, his father and elder brother conveyed to him the manʳˢ of Hovingham in Yorkſhire, Sages, and Upton Sᵗ Leonards, and their lands in Thornbury, and in fome other places in Glouceſterſhire, and the manor of Hinton in Cambridgeſhire

cartæ in caſtro de Berkeley 671

But the next year after his fathers death, hee for eight hundred marks fold away the manor of Hinton to Robert ffewrother a Goldfmith | of London and covenants it to beè—32ʰ p'annͬ old rent A fatall fortune that hath befallen this noble family for the fix laſt generations to enter upon their inheritance with a fale of part thereof, as after more fully will appear

About

About a year after that hee and his wife were fetled in Hovingham, (fhee then either great with child or newly delivered of her fon Thomas) they went in a kind of Pilgrimage to vifit divers religious houfes; And amongft others thofe at Yorke, where in recompence of their great bounty beftowed on the Covent of the ffryars mynors, fryar William the guardian thereof beftowed on them celeftiall prayers and bleffings, and by his deed granted unto them perpetuall participation of all their maffes, prayers, faftings, afperities, watchings, preachings, and of all other good things there done under his government, afwell in life as after their deaths; Adding alfo of his fpeciall grace, (the words of the Deed,) That when notice of their deaths fhall bee given to their Chapiter, the fame recomendations fhall bee made to God for them that is done for their own brethren newly departed the world.

Carta: 1508. 23. H. 7. in caftro de Berkel: Comp. hofpic: in caft: de Berkeley.

In the 18th of king Henry the 8th the warden of the fryars Mynors in Glouc. and his covent, did by their deed covenant with the lord Thomas and in their confciences bind themfelves thenceforth, to fay during the life of the faid lord, for the foules of his father and mother, and for the foule of his brother Maurice late lord, and of Katharine late wife of the faid brother, and for the foules of himfelfe and of Alienor and Cicely his wives, and for all chriftian foules, thefe divine fervices; viz! Every munday placebo and derige with nine leffons, And every teufday one maffe of requiem, And every thurfday placebo and derige with nine leffons, And every fryday a maffe of the five wounds, with the collect deus qui juftificas impium; for which this lord doth covenant to pay to them fower pounds by the yeare, The one half for the warden, and the other halfe for the pitances of the Covent to amend their fare.

Carta: 22. Marcij 18. H. 8. in caftro de Berkeley.

On the back of which deed one with a hand of fomewhat a later time hath written thefe words; If the Clergy could fell and make perfect fale of the remiffion of fins with affurance of the life to come, for money, they fhould fhortly have more coyne then the king; And 4ˡⁱ was too little for all thefe prayers; but cafuall ware is fold good cheap; God pardon us all, Thus the dorfe of the deed.

In the firft year of the raigne of King Henry yᵉ 8th, this lord had from the king a generall pardon, not procured to purge himfelf from offences comitted | againft the lawes, but out of providence taken up at the kings Coronation.

pat. dat. 1. ffeb. 1. H. 8. in caftro de Berkeley.

672

Hee was a Captaine over a bond of men, and a fpeciall comander at the great battle called fflodden feild, where was prefent 100,000 Scots, foughten the nynth of September

Annales Anglie in div'fis fcriptis Marten fol. 361. 362.

September Anno. 1513 in the 5th of Henry the 8th if histories may bee beleived, whereat 𝕵𝖆𝖒𝖊𝖘 the fourth king of Scots was slayne, whilst his brother in law the king of England, (with whom at the same time this Thomas his Elder brother the lord Maurice was in person, at the taking of Tyrwin and Tourney, and at the battle there fought with the ffrench,) And for his good service here at this battle of fflodden this lord Thomas received the honor of knighthood in the feild, by the hands of Thomas Howard Earle of Surrey his Cozen germane in the second remove, shortly after created duke of Norfolk.

<small>Pat. 15 Maij 6 H 8 in castr̃ de Berk:</small>

<small>Comp· Manerij de Alkington 9 et. 10 H 8. in castro de Berkeley</small>

𝕶𝖎𝖓𝖌 Henry the 8th in the sixth of his raigne gave this lord Thomas the Constableship and Portership of Berkeley Castle, and the keeping of the said Castle park called the Worthy, and of the palership thereof, And the keeping of the red and fallow deer in Chiselhunger and Redwood, and the fishings of Smethmore and of the gale in Seaverne, as amply as James Berkeley his brother now lately dead had held the same, with the yearly ffee of three pound duringe his life

<small>Carta sub privato sigillo 10 febr 13 H. 8 in castro de Berkeley</small>

𝕬𝖓𝖉 in the 13th of his raigne the king caused this lord Thomas to inlarge the said castle park called the Worthy by taking into it the grounds called Hamstalls and Coltenleys als Culverheys, the Twichen (where the scite of the old manor house of Alkington stood,) and Manmead, with a peece of the Oakleys called the Ragge, And to repair the pales of the residue, for that complaint by petition (saith the king) had been made to him of the great damage his deere did in the corne and grasse of his tenants; 𝕱𝖔𝖗 this family is to conceive That till this time that parke was not greater then the ground called the Worthy extending to Hurdpoole, scarce three-score acres 𝕬𝖓𝖉 forthwith after upon a second petition removed all those red deere which were in Redwood Cheselhunger and Branwood into that park, and into his park of Estwood which hee had the year before by the attainder of the Duke of Buckingham.

<small>pat 14. H. 8. in castro de Berkeley</small>

𝕴𝖓 the 14th of king Henry the 8th this Thomas was high Sherife of the County of Glouc, and kept his house at Mangotsfeild which not longe before hee had much repaired, and where his standing family for most part had continued since his returne from Hovingham in Yorkshire, | And now dies the lord Maurice his elder brother at Calais, before this Thomas was (as I conceive) discharged of his Shreevewick of Gloucester.

673

<small>Privat. Sigill 16 H 8 in castr de Berkeley</small>

𝕳𝖊𝖓𝖗𝖞 the 8th in the 16th of his raigne having proclaimed open warrs against Francis the ffrench king, whom hee called infestissimum inimicum suum, his most

deadly

deadly enemy, and wanting money to make good the warre, fendeth to this lord Thomas a Comiffion and withall private inftructions how to handle his fubjects in this County of Glouc., and to work them to the kings ends: which being matter of State, and not within the lifts of this hiftory, I leave, with this, That this lord laboured more then this his country then thanked him for.

In the 17*th* of king Henry the eighth, It was articled between Thomas Duke of Norfolke (whofe father dyed the year before) on the one part, and this lord Thomas on the other part, That Thomas this lords fon and heire, or if hee dyed before his age of nineteen years, then Maurice his brother before his age of fifteen years, fhould marry Katharine daughter of the faid duke, whofe marriage portion fhould bee one thoufand pounds, whereof 200^{li} at the fealing, and 200^{li} each year after at Martlemas, till the thoufand pound was p^d; And if by death or otherwife the mariage held not, then this lord Thomas to repay what hee had received by fifty pounds a yeare; And that this lord Thomas fhould make the faid Katharine a Joynture of five hundred marks, And allow fifty pounds a year for their maintenance, And this lord to leave his faid fon one thoufand pound a year land after his death; ffor performance whereof this lord Thomas gave a Recognizance of one thoufand pounds; Howbeit this marriage held not, as after doth appeare. *carta in papiro in caftro de Berkeley.*

fol: [702.]

It may bee written of this lord Thomas, that hee did not more really inherit his elder brothers honor and lands then his affection and defire of being a meer Gloucefterfhire man, and of being imbowelled into the foile of that County; accounted by them the proper and genuine Climate of their Anceftors, And in which meridian the fun had happily fhined by a fweet influence upon fixteen of their generations: And according to this his affection, having many fair poffeffions in other Counties, which hee accounted as forreigne, hee entertained fundry communications with divers gentlemen of other fhires having lands in this County of Glouc., of exchanging fuch his lands with them as lay in the counties where they dwelt, and more commodioufly for them; And therein amongft others proceeded foe farre with one Sr Richard Sacheve|rell, that this lord and hee, (then being togeather in London,) articled under their hands and feales of Armes for an exchange of all this lords manors and lands in the Counties of Leicefter and Warr. where Sr Richard dwelt, in lieu of Sr Richards lands in the County of Glouc.; But by whofe only means the fame brake of, let the tres of Thomas Try often before mentioned then dwelling at Callowdon, (very averfe thereunto,) written to this lord then at Yate and Mangotf-feild in the County of Glouc., in the faid 17th year of king Henry the 8th, tell this family

674

Div's L̃res bundled togeather in Berkeley Caftle.

2 G VOL. II

family in Mr Trys own words; viz*t*, **That** Sr Richard had said to him with great and high slanderous words and crackes, That hee would have this lords lands in those counties whether hee would or not: Telling this lord further by his Lres; That Sr Richard upon St Lawrence day sent a great company to keepe the faire at Melton Mowbray, jesting there, that hee had caught his Lordship within such a compass, that he could not start from him, and soe had enflamed in all the Country; **And** that Sr Richard had discharged all his Ldships officers in those manors, Which (saith Mr Try) greiveth mee full sore That Sr Richard should soe craftily delude you from sixteen lordships and seignories, warranted to your Lo*p* Ancestors by the kings noble progenitors under the great seale, with many other comodities: **As** unto the lordship of Segrave dependeth eight Advowsons, which are great, 40*li*, fifty marks, 40 marks, 20*li*, &c, besides your goodly foundations, that I know noe man (saith Mr Try) thereabouts have none such, if you regard them well, as at my coming to you I shall make declaration: **And** as touching your knighten fees, yee have . 300 . longing to yor honor, besides your other Lordships: **And** as for two of your said knighten fees, I trust to get you an hundred marks and better towards your charges, as I shall shew to your Lo*p* at my coming which shall bee shortly.

Mr. Try having by this and other like lres gained upon this lord as to pause upon this exchange, and to promise that hee would send his Counsell to him to Callowdon to consider fully of this buisiness, Hee by his other Lres, (returned by the same messenger as themselves do shew,) declareth his marvelous comfort therein, saying **That** then it shall appear before his Counsell the great deceit fallaxity and crafty waies cast and invironed to destroy and holy to an nyntyssement of your honor for ever, if God that is infinite, cui nihil incognitum est, had not lede the penne, for there was never man of honorable bloud soe near taken and trapped by perverse sinister and false meanes as your good lords*p* had beene, not only to your endles reproche, but also to the desolation hin | drance and decay of your noble successe after your departure, loosing two such baronies as Segrave and Mowbray is, whereby ye are lord Segrave and lord Mowbray, And thereby your stile of honor should bee lost from you and your honorable issue for ever; Therefore (saith Mr Try) insomuch as they falsly mindeth to deceive and dishonor your noble bloud, force your self with the help of Jhesu to retraite and annull their mischevous and froward purpose; And God will increase your honor and give you strength, and so shall daily bee my prayer for the increase of your honor, longe in good life to endure, written this 17*th* of this month of August, with the blotting hand of your humble servant.   Thomas Try.

Hereupon

Hereupon this lords Counsell came to Callowdon, where this honest and wise gentleman soe made good his informations, That the next Term this lord himself went to London taking with him these lres, as the words of this lords own handwriting on the back of one of them implies, whom Mr Try, (though then not recovered of a broken leg,) there mett; where followed a finall breach of this intended exchange, much furthered also by the duke of Norfolk, to whom Mr Try had free accesse on all occasions, as other lres of his do declare; And afterwards other exchanges intended likewise by this lord Thomas with other gentlemen fell of also.

And it is apparent That the Counsell here mentioned to bee sent by this lord were the Steward of his lands, the Auditor of his revenue, the receivor of his rents, and Sollicitor of his law causes, whom this lords son most comonly accompanied; and these once in the yeare visited all his manrs, and lands, And then not only held his courts and granted estates to his tenants in each manor where they came, but also took the accompts of the Bayliffes and Reeves, causing them there to pay in the moneys in their hands to the receivour; And from Callowdon at this time they went to Bretby and other manors of this lords.

Comp: receptor: et hospicij in castro de Berkeley.

In the 31th of king Henry the 8th was a suite in Chancery between Thomas Woodward and other inhabitants of Slimbridge plts. And Edward Trotman and others defts, touching the severall comonings of their sheep upon Slimbridge Warth, wherein from the depositions of divers witnesses therein examined appears the husbandly courses of this lord, who in the 20th of H. 8th, then dwelling at Mangotesfeild, built a sheep house on a pcell of ground by the Warth, And having hired common of Richd Hannis one of the coheirs of Rivers, kept there a flock of sheep, which hee afterwards withdrew, saith those depositions, upon remonstrance to him made by the inhabitants of Slim | bridge, (for at this time hee was not lord of that manor,) That noe person by the custom of the said Warth might have sheep going there unles hee personally dwelled in Slimbridge or fframpton parishes; which howsoever it went for currant in that suite, yet I am sure for forty years past the contrary hath been used, and still is. **But** this suite, (whereto this lord was noe party,) sets out his husbandly course of life, which is the end I Vouch it for.

Carta exempl: in castro de Berkeley.

676

His wives.

This lord Thomas in the twentyeth of king Henry the 7th not two years before his fathers death, maryed Alienor the daughter of Sr Marmaduke Conestable of Yorkeshire,

carta in castro de Berkeley.

Yorkeshire, knight, then the widow of John Ingleby Esqr, son and heir of Sr William Ingleby knight, by whome shee had issue a son called Will'm Ingleby; whose wardship of body and lands, this Thomas and Alienor the 14th of May in the third year of the Bishops translation, bought of the Bishop of Durham,[1] of whom the same were holden by knights service: Of which William is an honorable posterity with opulent possessions, flourishing at this day.

Carto. 14. Maij. a^o [1505] in castro de Berkeley.

The Joynture which this Alienor had for her life from her first husband, was the manor of Spridlington in Lincolnshire, and divers messuages and lands in Rowcliffe, Skelton, and Estharleisey, in Yorkshire, assured to her upon her first marriage in the 5th of Henry the seaventh; whereby I conceive shee was somewhat elder than this lord her second husband: And for her second Joynture upon this her second marriage with the lord Thomas, had assured to her the manor of Hovingham in Yorkshire, (where shee and this lord her second husband lived the most part of the first twelve yeares after their Marriage,) And the manors of Sages and Upton St Leonards in Gloucestershire, with some other lands.

Carta 5. H. 7. in cast^r de Berley.

Rec: mich: terme: 24. H. 7. rot. 327. rot. claus: in canc: 20. H. 7. m.

And the better to enable this younger brother for such a wife, his father and elder brother conveyed to him and the heires males of his body the said manors of Hovingham, Sages, and Upton St Leonards, and all their lands in Thornbury; And the manor of Hinton in Cambridge Shire; Some of which by new agreements were after reconveyed to the said Maurice his elder brother. |

carta in castro de Berkeley.

This Alienor was a mild and vertuous lady, taking great care for the education and marriage of those two sons and two daughters of whom this second marriage had made her ye mother, as by divers tres and muniments in Berkeley Castle may bee collected; Howbeit before shee could see those works performed, shee left her blessing to them, and her soule to God, in the 17th yeare of king Henry the 8th, having been baronesse near two years; And lyeth buried in the monastery of St Augustines by Bristoll, to whose side her husbands body was after brought, as followeth.

677

fol: [690]

The second wife of this lord was Cicely the widow of Richard Rowdon of Gloucester, Esqr and daughter and coheir of   whom hee married in the 18th of Henry the 8th; And whom againe after six years hee left a widdow, with her own estate shee brought, And the manors of ffenystanton, Hilton, Auconbury, Weston, Guiherne, Charters and Murrow, Bitton, and Upton St Leonards,

Volunt: 24. H. 8. 3. carta in castro de Berkeley.

Mich: rec: 38. H. 8. rot. 25. cum rem: thes:

---

[1] William Sever, who was translated from Carlisle in 1502. [ED.]

Leonards, in recompence of her Joynture and dower by him; which within fower months after her husbands death, shee assigned to his son and heire for the yearly rent of 142ˡⁱ 06ˢ 8ᵈ which was paid her till the last of Queen Mary, when shee dyed at Bristoll, where shee lyeth buryed; And for her continuall abode there was called my lady Cicely of Bristoll.

carta in castro de Berkeley.

Divers: compī ministr̄ in castro de Berkel:

By which later marriage of this lord hee hemmed in ffrances one of the two daughters and coheirs of the said Richard Rowdon to bee wife to Maurice Berkeley his second son, as followeth; (the other called Katharine being after married to Willm Read,) which alliance was partly the cause why this lady Cicely took part with the said Maurice in the unkind suites wᶜʰ his elder brother the lord Thomas, and after him the lady Anne his widowe, pressed against him, as after is related.

And it is truly said, That these two ladies Alienor and Cicely were the last wives to the lords of this family that have not had private ends for their own advantages upon their husbands affaires, and too often prevailed over them, As in the lives that follow to the end of this history will appeare: And like to hold for one generation further.

His issue.

This lord Thomas, by the lady Alienor his first wife, had two sons Thomas and Maurice, and two daughters Miriell and Jone, Of whom in order. |

1. **Thomas** the eldest was lord after his father, whose life followeth by the name of Thomas the sixth.

678

Maurice, the second son, had by the conveyance and will of his father setled upon him for his life, the manors of Dalby-Chawcombe, Mountforrell, Mangotsfeild, and other lands; And the manor of Aylmington, to him and the heires males of his body: wherewith hee had small quiet, through the suites that arose about them between his elder brother and his widowe the lady Anne, as in their lives appeares.

This Maurice married ffrances daughter and coheire of Richard Rowdon, brother and heir of Walter, sons of John Rowdon, after remarried to Richard Danvers, by whom also shee had issue remembred in the last will of Thomas lord Berkeley her father in lawe with a chaine of gold and other legacyes,) by which ffrances this Maurice had two sons, and fower daughters, viz!

Shee dyed. 4. Eliz: Ing: 5. H. 8. post mort Rowdon. Volunt: Thomæ de Berkeley. 11. Jan: 24. H. 8.

Edward

Anno 19 Eliz

Edward Berkeley of Bradley by Wotton, who marryed Elizabeth daug^r, and heire of Brice Berkeley of Bradley, and died without issue, and is buryed in the Chapple of Berkeley Church with this inscription, Here lyeth the Body of Edward Berkeley Esqr, who deceased the, 23th of March Anno Dom : 1576.

Maurice younger brother of the said Edward dyed also without issue

Matthewe

ffrances their elder sister was married to George Matthew, who had issue Thomas Mathewe, who by Judith his wife daugh^r of Henry Towensend of Oldbury hath left issue, Richard Mathewe that now is, Anno . 1628 And lyeth buryed in Portbury Church, with this mistaken inscription upon his tombe, Here lieth the body of Thomas Mathewe, gent . and cozen germane to the Lord Berkeley, who departed this life the 14th day of Decem^r 1615. For hee was in the third discent, And George now lord Berkeley (in whose time hee dyed) in the fourth discent from this lord Thomas, their common Auncestor.

Morris

Clifford.

Alienor, their second sister was maryed to John Morris, who had issue Mary since dead without issue As also is another sister of the said Alienor, married to James Clifford of fframpton, who lived not longe togeather, before death took her away without issue

Westley

Rowdon

Anne the fourth sister was marryed to Leonard Westley, who had issue ffrancis Westley borne after the death of his father, now of Cromhall in the hundred of Berkeley, who by Anne his wife daughter of William Trotman of Wotton hath issue Henry, now attendant upon George lord Berkeley, And after, the said Anne was remarried to Anthoney Rowdon of Bromyard in the county of Hereford, by whom shee had issue Richard, ffrancis, Isaacke, and Dorothy Rowdon - Which said Richard Rowdon, hath issue Edward, ffrancis, John, and Awdry, And the said ffrancis brother of the said Richard, hath issue Thomas, ffrancis, and John. The said Isaack is lately dead without issue ; And the said Dorothy their sister is lately Married to Mr Blunt of Wye in the County of Hereford, And this Maurice second son of this lord Thomas lyeth buryed in Temple Church by Bristoll, in a faire tomb, with his portraiture and Eschucheon of Armes thereupon, as I am informed

Throgm'ton of Caughton

3 **Miriell**: eldest daughter of this lord Thomas, was in the 18th yeare of king Henry the 8th maryed at Yate to Robert Throkmerton of Caughton in the County of War^r, (after knight,) son and heire of Sr George Throckmerton and of Katharine his

his wife daughter of Nicholas lord Vaux; 𝕿𝖍𝖊 marriage portion of Miriell was 750 marks, as by an Indenture containing many other covenants and agreements appeareth; And her Joynture, as the said Indenture sheweth, was the manors of Blacknonton in Worcestershire, and Birdbury in Warrwickshire; ffor payment of which marriage portion many acquittances remain on a file in Berkeley Castle: Where also it appeareth, That her wedding hose and shoes cost, 22^d. 𝕾𝖍𝖊𝖊 was a lady of a small stature, lived longe and vertuously; And saw ere shee dyed discended from herself—220—persons, as I have very credibly been informed, by such as undertook to recount them, Many of whom now follow; 𝖂𝖍𝖎𝖈𝖍 Sr George Throkmerton was son of Sr Robert, son of Thomas, son of John Throkmerton, who lived in the time of King Edward the third.

Carta: dat. 10. Nov: 18. H. 8. in castro de Berkeley.

Comp. Georg. Shipway senli. 18. H. 8.

𝕿𝖍𝖎𝖘 Miriell Berkeley and Robert had issue between them Thomas Throgmerton, Elizabeth, Mary, Emme, and Katharine, of whom in order.

𝕿𝖍𝖊 said Thomas Throgmerton maryed Margaret daughter and heire of William Horwood, Atturney generall to king Henry the 8th, by whom hee had issue John, Miriell, Mary, Margaret, Elizabeth, and Elleanor.

The said John the son of Thomas maryed Anne daughter of Thomas Wilford of Kent, who had issue Robert, Margaret, Ellenor, Winefred, and two or three younger sons. The said Robert first married Dorothy daughter of S^r ffrancis ffortescue of Buckinghamshire, And secondly married Anne daughter of S^r ffrancis Smyth of Leicestershire, by neither of whom hee had any issue. Of the said Margaret, Elleanor, Winifred, and the rest, I am not inabled to write.

Fortescue.
Smyth.

Myriell eldest daughter of the said Thomas Throgmerton and Margaret, sister to the said John, was marryed to Henry Berkeley of Stoke Gifford, of whose issue see before in the lives of Maurice the third, and of Maurice the fifth.

Berkeley of Stoke fol: 274. 275. 627. 628.

Mary the second daughter of the said Thomas Throgmerton and Margarett is not yet marryed. |

Margaret third daughter of the said Thomas Throgmton and Margaret was married to Rice Griffin of Dingly in Northton^{re}, who have issue Edward, Nicholas, Thomas, and Lucey; whereof the said Edward hath maryed the daughter of Mr Draycote of Staffordshire, who have issue, and the said Nicholas hath married Jane
daughter

680 Griffin

    daughter of Mr Edmond Peers of Warwickshire, who have issue, Thomas and Lucey are not yet married.

    Elizabeth, the fourth daughter of the said Thomas Throgmton and Margaret,
Griffith was married to Sr Henry Griffith of Wigmore in Shropshire, who have issue, Henry and Elizabeth; which Henry hath married one of the Coheires of S.^r ffrancis
Willoughby Willoughby, who have yet noe issue: And the said Elizabeth is married to S.^r
Boyton Matthew Boyton of Yorkshire, who have issue, 1618.

    Elleanor, the fifth and youngest daughter of the said Thomas Throgmton and
Jermingham. Margaret, was married to Sr Henry Jerningham of Cossy in Norfolke, who have issue John, William, Thomas, Katharine, and Elizabeth.

    The said John maried Mary daughter of S.^r ffrancis Moore of ffawley in Berk-
Saunders. shire, who have issue Henry, The said Katharine is maryed to Francis Sanders of Shankton in Leicestershire, Esquire.

    And the said Thomas and Elizabeth are not yet maryed.

    The said William is (Anno 1624) maryed to Mary the widow of Mr John Younge.

    The said Elizabeth eldest daughter of Miriell Berkeley and sister of the said
Goodwyn. Thomas Throgmton, was marryed to Sr John Goodwyn knight of Winchington in Buckinghamshire, who had issue two sons; John, who by Anne his wife daughter of
Stukeley. Sr John Baker of Kent have issue a daughter marryed to Sr Thomas Stukeley, between whom are divers children now living. 1618.

    And ffrancis Goodwyn knight, brother of the said John, who by the daughter of Arthur lord Gray, hath issue Arthur, and Edward who is dead without issue, and one daughter.

    And the said Arthur by Jane his wife second daughter of Sr Richard Wayneman of Tame Parke in Oxfordshire hath issue a daughter: And the said
Elmes. sister of Arthur Goodwyn, is marryed to William Elmes of Greensnorton in the County of Northampton Esqr 1618.

    The said Mary, second daughter of the said Miriell Berkeley and Robert
Arden. Throgmton, was maryed to Edward Arden of Parkhall in the County of Warrwicke
                                 Esquire,

Esquire, by whom shee had issue Robert, Katharine, Margaret, Myriell, Mary, and Elizabeth, who are married as followeth.

The said Robert Arden by Elizabeth his wife, daughter of Reignold Corbett, a Judge of the kings bench, hath issue S.ʳ Henry Arden, and Anne Arden; which S.ʳ Henry Arden by Dorothy his wife daughter of Basill ffeilding of Newenham in the county of Warrwick Esq̃, hath issue, Robert, Elizabeth, Judith, Dorothy and Anne: And the said Anne Arden was maryed to Walter fferrars Esq.ʳ second brother to S.ʳ John fferrars of Tamworth castle, who have issue, John, Walter, and Dorothy. <small>681 Ferrars.</small>

The said Katharine Arden sister of the said Robert, was married to S.ʳ Edward Deveraux of Castle Bromwich in Warrwickshire, Baronet, who have issue, Walter, William, George, Henry, Edward, Margaret, Anne, Howarda, and Grace; of whom, William, Henry and Edward are dead without issue. The said Margaret is maried to S.ʳ Hugh Wrothesly of Staffordshire; And Anne is maryed to M.ʳ Leighton of Shropshire; And Howarda is maried to Thomas Dilke of Maxtock castle in Warrwicksh.ᵉ; And the said Walter Deverox the eldest son maryed Elizabeth daughter of Thomas Knightley of Preston, in Northhamptonshire Esquire, who have issue Essex, Leicester, Katharine, Walter, Edward and John Deverox. <small>Deveraux. Wrothesley Leighton. Dilke.</small>

Margaret Arden another sister of the said Robert was first maryed to John Somerfeild, who was attainted of Treason in the 25ᵗʰ of Queen Elizabeth, by whom shee had issue Margaret and Elizabeth; And secondly to one De la hay. <small>Somerfeild. De la hay.</small>

Myriell Arden another sister of the said Robert, was maryed to William Charnells, who have issue Edward, Robert, Godfrey, Anne, Myriell, and ffrances Charnells. <small>Charnells.</small>

Mary Arden another sister of the said Robert, was maryed to ffrancis Wafery of London. <small>Wafery.</small>

And Elizabeth Arden the youngest sister of the said Robert was married to Simon Shugborrow of Shugborrow in Warrwickshire, who have issue, George slaine at the Isle of Ree, and two daughters. <small>Shugburrow.</small>

The said Emme another daughter of the said Myriell Berkeley and Robert Throgmorton was marryed to Ralph Shelden of Beoly in the County of Warwicke, by

Sheldon	by whom shee had issue Edward Sheldon, Elizabeth, Mary, Myriell, Margaret, Katharine, Phillipa, and Jone.

The said Edward Sheldon by Elizabeth his wife, daughter of Thomas Markam Esq.r hath issue William, who hath maryed Elizabeth daughter of William lord Peter, Ralph, unmarried, Edward Sheldon maryed to Anne sister of Thomas Morgan of Weston, Esq.r, Frances, Anne and Jone; which Anne is maryed to Henry Lucy of Pinchburge in the County of Hartford Esq.r; And the said Jone is maryed to S.r Henry Appleton of South benfleet in the County of Essex, Baronett, who have issue, Henry, Anne, and Mary, 1630.

<small>Lucey.</small>
<small>Apleton.</small>

The said Elizabeth Sheldon sister of the said Edw.d is married to S.r John Russell knight, who have issue S.r Thomas Russell knight.

<small>Russell.</small>

682 The said Miriell Sheldon an other sister of the said Edward is maryed to S.r ffrancis Clare of Worcestershire, knight.

<small>Clare</small>

The said Margaret Sheldon another sister of the said Edward is maryed to William Standen of Berkshire, Esq.r

<small>Standen</small>

The said Mary Sheldon, another sister of the said Edward is maryed to John fflower of Hambleton in the county of Rutland Esq.r

<small>fflower</small>

The said Katharine Sheldon another sister of the said Edward is maryed to ffrancis Trenton of Roceter in the county of Stafford Esq.r

<small>Trentan</small>

The said Phillippa Sheldon another sister of the said Edward is maryed to S.r John Sulliard of Wetherden in Kent.

<small>Sulliard</small>

And the said Jone Sheldon another sister of the said Edward is maryed at Andwerpe beyond seas.

The said Katharine, fourth daughter of the said Myriell Berkeley and Robert Throgmiton, was marryed to Henry Norwood of Leckhampton in Glocest.r shire Esq.r, by whom shee had issue William and Jane.

<small>Norwood.</small>

The said William Norwood, (who yet liveth, 1628,) by Elizabeth his wife daughter of William Ligon Esq.r had issue Richard, William, Henry, Raph, Thomas, Maurice, Elleanor and Elizabeth.

<small>see fol: 631.</small>

The

The said Richard Norwood son of William, by Elizabeth his wife daughter of Nicholas Stuard Doctor of the civill lawe, hath issue, Augustine, ffrancis, John, William, Richard, Edward, Thomas, Elleanor, and Dorothy, A⁰. 1618.

William Norwood brother of Richard, is dead without issue.

Henry the third brother of Richard, by Elizabeth his wife daughter of S.r John Rodney hath issue, Charles, Henry, and Jane, that now are, A⁰. 1618.

Raph the 4.th brother of Richard, liveth a souldier in the low Countryes. Anno. 1618.

Thomas the fifth brother of Richard, hath yet noe issue.

Maurice the sixth brother of Richard, is dead without issue.

The said Elleanor sister of the said Richard Norwood, was maryed to George Blunt of Sellington in the county of Worcester Esq.r, by whom shee hath issue, Walter, ffrancis, George, Elizabeth, and Elleanor.   Blunt.

And the said Elizabeth, the other sister of the said Richard Norwood, was maryed to Richard Moore Esq.r, by whom shee had issue divers children.   Moore.

The said Jane, sister of the said William Norwood, was maryed to M.r Bracebridge; who hath noe issue.   Bracebridge.

4. **Jone** Berkeley youngest daughter of this lord Thomas, was on Midsommer day in the nineteenth year of king Henry the 8.th maryed at Yate, her fathers house, to Nicholas Poynz, (after knight,) son and heir of S.r Anthoney Poyntz of Acton. knight, whose marriage portion was six hundred marks, whereof one hundred pounds at the marriage, and one hundred marks each year after; wherein the agreements were further, **That** if Nicholas dyed before the marriage, then shee to be marryed to his brother Giles Poynz: Each father at his own charge to apparell his own child after his degree: The charges of the wedding diet to be equally borne by either party: Her Joynture to bee—106.li 13.s 4.d by the year in land; And 280.li land by the year to bee by S.r Anthony settled upon the said Nicholas and the heires males of his body; If Jone dyed, then all payments to cease then unpaid; If by

Poynz:

Script: dat: 20:
Junij 19. H. 8. in
papiro in castro de
Berkeley.

the

the death of his fons this lords inheritance fhould difcend upon this Jone and her fifter, Then S:r Anthony to repay fo much of the portion as hee had received, and one thoufand pound more in lieu of that difcent; And if her fifter Myriell dye without iffue, whereby Jone becometh fole daughter and heire, Then S:r Anthony to pay . 2000:li and repay the 600 marks alfo: If differences arife, The fame to bee referred to Thomas then Duke of Norfolke: for performance of thefe agreements, S:r Anthony gave his ftatute of 1000:li with fureties; And the faid lord his bond of five hundred pounds: **What** fruite fprange from thefe two plants thus conjoyned, obferve in the vintage now following: **ffor** the faid Jone and Nicholas had iffue 1 S:r Nicholas, 2 ffrancis, 3 Edmond, 4 Anthony, 5 William, 6 John, 7 Anne, 8 Jane, and 9 ffrances, of each of whom in order: **And** this S:r Nicholas dyed in the third and fourth years of Phillip and Mary, And Jone furvived, and was in her Elder years marryed to S:r Edward Dyer, and dyed in the fixth of Queen Elizabeth.

1. **The** faid S:r Nicholas Poynz fon of the faid Jone and S:r Nicholas, by Anne his firft wife, daughter of S:r Raph Varney, had iffue S:r John Poynz knight yet living, and Mary, Anno, 1628.

The faid S:r John Poynz by Elizabeth his wife daughter of Alexander Sydnam Efq:r, had iffue Robert Poynz a knight of the Bath, who by ffrances his wife, daughter and coheir of Jervais Gybbon, Efq:r, hath iffue Grefill and Margarett, that now are, 1628; Enjoying the quiet contentment of a peacefull country life at Acton in the County of Glouc., the Auncient feat of his Anceftors fince S:r Nicholas Poynz in the time of king Edward the firft marryed Mawd the daughter and heir of S:r John Acton to his fecond wife, of whom the faid S:r Robert is lineally difcended.

And the faid Mary, fifter of the faid S:r John Poynz, was firft married | to ffrancis Codrington of fframpton upon Seaverne, by whom fhee had iffue Margaret, firft maried to Edward Bramidge, by whom fhee had iffue Ifaack, Mary, and Rebecca; And fecon[d]ly to John Sydnam, by whom fhee had iffue three daughters, viz:t Anne maryed to John Poynz of Surrey Efq:r, by whom is iffue; And Urfula maryed to Richard Molinieux Efq:r by whom alfo is iffue; And Elizabeth marryed to Poynz Mill of Harfcombe, by whom alfo is iffue.

And the faid S:r Nicholas Poynz by Margaret his fecond wife, daughter of Edward Stanley, Earle of Darby, had iffue Edward, Hugh, and Robert, yet living. 1618.

2. **The**

2. The said ffrancis son of Jone Berkeley, by [Ann] the daughter and heire of [. . . Stawker[1]] had issue Jone, marryed to John Wykes of Doddington, by whom is much issue disperfed in severall Counties. Wikes.

3. 4. 5. 6. The said Edmond John Anthony and William fower sons of the said Jone Berkeley are dead without issue.

The said Anne Poynz daughter of the said Jone Berkeley was marryed to S:r Thomas Heneage knight, of Cophall in the County of Essex, vicechamberlaine to Queen Elizabeth and of her privy counsell, who dyed, 1592. leaving issue Elizabeth only, maryed to S:r Moyle ffinch kn:t, and Baronet, by whom shee hath issue eight sons and four daughters, as followe; And surviving her husband, was in her widowhood created by king James, Vicountesse Maidstone; And after by king Charles, Countesse of Winchelsey, with qualification to all her children to precede as the children of Earles; Of which eight sons four are dead without issue, as also two of the said fower daughters; The rest have issue, as followeth, viz:t,

1. Thomas the eldest son is Earle of Winchelsey, and hath issue Heneage Finch vicount Maidstone, John ffinch, William ffinch, ffrances married to S:r William Strickland of Bointon in Yorkshire, between whom is issue Thomas Strickland: Other 4 daughters of the said Earle, viz:t, Anne, Cecill, Diana, and Katharine, are yet unmarryed, Anno, 1635.

2. John ffinch, second son of the said Countesse Elizabeth, married Anne daughter of M:r Walker, and left issue now livinge, John, and William.

3. Heneage ffinch, third son to the said Countess Elizabeth, knight and Recorder of the city of London, first married ffrances daughter of S:r Robert Bell of Norfolk knight, by whom hee had issue, Heneage, ffrancis, John, and Elizabeth marryed to the son and heire of Sir Raph Maddeson of Lincolnshire kn:t; And 2:dly marryed the widow of M:r Bennet of Lond, by whom hee hath issue left, ffrances and Anne. |

4. ffrancis ffinch 4:th son to the said Countess maryed Anne daughter and heire to M:r Walter of Suffolk, by whom was issue a son and a daughter, who died younge.

5. Anne,

---

[1] See Chancery Proceedings Queen Elizabeth, 16 Nov., 1590, William Hobbes of London, Yeoman, *versus* Francis Poyntz, of Mowbray, Gent., and Ann his wife. [ED.]

Twifden.

Cholmeley.

5. Anne, eldeſt daughter to the ſaid Counteſs, is married to Sr William Twifden of Eaſt Peckam in Kent, Baronett, who have iſſue, Roger, Thomas, William, John, ffrancis, Elizabeth, and Anne; Which Roger knight and Baronett, married Iſabella, daughter to Sr Nicholas Sander of Ewell in the County of Surrey knight: And the ſaid Elizabeth is married to Sr Hugh Cholmely of Whitbey in the county of Yorke, knight: And the ſaid Anne is married to Sr Chriſtopher Yelverton in the County of Northton knight, who have iſſue.

Wentworth.
Ld Gray.

6. Katharine, ſecond daughter to the ſaid Counteſs Elizabeth is married to Sr John Wentworth of Goſefeild in the county of Eſſex, Baronett, who have iſſue Cecill married to William lord Gray of Warke in the county of Northumberland; And Lucy Wentworth yet unmarried . 1634.

Strickland.

8. The ſaid Jane daughter of the ſaid Jone Berkeley was married to John Seimor Eſqr baſe ſon of Edward Seimor Duke of Somerſet, by whom ſhee had iſſue Sir Thomas Seimor of fframpton Cotterell knight, Jane and one other daughter; Which Sr Thomas Seimor by Jane his firſt wife daughter of Mr Webb, hath iſſue John Seimor knight, Gabriell, Elizabeth, and Anne; And by Anne his ſecond wife, had iſſue Edward, Elleanor dead without iſſue, Jone married to John Aſide, ffrances, Anne, and Mary dead without iſſue, and Elizabeth married to Sr Thomas Strickland of Yorkſhire knight, as followeth.

The ſaid Sr John Seimor by Alice his firſt wife daughter of William Pawlet Eſqr, hath iſſue Katharine, Agnes, and one other daughter: And by . . . . . his ſecond wife daughter of Mr Symes, hath iſſue Thomas, and others.

The ſaid Gabriel, brother of Sr John Seimor, by Katharine his wife daughter of Richard Cave of Briſtoll hath iſſue, Thomas, John and Mary.

Watkins.

The ſaid Elizabeth, ſiſter of the ſaid Sr John Seimor, was married to Edwd Watkins of Bridgewater, who have iſſue, Thomas, Elizabeth, and Anne.

Nuce.

And the ſaid Anne, ſiſter of the ſaid Sr John and Gabriell, is marryed to Thomas Nuce, who have iſſue: Hee lately dead in Virginia; ſhee there yet living, Anno 1618.

The ſaid Jone, ſiſter of Sr John Seimor, was married to John Aſide of Upton Cheyney his ſecond wife, by whom ſhee had iſſue fower ſons, and a daughter all dead without iſſue.

And

And the said Elizabeth, youngest daughter of the said Sr Thomas Seimor, was married to Sr Thomas Strickland of Yorkshire, who had issue 4 sons all dead w.thout issue, And Alice married to Sr Jno Webb of London, kn.^t who have issue. | Strickland. Webb.

9. The said Frances daughter of the said Jone Berkeley, was maryed to Sr John Berkeley of Beverston castle, knight, by whom shee had issue John Berkeley, Jone, Katharine and Margaret. Which John, by Mary his wife daughter of John Snell Esqr, had issue, 1 Maurice, 2 John, 3 Henry, 4 William, 5 Edward, 6 Thomas, 7 Mary, 8 ffrances, 9 Elizabeth, and 10 Anne. Whereof the said Maurice, by Barbara his wife daughter of Sr Walter Longe, hath issue Edwd; and others; And the said Mary his sister is marryed to Edward Conway of Gloucester shire, The other eight are unmarryed. 1623. As also is Jone the eldest sister of the said John Berkeley, leading a Nunnes life at Brussells, beyond seas; And now lady Abbesse there. 1630.   686 Berkeley of Beverston. See fol: 375. Conway.

The said Katharine, second sister of the said John Berkeley, by Thomas Symonds, a minister, hath issue Thomas, Anno. 1620.   Simonds.

And the said Margaret the other sister by Jesper Merricke of Berington, a minister, hath issue, Sibill, Anno. 1620.   Merricke.

His

His Seales of Armes.

This lord Thomas, a fewe years before his death, used (wherewith also hee sealed his last will,) a great broad Seale fower inches diameter, with the Armes of Brotherton, Berkeley, Warren, Mowbray, Segrave, and Breouse, quartered. The helmet for his crest with a lion passant on the top thereof: And two lions for supporters, circumscribed, Sigillum Thome Dñi de Berkeley, et Mowbray Segrawe militis.

And for his privy seale, A small lyon rampant. Behold the figures. |

His death and place of buriall.

687

Annis. 4. et. 5.
H. 8. et. 8. et. 11.
H. 8.

The lord Maurice elder brother to this lord Thomas, did by severall Deeds, fynes, recoveries and other assurances at severall times, estate Judge Brudnell and others in all his manors formerly mention'd, To such uses as before in his life hath been declared.

Carta. 30. Nov. 18.
H. 8.
Carta. 1. Julij. 19.
H. 8. in castro de
Berkeley.
Carta. 9. Julij:
20. H. 8. et. 12.
Nov: 20. H. 8. in
castro de Berkeley.

Now Katharine the widow of the said lord Maurice being dead, as also the lady Elleanor the first wife of this lord Thomas, And hee remarryed to the lady Cicely, And his sonns and daughters maryed, and ready to bee marryed, Hee now procures his brothers feoffees and Recoverors to grant over the same to Thomas Earle of Surrey and twenty others to divers uses: whereof

Volunt: 28 Aprill
24. H. 8. in castro
de Berkeley.
Triñ. fin: in scᵃcio
23. H. 8. rot: 19.

The manors of ffenystanton, Hilton, Auconbury and Weston in the county of Huntington: And Guyherne, Chatteryes, and Murrow in the county of Cambridge; And Bitton and Upton S.ᵗ Leonards, called Grove court, in the county of Glouc.; To the use of the lady Cicely his wife for her life, in recompence of all dower and Joynture that shee any ways might claime, And after her death, to his son Thomas in taile, with many remainders over, to his other son, daughters and neeces: **And** the manors of Dalby Chaucomb, and Mountsorrell in the County of Leicester, And the manor of Mangottsfeild in the County of Glouc., To the use of Maurice his second son for the terme of his life, the remainder to Thomas his eldest son in taile with like remainders over. **And** the manors of Melton Mowbray, Segrave, Sileby, and Coldoverton, and the hundred of Goscote in the County of Leicester; and the manor of Sages in the County of Gloucester, To the payment of his debts, and legacies, and performance of his will, And after to the use of Thomas his son and heire in taile, with the like remainders over, and the manors of Tetbury and Daglingworth in the County of Gloucester, To the use of Thomas his

his sonne and heire in tayle with like remainders over. **And** the Manors of Cotes, Thurneby, and Witherly, in the county of Leicester; The manors of Flekenhoe, Thurlaston, and Aspely, in the county of Warr̃, The manors of Bretby, Coton, Rostlaston, Repingdon, and Lynton, in the county of Derby, The manors of Bosham, ffuntington, and Thorney in the county of Suffex, and 14^{li}. rent going out of the man^{rs}. of Bromeley in Suffex, and Leigh in the county of Lincolne, Twenty two marks rent out of fframpton upon Seavern, and fower messuages and 170 Acres of Land in Thornbury, And the fourth part of the manor of Brok-|enbury in the County of Glouc., To the use of himself and his heires, and to performe his will.

Carta. 9. Julij. 20. H. 8. in castro de Berkel: **688**

By this will and other his deeds, hee gives these pensions and Anuities for the lives of the parties, his kinsmen, allies, servants, and well deserving freinds, vizt.

carta in castro de Berkeley. Vol: 24. H. 8. in p^{r}dict.

To John Arnold Esqr, his brother in lawe; Ten pounds, whom hee made high Steward of all his Manors and lands in England.

Carta. 4. Junij. 17. H. 8. in castro de Berkeley.

To Thomas Lane, 5^{li}.   To David Broke. 3^{li}.   To Thomas Hennege Esqr. 4^{li}. To Henry Weston. 4 marks.   To Henry Wikes. 40^s.   To Arthur Porter. 40^s. To Edward Chaple. 40^s.   To Nicholas Arnold. 40^s.   To Katharine Rowdon. 50^{li}. To Richard Arnold. 5^{li}.   To Richard Hawkins. 40^s.   To Robert Cockes. 53^s 4^d. To Maurice Denys, 40^s.   To Margaret Denys, 40^s.   To John Falkener. 40^s.   To Edith Martin, 66^s. 8^d.   To Bridget Paris, 20^{li}.   To Thomas Simonds, 20^s.   To Matthewe Bucke. 20^s.   To John Berkeley his unkle Thomas son. 10^{li}. w^{ch}, (saith his will) hee is bound in conscience to see him truly paid.

Inq: 29. H. 8. post mort̃ Thome dom: Berkeley

And by his said will hee further gave, Ten pounds towards the amendment of the highwayes at Mangotesfeild, where hee then dwelt. And Twenty pounds towards the repaire of Keinshams bridge fower miles off. And 100 markes towards the building of the high Altar at S^t. Augustines by Bristoll. And Ten pounds towards the repairing of the Cloister of the black ffryars in Bristoll; And divers other like legacies to his houshold servants, to the severall orders of fryars, poore prisoners in Goales in divers places, &c. **And** eight pound by the yeare for ten years to his godson Thomas Harcourt preist, to singe and pray for his soule: And to buy vestments for Mangotesfeild church eight pounds. **The** last remembred was his eldest son, to whom hee gave all his Armour and parliament robes; **And** of this Will hee made his three loving freinds, fitz James and Inglefeild Judges, his foresaid brother in law John Arnold, and Ciceley his wife, his Executors, to whom hee

gave

gave ten pound each; which fitz James was alfo one of his elder brothers the lord Maurice his executors, as before hath been declared.

2. Kings. 20. 1. **Thus** did this good and prudent lord Thomas followe the prophets counfell given to Ezekias, that pattern of Princes and their peeres, by fetting his houfe in order, in Aprill in the 24th of king Henry the 8th knowing, not as Ezekias from the prophet Efay, That hee fhould then dye, and not live, but out of a wife and religious meditation of mans mortality, his own old age, and the decaying conftitution of his body.

Vol: 28 Apr. 24. H. 8. in caftro Berkley.
689

In January following hee takes his chamber in his houfe at Mangottesfeild, And the 11th of that month reviews his will and approves it, made in Aprill before, And Adds thereto a Codicell, wherein (amongft other things) hee takes order for his Tombe and funerall; And then takes his bed and draws unto him company fitted for the longe journey hee was to take, the Abbot of S^ت Auguftines by Briftoll, the Abbot of Kingfwood, the Deane of Weftbury Colledge, the Doctor and pryor of the black ffryars in Briftoll, and fome other of the moft devout and learned divines of thofe parts; And on wednefday the 22th of that January, Anno. 1532. in the faid 24th year of king Henry the 8th in the midft of their prayers and bleffings, doth (as it were) clofe up his own eyes from the further fight of the tranfitories of this life, hereafter to fee with them God his creator and redeemer, and fuch things in his celeftiall paradife and third heaven (as St Paul fpeaketh) as are not poffible for man to utter, fuch as eye hath not feen nor eare heard neither have entred into the heart of man, even the things that God hath prepared for them that love him.

Vol: 24 H. 8. p^{rdī}. Comp: Señli hofpicij in caftro de Berkley.

Job. 19. 25. 27. 2 Cor. 12. 4. 1 Cor. 2. 9.

Thus lived this lord, thus dyed hee; dye ill hee could not, that lived foe well: well to God, well to the world, well to himfelf, well to his heire and pofterity, well to his friends, kindred and fervants; ever within compas, never exceeding his circumference, or the fphear of his revenue: Happy will bee his now grandchilds grandchild, if hee apply to himfelf the actions, life and death of this Anceftor for his example.

George Ld Berkley

As hee lived like a noble honeft lord, foe hee dyed like a Saint, yea hee did rather migrare quam mori; abire, quam obire; not dye, but fall afleep: Never hath my reading found any foe great a lord, that left this world more refolved, more prepared: As though hee had unbraced himfelf for his bed, rather than for his grave: **And** thus paffed hee from a mortall day to an everlafting morrow. Summum hominis

nis bonum, bonus ex hac vita exitus. The felicity of man is his good leaving of this life.

To the earthly happinefs of this lord, this may bee added, (greater then that of king Solomon,) That hee left behind him a wife fon to fucceede; A bleffing that that king had not; And honeft executors that performed his will.

The manner of whofe funerall and devotions for him done after death by preifts and fryars, read out of the accompt of his funeralls, deli-|vered by his Steward of houfhold, to his faid Executors, as breifly as I could abftract the fame; wherein note, that his body according to his will was firft buryed in the Church of Mangottesfeild where hee dyed, And after, as hee had appointed, it was removed to his owne tombe fet up in the church of the monaftery of S:t Auguftines by Briftoll, and there buryed by the fide of Alienor his firft wife, as his Will directed.

Comp: Señli: hofpicij 24. H. 8. 690 in caftro de Berkeley.

Vol. 24. H. 8. in caftro de Berkeley.

> To fower preifts to fay maffes the 24:th of January, the corps being then not buryed—16:d
> To thirty preifts and two clerks finging at the buriall—15:s 4:d
> To eight men ringing two dayes and a halfe—6:s 8:d
> To eighteen preifts for maffes—9:s
> To 24 preifts—12:s
> To poor people the day that the corps was brought to the church—38:s 8:d
> The fame day to forty preifts and twenty clerks—30:s
> To poore people in money doaled and given in Almes the day of the buriall of the Corps—6:li 13:s 4:d
> To S:t John Nelme preift for a derige and maffe at Slimbridge—2:s 1:d
> To men for ringing there—4:s
> To 8 preifts for each a maffe the wednefday the 29:th of January after the corps was buryed—2:s 8:d
> To 6 preifts the 30:th of January for 6 maffes—2:s
> To fower preifts the laft of January for 4 maffes—16:d
> To two preifts the fecond of ffebruary for 2 maffes—10:d this was candlemas day and thefe extraordinary maffes.
> The third of ffebruary to 4 fryars for 4 maffes—16:d
> The 4:th of ffebruary to two preifts for two maffes—8:d
> The 5:th of ffebruary to 4 preifts for 4 maffes—16:d
> The 6:th of ffebruary to 4 preifts for 4 maffes—16:d
> The 7:th of ffebruary to 6 preifts for 6 maffes—2:s

4:d was y:e ordinary price of a maffe, as certaine as 8:d is to a day laborer: or 20 eggs were for 1:d

The

The 8th of ffebruary to 6 preists for 6 masses—2ˢ
The 9th of ffebruary to 5 preists for 5 masses—20ᵈ
The 10th of ffebruary to 6 preists for 6 masses—2ˢ
The 11th of ffebruary to 4 preists for 4 masses—16ᵈ
The 12th of ffebruary to 6 preists for 6 masses—2ˢ
The 13th of ffebruary to 10 preists for 10 masses—3ˢ 4ᵈ
The 14th of ffebruary to 5 preists for 5 masses—20ᵈ
The 15th of ffebruary to 7 preists for 7 masses—2ˢ 4ᵈ
The 16th of ffebruary to 2 preists for 2 masses—8ᵈ
The 17th of ffebruary to 4 preists—16ᵈ

691

The 18th to 4 preists—16ᵈ
The 19th to 6 preists—2ˢ
The 20th to 9 preists—3ˢ
The same day being Sᵗ Mildreds day to poore people in Almes, 4ˢ 8ᵈ
The 21th to 4 preists—16ᵈ
The 22th to 4 preists—16ᵈ his monthes mind day.
To poore people in Almes the same day, the day of the months mind—
   10ˢ 10ᵈ Soe all masses ceased at Mangottesfeild.
To the Pryor of the black ffryars in Bristoll and his brethren for saying
   of masses—5ˢ
ffor derige, masses and services in the church of Berkeley, 13ˢ 4ᵈ
And soe in other places; And for tapers—wax, &c,—53ˢ 4ᵈ Thus the
   accompt of the Steward of houshold delivered to the Executors.

Hee dyed as hath been said the 22th of January, Anno, 1532. in the 24th of Henry the 8th then of the age of 60 years and upwards, whereof hee had sit lord nine years fower months and ten dayes; And lyeth buried under a fair tombe with his first wife Alienor, upon which hee appointed by his will forty pounds to bee bestowed: which was done. Where in the Sepulchre of his ancestors, (Gods servants,) waiting for the hope of Israell, the raising of their bodies in the resurrection of the just, hee sleepeth in peace. **And** posterity may not, without a spice of flattery call those that succeed after true and naturall branches of this excellent tree, that shall not in their times beare fruite somewhat relishing this roote, that gave such sap as his life and death hath done, for the imitation of his Posterity.

    Happy is hee whose Ancestors
     of vertue made profession,
    And from himself example leaves
     of vertue to succession.

The lands whereof hee dyed seized.

The lands whereof this lord dyed seized are under the laſt title before particularly mentioned, And were all the ſame in effect which | his elder brother left unto him, and hee to his ſon; ffor this family in this lord may bee ſaid neither to have ſuffered any remarkable eclipſe, or increaſe, but the moon in this lords hemiſpheare to have continued in the ſame aſpect as ſhee ſtood when hee firſt beheld her riſing upon the death of his elder brother.

And after this lords death, his eldeſt ſon found the favor to avoid the charge of finding of Inquiſitions; But the 12th of ffebruary following tendereth a ſchedule of the manors and lands with their yearly values, whereof hee deſired to take benefit by his ſpeciall livery and ouſter le maine, in the Counties of Leiceſter, Glouceſter, Huntington, Cambridge, Suſſex, Darby, Yorke, Warwick, Wilts, Lincolne, and Calais, all of the yearly value of——920^{li} in rents of aſſiſe, (beſides the demeſnes in hand,) or near thereabouts, And ſuch as were in ffeoffment to uſes; And the 24th of November in the 25th of the ſaid king procured the ſame under the great ſeale, which yet remaines in Berkeley Caſtle.

692

Sched: indent. dat. 12. febr: 24. H. 8. in caſtro de Berkeley.

Triñ. rec: in fc^{a}ĉio 23. H. 8. rot. 19.

Pat: 2 ps. 25. H. 8. carta in caſtro de Berkeley.

The Application and use of his life.

1. The courſe of this lords life verifies what is ſaid of learned men, That none ever ſaw a great ſcholler arrogant, for the more hee knows the more of his weakneſs hee underſtands; And that the leaſt knowledge is ever moſt proud: ffewe or none of this lords time in the county where hee lived milder or more provident, ever ſeeming rather deſirous to learne then to teach others: It was alſo in requeſt with this lord to ſay, Malo me divitem eſſe quàm haberi, better to bee rich then ſo accounted; Hee rightly underſtood the text of, vive tibi: Hee was ſoe lowly and moderate in his whole life That to the mean hee was freely affable, And to the gentry noe taller then a companion; whereby through humility and moderation of life, hee was honored of all: And (to tell truth to his poſterity) commanded without contradiction throughout the whole County of Glouc^r wherein for the laſt nine years of his life hee lived a Baron after his brothers death. |

2. Againe, having lived in the condition of a younger brother till ye 52th yeare of his age, And ſparingly bred in youth under his fathers and elder brothers huſbandly examples, hee little changed that frugality of condition whilſt hee lived a Baron and Peere of the Realme; And knewe, that for the regulating of an houſhold where the ruler himſelf runs at randome the ſervants will beare noe byas:

693

And

And that for order & thriving it was better to have in houſhold two too few then one too many: And having ſoe lived, his death could not bee but bleſſed, as you have read.

3. **Againe** by the example of this lords life, the words of his poſterity ſhould bee fewe but adviſed, forethinking whether that which they are to ſpeake bee fit to bee ſpoken; And rather to bee ſilent then ſpeake to an ill or noe purpoſe; And to let heart and tongue goe togeather in honeſty and truth; hating diſſembling in others and deteſting it in themſelves; the known vertues of this noble lord by the witnes of many that converſed with him living ſince the midſt of my daies: whoſe directions alſo to his ſteward of houſhold, (being lord,) were, That nothing ſhould bee ſpent which might honeſtly bee ſpared, nor any thing ſpared which might honeſtly bee ſpent.

4 **Againe**, this family may learn from the wiſdom and example of this their Anceſtor, how by following the counſell of his old and prudent ſervant Thomas Try hee avoided the baites and craft of Sacheverell, to his comfort and benefit of his poſterity: And not to ſcorne the advice of the aged and experienced, though ſervants of their own family: Or to thinke ſoe highly of their own abilities, as if they had a prerogative to bee free from error or overſight: What Rehoboam loſt by young counſell & flatterers, What hee had gained if hee had gone along with the advice of his fathers old ſervants let the ſpirit of God in the text tell for both, And let their practice bee thereafter.

1. Kings. cap. 12.
2. Chron: ea: 10.

5. **Againe**, This lords character I thus conceive; hee equalled not his father or elder brother nor many other of his ranke and time in proweſſe or in the depth of Worldly wiſdomes, neither did his education bowe him that way: But was not inferior to the beſt of them in an honeſt and religious life: Apt to beleeve well, loath to heare ill, farre from credulous aſſenting to a firſt tale never condemning any man unheard, and his accuſer face to face: many L̃res, and copies of his L̃res and reſcripts of others to him intimate his great diſlike of ſecret traducers, eſpecially when thoſe calumnyes or aſpertions | were in the generall: One of his L̃res hath thus, A falſe accuſer hides his mallice under generall words, as I have found this man did of thee. His diſpoſition ran neareſt parallell with his two Anceſtors, Thomas the firſt, and James the firſt, of any I have obſerved.

694

God grant his heires may runne
The race that hee hath done.

695 } blank
696 }

Finis Thome ejuſdem nominis quinti.

The Life of Thomas the Sixth

The life of Thomas lord Berkeley the fixth of that name; ftiled in Writings, Thomas Berkeley kn.t lord Berkeley Mowbray and Segrave: And was abavus, or as our Anceftors the Saxons called thirda fader, And wee at this day great grandfather, to George nowe lord Berkeley. And may bee called, Thomas the hopefull.

Contemporary with Henry the 8th, from 1532 . till 1534.

Whose fhort life I deliver under thefe nine titles viz.t,

1.—His birth and education, fol: 697.
2.—His Mifcellaniæ or various affaires . fol: 698.
3.—His lawe fuites, fol: 701.
4.—His wives, fol: 702.
5.—His Iffue, fol: 705.
6.—His feales of Armes, fol: 706.
7.—His death and place of buriall, fol: 707.
8.—The lands whereof hee dyed feized, fol: 710.
9.—The application and ufe of his life, fol: 713.

His Birth and education.

This lord Thomas was born at Hovingham in Yorkfhire in the 21th yeare of king Henry the 7th, about one yeare before his grandfather the lord Maurice the fifth dyed, And within one year after his fathers marriage with Mrs Ingleby; where hee continued till his parents returned into Gloucefterfhire about the 7th of king Henry the 8th, as hath been faid: At what time his unkle the lord Maurice the fixt, then newly made Leivtenant of the caftle of Calais, carried him beyond feas, where by his means, (accompting him as the heire apparent of his family,) hee was carefully bred up at S.t Omers in Artois, about 25 miles from Calais,

Ex relaĉone Henrici filii fui.

Calais, till himself dyed in the 15th of that king: And then returning, was till his marriage Termly imployed as his fathers Agent and Solliciter in his Lawe suites; And espetially about the restitution of Berkeley from the crowne, which his unkle the lord Maurice at his death left in such forwardnes, that his petition of right was signed by the king, as hath been noted in his life; And as testimonies of this lords towardlines and sufficiency in those unripe years, there yet remaine in Berkeley Castle divers of his Termes remembrances of his own hand writing; As, what suites were depending, how left at the former termes end, and in what sort to bee further prosecuted, And what of new was to bee begun, and the like: And of all his Ancestors wrote the best hand, and best understood the latin tongue, whereby it seemes hee made good use of the time hee spent at St Omers.

Diu'si compi et muniment in castro de Berkeley.

His miscellaniæ or various passages.

This lords father having left the manor of ffenystanton and others to the lady Cicely his second wife, for her life, as before appears; Hee within two months after gaines from her a grant of all the lands shee held of his inheritance, for threescore years if shee lived soe longe, at the yearly rent of—142ᶠ. 6ˢ. 8ᵈ.; whereby hee wisely wound in himself to have the manageing of his own lands in possession, And this hee wrought under the advantage of his second marriage with Anne Savage, as after will appeare.

Carta in castro de Berkeley. dat. 12 Maii, 25 H. 8.

In March, six weeks after the death of his father, hee obtained of king Henry the 8th a grant to bee Constable and Porter of the Castle of Berkeley, and keeper of the castle parke with the worthy enclosed in it, and to bee paler of the same; And to bee keeper of Hinton woods called Cheslanger and Redwood, and of the red deere there; And to have the fishing of Smethmore, (now excellent pasture ground,) and the fishing of the gale in Seaverne without rent, Taking the fees accustomed, which his father held for his life, as afore is written. At wch time, sith king Henry the 8th had been 24 years marryed to severall wives and had noe issue male, hee could not but cherish an inward expectation of a Reverter in fee of the wholl Barony of Berkeley, whereof hee now was glad to take a small morsell, at will.

pat: 8 marcij 24 H. 8.

Smeth is in the Saxon tongue plaine or smooth.

699

The 20th of May in the 25th of king Henry the 8th hee gave Thomas Cromwell Esqr, then Secretary to king Henry the 8th (after Earle of Essex) 13ˡⁱ 6ˢ 8ᵈ Anuity for his life, and then made him his high steward of Sileby, Thornby, Mountsorrell, and of Goscote hundred.

Comp. 29. H. 8. in castro de Berkeley. carta: dat: 20 Maij 25. H. 8. in castro de Berkeley.

And

Life of Thomas the Sixth

And 4ₗᵢ 13ˢ 4ᵈ yearly to the Earle of Huntington and to ffrancis Haſtings his ſon and heire, for exerciſing under him the office of high ſteward of his manor of Melton Mowbray, Segrave, Coldovton, Dalby, Thorpſachvill and Witherly. And on May day the ſame 25ᵗʰ of king Henry the 8ᵗʰ hee gave to David Broke of Briſtoll gent̃, for his good ſervice done to him, the fourth part of his manor of Brokenburrow in the pariſh of Almondſbury for his life at 4ᵈ rent.

Comp: 29. H. 8. ibm
carta: 25. H. 8. ibm
Inq: 28. H. 8. in canc.
carta dat. 1. Maij 25. H. 8. in caſtro de Berkeley

In Aprill before his death hee preſented Robert Derby for Abbot of Croxton, of the order of premonſtratenſes, which (as the Deed ſpeaketh) to his preſentation by Inheritance belonged, then void by the death of Attercliffe late Abbot there, commanding the pryor and covent of the ſaid monaſtery to receive and obey him as Abbot.

Inq: 29. H. 8. poſt mortem Thom̃ Dñi Berkeley in Canc.
Carta: 27. Aprill 26. H. 8. in caſtro de Berkeley.

And, this ſhall bee the place, whither I have often referred this antient and pyous family to viewe at once, the damage it ſuffered both in honor and profit by thoſe devouring Acts of the diſſolution of Monaſteries in the 27ᵗʰ and 31ᵗʰ yeares of king Henry the 8ᵗʰ, whereby and by the ſtatute of Chantries (amongſt other things) this family loſt the Advowſons and preſentations to divers Abbyes, Nunryes, and Pryories, As this of Croxton, and of Kirkeby, and of Chawcomb, and of Burton lazers, and of Sᵗ John Baptiſt in Melton Mowbray in Leiceſterſhire; Of Combe in Warrwickſhire, Of Sᵗ Auguſtines, and of Sᵗ Katharines, and of Mary Magdalens by Briſtoll, and Of Longbridge by Berkeley, and of Tinterne in Glouceſterſhire, Of the Pryories of Newenham and of Eppeworth in the Iſle of Axholme; Of ffountaines, Of the Abbey of Byland, and of the Pryory of Newburgh in the county of Yorke, and of divers others, as ſcatteringly appeares in theſe relations, where alwayes with ſolemn proceſſions and other honorable rights and ceremonies (I might ſay with incenſe and perfumes) they were received as founders, And where the memoriall of their honorable atcheivements were recorded; And of 80. knights fees at leaſt, which thoſe and other Ab-|byes and houſes of religion held of them, as Sᵗ Peters of Glouc., the Abbot of Kingſwood, the Pryor of Sempringham, the Abbot of Leiceſter, the Pryor of Lewes, The Pryor of Axholme, the Abbot de valle dei, the Pryor of Haverholme, the Abbot of Geroduu, [ſic] the Pryor of the hoſpitall of Sᵗ Johns Jeruſalem in England, the Pryor of Lawnd, the Pryor of Grace dieu, the Pryor of Nuneaton, the Pryor of Kirkeby, the Abbot of Sileby, the Abbot of Stonly, the Abbot of Myrivale, and of more then forty Chantries mentioned in theſe relations; for which, beſides their daily prayers for the happineſs and welfare of the livinge, (wherein was noe ſuperſtition,) they paid to this family many anuall rents and ſervices, and alſo paid

See before fol: [537]
Annis. 27ᵗʰ et. 31. H. 8.
Anno. 1. E. 6.
Claus: 52. E. 3. m. 28.
Pat: 7. E. 3. ps. 1. m: 15.
claus: 45. E. 3. m. 36.
Pat: 48. E. 3. m. 23.
Pat: 14. E. 4. ps. 2. m. 11.
Pat: 9. R. 2. ps. 2. m. 25. 26.
Eſch: 11. H. 6. poſt mortem Thom̃. ducis Norfolk.
pat: 14. H. 6. ps. 700 1. m: 6.
pat. 1. E. 4. ps. 6. m. ult.
P̃tita in ſc̃a c̃io. 13. H. 6.
pat. 19. R. 2. ps. 1. m: 26.
pat. 20. R. 2. ps. 2. m. 14.
pat. 20. R. 2. ps. 2. m. ult.
Eſch: 1. H. 4. poſt mort̃ Ducis Norf.

paid them releifes and efcuage, did them fealty and homage, fent their men to ayd and attend them in their voyages in the warrs, yeilded them aid and contribution for the marriage of their eldeſt daughters, and for making their eldeſt fons knights; brought up, and inſtructed divers of their children, received and kept as Corrodies, many of their old unferviceable fervants; fuch as old ffrañ Inchmore and Richard Cooke als Miller now are in the family of the lady Elizabeth Berkeley at Cranford; with other like duties incident to founders right, and to the tenures of the manors and lands and quantities of the knights fees which they held of them by knights fervice, and in focage, now extinct and devoured by thofe mercileffe Acts. **Neither** therein hath ended the damage which this noble family fuffered by thofe acts of diffolution; for the Crown having fince given and fold away not only thofe manors and lands holden of this family as aforefaid, but almoſt all the reſt of thofe monaſticall poffeffions, and therein referved tenures of themfelves by knights fervice in capite; now at this day each manor and almoſt each freeholder in each Village hath fome fmall pcell or other of that Capite land intermixt or inclofed with their elder poffeffions, formerly held of this family by knights fervice: whereby I have known this family within my memory to have loſt more then ten thoufand pounds, wch otherwife, but for thofe lands in cheife, had juſtly and legally accrued to it; A mifcheife alfo daily increafing to this and other great lords of Seigniories, through the frequent exchanges and inclofures, (the effects of peace,) And by ye parcelling out of Manors made by great lords upon fales to their feverall ten^ts, for ye better advancement of their prifes: whereby as not one wardſhip amongſt twenty now accrueth to this family wch otherwife had happened: foe, the Court of Wards and liveryes bringeth | an hundred fold more profit to the Crown then formerly before thofe Statutes it did, A growing perticular mifcheife likely to proceede to a generall inconvenience.

Margin: Efch: 27. E. 1. et. 35. E. 3. et. 1. H. 4. et. 1. E. 4. poſt mort de mowbraies claus: 11. H. 6. m. 8. fee before in ye life of Maurice ye 5th [615] And of James the firſt. fol: [537] Stat: 27. 31. et. 38. H. 8. et. 1. E. 6.

Margin: 701

His lawe suites.

Scarce was the laſt lord cold under the Tombe, before an unkind controverfy broke out between this lord and his only brother Maurice, about the poffeffion of the manor of Mangottesfeild, the place where their father gave up his foule to God, and that manor to them that now contended about it.

With Maurice, his brother in lawe Sr Nicholas Poynz and his mother in law the lady Cicely tooke part, And to the uttermoſt of their powers abetted his caufe, who made title by the expreffe words of his fathers will, proved by the Judges and others his fathers executors, and approved of by the lord Thomas himfelf, who alfo was a witnes thereto, and prefent at his fathers death and laſt confirmation thereof.

But

But this guift by will this lord Thomas would not admit, for that (faith hee) the feoffment of that manor made by the lord his father to the Duke of Norfolk and others, to the use of his last will and for performance thereof, was never executed in this manor of Mangottesfeild by the express inhibition of his said father; And on purpose soe to declare it hee kept Courts there in his own person and in his own name, and not in the name of the said Duke and his Co-feoffees, which was otherwise in all the rest of the manors comprized in the said feoffment; Alledging further, That his father builded upon Mangottesfeild house with the goods, knotts, trayles, carved works, and other ornaments of his, fetched from his house at Yate, which his unkle the lord Maurice gave him, to the value of two hundred marks, another manifest signe (faith this lord) that the lord his father never meant That his brother Maurice should have it, but hee whose goods had built and adorned it. And further alleadged, That whereas his father had allotted unto him in marriage with the lady Mary his wife, divers lands to the value of 100^{li} p ann̄: for their maintenance, his father retained fifty marks yearly of that hundred pound by the space of three years towards the building of Mangottesfeild house, which amounteth to one hundred pounds, Another declaration of his fathers mind (faith hee) That hee meant not that his son Maurice should have it; Also this lord Thomas alleadged further, that the manor of Mangottesfeild and the manor of Bitton doe adjoyne togeather, and have continued togeather in one mans possession many hundreds of yeares, And that there is an hill called charnells hill parcell of the manor of Bitton, and in the bottom of the said Hill is a great square poole called charnells poole adjoyning to Mangottesfeild hill, and in the end of the middle of the said poole his said father builded a newe mill from the ground, which is parcell of the manor of Bitton, which his brother since the death of his father hath entred into, and fished and destroyed the fish to the value of forty pound. And lastly (so farre prevailed hee) that hee caused the lady Ciceley, mother in lawe to them both, (yet shee tooke part with Maurice,) to avow That shee kept as well the Seale of Armes as the Signet of her husband by the space of five daies after his death, And in that time sealed two parts of the said will, being tripartite, (called Counterpanes,) with the said Seal of Armes. Thus, with much unbrotherly agitacōn was tost that controversy till the death of this lord, what time Maurice had the possession of the house and conigre,[1] and this lord of the rest of the manor; After whose death his widowe the lady Anne in behalf of her young son the lord Henry, banded this ball of discord anewe and with more bitternes, as after followeth; Declaring thereby, that her incantations had more powerfully prevailed

chartulæ in Castro de Berkeley

---

[1] Rabbit Warren. [Ed.]

prevailed with her husband then stood with the affection of a brother, or the honor of their fathers memory. Of which lady it now follows that I write, as the second of this lords wives.

His Wives.

His First Wife.

carta in castro de Berkeley.

fol: 673.

703

His first wife.

div'sa munimenta in castro de Berkeley.

div'si comp̄i in castro de Berkeley.

Inqu: in com. Glouc. 29. H. 8. p̃t mort Thom̃

Volunt: Thome de Berkeley: 24. H. 8.

originall: 25. H. 8. rot: 34. in fc̃āc̃io.

That it was intended and accordingly articled under seale That this lord should have marryed Katharine daughter of Thomas Howard Duke of Norfolk, and that part of the marriage portion was accordingly paid, hath been already written in the life of this lords father; But whether nearnes of bloud, they being cozens in the fourth degree, or the death of Katharine, or dislike either of | the parties to the other, or what else hindered the consummation of that marriage, I find not: But the same 17th yeare of king Henry the 8th hee tooke to wife Mary the daughter of George lord Hastings; the greatest part of whose marriage portion the lord Thomas his father in the second yeare after assigned over to Sr George Throgmerton, for payment of part of the Dowry hee gave with his daughter Mirriell Berkeley, marryed to his eldest son Robert, as hath been said: And for maintenance, this lord and his wife had one hundred pounds a yeare from his father; By her this lord had noe issue, though they lived lovingly togeather neare eight yeares; And dyed in the same 24th yeare of Henry the 8th about six weekes after this lords father; ffor whose Joynture and dower the said lord her father in lawe tooke spetiall care that it might bee quietly enjoyed by her, if shee survived her husband, without the impeachment of his own wife, As by his will made but a few dayes before his death appeares.

Howbeit, this lords sorrow for her death was not soe stronge or prevalent to hinder him many monthes from flying to the marriage bed of another as followes.

His Second Wife.

Stow et al.

The second wife of this lord Thomas, was Anne the daughter of Sr John Savage of ffrodsham in Cheshire knight, of whom Stowe, & others thus write; That on the 25th day of January in the 24th yeare of his raigne, king Henry the 8th privily married the lady Anne Boleine, what time Mrs Anne Savage bare up her traine, and was her self shortly after marryed to the lord Berkeley; which marriage seemes to have been contrived by the said King and Queen, or one of them.

The father of this lord dyed on the 22th of January as hath been said; The lady Mary this lords first wife dyed within less then two monthes after, And in Aprill following was this lords marriage with the said Anne Savage.

The portion which shee brought in marriage was five hundred marks in money, paiable at certaine days after, some whereof incurred not in her husbands life time.

Carta. 21. Maij 25. H. 8. in castro de Berkeley.

The Joynture assured by her husband in May next after mariage | were the manors of Melton Mowbray, Segrave, and Sileby in the county of Leicester; Bretby, Rostlaston and Coton in the County of Derby; and Callowdon in the county of the City of Coventry; which was after increased with the manors of Mountsorrell, Goscote hundred, and Coldoverton, And w:th the thirds of the manors of Sages, Tetbury, Daglingworth, fframpton, Manygford, Aspele, Hovingham, and of the lands in Calais, assigned to her in lieu of Dower.

704 Carta p:rdicta.

Esch: 2. 3. Ph: et. M. in Canc. Carta. 3. 4. Ph: Mar in Castro de Berkel: Comp: 20. H. 8. in castro de Berkeley.

Shee was a lady of a masculine spirit, over-powerfull with her husband, seldom at rest with her self, never wanting matter of suite or discontent to work upon, till the full age of that son which shee carryed in her womb nine weeks and fower days after the death of her husband: Shee was in the way to have proved a fruitfull lady, and to have replenished this family with males and females, whereof much scarcity hath in late discents been in the eldest line; for in the tenth month after marriage shee brought her husband as faire a daughter as lived in her time; And conceived againe the next night after her churching day, and brought a son, (of whom I am next to write,) as shee declared the time of her conception to him, and hee to mee, and as the sequell manifested to bee true, the birth being just forty weeks after, though the father lived not to see the day; Of complection shee was of a comely brown, of a middle stature, And, above all the ladies of her days, noted to bee most tender hearted to her children; And to them foe over and above reason indulgent, as not contentedly shee admitted them out of her sight, whereby they after com-playned of that want of Learning which a juster education should have afforded their estates and parentage; ffor whose sakes and the memoriall of her husbands love shee continued a widowe all her life: noe lady more constant to her religion, for from the instruction of her youth wherewith in the ten first years of king Henry the 8:th shee was seasoned, shee never would depart; which was the cause why Queene Mary and the Clergy of her time exceedingly favoured her.

Countes of Ormond: L:d Henry.

The places where most shee lived after her husbands death were first at S:t Augustines green by Bristoll, then at Yate, then at Kentish Towne by London, then at the Bishop of Bangors great house in Shewelane by S:t Andrews Church in Holborne, which shee held by lease. Then againe at Yate in Gloucestershire, And lastly at Callowdon by Coventry, where shee dyed intestate in October in the sixth yeare of Queen Elizabeth, A:o 1564. then of the age of 58. yeares or neare there-abouts;

Div:si compi hospic̃ in castro de Berkeley.

Ex. relaõne Hen: Dñi Berkeley.

Depos: in Canc: Sub mag: Sigillo in ca: de Berkeley.

abouts; And lyeth buried in the Church of S.t Michâll in Coventry; who may not foe sleep in peace, but that I must after and often call her suites and actions into question, in | the life of the lord Henry her son, to whose time I doe transmit many of them, as being prosecuted in his name, and concerned his inheritance.

<small>Administr: dat: 31 Jan: 7 : Eliz: 1564. sub sigillo in castr̃ de Berkeley.</small>

The administration of the goods and chattles of this lady was the 31.th of January following committed to the lord Henry her son, who for the honor of her memory, paid more then her goods which came to his hands amounted unto, which sometimes after, for his discharge, hee pleaded.

<small>Ex relacõne ipĩus Henrici: et Hancorne et Burbage tunc attendeñ.

Anne Gastrell her waiting gentle-woman.</small>

Country huswifery seemed to bee an essentiall part of this ladies constitution; A lady, that living at Yate, Callowdon, and other her Country houses, would betimes in Winter and Somer mornings make her walkes to visit her stable, barnes, day house, pultry, swinetroughs, and the like; Which huswifery her daughter in lawe the lady Katharine Howard, wife to the lord Henry her son, seeming to decline, and to betake her self to the delights of youth and greatnes, shee would sometimes to those about her, sweare, by Gods blessed sacrament, this gay girle will begger my son Henry: As the lord her son, and other of her servants have told mee: **And** if shee were to bee judged as Phillip de Comines doth King Lewis the 11.th his master, That hee was a good King because hee had more vertues than vices, I would soe conclude of this lady: But soe much remaines to bee said of her in the life of the lord Henry her son as I will leave my Judgment in Suspence.

And it might seem tedious to this family for mee to write soe largely of this lady as I have received from Anne Gastrell the widow of Thomas Harsfeild of Nibley, there living for ten years after I maryed into that towne, the nearest and eldest attendant about her of all this ladies gentlewomen untill her death.

His issue.

<small>Inqu: 29. H. 8. in scᵃcĩo: 1 year old post mort Thome Comp: Franſh recept 1. et 2. Eliz. in castr̃ de Berkeley.</small>

The children which this lord Thomas had by his last wife were only two; Henry born nine weeks and fower dayes after his fathers death, whose life is half a Volume of it self; And Elizabeth then scarce three quarters old, who was in the first of Queen Elizabeth marryed to Thomas Butler Earle of Ormond, whom in y.̃ 2.th of Eliz: shee followed into Ireland accompanied with her mother and brother from London to | Yate, thence to Bristoll, where shee tooke shipping for Ireland.

What portion the Earle had with her in marriage, I have not found; Howbeit having noe certainty left by her father, her brother gave her one hundred pounds by the yeare for many years togeather, both before and after her marriage.

Her

Her Joynture was altogeather of lands in Ireland, made in the 4ᵗʰ yeare of Queen Elizabeth: But afterwards fhee and her hufband not agreeing, An award was upon the labor of the lord Henry her brother made in the 11ᵗʰ of Queen Elizabeth between them, by the mediation of Thomas Howard Duke of Norfolk and of Thomas Ratcliffe Earle of Suffex, to whom their differences were referred; That fhee for her prefent alimony and maintenance, (then being feperate from her hufband meerely arifing from the antipathy of their natures,) fhould have 90ˡⁱ p Anñ out of her hufbands lands, which was duly paid by his Receivor during her life, which ended at Briftoll in the 24ᵗʰ yeare of Queen Elizabeth, Anno, 1582. leaving noe iffue behind her, nor for ought I could learne ever conceived by him: A lady whom the lord Henry her brother, and others of his old fervants, would report to have been the faireft that lived in the Courts of Edward the fixth and of Queen Mary, and foe noted in thofe dayes.

Carta in caftro de Berkeley.

Carta in caftro de Berkeley.

His Seales.

This lords time was fo fhort after his fathers death, And the name of Thomas one and the fame to them both, As alfo the ftile, That hee never altered either his fathers broad feale or privy Signet: Only I have obferved, That on the reverfe of his broad feale fixed to his laft will and Teftament, The privy feale or fignet, (being Mowbrays Lion rampant,) is five times imprinted, one, three, and one. See the figures in his fathers life. |

His death and place of Buriall.

Inq: in Canc:

Inq: in Sc̄cio:

I will satisfy this title with two records of Inquisitions found after the death of this lord Thomas, in one yeare in one county; The one at Wotton Underedge the 20th of August in the 29th of king Henry the 8th, by Commission in the nature of a Mandamus, the other at Marshfeild the 10th of October following, by the Escheator alone, virtute officij sui; The first returned into the Chancery, the other into the Exchequer. The first layeth down the recoveryes had by Judge Brudnell and others against this lords unkle in Ester Terme in the 4th and . 5th of Henry the 8th of the manors of Tetbury, Daglingworth, Sages, and the rest of his lands formerly mentioned, And how this lords father dyed the 24th of Henry the 8th indebted—627^{li} 3^s 6^d,—over and besides—488^{li} 16^s 6^d—in legacies given by his will; And the Anuities given by him for life, whereof many are formerly mentioned; And this lord Thomas his son dyed the 22th of September in the 26th of Henry the 8th Anno . 1534.

The second Inquisition layeth down the purchases of Bitton and Mangottesfeild, made by the lord Maurice of Mr Dormer in the 11th of Henry the 8th; And hee of Hussey in the 7th year of the said kinge; and how the said lord Maurice purchased the manor of Elmington of Mr Willm Hussey, son and heire of Margaret Blunt maryed to John Hussey, father of the said William, by fine in Ester Terme in the 12th of Henry the 8th; And how, when this lord Thomas dyed the 22th of September in the 26th of Henry the 8th Anno . 1534, Then Elizabeth was his daughter and heire, one yeare old; But that Anne his wife was then with childe, who since brought forth a son called Henry, the 26th of November following. **Thus** these Inquisitions.

This lord Thomas in the first yeare of his Barony, wisely taking into consideration the debts of his father and unkle wherewith the lands discended upon him were charged; And the Joynture and dower of the lady Cicely his mother in lawe of seaven of his manors, whereof mention hath been made in his fathers life; And the lands also which his younger brother had for his life: And having also some scores of his own uncut out incurred in his fathers life, in those eight years of his first marriage, what time hee had but one hundred pounds p ann̄. exhibition, for the maintenance of himself his wife and family, And part of that also not well paid as before appeares; And observing withall the many Anuities issuing | out of those lands given by his said Ancestors and himself still in being, And of the charge of children like to grow upon him, determined to cast off for a time the popular and

vaine

vaine fame of great houſkeeping, and the many expences incident thereto, And to ſojourne at a certaine rate, wᶜʰ hee would not exceed; And doth bargaine accordingly with the Counteſſe of Wilſhere, who then lived at Stone by Thames ſide, a mile from Dartford in Kent, for the lord of himſelf, his wife, two gentlewomen, and ſix men, at the rate of 25ˢ. 4ᵈ. the weeke for them all; And ſoe in June in the 26ᵗʰ yeare of Henry the 8ᵗʰ. ſets from his houſe at Yate in Glouceſterſhire towards London, and from thence comes to Stone the 15ᵗʰ of the next month, where, after a ſhort ſickneſs, hee dyes on Satterday the 19ᵗʰ day of September in the ſaid 26ᵗʰ yeare of the raigne of king Henry the 8ᵗʰ. Anno. 1534. And was there buryed the Teuſday after, the 22ᵗʰ of that Septʳ, which the ſaid Inquiſitions make the day of his death, then of the age of 29 years or neare thereabouts, whereof hee had ſit lord one yeare and eight months after the death of his father; And of all his anceſtors had the ſhorteſt life, yet longe, by the well imployment of his life.

div'ſa munimenṯ in caſtro de Berkeley.

Liberac: Thome dni Berkeley. 24. H. 8. et Henrici dni Berkeley 2. et. 3. Ph: et Mar̄.

In an accompt of one of his houſhold officers of that time, are theſe words, which I beſt beleive and followe; **Memorandum**, paid to my lady Wilſhire the 21ᵗʰ day of September in the 26ᵗʰ yeare of the raigne of King Henry the 8ᵗʰ in full conſideration for the board of my lord Berkeley, my lady, and all their ſervants, unto the ſaid twenty firſt of September in the ſaid year and raigne—12ˡⁱ. 13ˢ. 4ᵈ—which further ſhewes that hee came to ſojourne there the 15ᵗʰ of July before, himſelf, wife, two gentlewomen, and ſix men; And ſoe for nyne weeks till hee was buryed, paid as aforeſaid after—25ˢ. 4ᵈ. the weeke.

Comp: in caſtro de Berkeley et aī munimenta.

Concerning whoſe death and funerall are theſe further fragments, remaining in the accompts of his ſervants of that time, made to his wife the week after, which are all I have found of him.

Charges about the funeralls of my lord Berkeley the 19ᵗʰ day of September in the 26ᵗʰ yeare of Henry the 8ᵗʰ.

    ffirſt to a maſon for raiſing the foote of the herſe—10ᵈ.
    For making of his Cheſt—12ᵈ
    For half a hundred of boards—14ᵈ
    For 4 Buſhells of bran to lay within the Cheſt—12ᵈ
    For a winding ſheet—20ᵈ.
    For maſſes the 19ᵗʰ day of September at his death—3ˢ
    For dirige the ſame day—2ˢ

709

To

>   To the poore in Almes the fame day—12ᵈ
>   To Hall and three children for bearing of torches—12ᵈ
>   Itm at dirige on Thurfday 2. preifts—8ᵈ
>   Itm at dirige on Fryday 7. preifts—4ˢ 8ᵈ
> *A maffe conftantly rated at 4ᵈ a peece.*   Itm 5 maffes of the five wounds—20ᵈ
>   Itm. 3. maffes downe of the trentall—12ᵈ
>   Itm, remaineth more of the trentall—9ˢ
>   Itm offering pence—2ˢ 8ᵈ
>   Itm to the clarke—4ᵈ

And in another bill thus,

A place neare Stone by Thames fide.   Itm for the hire of a horfe from London to Stone in Kent, to ride to my lords month mind—16ᵈ

And in another bill thus

Itm received of my lady on Thurfday the 17ᵗʰ of September in the 26ᵗʰ of Henry the 8ᵗʰ xxᵈ whereof paid for a wherry for Doctor Nicholas a Phifition to Greenhithe —2ˢ For the doctors cofts at Greenhith all night—6ᵈ

I have been told from his fon the lord Henry, and by two other of this lords fervants, That hee dyed of a furfeit of cherries; which I beleive, though their feafon feem gone longe before his death; Neither is any of his anceftors found to bee better bred nor of greater hope, who for his fweet condition and for a mind as innocent as his years, and for his rare endowments, well deferves to bee commended to everlafting memory, that hee may bee permanent foe much the longer in the life of an Hiftory, by how much the thred of his naturall life was cut fhorter by the fates.

> Short was thy life, yet liv'ft thou ever,
> Death has his due, yet dyeft thou never.
> All well may wonder how foe youthfull years,
> Could frame a life where foe much worth appeares |

The lands whereof hee dyed feized.

710

The manors and lands which this lord Thomas left to difcend to Elizabeth his only daughter and heire at his death, And after to the lord Henry his fon, borne nine weeks and fower days after his death, were in effect the fame whereof his father and unkle dyed feized, vizᵗ

The

The manor of Melton Mowbray,
The manor of Segrave,
The manor of Sileby,
The manor of Coldoverton,
The manor of Mountforrell, called fuperior et inferior.
The manor of Dalby Chawcomb,
The manor of Thurneby,
The manor of Thorpe Sachevill & Twyford,
The manor of Witherley,
The hundred of Gofcote,
Divers Lands in Welby als Oleby.
} In the County of Leicefter.

The manor of Sages,
The manor of Bitton,
The manor of Ailmington, which was to Maurice his brother.
The manor of Upton St Leonards, called Grovecourt.
The manor of Mangottesfeild,
The manor of Tetbury,
The manor of Daglingworth,
The manor of Yate, was but a leafe for yeares.
The fourth part of the manor of Brokenburrow, in Almondfbury prifh,
Divers lands and Tenements in Thornbury, containing - 190 - acres,
A meffuage and divers lands in Berkeley,
Two and twenty marks rent out of fframpton upon Seaverne,
} In the County of Gloucefter.

The manor of ffenyftanton,
The manor of Hilton,
The manor of Auconbury,
The manor of Wefton,
} In the County of Huntington.

711

The

The manor of Chatterys,
The manor of Guyherne and Murroe. } In the County of Cambridge.

The manor of Bosham with Buckfold,
The manor of Thorney,
The manor of ffuntington. } In the County of Suffex.

The manor of Bretby,
The manor of Linton,
The manor of Coton,
The manor of Roftlafton,
The manor of Repingdon, } In the County of Derby.

The manor of Hovingham, in the County of Yorke.
The manor of Maningford Bruce, in the County of Wilts.
Certaine Lands and teñts in Thorpe, and Kingfton in the County of Nottingham.
The manor of Callowdon in the County of the City of Coventry and Warrwicke,
Divers lands and tenements in Stivechall, by Coventry.

The manor of Afpele, in the Parifh of Tamworth.
The manor of Thurlafton,
The manor of fflekenhoe. } In the County of Warrwick.

The moities of the Lo.ps of Catherlagh, Oldcroffe, and other lands. } In the Kingdome of Ireland.

Lands and Tenements in Calais of the value of—6^{li} 13^s 4^d of old rent.

ffowerteen pounds p.r Anñ out of Bromly, Lee, Gateborne, and Scothurne, in the Counties of Lincolne and Surrey.

Origin. 2. et 3.
Ph : et Mar.
ps. 2. rot. 73.

ffor thefe lands feverall Inquifitions, (in all or moft counties,) were found after the death of this lord in the 28th and twenty ninth yeare of the raigne of Henry the 8th, and in the third of king Edward the fixth ; And of them Henry lord Berkeley

Berkeley aforesaid, after hee had been one and twenty years in ward, sued his livery in the second and third of Phillip and Mary: And therein were valued to him at—992^{li} 18^s 03^d.

At which time also reverted unto him upon the death of king Edwd the sixth, for default of issue male of the body of king Henry the 7th, according to the entaile of Willm Marques Berkeley, as in his life is related, these manors, vizt

> The Castle and manor of Berkeley,
> The manor of Hame,
> The manor of Appleridge,
> The manor of Slimbridge,
> The manor of Hurst,
> The manor of Cowley,
> The manor of Alkington,   } In the County of Gloucester.
> The manor of Came,
> The manor of Wotton underedge,
>   with the Advowson,
> The manor of Symondsall,
> The manor of Hinton,
> The manor of Erlingham.

The manor of Portbury in the County of Somerset.
The 4th part of the manor of Tyborne als
Marybone, in the County of Middlesex.
The manors of Kington magna, and Kington parva, in the County
   of Warrwicke.
And these later were valued to him at—687^{li} 5^s

And also in the second yeare of Queen Elizabeth reverted unto him the manors of Kenet and Kentford in the Counties of Cambridge and Suffolk, for default of issue male of the bodies of Richard Willoughby and Edward Willoughby, according to the entaile of Willm Marques Berkeley made to them, as in his life hath been related; And these, in the livery which hee then sued, were valued at—34^{li} 6^s and then yielded in rent but—59^s 4^d more.

Lib: in cur̃ Ward: Spec: lib: 16 Junij 2. Eliz:

fol: 569.

> Soe all the lands for which Henry
> lord Berkeley sued livery m. 2.&.3.   }   li.   s.   d.
> Ph: & Mary, were valued at   1714 - 9 - 3

And

And alſo hee further had the Manor of Weſton iuxta Baldocke in the County of Hartford, recovered upon the ſuite in lawe from y:e patentees of king E. 6., (as after followeth in his life,) valued at 36 li. or thereab:ts |

713
Rate of his Livery

The fine which the lord Henry paid upon his livery for the lands diſcended from his father, was—496 li. 9 s. 1 d.

The fine which hee paid for the lands reverted to him after the death of king Edward the ſixth, was—343 li. 12 s. 6 d.

The Application and uſe of his life.

The uſe.

1. **In** Berkeley Caſtle on a file of bills, is one for the laſt ſuite of Clothes that ever were made for this lords wearing, which hee made at Stone, the 4 th. of September, but fifteen dayes before hee dyed, then in the 29 th. of his age ; Thus,

	s.	d.
Item paid for a yard and a quarter of black kerſie for my lords hoſe,	2	11
Item for two yards and a half of black fuſtion for a doublet for my lord,	2	1
Item for two yards of Lininge for the ſame doublet, - -	1	3
And ſo of the reſt of the parcells. In the whole makeing and all,	9	7

Sum—9 s. ,, 07 d.

Which I hope the divine providence hath reſerved for his poſterity as an example of moderation, and to avoid exceſſe in this kind : Poore is the condition of that man that muſt from his taylor take his reputation.

2. **Againe,** from the ſhort life of this lord his poſterity is admoniſhed, not to rely the everlaſting affaires of their life to come upon the gliding ſlipperines and running ſtreame of this uncertaine life ; Neither to ſojourne longe in ſinfull ſecurity, but to frame their premiſes as they would have the concluſion ; And by conſidering how the bud of this their Anceſtors life was cut from the ſtalk before it flowered, to meditate often on the fall of theire leafe, for none more likely than hee to have ſeen the ſeed ripened. And to deſire with this their anceſtor rather a good life then a longe, non quam diù ſed quam benè ; And to know with him that one day vertuouſly ſpent is to bee highlier valued then a longe life conſumed in vanity and prophanenes. |

714

3. **Againe,** when this family ſhall ſeriouſly conſider the generous fraternity and love that alwaies floured between this lord Thomas father and his elder brother the lord

lord Maurice, whofe individuall foules foe entirely comunicated their true affections each to other, that they feemed at once to bee all in all, and all, in every part of each other; And when in the next difcent this family fhall as ferioufly confider the bitter enmity of the two fons of the faid lord Thomas, this Thomas the fixth and Maurice his brother, which reconciled not till death, with the ill effects, It cannot but acknowledge, That tribulations and croffes waite and are let in as well at their doores as of inferior families: And therefore when they fee but one morrowe day to bee interpofed between fuch fweet affections and unnaturall difcords, It muft needs know it felf ftill fubject to the like adverfities, And beare theire faile thereafter.

715 } blank
716 }

Finis Thomæ, ejusdem nominis, Sexti.

The Life of Henry the First

The life of Henry lord Berkeley the firſt of that name, ſtiled in writings Sir Henry Berkeley knight, Lord Berkeley, Mowbray, Segrave, and Breouſe; never otherwiſe written from his cradle to his grave; **And** was Avus, or as our Anceſtors the Saxons called, eald-fader, And wee at this day grandfather to George now lord Berkeley.

And may bee called Henry the harmleſſe, or poſthumus Henry.

Contemporary with King Henry the 8th, Kinge Edward the 6th, Queen Mary, Queen Elizabeth, and King James, from 1534. till 1613.

The longe life of this lord Henry I deliver under theſe ſixteen titles;

1.—**His** birth and education, fol: 718.
2.—**His** reſtitution to Berkeley Caſtle and to the Barony of Berkeley: fol: 727.
3.—**His** lawe ſuites, fol: 741.
4.—**His** ſale of lands, fol: 817.
5.—**His** buildings, fol: 825.
6.—**His** recreations and delights, fol: 826.
7.—**His** hoſpitality, fol: 828.
8.—**His** rewards to Servants, fol: 832.
9.—**His** Almes and devotions, fol: 833.
10.—**His** miſcellaniæ or various paſſages, fol: 835.
11.—**His** Wives, fol: 849.
12.—**His** iſſue, fol: 863.
13.—**His** ſeales of Armes, fol: 875.
14.—**His** death and place of buriall, fol: 876.
15.—**The** lands whereof hee dyed ſeized, fol: 882.
16.—**The** application and uſe of his life, fol: 883. |

His

718

His Birth and education.

How piously the grandfather of this lord Henry left his life at Mangottesfeild in the 24th of king Henry the 8th, and peace (as hee supposed) between his two sons Thomas and Maurice; how his eldest son Thomas, this lords father, endeavored to wrest that manor of Mangottesfeild from the said Maurice his younger brother, and how the said Thomas dyed within two years after at Stone in Kent, in the 26th of that king in the midst of that catching contention; leaving Elizabeth a sucking infant not one year old, his daughter and heire; And the lady Anne great with child, delivered of this lord Henry nyne weekes and fower days after his death, To whom king Henry the eighth that gave his name was godfather; hath in part already been declared.

Comp. ministr. 14. Eliz: pat. 1 Sept. 34 H. 8. Mich. rec. 14 Eliz: rot. 72. cm rem thesaur in Sc̃c̃io.

It hath also formerly been written in the life of the said lord Thomas the 5th, this lords grandfather, how by his Will hee gave to the said Maurice his second son, (amongst other lands,) the Manors of Dalby in Leicestershire for his life in present possession, And also the manor of Mountforrell in the same county for his life also, after his will should bee performed;

Now after the death of the lord Thomas her husband, It was by the procurement of this lady Anne found by Inquisition, That her husband dyed seized of the said manors of Dalby and Mountforrell, and also of the manor of Thorpe Sachevill in the same County; which the said Maurice conceived to bee to his double prejudice, espetially this lord Henry son and heire of the said Thomas being then in minority and the kings ward: first becaufe Thorpe Sachvill is part of his manor of Dalby, which now is taken from him under the pretence of being a Manor of it self; secondly, becaufe by the said Inquisition the king is intituled presently to those two Manors of his: Whereas Dalby should presently bee to him in poss'ion, And Mountforrell also after his fathers will performed: Hereupon Maurice tenders his plea in Chancery in nature of a traverse, to avoid this part of the Inquisition soe unjustly found by meanes of this lady Anne his sister in lawe, who loved him not; whereupon issue is joyned between Maurice and the kings Atturney generall tryable by Jury, urged and defended by this lady Anne, in behalf of her self and her son Henry the Kings ward.

Inqu: 28. H. 8. post mort. Thome in Cancell.

Plita in Cancẽ. octabis martiñ 28. H. 8.

The

The Lady on the contrary maintained, That Thorpe Sachvill was noe part of Dalby manor, but a Manor of it felf, with a court baron | and a Leete yearly kept there; And alfo, that the tenants of Dalby never atturned to the feoffees, whereby Maurice could have noe eftate in that Manor from his father. And alfo, that there is both great Dalby and litle Dalby in that County, And in the feoffment which paffed by lre of Atturney it is not expreffed whether was meant unto him by his father great Dalby or litle Dalby. And alfo that Henry her fon was heir in taile to that manor, which Maurice claimed by vertue of a fine levyed by Maurice Berkeley his grandfather to himfelf and Ifable his wife, and to the heires males of their two bodies.

Breviats in Berkeley Caftle. 719

Fine: 10. H. 7. in banco.

Against Maurice alfo, for Mangottesfeild manor, fhee alleadged, That her hufband was feized of all that manor fave the houfe and the Conigre, and thereof dyed feized, And fo her fon (the kings ward) was in by difcent from his father: Against Maurice alfo, for the manor of Elmington given him likewife by his fathers will and to the heirs males of his body, fhee alleadged, That that guift was to him by a firft Will, which by making of a fecond was revoked: And that after the feoffment made by the faid lord Thomas his father to the ufe of his will, hee made a Leafe for lives of the manor place demefnes and Tenem^{ts}, referving a rent to him and his heires, with a claufe of diftrefs for nonpayment; Which rent muft refort to Henry her fon; Thus this lady Anne drew into fuite and queftion whatfoever lands this younger brother Maurice had in any County.

And becaufe her mafculine fpirit would beare noe coales at Maurices hands, whereas hee and his company had not longe before endamaged her hufband in fpoiling of Mangottesfeild poole and the Mill there, whereof hee had gotten the poffeffion, as hath alfo been faid; fhee incited James Berkeley of Bradley by Wotton, John Berkeley and Brice Berkeley his two fons, and thirty others who by her means they brought with them, the 12th of June in the 26th of Henry the 8th, immediately after her hufbands departure from Yate towards London, to reenter againe upon the faid Mill and poole, and riotoufly to break down the head thereof, And from thence to carry away tench and breames to the value of forty fhillings: For which fact by the purfuite of the faid Maurice, they were fhortly after indicted and fined. Which riotous deed the malice of the faid lady borne to Maurice foe well approved, That (her hufband dying the 19th of September following,) fhee the 28th of the next month, by an ample patent made the faid James Berkeley her Receivour, Surveyor, Auditor, and Woodward, of all her manors and lands in the

Carta in caftro de Berkeley.

Counties

720 Counties of Derby, Leicester, Huntington, and Gloucester, which shee either had in joynture or by leafe from the lady Cicely as Administratrix to her husband, as a reward for his said riotous fact.

And this is that Brice Berkeley whose daughter and heire Elizabeth was after maryed to Edward Berkeley son and heire of this Maurice, as formerly hath been written.

Pat: 1 Sept. 34. H. 8.
Mich: rec: 14. Eliz. rot. 72. in sc°cio cum: rem: thesaur̄
Comp: minis. 14. Eliz: in Sc°cio.

And for the wardship of this lord Henry, It was first granted by Henry the 8th to Robert Earle of Suffex his Chamberlen, with the exhibition of — 14li 6s 8d issuing out of fframpton upon Seaverne, and after by him assigned to this lady Anne.

Carta dat: 2. Januar: 26. H. 8. in castro de Berkeley.

It now followeth to declare, that forthwith after her husbands funerall the said lady Anne came to live at St. Augustines greene, and from thence returned to her house at Yate; And in the meane time, within one week after her churching, the more to increase the flame of the former fire (which by her addition of fuell had too much flamed between the two brothers,) shee wound in one Alexander Dowle of Thornbury, son of Walter, son of Thomas and of Alice his wife, daughter and heire of one Phillpot and of Alice his wife, to sell unto her in fee simple for twenty pounds in money a messuage and threescore acres of Land in Acton Ilger, which was wrongfully with power and force held from him by Giles Poyntz, (brother of Sir Nicholas,) And that hee being a poore man and not able to sue in the kings Courts for the same against the said Giles, did therefore sell his right and title to the said lady and her heirs; Thus the Deed speakes.

Ex relaçone H: dni Berkeley et diū. al.

Now whilst these and other suites travelled up and down Westmr. hall, Maurice on the other part, accompanyed with his brother in law Nicholas Poynz, and the said Giles Poynz his brother, to work like dispite to this lady, They one night specially, (as often they did the like,) with a riotous company of their servants and others, entred her parke at Yate, and having havoked her deere at pleasure sware amongst themselves, they would, to fret and damage her the more, set the great hay ricke on fire; meaning a great ricke of hay for winter provision inclosed with a high pale at the stable end adjoyning to the house, wishing the fire might catch the house and burne the lady with her werish boy in the midst of it, And then, Maurice (quoth Giles Poynz) thou shalt bee heire, and wee have an end of all our sutes.

721 It chanced at the same time another company of Hunters to bee in the same parke stealing also of this ladies deere; who perceiving a stronger pack of theeves then

then themselves to bee in place, and better provided, had drawn themselves secretly to shelter under the said hay ricke, where closely standing and hearing what was said and determined, and fearing either to bee descried or burned, presently ran away and fled; which being perceived by Maurice and his company, and by them thought to bee of the ladies family, and such as shee and her keepers had drawn togeather, They also, as loth to be descryed or taken, fled as fast another way; And soe by this chance was a great danger prevented, And Maurice and his company by the other company peached, and a Starchamber suite commenced. This, this noble lord Henry hath merily related unto mee, with many the like passages in those times by his unkind uncle Maurice, and his said brother in lawe; wherewith I might blot more leaves of paper and tell this family of divers of their strange actions, not (I think) before practised since the lawles daies of Robinhood; the remembrance of many whereof are yet of fresh memory in those parts.

In March the yeare after in the 29th of King Henry the 8th, Sir Nicholas Poynz aforesaid, John Butler, Edward Arden, Thomas Tovy, and others of his company, in a lewd riotous manner brake down the wall and head of Mangottesfeild poole aforesaid, which was now the said ladies, and destroyed the mill of late there built, and took and spoiled the fish and fry therein, to her very great damage, and the little profit of themselves; which was the third attempt upon this mill and poole; for which riotous fact, this lady Anne exhibits another bill in the Starchamber; And sending her man Thomas Stephens to serve the defendants with proces, the said Arden and others soundly beat him, for which battery and contempt of Justice, another newe suite was likewise raised and prosecuted.

Sir Nicholas Poynz and Maurice Berkeley being strictly pressed with the suits of this lady, for the riot committed upon the said mill and poole, somewhat to give colour to their fact, procured an Inquisition to bee privately found at Wotton by the Escheator, virtute officij, in the 30th yeare of king Henry the 8th, declaring how Henry the 8th in the 24th of his raigne leafed the Manor and Hundred of Barton to his father Sr Anthony Poynz for one and twenty years, whose executor hee was; And that the watercourse running between the manor and | hundred of Barton and the manor of Bitton was estopped by Thomas lord Berkeley the fifth of that name, when he new built that mill, And thereupon had overflown two acres of ground, one of the manor of Barton, the other of the manor of Bitton, which is now called Mangottesfeild poole a̶s Charnells poole, which Anne lady Berkeley now holds, but by what title they of the Jury say they know not: This presentment the lady traversed,

Inq: 30. H. 8. in scᵃcio.

722

traverfed, And hereupon fo many bills in divers Courts, Indictements and other Suites, were multiplyed between them, That at laft the faid lady to give fome eafe to her felf, fled to her old mafter king Henry the 8th, who granted her a fpeciall Comiffion under the great feale, to enquire heare and determine thefe riots and other mifdemeanors, and made her one of the Comiffioners, and of the Quorum; Whereupon fhee came to Glouc., and there fate on the Bench in the publique Seffions hall, impanelled a Jury, received Evidence, found Sr Nicholas Poynz and Maurice Berkeley and their fellowes guilty of divers riotts and diforders, and fyned them; And hence it is, that the common people in thofe parts of Yate and Mangottef-feild will with fome ftifnefs of opinion to this day, to the honor of this lady, (as they fuppofe,) maintaine that fhee was a Juftice of peace, and in the Comiffion of the peace, and fate with them upon the bench, But I have not otherwife obferved it, then as aforefaid.

Carta in caftro de de Berkeley.

I will not further weary this noble family with more of the braules and jarrs between thefe two families; I come to the end they tooke for the time; Sr Nicholas Poynz for two hundred markes, in the fecond and third years of Phillip and Mary, fold to this lord Henry the patent hee had from the Crown of the Rangerfhip and keeping of Kingfwood fforeft, which his Anceftors Anthony and ffrancis before had held, And which Maurice lord Berkeley the Sixth, before them had alfo held; for payment of which money the faid lady Anne became bound with her fon as a fuerty; And the next yeare this Sr Nicholas, leaving another Sr Nicholas his fon to fucceed him, dyed; the faid Maurice Berkeley his brother being dead before.

Efcheat: 13. H. 4. poft mort: Tho: Mowbray Com: Marefc.

723

Diverfa munimenta in caftro de Berkel: Div'fi compi inter record et fupervis: Tho. Jenifon, et Dñæ Eliz: nuper regine.

Soe troubled was this lady Anne with thefe diffentions at home, that fhee fuffered this lord her fon to fuftaine loffe of treble more moment abroad; for whereas by difcent of inheritance hee had the one moity of the feignories and lordfhips of Catherlagh, Oldcroffe, and divers other Manors and lands in the County of Wexford, (yea two baronies,) in Ireland, as a copercener with Thomas then Duke of Norfolk, A parliament was holden for that kingdome at Dublyn, the firft of May in the 28th of king Henry the 8th, whereat all lords and owners of lands were, by a law then made, under forfeiture enjoyned by a fhort day to come and inhabite upon them, whereby this lord became difinherited.

Of the Juftice of this act I will not fpeake, becaufe it was grounded upon reafon of State, as affaires then ftood; But, as to the lord Henry, then but feaventeen monthes old and the kings ward, and his whole lands under the kings rule and protection,

protection, and of his Courts, in refpect of his minority, it feemeth hard, and with fome unreafonable; And the more becaufe the Crown then feized upon them, and longe time after let them for yearly rents paid into the Exchequer there, untill king James fold them away in ffee fimple.

tempore Jacobi.

Neither would I have this family ignorant, that many lres and fome meffengers in the life of this lord Henry after his full age, and the marriage of his fifter with the Earle of Ormond, were fent to him about thefe lands; But what through the Jarre that fell between that Earle and his wife, and of the fuits that continued between Queen Elizabeth and this lord Henry, and with her potent favorites and patentees, till her end, and for feaven years after her dayes, and for many other troubles that preffed hard upon this lords eftate, as alfo through his own indifpofition for Court fuites, nothing was effected or brought to any apparent forwardnes for ought I have underftood: Since his death I remember the new Earle of Thomond had twice fpeeches with the lady Elizabeth Berkeley mother and gardian of his grandchild and heire touching thefe lands, whereof I think hee hath part, and of the act that did difinherite this lord Henry; And after wrote to her about a fearch to bee made amongft this lords evidences, but I knowe hee obtained nothing to the prejudice of her fon the lord George; To whom I can leave noe other hope herein, then that the Crowns injuftice, (if I may ufe foe harfh a word,) to his imediate Anceftor, may bee the ground for fome future fuite from his Matie.

Anno: 14. Jaco: et. 16. Jacobi.

Isable lady Berkeley, widow, having by her firft hufbands conveyance an Eftate in the manor of Callowdon for her life, And the revercōn after her death to Maurice lord Berkeley her fon in ffee, joyne in a leafe in the 5th year of king Henry the 8th of the faid Manor, to Thomas Try their Cofen and fervant, (often before mentioned,) for his life, paying for the life time of the faid lady—33^{li}. 18^s. 4^d And after her death lefs by twenty pounds a year to the faid Maurice and his heires; which leafe, the faid lord Maurice|enjoyned his heire by his will, fhould bee quietly enjoyed; After that ladies death the faid Maurice in the 12th yeare of king Henry the 8th, not only confirmed that former leafe made by his mother and himfelf, but granted twelve years more to the faid Thomas Try, to bee accompted from his death, in recompence of the great charges hee had been at, and the many good and faithfull fervices hee had done to him, at the feidges of Tirwin and Tournay, and other places; Thomas Try dies at Callowdon the Tenth of ffebruary in the 36th of king Henry the 8th; This Manor being part of this lady Annes Joynture, fhee comes now to take poffeffion, but is kept out by Walter Horton Efq^r, in behalf of his

finis: 10. H. 7. in banco.

Carta. 5. H. 8. in caftr̃ de Berkel:

Com̃. pleas: Pafch̃: 38. H. 8. rot. 448.

724

carta. 12. H. 8. in caftro de Berkeley.

Pleadings in Canc. 36. et. 37. H. 8.

his mother the widow and executrix of Thomas Try, by colour of the twelve years granted by this later leafe; This leafe the said lady Anne accufeth to bee forged, And exhibits her bill againft them in Chancery; they anfwere, Witneffes farre and neare are fetched and examined, and amongft others one Gerrard Try a Soldier from Bullen, a bafe fon of the faid Thomas Tryes; And the caufe coming to hearing was fent to bee tryed by action at comon lawe, which by extraordinary labour and

Pafch: 38. H. 8. rot. 448. in Comon pleas.

means paffed with the faid lady; And fo after two years and a half Strugling, fhee obtained the poffeffion and overthrew that leafe, I will not fay unjuftly: But knowingly, I may fay, favour and freinds much helped and prevailed; And in that fpace many forcible entries and riotous affaults were made, a part of the mote about that houfe filled up with faggotts, and foe affaulted by the faid lady, howbeit kept out both of the houfe and the greateft part of the Manor till tryall: After which the lady Anne to fortify her recovery fues out a fpeciall Comiffion in the nature of a Mandamus, to enquire what lands in the County of the City of Coventry her hufband dyed feized of; Whereupon an Inquifition was taken before Bradfhawe the kings Atturney generall and others, by jury, in the 3th yeare of king Edward the fixth, who found the faid firft leafe, and as much more fpeciall matter as would befreind the faid lady: All which, befides the records which fpeake at large, I have had from the relation of old Robert Burbage father of Thomas the now bayly of Gofcote hundred, then fervant to the faid lady, and many years after to this lord Henry her fon, and imployed in this fervice, with many other paffages by mee omitted.

carta in caftro de Berkeley.

725

This Thomas Try purchafed an houfe and certain lands in Binly by Callowdon, (wherein John Prowtinge and Hugh ffowler, two of this lords fervants, of late dwelt,) And by his will left the inheritance of it to the faid Gerrard his bafe fon, formerly mentioned, then at Bullen, | who having depofed moft advantageoufly in the former fuites for the f^d lady, loft him the love of his faid mother in lawe and of her fon Mr Horton; And alfo kindled in them a defire to doe him any mifcheife; And on the other part, the hatred the lady carried to the memory of his father Thomas Try for forginge the faid leafe, as fhee affirmed, (but untruly,) caufed her to caft injuftice upon him his bafe fon; for, having now the poffeffion of Callowdon fhee feized upon this houfe and lands at Binly as parcell thereof, under colour that they were by one and the fame man longe occupied togeather; Gerard Try comes from beyond feas, and petitions this lady for his right, but is rejected: Hee feeks to the Bifhop of Ely, then lord Chancellor, by petition, who refers him to the lady againe, efpecially charging him that hee fhould bee at quietnes with that good lady,

(for

(for such were his words;) whereupon hee went with his writings to Kentish Town by London, where at this begining of Queen Maryes raigne shee often lay with this lord her son, And telling her what the lord Chancellor had said, and the cause thereupon of his coming, hee declared to her his right to the land in Binly out of his evidence, which (as hee accuseth her) shee craftily catcheth up, and kept referring him to come to her to Callowdon where shee should bee sattisfyed; Thither shee repaires, and thither hee follows in lent after, where hee found her with Bishop Bond, that kept with her there that lent: Hee importunes, shee denies, And in the end giving him 20ᵈ to beare his charges because hee was come thither by her appointment, shee bids him begone, and trouble her noe more, for the land shee would have, or by Gods blessed Sacrament, (that was ever her oath,) shee would make him burne a fagott: And another time, upon his further importunity, shee charged him to bee quiet, or (swearing the like oath,) she would cause him to bee burned for his religion.

Gerrard packs againe to Bullen, and with the change of religion turns preist, and presently after the ladies death getts into possession of the said house, but by force; whom this lord Henry indictes at Warwicke Sessions upon the statute of the 8ᵗʰ of king Henry the 6ᵗʰ, of forcible entries: But hee (having his right favoured) avoids restitution of the possession. This lord thereupon brings his ejectione firmæ, whereupon issue is joyned whether this house and lands bee the freehold of this lord or of the said Gerrard: This suite being miscarried, this lord repaireth it by another, wherein hee prevaileth not; Gerrard now poorly beneficed at Childewickham in the said county, holding these multiplicity of suites for vexations, delivers a writing of his own hand writing to the proper hands of this lord Henry, wherein, (besides his laying down all the former passages,) hee plain|ly adviseth him not to inrich himself with wrongfull gotten goods, least it consume the rest of all his substance; for confirmation whereof hee vouches to him five texts of Scripture, (not unaptly applyed,) And tells him as plainly, That his father Tryes labour care and diligence redeemed to his Ancestors and him better than 1700 markes a yeare; And that hee himselfe came from Bullen to testify for his lordships mother in the title of Callowdon, whereby hee lost his mother in lawe, and Mʳ Horton her son; And was by them thrice maimed and hurt for answering of matters on her Laᵖˢ side, (hee means, I think, in the assaults given about the possession of the house,) who promised him fourty pounds by the yeare for those services, but never had penny of her, but in the end was forced to get over againe to Bullen.

10 Eliz:

Pasch: 10: Eliz. Rot: 238. in banco regis.

Trin. 12. Eliz: Rot: 430. ibm.

Manuscr: in castro de Berkeley. 726

Hee meanes the severall restitutions temp: H. 7. & H. 8. vide fols: [613, 674]

To bee short, Gerrard had good title but this lord had now the possession and was powerfull; Gerrard upon composition releaseth all his right and title, And in recompence had from this lord an Yearly Anuity of fourty shillings duringe life, and competent sum of money in hand: This is that house and land of late sold in fee to Edward Woodward and Henry Lucas, to the use of the countes of Bedford, and by her and them to the lady Craven of London by the lady Elizabeth mother and guardian of the lord George, for two hundred pounds, with whom hee joyned in a fyne in his minority: And thus is this ill got peece slipt from the rest, before the full age of the third heire.

<small>carta dat: 28 Maij. Anno. 20. Jacobi.</small>

It's noe unapt digression in this place to say, That its easy to find a staffe wherewith to beat a dogge: when a new Pharoe arose that knew not Joseph, it was easy to quarrell at the multiplication of his and of his fathers posterities: Howbeit Moses, from God, had told all generations of Josephs deservings towards Pharoes forefathers, and of their ill requitall of Josephs posterity: And the story of this Thomas Try, droppingly by mee delivered as occation required, in fower of the former lords lives, hath sufficiently assured this family of his great services to each of them in their successive generations. And now by the cominge of this lady Anne, who knew him not, as shee ought to have done, his reward for those services is quarrelled, and his fidelity and reputation wounded after his death, I may say, unjustly overthrowne: A fortune which I wish none other servant to this noble family may, without worse deserving ever find.

<small>Exodus. 1. v. 8. Acts: 7. v. 18.</small>

727

At this time, in the fourth of Q[u]eene Mary, Anno 1556, Cardinall Poole out of his Apostolicall authority and Legateship from the Bishop of Rome, absolved this lord Henry from all dangers of Excommunications, which in the late time of Schisme in England hee had incurred: And granted to him the faculty to use his Chappell in his manor of Callowdon, as of ancient time before the schisme his Ancestors had used the same: And to have there a portible Altar to say masse, to receive the body and bloud of Christ, and to keep the same in a box covered with a faire sindon or Linen cloth, with candle burning before it.

<small>Carta in castro de Berkeley.</small>

And by another instrument at the same time, the said Cardinall by like Authority, grants to this lord Henry to have all the Tithes to his said Chapple of Callowdon, which heretofore were granted by Pope Gregory; And which since have been accustomed to bee paid thereto untill the late most pernitious schisme in England happened, what time the grant of the said Pope was lost, which the Cardinall

<small>Carta in castro de Berkeley.</small>

Cardinall doth now by his said Apostolicall authority and legateship, repaire, renewe and restore.

His restitution to Berkeley Castle, and to the Barony of Berkeley.

Thus have I brought this lord and his active mother to the death of king Edward the sixth and entrance of Queen Mary, and him to the 19th yeare of his age; At which time such accidents fell togeather upon this family, as I shall seeme to those that read parcelwise and by broken houres, to relate them somewhat out of order.

I have not only in the life of William Marques Berkeley, but upon occasions almost in each lords life since him, touched in what sort that Marques for default of issue of his own body, entailed the greatest part of his Inheritance upon king Henry the 7th, and the heires males of his body, And for default of such issue male, the same to returne againe to his own right heires; And how the said Marques dyed in the 7th yeare of that kings raigne without any issue of his body, And how that king entred thereupon, and was seized, and tooke the profits accordingly.

I have also related in what sort Maurice the Marques brother and heire and Maurice his son were afterwards restored to part, and regained other parts of those possessions; Insomuch as of all those manors so by the Marques entailed upon king Henry the 7th, none remained in the Crown upon the death of king Edward the sixth, (the last of that kings issue male,) save the Castle, Manor, and Hundred of Berkeley, the manors of Hame, Appleridge, Alkington, Came, Hinton, Cowley, Wotton underedge, Simondsall, Erlingham, Slimbridge, and Hurst, in the County of Glouc., And the hundred and manors of Portbury and Porteshead in the County of Somerset, And the manor of Kington in the County of Warrwick: As for the manor of Weston iuxta Baldocke in Hartfordshire, which was granted away in fee by king Edward the sixth in the first of his raigne, it hath (as the case deserveth) a memoriall by it selfe.

I have also shewed how at the death of king Edward the sixth, this lord Henry was within age, and in ward to the king for his manors of Tetbury, Bitton, and other manors in divers Counties, which discended upon him by the death of the lord Thomas his father, holden by knights service in capite; whereupon arose a case of rarity and intricacy, which that venerable Judge of the Comon pleas, the lord James Dyer in his booke thus reporteth.

William

Dyer. Triñ Term. 1. Mar̃. fol: 102.

William Marques Berkeley levyed a fine of the manor of Berkeley to one Logge, come ceo que il avoit de son done, by which fine Logge rendred the said Manor to the Marques and to the heires of his body, the remainder to King Henry the 7th and to the heires males of his body, The remainder to the right heires of the Marques: That the Marques enters into the said manor and dies without issue, After whose death Henry the 7th enters, and was seized in taile, and dies; And the same discended to Henry the 8th, and from him to Edward the sixth, who enters and dies without issue: By reason whereof the remainder came to Henry lord Berkeley as Cozen and heire of the Marques, being within age and in Ward to Queen Mary: And that the said manor of Berkeley was holden by knights service in Capite; whereupon (saith Dyer) the question arose, Whether the said manor should bee in Ward to the Queen or not, by reason that the Seignory was suspended in Edward the sixth at his death; And at last (saith hee) it was resolved by the judges, That the Queen should have the wardship of the said manor, not by her prerogative because other his lands were holden in Capite, but by reason of the tenure which is revived by the death of Edward the sixth in the person of the Queen: And it ought to have escheated to her for want of heires of the Marques; Therefore (saith hee) the fee simple was in consideratione legis. Thus Dyer. |

729

Pr: Seale: Dat: 8: Sept: 1. et. 2. Ph̃. et Mar̃.

Pat: 11: Decr 1. et. 2. Ph̃. et Mar̃.

But to take away all scruples whether the Queen should have the profits of these manors thus reverted during the lord Henries minority or not, Shee the 8th of September in the second year of her raigne, awarded her privy seale, reciting therein the said case, and the doubt in lawe arising thereupon; And to take away that doubt doth command the master and officers of her courts of Wards to passe a speciall livery of all the said Manors to this lord Henry, though hee be not yet come to his full age: By which grace, clemency, and pitty, (for soe are Queen Maries words,) hee gained two whole years rents and more of these manors, as not coming to his full age till November in the third of her raigne.

Ind: dat: 6. Dec: 1. et. 2. Ph̃: et Mariæ.

Lib: sub: sigillo dat. 11. Dec. 1. et 2. Ph̃. et. Mariæ. Idem sub privato sigillo de dat̃ p̃d.

And for the more certainty of what manors and lands this lord was thus to sue livery and to take benefit by the said privy seale, hee in December following exhibited a perticular note of the names and values of each manor and lands as were to him reverted after the death of king Edward the sixth, and whereof hee meant to sue livery; which were not only the manors formerly mentioned in the Counties of Glouc̃: Somerset, and Warwicke, but also this lady Anne and her sollicitors ignorantly cast into the same livery the fourth part of the moitie of the manor of Tiborne als Maribone in the County of Middlesex, whereof noe benefit could bee taken,

taken, for that Maurice the fifth after restitution thereto had, amongst others, sold it away to the lord Burgeveny, as in his life hath been declared.

And in this livery, which is inrolled in six Offices or places of record, is laid down all the Marques Berkeleys fines assurances and estates by him created, as before hath been related; And how by the death of king Edward the sixth the said Castle Hundreds and Manors reverted to this lord Henry as right heire to the said Marques, which also Queene Maries Atturney generall, by the advice of the Judges of both benches, confessed to bee true. **And** thus entreth the lord Henry upon these possessions, being the whole lands of his Barony of Berkeley and more, whereof none of his fower last Ancestors had any possession, but had rested in the Crown for 61. yeares, 4. months, and 20. dayes; And which then were of the value of—687.5ˢ p Anñ, in old rent, not accounting the Parks and Chaces therein. **And** the more to fortifie his new gotten possessions, this lord had also a pardon and a release the 22ᵗʰ of February in the said third yeare of Queen Maryes raigne. |

Mich: rec: 1. Mar. rot: 50. in scᵃc̃io.
Orig. 2. ps. 1. et 2. Pħ. et Mař: rot. 68. in scᵃc̃io.
Orig: 2. ps. 2. & 3. Pħ: et Mař. rot. 73. in scᵃc̃io.
Mich. 4. 5. Pħ. et Mar: cum Auditoř bis.
Pasch: 1. Eliz. roť 36 in scᵃc̃io

Pat. dat. 22: ffeb: 2 et 3. Pħ et Mař.

And the 8ᵗʰ of January in the 4ᵗʰ of her raigne the said Queene, having recited fower of the old charters and grants of this Barony, as well of the lands as liberties, made by her progenitors, king Henry the second, Richard the first, king John, and Edward the third, (formerly by mee mentioned,) doth for her and her successors, for 33ˢ 4ᵈ fine, grant and confirme the same to this lord Henry and his heires: And by her other Charter of the same date confirmed likewise to him and his heires many of the old charters and grants of free warren within his demesne lands of Berkeley and all the hernesse nookes or corners thereof: And in Portbury and Porteshead in the County of Somerset.

730
2: Cartæ dat: 8. Jan: 3. &. 4. Pħ. et Mař. in casťř de Berkel:

But whereas this lady Anne and her agents in behalfe of this lord her son covenanted with the Master and surveyor of the Court of Wards, not only to sue livery of the forementioned Barony and of the manors and lands in the Counties of Gloucester and Somerset, which was well; But also of divers other lands in the counties of Sussex, Surrey, and Middlesex, (indeed the self same whereof Maurice the Marques brother had restitution in the time of Henry the 7ᵗʰ, And which hee shortly after aliened, as in his life appeareth,) It was a second grosse ignorance in them all, for which this lords purse smarted—220ˡⁱ.

Ind: 20: Nov. 1. et. 2. Pħ. et Mař.

Before I close up these passages, I must, though with some sorrow, recount to this noble family, That at such time as this lord was restored to these manors and lands

lands by Queen Mary, That title whereby this lord after loſt a great part of them was alſo in her by the Attainder of John Dudley Duke of Northumberland; which whether then perceived by this lords Councell, or out of their general providence to make all ſafe and ſure, with knowledge thereof in particular, I know not; but certainly they earneſtly adviſed this lady Anne and this lord her ſon to take them from the Queen, not by way of reſtitution, which was the longer way and more chargeable, but as of her guift by dedi et conceſſi, and with the uſuall words in all ſuch grants, of ex ſpetiali gracia, certa ſcientia, et mero motu, which was much ſhorter in time, labor and pleadings, more ſafe and leſſe chargeable; whereto Queen Mary her ſelf alſo more inclined, aſwell to enlarge her grace and favour the more amply to this lady Anne and this lord her ſon, As to oblige this lord the more

731 ſtrictly to her ſervice: But this lady Anne who then ruled all the roſt, (this lord her ſon then under one and twenty, unexperienced, indulgently foſtered, thinking on nothing but the delights of Youth,) would by noe perſuaſion aſſent thereto, out of a covetous purpoſe which ſhee had to avoid divers leaſes made of thoſe lands by king Henry the 8th, and Edward the ſixth, which, as ſhee was told by Counſell, were determined in lawe with the Crowns remainder; As both this lord himſelf, (out of greife for that groſſe overſight of his willfull mother,) hath told mee, and as I have heard from old Mr Thomas Denis of Glouceſter at that time Sollicitor in theſe buiſineſſes, and from divers others, and as the ſequell of her proceedings convinceth to bee too true: And therefore I may heare throw in the face of her memory thoſe evills which this family ſuffered by that her womaniſh wilfullneſſe, to the expence of above fifty thouſand pounds, as the reſidue of this lord Henrys life, his ſales of land, and other troubles, (nay all his troubles,) hence occaſioned and ariſeing, will mani-feſt to bee true, whereof I will not forget upon the cloſe of them, (for examples

fol: 793. ſake to poſterity,) to give her a ſecond reproofe by the double accuſation of this lord her ſon.

This lord Henry thus by way of reſtitution in poſſeſſion of the ſaid Caſtle Hundreds. and Manors, A generall veiwe, by vertue of his Comiſion directed to Hugh Denis and others, was taken the ſame yeare, declareing the eſtates that each tenant had in each part of the ſaid Manors lands and liberties, in the Counties of Glouceſter, Somerſet, and Warwicke, ſoe reverted upon the death of king Edward the ſixth, either by Copy, or by Indenture or at will, and digeſted into a folio booke,

Shellitoes booke. called Shellitoes booke, remaining to this day in Berkeley Caſtle; which paines of
2: Ma$\bar{\textrm{r}}$. theires, though not great, was largely rewarded to each one of them with one or more of the beſt of thoſe eſtates; Howbeit in ſome of thoſe officers this humor

abounded,

abounded, that much defired more, And fome of the old tenants muft bee thruft out of their beft leafes, made by kinge Henry the 8th. and king Edward the fixth, before their covetoufnes could creepe in, under colour and pretext That their eftates for years or lives were in lawe determined with the Crowns remainder by ye death of Edward the fixth without iffue male, as hath been faid: Six of thofe tenants (whereof fower had the Sirnames of Trotmans)|fpying the net, Joyntly fly by their petition to the feete of that mercifull lady Queen Mary; whereupon fhee addreffeth her lre to the lord Henry, fubfcribed with her own hand, telling him that fhee marvailed that hee would foe flenderly waigh the validity of her fathers and brothers leafes, confidering that hee foe lately enjoyed the inheritance of the faid lands by her liberality and favour, And therefore fhee being moved in confcience with the piteous complaint of the faid poore men, required him to permit them quietly to enjoy their faid lands according to the grants of her father and brother, And to doe fuch Acts for their further affurance, at their charges, as they fhould require, which would bee to her very acceptable and give the poore men caufe to pray for him. Thus the Queene.

732
Lre dat: 13. Maij
3. Mar. in
Berkeley Caftle.

The fruite was, noe more quarrells were picked againft their leafes, but this noble lord, (that out of himfelf never meant them damage,) permitted them to bee at quiett.

Before I enter upon the two unthrifty titles of this lords law fuites and of the fales of his land, I will deliver him to his pofterity in the other actions of his life, from the firft of Queen Mary forwards, (then in the nineteenth yeare of his age,) That the caufes of the faid unthrifty titles which next fhall follow may more groundly bee conceived.

Edward the fixth being dead in July: Anno. 1553. and Queene Mary fetled in the Crowne, her marriage was concluded upon with Phillip prince of Spaine, during which time this lords mother was bufied in regaining her fons forefaid Barony and poffeffions; And Sir Thomas Wiat and his Kentifh complices in raifing Armes againft that forraigne marriage, and the entry of ftrangers into the land: Brett and others of the Queenes captains and Subjects then alfo falling unto Wiat from their own faith and her Allegeance, the Queene, diffident of many of her nobi[li]ty, refolved amongft others, (partly out of the correfpondance of this lords mother with her felf in religion, and partly out of the bounty fhee then had and was in powring upon her fon then but nineteen years of age,) to truft him more then

many

many others more aged and experienced; Whereupon shee sends her lres to him togeather with her Commiffion, in January in the firft yeare of her raigne, | (hee then at Yate in Glouceftershire,) forthwith to Arme 500 of his truftieft tenants and fervants, and with all poffible diligence to attend her perfon then at Whitehall. **This** lord, to his great charges, readely prepareth armeth and apparelleth that number, All of them drawn out of the parts about Yate and Berkeley; for help whereto hee obtained a lone of money from his tenants from fourty fhillings to Twenty pound a peece, and gave bills of repayment, in like refemblance as kings by their privy feales borrow of their fubjects; And for further fupply pawned his mothers and Anceftors plate, (much of which was never after redeemed,) And having conducted thofe five hundred men about half the way towards London, (with many of whom I fince have talked,) the Queens Lres met this lord upon his way in the beginning of the next month, fignifying That Wiat was taken and prifoner in the Tower, and his complices difperfed, willing them to returne into his Country and with his utmoft care and induftry to keep the fame in quiett; Two hundred or more of which Armors yet remaine in Berkeley Caftle, rather as memorialls of this intended fervice then fit for any moderne ufe: Which forwardnes of this lord in his Princes fervice in a time foe wavering and unfetled, and in his minority, when fhee knew not well whom to command or where to truft, Queen Mary the next yeare both remembred and commended in the warrant fhee figned for this lords fpeciall livery of the reverted lands; makeing it a leading motive why fhee granted to him livery of thofe lands with their rents and profits from the death of her brother, two years and more before hee came to full age.

Priv: figill. 8.
Sept: 1. et. 2. Ph.
et. Mar.

in caftro de Berkeley.

And alfo the faid Queene fent other lres to this lord, fignifying That where fhee was by fundry wayes enformed That Thomas Wiat and fome others had of late by fpreading abroad moft falfe and vain rumors, procured to ftirre her fubjects of her County of Kent to arife againft her crown and dignity royall, Albeit fhee hath already taken fuch order as fhee doubted not fhall bee fufficient to repreffe and overthrow the unnaturall confpiracy, yet hath fhee neverthelefse thought good to require and charge him forthwith upon the fight hereof, to put himfelf in full order with as many of his fervants frends and tenants as hee can make, both on horfeback and on foote, to bee in a readines to march and fet forward upon one houres warning, either againft the faid rebells, or fuch other waies as fhall bee fignifyed unto him from her; And in the meane time, to have good regard to the quiet | order of the parts where hee dwells, caufing all fuch idle and lewd perfons as fhall either by fpreading abroad of untrue rumors, or by any other ways, attempt to ftirre or difquiet

quiet her loving Subjects, to bee apprehended and punished as the quality of their offences shall deserve; given at her Manor of S.t James the 26.th day of January in the first of her raigne, Mary the Queen, with her own hand.

Not longe after, (like a young lord left to much to the oversight of his own education,) hee came to London, setled at Tower hill, frequented the Court, and spent all his time at tenys, bowles, cards, dice, and in the company of his huntsmen and faulkeners, delights that drew on greater totalls in his Accompts at the years end then his revenue would support, espetially two Joyntures of his fathers and grandfathers widows draining a third part thereout.

In ffebruary in the second and third of Phillip and Mary, this lord sueth livery for all those manors and lands which discended to him after the death of his father, which, with their values are particularly mentioned in the end of his life: which noe sooner finished, but the lady Anne his mother bringeth against this lord her son her writt of Dower, wherein shee was soe quick that shee over ran her suite in time: but being an error betweene mother and son, and hee looking after nothing but his sports, and all his servants at her devotion, hee sealed what by her or them was tendered; And soe besides her Joynture made by her husband upon marriage, shee now in lieu of Dower from this lord her son, had the manors of Coldeverton, Mountforrell, and Goscote hundred in the county of Leicester, And the thirds of his manors of Sages, Tetbury, Daglingworth, and fframpton upon Seaverne in the county of Gloucester, And of Manyngford Bruce in the County of Wilts, And of Aspele in the County of Warr̃, And of Hovingham in the County of Yorke, And his lands in Calais; Which later this lord her son obtained after to rent of her at one hundred pounds p.r Anñ, for fourty yeares if shee lived soe longe; for true payment whereof hee gave her a statute of two thousand pounds; for it is to bee understood, That till the Statute made in the 27.th of king Henry the 8.th of transferring uses into possession, That Joynter might bee had, and Dower also, of lands soe transferred to possession; And thus with releases of actions one to another, the mother and her son parted their possessions. |

At this time, in the middle of Queen Maries raigne, what through this lords living with his mother at Kentish Town and Shoolane in London, and his daily hunting in Grays Inne feilds and in all those parts towards Islington and Heygate with his hounds, whereof hee had many and those excellent good, And what through the company of many gentlemen of the Innes of Court, and others of lower condition that daily accompanied him, And what through the fame amongst

those

Indent̃ dated: 10: et. 22. ffebruarij Orig: 2: ps: 2. et. 3. Ph̃: et: Mar̃. in scac̃io.

Carta: 5. Nov. 2. et. 3. Ph̃: et: Mar̃ Carta. 3. Marcij: 4. et. 5. Ph̃: et: Mar̃. Comp: 29. H. 8. in castro de Berkeley.

Stat: 27. H. 8. c. 10. Coke. 4: rep: fol. 1. Coke pla: fol: 171. 172. Dier fol: 61. 97. 228. 248. 266. 717. 340. cartæ in castro de Berkeley.

735

Plow: Com. fol: 223.

Check roll in Berkley Castle.

thofe ftudents of his cafes of Reverter of his Barony and lands, and of the cafe touching Wefton Baldocke, (reported by Mr. Plowden in his comentaryes,) and of others partly before mentioned, that termly walked all this Queens raigne up and down Weftminfter hall, and were points for every reporter and ftudents note bookes in thofe Innes of Court; And what through his marriage in one of the greateft families then of favor and obfervation, And of his one hundred and fifty fervants in livery, that daily then attended him in their Tawny coates, And the opinion of his mothers vertue and chaftity, then the only Sollicitor of her fex in her own perfon, in her own and fons caufes, hee was of as great note and hope as any of his age and of that time; But how longe that heigth of opinion held, and how by degrees it wayned, the reft of his life will tell his pofterity.

Mich: 5. et. 6. Ph. et. Mar: in banco. Plowd. Com. fol. 223.

Stat: 12. E. 1.

Liber: comp: caus: jurid: in caftro de Berkeley. 736

And in this time alfo began that great fuite in the Comon pleas, in an Ejectione firmæ concerning the manor of Wefton iuxta Baldock in the County of Hartford, between Henry Willon plt tenant for years under Sr. Henry Cocke, And this lord Henry defent; which continued from this time in argument and agitation at barre and Bench, through the power and means of the plts leffor, and the intricacy and confequence of it felf, untill the fifth year of Queen Elizabeth, when this lord had Judgment and recovered; wherein the principall point was, Whether the king was bound by the Statute of donis conditionalibus or not, arifing upon the entaile of this manor created in the 5th year of kinge Henry the 7th, by the Marques Berkeley to the heires males of the body of that king with the remainder to the right heires of the Marques, as in his life I have already mentioned; And upon the Alienation of his grandchild king Edward the 6th, (now dead without iffue male,) in the firft of his raigne to Sir Willm Herbert, after Earle of Pembrooke, and to his heires, who fold the fame to Sr. Henry Cocke afore faid; Than which the laws have not afforded a more learned cafe of that argument: **And** having out of the houfhold books of this lord yet remaining, obferved the lawiers fees of thofe daies, I find That what time two or three Sergeants at lawe | and other great counfell were drawn from their Chambers to conferences at a tavern in ffleetftreet, whereat this lord and his induftrious mother were prefent, there was given noe greater fee then ten fhillings the peece to any of them.

Whilst the former fuite depended, brake forth another in the third year of Queen Elizabeth, which had been fome former years in Hamering, And was grounded upon an old pretence of title pretended by this lord and his Anceftors to a place called Barrow Court in Tickingham in the County of Somerfet, with

other

other poffeffions there, fometime the inheritance of Phillip Mead of Briftoll and of Richard his fon, father and brother of the lady Ifable, wife of the lord Maurice the fifth, of whom I have written in his life, againft Roger Kemys of Wickwicke then in minority, forty years after receivour to this lord Henry; Infomuch as William Coneftable and Jone his wife mother of the faid Roger and Executrix to Thomas Kemys her former hufband exhibited their bill in Chancery againft the Maior and Aldermen of the City of Briftoll, And amongft other paffages fet forth, That two chefts of evidence of the faid Thomas Kemys were in the 37th of king Henry the 8th upon her departure from thence into Devonfh: committed to the fafe keeping of the Churchwardens of the parifh church of Ratcliffe by Briftoll, from whence, fhortly after, upon a tre written by Marques Pawlet after lord treafuror and then Mafter of the wards, to the Maior of Briftoll, the faid chefts were thence removed into the Town hall of the faid Citie, and fealed, with three locks; And was foe done upon a pretence of Title That Anne lady Berkeley in behalf of this lord her fon, then the kings ward, made to the faid lands; Anfwere was made to that bill, And the caufe coming to hearing, And the chefts by this lords means, (who put himfelf as a party into this fuite,) brought by order into the Chapple of the Rolls, and opened, and perufed by Cordell then Mafter of the Rolls in prefence of Counfell on both fides, This lord Henry was found to have noe title to the faid lands, but was barred by matter of record found in the faid chefts; Whereupon by order of Court the chefts and Evidences were delivered to the Complainants. A title, had it fo been known, that was fetled longe before in the 21th of king Henry the 8th by ffitz James and Porter Juftices of the Comon pleas upon a reference to them by Thomas the fifth then lord Berkeley and Arthur Kemys father of the faid Thomas Kemys; And this fuite was originally | rayfed through a certificate made by the Maior of Briftoll under the common feale of that City, declaring that the fifth of October in the fifth of Edward the fixth Thomas Pacy Alderman and juftice of the peace, and William Appowell, marchant, depofed, that they heard fay, That certaine lands difcended from one Phillip Mead fometime Maior of that Citie, lying in the faid Citie and Suborbs, which ought and fhould appertaine to the honorable lord Berkeley and his heires, And that they know that one Arthur Kemys deceafed held all the faid lands; And the lord Berkeley and Kemys were in contention for the fame, which variance was referred to ffitz James cheife Juftice, who awarded the poffeffion to Kemys for his life, And after to the faid lord and his heirs: But queftionles, this was a lying certificate in the materiall point, gotten by the faid lady Anne and made partially in her favour, as the originall award under thofe Judges hands which I have read plainly declareth, convincinge it of groffe falfhood.

Marginalia:
Bill in Cancell 3. Eliz:
Order: 3. Eliz:
Order: 19. Junij 3. Eliz.
Carta cum Arthur Kemys filio Rogeri 737 de Wickwick in com̃ Glouc̃.
Award with Arthur Kemys of Wickwicke.

Comp: Walter Shipw: señl: hofpicij 2 Mar̃. in caſtro de Berkeley.

In September in the ſecond of Queen Mary this lord maryed the lady Katharine Howard, at the Duke her grandfathers houſe in Norfolke, (of the life, death, and funerall of which lady Katharine I have much to write,) whom ſhortly after hee brought to his houſe at Tower Hill; from whence going by water to Greenwich, (where Queen Mary and her huſband king Phillip kept their firſt Chriſtmas,) to the Maſque on Twelvth day, theſe chargeable ornaments were provided, as the Stewards booke of houſhold hath them; vizt.; Paid for 2 pair of fine hoſen for my lady to weare on twelvth day—4^s. 8^d. for a Velvet hatt for my lord—3^s. for a fine boungrace and a mufler for my lady the ſame day—8^s. ffor two fine ſmocks—3^s. 9^d. And more, (the ſame yeare,) for two paire of hoſen for my lady—4^s. And being now accidentally entred into this lord and ladies Wardrobe, Take their apparell five years after made againſt the Coronation of Queen Elizabeth; vizt. for one Dublet of crimſon ſatten laid with ſilver lace, with ſilver buttons, lined with crimſon ſarcenet, And his breeches of crimſon velvet lined with crimſon ſatten; One other dublet of white ſatten, and breeches of white Velvet lined wth white ſatten, laid with ſilver lace; His points of black, white, and red ribbond; his hatt of crimſon ſilk and ſilver, And another hatt of velvet ſet with aglets, with a white feather, (ſome of which aglets I after ſaw with this lord;) The ſcabbards of his two rapiers and daggers were the one of white velvet, the other of crimſon; His guilt ſpurrs with velvet leathers of the ſame colours, And his ſhoes of crimſon and white velvet: As for the aparell of his wife, I obſerved only, (out of the ſaid Accompt,) That her petticote was of crimſon ſatten, And her gowne of cloth of gold, and her ſhoes of crimſon velvet.

Comp: Hofpicij. 1. Eliz. in Caſtro de Berkeley.

738

Comp: hofpicij 3. Eliz: in caſtro de Berkeley.

And two years after, hee furniſhed himſelf with a white ſpaniſh leather Jerkin laid with white ſilver bone lace, (ſoe are the words,) with ſilver buttons, and white leather buſkins.

And thus up and down all the time of Queen Mary removed this lord and his wife, with feldom leſſe (often more) then one hundred and fifty ſervants in livery, between Yate, Mangotteſfeild, London, Callowdon, and other places; And uſed to hauke as hee travelled thoſe waies, making his removes from thoſe places to London eight days at leaſt, and as many back againe.

Comp. hofpicij in eiſdem annis in caſtro de Berkeley.

Having in his firſt fower years after his marriage much over ranne his purſe, Hee in the laſt of Queen Mary and ſomewhat before ſojourned wth the Counteſſe of Surrey his wifes mother at Ryſinge in Norfolk, himſelf and his lady at ten ſhillings

the

the weeke, her gentlewomen at 4ˢ·—And their gentlemen and yeomen at 3ˢ· the weeke ; from whence they came to London the 5ᵗʰ of January, And thence returned againe the ninth of ffebruary by Ware, Barkeway, Newmarket, Soffam, and foe to Ryfinge, whither when hee had brought his wife, hee in fewe days after returned to London ; And living with his mother at her faid houfe in Shoe lane, fpent moft of his time at cards, dice, tenys, Bowling-ally, and hawking and hunting neere that Citie.

In July in the faid firft of Queen Elizabeth hee returned to Ryfinge, And from thence with his wife and family by the waies of Newmarket, Cambridge and Northhampton, came to Callowdon by Coventry : where the firft worke done was the fending for his buckhounds to Yate in Gloucefterfhire : His hounds being come Away goes hee and his wife a progres of buck hunting to the parks of Barkewell, Groby, Bradgate, Leicefter forreft, Toley, and others on that fide his houfe : And after a fmall repofe, Then to the parks of Kenilworth, Afhby, Wedgenocke, and others, on the other fide his houfe : And this was the courfe of this lord (more or leffe) for the thirty next fomers at leaft : not omitting his own at Callowdon and in the county of Gloucefter. **And** his wife being of like honnor and youth, from this firft of Queene Elizabeth to the beheadding of her brother the Duke of Norfolk thirteen years after, gave her felf to like delights as the Country ufually affordeth ; wherein fhee often went with her hufband part of thofe hunting Journeys, delighting her crofbowe : kept commonly a caft or two of merlins, which fometimes fhe mewed in her own chamber ; | which falconry coft her hufband each yeare one or two gownes and kirtles fpoiled by their mutings : ufed her longe bowe, And was in thofe daies amongft her fervants foe good an Archer at butts, as her fide by her was not the weaker : whofe bowes, arrowes, glove, bracer, fcarfe, and other ladylike accomodations, I have feen, and heard alfo her felf fpeak of them in her elder yeares ; which partly by the death of that noble Prince her brother, and partly by the troubles that then invaded her hufbands eftate, were broken of, and much difcontinued.

And thus lived this lord and his wife betweene London, the Dukes houfes in Norfolke, Callowdon, and Berkeley, never longe at one place, the firft thirteene yeares of Queene Elizabeth : **In** which their travells, (if both togeather,) they were feldom or never attended with fewer then one hundred and fifty fervants in their tawny cloth coats in fummer, with the badge of the white Lyon rampant imbroidered on the left fleeve ; And in coats of white frize lined with crimfen taffety in

the

739

See fol. 8.

the winter, This lord allowing only cloth, buttons, and badge; amongſt whom many were gentlemen and Eſquiers of remarkeable families and diſcent, and of alliance to this houſe; Many of whom I lived to ſee and know and to talke of theſe times: And have with ſome of them then in neareſt relation and place of his revenue, expoſtulated why they would ſuffer their young lord and lady his wife to runne yearly 1500^{li} at leaſt into expence above their utmoſt incombe, each year, (or ſecond at leaſt,) ſhortning the ſame by ſale of a Manor, having noe ſuites in lawe, nor daughters then marryed away, forraigne embaſſies, domeſtike ſervices in Court or Country, nor any other extraordinary cauſes of expence in the world; And not either as kinſmen out of affection, or as ſervants out of Duty, to advertize them thereof; And to pray them to think on the end in this their beginning and middle. Whereto Jeffry Ithell, (that lords Auditor from the firſt yeare of Queen Elizabeth till after the fortieth,) once gave mee this inſteed of anſwere; My prayer ſhall bee that you ſee not his ſon Sir Thomas (now your young maſter) doe the like, or worſe hereafter in a worſe manner then houſkeeping, and to bee attended with many followers; And (all they now dead) I reply, (after twenty ſix years ſilence,) and pray, That his ſon the now lord George may not after his full age tread in theſe unprofitable ſtepps of his father and grandfather: What Sr Thomas did, theſe relations will declare: What his ſon the lord George will doe, I hope himſelf (Julius | Cæſar like,) by his own comentaries of his own life, will tell that male poſterity of his, which I pray the God of heaven ſhortly to bleſs him withall; A true way to attaine the knowledge of himſelf, and to diſcerne the honor or errors of his own actions; But moſt ſure it is, That in the time of Queen Mary when this lord Henry entred upon his lands diſcended to him from his father, and alſo upon his Barony of Berkeley and thoſe manors which reverted to him after the death of king Edward the ſixth, as before hath been ſaid, That hee had many flatterers and ſicophants, as well of his own family as out of London, Captaines, Schollers, Poetts, caſt courtiers, and the like, That for their private ends humored him and his wife, making them to conceive that their eſtate and yearly revenue was greater then that they could exceed it; which would afford an expence at pleaſure, And to give without fear of want; whereto they liſtening with too open an eare, for facile credimus quod volumus, It came to paſs that within two or three years they were unknowingly caſt into a great debt, ere they came to diſcerne their eſtate; And to take off the ſame, (after borrowing upon mortgages, Statutes, and pawnes,) this lord began to ſell his land; A courſe hee overlonge after continued in, as that title too manifeſtly declares, expending one year with another all that time of Queen Mary and divers years after 1500^{li} p anñ at leaſt, as by the medium, (which I with ſome hours expence

div'ſi compī: Rec: et ał offic̃: in caſtro de Berkeley.

expence drew out of his officers accompts of those times,) appeares, above his ordinary revenue, and the fines and other casualties that his estate presented: The observation whereof I held the more remarkable through the knowledge I after tooke of his principall Officers which in those times managed his estate and affaires, as Thomas Duport, a wise man, Hugh Denis, Martin Petit, Walter Shipward, Thomas Denis, Thomas ffransham, Robert Cox, William Shillitoe, Anthony Corbet, Edward Bucknam, fferdinando Ligon, Henry Ligon, Richard Bedale, Thomas Jevais and Jeffry Ithell his Auditor; six of them his kinsmen, as in the proper places of their discents appeares.

In the second of Queen Elizabeth began this lord to present her Matie with ten pound yearly in gold at new years tide, and his wife with five pound; which course shee held during her life, And this lord the rest of the Queens daies: And was never unmindfull of yearly sending, Lamprey pyes, Salmon, Venison red and fallow, and other small tokens, to Judges, great officers of State, privy Counsellors and Lawyers, whereof hee reaped both honor and profit, an hundred times more than the charge. The same year hee sent the lord keeper for his new-years guift ten old angells, which gave him the mindfullnes of putting him into the Comission of the peace, wherein aswell in that County of Gloucester as in two others hee continued all the residue of his life; ffor which imployment, because through his mothers fault his education was not fitted, hee brought his servant Thomas Duport into equall authority with him, whereby his own unaptnes was less perceived, and the buisines of the Country not worse discharged.

Comp: Thome ffransham: 2. Eliz: in cast: de Berkeley.

Anno. 2. Eliz: 741

His Christmas, (as most part of this second year of Queen Elizabeth,) hee kept at Yate with great port and solemnity, as the extraordinary guilded dishes, the vanities of Cookes arts, (having none other guests but the gentlemen and ruralty of the Country,) served to the table on Twelvth day, well declare; whereof one was a whole bore inclosed in a pale workmanly guilt by a Cooke hired from Bristoll, as the Clarke of the Kitchens booke declareth: In perusall whereof, I could not observe how that dish was brought unto the table.

Comp Walteri Shipward in ijsdem temp: in castro de Berkeley.

In which yeare having in March extreamly heated himself by chasing on foot a tame Deere in Yate Parke, with the violence thereof fell into an imoderate bleeding at the nose, for the stay whereof by the ill counsell of some about him, hee clapt his whole face into a bason of cold water, whereby that flush and fulnes of his nose which forthwith arose, could never bee remedied; though for present help hee had
Physitians

Phyſitians in fewe daies from London, And for better help came thither himſelfe not longe after to have the advice of the whole colledge, and lodged with his mother at her houſe in Shoe-lane.

His Lawe ſuites.

I am by courſe of ſtory and promiſe now fallen upon the time wherein I ſhall deliver to this noble family the ſecond greateſt blow and wound that the poſſeſſions thereof at any time received; The roote whereof, (watered with the powerfull prerogative of the Crown,) thus grew up and bore theſe diſaſtrous fruits, as now followe.

742

The fifth of October in the firſt of Queen Mary, (her brother king Edward the ſixth being dead in July before,) began the parliament at Weſtm: which continued by ſeverall prorogations till the ſixth of December; In wch John Dudley Duke of Northumberland, John Dudley Earle of Warwicke, Sr Ambroſe Dudley knight, (after Earle of Warwicke,) Guilford Dudley Eſq^r and the lady Jane Gray his wife, Henry Dudley Eſq^r, Sr Andrew Dudley knight, and ſome others, having before been convicted and attainted by courſe of the Comon lawes, And the ſaid Duke (with others) executed the 22th of Auguſt before; their ſaid convictions and attainders were approved and confirmed, And they by this Act againe convicted and attainted of High Treaſon, and adjudged to forfeit all their honors, manors, lands, tenements, rights, &c. By reaſon whereof that right of entry (not of action) which the ſaid Duke had at the time of his attainder as heire to the lady Margaret Counteſs of Shroeſbury eldeſt daughter and coheire of Elizabeth daughter and ſole heire of Thomas lord Berkeley the fourth of that name, to the manors of Wotton, (comprehending the burrowe of Wotton, and the fower hambletts of Nibley, Sinwell, Combe, and Wortley, which make the manor of Wotton fforren,) Simondſfall, Erlingham, Sages, the third part of the manors of Came, Hinton, and Slimbridge, And to divers lands in Came called Corrietts, And to divers lands in Alkington called Holts, diſcended and came to Queen Mary; The pedigree of which Duke in the life of the ſaid Thomas the fourth from the ſaid Elizabeth that lords daughter and heire, is at large already there laid down.

fol: 480.

Paſch: 4. & 5.
Ph: et Mar: rot.
54. in ſc^{a}cio cum
rem regis.

Queen Mary upon this title againſt this lord Henry, (whom to theſe manors and lands, amongſt others, ſhee had reſtored not fower years before, upon his remainder for want of Iſſue male of the body of king Edward the ſixth,) exhibited an Information of Intruſion in the Exchequer for intruding thereinto without title.
This

This lord pleadeth thereto, And foe that fuite ftayed, upon what caufe I know not, neither could this lord remember, when a fewe years before his death I afked him, but thought, upon the death of Queen Mary; But the fame Terme Twelvemonth after, was the like Information put in in the name of Queen Elizabeth upon the fame title, And fomwhat better couched then the former; At what time Sr Thomas Parry then Treforer of the Queens houfhold and one of her privy Counfell, after mafter of the Wards, openly fhewed himfelf therein as an abettor of the fuite, as hee was in the former: It was the | wifdome of this lord and of Thomas Duport his fervant, whom only hee advifed withall, to put nothing to the hazard of a tryall, (efpetially fuch a Counfellor of State in the Queens behalf declaring himfelf an adverfary and Sollicitor). And thereupon a nihil dicit was entred, with a falvo jure for the Queen, and foe refted; which to mee would feeme more ftrange, fave that Sr Thomas Parrys eyes were blinded and his hands bound with a leafe of Simondfall farme made the 8.th of May that fame Terme this information came in, for three fcore years from Michaelmas 1578. at the rent of ten pound two fhillings; And a fine the next Terme leavyed by this lord for confirmation thereof, by the name of the manor of Symondfall and Wotton underedge; which I fuppofe liked him the better becaufe it adjoyned to his manors of Caldicote Lafborrow and others in thofe parts; Howbeit, it proved little beneficiall unto him, dying within two yeares after.

Pa: 1. Eliz: rot. 36.

743

Anno. 20. Eliz: Triñ. 1. Eliz: fub. figill. fol: 840.

For difcharge of which alienation by the faid fine, being without licence, A pardon was after pleaded; And the mouth alfo of Richard Hewes an Atturney then dwelling in Wotton, and the title bringer and Sollicitor to Sr Thomas Parry, was clofed by Thomas Duport aforefaid with an Annuity of ten pounds p.^r Ann̄ for his life; The death of which Hewes was after in a ditch upon London way by the bridge a mile and half on this fide ffairford.

Mich: 9. Eliz: rot. 169. cum rem thes: in fc̄ac̄io.

Thus flept this title, (what ever it was,) in the Crown, quietly without awaking, till Thomas Duke of Norfolke, (whofe fifter Katharine was wife to this lord,) was at the kings bench barre condemned for Treafon. the 16th of January in the 14.th of Queen Elizabeth; whofe fall, whether furthered by the policy of that prudent Statefman Robert Dudley Earle of Leicefter fon of the faid Duke of Northumberland, (as fome have written,) or not, I have not to determine; But when that great and affectionate friend and brother in law of this lords was foe caft down, (and his head taken off the fecond of June after,) forthwith came in the next Terme an Information of Intrufion into the Exchequer againft this lord, (longe before plotted and

Leicesr̄ comon welth fo: 164. printed: 1584.

Hillar: 14. Eliz:

and prepared,) for intruding into the said Manors of Wotton and Symondsall and for taking the profits thereof since the first of her raigne; wherein after pleading and issue Joyned, a tryall was by jury at the Exchequer barre, whereat the Earle of Leicester was present in person as the promoter and follower of that suite, who now like a storme amongst weakened waves wrought high, and all to bee ruffed this family into a some of fury, bringing with him divers other Courtiers of eminency to countenance the cause: Hee at this time having a private promise in writing under the Queens hand and signet to have this land, which I after met withall and is now in Berkeley castle. The verdict passed against this lord; (hereafter I shall shew how and by what means,) Judgement was given against him in Ester Terme in the 15th of Elizabeth, And the 18th of May removed out of the possession; But, veniet iterum, qui te in lucem reponet, dies;

<blockquote>Time againe will bringe the day
Of thy returne, to stay for ay.</blockquote>

The third of June following were these manors extended and valued by the Sherriffe at—251^{li} 3^s 4^d ob. old rent per Ann̄; And the first of July following was a perfect survey made of these Manors by Comission out of the said Court, by Sr Giles Poole and others, whereby also this lord was found to have unjustly received of the rents, fines, heryotts, woodsales, and other profits, 5024^{li} 12^s 8^d. Each tenant and occupier of any part being sworne to deliver his knowledge, for answering whereof this lord stood charged: The 7th of the said July by vertue of another Commission directed to the said Sr Giles Poole and others, the Queens title to these manors was found in this county by Jury at large, with all the mean conveyances, As Atfeilds old deed of entaile, The fine to the heires males in the 23th of king Edward the third, The particōn amongst the three lady-co-heires in the sixth of king Edward the fourth, the attainder of the said duke of Northumberland in the first of Queen Mary, And by her death discent and right of these manors to Queen Elizabeth.

This buisines thus prudently prepared, the Queen the 25th of the same July granted these manors of Wotton and Symondsall to the two sons of the said Duke, Ambrose then Earle of Warrwicke, and the s^d Robert then Earle of Leicester, and their heires. Which Earle of Leic^t shortly after, with an extraordinary number of Attendants, and multitudes of country people that resorted to him, (whom my neighbors parrallell to Bartholomew faire in London,) came to Wotton, And thence to Michaelwood lodge, casting down part of the pales which like a little parke

parke then enclosed that lodge, (for the gates were too narrow to let in his traine,) and thence went to Wotton hill, where hee played a match at Stoball; And a fewe days after this popular entry, having stayed at Wotton, departed from this ill gotten pur-|chase; And to tye cup and cover togeather, though somewhat out of time, both the said Earles of Warwicke and Leicester in the second year after the later recovery had against this lord Henry and Queen Elizabeths grant to them thereof made, came the second time to Wotton and to those new gotten possessions with a greater troup of Attendants then before; what time the said Earle of Leicester, the more to grace Sr Thomas Throgmerton, made him his daily coach companion; And amongst other visits they came to Rolls Court in Slimbridge, to remove that possession, which Arnold Ligon Esq, son of Henry Ligon oft before mentioned, a stout gentleman, there maintained against them, in right of his lease for life, which hee held under this lord Henry; which at that time they did not. But to returne.

745

All the year after this lord and his wife kept London and the Court, as petitioners for pardon of soe much of the foresaid meane rates and arrerages as were then unlevyed by Sheriffes, who had by proces out of the Exchequer shortly after the said recovery, extended all the lands of this lord in what County soever; So that (upon the matter) all his means for maintenance of his estate and calling was taken from him; And at last for 500^{li} paid into the receipt, obtained from the Queen a pardon for the same, dated the 23th of June in the 16th of Eliz: And, as I have heard this lord himself report, this Court suite cost him in the meanes hee used—1800^{li} in ten weekes: In one passage about which pardon, his Lordship added to mee, That what time his wife was upon her knees before the Queen delivering a petition touching these arrerages, Her Matie replyed, Noe noe, my lady Berkeley, wee know you will never love us for the death of your brother; meaning the Duke of Norfolke, beheaded about two yeares before.

Sexta ps. Patent. 23. Junij. 16. Eliz: sub sigillo.

And for defraying of this their excessive expence and payment to the Queen, they were enforced, (amongst other causes,) to morgage to Thomas Markam Esq, the manor of Alkington, extending welnigh to the walls of Berkeley Castle; which being by deed inrolled and without licence, and holden by knights service in Capite, this lord Henry was 28 years after in the 44th yeare of Queen Elizabeth, driven to his pardon, which cost 30^{li} in the Alienation office, besides other charges; And also by pleading the same after in the Exchequer in the office of the Treasorers remembrancer; And what other sales this lord now made, the list thereof hereafter mentioned will declare.

Indenture dated 27. Octob^r. 16. Eliz.
Pardon: 44. Eliz.

fol: 817

And

Carta in castro de Berkeley dat. 25. Nov: 3. Eliz.
746

And so deeply were his two principall officers Thomas Duport and Thomas Fransham, (besides others,) engaged for his Debts, That in the third of | Queen Elizabeth they had from this lord for their indemnity a lease of the Manors of Bosham, ffuntington, Thorney, Tetbury, Sages, fframpton, Daglingworth, Maningford Bruce, Auconbury, Weston, ffenystanton, and Hilton, for one and twenty yeares, with power to receive the rents of those manors, and pay the debts they were ingaged in for this lord; Which as they are scheduled then were above—2000ˡⁱ.

I am now, for ought I know to the contrary, almost left alone alive, that can testify the truth of this digression, (if a reall circumstance may soe bee called,) which, together with my love to truth, shall bee my motive to leave the same to the knowledge of this noble family; As namely, how one of the preparations or practices of the said Earle of Leic:, before the beginning of this suite, was his outward demonstration of great affection to this lord Henry, inviting him to his Castle of Killingworth, six miles from Callowdon, lodging him as a brother and fellowe huntsman with him in his own bedchamber, with semblance of great familiarity; gave him liberty without restraint over his Deere in his Parks and chace there; fairly relating unto him how it was his greatest honor, (as in deed it was,) to bee discended from his ancient house; desiring that the same by some good herald might by his means bee warranted unto him, with their matches, out of his evidence;

To a sweet note the fowlers pipe is set
When hee the bird betrays into the nett.

Anno. 12. Eliz: 1570.

This motion was assented to by this well meaning lord; One Harvey an herald, not longe after, was by the Earles lre commended for yᵉ service and sent to Callowdon, where after a small paines in perusall of those few evidences that then there remained, And some notes taken importing no other end but discents, Hee was thence with lres of Comission sent (as hee desired) to Berkeley Castle, where the maine body remained of those Berkeley evidence, having about him pfidious instructions to draw away from this lords evidence house some Deeds and exemplifications of records, (whereof the originalls was either lost, or taken from the files,) which the herald performed; And being somewhat in drinke, through the kind entertainment hee received at Berkeley Castle, in the house of one Thomas Bolton, then an Inholder (and an old brewer to this lord,) said unto him upon occation of speech, (as Bolton twice told mee and oftner others,) That this Journey by reason of what hee

747

had | found and had would bee his making for ever; which words I received from Thomas Boulton to whom Harvey spake them, upon occation of Boltons question, when hee would end his search. ffalse friends are the greatest enemies, worst when
they

they seem best, and most dangerous when they speake fairest; Ovid said truly; Ovidius

> Tuta frequensque via est, sub amici fallere nomen,
> Tuta frequensque licet, fit via, crimen habet.
> It is a safe and comon way, by freindship to deceive,
> But safe and comon though it bee, its knavery by yor leave.

And I my self doe here avow, That about twenty six years now past my self discoursing of these and the like words with Mr John Savage, hee told mee That this herald in his way from Callowdon towards Berkeley came to his house to Sainbury, (two miles from Camden, wth the lord Berkeleys lre of comendacon for his first nights lodging on the way, (as my self have often done,) where, having liberally supped, hee opened his portmanteau, and turning over a long roll of Armes to shew him the coate borne by the name of Savage, hee observed the coate of Berkeley, well known to him; And how that a note of paper was pinned over the same, which Mr Savage suspecting, (yet hee knew not what nor wherefore,) tooke a copy of the same out of the roll, whilst Harvey the herald slept in bed, (left by forgetfullnes in his parlor below;) And when hee could make noe construction thereof hee cast it into a cubbord in the same roome, amongst a heape of old cancelled bonds lers and the like trash; which note after some search I found, and thereby visibly discovered the treason; Quicquid sub terra est in apricum proferet ætas, This was in anno 12. Eliz: 1570

> Time will reveale each secret, sublunary thing;
> Noe hidden thinge there is, but time to light will bring.

And doubtles, one of the evidences then taken away was an exemplification under the great seale, of the office found in the first of king Edward the third in the county of Glouc., after the death of the lord Maurice the third, the originall whereof was not longe before filched from the file in the Tower; And one other concerning Erlingham, as the said note imported. **And** let mee by a short digression in this place ingeniously professe to this noble family, that by the happines of my poore endeavors, more then 300 peices of evidence have been returned into their Evidence house from many corners, but whether soe scattered by falshood or forgetfullnes, | or by what other accidents, I may not determine; But sure I am, that many of those peeces have been out of their possession since the death of Queen Mary: which is not here otherwise remembred, then to pray this noble family to bee carefull to whom they committ the keyes of their Evidence house; For such as St Luke mentions the unjust steward to bee will in great families bee found in all ages, that will serve themselves and theire own ends. This note is in Berkeley Castle

748

Luke. 16. v. 1.

After

After the said Informaçõn was put into the Court, and the issue in joyning, The Earle of Leicester sent for his inward freind Edmond lord Chandois, (esteemed in those daies as king of Cotswold,) And at Langly agreed of sixteen speciall freeholders names, to bee with others returned of the Jury for tryall of that cause; what time they had also the help of another knight since deceased, who gave the names of the other eight, whose name I forbear for his grandchilds sake, noe malevolent kinsman to this family; which twenty four soe corruptly packed, tryed the issue against this lord: And this was told mee in the hearing of Mr Edward Green vicar of Berkeley, (who is yet living,) in Berkeley Castle the 25th of September. 1603. by Mr Charles Hyet, which (as hee said) hee knew of his own knowledge to bee true; what time hee was very neare the lord Chandois in attendance; who then affirmed further, That Mr James Bramidge his familiar freind and neighbour after told him That hee was present as a speciall serv: by the death bed of the lord Chandois, (who dyed the 17th of March in the 16th of Elizabeth,) when hee heard him in that sicknes say, That nothing greived him more at that time Then what hee did about the Jury for the Earles of Warrwick and Leicester against the lord Berkeley.

[margin: Sr N. P. [Nicholas Poyntz]]

And further, on Munday the 18th of September in the first of king James, as William Chester of Almondsbury Esqr, my self, and Mr Edward Trotman walked togeather in Eastwood parke, (fower miles from Berkeley,) after dinner, whither Mr Trotman (then there dwelling and now living at Came,) had purposely at my request invited Mr Chester and my self, Mr Chester then told mee, (as a token of the love and friendship then by Mr Trotmans means purposely setled between us,) that hee being a page to the Earle of Leicesters chamber, observed the herald Harvies repaire unto him with Evidence from Berkeley; And that the Earles words to him, (which hee then heard,) were, That these titles had ever succeeded between | their houses, according to the kings favour in their times. And hee then further told mee, That Mr Henry Goodyeare, (after knight,) a gentleman in great trust with the lord Berkeley, held in this cause secret intelligence with the said Earle of Leicester, and brought him some evidence also about the beginning of this suite, as hee then observed also, waiting the more near to Leicester because hee was allied to him; Words heard by Mr Trotman as well as my self: I hate the tooth that bites the dead: But this gentleman, whom 34. years past I remember to have seen, and some of whose lres (admirably penned) written to this lord I have read, had his eare and his heart as much in those times as any man that lived; And was often present at this lords request at divers meetings and conferrences of his Counsell, as the

the said lord hath since told mee ; To whom I once related what Mr Chester had said to mee : But being againe to write of the like packing stuffe in another tryall and recovery, I will now returne from this digression.

After the Survey of these manors of the first of July in the 15th of Elizabeth was returned into the Exchequer, It appeared, (amongst other things,) to bee presented by that Jury under the title of woods, That the Queens Matie was seized of a wood called Michaelwood chace, which extendeth from the Towns of Nibley and Huntingford unto the redford, and soe going all alonge the said river or place where the water commonly runneth called redford, unto the woods end, unto Robert Jobbins house of the woods end ; Wherein the Maior and Burgesses of the Town of Wotton and the Inhabitants of Huntingford and Nibley doe comon with their Cattle ; And wherein the Inhabitants of Alkington, Woodford, and Wyke, have entercommon because of vicinage, That is to say, in respect of the Comon that the Maior and Burgesses of the manor of Wotton and the Inhabitants of the said Townes of Nibley and Huntingford have in the other part of Michaelwood over the red ford, being the Inheritance of Henry lord Berkeley : Which wood on this side the red ford is the free hold and wast ground of the Queens Matie, and parcell of the manor of Wotton, and extendeth as aforesaid, and is by estimation—207. acres. **Thus** the Survey.

In the composing of this survey it was soe partially carried, That Maurice Harding of Cowley, (yet living,) Richard ffourds of Pinelsend in Cowley, Robert Hale of Wotton, and Nicholas Cornock of Nibley, (grandfather to John Cornocke now servant in houshold to the lady Elizabeth Berkeley,) being of the Jury, would by noe perswasion or threats give consent to soe [untrue a presentment in the former point, which ready drawn by the Commissioners was tendred unto them, as the three first have often severally told mee ; whereupon their names, after they had been sworne, were strooke out of the panell from their fellowes who presented the same, being all of them tenants to this manor of Wotton : of which manner of proceedings wee have since had many times conferences togeather.

This Survey thus returned and remaining of record in the Exchequer, and the said manor the same month granted to the Earles of Warwicke and Leicester and their heires, as hath been said, They immediately thereupon placed one William Cecill as Ranger, to oversee their Deere in that part of Michaelwood chase soe presented to bee part of their manor of Wotton : Between whom and Dunning and Kimmerly

750

Div'se exam: in castro de Berkeley.
Diu'sæ lre Nichi Poyntz et Thome

Kimmerly his men, And the Ranger and keepers of this lord Henry, many bickerings often times happened, to the drawing of bloud, continuing in that troublesome course till the death of the said Earle of Leicester, 1588, in the thirtieth of Queen Elizabeths raigne.

<small>Throkm'ton Com de Warr: et Leicest 1578. 79. 80. 81. 83. in castro de Berkeley.</small>

Immediately upon whose death, this lord, relying himself upon the comon Justice of the Realme, (for potent Leicester only medled in these matters, and the whole manor survived to the Earle of Warwicke his brother then much infirmed with sicknes,) brought an action of trespas against the said William Kimmerly for treading of his grass in Michaelwood chase, and killing of a bucke there in July before the s:d Earle dyed, to his damage of ten pound; In which suite this lord recovered upon a non sum informatus.

<small>Trin : Pasch : 31. Eliz : rot. 462. in banco regis.</small>

This Kymerly some years after upon a suite in the Court of Wards prosecuted against this lord, and examined touching his behaviour in these times of his keepership in this part of the said Chase, deposed, That twelve years togeather hee was a keeper in that part of Michaelwood lying between Redford and Wotton, under William Cecill Ranger there to the Earles of Warwick and Leicester; And that all that time hee walked in great feare, and for the most part in the high waies, and durst not goe out of them into the said chace, but was always interrupted and threatned by the lord Berkeleys Rangers and Keepers, and had a warrant for a bucke taken from him by one William Hallam; And in that twelve years did not kill any Deere in that side of the chace where hee was appointed Keeper: And that afterwards hee was discharged from being keeper by Mr. Arnold Oldisworth, for that his Mrs the Countesse of Warwicke would not allow any fee for | any keeper to walk there, as hee said, since which time to this his examinacōn, there hath been noe keeper there by the said Countesses appointment.

<small>751</small>

These Manors of Wotton and Simondsall by the death of the Earle of Leicester coming by Survivor to the said Earle of Warrwick, as aforesaid, hee conveyed them (amongst many others) to Anne his wife and her heires, and dyed within two years after his brother the Earle of Leicesters death.

<small>Hill. 37. Eliz : rot. 92. eod. rot. 106. Trin : rec : 38. Eliz : rot ; 123. Mich : 40 : Eliz. rot. cum rem thes: in sc̄acio.</small>

It chanced shortly after, That Henry Parmiter then of Stone an Atturney at lawe, Giles Daunt then of Oulpen, George Smallwood then of Dursley, and seaven others, all men of mettall and good woodmen, (I mean old notorious deerestealers,) well armed, came in the night time with deere-netts and doggs to steale deere in this

this chace of Michaelwood, who Mr. Anthony Hungerford, yet livinge, then Ranger there for this lord, foone found in that part of the chace which was formerly prefented to bee part of the manor of Wotton, then the inheritance of the faid lady Anne Countes of Warrwicke; And prefently drew from Nibly and other bordering places nine or ten of his own tenants and friends, as good men with their ftaves as the hunters, whom they roughly fet upon in that part of the chace: betweene which two companies of true men and theeves, many fore blowes were exchanged, divers on both fides beaten to the ground, and much bloud drawn; which violence they ceafed not on either fide till the fall of Smallwood by his deaths wound, whereupon leaving him as dead, the reft of the Deereftealers fled: But by this means being known, And fuite commenced againft them in the Starchamber, the faid Counteffe of Warrwicke fent unto the faid Parmiter a copy of the faid Survey and prefentment, And earneftly by Arnold Oldifworth and other her officers, laboured him and the reft to juftifie their entry and hunting in the faid chace under her authority and licence; And the rather for that Parmiter being an Atturney of the comon place, and drawing his maintenance from his practice, might otherwife incurre noe fmall damage and fine alfo with imprifonment, with other like perfwafions: Howbeit the hunters having made their peace with this lord and his Ranger, And that practice of the Counteffe, (which Parmiter difcovered to mee with delivery of the copy hee had received,) not prevailing, And this lord having a good opinion of the juftnes of his title to that part of the chace, notwithftanding the faid prefentment, afwell as the reft, hee did in the 41th. of Queen Elizabeth, enlarge the enclofure which of old time had been about the lodge in the faid chace, And with a pale for the more comely proportion enclofed about 10 acres more then formerly was in the old enclofure; for which fact, (though not to the damage of the faid Counteffe or any of her tenants of 2d. by the year,) fhee caufed Robert George her Receivor and William Trotman one of her woodwards to fawe down the raile and pale in fuch places as the faid addition was made; And thereupon alfo brought her action of trefpas againft Thomas Hewes and other of this lords palers and workmen therein; During which fuite at the common lawe, fhee alfo exhibited her bill in the Court of Wards in Michmas Terme in the 41th. & 42th. of Queen Elizabeth againft this lord and Anthoney Huntley his fervt. and Woodward there, Setting forth therein how fhee was feized of a meffuage and one hundred acres of land called Holts, and of Comon of pafture thereto belonging in the faid part of Michaelwood; And alfo fet forth, That that part of the faid Chace which extended from the Towns of Nibley and Huntingford unto the river or water called the redford, and foe alonge the faid river or place where the water runneth commonly called the redfourd, unto the houfe late

of

Anno. 1598.

752

Mich: term. 41. et. 42 Eliz: in Cur Wardō Anno. 1599

of Robert Jobbins at the woods end, is parcel of her manor of Wotton underedge; And that this lord by the inſtigation of the ſaid Huntley had not only forbidden her farmer of Holts to have any Comon in the ſaid Chace, and driven back his Cattell, but alſo had incloſed about two hundred acres of that part of the chace with a pale, which did lye as aforeſaid and which was part of the manor of Wotton, with ſuch other ſuggeſtions as are too comon in Engliſh bills; To which this lord and Huntley made anſwer and ſhewed, That if any ſuch comon had of old belonged to the ſaid farme of Holts, that the ſame was extinguiſhed by an unity of poſſeſſion; And alſo, that the whole chace of Michaelwood was the inheritance of this lord, as in their anſwers at large is contained; Whereupon after both the defts had according to the uſage of that Court been examined upon Interrogatories, the plt replyed, and the defts rejoyned, And a Comiſſion was ſued out and executed at Wotton aforeſaid

September, 42. Eliz.

the nynth of September in the 42th yeare of Queen Elizabeth, whereat in fowerteen days were fifty witneſſes examined; And afterwards my ſelf and William Hallam (an old keeper) with the Examiner in Court: publication ſhortly after awarded, and copies amounting to—400. ſheets of paper taken; whereby appeared that both plt and defendants had aimed at one and the ſame end, by bending their maine proofes for the intereſt of the ſoile, and for the bounds of the ſaid manors of Wotton and Alkington, which was labored by as many ways means and devices as well might

753

fall into the hart of man: The concluſion was That the Counteſs finding her proofs overwaighed, ſuffered her bill without hearing to bee diſmiſſed: Neither would ſhee afterwards bee urged to proceed to tryall upon her action of Treſpas againſt Hughes, but diſcontinued it, and paid coſts.

Mich: terme. 43. et. 44. Eliz: rot: 382. et 383. in banco regis.

All which may more largely bee read in my parchment booke dedicated to this lord, Intituled a regiſter of the tenants by knights ſervice from the 378th leafe to the 388th leafe; And theſe two ſuites are both in Berkeley caſtle exemplifyed under the ſeales of thoſe Courts. Thus was the greater half of that Chace preſerved which the Counteſſe and her officrs had devour'd, with ſoe ſtronge an aſſurance that the ſales of the woods and timber were propoſed in the country, whereof the truer owner not longe after raiſed 2000li. Yet left the like value for his poſterity, as after followeth. But that compoſition which was afterwards made in the ſeaventh of

Michaelwood. Anno 8. Jacobi: 1610. fol: 792.

king James between this lord and Sr Robert Sidney then Viſcount Liſle, after Earle of Leiceſter, gave ending to theſe and many other ſuites; And thereby alſo the means of this lords ſale of all the trees in this chace growing without the ſaid Parke, (except—3000. of the beſt,) to one Thoms Hacket after a certaine rate by the Tunne for Timber and by the cord for fire-wood; which hee coaled, And errected

both

both a forge and furnace, bringing his iron oare out of the fforreſt of Deane ; And which hee, (having made little benefit,) aſſigned to Sʳ Wiłłm Throkmerton, And hee (as little,) to others : of which this lord Henry made. 2000ˡⁱ towards payment of the ſaid compoſition : **And** the end of that iron work begott the agreement that preſently after followed between this lord and the Inhabitants of Alkington, Comoners in this Chace ; which was, That this lord ſhould incloſe with a pale and keep in ſeveralty to him and his heires for ever, fower hundred acres on the South eaſt part of the Chace, at eighteen foot to the pearch, (accompting the forementioned little park and lodge therein to bee parcell,) free and diſcharged from yᵉ claim of Comon therein by any of the Comoners, And that this lord ſhould leave the reſidue of the ſaid Chace to bee a free comon for the Cattell of the ſaid Inhabitants of the manor of Alkington ; And the deere of this lord feeding within the ſaid parke or chace ſhould bee for ever excluded from that part of the chace and from their grounds adjoyning therto, which was agreed to bee left to the ſaid Comoners Inhabitants of Alkington for their ſaid Comon ; And that this lord ſhould leave ſtanding upon the ſoile of the Ground parcell of the ſaid chace, to bee | left out of the ſaid parke, one thouſand oaks (ſince marked out) for maſt and ſhadowe, which neither this lord nor the inhabitants of Alkington, freeholder or comoner, ſhould any otherwiſe uſe fell or diſpoſe of ; And that aſſurances ſhould accordingly bee made by indifferent Counſell on both ſides ; whereupon this lord forthwith encloſed his—400 . acres, And in Trinity Terme following exhibited his bill into the Chancery, ſetting forth the ſaid agreement between him and the Comoners, with ſuch other circumſtances as ſeemed dependant upon ſuch an agreement, And how thereupon hee had purchaſed other lands adjoyning for the circular and more uniforme proportion of his pale : **Whereunto** the defᵗˢ Comoners made anſwere, confeſſing the agreement. **And** thereupon by the conſent and deſire of both parties, It was decreed by the ſaid Court of Chancery That the agreement ſhould ſtand and bee inviolably for ever after obſerved of all parties, which at this day continueth accordingly, Aᵒ 1626. Which ſmall ſervice this lord ſo acceptably received, That in recompence of my contriving and finiſhing thereof hee by Deed granted mee a fee bucke and a fee doe yearly during my life, out of the ſaid new parke. **Yet** ſoe reſted not this chace or park, But that George lord Berkeley after his full age wholly diſparked it, And carried away the pales railes and poſts thereof for the mending of his three other parks of Whitcliffe, Newparke, and the Worthy ; And then demiſed the ſame for years to divers tenants, who forthwith at their charges according to their agreemᵗˢ with his Loᵖ, divided the ſame into many cloſes, grubbing up the thornes furres and other brambles thereof ; In the three firſt years of whoſe leaſes, the ſaid lord carried
thence

Triñ term : 1612. Annᵒ 10. Jacobi in Cancełł.

754

Anno. 1612. 10 : Jacobi.

thence alſo great ſtore of that timber for his buildings at Simondſall and at new-parke and at the grange by Berkeley, and at other places, And ſold much of the reſt, coleing alſo a great part of the firewood thereof and felling and burning the reſidue at Newparke and Berkeley caſtle, where hee then abode.

To this diſparking it may ſeeme the lord George was led by the preſident of his Grandfather, this lord Henry, who in the time of Queen Mary upon his firſt entry quite diſparked Hawe-parke by Wotton, and let the ſame at 6ˢ. 8ᵈ. the acre, taking a fine of 26ˢ. 8ᵈ for each acre | for one and twenty yeares; which a fewe years before Sʳ Thomas Thinne, under the then Protectors favour, had in the later days of king Edward the ſixth made thin, both of deere timber and woods therein growing.

755

Having thus purſued this recovery of the Manors of Wotton and Simondſall had againſt this lord, with ſuch Inquiſitions and circumſtances as followed thereupon, I now returne to a like recovery of other manors had in like manner ten years after, againſt this lord alſo.

Triñ Terṁ. 22. Eliz: rot: 124. in ſcᵃcio cum reṁ regis.

Queen Elizabeth, in the 22ᵗʰ of her raigne, exhibited another Informacõn of Intruſion againſt this lord Henry, (which was likewiſe proſecuted by the ſaid Earle of Leiceſter,) charging him thereby to have intruded into the Manors of Sages and Arlingham, and into the third part of the manors of Came, Hinton and Slimbridge, and into the ffarmes of Holts and Corrietts, Newleys, the warth, and other lands in the county of Glouc., from the firſt of December in the firſt yeare of her raigne untill the exhibiting of this information; And by all that time to have unjuſtly taken the rents and profits: **To** this Information this lord pleaded divers pleas according as his Counſell conceived his ſeverall titles to bee, All which for all the ſaid Manors and lands were in Hillary Term in the 26ᵗʰ of Elizabeth found by jury at the Exchequer barre againſt him, And next terme Judgement entred accordingly. The fifteenth of Auguſt following by vertue of a Comiſſion dated the 8ᵗʰ of July before, was this lord by the Sherriffe of the County put out of poſſeſſion, And the 20ᵗʰ of the ſaid Auguſt, the ſaid manors and lands were extended and valued to the Sherriffe. **The** 17ᵗʰ of September following by vertue of a more ſpeciall Comiſſion directed to the foreſaid Sʳ Giles Poole and others, a perticuler Survey was made of all the ſaid manors and lands, and of all the rents and profits received by this lord from the ſaid firſt of December in yᵉ firſt yeare of the ſaid Queen to that time, which, (beſides fines and all other caſualties,) amounted to the ſum of—3953ˡⁱ 15ˢ. 10ᵈ wherewith this

Anno. 26: Eliz:

Survey under ſeale in caſt: de Berkeley. Liber recogñ: hill. 28. Eliz: in ſcᵃcio.

this lord was charged. **Against** the payment of which meane rates and arrerages, this lord foe ftrugled, that I verily fuppofe noe one Terme for Thirteen years next following is without orders in the Exchequer touching the fame, befides the many petitions to her Matie, wherein at laft hee was much helped by Sr Edward Coke her Atturney generall.

The fecond of July following, the Queen granted all the faid manors and premifes foe laftly recovered againft this lord to the faid Earles of Warr. and Leiceft. and their heirs, to hold by the 4.th p.^t of a knights fee. | Anno. 27. Eliz.

The Earle of Leicefter dyed in the thirtieth of the faid Queen, Anno, 1588. without lawfull iffue, whereby all thofe manors and lands mentioned in thefe two recoveries had againft this lord furvived and came to the faid Earle of Warwicke, being his elder brother; who by his conveyances, (moft whereof is inrolled in Chancery,) in the 32.th of the faid Queen, granted the fame to certaine feoffees, To the ufe of himfelf for life And after his deceafe to the lady Anne his wife and to her heires for ever, as formerly hath been touched, And dyeth the 21.th of ffebruary the fame yeare; All which are at large found in the Inquifiton or office after his death the 15.th of December the yeare after in the 33.th of Queen Elizabeth. 756

By this office, the Queen was intituled to the moitie of a third part of all the faid Earle of Warrwicks lands during the minority of Elizabeth the daughter and heire of Sir Phillip Sidney, (after maryed to the Earle of Rutland,) as by the office at large appeareth: Upon returne whereof, the Queen by Indenture under the feale of the Court of wards and liveries dated the 4.th of June in the 33.th of her raigne, in confideration of Twenty pound fine and 26.^li 13.^s 4.^d yearly rent, demifed to the faid Anne Counteffe of Warr. the third part of the faid manors of Came, Hinton, and Slimbridge, the faid Newleys, the warth, Holts, and Corietts, in lieu of the moitie of the third part of all the Earle of Warrwicks lands, To hold during the minority of the faid Elizabeth Sidney then but fower years old, which was an Extraordinary favor that the greatnefs of this Counteffe found under a gracious Princefs, on whom in neareft place fhee waited, and of a freindly mafter of that Court, then William lord Burleigh, lord Treafurer alfo; By which favour this lord was as deeply prejudiced in effect as by the recovery had againft him in the Exchequer: for, being thereby under the prerogative of the Crown and the proceedings in that Court turned out of that poffeffion, which notwithftanding the recovery in the Exchequer hee had ftill maintained for the third parts of the Manors of Cam, Hinton, and Slimbridge, efpecially; And his poore tenants fent for daily

Inqu: 33, Eliz. poft mort: Ambr Com Warr.

Carta 4 Junij 33. Eliz.

by

by proces, and committed for their faithfull adhereing to their landlord, This lord to help himfelf and them exhibited even a world of bills, and made as many anfwers, whereupon, as alfo upon bills of Traverfes to the faid office, followed an Army of orders, Injunctions and affidavits for feaven or more yeares togeather; A fruitlefs refiftance of himfelf and his counfell in thofe times, whereby hee not only loft all

757 that was demanded againft | him, (for what the faid Counteffe would fhee obtained,) but alfo with the exceffive expence and payment of cofts, exhaufted his coffers; Suits much better not to have been defended at all, then not defended in the fucceffe; And if better times fhould ferve, the regaining made more difficult.

I should make the life of this lord a volume of it felf if I fhould perticularize but a fowerth part of the toiles and turmoiles, troubles and difquiets, that arofe about the poffeffions alfo of the faid Newleyes, Holts, and other of the faid lands, kept

33. Eliz: loft and regained, and loft againe, by this lord and his fervants: of the indictments
Sr Henry Winfton and traverfes that followed thereupon at Gloucefter and other places, purfued by
Hill: 33 Eliz. Sr Henry Winfton efpetially in behalf of the faid Counteffe: And of the multitude
Trin. 32 Eliz. of Starchamber bills in thofe years alfo exhibited by her againft this lord, Rich.^d
Mich: 32. et 33. Thomas, Anthony Huntley, and other of his fervants and tenants, touching entries
Eliz. ryotts and forces, Termly attendants in the chamber of Mr Thomas Chamberlayne, then this lords Sollicitor, (after a Judge;) And how this lord by the injurious fuggeftion of the faid Counteffe was twice convented before the Counfell table at Whitehall, to anfwere fuppofed mifdemeanors by her objected, which could not bee proved; And at another time at Oatlands, where the 16th of Auguft. 1590. in the 32th of Elizabeth hee was ordred to enter into a recognizance of ten thoufand marks, That hee his fervants followers and freinds fhould from thenceforth keep the peace towards the tenants fervants followers and freinds of the faid Countefs during the controverfies between them: At what time alfo another recognizance of 500 marks was taken of Humphry Alfop this lords then Steward of his Gloucefter- fhire lands, and one of the Sollicitors of his lawe caufes: As alfo of the many proceffes ferved upon many of this lords fervants and tenants at thefe times to appeare in the kings bench and Crown office, to give bonds for their good be- haviours, with an endles number of brawles and broiles about thefe times raifed and purfued by the faid Sr Henry Winfton and Arnold Oldifworth her greateft Agent and Sollicitor.

This is that lady of Warrwick whom Mr Rowland Vaughan, in his booke of Waterworks, reporteth, That to ferve turnes was able in Court to work miracles in

lay

lay matters; which this lord Henry found true, to his extreame coſt and trouble, as herein appeares.

 I forbear alſo to ſpeake of the action brought by this lord in theſe times againſt the ſaid Sr Henry Winſton, upon the Statute de Scandalis magnatum, who malitiouſly and falſly had given out That this lord ſaid hee would come | with . 140. men, and get his poſſeſſion againe of the Newleaſe with the ſword; **As** alſo I omit to write of the bill Anſwere proceedings and decree in the Court of wards, touching the watermill and carucate of land called Corietts, in Cam, wherein who deſireth to bee inſtructed in the learning of favour and prerogative, and to ſet a fair gloſſe upon a foule Text, may have recourſe to the ſaid decree, which paſſed in Eaſter Terme in the 42th of Queen Elizabeth in the Court of Wards for the ſaid Counteſſe againſt this lord and his tenant John Somers, thereby caſt out of poſſeſſion; A ſuite ſollicited by the wily diligence of the ſaid Arnold Oldiſworth then interreſſed in the ſame for many years by her demiſe, who, (after the compoſition in the 7th of king James with the lord Liſle,) having purchaſed the fee farme thereof of this lord Henry, ſhortly after ſold the ſame to W^{ill}m Harding and his heires, As not longe after hee did all the reſt of his eſtate to others, And yet ſattisſyed not his debts by—4000^{li.} at the leaſt; And laſtly dyed in Virginia.

 Neither doe I here remember the extents upon all this lords lands in what County ſoever hee had any lands for the leavying of the ſaid meane rates, nor the great ſums which in part payment thereof hee paid into the Exchequer, nor the recognizance of—4000^{li.} which hee was by orders in the Exchequer inforced to enter into, with condition to pay all the rents and profits of the ſaid manors and lands ſoe recovered againſt him; wherein the preſſures were farre more violent upon this lord then the uſuall courſe, either of the Crown, or that Court ordinarily inflicted upon the ſubject, in regard the one moitie of the ſaid arrerages or meane rates was granted by the ſaid łres patents to the ſaid Earles with the lands, with all the means which the Crowns prerogative had to recover it, and ſo came to the ſaid Counteſſe, who not only with the ſame coveted to defray the charges of theſe ſuites, but to reward the diligence of her ſervants, freinds, and Counſell employed therein: And this guiſt of the moitie of the meane rates filled five years vacations with Inquiries in this County of Glouc. by Juries, to find out the value and profits of the lands recovered, in rents herriots fines and woodſales received by this lord, to the extreame expence of both parties: ffor ſome eaſe and releife wherein, this lord exhibited his petiton to the Queens perſon, preſenting alſo his greiſe therein by word

Anno. 32. Eliz:

758
Mich. 40. et. 41.
Eliz. 1599.

Paſch. 42. Eliz:

Hill. 28. Eliz:

Annis 28. 29. 33.
39. et. 41. Eliz.

Anno: 36. et al.

word of mouth to her Matie For the countermining whereof, and to fruſtrate that court ſuite which to this lord was both tedious and coſtly, the ſaid counteſs exhibited alſo her petition, (for ſhee that perpetually waited next her perſon, could not be any ſmall time ignorant thereof,) praying the Queen to | have allowance by her privy ſeale of the ſaid arrerages according to her Ma^ts grant under the great ſeale; And that the further diſpatch thereof might bee referred to ſome of her Officers, To the end the debts of her late huſband the Earle of Warrwicke might the ſooner bee paid by her his executrix; Which being referred to Buckhurſt lord Treaſorer, hee certifyed almoſt all the former proceedings in perticularity, but in ſuch ſort as this lord gained nothing but further loſſe for all his paines and expence.

759

Cert: dat: 26. Maij 1599. 41. Eliz.

Neither doe I here, other then in curſary manner, ſicco pede, remember how this lord Henry after the ſaid verdict and Judgement upon the ſaid Informacon given againſt him, often moved that Court of Exchequer to have allowance of certaine errors to reverſe the ſaid Judgement and verdict, and to have his writ of error ſigned by Sr John Popham then atturney generall; who after counſell at ſeverall times heard on both ſides, held them to bee errors unanſwerable: but his remove to the place of Cheife Juſtice hindred the ſame: whom Sr Thomas Egerton ſucceeded, who, all his time of Atturney generall delaied it: After him Sir Edward Coke ſucceeded, To whome upon new motions the Court referred the examination of the errors anew, who alſo for his better reſolution before hee would deliver his opinion, heard Counſell on both ſides, And at laſt in Court told Peryam cheefe Baron That if ſuch errors were depending in any other court, hee thought them ſufficient to reverſe judgment, but what they were in this Court, hee referred to his Lo^ps conſideration.

At laſt, after long preſſures, the ſaid lord cheife Baron referred this lord to his petition to the Queen for allowance of the ſaid writ of Error; her Matie referred the conſideration of the ſame to the two cheife Juſtices, the maſter of the Rolls, Egerton, and to her Atturney generall, who with much Sollicitation met in Hillary Terme in the 37th of Elizabeth, and having heard Counſell on both ſides, reſolved, that the proceedings upon the ſaid Information were erronious: But notwithſtanding directed this lords Counſell firſt to ſearch for preſidents in the Exchequer from the time of king Edward the third, wherein any writ of Error had been brought for any matter of forme, or for miſjoyning of iſſue, or tryall, or pleading; And alſo to ſearch for petitions, whether by the Statute of 31. E. 3. a writ of Error may bee brought between her Matie and a Subject without a petition; And to ſee alſo the manner of

the

the petition for the proceeding therein in forma juris, And then they would certifie their opinions.

Search, (the coftly work of a longe time,) was made accordingly, And many prefidents found wherein the fubject had been allowed his writ | of error in that Court, both by and without petition; Copies thereof were praied by this lord Henry: Anfwere was made, None might bee given without an order from the lord cheife Baron: Hee being by this lords Counfell often moved thereto, finally anfwered, hee fhould have none except it were by warrant from her Matie, feeing the prefidents intended the fubvertion of the eftate of the Queens patentees, (meaning his deareft lady and freind the Countefs of Warwicke,) and therefore this lord fhould ufe his petition to the Queen if hee would have any; which referment of his is entred of record in the booke of orders of that Court; whereby Certificate was never made.

760

Liber ordinum in fine term̃ Michīs 37. et. 38. Eliz.

A marriage at this time went on between Thomas the only fon of this lord and Elizabeth the only child of Sr George Carey knight marfhall, fhortly after lord Hunfdon and Chamberlaine to her Matie. To whom a breife collection with the orders annexed of all thefe proceedings was delivered; hee undertooke with the Queen, and effected it: The cheife Baron by like art, as hee had delayed, deluded the faid writt of error: And after, this lord turned himfelf to looke after other Counfells and Courfes that gave at laft a winding out from thefe irkfome laborinths and perplexities.

And I remember a Sollicitor of the lord Berkeleys in the clofe of that day caft before thofe referrees, the confideration of the Statute of the 33th of Henry the 8th, which giveth the actuall poffeffion of the lands of perfons attainted without any Office found, Saving the poffeffion of all Strangers: which, faid hee, is expounded as if an office had been found at Comon lawe: And if the office at the comon lawe had found the feifin and diffeiffin, yet the king could not have granted away the land before feifin, or a Scire facias fued; Inferring thereby, That noe informaco͠n of Intrufion at all would lye againft the lord Berkeley by reafon of the favinge in the faid Statute: which they (not difliking) held worthy of further confideration, but, I fuppofe, forgott it foone after.

Cokes rep: Doughties cafe.

My defire in thefe relations is nothing more then to informe the now lord George truly, though with prolixity, of the paffages of this his immediate anceftor in thefe paper warrs; whereby I will looke back to the Jury that tryed this laft
iffue

issue in the 26th of Queen Elizabeth in the Exchequer againſt this lord, And tell him truly, as I have done in the former recovery, That they were likewiſe plotted | and named by the ſaid Earle of Leiceſter, with the aſſiſtance of Sr. Thomas Throkmerton and Sr. Nicholas Poynz, (then at enmity with this ld.) And the whole 24 names ready written were delivered by the firſt of them to Richard Adams of Wotton ſervant to the ſaid Earles, And by him delivered to Mr. Hall then underſherriffe to Thomas Baynham of Clowerwall Eſqr, as ſent with them from the ſaid High Sherriffe, with a comandment in the name of the ſaid Earle of Leiceſter that hee ſhould ingroſſe and returne them, mixed with the delivery of forty ſhillings then given to Hall, and ſome threats if hee did not: And this did Hall himſelf out of remorſe of conſcience, (when hee ſaw the ill effect,) make known to Humphry Alſop then ſollicitor to this lord, who thereupon, to continue the memoriall thereof, exhibited a bill againſt the ſaid High Sheriffe and Underſherriffe for this miſdemeanor in the Chancery, (not in the Starre chamber as hee ſhould have done,) whereto they made anſwere and confeſſed the whole matter as aforeſaid, this being the next yeare after the tryall; And ſoe it reſted; Whereof the Counteſſe of Warwicke having notice ſome years after, And knowing well how deeply this packing and nomination of a Jury, (though in the Queens caſe,) might trench into her title, that ſtill continued reſtles and in Termely agitation, Shee to damme this bill and theſe anſweres, complained in Chancery in Micħmas Terme in the 36th of Queen Elizabeth: Whereupon Hall and Alſop being examined at the ſuite of the ſaid Counteſſe, confeſſed upon oath the truth of the premiſes, which to this day yet remaineth with the ſaid examiner. But in regard that her title was hereby ſcandalized, and for other reaſons, movinge the court, After order upon order, this lord Henry was compelled to bringe in the Exemplification of the ſaid bill and anſwers, which hee had under the great Seale, into the Court, where it was broken and cancelled, and bill and anſwers orderd alſo to bee taken from the file and cut to peeces, wch was done: howbeit true copies were taken and ſufficiently teſtified and caſt into the Evidence houſe at Berkeley Caſtle, where they yet remaine: About ſower years after, my ſelf ſerved Mr. Hall with a Subpena to teſtifie his knowledge herein upon a tryall at the comon pleas barre, touching ſome of theſe lands, (whereof I ſhall after write,) thereby to extenuate the validity of the former verdict; what time hee told mee and others the whole matter, with all the circumſtances aforeſaid; And accordingly appeared, but in regard his anſwere had been damned by Decree in Chancery as aforeſaid, the Court would not heare him upon oath, but left the conſideration to the | Jury of what they had heard by this lords Counſell at the barre, wch I know did noe harme. As for Richard Adams, (who dyed ſhortly after,) the

the inſtrument of this unconſcionable and unjuſt practice, returning from London to Wotton, where his dwelling was, having failed after much ſuite in obtaining of a protection to preſerve him from divers creditors, to whom hee ſtood indebted, the next day after his returne dyed with thought and greife, as publickly then reported, and ſtands yet beleived. Neither could the freſh labour of Thomas his ſon obtaine more favour after his death then an increaſe thereby of his fathers ingagements, and his own leſs means to pay what himſelf as ſuerty for his father ſtood alſo bound for; who being now alſo dead, after much penury, hath left a miſerable male and female poſterity, not of worth to divide five pounds amongſt ſeaven of them: And his wife at this day 1626. by my meanes an Almeſwoman in the hoſpitall of Cheineis.

And to knit the Cup and Cover here togeather, the ſaid Rich.d Hughes, firſt an Atturney at lawe and of the ſtanding fee of this lord, then dwelling at Wotton and this lords Steward there, hee falſly turned away to this lords Adverſaries with a perfidious revealing of all his ill gained knowledge; And after a ſecond regaining, thirdly revolted; And laſtly miſſing of his promiſed (at leaſt hoped,) reward, preſſed with poverty, returned from Diſtaffe lane and other places in London where hee had ſome years covered himſelf, towards Wotton, periſhed in a ditch on this ſide Fairford in Glouceſterſhire, as hath been ſaid, where hee was found dead early in a morning; whoſe children, (long ſince in the condition of beggars,) have nothing remaining to them but the ignominy of their father; Of whome, not the leaſt unhappy, was John Hughes, made, ſoone after the firſt recovery, a woodward of wotton, who ſhortly after, (grown not worth the bread hee wanted to eat,) dyed bellowing and roaring in Wotton, whereof hundreds yet living give teſtimony.

And to touch but light[l]y on Thomas Trotman of Stancombe, an other prime ſervant and trader in theſe practices, rewarded after the ſaid recovery of Wotton with a baylywick and woodwards office, being at a faire in Wiltſhire, and offering (perhaps in drinke) to put his foot into the ſtirrup with intent to ride home, ſodainly died; of whoſe eldeſt ſon Wm, lately departed his houſe for debt, I forbeare to write what juſtly is occaſioned; my ſelf diſlikeing thoſe juſt occaſions that have through truth of ſtory, caſt mee upon ſoe unpleaſant relations, eſpecially wherein the perſon is taxed or aſperſed.

ffor more aſſurance of the packing and plots about this Jury that tryed the ſaid cauſe, heare a tre of the proper hand writing of Sr Thos Throkmton, directed to his loving Nephewe Mr John Tracy, (then a ſervt to the Earle of Leiceſter, now knight,) and

tre in caſtro de Berkeley dated at Tortworth. 30. Jan: 1583. 26. Eliz.

and who after had an eftate given him in Rolls Court in Slimbridge, and yet liveth at Tuddington.

Good Nephewe, according to my good lords defire, I have fent up a fufficient Jury for the tryall of the matter between the Queen and y*e* lord Berkeley, And to the end their appearance may bee the more ready, I have fent up this bearer to attend upon them; If I had thought mine own fervice there in any fort neceffary to the behoofe of my lords, I would not have fpared my travell, thinking it un-neceffary to make a greater fhew of good will then needeth; And that I have fufficiently performed what I have undertaken for the apparance of the Jury it fhall well appear; And leaft the apparance of S*r* Thomas Porter fhould bee requifite, what pollicy I ufed for the fame this bearer can informe you; All which I pray you informe both my good lords the Earles of Warrwicke and Leicefter, As alfo I pray you informe them that they are to give thanks unto S*r* Nicholas Poyntz and your father, for the apparance of fome of the Jury, whofe names this bearer will informe you; further I pray you credit the bearer, And foe commending mee heartily unto you, and your brother, I comit you to God. At Tortworth the 30*th* of January. 1583.

Your loving Uncle
Thomas Throkmorton.

John Garlicke was the bearer.
Earles of Warr̃ & Leicr.

Old Sr John Tracy.

Anno: 26. Eliz.

It is not yet three months fince I talked of thefe paffages with John Garlicke, that's mentioned to bee the bearer, of what hee had to deliver upon the credence given by this l̃re unto him; It fuffices the plot and pack was foule; what before is written was too true for the lord Berkeley: for the verdict of the faid Jury turned him out of his ancient inheritance, And fome of it, (as Cam and Hinton,) fuch whereof hee and his Anceftors and thofe who held under them had been in quiet poffeffion, and never year or month out of poffeffion, fince the begining of thefe relations in the lord Robert the firft of that name. |

At the fame time went alfo the l̃re of S*r* Nicholas Poyntz to the Earle of Leicefter himfelf, wherein hee intimateth that convenient means is now offered, by change of Officers in Ireland, to benefit M*r* Throkmorton of Tortworth, than whom an honefter man liveth not, very wife to govern in place of Juftice, and is intirely your lordfhips: I write the very words of his proper hand writing, The reft need not; It fufficeth hee was an old Courtier, And wholly alfo the Earle of Leicefters, And dyed in fewe weeks after.

764
L̃re in caftro de Berkeley

In these times also, was one Edward Andrews of the county of Leicester, an utter barrester of Graies Inne, of Counsell in these and other suites with this lord Berkeley, who was wrought to bee false to his Client, and to make known before hand his Evidence and breviats to the adverse party; which as M.r Alsop hath told mee, yet living and then this lords sollicitor, and the discoverer thereof, hee did to have the said Earles favour in his own great and tedious suite with the lord Cromwell for the manor of Allexton in that County, wherein at last, (out of the wilines of his own brain,) hee was overtaken with loss of the Land, after that fower or five verdicts formerly passed for him; which case is reported in print by S.r Edward Coke in the second part of his reports.

<small>Cokes rep. 2. pts fol: 69.b
Burtons descripčon of Leic.t Shire fol: 10: 11.</small>

And heere, (though somewhat out of place and order,) may bee remembred the often references that were to freinds, and their meetings thereupon, to have (by way of arbitrament) determined these suites, aswell before as after the second recovery; As to Phillip Earle of Arundle, Thomas Earle of Sussex, lord Chamberlain, and S.r Christopher Wray, cheife Justice, for this lord Berkeley; And to Henry Earle of Huntington, S.r Christopher Hatton, and Judge Anderson, cheife Justice of the Comon pleas, for the said Earles; and of their often meetings and hearing of Counsell on both sides, at Ely house in holborne, at Leicester house in the Stran, And in the Inner chamber of the Starchamber, and other places: and how upon the death of the said Earle of Sussex, which happened in June 1583, A.o 25. Eliz., this lord Berkeley chose Henry Earle of Northumberland, who also after divers meetings concluded of nothing: And soe breaking off, the tryall went forward in the 26.th of Elizabeth, at the Exchequer barre, whereof it now followeth that I write; with this remembrance to posterity, That these meetings of soe great lords were solicited and procured by the personal travell of the lady Katharine this lords Wife, of whom I have after to write. |

<small>Annis. 22. Eliz. et. 24. Eliz. et. 25. Eliz: 1583.

Leic.rs comon wealth fol: 33. 43. 59. printed: 1584.

Div'sa munimenta in castro de Berkeley.</small>

Having somwhat outrunne the order of time, the better to avoid such fractions as the multitudes of suits and occurrences that came togeather would otherwise have cast mee into, I now returne to declare, That amongst the manifold lawe-suits of this lord Henry, none was of greater consequence, nor wherein his honor more suffered, then that for the Tythes of Oldminster in Hinton within the parish of Berkeley, between himself and the said Thomas Throkmton of Tortworth Esq̄ure, after knight, father of S.r William the now Baronet; nor prosecuted with more violence and discontent both between the parties themselves and also their sollicitors and servants; which took begining about the Twentieth of Queen Elizabeth. **This** lord

<small>Annis: 19. 20. Eliz:</small>

lord was in possession of the lease thereof as administrator to the lady Anne his mother, who about two years after the death of the lord Thomas her husband, did, in the 28th yeare of king Henry the 8th take a lease thereof from one Burton then Abbot of St Augustines by Bristoll, for threescore years, at eight pound rent, who, the next year dying, Abbot Morgan him succeeded in that Monastery; In whose government two years after, that Monastery was by king Henry the 8th dissolved, And three years after that, by the said king, converted into a Bishoppricke, Deane, and Chapiter, as formerly I have written; from which lease, (not expired at the time of this suite,) this lord Henry made his title; And Sr Thomas Throkmerton claimed by a lease made by the said Deane and Chapiter in the time of Queen Elizabeth in reversion of the former lease: The suits raised between them were many, and in most of the Queens Courts togeather, whereof the Starre chamber in the 22th and 23th of Elizabeth was at one time possessed with thirteen severall bills, The kings beanch and Comon pleas with twelve, And the Chancery had her share: Tryalls by Jury both at the barre and Westminster and in the proper County at the Assises were more then too many: Inditements for riots and forcible entrie at severall assises and Quarter Sessions, held at Gloucester Cirencester and Tewksbury, were almost numberles, wherein at one time in fower inditements forty of this lords servants were indited and fined: The successes of both partes were variable, but much the worse fell on the part of this lord and his forwardest servants, who much smarted by censures in the Starchamber; wherein over many of them, (whereof their children and themselves yet complaine,) were (otherwise then this lord had promised by his tres,) left to themselves and payment of their fines, And this lord to the losse of his lease for all the years hee had to come: | And yet, without doubt, the title of this lord thereunto was good and unavoidable, had his Sollicitors understood as they should: The maine question, upon issues joyned between them, was, dimisit, or non dimisit; whether Abbot Burton made such a lease to the lady Anne Berkeley, or not: Sir Thomas Throkmerton surmising, That if any lease under Burtons name were at all made, it was made by the kings Comissioners without any authority after the dissolution of that Monastery, which in that year wherein this and other Monasteries were dissolved, was too often practiced; And that noe possession was had by the said lady Anne till after the dissolution; proofes of which surmises, hee had none at all that were direct, And taken in their best condition were but weak probabillities, uncertaine and in themselves meerly false: Howbeit (whereof I would not write but truth enforceth, (for I hate to scratch the dead) this lords cheife Sollicitors that then in this County of Gloucester governed his affaires, (himself and family then abiding at Callowdon,) were Henry Grantham, a better Italian then lawyer,

tre dated at Callowdon. 1 Aug: 1578. A° 20. Eliz:

Hill. 22. Eliz: rot 596. in banco. inter Thom: Throkm'ton plt et Bourcher defendant.

lawyer, And Anthony Huntley th'elder, then alfo in the beginning of thefe fuites his high Steward in this County, whofe falfe orthography in more then an hundred of his lres yet in Berkeley caftle will affure all that read them that hee underftood not a line of latin; who ufed to keep his Courts with a white feather in his cap, and to read his charge to the Jurors at the Courts hee kept out of his papers; A man fitter for ffaires and Markets of Cattell and fales of wood, wherein hee had good fkill, then to graple with foe watchfull an adverfary in the combates of Littleton, who knew how to take all advantages, but to give none. As for Humphry Alfop aforenamed, (yet living,) hee was then an unexperienced young man, and in Trinity Terme in that 22.th yeare firft preferred into this lords fervice, from being a Clarke to Mr. Lewkner then this lords Steward of Bofham manor in Suffex; All wch took their directions, (when they pleafed to travell foe farr as Glouc.r for them,) from old Thomas Denys, (father of him of the fame name that yet liveth there,) a true hearted gentleman to this family, (though neither read nor practiced in thefe affaires,) then receivour of this lords Revenue, and allyed to him in the fourth degree, of whom I formerly made a double mention; And to have proved the iffue | whereupon the leafe was loft, this lord Henry then had amongft his Evidences both the leafe of Abbot Burton under the covent feale fubfcribed with his own hand, who dyed two years before the diffolution, And five or fix Acquittances for each half years rent both under the faid Abbot Burtons hand, and Morgans his fucceffor, upon whom the diffolution came, with a conftant unqueftioned poffeffion to the very time of thefe fuits: of which leafe it felf and the acquittances thefe ignorant Sollicitors were ignorant, relying only upon teftimony of Witneffes, viva voce, which after forty three years could not bee certaine or direct; In my fortings of the evidence of this lord, finding thofe and other evidences, (which in all Tryalls this lord Henry was ftill urged to fhew forth or directly to prove,) And which done (as done it might have been) had ended the controverfy And knowing that the charges of fuits And the payments of fynes coft this lord above—1500li, befides the loffe of the leafe and the difhonor which thefe overthrowes caft upon him, And the damage done to freinds whom this lord embarked in thefe fuits, and confequently loft; And alfo how the eftates of many of his tenants whom the faid follicitors led into ryots were never able to pay the cofts of fuite damages fees and fynes, wherein they were condemned, and wherein they were left to themfelves, as hath been faid: And knowing alfo how this politick gentleman Sr Thomas Throkmton, by many wily devices, put on the forefaid Exchequer Information of Intrufion in the 22th of Elizabeth with the Earle of Leicefter, as a diverfary means to fhorten his own fuite, wherein this lord received one of his greateft loffes; knowing, I fay,

Anno: 1618.

767

thefe

these and other crosse accidents after happening which hence took sapp and rooting, I cannot but bewaile what's past, And for the time to come advise the now lord George and his heires after him, to serve themselves with wise and understanding men, trained up and professing the same faculty; (my selfe already entred into the suburbs of my grave, and a derelict of that profession:) for if the Sollicitor bee not at home with himself, If ignorant or carelesse, Counsell that are strangers to the cause and must take up their knowledge at the second hand cannot bee instructed; neither can breviats for them (especially in matters of title) bee drawn really and to life, wherein much of good successe in each tryall consisteth; I could never in this later half of my life perceive otherwise but that the | life or death of the suite, as well in instructions for pleadings, as for evidence, was in the Sollicitor: His following, his follicitation in all Courts, especially in the English, maketh or marreth; yea often in a bad cause it gaineth, and in a good, looseth; Let others think what them listeth, I write what I have seen eaten and digested; Clyents witnesses Jurors Counsell and Judges, are men and noe angells, the sons, as the poets allude, of Prometheus, not Epimetheus, neither will bee otherwise soe longe as men are men, neither may a paradice bee expected to bee where any man may innocently fall by the lawe, As by ignorance or misprision; by his Atturney or Counsellor; by practice or combination of the adversary; by perjury of witnesses; by forgery of Deeds; by subornacon or corruption of witnesses Jurors or officers in Courts: by affection, inclination, or corruption of the Judge; and by many other by and black ways, whereof many men have made experience, in lesse or greater measure, sufficiently veryfying what I write.

After such time as a reconciliation was wrought between this lord Henry and Sir Thomas Throkmton in the later end of Queen Elizabeths raigne, by the means of his wives father S:r Richard Berkeley; In the first seaven years of king James that now is, what time hee did good offices towards this lord in his suite against the lord Lisle, And was to mee an intelligencer of times passed, I often talked hereof, both with this lord Henry and with S:r Thomas, And told them at severall times, what evidence I had found, and bound up togeather with the former unhappy papers, which both of them seemed earnestly to wish they had at first, or before the suits, been found; for then, (said this lord Henry,) I had saved many waies much, and kept my leafe and prevented other mischeifs that fell upon mee, and my house. **And**, quoth S:r Thomas, I had then saved what I spent in these suits, more by one thousand pounds then the leafe I overthrew was worth; besides that some great freinds of my lord Berkleys deeply afterwards revenged his quarrells upon mee in other

other law suites I had; and oppofed my preferrment at Court with ye Queen; | with other like words on either part: **And** both of them blamed the provocations of their fervants; And (as this lord then told mee) the reprochfull words caft out by Sr Thomas Throkmerton againft Henry Grantham, calling him bottle nofed foole, wherein hee reproched the worke of nature in his face: And objecting to Anthony Huntley, beggarry and the illegitimation of his birth, with rudenes of condition; And taunting the youth, forwardnes and religion of the faid Humphry Alfop, foe overheated the two former, That they multiplyed fuits againft Sir Thomas like the heads of Hidra: Soe farr forth fuffering their paffions to tranfport them, That infteed of rakes and Sheafpikes to gather Tithe in Harveft in the 22th of Elizabeth, they carried their workfolks out of Berkeley Town armed with fwords and bucklers, halberds and fuch like weapons; By which improvidence they gave great advantage to their adverfary, whofe warines quickly apprehended it, And caft upon forty of themfelves, the fortune to bee juftly endicted at one Seffions and fined for their folly. **And** afterwards when the right of the leafe in point of title came to receive tryall at the kings bench barre, This lords faid Sollicitors thought it fufficient to give in Evidence fower or five witneffes, (of hearfay and credibly beleiving,) exemplifyed under the great Seale; And never looked at or after thofe materiall proofes, (omni exceptione maiores,) before mentioned; Nor into the certificates, Nor Surveyes of thofe Commiffioners imployed by king Henry the 8th at the diffolution of that Monaftery, Nor into the accompts of the lady Anne Berkeleys receivor in the firft fower years of her leafe, Nor afterwards in the Court of Augmentations till the erection of that Bifhopricke, Deane, and Chapiter, where they might have found both the leafe proved, and the rent alfo each half year paid.

[margin: 769]
[margin: Hill: 22. Eliz. rot: 596. in banco regis.]

After the faid Tryall at lawe at the barre in Efter terme in the 22th of Elizabeth, thofe two Sollicitors, Grantham and Huntley, complained to this lord of the partiallity of the Jury, wherein they further erred, for they fhould have complained of the indifcretion and infufficiency of themfelves, as meerly unable to make head againft foe powerfull and plotting a gentleman as they had to buckle withall; And I have heard the faid Humphry Alfop, (who after grew to a better underftanding in the lawe fuites and tenures of this lord,) expreffely cenfure Grantham and Huntley out of his knowledge | to have both foolifhly and infufficiently followed thefe caufes: which Alfop fhortly after did this lord Henry good fervice in caufing him to depart from a propofition made by the Earle of Leicefter, clofely put on alfo by Sir Thomas Throkmton, for an exchange of thefe and more lands of this lords in the county of Gloucefter, parcell of his Barony of Berkeley, for longe Itchington

[margin: Banco regis 22. Eliz: Hill: rot. 596.]
[margin: 770]

Itchington and other the said Earles lands in the County of Warwicke, which was likely by their wilines to have taken effect, whilst this lord Henry and his lady lay at Ivy-bridge, at that time commanded by Queen Elizabeth to attend the cominge of Monsieur out of ffrance; An attendance which in thirteen weeks cost this lord and lady two thousand five hundred pounds.

<small>Anno. 1581. 22. et. 23. Eliz.</small>

Before these suits began there were some others precedent concerning certaine Trees which Sir Tho. Throkmton had cut down upon his lease of Appleridge by newparke, which hee held of this lord for one and twenty yeares by a demise in the 12th of Eliz:, raised somewhat harshly against him, those times considered.

<small>Pasch. 19. Eliz: rot 324. et. 224 in banco regis.</small>

And after these suites, (as a fiery comet drawes her taile,) pulled on many more, for huntings in this lords parks by Sr. Thomas and his servants and others in relation to him, which in the Starchamber and Marches of Wales were not quenched of seaven years after.

<small>Annis. 29. et. 30. Eliz.</small>

And besides, when, upon a spetiall verdict given, the said Sr Thomas Throkmton perceived the Court upon the first argument or reading of the record to encline against him, hee corrupted one Green, (as this lord Henry then charged him, and like enough to bee true,) his then Atturney, to suffer Judgement against him for want of looking after; Notwithstanding the Court in favor of this lord and of that cause, whereof they had well conceived, gave rule upon rule for divers termes togeather.

And two of these Sollicitors, (as this lord longe after told mee,) caused to bee burned in his chamber in his presence, a great bundle of Court rolls Accompts and other Evidences, as seeming hurtfull to that title; which in the 26th of Elizabeth (formerly mentioned) was in the Exchequer tryed against him; and especially about the Leet of the upstarted hundred of Wotton; whereas to one that knew how to handle those weapons, they were stronge defences in his hands, and to have been turned to the adversaries reproofe; As some of the like kind which escaped that fire were in the first six years of king James, as after will appear.

<small>Hum: Alsop Tho: Dennis</small>

This I know, that as I once expostulated this unadvised martirdom of those evidences with one of those Sollicitors, who yet liveth, whose advise especially condemned them to the fire, which hee could not then defend, Soe I now misse them for the more compleat enlargmt of these relations in the lives of those lords that
lived

lived in the time of king Henry the fixth, Edward the fourth, and king Henry the feaventh: And to make more apparent foe much of thefe former paffages, (which, with diflike, I confefs to fcrape fomwhat harfhly upon the dead,) I have within two years laſt caſt into the evidence houfe at Berkeley divers breviats, notes, ł̃res, and copies of Łr̃es, written by this lord, Sir Thomas Throkm̃ton, Sir Nicholas Poyntz, and others, to Judges, honorable freinds, Officers and fervants, received from John Garlicke, in theis times fpecially imployed by Sir Thomas Throkmerton, whofe follicitor and underfherriffe hee was; and principally alfo imployed in thofe affaires under Sir Nicholas Poyntz his firſt mafter, who (as his ł̃res declare) made himfelf a freind and party in favor of Sir Thomas Throkmerton againſt this lord Henry; and laſtly was fervant to this lord Henry by my preferrment, as Clark of his Kitchen at the time of his death, and yet living at Tortworth; which make good all and more, (eiufdem farinæ, of the like courfe bran,) then is formerly written; two of which ł̃res, the one from Sir Thomas the other from Sir Nicholas, I have inferted verbatim a few leaves before.

Anno 1616.

Anno. 1618.

fol: 763. 764.

After Queen Elizabeth had in the 26ᵗʰ of her raigne granted to the faid Earles of Warwicke and Leicefter and their heirs (amongſt other lands,) the third parts of the manors of Came Hinton and Slimbridge, as before is written, They in the year following brought againſt this lord a writt of Partition, to have the faid Third parts of the faid Three Manors allotted to them in feveralty; whereto this lord pleaded, non tenet infimul et proindivifo, And upon tryall at the comon pleas barre the Jury gave a fpeciall verdict, which being of length, (this lord nothing haftning himfelf in a bad market,) the Earle of Leiceſtᵣ, before it could bee entred of record, dyeth the fifth of September in the thirtieth of Elizabeth, and foe that fuite abated: Howbeit to the end that that verdict might bee in one kind or other of record, A bill was afterwards in the 42ᵗʰ of Elizabeth exhibited into the Court of Wards by the faid Anne Countefs of Warrwick againſt this lord Henry and others, wherein this longe fpeciall verdict was made an I[n]terrogatory, (the longeſt I think that ever was,) And Mʳ Scot the prothonotary, Mʳ Waller then his Secondary, (now in like office to his mafter,) and Mʳ Ethrington a clarke of that office, were examined thereupon as witneffes; by that means to make the fame of record to pofterity, which afterwards the faid Counteffe exemplifyed under the Seale of that Court, and is now amongſt the lord Berkeleys Evidence in Berkeley Caſtle.

Trin̄. 28. Eliz: roł̃ 639. in Scots office

Anno. 1588.

772
Anno: 42. Eliz: in Cur̃. Wardorum

And truth bids mee tell this family from the mouth of the forenamed Humphry Alfop, then this lords Sollicitor, and of old William Bourcher then his Atturney in
this

this Exchequer Court, That upon this tryall in the 26th of Elizabeth the Queens Counsell at the barre waved all the quillets, saying they would give noe evidence for them; Howbeit by practize and greatnes becaufe they were in the Information they were foisted into the verdict, which themselves drew up and entred of record, whereby without any evidence or verdict given, Judgement was entred, and this lord turned out of Corriets, Holts and other parcells, which hee could never help; Whereat let thofe only marvaile that knew not the parties, plt and deft, nor what time and Court greatnes can doe in the Exchequer court in the kings cafe.

Hill: 39. Eliz: rot 327. in cōi banco.

vide antea fol: 8. et 81.

How thefe lands with many others after the deaths of the faid Earles of Warrwick and Leicefter came to the faid Counteffe of Warr and her heirs, I have before written; who defiring as the faid Earls had done to have the faid third parts of the faid three manors of Cam Hinton and Slimbridge fet out in feveralty from this lords other two parts, thereby the better to make her profit, fhee likewife in Hillary Terme in the 39th of Elizabeth, brought a writt of partition againft this lord, who pleaded as before a non-tenure in comōn; the Jury at the barre the 22th of November in the 40th of Eliz., being all knights and Efquires of remarkeable houfes, found fpecially as the former Jury had done twelve years before; After argument by Counfell on both fides Judgment was given, That partition fhould bee made for the third parts of the two manors of Cam and Hinton, but not for the third part of the manor of Slimbridge, wherein the law fell out for this lord: At which tryall was this lord Henry himfelf, accompanied with his brother in lawe the lord George Hunfdon lord chamberlaine to her Matie, and others; As alfo were many honorable perfons on the behalfe of the faid Counteffe: The evidence at barre lafted from eight in the morning till fower in the afternoone, nothing I think left unurged or defended that art or learning might afford, or at Barre or Bench bee uttered: The Sollicitors on both fides had the publicke commendation of the Court and of the parties, wherein though this lord Henry prevailed only for Slimbridge, yet

——————— Careat fucceffibus opto,
Quifquis ab eventu facta notanda putat.
Ever let him want an hopefull happy end,
Which by the iffue, doth the Act comēnd.
The event is noe juft mete-wand of mens endeavours.

One of which Jury was ffrancis Heydon, an Efquire dwelling in Hartfordfhire but a ffreeholder in the County of Gloucefter, (as many others were refident in feaven other Counties,) fomtimes a Counfellor at lawe, which was not unknown to

this

this lord Henry nor his Sollicitor, And therefore had been challenged, (upon other fufpition of not ftanding indifferent,) but that one Willm Cotton, a gent depending wholly on the faid lord Hunfdon, undertooke for his indifferency yea and favour as for his own foule, for foe to my felf were his words when I told him the caufes of my fufpition of him; whereto againe hee replyed, That if hee were challenged wee above meafure weakened our tryall and good hopes, And that for him hee would undertake at his perill, with other like confident words, wherein I affure my felf hee meant faithfully, though hee was extraordinarily deceived: But furely many of this Jury were beforehand acquainted with the caufe by both parties, which was not unknown to either fide: After their departure from the barre and longe debate amongft themfelves, they all agreed to find for this lord Henry the tenant a non tenet pro indivifo generally for all the three manors, whereto this Mr Heidon gave confent with his fellowes: Howbeit telling them That to find fpecially as hee would draw it up in notes would amount to as much for this lords benefit as a generall non tenet would, And foe alfo fhould they deale refpectively towards the memory of thofe Jurors who had in former tryalls found otherwife, And | alfo more modeftly towards themfelves in not taking upon them over boldly to determine the lawe in points that feemed fomwhat doubtfull, And alfo lefs offend the loofing party: whereto they affenting, hee purpofely (doubtles having the fame formerly prepared,) foe drew up the note of their verdict That the law fell out againft this lord for Came and Hinton, as hath been faid; And foe (by his advantage of learning) abufed the truth of his own confcience, and of all his fellow Jurors: ffor which Tracy, (now baronet,) Pleadall, Lambert, Carter, and Webb, Efquires of good underftandings, his fellows in that Jury, termed him a devill in their joynt and particular conferences afterwards with mee and fome others, gentlemen; with whom many years before and after I familiarly converfed, And with the fifters daughter of Mr Webb, after maryed.

774

In Hillary Terme in the 41th of Elizabeth went out the writ to ye Sherriffe, then Sr Edward Wintour of Lidney, to make partition of the faid Manors of Cam and Hinton, which hee in perfon began to execute affifted by a fubftantiall Jury the 27th of March, continuing his paines therein till Efter Terme, with fuch uprightnes as I could not in all that time, though daily prefent, obferve to whether party hee inclined; yet was hee challenged from of the principall pannell in this tryall for kindred by his wife, daughter to the Earle of Worcefter, to the demandant; The verdict of which Jury, which containeth a perfect Survey of thefe two manors, refteth filed in the office of the faid Scot the prothonotary.

Terme Pafch 41. Eliz.

The

Trin: 41. Eliz:	**The** next Terme after, this lord brought a writ of error removing the record into the kings bench, hoping to reverfe the Judgement formerly given for the third
Pafch: 1. Jacobi	parts of Came and Hinton, and affigned errors which were in Efter Terme in the firft year of king James that now is, argued by Mr. George Crooke and Mr. John Dodderidge, (after Judges in the fame Court,) and Sr. Edward Coke then Atturney generall, (after lord cheife Juftice and Counfellor of State,) for this lord Henry; And by Mr. Thomas Stephens, (after Prince Henries Atturney,) and Serjeant
Trin. 1. Jac.	Tanfeild, (now lord cheife Baron,) for the faid Counteffe of Warrwick: In Trinity terme after, the Judges themfelves purpofed to have argued but that Terme was
775 Term: Michis 1. Jac.	adjourned in regard of the plague then | raginge in London, And alfo the greater part of Michmas Terme was cut off for the fame caufe, and the refidue adjourned
Hill: 1. Jac.	to Winchefter; whereupon the Judges were againe moved to have argued in Hillary terme following, which was prevented by the death of the faid Counteffe the demaundant, happening on the ninth of ffebruary; whereby the faid writ of Error abated.
Sept. 1. Jac.	**And**, (as by office after her death found in Her[t]fordfhire in Septr. following appeared,) all the Manors and lands formerly mentioned to bee recovered upon
Carta fub figillo in Caftro de Berk:	both the faid Informations againft this lord Henry, were by her conveyed to Sir Robert Sidney then lord Sidney, after vifcount Lifle, and now Earle of Leicefter, and his heires; Againft whom this lord to the utmoft of his Strength purfued his Weftminfter hall warrs, hoping to change his fortunes with the change of time and perfons; The faid Counteffe having charged thofe lands with payment of Thirty pound p ann̄ for ever towards the releife of twelve poore men and women in her hofpitall of Cheyneis, whereof it is of late agreed, That two men and one woman fhall perpetually bee taken from this lords markett town of Wotton and fucceed one another.
	As well at the death of Queen Elizabeth as at the death of the faid Countefs of Warrwick, eleaven monthes after, were divers fuits in divers Courts depending, not only between this lord Henry and the faid Countefs in their own names, but in
Banco regis. Michis 1. Jac: rot. 147.	the names of their freinds tenants and fervants alfo; whereof one was brought by my felf againft John Denton and Thomas Horfman, two under baylies to the faid Counteffe of her pretended hundred of Wotton, wherein the iffue was, Whether any hundred called Wotton hundred was within the County of Glouc., or not: They affirmed it; I denyed it, whereby the proofe refted on their parts being defts; The
Michis 41. 42. Eliz:	other was brought by Thomas Payne of Uley againft the faid John Denton and one John

John Morris another of the said Countesses underbailies of her said pretended hundred, wherein the issue was Whether that village of Uley was within the Leete of her manor of Wotton, and within the hundred of Wotton, or not; Payne, the Pl:t denyed it, the def:ts Morris and Denton affirmed it, whereby the Proofe also rested with them. Of both which it after followeth.

rot. 25. 56. in c͞oi banco.

After Queen Elizabeth had recovered the manor of Wotton, and had granted the same to the Earles of Warwick and Leicester in fee, | and that they had extended the same to consist of the Burrow or market town of Wotton and of the fower villages and hamletts of Nibley Sinwell Comb and Wortley, They endeavoured also to erect a liberty therein and to call the same the hundred of Wotton, and to make such an hundred appendant to their manor of Wotton; wherein they at last prevailed, And an hundred of Wotton was really in esse, And an high Bayly, underbailies, high Constables, high Steward, and understeward, and all other officers appertaining to such a liberty were elected and erected, who executed their severall Offices and places the space of thirteen years or thereabouts: And the like officers of this lord Henries within his hundred of Berkeley were inhibited to intermeddle in any service appertaining to any of their offices or places within the parrishes and villages of Wotton, Simondsall, Nibly, Bradly, Huntingford, Combe, Wortley, Sinwell, Oulpen, Erlingham, Uley, Cam, Cowley, Dursley, Woodmancote, Cromhall, Kingscote, and Warrens Tenants in Nibley; As though those Townships had been removed out of this lords ancient hundred and liberty of Berkeley and setled within this new created hundred and liberty of Wotton.

776

By mariage of the widowe of John Drewe Esquire in October in the 39:th of Elizabeth my self setled in Nibley aforesaid, and all I could opposed daily in all meetings in the County against this Usurped hundred of Wotton, the rather because I was then become acquainted with the law suites of this lord, quarum pars parva fui, and his lord:ps Steward of his liberty and hundred of Berkeley, under his fee: And not only an hundred or liberty of Wotton was thus erected, but a Court of pleas also for tryall of all actions every three weeks at Wotton where the debt or damage exceeded not forty shillings, And also a Court Leete or view of frankpledge of the resiants within almost all of the foresaid parishes and villages, to the great dishonor and diminution of the inheritance of this lord, his profits and regalities: Against these usurpations I oftentimes upon occasions publikly protested, aswell before the Judges and Justices of the peace at assizes and quarter Sessions, as at other meetings; And somtimes, (which I commend not,) I fell upon the persons

Paine v'sus ffouch Hill. 40. Eliz: rot. 1154. in banco — touching this Court of pleas.

of

of those officers and servants, telling them, partly plainly partly ironically, what dangers they cast themselves into by this usurpation over the kings subject, ministring oaths at their Courts and otherwise without authority, having neither warrant by Comission nor prescription soe to doe. By which means many Inhabitants in those places withdrew themselves, and the whole building began to totter, and much

777 talk was of these | their and my proceedings; whereupon by direction of the said Countesse or her said learned Counsell in London, or by her officers in the County of Glouc., an action of debt, (meerely imaginary,) of a beggerly sum of sixpence was in the name of Ambrose Jobbins, a tenant to the said Countesse and dwelling in Nibley, scornfully entred against my self in the hundred Court held each three weeks at Wotton for that hundred, where they were assured I would not appeare: Somoned I was with a loud voice to appeare in the hearing of all my neighbours as I came out of my parish Church on a sunday; And my man at the same time arrested at my heeles in the churchyard upon noe better a ground then the former action, by vertue of a Warrant from the Sherriffe directed to the Bailies of the hundred of Wotton: The Court day came, I appeared not; An Attachment was awarded and two of my cowes taken by the said Denton and Horsman, to draw mee to appearance; for which taking and chasing of my kine I brought the said action against them, wherein the issue was as before is mentioned, I denying that any such hundred as Wotton hundred was in the County of Glouc.; And if the now lord George or his posterity shall desire to understand what proofes either party had, they to prove their Wotton hundred, I the negative that there was noe such: but that aswell the markett Town of Wotton it self as all the other parishes and villages were within the hundred of Berkeley, I referre them to the large breviats which with the pleadings I have bound togeather and cast amongst the Evidences at Berkeley; And if they Judge the proofs overlarge in each kings time, from the Conquest to the 37th of Elizabeth, let them think that my reputation was ingaged in the suite, and the purse this lords that defrayed the charges of those searches and exemplifications; This issue was joyned in Michaelmas Terme in the first of king James, And by the def.^{ts} motion ordered to bee tryed at barre in Ester Terme following; but in Hillary terme before, the said Countesse dyed, as hath been said: The Jury appeared in Ester Terme according to their sommons, And being ready to bee called, the lord Sidney being himself in Court, prayed by his Counsell to have the tryall deferred till Michmas Terme following, for that the title thereof by the conveyance of the said Countesse now appertained to him, And that none of her Evidence that should prove this issue were yet come to his hands, with divers other allegations; wherto I did in open Court assent, foe that this lord might exhibite his

bill

bill in Chancery | againſt the lord Sidney, and that hee would without proces forth- 778
wᵗʰ appear and anſwer thereto, And that the Witneſſes which then were brought up
out of the County, being very aged men, might bee examined thereupon and publication forthwith granted, All which was by the Court ordered accordingly: The bill
was exhibited, Anſwere made, and eight witneſſes on the part of this lord Berkeley
examined that Terme upon Interrogatories, who depoſed fully and directly to many
excellent purpoſes touching Berkeley hundred and the liberties therein uſed, in
granting Replevins, felons goods, &c. And touching Wiłłm Cheſters divideing of
Berkeley hundred in the 37ᵗʰ of Elizabeth, then high Sherriffe of the County
of Glouc., and his eſtabliſhment of Wotton hundred, not fully before created,
And of this lords tres and meſſengers to him about the ſame, and his anſwers
thereto, with other neceſſary matter, which otherwiſe then by this means had never
remained to the knowledge of poſterity: All which are exemplified under the great
Seale, and reſt in the evidence houſe in Berkeley caſtle, whoſe materiall uſe alſo for
other purpoſes elſwhere is declared in theſe relations; but on the part of the lord
Sidney was noe witnes at all examined.

In the beginning of Michaelmas Terme following, the lord Sidney twice in
perſon, Sʳ Robert Wroth his brother in lawe, and Sʳ Henry Mountague his cozen,
(now cheife Juſtice,) came ſeverally to the black fryars in London, where Sʳ Thomas
Berkeley this lords only ſon and the lady Elizabeth his wife then dwelt with her
mother the lady Hunſdon, and earneſtly ſollicited an end of this and other like ſuits
then depending; And at my coming to London from labouring my Juries apparance
ten daies within the Terme, ffrancis Woodward the ſaid lord Sidneys Sollicitor came
divers times to my chamber in the middle Temple, and in his lords name moved
mee to have theſe ſuits referred to the ending of freinds, alleadging the love that
was between this lord Henry and his lord: how kindly in extraordinary faſhion his
lord tooke the noble entertainment which the lord Berkeley gave him at Berkeley
Caſtle not ſeaven weeks before, And how this reference was like to draw to concluſion all other titles of land between them, with the like pʳſwaſions: The end was,
That the evening next before the tryall ſhould have been at the barre, all matters
touching the ſaid liberty and hundred of Wotton, and | the Leet aforeſaid, and 779
returne of Writts, were by the over-rulinge hand of Sʳ Thomas Berkeley and his
wife, referred to the arbitrement of Sʳ Thomas Foſter Serjeant at lawe and the ſaid
Sʳ Henry Mountague; And as well that Jury of mine as one other which was the
ſame Terme to have appeared in the Comon pleas upon like iſſue between the ſaid   Com. pleas. 45.
Jobbins plᵗ and Oty and Benyard, two of this lords undʳ-Bailies of his hundred of   Eliz. rot. 637. de
                                                                        Berkeley,   term Hill:

2 T VOL. II

Berkeley, def.ts, to bee difcharged. Of the Jury wherein I was pl.t, nyneteen the next day upon calling appeared; To every of whom by affent was given twenty fhillings by this lord Henry and ten fhillings the peece by the lord Sidney, towards their charges, and foe returned into their Country.

<small>Judic: de Pafch 2. Jac: Scot</small>

The two arbitrators met three times that Terme at the faid black ffryars, and twice in the vacacōn following, and heard Counfell on both fides; At which times were prefent both the lord Sidney and S.r Thomas Berkeley and his wife; And after perufall of all evidence fhewed on either part, and moft affured I am, of all that could bee fhewed for the lord Sidney, (though I kept back half at leaft, I mean five hundred deeds and peeces of evidence, which I had drawn togeather in feverall ages from the Conqueft, fearing noe end would have enfued in the liking of this lord Henry;) An award after much turmoiling was agreed upon and fealed, dated the fifth of March following, wherein it was awarded and declared That all the Villages and Hamletts pretended to have been within the hundred of Wotton were within the hundred of Berkeley; That there was not nor ought to bee any fuch hundred of Wotton in the County of Glouc: That the liberty of returne of writts, afwell within the hundred of Berkeley as within the fuppofed hundred of Wotton, did of right belong to this lord and his heirs: That the lord Sidney nor his heires, fhould not keep nor ufe any hundred Court, or Court of pleas, with other branches, as by the fame appeareth; both parts whereof are now in Berkeley Caftle.

<small>March: 2: Jac: 1604.</small>

Upon the conclufion whereof, the bailies high Conftables Stewards and other officers of the faid Hundred of Wotton and Courts thereof, by verue of the lord Sidneys L.res fent to them, (whereof I had the cariage,) furceafed their places and all further intermedlinge: And thus was the fall and ending of that pretended liberty leet and hundred of Wotton, and of all the officers and Minifters thereof, which had for twelve years | or more extreamly troubled the Country at each affize and Quarter Seffions, and in eight or ten bills at leaft before the Counfell in the Marches of Wales: And the lord Sidneys receivor had direction to pay mee for my two kine, And the faid Thomas Payne for two young beafts of his, for which hee brought his forefaid action: which was performed.

<small>780</small>

This Thomas Payne brought, in behalf of this lord, one other action againft John ffouch an underbaily to the faid Counteffe, for breaking his houfe at Uley within the hundred of Berkeley, and thence taking away his gelding; Wherein the iffue was, Whether Paynes houfe in Uley was within the hundred of Wotton or not:

<small>Hill: 40: Eliz: rot: 1154. in cōi banco.</small>

not: In this suite, a repleader was awarded, and afterwards a demurrer: Afterwards, by unusuall pleadings, this matter came about againe, And in the end Payne had Judgment upon the former issue: In this suite the labor was laborious and costly, as the large breviats, foe plentifull of records and proofs on Paynes part, which remaine in Berkeley castle will witnesse.

Michis: 43 et 44. Eliz: rot: 2447. in coi. banco.

In the times of the former suits the said Countesse of Warrwick exhibited her bill in the Court of Wards against this lord, Humphry Alsop, and my self, touching a supposed razure of a Deed of the Manor of Slimbridge, made by Alice de Berkeley the widow of Maurice the first unto Robert her son and heire, whereby shee destroyed the guift of frankmarriage of that manor; wherein witnesses were examined, and much labor and money spent, And in the end dismissed; whereby the title of this lord Henry to that manor was the better strengthened. And in the five last years of Queen Elizabeth were many other suits in severall Courts, put on aswell by this lord Henry as by the said Countesse, both in their own names, and in the names of their freinds, servants and tenants, both touching the said upstart hundred of Wotton, and other their possessions; As the said Ambrose Jobbins was pl: against James Oty and Thomas Benyard two of this lords underbailies of his hundred of Berkeley, wherein after issue joyned, which was whether a place in Nibley called Moore close, wherein the def:ts distrained the pl:ts oxe, was within the hundred of Berkeley or not; and the apparance of seaventeen of the jury at the comon pleas barre the 2th of May in the second year of king James, the pl: before evidence became nonsute, and paid costs. |

Trin: Terme. 41. Eliz: in Cur wardo3.

See fol: 771. 772.

Hill: 45. Eliz: rot: 637. in banco michis. 42. et. 43. Eliz:

In the 39th of Elizabeth, Thomas Crofts of Arlingham who is by custom perpetuall tythingman of that Township, by the instigation of the Countesse of Warrwick his landlady, brought an action of trespasse against William Atwood this lords Baily of his hundred of Berkeley, for entring his house and taking thence his goods: Atwood answereth That the pl: dwelling within the leet of Berkeley hundred was thereat amearced for non-apparance, for which amerciament hee entred his house and distrained, as was lawfull for him to doe. Atwood died in January the next yeare, by whose death that suite ended.

781 Hill: 39. Eliz: rot. in banco regis. Glouc:

And the said Countesse of Warwick was pl:t in the kings bench against Thomas Williams another of this lords underbailies of his hundred of Berkeley, in an accon of the case, for infringing her supposed hundred and liberty of Wotton; wherein a non vult prosequi was had against her, and costs of suite awarded to the def:t which shee paid.

Mich: 38. 39. Eliz: Glouc: rot. 313. in banco regis.

Also

Pasch. 41. Eliz: Glouc: rot. 331. in banco regis.

Also the said Countesse of Warrwick was plt in the kings bench against William Davis this lords high-baily of his hundred of Berkeley, in an accōn of the case for his entries into her hundred of Wotton, in execution of his office as Baily of the hundred of Berkeley, wherein shee after much struggling, fearing tryall by Jury, entred a non vult prosequi.

Pasch. 40. Eliz: rot:

Also this lord Berkeley, in the fortieth of Elizabeth, was plt against John Denton an Underbaily to the countesse of Warr̃ of her supposed hundred of Wotton, for serving of proces within his hundred of Berkeley, whom this lord punished by that action.

Pa: 2: Jac: in banco regis, et in al̃ term̃ 1. et. 2. Jac: in banco et in banco regis.

Also, in the first and second years of king James, Richard Browne of Cam and Edward Trotman of the same, John Andrews and others of Cowley, tenants to this lord Henry, were plts severally against the s̃d. Denton for entring their houses at Came and Cowley, somoning them by vertue of his office to appear at the Assises and Quarter Sessions; at what time my selfe in Trotmans house was holding the Halimot Court of that manor; which hee justified as Baily of Wotton hundred, and that Came and Cowley were within the same hundred: **In** which times the wily officers and freinds of the said Countess closely endeavoured the inditing a Sollicitor of this lords at Gloucester Assizes upon the Statute of 8. Eliz: cap. 2. but prevailed not.

Stat: 8: Eliz: ca: 2.

782

Which Sollicitor, (studying for mettall of the like refining the better to | repay his debt with like coine,) observed that one John Goodman, an ancient Barrister of Lincolnes Inne, who had for divers years been a sollicitor and of Counsell with the Earles of Warrwick and Leicester in their said suits against this lord, and after steward of their Courts, had for divers years been neglected and of late disgraced by one of those officers under the said Countess, repaired privately to his Chamber, and at last soe fairly agreed with him That hee became of Counsell with this lord Henries son and heire; and soe well conceived of the language which this lords said Sollicitor used, That shortly after hee gave him leave to search, aswell amongst the papers in his study at Lincolns Inne, which were very many, as at his house in Hartfordshire, from whence a servant of that Sollicitors brought at severall times a great Cloke-bag-full of Deeds under seale, exemplifications of records, accompts, courtrolls of those Manors soe recovered of this lord, breviats prepared for Counsell and other mynuments, with many l̃res and copies of L̃res, copies of Accompts of the said Earles, lawe charges against this lord, and notes of what rewards the said

Earles

Earles of Warrwick and Leicester gave to every Juror that tryed that issue in the 14th of Elizabeth against this lord Henry; whereby the evidence house in Berkeley castle is restored to what it had formerly lost; And these relations the more inlarged and better warranted then otherwise they could have been in those works of darknes thereby made manifest to this family.

And it may not bee omitted, That the said Mr. Goodman and one Mr. Nuttall the two Stewards to the said Earles of Warrwick and Leicester, at the first Courts of Recognition which they held after the said recovery, did by direction of the said Earles draw into their hands from each tenants of those lands and Manors not only all the leases and Copies which any of them had by grant of this lord Henry, but also all the Deeds Court Rolls and other evidence they possibly could get wherein the name of Berkeley was mentioned, with intent to extinguish the memoriall thereof from out of those manors for ever, as Mr. Goodman said; which being near fower hundred peeces soe drawn in are now by the divine disposall of the Almighty in the possession of this lord Henrys grandchild, whereby his name is by that their act the more perpetuated to posterity; And not one tenant now living | holding any parts of those manors that hath not that name of Berkeley in the forehead or frontispeece of such their lease or Copy: whereas on the other part there is not one Lymme discended from the loynes of either of those Earles to pisse against a wall; And the booke also by them then made ingrossed in Vellam, with all their glorious titles in Rubricks and guilt letters, is now likewise in the evidence house of this family.

See after fol: 838. 839.
783

About this time also it was, That the said Sollicitor observed in this lord Henry (then in the 70th year of his age) a disposition to cast off all further suits in lawe, and to leave these titles to his son and posterity; which to prevent, the said sollicitor obtained of his Lop. to draw to a Conference at Callowdon two or three of his freinds and as many of his Counsell, with some other of his officers; before whom the said Sollicitor opened such new matter not before known or given in evidence in any former tryall, as this lord, by their unanimous advice, resolved to call againe the wholl lump of all that had been lost by him into question, by severall actions according to the diversity of his titles; And to begin with the manor of Sages; And thereupon made a lease for years to his servant John Machin, for the bringing of an accon of Ejectione firmæ in the Comon pleas for part of yt Manor against Edward Beard, a Copy hold tenant of parcell thereof under the said Robert Sidney viscount Lisle; who pleaded not guilty: wherein to the Jury at the barre

Sages.
Pasch: 3: Jac: rot: 744 in Com̃ banco.

were

were delivered more then three hundred peeces of evidence in that six hours the tryall lasted; whereat were present both this lord and the said viscount Lisle, with divers honorable personages which came as freinds to the hearing thereof; wherein the plt Machin recovered; At what time Sr. Thomas Walmesley one of the Judges of that Court, speaking as much almost at the bench on this lords behalf as any of his Serjeants at the barre, gave this for answere publickly, That having been of this Ld Berkeleys Counsell from the 13th of Queen Elizabeth, and thereby privy to all the passages of his suits till hee was made Judge, hee held himself bound in conscience to direct the Jury as hee did, which was a great furtherance of the Verdict: At what time this lord towards the end of the Evidence demanded of his said Sollicitor where hee thought the verdict would bee; who answered, wee are beaten from all our discents whereon wee mainly relyed, and have cast it upon

784 equity and the deeds of dures, And therefore the Jury may goe either way | with safety; Then, quoth hee, I shall the better judge of your labors and my Countries love if I have the verdict; as the next morning hee had.

Pasch: 5: Jac. rot: 20. in banco regis.
Mich. 4. Jac: rot. 547. in banco regis.
Hill. 4. Jac: rot. 6. in banco regis.

After Judgment was given upon that verdict, the lord Lisle brought in an Attaint in the kings bench against the Jury, being much unsatisfied with their verdict, wherein after some strugling a Jury of knights and Esquires was returned; which Attaint having depended two years was discontinued by him, though this lord Henry and the first Jury urged him by many provocations to proceed, which noe doubt out of prudent grounds and observations hee thought not fit to doe, hee being in his own person a very able lord and a dilligent sollicitor: The Evidence house in Berkeley castle will witnes to after ages the preparations towards the tryall in the attaint by severall sorts of Collections from lawyers, Antiquaries, Sollicitors, and others, and what sorts of breefes for lawe, presidents, reason, fact, and equity, were delivered to each of the petite Jury, and by them to others, containing also the reasons that moved them to give their verdict for the plt, as they did.

Pa: 4: Jac: in Cancell:

This lords now thinking the times more opened towards his titles, resolved to loose as little thereof as hee could; And thereupon exhibited his bill in chancery against the said viscount Lisle, setting forth That in the 12th of Elizabeth and longe before hee was seized of the Manors of Simondsfall, Wotton, Arlingham, and Sages, the third part of the manors of Cam and Hinton, and of lands called Holts, & Corriets, and divers others in the County of Glouc.; That about the 15th of Elizabeth the Earles of Warrwick and Leicester wrongfully entred into, and expelled him out of the same; And that they have since levyed or caused to bee

levyed

levyed divers fines of the premisses, thereby to barr his right and title; Into which manors and lands, hee to preserve his right and title, hath made entries in the presence of honest witnesses which will testify the same: That the Earle of Leic: dyed, And the Earle of Warwick him survived and conveyed the premisses to Anne his wife and her heires, and dyed; That shee likewise conveyed the premisses to the def't, And that likewise both the defend: and the said Countesse have levyed fines to barre the plt as aforesaid; And that hee, for like preservation of his title, hath made like entries in the presence of honest witnesses willing to testifie the same, | who are soe aged that they are not able to travaile to any Court of Justice to testifie the same, whose testimony not being had would greatly prejudice him, And therefore this lord prayed that his witnesses might bee examined: **Whereto** the viscount Lisle after many delaies on his part and as many pressures on the plts, made answer in November following, setting forth all the particular verdicts in effect which had been had against this lord, and all the other proceedings formerly mentioned, And concluded thereupon That if hee had any right the same by that means was bound, And soe demurred: But the demurrer at last was overruled and many Witnesses were examined both by Comission and in London by the examiner, And soe rested, which was the sole end of the suite: Amongst which entries one was proved to bee by this lord himself in his own person into Westridge woods in the most conspicuous place of all that manor, attended with too many for that buisinesse, though not for the honor of his Nobility.

785

Ordo: 26 Nov. 5. Jacobi Robinson examiner.

At this time also William Bower servant to this lord, brought an action against John Willis Willm Trotman and others, wherein the title of the messuage and lands called Holts came in question; which by Jury was tryed at the barre the 21th of May the year after, wherein the plt recovered his damages to 15li, after abated by the Court to—10li And 13li. 11s. for costs of Suite.

Trin. 3: Jac: in banco regis. rot.

Term Pasch 4: Jacobi.

And in Michaelmas Terme next after the former action, the said Willm Trotman brought his action in the same Court against William Bower for a trespas on the same grounds called Holts, wherein the pleadings were curious, but proceeded not to tryall; And before those, between the said Trotman and Richard Thomas, were also suites in the Marches of Wales, and many Witnesses examined between them touching the said lands, wch in the end was dismissed that Court.

Mich: 3. Jac. in banco regis.

Anno primo Jacobi

The same Michmas Terme, James Atwood a servant to this lord was Plt against Thomas Gilman a Copihold Tenant of the said Manor of Sages, wherein

Pasch. & Mich 3. Jac: in banco regis.

after

after longe pleadings upon the title, they at laſt grew at iſſue, which came not to tryall.

Micħ: 3. Jac: rot: 111. in banco regis.

The ſame Terme William Mallet ſervant to this lord was plt againſt the ſaid William Trotman, Wherein the iſſue was Whether Shobenaſh park in Hinton was the freehold of Robert Viſcount Liſle, (whoſe tenant Trotman was,) or of this lord, who had leaſed the ſame to Mallet, which was never tryed through the default of Jurors, and after diſcontinued by the plt.

Trin. 4. Jac: rot. in banco regis. 786

And the like iſſue, upon the freehold of the ſaid parke, was next yeare joyned between John Merrit plt and the ſaid Mallet and others def'ts, wherein are pleaded the conveyances from the Countes of Warwick to the lord Liſle.

Hill. 4. Jac. rot: 848. in cōi banco.

In the 4th of king James, William Knight a tenant to this lord broʰ an action of treſpas againſt John Green Sollicitor to the lord Viſcount Liſle and Edward Horwood his tenant for part of the Manor of Sages, who juſtifyed their entry under the recovery of Queen Elizabeth in the Information in the 26th yeare of her raigne, and of her conveyance to the Earles of Warr and Leiceſter, and from the ſurvivor of them by mean conveyances to the lord Liſle their maſter: Knight replies, That Maurice lord Berkeley brother of the Marquis dyed thereof ſeized, and the ſame diſcended thereby to Maurice his ſon and heire, And ſoe to this lord as heire, and

6: Jac:

ſoe confeſſeth and avoideth their plea; But after theſe and other pleadings, which were large learned and chargeable, they ſecretly corrupted the plt Knight, And the 17th of November in the ſixth of king James obtained of him a releaſe of all actions and demands, which in Hillary Terme after they pleaded of Record, And ſoe ended that action with the infamy of the plt; whoſe perfidious treachery cauſed this lord

Paſch: 7. Jac: in banco regis.

ſhortly after to bring his accōn of the caſe againſt him, for falſly delivering up the poſſeſſion of a Meſſuage and divers lands parcell of his manor of Sages to the lord Viſcount Liſle, which hee had taken for three years; To requite which ſuite the ſaid Viſcount, in the name of his ſaid Tenant Horwood, exhibited an angry bill in chancery againſt a Sollicitor of this lords and one William Cloterbooke, then tenant to the ſaid meſſuage, whereto was made ſuch an anſwer the ſame Terme, as that hee in that ſuite proceeded noe further: And theſe were folded up in the Compoſition made between theſe two lords in Micħmas Terme following, to the private loſſe of that Sollicitor of—80li and more, through the interreſt hee had purchaſed in that ſaid Meſſuage and lands; to the loſſe whereof hee rather gave way then to hinder the ſaid Agreement between the ſaid lords.

As

As for the longe and tedious suits touching the new warth and new grounds in Slimbridge, raised by Arnold Oldisworth and George Thorpe Esq.^rs tenants to the said viscount, against the Inhabitants of fframpton upon Seaverne upon the close of the said composition, I have mentioned them before in the life of Thomas ye 2th | fol: [225]

The said John Machin servant to this lord was in the second of king James plt against James Dangerfeild and John Hobbs in an Ejectione firmæ touching Hawpark at Wotton, which upon bringing the writs of right for that Manor was in the fifth of king James discontinued by the plt.   787 Trin: 3. Jac. rot: 114. in banco regis.

Also the said John Machin was plt in the Comon pleas against Thomas Adams Willm Trotman and Richard Trotman three of the said lord Lisles servants, concerning another part of Sages Manor; wherein they largely pleaded all the meane Conveyances of their lord, whereof good use may bee made; The entry whereof taketh up fower rolls of parchment at the least, which came not to tryall through the writs of right which at this time were by this lord brought for ending of all suits, as after followeth.   Pa: 4: Jac: Trin: 5. Jac: rot. 1943. in banco regis.

William Machin was plt, John ffouch and John Morris two under bailies of the lord Lisle of his hundred of Wotton defendants, for an arrest made upon the plt at Berkeley, and consequently a false imprisonment of him, the place being in the hundred of Berkeley; Judgement was given for the plt, and damages to— 26^li 13^s 4^d After by double rules in Court qualifyed to ten pound damage, and —3^li 15^s 6^d costs which was paid.   Mich: 4. Jac: in cōi banco: rot. 1656.

At the same time this lord was plt against the said ffouch and Morris for infringing of his liberty in the hundred of Berkeley upon the former arrest, wherein the plt recovered 20^s damages and his costs to 7^li.   Mich: 4. Jac. rot. 1655. in banco cōi.

At this time also this lord in my name prosecuted an Ejectione firmæ against Charles Clough and William Clough tenants to the grounds in Slimbridge called Newleyes, which after was compounded.   Mich. 4: Jac: in banco regis.

In this tossed and restles manner many parcells of these controverted possessions having been banded by each party against other, as either of them held most advantageous to gaine profit or reputation upon the other; This lord Henry now prudently observing that time with a fairer countenance smiled upon him then formerly it had

done,

2 U VOL. II

done, And that his Counsell and sollicitors had dived deeper into the abstruse understanding of his title then heretofore, resolved with his Counsell and freinds to hazard the wholl at the next cast; And thereby either to bring back all his lands into the old sould, or else unrecoverably to loose them, and soe to end his daies in freedom from suits; And thereupon according to the three fold difference of his titles to the manors and lands formerly recovered against him, hee sorted the same | into three severall writs of right, which hee now sued out against the said Viscount Lisle, as being the last highest and finall suits of the laws of England, and such as none can bringe but tenants in fee simple.

Pasch: 7. Jac: rot. 172. in cõi banco.

In the first writ was comprehended the manors of Wotton and Symondsall, and the third parts of the manors of Came and Hinton.

Eisdem terme et rotulo.

In the second, the manors of Arlingham and Sages and newleys, and the warth in Slimbridge.

Trin. 7: Jac: rot: 123.

And in the third, the lands of Holts and Corriets, by the names of a messuage and two hundred acres of land in Alkington and Cam: In all which somons was solemly given, and proclamations at the parish Churches doors made in formall maner, according to the laws; which though the wise and prudent tenant, the lord Viscount Lisle, seemed to Sleight and to bee glad of, as whereby hee would finally barre this lord Henry, and soe hold these manors and lands at quiet; Yet this lord Henry had assured intelligence by a sollicitor of his, That hee was much troubled thereat. And the more, because by the unexpected coming of Thomas Adams, (the son of the former false Adams,) into the Chamber of the said Mr. Goodman of Lincolnes-inne, somtimes Thomas Adams master, and whom of seaven years before hee had not seene, (such are the chances of humane things,) yet hee found this lords said Sollicitor secretly in his inward chamber, perusing of such old breviats and other writings as Mr. Goodman had, (upon a precontract between him and the said Sollicitor with the privity of the said Sr. Thomas Berkeley,) drawn togeather, as before is touched; from whence also by secret watch not possible to be prevented, because unsuspected, The said Thomas Adams saw John Cornock the said sollicitors then servt. to bring away a Clokebaggfull of evidence and papers, as before also hath been mentioned: All the delaies that either the laws admitted in such reall actions, or which learning and experience could devise, were used on the part of the lord Lisle, But in the end severall issues were joyned upon the meere right, Whether the tenant the lord Viscount Lisle had more right to hold the lands as now hee held them,

them, or the demandant this lord Henry to have them in such sort as hee demanded them: The principall Elizors who appeared | with their swords and spurrs to returne the three Juryes for tryall of the said issues, in the beginning of Micĥmas Terme in the 7th of king James, were Sr Henry Poole, Sr Edward Wintour, Sr Wiℓℓm Cooke, Sr George Huntley, Sr William Throkm̃ton, and Sr Thomas Escourt, knights: These earnestly labored an end by applying themselves to the said Viscount Lisle, and to Henry lord Howard Earle of Northton, whose sister this lord had maryed, and who openly shewed himself a favorer of his brother in laws suits, this lord Berkeley himself then being at Callowdon; with each of which Elizors my self had often conferrence, as also with the said Viscount Lisle Sr Thomas Tracy and others, from him: **In** the end by their mediation an accord was made, and Articles drawn and signed the same Terme bearing date the last of October in the said seventh yeare of king James, made between the said Viscount Lisle on the one part, and this lord Berkeley on the other part, by the mediation of the said Sr Henry Poole, Sr Edward Wintour, Sir William Cooke, Sr George Huntley, Sr Wiℓℓm Throkmerton, and Sr Thomas Escourt, knights; Whereby it was agreed,

789

Micĥas. 1609.
7 : Jacobi.

Articl: dat: 31 :
Octobris. 1609.
7 : Jac:

1. That all the manors, lands, liberties, and hereditaments of the said lord Lisle sometimes belonging to the said lord Berkeley or his Ancestors, and then in question between the said lords, should bee assured to this lord Berkeley his heires or assignes by the said lord Lisle, as Counsell should devise.

2. That all estates rents and Annuities granted in writing by the late Earles of Warrwick and Leicester, or the late Countes of Warr̃, or by the said lord Lisle before Micĥmas last, contained in a schedule, to bee allowed and enjoyed in like strength as then they were.

3. That the lord Berkeley shall pay in two years next at certaine daies expressed—8333li 6s 8d. which was after agreed to bee paid in hand, And—7320li. to bee accepted in lieu of such ready payment, whereby much labour was saved in drawing up the assurance in that point; wherein some of the lord Lisles Counsell declared themselves more than desirous to break off the said agreement. And conveyances were drawn up and sealed accordingly, whereby aswell the said Viscount Lisle and William his then son and heire, (since dead without issue,) as the lord Henry, joyned in the conveyance of all the said Manors and lands to Wiℓℓm Dutton Esquire and my self, for the better uniteing of both titles, and securing our engagements for all that money; And was executed by livery of

Carta 27 Novemb.

seizin

seizin the 23th. of December following on Westridge Hill, the most conspicuous place of all those Manors by | the fower Atturnies therein named, in the presence of one hundred persons at the least, Whereof the Maior of Wotton and thirty three others in the same place subscribed their names as Witnesses, as by the indorsment of the Deed appears.

ffine: Hillary 7: Jac:

In Hillary Terme after, aswell the said Viscount Lisle and the lady Barbara his wife and the said Willm their son, As also the lord Henry and Sr. Thomas Berkeley his son, leavyed a fine, aswell of the said Manors and lands thus moving from the said Visct., as of the Manors of Cam, Hinton, Cowley, Slimbridge, and Hurst, to the said William Dutton and my self; **And** in Ester Terme following was a comon recovery of the said Manors and lands wth. a double Voucher against the said lord Lisle alone; for the better perfecting whereof, Surrenders upon Conditions were had of all the tenants for lives of any of the said lands; And the kings Licence for these alienations was dated the first of December before.

Recovery. Paschi: 8. Jac: rot. 57.

Licence. 1. Sept. [Dec. ?] 7. Jac.

And thus these manors of Wotton and Symondsall contained in the first Information, after thirty eight years; And the manor of Sages and the others contained in the second Information, after. 24. years, And the foresaid Hundred and liberties by violence for. 15. years, wrested from this lord Henry, returned againe into their old sheep fold; whereby this lord was as it were of new reinvested in those his Ancient inheritances, being essentiall parts of his barony of Berkeley, then valued to bee worth—35000li. Which composition money soe paid for the same, this lord raised againe with the interest in the next fower years, out of rents fynes and other casualties of the same Manors and lands, as by a particular accompt delivered unto him, and now in Berkeley Castle, appears. **And** the Records heere marginally quoted will declare what conveyances were made by every of the owners of every of them in their severall times after the lres patents of Queen Elizabeth; And how all Allienations without licence, and meane rates and issues, were discharged and pardoned, very necessary to bee known, aswell for avoydance of Exchequer troubles, as repose of the title. And a pardon in the 3rd. of King James to Robert Viscount Lisle of all arrears inrolled in memor scacij. 5. Jac: ex parte Rem Thesaur, and with 5. Auditors. |

Trin rec: 38. Eliz: rot: 123. in scacio
Hillar rec: 37. Eliz. rot: 52. et. 106. in scacio.
Mich rec: 40. Eliz: rot: in scacio
Origin 1: 2. Ph: Mar ps. 2. rot. 68 in scacio.
Trin. 5. Jac: rot. 1943. in coi banco. et 4 Jac. rot. in banco regis.
Hillar. 4 Jac. rot. 848 in coi banco.

791

192: years title.

And thus ended that trita et vexata questio, that old intricate and perplexed title, as it was usually in all Courts called, that had continued the space of 192. years, from the 5th. of king Henry the fifth to the seaventh of king James, between the heires

heires generall and the heirs males of this noble family; wherein besides more then fower times the value of the inheritance of the lands, that had by both parties in that longe tract of time been spent, the bloud of divers eminent persons on both sides had been spilt, from the guilt whereof, (more then fower generations on either side now being passed,) good God effree and deliver all the discendants and branches on both sides to all posterity, Amen,

In the close whereof, the forenamed Sollicitor in that cause received this comfort, that his endeavours were accepted and valued by this noble lord Henry above their deservings, who recompenced the same with an Anuity of ten pound p^r ann͠ during his life; with this his further testimony, That had not his perswasions been, hee had never looked more after these lands nor now had had them; And from the said lord Lisle had these words, That if hee had dyed in the year before in his sicknes at Glouc., hee would not have given this lord Henry 200^{li} for his releafe; which, (as conscious of his faithfull and utmost endeavours, is held noe arrogance here to bee written,) was publickly spoken by him in Serjeants Inne hall in ffleetstreet upon the lord Cokes commendations, (then lord cheife Justice of the Comon pleas,) of the cariage of a branch of this cause then referred to his opinion and other Judges, whereat both these lords were present: As also they had been at fower or five other meetings of Counsell on both sides in the same place, in the months of June October and Novem^r 1607, Anno quinto Jacobi regis; what times all differences of titles were referred by these lords to ffleminge and Coke cheife Justices, Tanfeild cheife Baron, and Judge Yelverton, when after great debates on both sides, falling from all hopes of peace by compromise, those writs of right were forthwith resolved on to be brought; which in the second year after, rendred an end to a perplexed title of 192. years agitation, as formerly hath been said.

Not longe after, this lord, (partly the better to pay the said composition money to the lord Lisle, and partly to pursue the presidents of his Ancestors, then shewed to him,) had a benevolence from all his tenants, whether holding by Copy of Court roll, or by Indenture: And also Aid pur faire fitz chivaler, according to the Statutes of. 3. E. 1. | and. 25. E. 3. from all his freeholders, whether holding by knights service or in socage, whereby the sum of—700^{li} and upwards was raised, And for any thing I perceived, (being a Comissioner in both the services,) willingly paid. — Benevolence money / Aid money / 792 / Annis. 9. et. 10. Jac: 1611. 1612.

Hee also at the same time bargained with one Thomas Hackett for all his Timber and firewood in Michaelwood chace, not growing in the parke there, excepting — Aprill. 8. Jac: 1610.

v'e fol: 753. 754.

excepting alfo three thoufand of the beft Timber trees in the Chace, which this lord referved to himfelf; whereby was raifed above three thoufand pound towards this Compofition money and his other debts; which the faid Hacket affigned over to Sir Wiłłm Throkmerton then of Tortworth, after hee had, to his loffe as was generally conceived, more then one year ufed the fame in making of iron, bringing his oar out of the faid fforreft; And which alfo the faid Sr Wiłłm with the loffe of one thoufand pound, (as hee hath written and protefted,) affigned over to two Citizens of Briftoll: A courfe that was taken in the fame place and in the lordfhips of other men in their manors adjoyning in the times of king Edward the third, as appeareth in Accompts of that time; whofe Sinders and other remains of thofe old works, at this time in many places digged up, was now both ufefull and profitable.

Against which iron making Sir Edward Wintour of Lidney, partly through the difpleafure that then raged between the faid Sr William and himfelfe, And partly for Sr Williams entring into his trade of iron making foe near his doors, from whence alfo hee fetched his oare, oppofed by private łres and informations fecretly delivered, which in the end brake forth to objections and anfwers, untill thofe premifes brought forth this certaine conclufion, which pleafed both parties, That this lord Henry gained, Sir Wiłłm and his affignes loft: And when thefe Michaelwood woods failed Sr Wiłłm was deftitute of other woods to continue them: **And** of thofe three thoufand choice trees foe left, the lord George in the fower firft years

v'e folio. 753. 754.

after his full age, made his profit by fales; And for his buildings at Simondfall, Newparke, the Grange by Berkeley, And at Brownfmill, Berkeley town mill, The Inne by Berkeley Caftle, and other places, as before hath been touched, befides what hee gave to Wotton and Nibley Churches, and to the Vicaridge houfe in Berkeley. |

793

Hitherto I have in the laft 60. pages related in a continuall feries thofe law fuits without interruption, which concerned the title of Wotton and thofe other Manors and lands, parcell of the Barony of Berkeley, with the confequences which thereupon followed, afwell for avoiding of fractions that otherwife would have interrupted that entire narration, As that this noble family might difcerne running what travaile and expence for 38. years togeather this lords mother the lady Anne, by

v'e fol: 731.

her over-ruling will, in a learning wherein fhee had not been bred nor experienced, threwe upon this lord her fon, and confequently upon her own pofterity; by her willfull refufall to take thefe manors and lands with the refidue of this lords Barony from Queen Mary by dedi and conceffi, contrary to the advice of her Counfell and

the

the defire of that Queen, as before is noted; upon which lady this lord her fon, fhortly after this compofition, faid to my felf and others That hee might juftly caft all the blame thereof; And then alfo, (turning to my felf,) further faid, That hee would make mee judge whether hee had loft or gained by following another perfwafion of his late wife, and neglecting the advife of a noble and faft freind of his, who a few daies before the firft Exchequer tryall in the 14th of Queen Elizabeth privately came to him, and earneftly advifed that hee fhould in noe wife give any evidence or make any defence at all, but to fuffer his land to bee loft by default; rendring many great reafons for fuch his Counfell, whereto of my felf, faid this lord Henry, I did incline; Howbeit, the great fpirit of my wife whom I privately acquainted therewith would not fuffer that advice to bee followed, though fhee refted affured of the true heartednes of that noble freind, and hee knew much of the Earle of Leicefters clofe workings of the caufe; And the more to divert mee, faid this lord, my wife drew Thomas Walmefley then of my fpeciall Counfell to bee ftrongly of her opinion, who in her prefence told mee That my title was foe cleere that I fhould not fear the verdict what ever the Jurors were; Adding further, That the remembrance hereof was noe doubt a fpeciall motive for Mr. Walmefley, (come to bee Judge of the Comon Pleas,) to bee foe affectionate to my caufe, as at the laft tryall you faw hee was: And indeed, quoth this lord, hee only ftucke to mee at that firft tryall with great boldnes when | all other of my Counfell were drawn away, on whofe brother I conferred the Viccaridge of Tetbury; The name of this noble freind I could never obtaine from this lord, but by circumftances I conceived it was his wives kinfman Thomas Ratcliffe Earle of Suffex, lord Chamberlaine to Queen Elizabeth; who ten years after, told the faid lady when in perfon fhee follicited an end by Compromifes, That fuch was the potency of her adverfary the Earle of Leicefter both in Court and Country, and his reaches, That what hee had hee would keep, And that it was gaine to her to win him not to feeke for more, And that his drift by yeilding to referrences was only to dive into her hufbands evidence and noe other; This is that Earle of Suffex whom Cambden in his Britania ftorieth to bee a moft worthy and honorable perfonage, in whofe mind were feated joyntly both policy wifdom and martiall proweffe, as England and Ireland acknowledged; who dyed in June the 25th year of Queen Elizabeth; Anno, 1583. But inftead of anfwere, I obtained pardon; And here alfo both time and place and refemblance of matter call upon mee further to informe this noble family, That in the 13th yeare of Queen Elizabeth, before the firft fuite for Wotton began, (what time this lord Henry had by his wives means fetled all his manors lands and Barony upon his daughters,) An overture was made from the Earles of Warr̃ and Leicefter for a

of this tryall fee in Leicefters comõon welth printed. 1584. fol: 34. et. 89.

794

Leicr̃ comon welth fol: 80. printed 1584.

Cambden. fol: 321. in Suffex. Leicr̃. com̃. welth fol: 52.

double

double marriage, between Sr Philip Sidney and Sr Robert Sidney their sisters only sons and this lords two eldest daughters, Mary and ffrances; which being more slighted by this lords wife then either reason or direction warranted, soe offended the said Earles and others of their bloud, That her brothers trouble Thomas Duke of Norfolke went on, and his head off; And the same month of his Attainder the Information against this lord Henry touching Wotton and Simondsfall was exhibited against him by their means and prosecution, as formerly hath been written: whereupon judgment being given against this lord in Ester Terme, Anno 15th Eliz: and hee shortly after turned out of possession of those manors; And the like black cloud being by a wise servant of this lords discerned to bee in gathering, (who prudently was willing but unable to resist the will of a woman, who as before shee liked not, soe now hated | the Earles bloud in their two nephewes,) wrought soe farr with this lord Henry to ask the advice of his best kinsman and freinds touching the said overture, which that prudent servant and freind secretly knew would againe come on, if intended to bee accepted;. Whereupon this lord by his lre prayed the advice and Counsell of Sr Nicholas Poyntz, Sr Giles Poole, Sr Richard Berkeley, and of Sr Thomas Throkmerton, his nearest kinsmen and allies, and all of them at that time in perfect freindship with him, and the cheifest in reputation of that County: who, the 26th of October 1573 15th Eliz: returned this grave and solid answere and advice.—**There** shall come from us noe advice (in our own judgements) unfit for your Lo:^p to follow: yor good and prosperous estate is the thing wee desire; Assured freinds doe sufficiently declare themselves by plaine speeches and freindly actions: Every man may behold good policy to bee your surest defence: We will not nor may not devine what should bee the cause of your Lo:^{ps} late great losses; but by considering the circumstances of that is past, wee may fear what will followe, and advise you in time to prevent the same: And because your lo:^p is overresolutely determined to leave your daughters to inherit your land, not to give the same to any heire male of your house, (which is great pittie,) Wee therefore think it nescessary for you upon resonable conditions to accept the offer of Mr Phillip Sidney if the same bee again made: if also a further offer bee made of Mr Robert Sidney for one of your younger daughters, wee likewise hold the same nothing necessary for you to refuse: Your lo:^p cannot bestow your daughters more honorably in this land, as wee think: for their possibillities are in very deed certaine, or to bee made certaine: the Earle of Leicester greatly tendring the younger son for that hee is his godson and beareth his name: That match cutteth of all lawe and losse that may followe; bindeth those to favour you and yours that may doe good to whom they list; Seeing therefore it is honorable rich safe and strong for you to bee affected that way, if

ill

ill Counsell or wilfullnes draw you back, we shall bee sorry, and shall hope you will strongly appoint your self by patience to beare those burthens that are like to bee laid upon you: ffor our parts, wee bee assuredly your lordships freinds, foe can the same doe you noe service, for our acts will bee but shewes and shaddows; Wee speak not this that you should spare to command us, | or that wee will bee cold to execute what is reasonable and meet for honest freinds and kinsmen, but you may make your accompt before hand; and wee are doubtles assured there will bee nothing offered against you that your Lo: and all your freinds can defend: In these sewe lines wee shewe your Lo: what wee wish you should neither sue for nor lightly esteem, if it bee offered; and doe commit your Lo: to the protection of Almighty God, this 26th of October, 1573; your Lo^{ps} assured. N: Poyntz, Giles Poole, Richard Berkeley, Thomas Throkmton. Directed, To the R: Honorable our very good lord, the lord Berkeley. But the same womanish power that quasht the first motion queld also this second sound Counsell, Alliened by degrees her husbands affection from those freinds that foe really advised, And foe frowned upon that prudent servant that wrought herein that hee retired himself to his paternall inheritance, and but once in fifteen years after, eare hee dyed, came to Callowdon; Howbeit had this advice been followed, her two daughters had enjoyed two as eminent gentlemen for their husbands as England afforded, And they not stayed 14. years after for meaner preferrments; The great lump of land that after was lost, (according to the propheticall foresight of those freinds,) prevented: her self and husband freed from a world of sorrow attendance travell and expence: And yet this lords land and Barony had, as it was then setled, wholly fallen to her son Thomas, borne within two years after.

And now I transmit the Judgment to this lords posterity upon confideration of what followed, in the said thirty eight years till this composition; whether hee suffered not extreamly by being thus doubly over-ruled by his wife; And whether the will of this wife was in mariage foe given up to her husband, as that shee was noe longer her own but at her husbands disposing.

It's now time to turne to such other of this lords law suits as seems most materially to import the knowledge of his posterity, not formerly mentioned.

Other lawe suites.

In the seaventh of Queen Elizabeth this lord humoring the greatnes of his wives mind, (whom about the same time Queen | Elizabeth called her golden lady,) bought a lute of mother of pearle, (her self an excellent lutist,) for which the Queen formerly had offered one hundred marks; for this lute this lord paid a

sum

fum of money in hand, and gave a recognizance to pay to Beft the owner thereof three pound a year more during his life, which for ten years after was duly paid; what time this lord growing either negligent or weary of the payment, neglected it, whereby his recognifans becoming forfeited, Beft fued out a Scire facias and foone had judgment thereupon: This lord for releife flyeth into the chancery, where after bill and anfwer and witneffes on both parts examined, thefe offers in Court were made to Beft by this lords Counfell; Either to take twenty marks in money for the only default of one three pounds, and the paym.t to bee continued after; Or to take 32^{li} 13^s 4^d —in ready money, and the Anuity to ceafe; Or to bee quit of the 34^{li} which already hee hath received and to have the lute againe to his own ufe, as fafe and faire as at firft it was; Or to referre the caufe to the ending of any two Aldermen of London whom himfelf would chufe; Or to his own two Counfellors Bell and Puckering, (the one after Baron of the Exchequer, and the other lord keeper,) fetting lawe and affection toward their Client apart: None of which Beft would accept of, but refufed all; whereat Bacon then lord keeper being moved, awarded an Injunction and ftayed him from taking any benefit by the faid recognizance untill the caufe fhould otherwife bee ordered in that Court; Afterwards Beft accepted of much lefs then was formerly offered.

Order: 18. Nov:
18. Eliz:

This Lute, this lord, about two years after the death of his faid wife, gave to the Dowager Counteffe of Derby, whom in his widowers freedom hee called miftris; and hee afterwards almoft maryed M.rs Ratcliffe one of her gentlewomen.

Much about this time this lord had brought home to him by one Holloway his tailor a fuite of clothes, of doublett, breeches w.th panes, and jurkin without fleeves, laid very thick with filver lace; And withall the tailors bill was delivered by his direction to Giles Yate one of the grooms of his chamber, who on the next day well obferving his imodarate proportion of ounces of the filver lace, (which the tailor himfelf had bought, as alfo hee did all the other ftuffe of the Suite,) waighed the wholl fuite, which was not foe many ounces of like waight as the bill made the lace alone to bee: And thereupon | fecretly, unknown to this lord, caufed all the lace to bee ripped off and weighed alone, And found the bill falfe by more then fower fcore ounces: whereupon for nonpayment of noe part of the bill, a fuite was longe time after commenced by the Taylors executor againft this lord, which was compounded.

Robert Burton of Linley dyed feized of the Manor of Lindley in the county of Leicefter, leaving Ralph his fon and heire within age, whofe wardfhip this lord

Henry

Henry gave in the second of Queen Elizabeth to Thomas Duport his servant, a prudent man: Duport after assigned to Puresy, and hee againe to Agard, who brought a Valore maritagii[1] against the said Raph Burton, tried at the Assizes holden at Leicester about the tenth of Eliz. and recovered; which I had the relation from William his son and heire, Author of the description of Leicestershire. And this grant from the lord Berkeley is entred in his great black booke of Inrollments.

This lord had a cheise rent of five pounds p Ann̄ paid to him as to his Manor of Weston near Baldocke in the county of Hartford, issuing out of certaine lands called Broughtons, in Toddington, the inheritance of Henry lord Cheney: which this lord Berkeley, (out of what humor I know not,) reserved to himself in the conveyance whereby in the 14th of Queen Elizabeth hee sold Weston to Mr. Burgoine, who then for that rent, (as this lord told mee,) would have given him one hundred pounds: This rent was somwhat before detained: whereupon many tres and references to Counsell passed between this lord and the lord Cheney, as the tres yet extant doe shewe, wch coming to noe effect, this lord in the said 14th of Elizabeth exhibited his bill in chancery, wherto the lord Cheney made Answer; But after replication and rejoynder and witnesses examined, the lord Cheney before hearing dyed: And soe hath rested ever since. *Carta. 28 Novr. 14. Eliz: Anno: 1569. 11. Eliz. tres in Berk: Castle. Canc: 14. Eliz. See after fol. 819.*

In the 17th year of Queen Elizabeth was a troublsome suite in Chancery between this lord plt. and one Mr. Yaxley, which I touche noe further upon, for that it concerned lands in Derbyshire which this lord hath longe since sold away. *Cancellar̄.*

In the 19th of Queen Elizabeth this lord brought an Action against | Edward Bucknam somtimes an officer much trusted and imployed by him, for not accompting for the rents and profits of the Manor of Callowdon, (whereof hee was Baily,) for . 7 . years next after the death of this lords mother, when to him it fell in hand: wherein it was found by verdict, That Bucknam had formerly accompted for the first six years, but not for the last of the seaven; for which last year hee after accompted in prison, as the record speaketh; which suite I the rather here remember, for that it containes a resonable survey of the perticulars of that Manr. *799 Civiī Coventry Hill: 19. Eliz: in banco regis. rot.*

In the 39th of Queen Elizabeth, in the same Court of kings bench, was an action depending prosecuted by ffrancis Smyth Esqr, after knight, against Henry Shipward *In banco regis Leicr*

---
[1] A Writ by which a Lord was entitled to sue an infant tenant, who had refused a suitable marriage offered to him by the lord, for the value of his marriage. [Ed.]

Melton — Shipward Baily of Melton Mowbray, upon a diftres taken by him for Toll; wherein though the pleadings were much laboured by great Counfell, yet the Court upon argument found error in the Avowry of Shipward, which to know may bee of ufe hereafter.

Anno: 25. Eliz: — In the 25th of Queen Elizabeth William Brown being keeper of Cam woods under this lord, impounded the Sheep of Richard Tindall Walter Hampton and Richard Nelme of Stinchcomb, and of Thomas Trotman and John Selman of Stancombe, for which they preferred their bill in the Marches of Wales againft Browne; And thence had a Comiffion to Richard Pate Efq.r, lord of the manor of Stinchcombe, and one of the Counfell there, to examine witneffes; who in January in the 26th of Elizabeth examined Tindall, Trotman and Selman aforefaid and others interefted as parties and Commoners; who depofed the ufage of their comon in the

Anno: 26. Eliz: — faid woods time out mind. ffor which perjury this lord in the 26th of Elizabeth exhibited his bill againft them in the Starre chamber; And alfo againft Edward Trotman Henry Parmiter John ffrancombe Simon Codrington and others, (creatures to Sr. Thomas Throkmerton,) for hunting and killing his Deere in Whitcliffe park New park and Michaelwood. In the Court of the Marches of Wales it was, the

Anno: 27. Eliz: — firft of July in the 27th of Elizabeth, at Salop, ordered, That the plts fhould ufe their Comon for their Cattell and pawnage for their fwine in the faid woods untill the fame fhould bee difproved; which order in their anfwers in the ftar chamber they fett out; And how it was not Edward but Richard Pate that examined the witneffes; And foe took advantage of the plts miftaking in this bill; And this order is carefully preferved amongft them to this day; but certainly in right they have noe Comon in thofe woods, which is like hereafter to come in queftion.

Bill in the Excheqr chamber: 27. Eliz: — In the 26th of Elizabeth this lord diftrained Henry Goldefon for an amerciament of fower pence impofed for his not appearing at this lords leete holden for his Manor of Melton Mowbray in the county of Leicefter; whereupon Thomas Chancey als Giles whofe tenant the faid Goldfon was, exhibited his bill in the Exchequer chamber againft this lord Henry, fetting out that hee had a Manor in Melton called the manor of Lewes, which was of late belonging to the Prior of St. Pancraffe of Lewes in the County of Suffex, to which manor was a leete or viewe of frankpledge belonging; which Pryor and Covent, by their Indenture dated the 17th of Aprill in the 23th of Henry the 8th, demifed the fame to Willm Gonfon Efqr, for fifty five years, whofe eftate for the terme to come, hee the plt hath, the reverfion to the Queen that now is: And that Henry lord Berkeley having another manor in Melton,

800

Melton, goeth about to conftraine the Queens tenants of her faid manor of Lewes to doe fuite to his manor and Leete, and hath amerced fome of them for refufing the fame, &c. Whereto this lord anfwereth, That to his Leete in Melton all refiants whatfoever in that Town have ufed to come, And for that the faid Goldfon made default, hee was amerced at 4.^{d} for wch hee being diftrained, hee replevyed, which is now ready for tryall at lawe; And traverfeth the Pryors leete and the reft of the bill: **In** which fuite Witneffes on both parts were examined in September in the 27th of Elizabeth, who fwore pro et contra, And upon hearing it was ordered that [refult not given. ED.]

Rotul: 4. E. 4. in recept̃ Sc^{a}c̃ij coram Rogero de Saham.
Rot: cart. 16. E. 4. m: 5. et. 6. et ultima in arce Londin:
Efchaet.p^t mortem Joh̃is de Mowbray 16. E. 3.
Rot: pat: 18. E. 3. pars. 2. m: 8.
Rot. claus. 2. E. 3. m: 14.
Rot: Romæ. 2. E. 3. m: 2.
Efchaet: 2. E. 3. n⁰ 73. Pro priore de Lewes.

And this is now, Anno 1628, the inheritance of Robert Hudfon of London this lords Baily of Melton aforefaid, And was purchafed of Queen Elizabeth the 27th of October in the 23th of her raigne by Edward Downinge and Peter Afhton, and foe by meane conveyances came to him. Touching which fuppofed manor of Lewes and of the originall guift thereof to the faid Pryory, fee my tract of Melton Manor in a book by it felf, where is matter enough to break the neck of this fuppofed Manor of Lewes and of the Leete thereof, Whereof Humphry Alfop who followed this fuite, and then Steward to this lord of this Manor, was altogeather ignorant. And in the mean time take thefe marginalls, which are unanfwerable.|

801

This lord and his Anceftors for. 300. years and more had received a cheife rent of three pound ten fhillings out of the manor of Acton Ilger, paid by Sr Nicholas Poyntz and his Anceftors to the Reeve of this lords manor of Hame, and reputed as parcell of the fervices thereof, as by many records deeds rentalls accompts Courtrolls and other evidences appeareth. This rent Sr Nicholas Poyntz, though cozen german to this lord yet then at enmity with him, and pertaking with the Earles of Warwick and Leicefter and Sir Thomas Throkmiton in the fuits aforementioned, denyed any longer to pay; whereupon this lord in the 26th of Elizabeth exhibited his bill in Chancery, whereto Sr Nicholas anfwered, And after replication, rejoyned; in which rejoynder Sr Nicholas having the faid Earles Counfell of Counfell with him, intitled the Queen thereto by the attainder of their father the Duke of Northumberland in the firft of Queen Mary, To the Anceftor of which Duke faith hee, the fame was allotted in p̃tition in the fixth year of king Edward the 4th whereof I have formerly written, afwell in the life of this lord as in the lives of James the firft, and William Marques Berkeley his fon; By which means upon the motion of Sr Nicholas, the fecond of June in the 27th of Elizabeth, It was ordered That the Queens Counfell fhould firft bee confulted with, before any further

See fol: 200

Anno: 26. Eliz:

Order. 2 Junij 27. Eliz:

proceedings

proceedings were had: And Sr Nicholas dying in ffebruary next after, the suite abated. But after such time as Sr John Poyntz his son and heir had sued his livery, this lord sensible of the manifest wronge offered him in detaining of this rent, did in Hillary Terme in the 32th of the said Queene, exhibite another bill in the said Court (by way of reviver) against him for the said rent unpaid for Ten years in the life of Sr Nicholas his father, and five years since by himself; who in his answere denyed that any such rent was going out of his said manor of Acton Ilger to his knowledge; what further became hereof I find not: But of this I am assured, That this lord had and his grandchild the lord George now hath, (if the Statutes of limitation prejudice him not,) as good right thereto as to his manor of Hame, whereof the said rent is pcell.

<small>Hill. 32. Eliz: 1589.</small>

<small>vide comp: man'ij et libert. de Wotton. 12. 14. 15. H. 6. in castro de Berkeley. Anno; 31. H. 8. et 1. Jacobi.</small>

In the 29th of Elizabeth a suite in Starchamber arose between this lord and his then neighbour Sir John Harrington of Combe, (after lord,) and other of his servants and tenants of Binley, who committed a great ryott by night in cutting down all the corne that grewe upon a tenement of this lord there, let by him to Edward Jones a blacksmyth, upon whom, for not payment of his rent and not doing his farriers work, hee re-entred; who had assigned his terme to Walter Pyle, and hee to Sr John Harrington; which discurtesies were agravated by the reapers scoffingly setting up an handfull of corne at each lands end, like a poesy; which this lord conceived to bee in mockery and despite: But this was never brought to hearing: And this is that house and land which formerly in this lords life I have noted to bee unjustly gotten by this lord and his mother from Gerrard Try, that like ill gotten goods never prosperred in his hands.

<small>Starch: 29. Eliz:</small>

<small>802</small>

In the 30th of Elizabeth this lord brought an accon of covenant against Nicholas Brown of Melton for not payment of his last half years rent, and not repairing of the comon bakehouse in Melton with the Ovens there, in such sort as by this lease, then ended, hee was to have done, As also for not baking at the said ovens, who reformed and made his peace.

<small>Mich: 29. et. 30. Eliz: in banco regis rot: Hackburne cum quer. Shirborne cum def^ts</small>

And touching this bakehouse, Abraham Sheldon lessee to this lord, brought his action of the case against William Archer of Melton for not bakeing his bread thereat according to the custome of the said Town: which I mention because the Declaration was curious; And the action is like to prove frequent, for the lords Court there is scarce able to preserve his inheritance in this custome of bakeing.

And in 8° Jac: this lord exhibited a bill in the exchequer chamber against Edward Wormwell

<small>Trin. 5. Jac: in banco regis rot. Bryan pro quer Brown pro def^t Claus: 35. E. 3. m. 3. et. 4. in dorso. mich terme. 8. Jac. A bill in ye Exchequer Chamber.</small>

Wormwell and three others, for not baking at the said comon oven or bakehouse, who thereupon conformed and made their peace.

In the said 30th of Elizabeth arose divers suits both in the Chancery and at the comon lawe, between this lord and Arden his tenant at Mangottsfeild house parke and conigre, whereof followed much trouble and expence; And the violence at severall times used between the servants of this lord, and the said Arden drew often bloud, with much danger in taking of distresses rescouffes[1] and possessions, which lasted six years; Howbeit I pass them over in generallity, becaufe that manor is since sold away, as after followeth under that title.

<small>Anno: 30. Eliz:
Order: 14: Junij.
34. Eliz:
pasch: 32. Eliz:
in Cancell.
Peport: 7. ffebr.
36. Eliz:</small>

In the 33th of Elizabeth Willm Bower in behalf of this lord pursued an accon against John Birton, tenant to an antient messuage called Baffetts Court in Nibley, for a cheife rent of 33s. 4d. which since the 7th year of king James hath been duly paid to the manor | of Wotton fforren, and the services acknowledged, of which messuage and the first creation of that rent, see before in the life of the lord Thomas the second.

<small>Mich. 32. et. 33.
Eliz. rot. 808. in
cōi banco.

803
fol: 171.</small>

The same year this lord recovered in an action of Wast against Thomas Printhorpe for cutting down divers trees in a close called ridhay alias Callowdon close in Exall in the County of the City of Coventry, And an Inquisition for the damage thereof returned accordingly.

<small>Anno: 33. Eliz:</small>

In the same 33th of Elizabeth Thomas Chamberlin of Graies Inne, then an utter Barrister and after knight and cheife Justice in the Marches of Wales, became follicitor to this lord, under his fee of 15li. p Ann, And the first suite he travelled in was an Assife of Comon brought by Richard Barker of Austy against this lord by the name of Henry lord Berkeley, in regard of an Enclofure not longe before made in Sowe wast parcell of his manor of Callowdon, to the plts dissensin, who claimed to have Comon of pasture therein; whereto this lord pleaded, nul tort, nul disseisin; In which Barker had to prove, first his title to the messuage and Yardland and an halfe whereto hee claimed his Comon. 2dly That the yardland and halfe had alwaies been belonging to the said Messuage and to none other. 3dly his prescription modo et forma, as hee laid it down, 4th That the comon of pasture was belonging to the messuage and yardland an half undivided, for if the comon bee certaine to every yardland, Then hee failed in his prescription, in that it was laid joyntly; whereas it should have been laid severally for the number of cattle to every yard, and half yard of land. 5thly The disseisin of this lord of the said Comon of pasture, who had

1
2
3
4
5

left

---

[1] Rescues from *Rescous*. a. n.=Rescue. [ED.]

6 left sufficient gaps in his inclosure for the cattle of the Comoners. And lastly, whether the land were sowen or not at the time of the disseisin: The verdict passed against this lord, but partially, which hee afterwards avoided by the mistaking of his name, for hee was a knight of the bath and therefore should have been stiled Henry Berkeley knight lord Berkeley: Many other good notes arose upon this suite for the instruction of young practicers; As that the messuage and yard land and half were purchased by the pl:t of severall persons; That some of it was in lease for years or life; That hee had noe cattell of his own but borrowed other mens, and the like. About the time of this tryall was the ditch of this inclosure riotously cast down in the night time by Peers, Pettifer of Austy, and others, whereof followed a troublesome and un- | profitable Starchamber suite; In perusall whereof I gained this knowledge, That a child of fowerteen years old may bee made a defendant in that Court; All which were afterwards in the 35:th of Elizabeth concluded by arbitrement: And that agreement upon Barkers bill in Chancery and this lords Answere, acknowledging the agreement, ratifyed by the Decree of that Court, That hee and others should have Comon when the corne is out, and the enclosure to stand; This cause was as well pressed and defended by both parties as I think lay in the power of learning.

Mich: 32. et. 34. Eliz:

804
Order in Hill terme 33. Eliz: Anno: 35: Eliz:

In the 32:th of Elizabeth, Thomas Clark recovered against this lord an action of the case for not paying him—49:li 13:s 4:d, after the rate of 6:s 8:d by the day, according to promise, for Surveying and measuring the Manors of Sileby, Melton, Mountforrell, and Segrave, in the county of Leicester: for reversall of which Judgment, this lord brought a writ of Error, But not prevailing, Clark by Elegit took in execution the Manors of Melton, Coldoverton, Segrave and others. Howbeit this lord in Hillary terme in the 32:th of Elizabeth, brought Clarke into the Starchamber for subornation of perjury in the former proceedings, whereby they came after to composition.

Mich: 32. &. 33. Eliz: in coṁuni banco.

Hill: 32: Eliz: Starchamber.

In the 35:th of Elizabeth or near that year, William Harvar of Keinsham yeoman was at Bitton leete amerced—23:s 4:d for surcharging the Coṁons in Bitton with his sheep: ffor which John Brittaine Baily there distrained a gray gelding of the said Harvars in Sidnam mead, impounding him in the common pound at Bitton: Harvar replevyed, The suite from the county court was removed into the common place: By Harvars default a writ of Withernam[1] was had, and two of
Harvars

Anno: 35. Eliz:

---

[1] *Withernam* is where a Distress is driven out of the County, and the Sheriff upon a Replevin cannot make a deliverance to the party distrained: In this case a *Writ of Withernam* is directed to the Sheriff for the taking as many of his beasts or goods that did thus unlawfully distrain into his keeping until the party made delivery of the first distress. [ED.]

Harvars kine taken in that meade: whereupon hee acknowledged his offence, paid the 23ˢ 4ᵈ amerciaments, and 40ˢ for costs of suite.

In the 37th of Elizabeth this lord was plt againſt William Deane and Robert Deane for a treſpas comitted upon a cloſe called Potters green, part of his manor of Callowdon, which was tryed againſt him at Coventry aſſizes, but without all colour of truth; for noe manner of evidence was given on the defendants behalfe, which I write out of knowledge, being preſent; For which groſſe perjury this lord Henry brought the jury into the Starchamber, who were upon motion difmiſed with coſts, becauſe they were charged | fix and fix in two bills, and Mr Chamberlyn the Counſellor reprehended that foe drew thoſe bills and marſhalled them; hee then a young barriſter of Graies Inne and this lords Sollicitor, as hath been ſaid. *Trin: 37. Eliz: banco regis. rot. Paſch: 38. Eliz: 805*

In the 38th of Elizabeth this lord Henry was plt in two ſeverall actions of treſpas againſt John Brock John Champion and others for cutting and carriage away of divers loads of wood out of Woolcombe and other places, parcell of the Downs or waſt grounds of his Manor of Portbury in the County of Somerſet; which fact the defts ſeverally juſtifyed under John Wake Efqr as holding in comon with this lord, in regard of a manor called Portbury Pryor which hee had in Portbury purchaſed by Godwyn his wifes father of king Henry the eighth, and late belonging to the pryory of Brimmore in Hampſhr upon which tenancy in Comon the iſſues were joyned, And the two records of Niſi prius taken out: whereupon John Creſwell ſteward of houſhold to this lord and cozen to Mr Wake, labored an end, And wth faire words and ſattisfaction for the wood made the defts peace, the very day that I ſhould have ridden from Callowdon towards the aſſizes about thoſe tryalls then holden at Taunton. *Mich: 38. & 39. Eliz: in banco regis.*

At the fame time this lord brought an action of dett for five pound againſt Richard Baily, declaring That hee being ſeized of the hundred of portbury, had time out of mind uſed to have a veiwe of frankpledge belonging thereto, To which the Tythingman of Clyvedon and fower men with him, (called his fower poſts,) have alwaies accuſtomed to come, And upon oath to preſent ſuch things as are preſentable in a Leete; And becauſe the defts refuſed to bee ſworne and to preſent, the Steward impoſed upon him the fine of five pound: for which hee brought this action: The ſaid Mr Wake lord of Clyvedon defended the ſuite, and alleadged That the Thirdbarrow or Tithingman ought to come to Portbury Leete, and pay 4ᵈ in name of his fower poſts that come with him, but not to preſent any offences. *Mich: 37. et. 38. Eliz: in banco regis rot.   Somſet.*

This

This came to a communication before Serjeant Nicholls, after Judge, his freindly neighbour, who was foe well Sattisfyed with the evidences which this lord shewed since the Inquisition in the 12th of Edward the first, That hee openly advised him to acknowledge the suite to bee just: which with payment of costs of suite and the perswasion of Mr. Creswell satisfyed the plt, the service ever since being duly performed.

<small>806
Hill: 39. Eliz: rot coi banco. Scotts office Gloucester.</small>

In the 39th of Queen Elizabeth, Thomas Phelps lessee to John Yowen and Mary his wife, tenants for life to John Harvy of Bradston, of Divers lands in Bevington within ye manor of Hame, brought an action of Ejectione firmæ against William Danfeild servant to John Huntley and Jone his wife, Copihold tenants to this lord of a messuage and divers lands in the said manor, supposing they withheld from him nineteen acres of his land under colour of this lords copyhold graunt to them; upon tryall whereof one small parcell of a close called gromballs hay containing about a quarter of an acre, (whereout this lord hath a cheife rent of 3s. 4d. p Ann, and whereon the lease was sealed,) was found for the plt; for all the rest the defts were found not guilty, And soe ever since hath slept at peace: Howbeit in

<small>Mich: 31. et. 32. Eliz: rot: 524. Glouc:</small>

the 31th of Elizabeth was a verdict for much more against this lords then tenant, but the plt dyed before judgment: And likewise a troblesome suite was shortly after at the Counsell in ye Marches of Wales, whereat many Witnesses were examined, but without fruite.

<small>Mich: 40. et. 41. Eliz: rot: 3127. et Trin 41. Eliz: com. pleas.</small>

In the 40th of Elizabeth Mary Gawsell widowe, late the wife of John Willoughby, brought a writ of Dower against Sr. John Peter for the third part of the manor of Kenet in the County of Cambridge, which this lord in the third of Elizabeth sold to Sr. Willm Peter his father, wherein this lord is by Sr. John vouched to Warranty: who pledeth the grant of king Edward the second made the 16th of Decemr in the sixth of his raigne, of this manor (amongst others,) to Alice Bigod widow, late wife of Roger Bigod Earle of Norfolk, for her life, the remainder to Thomas of Brotherton his brother and the heires of his body; which Thomas had issue Margaret maryed to John lord Segrave, who had issue Elizabeth maryed to John lord Mowbray, who had issue Thomas lord Mowbray created Duke of Norffolke, who had issue Thomas, John, Margaret, and Isable; which Thomas died without issue, And the said John had issue John, who also was Duke of Norfolke, and had issue John, who also was Duke of Norff, and had issue Anne maryed to Richard Duke of Yorke second son to king Edward the fourth, who dyed without issue: That the said Margaret was maryed to Sr. Robert Howard, who had issue

John

John Howard created duke of Norfolke; And that the said Isable was maryed to James lord Berkeley, who had issue William after Marques Berkeley, and Maurice lord Berkeley: That the said Willm Marques Berkeley had this manor, (amongst others,) alotted to him by ptition with the said John Duke of Norfolk, And afterwards conveyed the same to Richard Willouhby and the heires males of his body, The remainder to Edw.d Willoughby & the heirs males of his body; which Richard dyed without issue, And the said Edward entred and had issue John Willoughby, who maryed the said Mary Gawsell, and after dyed without issue male: After the death of which John Willoughby this lord Henry son of Thomas, son of Thomas, brother of Maurice, son of the said Maurice, entred, And by fine in the third of Elizabeth alyened the same to Sr. William Peter father of the said Sr. John Peter, And soe demandeth judgment of the Court, whether by lawe shee ought to bee endowed. The widow Gawsell confesseth all the former pleadings to bee true, but further saith That the said Edw.d Willoughby by Izable his wife had issue John her husband, And that the said Edward enfeoffed one Logge parson of Wotton, against whom in the 22th of Henry the 7th a comon recovery was had of the said manor, (amongst others,) to the use of the said Edward and Isable his wife and of the heires of his body, The remainder to the said Maurice brother of the said Marques Berkeley and of his heires; whereupon it appeared that shee was dowable, neither would shee henceforth accept the 11li. 10s. which till then had sattisfyed her from the death of her husband for near forty years; And thereupon this lord through the strictnes of his covenants in his conveyance to Sr. William Peter was inforced to compound with her for——18li. 10s. p Anñ for her life, which hee paid her about five years ere shee dyed.

vide antea, fol: [587, 596] 807

Terme Pasch: 3. Eliz:

Rec: 22. H. 7.

And this action and pleadings I have the rather here mentioned because the manor of Bosham is at this day enjoyed by the lord George under the same entaile of the 6th of Edward the second. Yet such was the ignorance of the sollicitors and Counsell of this lord Henry in those times, That they suffered him to covenant with Sr. Willm Peter That hee was seised in fee of that manor And that noe revertion was in the Crown; which were two untruths, and a double breach of his Covenant; By which ignorance this further inconvenience happened, That Sir John Peter finding the said covenants broken and that the reversion was in the Crown, brought his action upon the said Covenant, laying down the grant and discent as aforesaid, concluding thereby that this lord was seized in taile and not in fee; whereupon this lords manor of Alkington in the County of Glouc., (whereof hee as Humphry Alsop his then Sollicitor deposed was seized in fee,) was recovered over in Value and warranty,

Mich: 29. et. 30. Eliz: in Ester: com pleas.

808	warranty, ut tunc pro nunc, et nunc pro tunc, with fifty two pounds costs, which this lord paid.

Hill: 28. Eliz: in banc: regis: rot. 838.
Mich: 27. 28. Eliz: in banco regis. et. 26. &. 27. Eliz: rot. 474.
Hill. 5. Jac: in banco regis.
Pa: 3. Jac: rot. 399. in banco regis.
Mich. 3. Jac: rot. 110. in banco regis.
Pasch: 5: Jac: rot. 404. et pars 2. in banco regis.
Hill: 5. Jac: rot. 810. et. 811.
Hill: 28. Eliz: in banco regis.
Bill in canc: in Mich: 3. Jac:
Certificate in chancery 30. Jan:ry 1608.

Thomas Estcourt of Tetbury a bencher of Graies Inne, father of Sir Thomas Estcourt knight and of Edmond Estcourt, set on foot two suits against John Savage gent a farmer to this lord Henry, touching comon of pasture in the feilds of Tetbury for a flock of Sheep of 400. or more called the lords flock, never used to bee stinted, as all other freeholders sheep are within the manor; And (by mistaking the prescription) had two verdicts and Judgments against the said John Savage: Thomas Estcourt dying, left his lands in Tetbury to the said Edmond his younger son and his heires, who all his life for many years permitted the continuance of the said flock (as his father also had done after the said verdicts;) Afterwards, George Estcourt a younger brother to the said Thomas, an other freeholder in Tetbury, set on foot three or more the like suits against the said John Savage, and had like verdicts upon Severall Tryalls at lawe. After divers years, (when all issues that might well be joyned upon any prescription were foyled,) M:r Savage acquainting a Sollicitor of this lords with the former proceedings, and of the vexations of the said George Estcourt still continuing, was advised by him to seek peace by a bill in Chancery; which in the name of this lord was exhibited against the said George Estcourt; whereupon many witnesses were examined, And amongst others, these points fully proved. 1.st That the said lord and his Ancestors and their tenants time out of mind have used to have pasture or feeding in the feilds of Tetbury for a flocke of sheep called the lords flocke, of about. 400, all the year longe when the feilds lye fallow; And when the feilds are sown, then from S:t Lukes day till they bee sown againe, peaceably enjoyed without interruption of any, save the def:ts George Estcourt and his brother Thomas the lawyer, proved by 25. witnesses 2.dly That the lords flock was never stinted, though all others were stinted after three sheep for an acre. 3.dly That the said flocke hath used to depasture in a place called the sleight w:th in Tetbury warren from Holliroode day in May till holliroode day in Septem:r, And from thence till the Annunciation of our lady. And none elce

809

Throkm'ton. pl:t Estcourt def:t Mich: 3. Jac: rot. 110. in banco regis.

to have any Comon of pasture there at those times. | 4.th That every person holding a burgage house in Tetbury hath accustomed to have pasture for three beasts within the Stubble feilds of Tetbury from the 13.th of September untill Mictimas eve. 5.th That the lords flock may not feed in the said Warren out of the sleight between Holliroode day in May and Holliroode day in September, nor in the Stubble feilds from Holliroode day in September till Michaelmas eve, Nor in south hayes till the town herd of cattle have first grazed it, with divers other particularities incident to

a

a suite of this angry quallity. What strong resistance the defendant made appeareth by the orders of the 12th and 19th of November in the 4th of king James, And of the 28th of January, and 4th 6th and 18th of ffebry following, And of the 29th of Aprill in the 5th of king James, and divers others: But in conclusion, in Michmas terme in the 6th of king James, the cause was heard, And the flock was established with this lord till hee should bee evicted by order of lawe, and soe continueth to this day. All which proceedings in Chancery remaineth exemplyfyed with the executors of the said John Savage, As also doe the verdicts with the heires and assignes of the said Estcourts; The successe whereof and the paines of the said Sollicitor who advised this suite, the said John Savage gratefully requited by a guilt boll of twenty Nobles price, bequeathed by his last will a fewe years after to the said Sollicitor.

Mich: 6. Jac. in Canc: Certificate in chancery 30. Jan. 1608. Exemplified the 9. Jac: 1611. under 2 seales, cum Carolo Savage de Tetbury.

This George Estcourt being tenant to this lord of the Tolsey and weights in Tetbury brought divers actions upon the case against John Lany and others, touching the custome of the Toll taken for weighing of woole, yarne, and the like merchandise; The proceedings wherein the records marginald will declare, whereof that of Ester terme in the 39th of Elizabeth may bee a good president for posterity, whereof much use is like to bee.

Hill: 39. Eliz: rot. 73. in banco regis.

Pasch: 39 Eliz. rot. 180 in banco regis.

In the 17th of Queen Elizabeth was an exchange of divers lands in Callowdon and in Wiken a village adjoyning, between this lord and Sr ffrancis Willoughby knight lord of Wiken, whereby this lord with much conveniency drew his out lands together, neare to his mansion house at Callowdon; And Sr Francis enabled himself for enclosing divers parts of Wiken with like profit and conveniency; which shortly after hee sold to Richard Greene his servant, then tenant to a farme in Wiken, against whom in the 41th of the said Queens raigne, this lord | Henry exhibited his bill in Chancery, thereby to stay his suite at comon lawe, upon a counterbond hee had to save himself harmless from a bond of this lords entred into to Mr Edward Deveroux for one hundred pound hee had borrowed of him: wherein Green was never damnified nor sued, nor the originall bond, at the time of his processe sued out, forfeited: which unneigbourly course of Greenes, drewe on shortly after other suits and questions between this lord and him touching Tythes Comons wayes and divers parcells of land intermingled in each others said manors of Callowdon and Wiken: some of which differences brought forth also Inditements at Coventry Sessions; And after followed peace by another agreement and exchange of other lands, one with the other in the 43th of Elizabeth. And afterwards againe in the 8th of king James brake out new suites at lawe, and crofs bills in Chancery; In which

Carta in castro de Berkeley dat. 1. Sept. 17. Eliz:

Hill. 41. Eliz. in Canc.

810

Carta. 20. October 43. Eliz. in castro de Berkeley.

Canc: Hill. 8. Jac:

which I was a Comiſſioner for this lord, ryding purpoſely from my houſe in Glouceſterſhire to Coventry for execution thereof; And theſe alſo tooke ending by arbitrement in the tenth of king James. 1612. At what time by mediation of the Comiſſioners an other exchange of divers parcells of lands and tithes was had between them, in either of their ſaid Manors of Callowdon and Wiken; In penning whereof more then ordinary curioſity was uſed on both parts, as by the ſame will appeare.

Carta: 21. Julij 19. Jac: in caſtro de Berkeley.

In the 43ᵗʰ of Elizabeth this lord was plt againſt Hunt defᵗ in an¹

Paſch: 43. Eliz: rot. 2084. in com̄ banco.

In the ſame yeare James Atwood an underbaily to this lord was plt againſt William Millard in an¹

Hill: 43 Eliz: rot. 250. in banco regˢ

In the ſame yeare this lord Henry was plt in an action of det upon a bond of one hundred pounds againſt William Davis his | Baily of Berkeley hundred, whoſe courſe was to receive all that was levyable upon his extracts, if not more, but to accompt for little; wherein this lord recovered upon a nihil dicit.

Trīñ: 43. Eliz: rot: 46. in banco.

811

In the 45ᵗʰ of Queen Elizabeth, upon a diſtreſs taken by Henry Shipward baily to this lord of his manor of Melton Mowbray, for a releeſe of ten pound due by Thomas Mackworth for his manor of Epingham in the county of Rutland, holden of this lord as of his manor of Melton Mowbray by two knights fees, whereof George his father dyed ſeized in fee, Hee thought to have helped himſelf by the lawe, for that hee the ſaid Thomas was for other lands holden by knights ſervice in Capite in ward to Queen Elizabeth after the death of his ſaid father; And therefore conceived the lawe to bee That hee was not to pay releeſe to any other lord at his full age, after his livery ſued: And ſoe demurred upon the plea of Henry Shipward, which upon argument both at barre and bench was adjudged againſt Mackworth; And was the firſt expreſſe Judgment in the lawe in that point as was then affirmed, whereof Many Students then preſent in Court have ſince had the number roll.

Mich: 44. et. 45. Eliz: rot. 32. in banco regis.

In

[1] Not completed. [Ed.]

In the 44th of Queen Elizabeth, James Hervey an Underkeeper to this lord in Newpark, did with a forker out of his crofs bowe in the night time, cut the throat of one William Olive then with Richard Haynes and others paffing through his parke; whofe intentions were, (as after appeared,) firft to fteale fifh out of putts and weeles at Seaverne, And in their returne to Steale Deere in Whitcliffe parke: Harvey by a notable plott clofely carried was at the next affizes at Glouc., on a fodaine indited of Murder: And imediatly thereupon, (the purfuants knowing him to bee in the Seffions Hall,) was called by proclamation upon the inditement againe and againe; And the Judges being informed of his being there caufed that call to bee redoubled: Hervy by chance being by mee, And I by more chance then there by him, charged him to kneel down and fhade himfelf under my cloke, (being not leffe in Stature then in Courage a Coward,) and not to fpeak a word or elfe hee would with all help to the contrary bee hanged: The calls ended, away I fent him inftantly out of Glouc. as faft as hee could ride: forthwith that inditement was removed, And hee the next Terme at the kings bench barre, difcharged from his offence, which was held by the Court not to bee foe much as a breach of the peace: The Coroners inqueft taken the 8th of Auguft in the 43th of Elizabeth found the death of Olive to bee by Harvey, the 6th of that month, per infortunium; And this plot was practiced againft him the lent affifes after.

44 Eliz: in banco regis.

Stat: de malefactoribus in parcitt 21. E. 1.

812

In the fecond of king James, William Thorpe leffee to Thomas Chamberlyn was plt againft George Jerrat and others defts in an action of Ejectione firmæ for an acre of land in Mountforrell in the County of Leicefter; upon not guilty pleaded, and evidence by the deft that the fame was parcell of this lords manor of Mountforrell, the Jury found for the deft, and foe this lord enjoyeth it to this day.

Pafch: 3. Jac: rot. 911. com pleas Brownloe.
Mich. 2. Jac: in banco. inter p̄tes verdict: rot.
Hill. 3. Jac. in cōi banco.
Pafch: 5. Jac: in banco.

The fame year a fine of five pound was impofed upon one Edward Ithell of Slimbridge for a contempt committed by him in the leet held at Berkeley, for which this lord brought his action of debt: Ithell confeffeth his offence gave fattisfaction, And foe ceafed that fuite.

Pafch: 2. Jac: in banco regis.

In the third of king James, this lord Henry brought his Writ of ravifhment de gard[1] againft Robert Hill Clarke, for taking away the body of John fon and heire of Godfrey Goldefborrowe late Bifhop of Glouc., who dyed feized of the manor or farme

Pafch. 3. Jac: in banco rot: 745.

---

[1] *Ravifhment de gard* was a Writ that lay for the guardian for Knight's-fervice, or in Socage, againft a perfon who took from him the body of his ward. By Statute 12, Charles II. c. 24, this writ is taken away as to lands held by Knight fervice, &c., but not where there is guardian in Socage, or appointed by will. [ED.]

farme of Goffington in the parifh of Slimbridge, holden of him as of his manor of Berkeley by knights fervice: Not guilty was pleaded, And upon a tryall at Glouc. Affifes the Jury found for this lord, And gave damages to 400. marks, And Judgment was after entred accordingly.

Hill: 3. Jac: rot: 171. in banco regis Trin: 4. Jac: the writ filed.

And afterwards, this lord brought an acc̃on againft William Clutterbooke tenant to the faid farme for the meane rates, wherein hee recovered alfo; And upon a writ to inquire of damages had threefcore pound given him by the jury.

Hill: 3. Jac: rot. 172. in banco regis Pafch. 4. Jac. the writ to inquire of damages.

The fame year this lord Henry brought his Acc̃on of the cafe againft one Bendall for infringing his liberty of Berkeley hundred and arrefting one Cafwell at Berkeley, wherein hee recovered his cofts and damages: In the pleadings whereof are perfectly laid down the grant of king Edward the third, in the 4th of his raigne, of returna brevium, to Thomas lord Berkeley the third of that name, and his heires; And how afterwards hee entailed the fame to himfelf and the heires males of his body, with all the | meane difcents after to this lord Henry; which may bee of frequent ufes in the like cafes, I having purpofly omitted many others of the like nature.

813

Pafch: 3. Jac: rot: in banco regis.

The fame year Henry Shipward, Baily of Melton, diftrained the Goods of Thomas Grococke of Eftwell in the County of Leicefter, fuppofing the tenure of that manor to bee of this lord as of his manor of Melton by knights fervice: After iffue joyned upon the tenure, S.r Edward Brabazon owner of the faid Manor of Eftwell fled for fuccour into the Dutchy court, and there exhibited his bill againft this lord and Shipward for ftay of the fuite, fuggefting the tenure to bee of the king as of the Dutchy of Lancafter, by the fourth part of a knights fee; which the def.ts anfwering in Hillary Terme after, an Injunction was awarded to ftay the fuite at lawe, and foe hath refted.

Hill: 3. Jac:

Trin̄: 4. Jac: in banco regis.

In the 4th of king James, John Driver this lords Baily of Tetbury was pl.t againft William Tamer def.t, for carrying away without the lords leave the dounge or foile out of the waft ground called the Cheeping, (the golgotha of that markett Town,) which Driver under the prerogative of his office would appropriate to himfelf, wherein Driver had compofition from the def.t.

Trin: 11. Jac: rot. Comon pleas. Bolton att. pro quer̄.

In the 11th of king James this lord was pl.t againft John Huntley, a man of wit but void of honefty, his lo.pp coppyhold tenant in Bevington, for killing a brace of of Bucks in Whitcliffe Parke, near the pale whereof Huntley dwelt; who after hee had before this lord and other Juftices of the peace with incredible impudency forfworne the fact, And with bafe and upbraiding termes infulted over thofe underkeepers who firft drew him into fufpition; whereof they complayning to a Sollicitor of this lords, and hee taking it to heart, found means by Huntleys fervants that then were, (for great guifts are like Gods,) to difcover not only who fetched the bucks out of the park to Huntleys houfe, but to whom hee gave feaven quarters of them, and by whom fent: Which they upon examination acknowledging, And Huntly confronted, Huntly for anfwere and excufe faid to the Sollicitor, That it was held a rule and noe offence with deereftealers to forfwear the fact and out brave the keepers, as hee formerly had done; But the pl:s death and Huntleys alfo not longe after happening, took off a great part of that punifhment which | otherwife moft defervedly had been inflicted upon foe ungratious a man.

814

In the fourth of king James this lord exhibited his bill in Chancery againft William Dunning and five others, concerning his liberties of fifhing in the river of Seaverne within his hundred of Berkeley: which in the end of ffebruary in the 7th of the king were decreed for him: In this fuite is contained a full declaration of all the liberties and jurifdictions which the lord George now claimeth in Seaverne, which is like to bee of great ufe to his pofterity: And more then one other fuite which was in the 34th of king Henry the 8th, between Richard Williams ats Cromwell pl: And Richard Byriat and others def:s, I have not mett withall, touching thefe liberties of fifhing, whereof in the forefaid fuite good ufe was made.

Mich: 4. Jac. 1606. in Canc:

Cur Augm̃. 34. H. 8. et in caftro de Berkeley.

In the fame year Willm Chamberlyn brought an Action of Ejectione firmæ againft George Jerrat of Mountforrell for two acres of land there; the evidence of the def: was That it was the inheritance of this lord Henry, parcell of his manor of Mountforrell; And of the pl: That it was parcell of the land of the feoffees of that Town, called the Town land; wherein the pl: after evidence became nonfuite; And hath quietly been enjoyed ever fince as the inheritance of this lord, more land ftanding upon the fame title.

Hill: 4 Jac. rot. 1907. com̃ pleas. Mich. 4. Jac. rot. Com̃ pleas.

And for fetling divers cheife rents in Mountforrell amounting to 24s. 4d. claymed by this lord Henry and denied by divers the inhabitants there, This lord in the 8th of king James exhibited his bill in Chancery againft Nicholas Fowler John Hood and Thomas Monke, wherein hee prevailed, and fet his faid rents afoot, now paid accordingly: In which, other wrongs offered to this lord in that Town were alfo contained and certified.

Mich: 8: Jac: in Cancell.

In

Anno. 4. Jac:	In the fame fowrth year of king James, the grand-jury at Coventry Seffions indicted this lord Henry for not repairing the way in Callowdon lane between Afhmore gate and Wiken lane: The inditement was removed and avoided; A work that ought to bee done by the County or the parifh of S.t Michaells and not by the particular charges of the owner of Callowdon manor.
Crown office. 5. Jac:	
Hill. 4. Jac: Starchamber. 815	This yeare alfo this lord exhibited a bill in Starchamber againft Thomas Mainfton John Cerney John Weft and divers others,	a compact neft of deereftealers, for hunting and killing his deere in Michaelwood chace; for which their purfes after fmarted, And bonds with fureties taken of them and above twenty others, (whom they peached,) to bee afterwards true to all his Lo.rs games; By the diffolution of which knot of Deereftealers his games refted more quiet then in fifty years before they had done.
Pafch: 6. Jac: rot. 1559. in cōi banco: or 1159.	In the fixth of king James this lord brought his writt de valore maritagij againft Thomas Bowfor, brother and heire of Anthony, who dyed feifed of divers lands and tenements within the Manor of Hame, parcell of the manor and lands called Serjeants lands: The iffue was whether the faid Thomas Bowfer was within the age of one and twenty years at the death of his brother or not: The pl.t finding afterwards that hee was a weeke above one and twenty at his brothers death, who dyed beyond feas, proceeded noe further, though hee had taken out his writ of Nifi prius for tryall thereof.
Com. Pleas Pafch: 6. Jac. rot. 1141. Suffex in cōi banco. lib: Ward: fol: 16. in caftro de Berkeley.	In the faid fixth of king James this lord brought his Writ of ravifhm.t of ward againft Agnes Payne widowe, for keeping from him her fon Thomas Payne from the death of Thomas his father, for that hee dyed feized of the Scite of the manor of Southmundam called Bowley ffarme, and of. 120. acres of land thereto belonging in the parifh of Pagham in the County of Suffex, holden of this lord as of his manor of Bofham by knights fervice, wherein hee recovered great damages, as by the record appeareth.
Pafch: 8. Jac. rot. 1752. comon pleas Waller.	The Inhabitants of fframpton upon Seaverne clayming comon of pafture for their fheep upon Slimbridge old warth, encouraged John Savacre the vicar there to put in his fheep alfo: which Richard Byford an Attorney, noe lefs factious in Slimbridge then the minifter contentious, impounded as a Comoner; And not only brought him but many others of the faid Inhabitants upon colours of Surcharges, to compofitions, Taking of fome ten fhillings, of fome. 30.s, of fome 3.li, and of fome

some others more, to the value of ten pound in the year; whereby for three or four years whilst this course lasted they were reconed Byfords tributaries.

An action of Accompt was by this lord brought against Cyprian Wood one of the Groomes of his first wives chamber, suppofeing hee had remaining in his hands one hundred pounds, received from her a fewe daies before her death: wherein after pleadings, Auditors | were affigned by the Court, before whom hee accompted, and paid what was found by them to remaine uniffued in her life time: A fuite the rather profecuted upon advertifement given to this lord that two trunks of his fineft Linnens were by him, (as an inftrument to a gentlewoman in that houfe,) to have been conveyed away by night; The truth whereof was That the trunks being to bee ferryed over the mott at Callowdon in one of the brew houfe coolers, the bunhole in the midft fell open, and foe the ferry boat being heavy laden began to finke ere it was two yards from the fhore; whereof this lord had early notice by fuch as lay in waite to have intercepted them, And foe faved his linnens and other things therein, but never difcover'd that his intelligence came from a Sollicitor of his, one of the watchmen in that dark night.

Trin: 38. Eliz: in banco.

816

Upon the death of Thomas Tomfon rector of the Church of Sutton iuxta Bonyngton in the County of Nottingham, Chrift church Colledge in Cambridge who pretended title thereto prefented Edward Barwell as their Clerke, in the 21ᵗʰ of Queen Elizabeth; And this lord Henry prefented John Savage, who being refufed by the ordinary this lord brought his Quare impedit and recovered; upon which recovery the colledge brought a Writ of Error, wherein the former recovery and Judgment was affirmed, and this lords Clerke eftablifhed, ftill the Incumbent there; Hereof I have more largely written in another booke ufefull to this family, in a tract of the Manor and Barony of Segrave by it felf.

Trin: 22. Eliz: rot. 976. in banco cōi.

Hill: 30. Eliz: rot. 484. in banco regis.

Upon the death of Richard Smyth Rector of the church of Howby in the County of Leicefter, Sʳ George Villers of Brokefby prefented thereto John Bifhop; And this lord Henry prefented Willm Read, in the 22ᵗʰ of Elizabeth; who being refufed, this lord brought his Quare impedit and recovered, And Read this lords Clerke eftablifhed, who ever fince hath been incumbent there; **In** the longe pleadings whereof, the difcents afwell of this family as of the lord Mowbraies, And the ptition of the Mowbraies lands between the family of Berkeley and the family of the Howards, are foe errioufly laid down and pleaded on both parts, that each party might thereupon have trounced the other, | Howbeit ignorance being alike comōn

Pafch: 22. Eliz: in banco.

Trin: 23. Eliz: in banco.

817

comon to the Counsell and Sollicitors of both sides, neither party was able to reprove or take advantage of the others errors or mistakes, And soe a double falshood had by ignorance the passage of a double truth. Of this Advowson I have more largely written in my other booke lastly mentioned.

And thus endeth this longe title of this lords lawe suites, of . 85 . pages ; the most toilsome of all my labors, yet pleasing in the finishing, becaufe likely to bee of much use to this noble family in this and ages to come.

His Sales of Land.

Having ended the longe title of lawe suites, I now returne to a shorter but worse, the sale of lands ; too soone begun and too longe continued.

carta : 16. ffebr̄ :
3. Eliz :

In the third yeare of Queen Elizabeth in consideration of 893^{li}. 19^s. 4^d, this lord sold his manors of Kenet and Kentford in the counties of Cambridge and Suffolke, with the Advowson of Kenet, to S^r. William Peter and his heires ; And covenants them to bee of the yearly value of . 37^{li}. 5^s. 4^d. And that noe reversion was in the Crown ; whereupon that trouble and expence arose which I formerly have mentioned amongst the lawe suits of this lord ; And these were those lands that reverted to this lord for default of issue male of the body of M^r. Willoughby according to the entaile of William Marques Berkeley, And whereof hee had sued livery but in June before as formerly hath been said.

fol : 806.
818
Revert. Nov. ye 26.
2. Eliz :
Liberac : 16. Junij.
2. Eliz :

carta : 20. ffebr̄ :
5. Eliz :

In the fifth year of Queen Elizabeth in consideration of 2050^{li} this lord sold the manor of Hovingham in the county of Yorke to Sr Thomas Gerrard and his heires, the mansion house of his grandfather the lord Thomas, as in his life appeareth.

carta 30. Oct :
6. Eliz :

In the sixth yeare of Queen Elizabeth in consideration of . 200^{li} this lord sold all his messuages lands and tenements in the hamletts or parishes of Brokenburrow and Almsbury in the county of Gloucester, accounted the fourth part of that manor, to John Hollister Thomas Harper and Margaret Wade, and their heires.

carta : 26. Maij.
7. Eliz :

In the seventh year of Queen Elizabeth in consideration of . 600^{li}, this lord sold the lease of Yate in the county of Glouc^r to Sr Nicholas Poynz, wherein hee had forty two years to come, the ancient habitation of his father grandfather and great unkle, and where they had bestowed great charges in building, as in their lives hath been delivered.

In

In the same yeare in consideration of . 1000ˡⁱ this lord sold the Manor and Advowson of Maningford Breouse in the county of Wilts, to Edward Nicholas and his heires.   carta : 8. ffebr̃ : 7. Eliz :

In the eighth of Elizabeth in consideration of—300ˡⁱ this lord sold a rent of 14ˡⁱ p Añ reserved for equallity of ptition out of the manor of Bromley in Surrey, and out of Lea Gateburton and Schothurne in the county of Lincolne, in division of Breouses lands, to Thomas Duke of Norfolke his wifes brother and his heires.   carta : 28. October 8. Eliz :

In the nynth of Elizabeth in consideration of 450ˡⁱ this lord sold the manor of Aspele in the county of Warrwicke | to Charles Raynesford Esquire, and his heires.   carta : 14. Novr. 9. Eliz : **819**

In the Tenth of Elizabeth in consideration of 304ˡⁱ 10ˢ this lord sold the manor of Cotes with the members of Prestwold and Houghton, and all his lands in Wimeswold Thurmaston and Burton on the olds, in the County of Leicester, and in Stanford in the County of Nottingham, to Henry Skipwith Esqʳ and his heires.   carta, 25. Aprill 10. Eliz :

In the eleventh of Elizabeth in consideration of 2220ˡⁱ this lord sold the manors of Rostlaston Coton and Linton in the County of Derby, And all his lands in Greisly, Caldwell, Durandsthorpe, Lollington and Walton upon Trent in the counties of Derby and Leicester, to Sʳ William Greisly and his heires.   Carta. 10. Decem. 11. Eliz :

In the 14ᵗʰ of Elizabeth in consideration of . 3200ˡⁱ this lord sold the manor of Weston near Baldocke in the County of Hartford, to George Burgoyne and his heires, excepting a cheife rent of five pound p Añ going out of Broughtons lands in the County of Bedford the inheritance of Sʳ Henry Cheney knight ; of which cheife rent I have before written amongst this lords lawe suites.   Carta. 28 Novr. 14. Eliz :

fol : 798.

In the same 14ᵗʰ of Elizabeth in consideration of 336ˡⁱ 7ˢ 1ᵈ hee sold the manor of Thurlaston and all his lands in Dunchurch in the County of Warrwick, to Alice the widowe of Sʳ Thomas Leigh knight late Alderman of London, And covenants the same to bee 6ˡⁱ 14ˢ 6ᵈ ob. p Añ of old rents.   Carta : 6. Decemʳ 14. Eliz :

In the   of Elizabeth in consideration of 800ˡⁱ hee sold the manor of fflekenhoe in the said County of Warrwick to Mʳ Broughton and his heires.   Carta

In the 15ᵗʰ of Elizabeth in consideration of 84ˡⁱ 14ˢ hee sold to Thomas Walton and Michael his son and theire heires, two messuages and three yard land and an half in Thurneby in the county of Leicester.   Carta. 4 : Nov. 15. Eliz :

Carta. 4. Nov.
15. Eliz:
   In the same 15th of Elizabeth in consideration of 24li. 4s. hee sold to Robert Read and his heires, a messuage and certaine lands which | hee held in Thurnby aforesaid.

Carta. 6. Nov:
15. Eliz:
   In the same 15th of Elizabeth in consideration of—160li. hee sold all his lands Tenements and hereditaments in Welby als Oleby in the county of Leicester to William Digby and his heires; whereby through the ignorance of his officers the tenure of Welby it self, being by knights service of the manor of Melton Mowbray, was released, which was not intended to passe.

Carta: 1. ffebr.
16. Eliz:
   In the 16th of Elizabeth, in consideration of 420li, hee sold the Manor of Thorpe Sachevill and Twyford in the County of Leicester, to Thomas Cave Esqr and his heires.

Carta: 30. Apr.
16. Eliz:
   In the same 16th year of Elizabeth, in consideration of 500li, hee sold the manor of Witherly in the County of Leicester, to Michael Ludford and his heires.

Carta: 3 Sept
17. Eliz:
   In the 17th of Elizabeth, in consideration of—720li, hee sold the manors or hamletts of Kington parva Brockhamton and Combroke, with all the lands hee held in Kington magna, in the county of Warrwicke, to William Burton and his heires, except the wood there called Kingswood.

Carta: 3. Sept
17. Eliz:
   In the same 17th of Elizabeth, in consideration of—520li, hee sold to Francis Aylworth and his heires the manor of Kington magna in the County of Warrwicke.

Carta: 28. Julij
17. Eliz:
   In the same 17th of Elizabeth, in consideration of 40li, hee sold a messuage and three closes adjoyning in Thornbury in the county of Glouc., to John Davis and his heires.

Carta: 21. Maij.
18. Eliz:
   In the 18th of Elizabeth, in consideration of—300li, hee sold the wood called Kingswood in Kington in Warwickshire, (excepted in William Burtons conveyance,) to Andrew Ognell of Badesly Clinton and his heires.

Carta. 7. Julij
20. Eliz:
   In the 20th of Elizabeth, in consideration of—37li. 6s. 8d, hee sold three houses in Thornbury, (then in lease to John Tayer at 7s. rent for divers years to come,) to John Hilpe and his heires, who was the great grandchild of that Richard Hilpe present with William | lord Berkeley and his two brethren at the death of the Viscount

Viscount Lisle, slaine at Nibley Greene, and against whom Margaret his widow brought her appeale, as before is declared in the life of the said lord William. fol: 548.

In the 22ᵗʰ of Elizabeth, in consideration of 1700ˡⁱ, hee sold the Manor of Elmington and all his lands in Henbury in the County of Glouc., to Thomas Wilmare and his heires: Which manor and lands this lord but the Terme before had drawn from Edward Berkeley of Bradley and Elizabeth his wife, to whom in recompence, hee gave forty pounds p Añ for theire lives: And which this lord in the first of Elizabeth had conveyed, (for better strengthening of his grandfathers entaile before remembred,) to the said Edwᵈ and the heires males of his body, the remainder to Maurice his brother and the heires males of his body, The remainder to Frances their mother for life, wife to Richard Danvers, the remainder to his own right heires. Carta: 8. m'cij 22. Eliz: fine Hill: 22. Eliz:

The same year in consideration of 160ˡⁱ, hee sold all his lands in Stichall in the county of Warrwicke and in the County of the Citie of Coventry to Arthur Gregory and his heires; And these formerly were sold to Richard Turner, and after repurchased and sold as aforesaid; And were esteemed as a member or Hamlett of Callowdon Manor. Carta: 4. Nov: 22. Eliz:

In the 27ᵗʰ of Elizabeth, in consideration of 2560ˡⁱ, this lord sold the manor Castle and lordship of Bretby and all his lands in Repington and other Hamlets there in the County of Derby, to Edmond Scarlinge and Lawrence Wright and their heires, persons trusted by the lord Stanhope, whose now it is; Of the parke whereof this lord in the eleventh of Elizabeth had given a lease for 21 years to his servant Thomas Duport, which was excepted in this sale. Carta. 22. Apr̃: 27. Eliz:

In the 29ᵗʰ of Elizabeth in consideration of 2500ˡⁱ this lord sold the manor of Dalby Chawcombe, and all his lands in Ardeburrowe South croxton and Kirkby belers, to Sʳ John Burrow knight and his heires. | Carta: 14. Aug: 29. Eliz:

In the same 29ᵗʰ of Elizabeth, in consideration of—3200ˡⁱ, this lord sold the manor of Sileby and all his lands in Thurneby in the County of Leicester to George Shirley Esquire and his heires; who in the same year had maryed his daughter ffrances Berkeley, As after in the title of this lords issues followeth. 822 Carta: 20. Octob: 29. Eliz:

In the 42ᵗʰ of Elizabeth in consideration of ten thousand pounds all paid in hand, this lord sold to Sʳ John Spencer Alderman of London and his heires, The Carta: 18. m'cij 42. Eliz:

manor

manor of Coldoverton (3000ˡⁱ) with the Advowſon thereof in the County of Leiceſter, And the manors of ffenyſtanton (3000ˡⁱ) and Hilton, And of Auconbury (4000ˡⁱ) and Weſton in the County of Huntington; **And** in regard that 3000ˡⁱ the price of Coldoverton, came wholly to his ſon Sʳ Thomas Berkeley, It was by Deed concluded between them That the ſix hundred pound Annuity agreed upon at his marriage ſhould thenceforth bee but—533ˡⁱ 8ˢ; Howbeit the 4000ˡⁱ received by this lord for the price of Auconbury and Weſton ſlept not ſoe quietly in his purſe, but that (through the generall warranty hee gave to Sʳ John Spencer) hee departed with—400ˡⁱ thereof beſides charges to kingē James upon a compoſition for a cloſe of—480. acres, parcell thereof, called great ſartfeild and other lands, wherto his Maᵗⁱᵉ made title as parcell of his fforreſt of Sapley and Weybridge in the ſaid County, And ſometime aſſarted thereout: And the ſaid Sʳ John Spencer for his better aſſurance did afterwards bring againſt this lord and his ſon, two writts of Warrantia chartæ.

Carta: 7 Maij 42. Eliz:

Comp: cum Oth: Nicholſon: 1609. 7. Jac. Regis.

Triñ: and Mich: terme. 7. Jac. in cōi banco

In the 44ᵗʰ of Elizabeth, in conſideration of 1320ˡⁱ, hee ſold the Manor of Daglingworth in the County of Glouceſter to Sir Henry Poole and his heires; And this money coming alſo to his ſon Sʳ Thomas Berkeley, (for payment of whoſe debts hee joyned in ſale thereof,) It was agreed That Thirty three pounds and eight ſhillings of his Anuity ſhould bee abated, And the ſame thenceforth to bee but five hundred pounds by the yeare.

Carta: 12. Maij 44. Eliz:

In the nynth of king James, in conſideration of 2225ˡⁱ, hee ſold to Phillip Langley Eſqʳ and Mary his mother and their heires the manor of Mangotsfeild in the County of Glouc.; To which grant Sʳ Thomas Berkeley and the lady Elizabeth his wife were alſo parties. |

Carta. 16. Septemʳ 9. Jacobi.

In the 8ᵗʰ of king James, in conſideration of 800ˡⁱ, hee ſold to Thomas Yate and his heires the manor of Erlingham in the county of Glouc., which was part of that land hee had by compoſition the year before from the lord Viſcount Liſle.

823

Carta. 20. Nov. 8. Jac:

In the ſame year alſo for ſatisfaction of that ſum of money which hee paid to the ſaid Viſcount Liſle, and for diſcharge of his own former debts, hee raiſed—1183ˡⁱ by the ſale of twelve tenements in Wotton, Nibley, and Cam, in ffee farme, which hee ſold to Walter Oſborne, William Ven, John Staunton, Arnold Oldiſworth, Thomas Perry, Thomas Adams, Robert Dawe, Robᵗ Smyth, Thomas Trotman, William Marten, John Wilkins, and Edward Trotman junʳ; In all which this lord

reſerved

reserved the former old rents Heriots suite of Court and all other services before paid or done.

And at the same time for the same causes hee sold certaine outlands in Horton Kingscote and Minchinhampton to Arthur Came, William Shipton, and Edward Barnefeild, for which hee had six hundred pounds.

As for the lands in Calais, they were lost when that Town was in the time of Queen Mary taken by the ffrench. And the lands in Thorpe and Kingston in the County of Nottingham hee gave to Thomas Read his bayly of Segrave; which were after swallowed up by the great manor of the Earle of Shrewesbury, wherein they were.

And in place of all these manors and lands thus sold for—41399^{li} 13^s. hee purchased of M^r. Beconsale in the 13th year of Eliz. the little poor manor of Canonbury, of the value of—5^{li} 11^s 8^d p Ann., out also of which is issuing to the Crown an yearly tenth of 2^s 4^d; sometime parcell of the possessions of the oft mencõned Monastery of St Augustines by Bristoll, of the foundation of the lord Robert the first, late Thomas Sackviles lord Buckhurst; which is all the land heretofore given to any monastery or other religious use which this family hath had since the first suppression of Monasteries or | other religious houses; Whereby this noble family seems plenarily absolved from that black observation of divers modern historiographers and divines, who write to have observed many great families, purchasers of church lands, to melt to nothing; And wish that the residue might bee observed in times to come, whether they also consume not by riot or improvidence.

824
Heyward in vita E. 6. fol : 155. et div'si alij.

As for Tythes heretofore belonging to Church or Monastery, this family hath none at all, no not in their own manors; whereby none of the sharpe pens of divines censuring those as sacrilegious persons that receive tythes or any other thing that hath heretofore been set apart and confecrated to Gods service; making it sin and sacriledge to take or keep them from Gods Ministers, doe at all smutt or point at this family : Neither did the minority of this lord Henry, (although then a Baron,) permit him to bee any of those parliament men in the 27. 31. and 38. H. 8. or in 1. E. 6., (all those times under fourteen years,) that suppressed religious houses and Chanteries; cryed down in print by Armies of divines in these daies, to have done like wicked Judges, who banished the theeves but took the stolen goods unto themselves.

Yet

yet was, upon a title pretended to this wholl manor of Canonbury by the Crown, a new patent enforced to bee procured in the end of Queen Elizabeth, whereby this lord welnigh made a new purchafe thereof, in the name of John Denis and others.|

His Buildings.

Warrant under feale in Berkeley Caftle.

The 27th of March in the tenth year of Queen Elizabeth, Anno 1568, this lord from Callowdon directed his warrant to his fervant Henry Ligon to new build a Lodge in that part of Michaelwood upon the hill where now it ftandeth, called the park hill; for that the old is the former place and one other in another place of that chace were grown into utter ruin and decay, (faith the warrant,); which was done, and paid for by William Lawrence his then Receiver who likewife had a warrant to iffue out the money.

About the 22th of Elizabeth was the porters lodge, the buildings towards the great poole on the northweft part, of Callowdon houfe, with the brewing houfe, the ftables, and many other out houfes both within and without the mot, built of new; And the roofs of divers of the houfes of thofe old caftle buildings taken down and foe far altered that the whole houfe might bee faid to have been moulded and made new; But for the banquetting houfe on the northfide of the faid poole, it was the polite work of the lady Elizabeth wife of Sr Thomas Berkeley in the fortieth and one and fortieth years of Queen Elizabeth, And the retired Cell of her foules Soliloquies to God her creator.

Annis. 35. et. 39. Eliz:

At other times this lord built all the new timber buildings at new park lodge with fome of the out houfes, whereto his grandchild the lord George hath lately given a fair addition; And put alfo the lodge in Whitcliffe parke into that comlines it now rejoyceth in.

Anno. 29. Eliz:

This lord alfo made of new the ftone bridge leading into Berkeley caftle, which before was a draw bridge of timber; And fet | up thofe faire ftone pillers and buttreffes, whereby the Keepe and great kitchen feeme fupported.

Others of like condition at Yate Mangottsfeild and other places hee repaired, which being now fold away I pafs over, and come to the title of this lords recreations and delights, wherein hee tooke too great a delight.

His recreations and delights.

How this lord entred upon his pleasures, or rather his pleasures upon him, so soone as his youthfull years were capable of delights, it hath already been related in the title next before his law suits.

The hours may seeme too many which this lord spent in his best ages at bowles tenis Cockpit Shusgrote cards and dice, especially when hee liked the company; **And** I will, without blemish to his honor, tell his posterity, That his longe and slender lady-like-hand knew a dye as well and how to handle it as any of his ranke and time: Insomuch as once about twenty years agone at Callowdon, playing at the Irish game at tables with Francis Stafford one of the yeomen of his great chamber, for three pence a game, And having the game in such assurance That almes-ace would have carried all his table men, hee turned his face to my self and others then standing by, and merily said, will you see mee loose this game by throwing lesse then Almes-ace? And so hee did indeed, by casting one dye upon the other in the corner of the tables, and the ace peepe upwards, on the other dye; whereat when wee wondred, hee said that hee had not done the like, (though often assayed,) of many years before. **But** his cheife delights wherein hee spent near three parts of the yeare, were, to his great charges, in hunting the hare fox and deere, red and fallow, not wanting choice of as good hunting horses as yearly hee could buy at faires in the North; And in hawking both at river and at land: **And** as his hounds were held inferior to no mans, (through the great choice of whelps which with much care hee yearly bred of his choicest braches, and his continuall huntings,) soe were his hawks of severall sorts; which if hee sent not a man to fetch from beyond seas, as three or fower times I remember hee did, yet had hee the choice as soone as they were brought over into England, keeping a man lodging in London, in some years a month or more, to bee sure of his choice at their first landing; espetially for his haggard falcons for the river, wherein hee had two that fell in one after the other, and lasted twelve or more years, the one called stella, and the other kate, that were famous with all great faulconers in many counties, and prized at excessive rates, esteemed for high and round flying, free stooping, and all other good conditions, inferior to none in Christendome; whom my self in my younger years waiting upon his son Thomas, then not twelve years old, at Binly Brooke, have in the height of their pitch, lost the sight of, in a cleer evening: **And** for huntsmen and falkeners, noe man could bee better served than this lord; Of whom I may not omit the naming of Tooly and Guy Good, men singuler in their professions, And (as may bee said) borne and bred for the delights of princes and

their

their peeres : **But** being in a title whereto my felf was neither born nor bred nor ever much delighted, and loth to borrow words for adorning of thefe his fports out of the books of thofe who have extolled thefe recreations, I will conclude a world of matter which mine eye and ear could fpeake hereof with the old verfe, Omne tulit punctum qui mifcuit vtile dulci,

> Hee of all others is the noblest wight,
> That intermixeth profit with delight.

828   And I remember that in the 39th of Queen Elizabeth, after the | death of his wife and before his fecond mariage, at the firft coming of John Crefwell his Steward of houfhold, giving him authority of difplacing whomfoever hee found in his houfe diforderly, hee by fpeciall words exempted his Cookes Huntefmen and faulkeners ; which intimated to the obfervation of all his family then prefent his inbred inclination to his fports, and to hofpitallity, which was generaly applauded.

His Hospitallity.

What houfhold port this noble lord for his firft twenty years after full age, that is till the beheadding of his brother in lawe the Duke of Norfolke in the 13th of Queen Elizabeth, had kept, hath before appeared ; About which time the tide began to turne with this family, And their full fea ebbed ; Efpetially when the power of Robert Dudley Earle of Leicefter, often before mentioned, under his Court greatnes and Queen Elizabeths title, and the fale of eight or more manors by that time fold away, had drayned foe great a portion of their poffeffions : from which time, upon this lords returne from fojourning with Sr Thomas Ruffell at Stranfham, the check roll of his fervants was fhortened forty perfons at the leaft, and many un-ufefull people pared of ; Howbeit the faile this family ftill bore for the next twelve years or near thereabouts, feemed full, and the gale faire ; And his hofpitallity much renowned in all the neighbourhoods of his abodes ; But then about the 26th of Elizabeth, upon the fecond recovery of Arlingham with the other manors and lands contained in the fecond information, formerly alfo mentioned, And the further fales of feven or eight other manors that had in that time been

829   done away, upon this lords returning from fojourning with Sr John | Savage of Baraper, the former checkroll of his houfhold fervants was againe further fhortened twenty perfons at the leaft, and a fecond paringe of other unufefull drones : Howbeit, removing from Baraper to the white ffryars in Coventry, And my felf at that time firft becoming a member of that houfhold, I well remember the number then was about three fcore and ten of all forts ; In which condicōn it continued till

within

within a year or two before his wife the lady Katharine dyed, and the mariage of his eldeft fon to the daughter and heire of George lord Hunfdon, as after followeth: And thence forth till his death in the Eleventh of king James, whether hee lived with his fecond wife at her houfe in Barbican in London, or at Callowdon (as moft hee did,) it was very honorable and praife worthy though fhort of the former greatnes : And I write what more then . 200 . times I have obferved, That noe monies went foe cheerfully out of the purfe of this noble lord as thofe which were delivered to the Steward, Clarke of the Kitching, Purveyor or Cator, for the provifion of his family : And in what honorable fafhion this lords family flourifhed at Callowdon till the day of his death and fome weekes after is not unknown to my dedicatees, at their breaking up of that family and their departure, the mother and fon for London, And the lady her daughter with S.r Robert Coke her hufband for Coventry ; And for the regulating of this family let thefe ftanding orders enfuing fpeak for all, compofed by M.r George Savage then Archdeacon of the County of Glouc. and M.r Cheney, fometimes Stewards of houfhold, M.r Payne the old ladies gentleman ufher, and two or three others of this lords officers, And by both lord and lady approved of, as followeth, viz.t,

1. The gentleman ufher to bee in the dininge chamber in fummer by feven and in winter by eight of the clocke, or fooner if ftrangers bee there, and to fee every thing therein fet in order, according to the feafon of the year : That himfelf bee not only at fervice, but doe fee the reft of the gentlemen to bee there alfo to heare fervice, when and foe often as any fhall bee either in the great Chamber or Chapple.

<small>Gent. ufher and Gentlemen:</small>

2. That noe gentleman come into the great chamber without his cloake | or livery coate ; And when there are ftrangers, to bee all or moft part in the dining chamber after dinner and fupper, to fhew themfelves and doe fuch fervice as caufe fhall require.

3. That noe gentleman bee abfent at dinner or fupper times without fpeciall lycence, and then not to break their time appointed for their returne.

4. The faid gentleman-ufher to fee all ftrangers of worth and that fhall bee admitted the great Chamber well entertained for the hon.r of the houfe, and that they want nothing neceffary at their Chambers ; And when any gentleman of quality fhall come, that hee and the reft of the gentlemen bee ready to bring him into the great Chamber, and when fuch a one goeth away to bring him to his horfe.

5. That

5. That noe gentleman (the gentleman usher excepted) shall come into any of the Offices besides the buttry or cellar, in absence of the gentleman-usher, to give entertainment to strangers.

6. The gentlemen to come to the dresser at the first call of the usher, and there to behave themselves decently without noise or uncivill behaviour.

7. When the lord himselfe rideth abroad, the gentleman usher to see the gentlemen to ride before, two and two, decently without any lewd speech or other rudenesse.

8. If the Usher of the hall, hearing great noise at Dinner or supper times, shall bid make lesse noise, noe gentman to seeme to scoffe or jest at him, but orderly to use moderate speach for the better example of others.

Yeomen.
9. All the Yeomen to bee ready in the Hall before the time of service, and to goe up with the Yeoman usher to prayers, and none to bee absent without speciall licence or other earnest imployment.

10. Noe Yeoman to lye out any night, but to bee in their lodgeings by 9. of the clock at night.

831
11. Noe Yeoman to come into the buttry, pantry, cellar, kitchen, scullery or other offices, except they shall have buisines there by | their lords imployment, nor to give any ill language to any Officer that shall reasonably tell them thereof; And each disorderly person therein upon proofe made by the officer before the steward of houshold, to loose his service, or undergoe other punishment.

12. All the Yeomen to come at the first call to the dresser, and there to behave themselves civilly, and without noise and rudenes, but to carry themselves as in duty becometh that service.

13. The Yeoman usher, yeoman of the great chamber, and usher of the hall, to bee directed by the gentleman usher how they shall use their offices, by whose authority they are to bee commanded touching their orderly services.

Porter.
14. The Porter to let in noe strangers but by the appointment of the Steward of houshold, except gentlemen or men of good sort.

15. The

15. The yeomen of the dininge chamber daily to ftrew the rufhes: to take out all fpotts as fhall happen in the carpetts, chaires, or ftooles; to duft the cufhions; In the winter to have fire in the chimney, and in the fommer flowers in the windows: either both or one of the yeomen to bee there continually waiting, to remove ftooles, fnuffe the lights, and to light gentlemen ftrangers to their chambers, when they fhall goe from thence to bed; And that they fuffer noe doggs to come into the dyneing chamber. *Yeomen of the dyning chamber.*

16. No yeomen to bee abfent at ferving up of liveries in gentlemen ftrangers chambers, if any ftrangers bee there. *Serving up of Liveryes.*

17. When the lady fhall ride abroad, the yeoman ufher to difcharge his duty in caufing the yeomen appointed to ride to keep togeather, without tarrying behind their company and fcattering abrode; And when they come through any Town, the yeoman ufher to place them by two and two orderly. *Riding abroad.*

18. Noe yeoman upon leave obtained to ride abroad to break the day appointed for his returne, without fome fpeciall and manifeft caufe thereof. *Keeping of daies.*

19. Such yeomen as fhall bee appointed by the gentleman ufher to waite in the dyninge chamber, when my lady fitteth abroad, | fhall with due reverence and diligent attendance doe fuch fervice as they fhall bee appointed by the gentleman ufher in each refpect. *Keeping of daies.*

Other orders there were, particulerly reflecting upon this lords wife, here omitted, little defiring to meddle in the matter of woemens greatnes.[1]

His rewards to servants.

I will not come too neare the heeles of this title, nor draw a needleffe envy from the fons and furvivors of fuch whom the bounty of this lord Henry raifed and rewarded in the firft ten years after his full age and reftitution to his Barony of Berkeley, what times the leaft deferving of twenty or more then in relation to this family in the feverall Counties of Glouc., Somfet, Leicefter, Darby, Huntington and Suffex, had their barren feilds watered from this lords bounty, fome for years, others for lives, with the value of 60^{li} 80^{li} 100^{li} 150^{li} 200^{li} and 300^{li} a peece by the year

[1] Certain Orders for the regulation of the Houfehold, found at Candover Hall, were in 1601 given by this Lord's fecond wife.—See Appendix to this Life. [ED.]

year and more, above the rents referved upon fuch leafes, fome of which determined not till within three years now paft; the moft of them rather bred to drink fport and play, then for merit or imployments; Neither grew this lords bounty much dryer to fundry others in the riper part of his life, As the living may witnefs, and the Annuities left iffuing out of his lands at his death doth teftifie, And as in his laft will and the Office found after his death hereafter mentioned is fpecifyed: Only of my felf I will write in particular, that the faire afpect of this lord for almoft thirty years | before hee dyed, and alfo of the lady Katharine his firft wife and of their fon and granchild the now lord George, with the lady dowager the grandchilds mother, have by a liberall influence fhoured by former and later raines more bounties upon mee then I have either means or daies remaining to deferve, otherwife then by this humble and thankfull acknowledgment: Into which bountifull catalogue conferred on my felf, let mee alfo bundle up the noble curtefy of this lords vifiting mee at Gloucefter, in my dangerous ficknes of fix weeks continuance in Auguft and September, 1608. Anno, 6to Regis Jacobi, what time I loft the ufe of reafon and all mens hope of recovery; And by a gratefull memoriall acknowledge the unicornes horne Befaar ftone and exquifite Jellyes, often by him fent unto mee, whereby my daies feeme repryved to this prefent; And I defire this humble digreffion may reach alfo by like thankfulnes to the aforenamed lady Dowager, mother of my lord George, acknowledgeing her like noble curtefy of travelling many miles to Wotton Underedge 12. years after, to vifite mee in another ficknes, which report had declared likely to bee the clofeing of my pilgrimage. By the memoriall of which memorable curtefies, my defires have inlarged my travailes about thefe relations.

His Almes and devotions.

The former titles of hofpitallity and of rewards to fervants, challenge this of this lords Almes and devotions in the next place.

As touching this lords Almes to the poore, it was three daies in the weeke wherein the poore of 4. 5. and fix country | parifhes and villages next adjoyning to Callowdon were releived, with each of them a meffe of wholfome pottage with a peece of beoffe or mutton therein, halfe a cheate loafe,[1] and a kan of beere; befides the private Almes that daily went out of his purfe, never without eight or ten fhillings

---

[1] The fecond fort of wheaten bread, ranking next to manchet. There were two kinds of Cheatbread, the beft or fine Cheat, and the coarfe Cheat, ravelled bread. The fecond fort ufed in the Halles of the Nobility Gentrie onelie.—*(Halliwell.)* [ED.]

shillings in single money, of 2ᵈ 3ᵈ and groates, And besides his Maundy each thursday before Easter day, wherein many poore men and women were clothed by the liberallity of this lord and his first wife, whilst they lived: And besides twenty marks or twenty pound or more, which thrice each yeare against the feasts of Christmas, Easter, and Whitsontide was sent by this lord to two or three of the cheifest inhabitants of those villages, and of Gosford street at Coventry, to bee distributed amongst their poore according to their discretions; All which to bee true, besides mine own knowledge, the living and graves of the dead that relished this his pious Almes and charity, doe testifie with mee.

And for his publike frequenting of service and sermons, and for his private devotions in his chamber, I have many and many times seen and observed him assoone as hee was out of bed and clothed, to bee upon his knees in his bedchamber, calling upon that God for mercy and forgivnes to whom his soule is now singing alleluia for the mercy and pardon it hath received; And many and many times hath this right hand of mine that thus transmitteth this passage to his posterity, laid his cushion and brought his prayer books, and againe taken away the same: And often and againe have these feet of mine attended at his chamber doore for accesse whilst thus piously hee hath been in his Soliloquies with God: This I tell his children, and let them tell their children, and their children another generation, That this was the pious practice of this their Ancestor; who out of the fervency of these his devotions still seemes speaking to his grandchild and heire, as king David in his old age a few dayes before his death did to Solomon his son; And thou George my son, know thou the God of thy father, and serve him with a perfect heart and with a | willing mind: for the lord searcheth all hearts and understandeth all the imaginations of the thoughts: if thou seeke him hee will bee found of thee; but if thou forsake him hee will cast thee off for ever.

Joel 1 vers 3.

3 Chron. 26. vers. 6

835

His Missellanies, or various passages, not reduceable under any of the former titles.

1. In the yeare 1593. the Inhabitants of Howby in the county of Leicester, by their petition in writing, complayned to this lord Henry against Sir George Villers knight for a great inclosure by him unjustly made of their Cow pasture and of a great part of their arrable lands and Comon feilds, wherein hee had also inclosed part of this lords land, and part also of the gleabe land of the Rectory of Howby whereof this lord was patron: Hereupon my self was sent to enter and dig down part of the ditch and quick set, which I did in severall places: Sir George came

came thereupon to this lord at Callowdon, And promifed foe fair to recompence each party greived, that further proceeding was not, untill another petition or remonftrance came under the hands of moft of the faid inhabitants efpecially of thofe holding of Mr. Brokefby, that they were fatisfied by exchanges and otherwife; Howbeit fith noe writing touching that conclufion was amongft them, nor yet is, It is not unlike but in time to come fome prejudice to this lords pofterity and to thofe Inhabitants may grow thereby; the caufe why this memoriall is here fet down.

2. In the year 1597, one Edmond O-nele, who pretended himfelf to bee a Romifh Bifhop of Ireland, was apprehended at Nuneaton not farre from Callowdon where this lord then lived, as a forraigne fpye or intelligencer; One Edward Pynne then a fchoolmafter in Nuneaton, publiquely before two Juftices of the peace affirmed That O-neale fhould in private requeft him to | goe to this lord Berkeley in his name, and bid him come and help him, hee then going towards the comon gaole: which brought this lord fome trouble and danger: but in the end hee was difcharged by the privy Counfell, And Pynne the Schoolmafter laid open to bee a lewd and factious knave.

3. The greateft part of this lords abiding after his mothers death, happening in the fixth year of Queen Elizabeth, was at Callowdon till his own death in the eleaventh of king James; from whence once in two or three years hee ufed in July to come to Berkeley, not comonly by one way, lodging in his journeys at the houfes of gentlemen his freinds and acquaintances, As at Claredon, Milcote, Clifford, Sainbury, Shirborne, Saperton, Lackhampton, Caffies Compton, Gloucefter, Ellmore, ffrocefter, Laffeborrow. Downamny, and fome others, by bending his journeys fometimes on the one hand and fometimes on the other. It was an innate difpofition in him to avoid lodging at Comon Innes; In his laft daies Journey to Berkeley I have often attended, when I have obferved him met by the way and accompanied with 300, 400, and 500, horfe of his kindred freinds and tenants ere hee came to Berkeley town, though he ufually fet forth from Callowdon with feldome above fourteen or fixteen; which confluence of trayne, how it daily doth and more is like to degenerate, let his pofterity obferve and declare to their generacõns.

4. King James the 14th of Auguft in the firft of his raigne, Anno 1603, made this lord Henry Lievtenant of the County of Glouc.; whofe deputies were, Sr.
Richard

Richard Berkeley knight and William Dutton of Shirborne Esqr, authorized from him by his severall writings of deputation under his hand and seale.

And the 26th of May in the 7th yeare of his raigne, the said king James by his other ħes patents of new granted to this lord the said Office of Leivtenancy within the said County and within the Citie of Gloucester, more amply then at first: Both which remaine in Berkeley Castle under the great seale of England.

5. **Touching** all passages in that office and authority of Leiv- | tenancy his Sollicitor for his better dispatches kept certaine books, wherin all ħes from the king the privy Consell or any others and his answers were entred; and also how each particular gentleman and other inhabitants of that County, and in the County of the Citie of Glouc., aswell of the Clergy and Laity, were charged with armes, foote, or horse; And of what age Stature and abillity each one in that county was of, were likewise particularly expressed, with such other remembrances as seemed incident to that honorable office; And also what soldiers were during his leivtenancy sent into Ireland, and how furnished and at what rates and how raised; wherein to y[e] honor of his memory I will tell his posterity, That in sending of one hundred soldiers in the sixth of king James for Ireland, hee observed that some were pressed out of malice and displeasure, and for other unapproveable ends; whereupon calling all the soldiers togeather to Glouc., then accompanied with one hundred gentlemen at least of the county, hee openly published before them all, That if hee might understand of any that had given money to stay, hee should stay, for hee would not have any to goe and loose his money alsoe; And if any there could prove himself to bee pressed by Constable or other for malice or displeasure, or for other private ends, hee should not goe; By which means hee having discovered many of both kinds, hee caused restitution of the money taken to bee made to a peny, but sent that soldier that gave it; And released divers of such as appeared to bee maliciously pressed, saying, (then in sadnes without dissembling,) That none of what quality soever should make his authority an instrument of quittance or revenge: **And** lastly, as each of those soldiers was called by name and deliver'd to their conductor, hee caused my self to put 12[d] the peice into the hand of every soldier out of his own purse; which course drew upon him a world of good words praises and prayers from each one present: **And** I also remember that at that instant of departure, one of the soldiers openly greived and wept at his going, which all

837

4 libri in Castro de Berkeley.[1]

---

[1] This interesting Volume is now in the possession of Reginald Cholmondeley, of Condover Hall, Co. Salop, Esq., Smyth's lineal discendant.—See Pedigree, Vol. I. Preface. [ED.]

all the other 99 obferving, they fell upon him with opprobious words, of Coward, Cotquene,[1] milkfopp, diſhwaſh, and the like, and with one unanimous requeſt befought this lord That fo bafe a Coward might not bee of their bond; whereupon, having been difrobed of his Armes, hee was with much reproach | fent home, and another put into his place: for which fupplies, if occafions fo required, this lord had to that inſtant kept three or fower in ſtore.

6. **The** Maior of Wotton hath ufually a Mace of filver borne before him by the Serjeant of that burrowe, with the Armes of the lord of that Town on the lower end thereof; which were the lord Liſles, And fo had from the time of Henry the fixth continued till the firſt of Queen Elizabeth, when that old Mace was fold, and a new made with the Armes of this lord engraven that year upon it: which againe in the 15th year of that Queens raigne, upon the loffe of that burrowe town was defaced, And a new Mace made with the Armes of the then Earles of Warr̄ and Leic: engraven thereupon, which continued till the 8th year of king James; And then was that mace againe excluded, and a new bought, (much longer then any of the reſt,) with the Armes of this lord Henry engraven thereupon. **To** which laſt alteration my advice was guided by the prefident of the fifteenth of Elizabeth formerly mentioned; what time alfo the prudent officers of thofe two Earles drew into their hands each leafe and Copy formerly made in any of thofe manors, then recovered againſt him, whereto the name of Berkeley was, to extirpe the rather the memoriall of that name: Howbeit that divine providence that often turneth the actions of men to other ends then they were intended, hath of late years brought all the fame into Berkeley caſtle in great files and bundles, to the perpetuating of that name whereof they intended noe memoriall, as in part is before touched amongſt the law fuits of this lord.

7. **Charles** Howard Earle of Nottingham, high Admirall of England, by his patent dated the 14th of November, 1603, in the firſt year of king James, conſtituted this lord Henry his vice Admirall upon the river of Seavern throughout the county of Glouc.; which hee enjoyed till his death. Whofe Steward my felf was therein.

8. **In** May - 1609. in the 7th year of king James this lord caufed a view to bee taken of all manner of trees growing upon any of | his tenants lands holden of him, by Indenture or by Copy, in the counties of Glouc. and Somſet, and upon what ground

---

[1] A man who bufies himfelf with women's affairs. [ED.]

ground, with an eftimate of their value; And what trees had been cut by any tenant within three years before, and how they had been imployed; which providence begot a faire book fhortly after written by Willm Archard one of my Clarks, and prevented many of thofe wafts that tenants ordinarily do comitt, and lords neglect to punifh.

9. **I doe** afcertaine this noble lords pofterity that I fpent a month and more, in tumbling over all fuch bookes of Officers and Minifters accompts as might informe mee and I them, what the totall fum was of all moneys which came to this lords hands, and were raifed in rents, fines, heriots, fales of Coppice woods, and of timber, and in the fales of the lands hee made, in the benevolences of his tenants thrice given him, and lones (never repayed,) And in the Aydes hee had from his freeholders, monies paid for Confirmation of Cuftoms of Bofham, Auconbury and ffenyftanton manors, And for fuch wardfhips, releefes, and other cafualties as happened and came to his Coffers and were put into accompt, from the firft of Queen Mary to his death in the eleventh of king James, the fpace of threefcore years; And that the totall thereof cometh to two hundred and fixty thoufand and five hundred pounds: **And** withall, that I am confident (out of the induftry of my labors therein) that I have not erred two thoufand pounds: Telling alfo his pofterity out of mine own knowledge, for thirty years before hee dyed, That whatfoever money this lord received or after iffued out, it was exactly fet down in writing, And at his generall Audit at the years end caft into the Accompt of his receivor generall: And that for fuch ready monies not otherwife iffued but delivered to himfelfe, which was the half of his yearly revenue at the leaft, That hee not only kept with himfelf a booke of the receipt thereof, and from whofe hands it came, and of what nature it was, but alfo how each peny thereof was paid out by himfelf againe, whether deliver'd to the Steward of the houfhold, purveyor, Clarke of the Kitchen or Cator, or otherwife iffued, for which they againe accompted: Only what thereof hee would fhould bee concealed, hee entred (as being put into his purfe;) Some of thefe books and accompts are in Berkeley Caftle, but more of them came after his death, (much againft | my defire,) to the hands of his two executors, Sr William Cooke and Sr Thomas Eftcourt; with whofe executors the fame ftill remaine as I conceive: The ufe and application whereof I leave to his grandchild and heire and his pofterity, as under that title after followeth.

Monies raifed.

840

fol: [885]

10. **I may** not omit the mentioning of this lords fynes recoveries and other conveyances for the eftablifhment of his own lands, becaufe the ready finding thereof

Fines & recoveries

thereof in one bundle togeather cannot but bee very usefull to his posterity, whereat I only ayme.

exempl: in castro de Berkeley. Michas rec̃ in sc̃acio cum rem̃ thes : 9. Eliz: rot. 169.

See fol : 743.

As how in Trinity terme in the first year of Queen Elizabeth this lord leavyed a fine sur conusans de droit of the manor of Simondsall, to Thomas ffransham and William Porter, by the names of the manr̃ of Symondsall, And of 1200 acres of land, 100. acres of meadow, 500. acres of pasture, and of 200. acres of wood, with the appurtenñts, in Symondsall and Wotton underedge; which was for confirmation of a lease for three score years made to Sr. Thomas Parry of Symondsall farme, in reverc̃on of one other then in being for divers years to come.

Licent. dat : 16 : Apr : 7 : Eliz : Pasch : rec : 8. Eliz : rot. 73. cum rem̃. thesaur̃ in sc̃acio.

In Michmas terme in the 7th. and 8th. of Elizabeth this lord levyed a fine to William Porter and ⸻ Savage of his manors of Slimbridge, Hurst, Came, Cowley, and Sages : And granted by an Indenture dated the 20th of May in the same yeare, an Anuity of forty pound p Anñ, out of those manors to Edward Berkeley of Bradley and Elizabeth his wife for their lives, in recompence of their surrender of the custody of Hawpark, which with the herbage at ten pound rent this lord had formerly given unto them; The licence of which fine cost this lord— 82li 15s. 06d.

Trin̄ : 13. Eliz : rot: 1055. in banco. Ind: irrot. in Canc̃ 15. Eliz: et. 16. Eliz : ps 36. claus : rot : michas: 15. Eliz : rot: 1960. in banco.

In Trinity Terme in the 13th. of Elizabeth this lord suffered Com̃on recoveries of the Castle and hundred of Berkeley, and of the manrs. of Berkeley, Alkington, Ham, Hinton, Wotton underedge als Wotton Serjeant, and of Wotton als Wotton fforren, and Erlingham : And in Michmas terme in the 15th of Elizabeth of the manors of Daglingworth, Tetbury, Bitton, and Hannam : The uses whereof by severall Indentures were to himself in taile with remainders to his daughters, (his son Thomas not then born, nor hoped for.) |

841

Hill : 37. Eliz : rot. 106. in sc̃acio. Trin̄ rec : 38. Eliz : rot : 123. c̃m rem̃ thesaur̃ in sc̃acio. Pardon 6. Junij 36. Eliz : in Canc.

In the 22th of Elizabeth a fine sur conusans de droit was leavyed (inter alia) by Robert Earle of Leicester to Sir John Huband knight, John Dudley and John Nuthall Esqrs, of the Castle and manor of Kellingworth and divers other lands in the County of Warr̃, and in other counties, And of the moitie of the manors of Wotton underedge and Simondsall, And of the moitie of the Burrow and forren of Wotton with their rights members and appurtenants in Wotton, Nibley, Cromhall, or elsewhere in the County of Gloucester.

Hill : 37 : Eliz : rot : 92 : c̃m rem̃ thesaur̃ in sc̃acio.

In Trinity Terme in the 34th of Elizabeth a fine was leavyed of the moitie of the manors of Wotton and Symondsall by Sr. Christopher Blount and the lady

Lettice

Lettice his wife, Countes of Leicester, to Edward Barker and John Wakeman Esq.rs, of the estate for life of the said Lettice of the moitie of the manors of Wotton underedge and Symondsall, and of the Burrow and Hundred of Wotton, and of 300. messuages, 200. cottages, 6. mills, 6. dovehouses, 200. gardens, 200. orchards, 1000. acres of land, 400. acres of meadow, 400. acres of pasture, 800 acres of wood, and of 1000. acres of furres and heath, with their appurtenants in Sinwell, Combe, Wortley, Nibley, Serncliffe, Cromhall, Horton, and Baies in Horton, Wotton underedge, Simondsall and Wotton, And of the moitie of the advowson of the church of Wotton.

In the 39th of Elizabeth, a fine was leavyed by Anne Countes of Warrwick to her servants Vincent and Vaughan, of three messuages, three mills, and 330. acres of land, in Berkeley, Cam, Alkington, Wike, Newport, Stinchecomb, and Dursley; which in trinity Terme after was pleaded in the Exchequer to bee for the confirmation of two leases made by her to Arnold Oldisworth and Richard Danford, of the two messuages of Corrietts in Cam, and of Holts in Alkington.

Trin: 39. Eliz: rot : 91. c̃m rem̃. thesaur̃ in sc̃acio.

In Micl̃mas Terme in the 44th and 45th of Elizabeth, A fine sur conusance de droit was levyed by Thomas Stephens and John Hunt to Thomas Gaddesden and Eustace Grubb, of the manor of Sages, Rowles Court and new leyes, by the names of eight messuages, three cottages, three tofts, two dovehouses, nine gardens, ten Orchards, 300. acres of land, 100. acres of meadow, 200. acres of pasture, six acres of wood, and twenty shillings rent, in Slimbridge, Kingston, Cam, Gossington, Hurst, Berkeley and Hinton. |

Hill: 45. Eliz: rot in sc̃acio. Mich̃as. 44. Eliz: in banco : rot: 10. Licent : dat. 1. Sept. 44. Eliz: irrotulat̃r in terme hillar̃ postea in sc̃acio

In Hill: terme in the 7th of king James Robert Sidney knight, viscount Lisle, and Barbara his wife, and William their son and heire, (since dead without issue,) and this lord Henry and Thomas his son and heire, levyed a fine sur conusans de droit to William Dutton Esq.r and John Smyth, of the manors of Wotton, al's Wotton underedge, al's Wotton fforren, Symondsall, Came, Hinton, Cowley, Erlingham, Slimbridge, Hurst and Sages, And of the Burrow of Wotton, and of two water mills, 800. acres of land, 500 acres of meadow, 1000. acres of pasture, 200. acres of wood, 500. acres of furres and heath, 10li. rent, views of frankpledge, goods and chattells of felons, and of fugitives and outlawed persons, deodands, free warren, faires, marketts, and wrecks of Sea, and piscaries, with their appurtenants in Wotton al's Wotton underedge, al's Wotton fforren, Simondsall, Erlingham, Slimbridge, Sages, Hurst, Gossington, Cam, Cambridge, Holts, Berkeley, Hinton, Alkington, Wike,

842
Hill: 7. Jac: Recovery: Pasch̃ 8. Jac: rot. 57. Licence to alien 1 Sept : 7. Jac:

Wike, Stichcomb, Stancombe, Nybley als Northnybley, Serncliffe, Uley, Durſley, Combe, Wortley, Huntingford, Sinwell, Bradley, Kingſcote, Cromhall, Horton, Horwood, and Baies with their appurtñnts in the County of Glouc.; And the next Terme after a recovery of the premiſes.

<small>Inq : 11 : Jac poſt mort Henrici dni Berkeley in Canc. Licence to alien, dat. 1. Julij. 10. Jac. in Canc : Trin : Terme : 11. ac : in ſcᵃčio c̃m rem̃ thes: all alienations are pleaded and diſcharged.</small>

William Dutton Eſqʳ and John Smyth in Micħmas Terme in the 10ᵗʰ of King James levyed a fine ſur conuſans de droit to Thomas Spencer Eſqʳ and Thomas Ligon, To the uſe of this lord Henry and his heires, of the manors of Wotton als Wotton underedge als Wotton Forren, Simondſall, Cam, Hinton, Cowley, Slimbridge, Hurſt and Sages with the appurtenants; And of the burrow of Wotton, and of the other p̃ticulers as in the fine to them formerly mentioned is expreſſed; many of which, (beſides the originalls which are in Berkeley caſtle,) are alſo found in the offices of Sir Thomas Berkeley and of this lord Henry after their deaths in . 9 . and 11°. Jacobi Regis.

<small>Hiſt : 10. Jac : in Scᵃčio c̃m rem̃ theſaur : rot.</small>

In the 10ᵗʰ of king James was put into a plea into the Exchequer for avoiding a charge upon Oakley park, Wotton, Hackmill, &c., as Seymors lands exchanged with king Edward the ſixth, which to know, is like to bee of uſe.

<small>Sojournings
843</small>

11. **Neither** may I omit the divers ſojournings of this lord at the houſes of his kinſmen and freinds, whereby hee both eaſed his purſe and tooke | a cleanly occaſion aſwell to ſhake of ſuch impudents as hanged overlonge and unmannerly upon his table and ſtable, as to rid his houſe of waſtfull and diſorderly ſervants; and ſuch as were not conformable to his tenets in religion, whom the popiſh inclination of an ancient gentlewoman many years attendant on his wife, and extraordinarily favored by her, had drawn into his family; not otherwiſe without an houſhold ſtorme to have been ſoe calmly put of. **As** firſt in the time of Queen Mary this lord and his wife ſojourned with the old Duke of Norfolke till hee dyed, at Keninghall in Norfolke; And after his death for the laſt year of Queen Mary and ſomewhat before, with the Counteſ of Surrey his wives mother at Ryſing in Norfolke aforeſaid.

In the 11ᵗʰ and 12ᵗʰ years of Queen Elizabeth this lord with his wife and family ſojourned with Sʳ Thomas Ruſſell at Stranſham. **In** the 26ᵗʰ and 27ᵗʰ of Elizabeth this lord with his wife and family ſojourned with his cozen germaine Sʳ John Savage at Baraper in Hampſhire; And in the 41ᵗʰ and 42ᵗʰ of Elizabeth with Mʳ ffeilding at Newnham.

Laſtly,

Lastly, for moſt part of the fourth, fifth, ſixth, and ſeventh years of king James, hee ſojourned with Mr. Peito at the white fryars in Coventry; and at Stoke, a mile from Callowdon; at which times hee was maryed to his laſt wife.

Some other ſhort removes this lord had with other of his freinds, here omitted, but not for above half a years continuance at a time: one of which was occationed upon a letter which in the later daies of Queen Elizabeth hee received from that reverend prelate Doctor Whitguift Archbiſhop of Canterbury, gravely adviſing him to take notice of the diſpoſitions of his ſervants and his wives waiting woemen in matter of their conformity in religion; And how comely and honorable it would bee to ſee himſelf and his wife attended upon at ſervice and ſermons by his wholl family, praying his lordſhip to take from him the occation of a ſecond admonition, which hee by the means aforeſaid fairly did: which lre this lord once ſhowed mee.

12. **Maurice** lord Berkeley the ſixth of that name did in the 7th of king Henry the 8th give the Rectory of Kegworth to Chriſt Colledge in Cambridge, now worth 250li. p Anñ; In which grant it was agreed, That as often as the church ſhould become void the Colledge | ſhould within one month name two able Clerkes of their Colledge to the ſaid lord, and his heires, by writing under their comon ſeale; which lord ſhould within ſix days after by his writing appoint one of them two to have the ſaid benifice: Hawford the Incumbent dies in the 25th of Elizabeth, And the Colledge raiſed a queſtion whether their two Clerks ſhould come perſonally or not, And thereupon ſent their nomination to this lord in writing, neither of whom hee would make choice of without ſight of their perſons: At laſt this difference coming to the determination of Gawdy and Ailyffe the two Judges of that circuite, they determined, That as often as the ſaid Church of Kegworth ſhould bee void, the Colledge ſhould ſend with their writing of nominacon the ſd. two Clerkes perſonally to this lord and his heires, being in England, and not in ward; which I remember was in the 4th of king James ſoe done, when Barwell, yet there living, obtained the nomination from this lord.

<small>Kegworth Advowſon.</small>

<small>844</small>

13. **This** lord about the 16th of Queen Elizabeth adviſing with Jeffry Ithell his Auditor and two others his ancient officers touching his houſhold affaires, was by Ithell amongſt other Counſells adviſed to be attended with none of his kindred, if hee could avoid them; for, quoth hee, experience tells, that ſuch will doe little, and expect much, and think a great reward too ſhort, tho' the merit of their ſervice bee none at all; which ſpeech coming to bee divulged amongſt the ſervants in the houſe,

houſe, malice forthwth added, That Ithell alſo adviſed this lord never to keep ſervant above two yeares, for afterwards their diligence would abate and they bee ever begging; words hee ſpake not: But being from hand to hand delivered and beleived by credulous ſervants, Ithell ever after had each officer of houſe and ſtable againſt him and his horſes, when ever hee came for thirty years after; Which I here remember as a double caution for after Counſellors to private lords, To keep more ſecret their adviſes, And to overlooke the company before they ſpeake freely.

845
Wages and Liveries

14. The ſtanding yearly wages of this lord to his houſhold | ſervants were ordinarily five marks to a gentleman, fower marks to a yeoman, and fourty ſhillings to a groome, with a tawny coate for ſummer and a white frize coat for winter lyned with crimſon tafaty; which I note for difference between times ſo lately paſt and theſe I write in, and which this family is further like to ſee in it ſelf: And thereby with more caution to regulate their revenues: and yet fewe Peeres of this lords time were ſerved with better qualifyed gentlemen and yeomen then I have known this lord to bee; which I might the better note, for that I was his ſteward of houſhold from the death of his firſt wife till my marriage, and the coming of Mr John Creſwell who ſucceeded mee.

Worthy Parke Red Deere

15. Queen Elizabeth in her progreſſe time in the fifteenth of her raign came to Berkeley Caſtle, what time this lord Henry had a ſtately game of red deere in the park adjoyning called the Worthy, whereof Henry Ligon was keeper; during which time of her being there, ſuch ſlaughter was made, as—27. ſtagges were ſlaine in the Toiles in one day, and many others in that and the next ſtollen and havoked: whereof when this lord Henry, then at Callowdon, was advertiſed, having much ſet his delight upon that game, hee ſodainly and paſſionatly in diſcontent diſparked that ground: But in fewe monthes after, hee had a ſecret freindly advertizem^t from the Court, That the Queen was informed how the ſame was ſoe diſparked by him in repyning at her coming to his houſe, (for indeed it was not in her Jeſts,) and at the good ſport ſhee had in that parke; Adviſing this lord to carry a wary watch over his words and actions, leaſt that, that Earle (meaning Leiceſter) that had contrary to her ſet Jeſts drawn her to this Caſtle, and purpoſely had cauſed that ſlaughter of his deere, might have a further plott againſt his head and that Caſtle, whereto hee had taken noe ſmall liking, and affirmed to have good title thereto, And was not farre from his manor of Wotton, lately recovered againſt him: whereof when this lord Henry many years after told mee, I remembred him of the ſtory of Thomas Burdets white bucke in his park of Arrow in Warrwickſhire, which hee greatly eſteemed,

esteemed, killed by king Edward the fourth in the 18th yeare of his raigne; upon the first hear- | ing whereof Mr Burdet in discontent wished the bucks head and horns in the belly of him that moved the king to kill it; and how that upon the misconstruction of those words hee was accused of treason, attainted and beheaded; whereto this lord, more perfect in the story then my self, replyed; Like soddaine passions made little difference between our words and wishes; but that Burdet had been a great freind and Counsellor to the Duke of Clarence the kings brother, when between them there was bitter enmity, which to revenge, the king (said this lord) made these words but his colour to take off Burdets head.

16. **About** the 23th of Queen Elizabeth, the lady Katharine wife to this lord, by ill advice, wrote a secret l're to one old Bourne, then dwelling in the forrest of Arden in Warrwickshire, who (though falsly) was with many reputed a conjurer, witch, or foreteller of events, and of the periods of Princes lives; sending the same by John Bott her servant, with direction to see her l're burned, and Bournes answer to bee returned in writing. Bott ignorant of the contents most dishonestly opened the l're, and kept it to himself, delivering the substance thereof to Bourne by word of mouth, with the reward sent to him; what answer Bot brought back (a lye noe doubt) or what hee changed, or added thereto I know not: But this I know that a fewe years after, Bot was cast out of service, and by this lord Henry called to accompt about his receipts and disbursments in the new buildings adjoyning to Callowdon house, and of the gate house and other outhouses whereof hee had the oversight; And touching his purveyance of Beoves and muttons, which hee for many years had made for this lords house: Bot, not able as it seemed to cleare his reconings, caused this lady by a gentlewoman ever near and deare unto her, and who had urged and perhaps wrote that l're, to understand that unles shee would take him off from those accompts, hee would reveale her l're written to that wizard Bourne where neither her lady nor her self should answer it. The lady and her gentle- | woman supposing that Bourne had both received and burned the l're, desired of Bot to see it, not seeming to remember the contents thereof: But Bot, not intending to trust either of their hands therewth, offered for satisfaction to shewe the same to Mrs Anne Try, another Ancient waiting gentlewoman, and in good favour also with her lady, and cozen to the other, but could badly read; which being accepted, Bot freindly invited into his chamber a younge man under 18. years of age, and lately become a servant to the ladies son by Botts meanes, at whose fathers house hee had often lodged as hee travelled to faires and marketts in those parts; and obtained of him secretly to copy out that l're, in a like Romane hand, not imparting

parting to him more then barely to copy it out; But that younge man fufpecting fomewhat then and getting a little more inckling forthwith after, having obferved where Bot laid up the originall lre, fecretly got into Botts chamber found the lre and forthwith burned it indeed; Mr. Try made relation of the contents, which being well enough remembred, the lady made Bots peace with her hufband; But when it appeared that hee had not the originall lre to deliver up, as hee had vowed to do, the whole buifines was difavowed and Bot threatned with punifhment as the author of foe great a fcandall; yet at laft hee was difcharged, and all couched under filence; The copy alfo was burned, it never being further known either who wrote it or what became of the originall lre. The profitable ufe that may bee gathered herehence fhall appear under the proper title.

fol: 886

dangers efcaped

17. **This** Lord Henry had three great deliverances from iminent death, as in his middle age hee would often comfortably remember; The firft whereof was in Kingfwood chace neare Briftoll, (where himfelf under Queen Elizabeth was ranger,) as hee was gallopping upon a full fpeed through the fearne and brakes there to have rated the forehead of his hounds then in chafe after a wronge bucke. The fecond was not farre from his manor of Callowdon in Warrwickfhr then alfo in a fwift gallop after his hounds hunting the hare. At both which times, the gelding hee rode on, called Brimfley, | (than which, I never knew a better,) being within lefs then his length firft of an old Colepit unfilled up, hid from fight by thofe brakes, fudainly (in an inftant as it were) upon the glimpfe thereof threw himfelf flat upon his fide: As likewife the fecond time the fame gelding did, upon the like glimpfe of a deepe pit of water like a well, kept alfo from fight by like fearne and weeds; no other way in mans reafon (as himfelf would fay,) being for his prefervation then the geldings foe cafting down himfelf, without hurt at either time to his rider; neither of thofe pits being by this lord difcerned till hee was tumbling on the ground: The third was neare Holborne bridge in the parifh of St Andrewes in London, what time his Coach horfes in a furious courfe down Holborne hill, having caft off the Coachman, had run the coach and themfelves befides that bridge into a defparate downfall, (as the paffage at that time was,) if Laughan his Irifh footman, (a man of extraordinary ftrength and footmanfhip,) had not by as fwift a courfe and ftrength overborne the foremoft horfes againft the coine end of a wall, which at that time ftood neare the faid bridge: Whereunto may bee added a fourth prefervation, not much inferior to the former, not 4 months before his death, which fee in the title of his iffue. This Laughan is that footman which 40 years paft, upon the ficknes of the lady Katharine this lords wife, carried a lre from Callowdon to old

848

fol: 872

Doctor

Doctor ffryer a phyſicion then dwelling in little Brittaine in London, and returned with a glaſs bottle in his hand compounded by the Doctor for recovery of her health, (a journey of 148. miles performed by him in leſs then 42 houres,) notwithſtanding his ſtay of one night at the phyſition and Apothecaries houſes, which noe one horſe could have ſoe well and ſafely performed; for which the lady ſhortly after gave him a new ſuite of Clothes.

18. Such was the humanity of this lord, That in times of Chriſtmas and other feſtivalls when his neighbour Townſhips were invited and feaſted in his hall, hee would in the midſt of their dinner riſe from his own, and going to each of their tables in his hall, cheerfully bid them welcome: And his further order was, | having gueſts of honor of remarkeable ranke that filled his own table, to ſeat himſelf at the lower end; And when ſuch gueſts filled but half his bord, and a meaner degree the reſt of his table, then to ſeat himſelf the laſt of the firſt rank and the firſt of the latter, which commonly was about the midſt of his longe table neare the ſalt; This I tell his poſterity, the better to knowe the practice of that time, and the poſture of this their noble anceſtor beloved by all good men.

849

19. This Lord having Mr Lapworth his accuſtomed phiſitian, (father of Doctor Lapworth of Oxford that now is,) at his houſe, (himſelf keeping his chamber,) commanded his Steward of houſhold to bee carefull of his entertainment; ſaying, that hee would not have his phyſitian for his health ſake, his ſollicitor for his eſtates ſake, nor his chaplin for his ſoules ſake, to bee unregarded: which not well reliſhing with his cholloricke Steward, becauſe himſelf was not ranked in that Cattalogue, hee uſed ever after to welcome them, as perſons priviledged from his lords diſpleaſure, but their horſes with noe better provender.

His Wives.

This lords mother having bought the wardſhip of the body of this lord her ſon of Thomas Earle of Suſſex, to whom Henry the 8th had granted the ſame as hath been ſaid and already written, provided for his wife Katharine, third daughter of Henry Howarde Earle of Surrey and of ffrances his wife daughter of John Vere Earle of Oxford; which Henry was beheaded at tower hill (in the life-time of Thomas Duke of Norfolk his father, then alſo priſoner in ye Tower,) the 19th of January, 1547. in the 38th of Henry the 8th, but nyne daies before the death of that king. |

Mich: rec: 14.
Eliz: rot: 72. in
ſcᵃcio.
fol: [720]

This Lady Katharine (then of the age of ſixteen) hee married at Kenynghall in Norfolke in September in the ſecond year of Queen Mary; And (as I have been informed,

850
Anno: 1554.

informed, by the bed fide of the faid noble Duke her grandfather, who gave her in marriage as hee lay in bed, then grown weake with age and ficknes; who having been toffed to and fro between the reciprocall ebbs and flowes of variable fortunes, not longe after finifhed his race of mortality in the fame place.

<small>Act in Berkeley caftle under the great Seale.</small>

This Lady Katharine was, at the parliament in the firft year of Queen Elizabeth, by an unprinted act reftored in bloud, occafioned by the attainder of her faid father.

<small>Act: parl: 13. Eliz: in Canc:</small>

The portion which fhee brought in marriage was not great, neither had fhee any Joynture affured to her before the 13th of Elizabeth; At what time by act of parliament were fetled upon her for her life in lieu of Dower, the manors of Segrave, Sileby, Mountforrell, Melton Mowbray, Dalby Chawcomb, Coldoverton, Witherley, and the hundred of Gofcote in the County of Leicefter; And the manors of Auconbury, Wefton, Fenyftanton, and Hilton in the County of Huntington; And the manors of Bofham, Thorney, and ffuntington in the County of Suffex; And the manor of Callowdon in the County of the Citie of Coventry; And the manors of Kington magna, fflekenhoe, and Thurlafton in the County of Warr̃; And the manor of Bretby in the County of Derby; And the manors of Bitton and Hannam, Mangottesfeild, Daglingworth, Tetbury, and newparke, in the county of Glouc.; And the manor and hundred of Portbury in the County of Somerfet; Which Joynture was two years after enlarged with the manors of Ham, Arlingham, and fome others.

<small>Carta: 8. Nov: 15. Eliz: irrot̃ in Canc. 15. et. 16. Eliz: 36 ps. claus: rolls.</small>

At which time this lord having only three daughters, eftated the inheritance of his whole lands to difcend upon them for defalt of iffue male of his own body, under which vaile hee wrought that inlargement as after more perticulerly is mentioned.

Of Stature this lady was fomewhat tall, of complection lovely both in the fpringe and autumne of her life, but a little inclin-|ing towards an high colour; her haire fomwhat yellowifh; of pace the moft ftately and upright all times of her age that ever I beheld; of ftomacke great and haughty, no way diminifhing the greatnes of her birth and marriage by omiffion of any ceremony, at diet or publike prayers; whofe book I have ufually obferved prefented to her wth the loweft curtefies that might bee, and on the knees of her gentlewoman: of great expence and bounty beyond the means of continuance, of fpeech paffing Eloquent and ready; whom in many years I could never obferve to mifplace or feem to recall one miftaken,

taken, misplaced or mispronounced word or sillable; And as ready and significant under her pen; forty of whose letters at least at severall times I have received; her invention as quick as her first thoughts, And her words as ready as her invention; Skillfull in the french, but perfect in the Italian tongue, wherein shee most desired her daughters to bee instructed; At the lute shee played admirably, and in her private chamber would often singe thereto, to the ravishment of the hearers; w^{ch} (to her knowledge) were seldom more then one or two of her gentlewomen; Howbeit I have known divers of her servants secretly hearkening under her windows and at her chamber doore; whom her husband hath somtimes there found, and privately stayed amongst them; of which number three or fower times my self hath been one.

And the more to verify what is written of this lady Katharine, I will insert verbatim one of her tres written to my self during the treaty of the marriage about her only son, which her posterity shall find cast by mee into their evidence house in Berkeley castle. John Smyth, I have received your tre, but doe not think good to shew it to my lord least hee should leave his suits in law wherof I have soe good hope to a dangerous event, with an imagination that out of his own Judgment hee could conclude a profitable end upon the overture now made: These imaginations you know have not produced the best effects: If the motion for my sons marriage proceed, I doe then beleive the politicke lady will bee glad to come to an end; yet doe I fear her proffer rather proceeds of policy then from sincere meaning: I have observed that when shee sees any thing bending to our good, then shee proffers an agreement, and yet proceeds in lawe with all extremity. |

An: Co: of War:

Write weekly by the carier what is done with Sr George Carey; I beleive shee hath heard somwhat of that motion about our children, which makes this fained proffer of reference, but in any wise goe on with such circumspection in our law suites that shee may take noe advantage, and then leave the successe to God. I am very desirous to know what Sr George Carey intendeth to doe, not that I would have him know that I doe earnestly seek his resolution, for such forwardnes in mee will make him the more sparing in his offers: I doe affect the motion with that discretion, that I wish it as well for my lords comodity as my sons, but to the last I have the greatest regard.

852

My lord now writes to buy a suite of apparell for my son, wherein I would have good regard used, to bee of the fashion, sightly, fit for a young man, and of

a good

a good fhewe; not too coftly, not too meane, rather coftly then too meane; I hope it fhall bee ufed for fome caufe of comfort.

I have fent you here enclofed——10ˢ. to buy Ciceroes fentences, bound faire and of a good print; bee carefull of the reft of my books, and follow my lords fuits with diligent endeavours.

I hope Mr. Chamberlaine will ufe the matter according to my laft fpeech with him, that my lord fhall not bee fent for to come to London: If hee doe, his expences will bee great and his caufes rather hindred then furthered, not only law caufes, but the motion for my fon; hee is plodding upon many changes of devifes, not of the beft, which I feek to remove what I may; fome of them, if they fhould bee put in practice, would dafh all proceedings; being here with mee I can perfwade fomwhat, but at London younge crafty Courtiers will lay baites which will bee fwallowed with danger; the fafeft way is to keep him from London, foe tell him. Callowdon this prefent funday in hafte. May. 1595.

And in another of her tres to mee a few weeks after, hath thus; Whofoever intends to match with my fon fhall only deale with my lord and mee: Meanes of motioning of marriages there muft bee, and that hath been Mr. Chamberlyn from Sr. John Spencer, And now the wholl proceeding fhall bee by my lord and mee, and Sr. George Carey; hee is my kinfman whom I love, and ever have found freindly; ffor conclufion, if all offers bee performed, with direct dealing, upon their motion, to my lord and mee, by fome fufficient freind on their fide, my good will fhall appear in all reafonable fort, being not to my lords prejudice, and the parties likeing upon fight: Let my anfwer bee delivered according to the contents of my tre without either adding or diminifhing, my intent is honorable and plaine.

In the firft twenty years after her marriage fhee was given to all manner of delights befeeming her birth and calling, as before hath been touched; But after the beheading of the Duke of Norfolke her brother, and the frownes which State government had caft upon the reft, and others of her deareft kindred, with the harfh recoveries (or rather wreftings) of her hufbands poffeffions, as hath been declared, (then grown towards thirty eight or forty years,) fhee retired her felf into her chamber and private walks; which each faire day in garden, park, and other folytaries, for her fett houres, fhee conftantly obferved: not permitting either her gentleman ufher, gentlewoman, or any other of her houfe to come nearer

to

to her then their appointed diftance; When the wether permitted not abroad, fhee obferved the fame order in her great Chamber or gallary.

In her elder years fhee gave her felf to the ftudy of natural philofophy and Aftronomy. And (the better to continue her knowledge in the latin tongue) in reading over her grammer rules hath three or fower times called mee to explaine fomething therein, that fhe feemed not fully to apprehend; And in Hillary Terme A° 37. Eliz. I bought for her a globe, Blagraves mathematicall Jewell, a quadrate, Compafs, Rule, and other inftruments, wherein fhee much delighted her felf till her death.

I remember about three years before her death, one of her fingers in the two foremoft joynts put her to much paine, which caufed her to fend for an excellent Chirurgeon from Coventry, who told her plainly, That either it muft bee cut of by the palme of the hand, or elfe be launced all alonge to the bare bone; which latter though farre more painfull fhee made choice of; At the time appointed her Surgeon defired her to fit, and that fome of her ftrongeft | fervants might hold her, for the paine would bee extreame: To whom fhee replyed, fpare not you in performing your part, and leave the reft to mee: Shee held out her hand, hee did his office, fhee never blenched or fo much as feemed to take notice of the paine; At which Romanlike magnanimity and fortitude of mind, the Surgeon feemed incredibly to wonder, as often after hee told my felf and others.

Being in the 16th of Elizabeth the mother of three daughters, and almoft without hope of more children, efpecially of a fon, which fhee for continuance of her houfe and hufbands name much defired, extreamly greiving that the male line of this ancient family fhould end in her default, as fhee accounted it, Shee acquainted Mr Francis Aylworth therewith, then of Kington magna in Warwickfhire, a little old werifh man, but an excellent well read and practiced Chirurgeon and phyfitian, And for many years a gentleman living in her houfe; hee gave her hope of Conception, yea of a fon, if fhee and her lord would for a few months bee ruled by him; This in a private conference between them three was agreed upon and promifed to bee obferved.

    Children are given to men
    It's God that giveth them.

Shee conceived and within one yeare after this communication brought forth a fon called Thomas, father of the lord George of whom I am next to write, to her un-
                        fpeakable

speakable comfort, but never conceived after; what time M:̲ Aylworth told mee this story about ten years after at Callowdon, (which I have at second hand heard also that this lord hath privately told some others,) hee added, That some month or thereabouts before her time of delivery, shee sent for him and kept him with her, And hee, (out of what observation I know not) being confident shee went with a son, offered to wage with her ten pound to thirty pound, that soe it was; Shee accepted the offer, (most willing noe doubt to loose had the wager been thirty hundred;) Assoone as shee was delivered and understood it was a son, the first word shee spake was, carry Aylworth his thirty | pound, which purposely shee had laid ready in gold in her Chamber: This being the eleventh of July, Anno, 1575. Shee also prevailed with her husband to sell him the said manor of Kington magna in September following, for 520^{li}· which hee then held in lease for years, formerly by mee mentioned amongst this lords sale of his lands.

855

Anno: 17. Eliz:

fol: 820.

ffor the awing of her family, (I say not regulating the expence according to the revenue,) and the education of youth, shee had noe com-peere, which I could much inlarge by many perticulers: I will only mention one instance, That as my self, in the 26th of Elizabeth (then about seventeen,) crossed the upper part of the gallery at the ffryars in Coventry where shee then dwelt, and walked, having a covered dish in my hands with her sons breakfast, wherewith I was hastening, and thereby presented her, (then at the farther end,) wth a running legge or curtesy, as loth too longe to stay upon that duty, shee called mee back to her, and to make, ere I departed, one hundred leggs (soe to call them) at the least, And when I had done well and missed the like in my next assay, I was then to begin againe; And such was her great noblenes to mee therein, (then a boy of noe desert lately came from a Country Schoole, and but newly entred into her service,) That to shew mee the better how, shee lifted up all her garments to the calf of her legg that I might the better observe the grace of drawing back the foot and bowing of the knee: At this time the anticke and apish gestures since used in salutations, nor the ffrench garbes of cringing, were not arrived nor expected in England: But which is worse, your humble servant in subscriptions of lres, hath since that time almost driven your loving freind, quite out of England.

It cannot bee said That any apparant vice was in this lady, But it may bee said of a wife as of money, they are as they are used, helpers or hurters; money is a good servant but a bad master: And sure it is that shee much coveted to rule her husbands affaires at home and abroad, And to bee informed of the particular passages

of

of each of them, which somtimes brought forth harshnes at home, and turning off
of such servants as shee observed refractory to her intentions therein: As farre as
was possible, shee had in her middle and elder years a desire to bee informed from
the | grooms of her husbands bedchamber and otherwise, of his speeches, dispatches, 856
and purposes; few fines or Incombes from his tenants were raised, and never any
land sold, but shee had a fixt, 8th, or tenth thereout, unknown to him, so strictly held
shee obliged to her the servants and Officers imployed under her husband. (I write
mine own knowledge, for many of her last years,) And received the usage of former
times from my fellow Comissioners imployed in that kind many years before my
observations; by us all disliked, but by none of us to bee helped. Most just it is,
that all Toll should come into the right Tolldish: For the most part it falleth out
That where wives will rule all they marre all, words I lately heard from wise lords
in the Starchamber in the cases of the lady Lake, the Countesse of Suffolke, and
some others: These verses are ancient;

>Concerning wives, take this an certaine rule
>That if at first, you let them have the rule
>Your self with them at last shall bear no rule
>Except you let them evermore to rule.

For many of her first years after marriage, shee was allowed from her husbands
purse and his Receivors what shee spent and called for, but that proved more
burthensome then her husbands revenues could beare: After shee undertooke to
amend much that was amiss, and became his Receivor generall, to whom all officers
forraine and domestick made their Accompts, But that proving more unprofitable,
soone blasted: Lastly shee had . 300ll. by the yeare for her apparell and chamber
expences, which allowance continued till her death.

After this lady had seen her son, and two daughters maryed, growing by
degrees into a kind of Dropsey or watery timpany, shee departed this life the 7th of
Aprill in the 38th of Elizabeth, Anno, 1596. at Callowdon aforesaid, then of the age   Anno: 1596.
of ffifty eight years or thereabouts, And was buryed on Ascention day following,
then the twentieth of May in Saint Michãlls Church in Coventry with the greatest
state and | honor that for many years before had been seen in that Citie, or in those 857
parts of the kingdome, The manner whereof by direction of this lord Henry for his
private satisfaction (mourning all that time at Callowdon in his private chamber) I
put into writing, A labour the more readily undergone, as the last service I could
perform to the memory of her, who had to my younge years and education, both in

her

her houfe, at Oxford, and in the middle Temple continued my benefactrix by the penfion of Ten pound per Ann: which here I prefent Verbatim, out of my rough draught as I delivered it fairer written to this lord Henry, the third day after the funerall, viz*t*:

A Declaration of the funerall of the lady Katharine Berkeley, as it was performed on Thurfday the 20*th* of May, 1596. being Afcention day.

Her Corps having continued at Callowdon in the Chamber where fhee dyed, honored with all accuftomed Ceremonies afwell by night as by day, from wednefday the 7*th* of Aprill before, on w*ch* day fhee dyed, untill the fecond evening before the funerall, when the Coffin with her whole body inclofed was privately by perfons of good quallity conveyed by night to Coventry to the houfe of Sampfon Hopkins in the end of Earles Street; where honored with like ceremonies, it continued untill the funerall houre, which was in manner following.

The wholl traine being, as travellers from Callowdon and other places, affembled by ten of the clock in the forenoon, were by Garter king at Armes and Chefter herauld, fet in order and directed thus to proceed from the faid houfe to the Church of S*t* Michaell, in this manner.

ffirst went fix of your principall yeomen called the conductors of the traine, in longe black clokes, with black ftaves in their hands, directed to conduct the traine all the length of that ftreet, to the Barre yates, and thence to croffe cheeping, and foe through the north fide of Trinity churchyard, to the great weft doore of S*t* Michaells church: Both fides of which paffage neare a quarter of a mile longe, was impaled by many thoufands of people affembled to behold the honor thereof; Next after thofe fix conductors, in mourning gownes and Holland kercheefes, came 70 poore weomen; Then came thirty gentlemens fervants in black coats, Then followed the fervants of gentlemen and Efquires in black clokes; Next them the fervants of knights in black clokes alfo; Then came your Lo*rs* yeomen, And after them your gentlemen (all two by two) with fome of the lady Stranges gentlemen interplaced with them, yours being 74. whereof my felf went as one of her fecretaries; Then the officers of your houfhold, as Clark of the kitchen, gentlemen of the horfe, Auditor, and Steward, in their gowns and hoods, your Steward bearing a white rod in his hand: Next behind the Steward came M*r* Henry Beamont bearing the great banner of honnor; After him followed the Efquires and cheefe gentlemen of the Country, as M*r* Clement ffifher, M*r* William Cotton, M*r* Elmes, M*r* ffulke Butteris,

young

young Mr. Beamont, &c. Then came your Lopr. Chaplins, And after them, and next before the Coffin, went Chester herald affisted by Mr. Walter Denis as a neceffary marshall to the better direction of the traine. The Coffin was borne by eight of your cheife gentlemen and yeomen, and fupported by fower other gentlemen of moft note; vizt. Mr. Edward Deveroux, Sr. John Spencer, Sr. Thomas Leigh, and Mr. George Shirley your fon in law.

Neere to the fower corners whereof, went fower Efqrs. vizt., Mr. Robert Spencer fon and heire of the faid Sr. John, Mr. Bafell ffeilding of Newnham, Mr. Samuell Marrowe, and Mr. William Norwood, each of them bearing a Baneroll, with her Armes and your Lopr. quartered.

Next behind the Coffin came Mr. Richard White as her gentleman ufher, with a fmall white rod in his hand, accompanied with the gentleman ufher of the lady Strange, both of them bareheaded, between whom went Garter in his kingly Coate of Armes. |

Next after them came the lady Strange, eldeft daughter to the late Earle of Derby, and for this day principall mournereffe, in her gown, mantle, trayne, hood, and tippet of blacke, and in her parys head, tippet, wimple, vaile, and barbe of fine lawne; on whofe right hand went your fon Sr. Thomas Berkeley, and on her left hand your brother in law Sr. George Carey, fupporting her by the Armes, called the two principall affiftants, who were apparelled in their gowns, hoods and tippetts of fineft black: Then came Mrs. Audeley Denis bearing the trayne of the principall mournereffe, apparelled as an Efquireffe in her gowne and lyned hood of black, with a pleated kercheefe and barbe of lawne.

Then came Mrs. Elizabeth Berkeley your daughter in lawe, and the lady Carey, fide by fide, apparelled as Baroneffes, and in all points futable to the principall Mournereffe, fave that their traines were tucked up and not borne.

Then followed in femblable order Mrs. Deveroux and lady Leigh, apparelled as knights wives, in their black gownes, hoods, and tippetts, and in their round parys heads, boungrace, and barbes of fine lawnes.

In anfwerable order, next came Mrs. Beomont and Mrs. Spencer apparelled as knights wives like the former; which feaven were called the feaven principall mournereffes and eftates of the funeralls.

Next

Next after whom in like correspondency, two by two, came fower Esquiresses, viz*, M***. ffeilding, M***. ffisher, and her daughter, and M***. Dilkes, apparelled as the trainbearer, save that they wanted hoods.

Then followed your late ladys gentlemen, the principall mouneresses two gentlewomen, knights and Esquires wives gentleweomen, all like apparelled in black gownes, kercheefes, and barbes of lawn, to the number of fourteen; And next after these came eight Chambermaids, servants to the estates and ladies aforesaid, in gowns and kercheifs of lawne only, All which were furnished at the only charges of your L.^dship.

After all these and last of all came M^r. Maior of Coventry, the Sherriffs, Aldermen and Comons in great number, & great proporcõn. |

In this order passed this traine with slow steps and frequent pauses to the church aforesaid, In the first Isle whereof stood the foresaid 70. poore weomen paling the passage on either side, through whom passed the whole action up to the east end of the church, where the pulpit was purposly placed, and also the hearse.

The 7. principall mouneresses were placed by M^r. Garter king at Armes within the inward raile of the hearse with their faces towards the same; And the rest of the Gentlemen, ministers to the funerall, were placed in the utter railes about two yards distant from the Pall of the Coffin; All others in seats next adjoyning.

The company thus placed, And the psalme ended, (which had received the corse at the entrance into the Church,) your Chaplyn Edward Cowper ascended the pulpit, And towards the end of his learned sermon tooke a fit occation to speak of her learned and virtuous life, (a lady never known to dissemble or heard to swere, which speech (modestly carryed,) sealed also with the knowledge of many hundreds there present,) wrought such effect, That seldom hath been beheld a more sorrowfull assembly at a subjects funerall, nor teares more droping down.

The sermon ended another psalme was begun, during which all such mourners as before are said to weare heads of lawne, togeather with the two assistants, walked in procession wise about the hearse: In which procession the waiting gentlewomen and chamber maids were severed from the rest, and aptly seated on one side the Isle extending to the offertory, where they continued till all ceremonies were ended:

But

But all the reft by their circuler walk were feated in their former places; which done, the offertory began, firft by the principall mournereffe, and after by the other fix each conducted by M: Garter. Then were the banners offered up by fuch as formerly I have noted to beare them; which finifhed, M: Berkeley your eldeft fon, was by M: Garter led to the offertory and there by him invefted with the honor of his deceafed mother, by delivery and acceptance of the banners and | other ceremonies; which done, and hee folemly conducted back to his former place, Then were next brought before the herfe the two principall officers of houfhold, the fteward and gentleman ufher, who after many obeyfances and humble reverences, brake their rods, commending them to the cuftody of the corps and herfe: which ceremony ended, the whole company arofe, And in the order they came returned to M: Hopkins houfe aforefaid, and thence to Callowdon, where your Lo:P for them and many hundreds more had foe plentifully provided, That the exceffe herein appeared, when with fuch difhes as for the moft part paffed untouched at former tables, more then one thoufand poore people were plentifully fed the fame afternoone: And thus have you performed that part of your late lre to her brother the lord Henry Howard, That as her life was honorable, foe you intended her funerall fhould bee. Finis. Thus the paper I delivered to this lord.

Her body was after interred in a vault in the northeaft corner of that Church neare the drapers Chappell there; And I think it hardly poffible to have all things better performed then were at this funerall, and after at the feaft, wherein noe error was by any obferved to bee committed, foe carefull were the fervants of this lord in their feverall offices and charge comitted to them; who alfo for more comlines had attired themfelves, the gentlemen in black fattin fuites and black filk ftockings with gold chaynes folded in black fcarfes, And the yeomen in filk rafhes,[1] grograns,[2] and taffetyes, of black colours.

<blockquote>
Reliquit nomen, narrantur laudes.
God graunt us all fuch race to runne,
To end in Chrift, as fhee hath done.[3]
</blockquote>

His

---

[1] Rafh, a kind of inferior filk.

[2] Grograin, a coarfe kind of filk taffety ufually ftiffened with gum.

[3] Sir Gilbert Dethick, who at this time held the Office of Garter King of Arms, and Marfhalled the proceffion, has left in his "Funerals of Nobility," (1584—1603, Vol. II., pp. 528, 531, MS. in Heralds' College,) an account of this Funeral, for Notes from which we are indebted to the courtefy of S. I. Tucker, Efq., *Somerfet Herald*. The defcription agrees, except flightly in the number of perfons prefent, with that

His second wife.

862   **His** fecond wife was Jane daughter of Sʳ Michaell Stanhope | and widow of Sir Roger Townfend, whom before hee had two years continued widower hee maryed at Sᵗ Giles Church without Creplegate in London, the Ninth of March in the fortieth of Elizabeth Aᵒ 1597, then aged about 64, who furvived him, And after dyed at her houfe in Barbican on Satterday the third of January in the 15ᵗʰ of king James, 1617, in as ripe an age, loaden with many honorable and well reported daies.

Carta in caftro de Berkeley dat. 8. marcij : 40. Eliz :

Howbeit, fuch was not alwaies the accord, but for this lords not performance of fuch Covenants as hee had entred into the day before his marriage, to the lord Thomas

of Smyth in the text, but it gives an account of fome of the charges on fuch occafions, which may be read with intereft. The following is the Bill of the Heraldic Painter :—

The Painters Bylle for the funeralle of the Righte Honorable the Ladye Berkley—

Item for a great banner of Armes	2 10 0
Item for iiijᵒʳ Bannerowles at xxvjˢ viij the pece	5 6 8
Item for iiijᵒʳ Dozen penfcles at xˢ the dozen	2 0 0
Item for iiijᵒʳ Watertables wᵗʰ fupporters and Crefte	2 0 0
Item for iiijᵒʳ Comptement Efcutcheons one pafte borde	1 0 0
Item for vj Scrowles wᵗʰ words one pafte borde	0 18 0
Item for one dozen of great buckram Efcutcheons	1 4 0
Item for one Dozen and a halfe of fmalle buckram Efcutcheons	0 18 0
Item for v. Dozen of pap Efcutcheons on meatale	5 0 0
Item for v. Dozen of pap Efcutcheons in Cullers	4 10 0
*Item the Irons and black ftones	[0 3 4]
Som is	25ˡⁱ 10ˢ 0

Robert Hooker

To which muft be added the following—

Mʳ G[arter] fee	xˡⁱ
Gown and Liveries	xˡⁱ
Tranfportañ	vij. viijˢ

Dettes and Charges

To Chefter [James Thomas, Efq. was Chefter Herald at this time]	iiijˡⁱ vjˢ viijᵈ
Gown and lyveries	iiijˡⁱ xvjˢ viijᵈ
Tranfportañ	iijˡⁱ xivˢ
*The velvete pall and hearfe	
The paynters charges for Banʳˢ etc.	xxvj xiij iijᵈ

Mr. John Smyth fervant to the Lo. Barkeley hathe a note of a pedigre of me.   [Eᴅ.]

* The amounts of thefe items are not filled in. In the firft cafe 3ˢ 4ᵈ is required to make the total correct.

Thomas Howard, (after Earle of Suffolke,) and to her brother Sir Michaell Stanhope and others, which hee was charged in many tres and rescripts to have broken; They at her request and pressure, extended his lands in Gloucestershire upon a Statute of ten thousand pounds given by this lord for performance of those covenants, As by the Inquisition thereof taken at Berkeley the 15th of January in the 42th of Elizabeth appeareth; Whereupon shortly after followed such an agreement, as occationed the sale of all the manors and lands which this lord had in the County of Huntington, to Sir John Spencer an Alderman of London, as before is written.

Rescripts. 1599. et al annis.

fol: 822.

Many learned men have longe since censured this amorous humour or dotage in old men. And Ovid in this disticke,

> Militat in teneris annis amor, hospes amænus,
> Est in canitie ridiculosa venus.
> In young men love is pleasant to behold,
> But t'is rediculous, in one that's old.

And divers Canonists doe hold, That an old man cannot lawfully bee marryed, for say they, The end of marriage is only twofold, for procreation of Children, and avoidance of fornication; And that if but one of these two ends bee only aymed at, the marriage is not good.

Seneca Plutarch Comes purtilcar Ovidius Naso.

Portius institut: Secinus cons: et al.

And St Ambrose in his comentary upon St Luke, And St | Augustine, say That such a mariage without hope of Children, non matrimonium sed concubium dici debet, is not to bee called an holy wedlock, or mariage, but a copulation or coming togeather; But I write the words of others, my self being farre from censuring this honorable couple: Howbeit, neither of those two ends could bee in this marriage, nor the third, Of mutuall society help and comfort; ffor as they never bedded togeather that any of their attendants could observe, whereby they might have become one flesh; soe were themselves and their families for most part as farre asunder as Barbican in London, and Callowdon by Coventry: neither medled hee more with her lands or goods, or ought else that was hers, then with her.

863
Ambrose. Augustine. Burtons descr: of Leicrshire fol: 217:

His Issue.

By the lady Katharine this lord Henry had issue, Thomas, Mary, and ffrances, of whom it followeth; And also fferdinando, born at Yate in the second year of Queen Elizabeth and was buryed in the Chancell of that church about two years after:

after: Katharine there alfo borne about two year after her brother, who alfo dyed young: And Jane born about the 8th of Elizabeth at Callowdon, and dyed in the 16th of Elizabeth and is buryed at Sowe Church by Callowdon; whofe untimely death, (If I have been truly informed,) was occationed by mifeating part of a rofted apple prepared with Arfnicke for the poyfoning of rats; An accident with great fecrefy concealed from the parents.

Thomas.

Thomas eldeft fon of this lord Henry is of right to bee numbred in the honorable Catalogue of his forefathers, And juftly in thefe Collections to bee one of the one and twenty in their | generations, hee being the maine bridge by which the Caftle, honor, and Barony of Berkeley, is conveyed to the lord George his fon and his fucceffion; Neither doth his death in the life of his father, prejudice the number; whom for diftinctions fake I will call, Thomas the fhort liver.

864

fol: 854.

Hee was born at Callowdon the 11th of July in the 17th of Queen Elizabeth, 1575. as formerly it hath been written; at what time Queen Elizabeth was at Kenilworth Caftle the houfe of the oft named Robert Dudley then Earle of Leicefter, fix miles thence, whereby fhee by Anne Countes of Warrwick her deputy, became his godmother: The moft part of his education was at Callowdon under the indulgent inftruction of his mother and her waiting gentlewomen, whom in nine years they had only taught to fpell and meanly read a little Englifh: Then was hee provided of the faid Edward Cowper from Trinity Colledge in Oxford, to bee his Schoolmafter, who after made his mothers funerall fermon; what time this lord being with his family newly returned from fojourning with old Sr. John Savage his cozen germaine at Baraper in Hampfhire, continuing at the ffryars in Coventry, which for three years hee had taken by leafe of one John Hales Efqr.

Anno: 26. Eliz: 1584.

To this place the 10th of November, Anno, 1584, a fewe daies after Mr. Cowper, my felf then feventeen years of age, happily came from the ffreefchoole of Derby to attend to Sir Thomas Berkeley in his chamber; what time alfo came William Ligon (formerly mentioned amongft the iffues of the lord Maurice the fifth,) for the fame intent, with hopes alfo that one of us might benefit the other at our books: Here wee all continued for two years more as fervants and fchollers with him; At which place as hee (with fome others) played togeather in the paved cloifters, by a fmall flipp of his foot hee fell and brake his channell bone foe notwithftanding borne out by him, That the caufe of his ficknes was not perceived, till it fo drew his head and neck awry that it was difcernable all his life after.

fol. 629

ffrom

ffrom hence this lord his father removed with his family to his | own houfe at Callowdon; from thence hee with his tutor, Wittm Ligon, and my felf went to Magdalen Colledge in Oxford in ffebruary, Anno 1589, in the 32th year of Elizabeth where after three years, leaving them, I removed to ftudy the Comon laws in the Middle Temple in London; After my departure from Oxford, a dangerous ficknes befell him in the nature of a burning feaver, (as alfo did a quartan ague his Tutor,) from the dreggs whereof his future days were never cleared: Being from Oxford returned to Callowdon, and coming from thence to London with this lord his father in Michaelmas Terme, Anno, 1595. fuch affection (upon motion formerly made) grewe between him (then lodging with his father at Thomas Johnfons houfe in fleet ftreet,) and Elizabeth Carey only child of Sr George Carey, then knight marfhall and governour of the Ifle of wight, then living at his houfe in the black ffryars, That on Thurfday the 19th of ffebruary following, Anno 1595, in the faid 38th of Elizabeth, they were maryed togeather: The articles of agreement concerning wch marriage were drawn and fealed the fame morning, whereof I fhall fomwhat afterwards write; And on Thurfday the 29th of July following dyed the lord Henry Hunfdon father of the faid Sr George, whofe authority and greatnes in the Comonwealth know by his ftile, which in dedications was in thefe words; To the R^t Honble Henry Carey, of the moft honorable order of the Garter knight, Baron of Hunfdon, lord governour of her Maties Town of Berwicke, lord Warden of the Eaft and middle marches of England againft Scotland, Captaine of Norham Caftle, Captaine of her highnes gentlemen pentioners, Juftice of Eyer of all her Maties Forrefts, Parkes and Chaces on this fide Trent, Lord Chamberlaine of her Maties houfhold, and one of her highnes moft honorable privy counfell: And for his approved fidelity, wifdom, valour, and circumfpection, (the words of the patent under the proper hand of Queen Elizabeth,) was on the 29th of July in the 30th of her raigne, Anno, 1588. made Lievtenant, principall Captaine and governour of and over the Queens Army then affembled for defence of her royall perfon, againft that fearfull Invafion of the Spaniard, with as ample power as the State and neceffity of that time required, | or could by termes of lawe bee given; And the 11th of May in the 36th of the faid Queen was made Leivtenant of the Counties of Norfolk and Suffolke; Then whom a more loyall fubject to his Prince lived not in his daies; To whom hee was cozen germaine, As being fon of William Carey and of the lady Mary his wife, fecond fifter and co-heire to Anne Bullen, fecond wife to king Henry the 8th mother of the faid Queen Elizabeth: And they the faid Mary and Anne were daughters and coheires of Thomas Bullen Earle of Ormond and of Wiltfhire, and of the lady Mary his wife daughter of Thomas Howard Duke of Norfolke:

which

Margin notes:
Anno: 37. et. 38. Eliz:

Articl: dat. 10. ffeb: 38. Eliz: Conveiance: dat. 6. Maij: 39. Eliz:

carta in caftro de Berkeley.

Carta in Caft: p^{r}dict.

which Thomas Bullen was son and heire of Margaret one of the two daughters and coheirs of Thomas Butler Earle of Ormond,

> This happy lord, still loyall to the Crown,
> Hath left an heire, heire to his renown.

<small>Anno: 39. Eliz: 1597.</small>

For the said Sr George Carey, now by the death of his father become Baron of Hunsdon, was the 17th of Aprill following sworn of the privy Counsell and made lord Chamberlaine of the Queens houshold, And on St Georges day after, knight of the most honorable order of the Garter, which (with other eminencies of honor and authority) hee enjoyed till the 8th of September in the first of king James, Anno, 1603, when hee left this life, And lyeth most honorably buryed in the midst of St John Baptist Chapple in Westm.^r, a place of buriall for the family of the Careys; A lord of such perfection of person and inside, that I cannot parralell his character; I would render him the right of honor hee deserved, but for robbing his daughter of that memoriall shee oweth to the life of soe learned and prudent a father.

<small>His motto was Comme ie trouve</small>

The said Elizabeth was born the 24th of May in the 18th of Queen Elizabeth, Anno 1576, who was godmother to her, as before shee is said to bee to her husband.

The fruits of the marriage appeared by the birth of Theophila their daughter, born at the said black fryars house on saturday half an hour after six in the morning, the 11th of December, 42 | weeks and 2 daies next after their mariage, Anno 1596, And was christened the 30th of the same month; To whom also the said Queen was godmother, And Robert Deveroux Earle of Essex was godfather; from which Stock issued also George now lord Berkeley born the 7th of October, 1601. in the 43th of Elizabeth, As after more fully followeth.

<small>867</small>

The portion which the said Elizabeth brought in money, was 1000^{li}, and of land near to the value of 1000^{li} p Ann, in Tunbridge and Hadlow in Kent, which was estated upon her and her heirs after the death of her father and mother, besides what shee might further expect from either of them, as being their only child and heire; In returne whereof, this lord Berkeley then covenanted to convey, (which in the next year he performed,) those manors and lands hereafter mentioned in the last title of his life, whereto the Termes, yeares, and number rolls following, will guide his posterity to such parts of those assurances as are inrolled, or of record; vizt, The licence to alien is dated the 2 Aprill. 39. Eliz: enrolled in the Chancery that yeare; And also inrolled in the Exchequer in Trinity. 16. Jac: ex pte Rem̃
Thesaur̃:

Thesaur̄: And the bargaine & sale made to Sir John Spencer and Arthur Mills is dated 20 Aprill 39. Eliz: inrolled in Chancery also.

The Recovery of Callowdon is; Terme Pasche 39. Elizabeth, Rot: 105.
The Recovery of the honor Castle and Barony of Berkeley and of all the Gloucestershire lands, is Terme Pasche 39 Eliz: also. Rot: 113.
The Recovery of Portbury and Porteshead is eod̄ anno et Terme Rot. 105.
The Recovery of Leicestershire lands is eod̄ anno et terme. rot. 104.
The Recovery of Sussex lands is eod̄ anno et terme. rot. 104.

Upon the death of Queen Eliz: this Thomas went into Scotland to carry king James newes of being proclaimed king, whom his wife with other honorable ladies shortly after followed; And at the Coronation of king James this Thomas was created knight of the Bath: And for the Parliament begun the same year was chosen one of the knights for Gloucestershire, wherein hee served.

Truth of story tells this family, That this noble knight S.r Thomas was profuse in expence beyond his ordinary means: for support of which excesse, hee sold (without consent of this lord his father) the remainders in the manor of Upton S.t Leonards by Glouc. to S.r Arthur Ligon for——1100.li And in the three parks of Portbury manor with ffluellins farme adjoyning, to S.r Edward Gorges for——1400.li And in Upton farme by Tetbury to M.r John Berkeley for——330.li And had also——4320.li raised upon the sales of Coldoverton and Daglingworth, wherein his father joyned in the Conveyances, as formerly is mentioned amongst his Sales; And some other moneys were raised by him upon demises in Tetbury, Hame, Melton, Bitton, Binley, Sowe and Wiken: which when all those monies sufficed not, (that amounted to——7400.li,) his wife also in May in the fourth of king James gave free way to the sale of his revertion in Tundridge and Hadlowe, for which shee and her husband received of S.r John Kenedy——8450.li The greatest part whereof sufficed not for clearing of debts: So that it is truly transmitted to their posterity, That in the first fourteen years after their marriage, (Accompting the composition monies received of the lord Rich and some others for Bullens title, which the said lady pretended as heire to Queen Elizabeth on the mothers side,) they spent each year more then——1500.li above that Anuity of——600.li proportioned unto them upon their mariage to have sufficed for their parents lives. **And** I well remember, that the said lady Elizabeth Berkeley having, in a private accompt of her own hand writing, set down how and to whom and for what causes——6955.li 7.s of the foresaid——8450.li was paid away

away and gone, Shee fubfcribed under that accompt privately to her felf thefe very words; Of which I hope in God the like will never bee again; whereof I the rather took notice, To the end I might often there to the better fay, Amen. Amen.[1]

[1] It was probably thefe circumftances which led to the following agreement for the retrenchment of expenfes, a copy of which we found at Condover Hall:

Articles agreed upon between Sir Thomas Barkly knight, and the lady Elizabeth, his wife, and John Smyth gent. the 16th day of December 1609 Annoque Septimo Regis Jacobi, touching the expenfes and government of his houfhold at the lodge in Newparke in the county of Gloucefter.

1.—Imprimis, it is agreed that the faid family fhall not exceed the number of 18 perfons over and befide the faid Sir Thomas Barkly and his lady and their children.

2.—Item, the faid Sir Thomas Barkely promifeth hereby to deliver every year to the faid John Smyth towards the charges of the faid houfe the fum of ccccli, by two equal payments to be made within one month after the feveral feafts of the Anunciation of our lady and of St. Michael tharchangel, fave that £65 of the firft payment is now to be delivered to the faid John Smith, which at this prefent remaineth in the hands of the Right honorable the lord Barkely, being the money of the faid Sir Thomas.

3.—Item, the faid lady Elizabeth and John Smyth hereby promife to maintain and keep the faid family in that eftate degree and calling, that ftandeth with the reputation of a knight and his lady, being both of them defcended of honourable parents, with all manner of neceffaries for houfkeeping in bread, beer, wine, acates,* fire wood, hay, litter and oats.

4.—Item, the faid Sir Thomas promifeth not to keep in his ftable at one time together above the number of four horfes, geldings and mares.

5.—Item, the faid Sir Thomas promifeth on the word of a true gent., that after one or two admonitions and no amendment he will not keep in his faid family any drunkard, fwearer, incontinent or any other diforderly perfon, but will give credit to the information of the faid John Smyth touching the fame.

6.—Item, it is agreed that the faid lady and John Smyth fhall not be charged with reparations of the faid houfe or ftable, nor with finding any linens, brafs, pewter, implements or furniture of houfhold, but that the fame is to be at the charges of the faid Sir Thomas or the faid Lo: Barkely.

7.—Item, it is agreed that this agreement fhall ftand during the life of the faid Lord Barkely unlefs the faid Sir Thomas fhall give three months warning for the diffolution of his family.

8.—Item, it is agreed that the faid lady and John Smith fhall keep all the year long fix couple of hounds for the faid Sir Thomas' delight and recreation with the huntfmen.

Signed by T. BARKLY, ELIZA BARKELY and JOHN SMYTHE.

* Provifions purchafed.

I, and all choice that plenty can fend in;
Bread, wine, *acates*, fowl, feather, fifh, or fin.—*Sad Shepherd*, I. 3.

[ED.]

It may not bee denyed, That this noble knight was inconstant | and too **869** sodaine in his determinations: **In** the years, 1600, 1608 and, 1610, hee thrice posted into ffrance, to Paris, Roan, Orleance, and over the Alpes, visiting Rome, Naples, Venice, and many other the cheifest Cities of those States and Kingdomes; And in their returnes, Brussells and many principall Towns in the united provinces; from the last of which voyages, (much shortened by the lres of his wife sent after him by William Ligon before named, whom for that service shee did reward with *Willm Ligon. pat.* an Anuity of ten pound p Anñ,) hee returned not a year before his death; whom *dat: 24. Apr: 1611.* also hee himself had formerly rewarded with a lease for one and twenty years of Appleridge grounds in Berkeley parish, by fine in revercōn of the estate for life held *fine: 43. Eliz: to* by his unckle Walter Denys; which fine soe levyed without Lycence, longe after *Norwood.* brought trouble and expence in the Exchequer, the tenure thereof being by knights *Licence 3. ps.* service in Capite. *origiñ 44. Eliz: rot. 155. cm rem thesaur̄.*

And having with much weaknes passed over the later part of Summer after his said returne, at Berkeley Castle with this lord his father, (from whence for change of air and hope of better health it vouchsafed him to remove to my house at Nibley, three miles of,) hee returned with his wife and father in the end of September to Callowdon; where hee yeilded to nature the 22th of November following, in the 9th of king James Anno 1611, then of the age of thirty six years fower monthes and eleaven daies; And was buried in the northeast corner of St Michaells Church in Coventry, within the same Iron grate wherein his mother lyeth: whose tombe (beautifully erected by his sorrowfull widow) hath this inscription: Here lyeth *Epitaph* expecting a Joyfull resurrection the body of Sr Thomas Berkeley, kn^t, only son of the R^t Honble Henry lord Berkeley and of the lady Katharine his wife sister of Thomas Howard Duke of Norfolke; who by Elizabeth his wife sole daughter and heir of the right honorable George lord Hunsdon, lord Chamberlaine to our late Soveraigne lady Queen Elizabeth, left issue George and Theophila the only children of six whom death had spared to attend their fathers funeralls and to bee the comfort of their mother; | to whose perpetuall memory shee hath erected this her **870** husbands monument: In which also lyeth the body of Henry the youngest of their *born after his* children; The said Sr Thomas Berkeley deceased the 22th of November, Anno, *fathers death.* 1611, ætatis suæ, 37°. And the said Henry his son deceased the 4th of March *Anno. 9. Jac:* following. Soe the Tombe.

The manner of whose death read out of an Almanack of that year, written with the proper hand of the said lady his wife, in these words; **This** 22th day of November

November between one and two in the afternoon, it pleafed God to take my deare hufband from mee, by a moft gentle and milde death without groane or ftruglinge, to encourage all the lookers on of Gods great mercy towards him, who like a lambe left this troublefome world to enjoy perfect reft in God, I truft. Jefu reft his foule. Thus the Lady.

Somwhat more remaineth of the life of the noble knight, which I leave to the relation of his lady (ftill his widow) whereof to informe her fon, if fhee foe pleafe: The way hee walked in to mee feems fomwhat foule, which becaufe I will not wade through I will leap over and foe avoid: Only adding, That after his death a fecret paper of his own hand writing was found in his Cabinet, amongft other private remembrances, wherein his nativity by a grand Impoftor beyond feas feemed curioufly and exactly calculated, in quality of a journall of each years accidents and fucceffes which fhould befall him, with an affured promife of a longe life and an happy old age; whereon though hee too much relyed, yet underneath the fame paper himfelf had written thefe very words; But although thefe planets doe promife good fortune, as minifters that doe demonftrate the glory of God, and are altogeather over ruled by him, and have noe influence or vertue without him; To his power and mercy I only comit my felf, affuring that hee never faileth thofe that put their truft in him; To whom bee given all honor glory and praife for ever, Amen. Thus the writing, which I copyed out verbatim. |

871

His foule afpiringe to an higher fphere,
Is glad that it did reape noe comfort here.
Conditione pares, mortales nafcimur omnes,
   Nos rapit et fatum, conditione pares;
Conditione pares, quamvis non vivimus omnes,
   Nafcimur et morimur, conditione pares.

Theophila.

The education of the faid Theophila was both in Court and Country under the fole direction of her mother: Towards whom (with thofe that have the means truly to obferve) is drawn an admiration of her vertues and perfections. A lady whofe hourly life adds a dayly luftre to the noble families from whence fhee is extracted: At the maryage of the lady Elizabeth to the Prince Palfgrave fhee had the honor to bee one of her Bridemaids.

Anno. 1613.

On Thurfday the 12th of Auguft in the 11th of king James in the forenoone, fhee was at Berkeley Church marryed to Sr Robert Coke knight fon and heire of
                                                                   Sr Edward

Sr Edward Coke then cheife Juſtice of the comon pleas, and of Bridget his wife daughter and coheire of John Paſton Eſq.^r, ſon of Robert Coke and Winifred his wife, daughter and Coheir of William Knightley, ſon of Robert Coke and of Anne his wife, daughter of Thomas Woodhouſe, ſon of Thomas Coke and of Alice his wife, ſiſter and Coheire of Thomas ffolchard, ſon of John Coke ſon of Robert, ſon of John Coke who lived in the time of king Henry the fifth. **In** the treaty of which marriage I had the honor of imployment between Callowdon and London, (where the parents and freinds of both parties interreſſed then remained,) in divers Journeys for fower months before, (eſpecially under her mothers directions,) with equall truſt of all parties: ſome paſſages wherein might not unprofitably bee derived to poſterity, ſave that all the perſonages themſelves, (this lord excepted,) with the matter negotiated, yet live the moſt aſſured memorialls to themſelves. But how contenting on this lord Berkeleys part this mariage of his grandchild was, by this may bee collected, | That when Henry Briggs his chaplin demaunded in the time of mariage, who giveth this woman to bee maryed to this man, Hee coming out of his ſeat in the Church, (where hee ſate with Sr Edward Coke,) taking her by the hand, That doe I, quoth hee, with all my heart: By which ſweet addition of the words (with all my heart) hee not only declared the contentment of his own, but drew tears of joy from the eies of the Bridegroomes father, to both which mine eares and eyes were witneſſes.

872

And the lord Coke the ſame day after dinner retiring into his chamber, forthwith brought forth theſe latin verſes by him then made, alludeing to the maryage and the day, being St Clares day,

        Clara dies Claræ, virgo quâ clara marita eſt
        Clara priùs virgo, clarior vxor erit.

And alluding to the planets of that day,

        Ecce hodie coeunt cæleſtia ſidera, phæbi
        Pulchri cum pulchra virgine ludit amor.

And againe alluding to their names,

        Clara dies Claræ, conjunxit pignora chara,
        Clarum Theophila et nomen et omen habet,
        Et prolem numeroſam (clare Roberte) precatur,
        Sanguis uturque tibi, et magna caterva virum.

A day ſtill honored with a feſtivall memoriall wherever the Bride and Bridegroome hap to bee: A wedlock bleſſed with ſuch a mutuall Sympathy and ſweetnes, that they ſeem to live one in the other. **Other** the like ſongs of joy and contentment
                                                                                     proceeded

proceeded from that learned phyſition Doctor Edward Lapworth, and other ſchollers then preſent; which if I had preſerved, aſwell as the catalogue of the 24 names of gentlemen of honor and Armes then preſent, and delivered by mee upon the requeſt of the ſaid cheife Juſtice, they had herein alſo appeared.

fol: 848.
873

Lr̃e in caſtro de Berkeley.

Neither ſeemeth it a digreſſion to remember, That as this lord brought his noble gueſts on their way towards Cirenceſter about a week after the mariage, hee and the lord Coke riding in one Coach togeather, the ſame was by the violent courſe and fury of the ſower | Coach horſes overthrown and dragged by their force a good diſtance on the ground: Out of which when they were taken, And conſideration had of the great danger their lives had eſcaped without hurt, It moved one of them preſently to ſay, and the 24ᵗʰ of the ſame month to write from ſtoke in Buckinghamſhire with comfort, That hee never heard That out of ſoe great danger there iſſued ſoe little harme, eſpetially to perſons ſo farre ſtepped in yeares.

Mary.
Comp: hoſpicij in caſtro de Berekely.

Mary, eldeſt daughter of this lord was born at London, whither her mother was brought in a litter from Yate the ſecond of October in the 5ᵗʰ of Queen Mary, with her midwife fetched from Chedder in Somꝛſet ſhire, whoſe reward, for her ſervice in that perill of childbirth was—6ˢ 8ᵈ at her departure; And chriſtened the 19ᵗʰ of November following in the ſaid 5ᵗʰ of Queen Mary, to whom Queen Mary was godmother: And this Mary was after maryed at the white ffryars in Coventry the 14ᵗʰ of ffebruary (being Sᵗ Valentines day) in the 27ᵗʰ of Queen Elizabeth, Anno 1584, to John Zouch Eſquire, (after knight,) then ſon and heire apparant of Sʳ John Zouch of Codnor caſtle in Derby ſhire, who dyed ſhortly after; hee then of the age of twenty and ſhee almoſt thirty: whereby out of an youthfull appetite hee afterwards diſcontentedly objected that hee was ignorantly married to his mother.

Her portion was—2500ˡⁱ in money, beſides—500ˡⁱ for her apparrell, and jewells for the ornament of her perſon.

Her joynture after his death was at her marriage agreed to have been 500ˡⁱ p Anñ, but the error of thoſe of Counſell therein, much leſſened the ſame. A marriage whereat no ſinging was of I-opean, nor epithalamians to Juno the goddeſſe of marriage, for it was only bleſſed in the birth of their two children John and Anne, which were in fewe years born unto them.

It was not fower years after marriage before unkindnes aroſe between them; And when (moſt cauſleſſly) ſhee had been repudiated by him, hee in the 33ᵗʰ of
Elizabeth

Elizabeth granted her an Anuity of 200ˡⁱ p annum for her prefent maintenance, which being not more malevolently yeilded | unto then worfe paid, many fuits arofe againft him by this lord Henry and her freinds put in truft therein; who alfo extended his lands upon a Statute given and forfeited by him, And after obtained a Decree in Chancery for better payment of the 200ˡⁱ Anuity.

874

Hill: 33. Eliz:

Neither found the lady Elleanor Zouch his mother much better favor from this her fon, as the fuits between them in Chancery and other Courts, whereto fhee was enforced for her Joynture, doe declare; And in the end having prodigally confumed his patrimony, felt the heavy waight of want, and dyed in the 8ᵗʰ year of king James, leaving iffue the faid John and Anne; which Anne after dyed without iffue: And the faid John (now knight) of Codnor Caftle aforefaid, which hee by fuite recovered after his fathers death, maried Ifable daughter of Patrick Lowe of Denby in the faid County Efqʳ by whom hee hath iffue, John, Katharine, Ifable, and Elizabeth, Anno, 1624.

Frances, youngeft daughter of this lord Henry was borne at Yate in the third year of Queen Elizabeth, And from thence brought in a litter to Callowdon in June in the 7ᵗʰ yeare of the faid Queen, And there married to George Shirley of Aftwell in the County of Northton Efqʳ, (after Baronet) the 22ᵗʰ day of ffebruary in the 29ᵗʰ of Eliz: 1586.

Frances.
Comp: Willi Lawrence 7. Eliz: in caftro de Berkeley.
The licence dated 12. ffebr: 1586. for their marriage.

Her portion was—2500ˡⁱ· And in apparrell and Jewells as her elder fifters: of the provifions made for Joynture of the wife, and for children, I need not write, fave that each of their daughters was by the bond of Mʳ Shirley to have—1500ˡⁱ a peece.

I have feldom known a more true wedlocke nor more tender love in marriage then was between them, nor an hufband more truly forrowfull for his wifes loffe then hee for hers: whofe eies I have feen in his elder years (many times after her death) to ftand with tears as hee hath talked of her with my felf; Shee was a gentlewoman as really allied to vertue and devotion as lived in her time: Hee after married Dorothy daughter of Sʳ Thomas Wroughton knight and widdow of Sʳ Henry Vinton of ffarington in Berkfhire, between whom was not always foe fweet an agreement.

By the faid ffrancis hee had iffue Henry Shirley now Baronet, Sir Thomas, and Mary. |

1. Sir

875   1. Sir Henry hath married Dorothy second daughter of Robert late Earle of Essex, by whom hee hath issue Charles and Leta.

2. Sir Thomas Shirley knight of Botulph bridge in the County of Huntington hath married Mary second daughter of Thomas Harper Esq:, by whom hee hath issue, Henry, George, John, and Mary; The incouragement of which Sir Thomas to these relations, I thankfully acknowledge.

3. Mary sister of the said S: Henry and S: Thomas, is lately dead without issue.

His Seales.

In the time of Queen Mary and for twelve years after, this lord sealed with Mowbrayes lion rampant without crest or supporters, circumscribed, Sir Henrie lord of Berkeley, somwhat more then an inch diameter.

And in the ninth of Queen Elizabeth and for six years after, with the said lion circumscribed with this motto, deus me respicit, of like diameter.

And in the 15th of Elizabeth and after, with the like lion of the same diameter, but circumscribed virtute non vi. Howbeit his more ancient word is, dieu soit avec nous. And that of Mowbray, Sola virtus invicta.

And also in the 40th of Elizabeth used another like seale of the lion without any motto at all, of like bignes: Soe that in his seales of Armes hee seemed wholly to rellish of the wife and her family.

vetus manuscript.   And whereas in old verses of the bearings of divers noble families, there is given to this, (Berkeleij vigor,) from thence it may seem came the words, (virtute non vi.) Behold the figures of the former Seales; |

876   ### His death and place of buriall.

After the death of Sir Thomas this lords only son, in those two years hee survived him, his care most seemed to bee for his two grandchildren, George and Theophila;

Theophila; whom their father dying inteſtate and in debt had left foe much neglected, That his wife as Adminiſtratrix, paid for the acquitall of his memory divers great ſums more then his perſonall eſtate amounted unto.

ffor the obtaining of the wardſhip of George, (the prime arch and hope of his houſe,) this lord preſently upon his fons death, by ſpeedy łres, put the Earle of Northton his brother in law, lord privy ſeale; ſuggeſting as truth by ſtraining proved, That for his body his ſaid grandchild would forthwith bee in ward to the king, And for his lands after his own death: Upon conſultacon hereof with his daughter in lawe the lady Elizabeth, (when theſe łres were to bee diſpatched,) two things were with them in Ayme and hope; the one, that ſoe powerfull a privy Counſellor would without competition of any other Courtier, (eſpetially having the firſt notice,) obtaine the wardſhip from all others, And would afterwards caſt the wards education upon the tender care of her the mother; which, to the comfort of this lord Henry, proved true. The other, That the ſaid Earle having neither wife nor child, And this infant the grandchild and heire of his deareſt ſiſter, hee would in likelihood not only beſtow his wardſhip and mariage portion freely upon him, (whether hee lived or not lived till his full age or mariage,) but alſo a greater bounty: Neither was it in this conference (whereat my ſelf was preſent) unremembred, That the lady Katharine the infants grandmother had for twenty ſix years and more before her death given to him an annuall exhibition of 50ˡⁱ p ann̄, when left, ſlipped from the allowance ſhee received of her huſband; And therefore might probably expect the Inning of their hopes, if not by way of repayment, yet of a conſcious retribution; which alſo the Earles łres from his houſe at charing Croſſe (then in building) ſodainly and frankly ſeemed to aſſure; But how performed, it after appeareth, ſoe that that firſt care was taken off and turned into comfort.

verba vlī volunt̄.

877

As touching Miſtris Theophila, the other Arch of this lords houſe, this lord in December after that wardſhip of Mr. George obtained, (and almoſt a year before his own death,) having in July before taken back into his own name his ffee ſimple lands, and increaſed his ſaid daughter in laws joynture, made his Will; And thereby beqūathed towards her mariage portion. 3000ˡⁱ to bee levied out of his fee ſimple lands: But her mariage with Sir Robert Coke following in Augt after, as hath been declared, his further care for her was likewiſe comfortably taken off, And a greater portion by Articles enterchangeably ſealed agreed upon to bee paid in land, with the great liking of her mother; which after coſt the manor of Portbury in the County of Somerſet, worth—8000ˡⁱ And thereupon a few daies after that mariage

Carta: 20 Julij 11 : Jac:

at

at Berkeley Castle, he took his former will (as it was in parchment under his hand and seale) in my presence to one Ambrose Cowper, directing wherein to have it altered at his coming to Callowdon, with whom by that means it remained at the time of his own death in November following : To which effect also, my self was not only moved by him, but desired afterwards by lre in Michaelmas Terme following to return that way from London, where I then was, about the perfecting the assurances on all parts according to the said Articles, which were agreed upon and ingrossed : And the writ of dedimus potestatem sued out, whereby this lord was to have acknowledged a fine before Judge Warberton in his way homewards through Coventry, in the end of that Terme ; And the two thousand pounds which the lord Coke was also to have paid to this lord for Portbury, told out, all or the most part which by George Lord Berkeley was after remitted.

Howbeit death prevented whatsoever was intended, for this lord having at dinner on fryday the 12th of November, taken liking to the tast of small custards then served to his table, hee willed that some of them should bee reserved for his supper : whereupon feeding, surfeited, so that the same not well digesting, hee grew distempered in the night following, sicknes by degrees increasing upon him till that day fortnight after the 26th of that month : In the evening | before in his private prayers hee cryed, come, come, lord Jhesus, which hee often doubled till the morning ; And when his weak breath caused the words (lord Jhesus) to bee unsounded, Then only was heard, come, come, And after when the letter (C) became somwhat too harsh, hee was heard to say, Tome, tome, the letter (T) being more soft and easy of sound ; And soe without any plunge motion or stirre of body, at five of the clock in the morning the said 26th of November 1613, in the 11th year of king James, rendred back his spirit to him that gave it, his chaplin Henry Briggs (a learned divine) then on his knees in prayer by him : And thus having the comfortable memory of a well led life, hee beheld death without dread, and the grave without fear, And imbraced both as necessary guides to endles glory : And in this sort did this pious peere, in this navigation of his life, lett fall his fatall anchor that never can bee wayed up againe.

It pleased the lady Elizabeth Berkeley by her lres to presse my coming to Callowdon, where I attended her the third day after this lords death ; whereupon lres were forthwith directed to Sr George Shirley, Sr William Coke, and Sr Thomas Estcourt, named for his executors, of whom Sr George refused to intermeddle : The others promised their repaire thither, but before their arrivall (in regard of their protraction)

protraction) the said lady Berkeley with the lord George her son, were with their family departed for London, And Sr Robert Coke with his lady for Coventry, where some years after they remained, as is before touched. The Executors Sr William Coke and Sr Thomas Estcourt having after their coming informed themselves of the personall estate of this lord, entred into the execution of the will, and sattisfyed all debts and demands in those parts ere they departed thence: And having in fitting manner provided a Coach and all things necessary for conduction of the Corps to Berkeley Castle according to his will, the 21th of December set forward with it, attended with a fair troope of his and their own servants, to Warwicke; thence the next day to Campden, thence the next day to Tetbury, thence on Christmas even to Berkeley Castle; | in the Chappell whereof it remained till a air Tombe (after some months) was set up in his own Chapple and place of buriall, adjoyning to the Chancell of the said Church, (his wholl body and bowells laid thereunder,) with this inscription.

Here lieth the body of Sir Henry Berkeley knight lord Berkeley, Mowbray, Segrave, and Breouse, lord Leivtenant of the County of Glouc., who departed this life the 26th day of November in the year of our lord God, 1613. being the day that hee accomplished the age of ffowerscore years: Hee first maryed Katharine, sister to Thomas Howard, Duke of Norfolke, by whom hee had issue, Thomas, Mary, and ffrances; Thomas being a knight of the Bath maryed Elizabeth only daughter and heir of Sir George Carey knight lord Hunsdon, Mary the eldest daughter was maryed to Sr John Zouch knight, And ffrances the second daughter was maryed to Sir George Shirley Baronet: Hee seconly maryed Jane the widowe of Sir Roger Townsend knight, yet living, by whom hee had noe issue.—Thus the Tombe.

Of which monument it may rightly bee said—Sic oculos, sic ille manus, sic ora ferebat: The resemblances of both Henry and Katharine are to life: And hee whose coming was to find the lost sheep, to bind up the broken hearted, to call sinners to repentance and by it unto salvation, save and have mercy upon them, mercifull in their lives to many.

Hee sate lord from the first to the last of his life just 79 years, not 80 as his Epitaph hath. A misinformation of those that waited in his sicknes, Telling his Executors how hee oft told them, That if hee lived till fryday the 26th of that November hee should bee just 80 years old.

Hee

Hee had a longe life with an happy death, the moſt pretious guift of Heaven, which all the gold the ſun hath made and ſhall make, will never bee able to buy.

A mile before the body of this lord came to Tetbury, it was met by 150, at the leaſt of the better ſort of his old Tenants, out of Berkeley hundred (without any notice given) out of the deſire they had to condole over the Coffin, the loſſe of ſoe noble a lord; And ſurely I never ſaw the eyes of Tenants (uſually otherwiſe affected) more really mourning: Which number in the next daies journey to Berkeley, much increaſed: who, being by my ſelf, in the name of his executors, called up into the great chamber in the Caſtle of Berkeley (which his Coffin out of the Coach was firſt brought) to refreſh themſelves with wine and the like, I ſaw. 100. pair of Eyes at leaſt pouring out (before that Coffin) ſuch paſſionate and ſorrowfull tears, as if their ſpirits ſhould have followed thoſe teares: which to behold (with the remembrance of my youths education, and the daily favours I had from him, teſtified alſo by his legacy of his ſilver watch as a teſtimony of the good and faithfull ſervice I had done unto him, they are his own words in his will) drew a floud from my ſelf: This being their generall teſtimony, That they had loſt the beſt landlord that England had, whoſe like might not after bee by them expected.

It is baſenes to flatter his memory, but I truly tell his grandchild and poſterity, honeſtè vixit, neminem læſit, ſuum cuique tribuit; Hee lived an honeſt man, without hurt to any, rendring to each man what was their right: none in his time was found more ready to render juſtice to all alike.

Of body, hee was tall and ſlender, as were his father and grandfather, as both from himſelf and more eſpetially from divers of their attendants I have been informed; ſaid alſo to bee the naturall poſture and compoſure of the name and family;[1] Of a found conſtitution, his hearing good, his eyes not more dimme then in his youth: Reading much, yet never uſed ſpectacle or other help: hee knew not what the gout, ſtone, Ache, or other greifs incident to age did meane: In the courſe of his wholl life none could bee more temparate, ſpare of ſpeech, better conceiving then expreſſing; Nothing beholding to his youths education, as himſelf would complaine: enclining to pitty: ready to releive: exceeding apt to forgive, and to bee reconciled: And being reconciled, would imbrace them without ſcruple or remnant

of

---

[1] In the margin of the manuſcript is the following note in the handwriting of Lady Elizabeth Germain, dau. of Charles Earl of Berkeley, and wife of Sir John Germain, of Drayton Co. Northampton, Bart:— "Exceedingly degenerated for we are all but a low Race now." [ED.]

of gall; his face was the frontispice of his mind, hee knew not how to dissemble a thought: ffor frank well ordered | and continuall hospitallity, hee equalled, if not **881** outwent, all others in the parts where hee lived: In a word, Noe man (that ever I could hear, hee, living or dead,) could say That hee ever descryed in him any notorious vice: Only, it may truly bee said, that hee was too great a lover of law, knowing it noe better: And that hee did not alwaies soe lend one eare to the accuser, as that hee kept the other for the accused.

> Gratior est virtus veniens a corpore pulchro.
> Vertue is more lovely much more acceptable,
> Proceeding from a personage amyable.
>
> God grant thy grandchild such a race may run,
> As thou throughout thy life hast nobly done. |

His lands whereof hee dyed seized.

882

The lands hee left unto his heire, (whereof only little Canonbury scarce worth ye naming was purchased by him) were these,

The Castle burrow hundred and manor of Berkeley.	
The manor of Hame,	
The manor of Appleridge,	
The manor of Alkington,	
The manor of Hinton,	
The manor of Hurst,	
The manor of Slimbridge,	
The manor of Sages,	In the County of Glouc.
The manor of Came,	
The manor of Cowley,	
The manor of Wotton,	
The manor of Wotton fforren,	
The manor of Symondsall,	
The manor of Canonbury,	
The burrow and manor of Tetbury,	
The manor of Bitton & Hannam	

The manor and Hundred of Portbury	In the County of Som{r}set.
The manor of Porteshead,	

The

The manor of Callowdon,	In yᵉ county of the Citie of Coventry and of Warwicke
The manᵣ of Me[l]ton Mowbray The manor of Segrave, The manor of Mountforrell, The manor of Goſcote	In the County of Leiceſter
The manor of Boſham, The manor of Thorney, The manor of ffuntington, The manor of Buckfold,		In the County of Suſſex.

883   The Advowſons of the Churches of Segrave, Howby, Sutton Bonington, with Sᵗ Anns, Kegworth, and Tetbury Vicaridge, as in his life are mentioned.

Inquiſitio poſt mortem Thome Berkeley. 10. Jac. Inqu: poſt mortem Henrici dni Berkeley 11ᵒ Jacobi.

Of all which a dying ſeized by Inquiſition was found in the County of Glouc., in January following his death: As alſo one other Inquiſition had been in the ſaid County almoſt two years before, after the death of Sᵗ Thomas his ſon and heire, wherein the forementioned conveyances and anuities are ſpecified: And for the foreſaid manors of Tetbury, Bitton, and Hannam, in the county of Glouc., And the manors lands and Advowſons in the Counties of the Citie of Coventry and Warwick, Leiceſter, and Suſſex, I have at large written of each of them, And how, and when they firſt came into this family, with each antiquity to them belonging, in a book by it ſelf finiſhed with this hiſtory, which may bee of uſe to this family.

The Application and uſe of his life.

The uſe.

1. **This** lord Henry in the laſt and immediate Anceſtor preceding the lord George, clothed (by this lords death) with honor of twenty former generations: Hee had much, ſpent much, yet left enough to continue the like honorable port, if regulated after that method which hee obſerved in the later half of his life; whereby hee knew to a peny what quarterly hee was to receive, And for what the ſame came in, And how it was againe iſſued out; And was able at the end of each year in the cloſing of his Audit to ſay, That ſuch and ſuch ſums and expences might have been avoyded by providence, but being paſt hee would amend it in the year following: If like providence bee not hereafter found in his heire, that portion which now diſcendeth will bee found ſhortened in the next generation: which, my wiſh is, may in time bee ſeriouſly thought upon. |

2. Againe,

2. **Againe**, this family from the example of this lords first wife, may learne That nothing is more necessary in the person of a master of a family, according as his estate and greatnes shall bee, then Majesty: which, (having moderation and judgment how to order it,) is then of excellent beauty and use. And herein let every master remember Esops fable of the frogs, how contemptibly they esteemed their heavy and blockish king. And that, nimia familiaritæs parit contemptum; The masters awe is often the levell of his servants life and manners. 884

3. **Againe**, this lord having in the length of his longe life often outspent his purse, betooke himself to sojournings with his kinsmen and freinds, (as before is mentioned,) the better thereby to bring the unruly tide of his former overflowings into a more orderly channell, and to shake of at once togeather such needless and disorderly attendants, old Captaines, old Courtiers, unusefull Schollers and companions, as could not otherwise soe fairly bee put aside: whereby (as himself hath said) hee saved a good portion of his land, and ridd his house of some persons dangerous to have been kept, and different from him in religion, drawn thither by such as had over great a power in his family; A phisicke by which his father and grandfather had cured their estates, And may againe bee of use to his grandchild in his riper years, for whose sake this his Ancestors modle is here shaped unto him. fol: 842

4. **Againe**, from the sojournings of this lord his posterity may take example how to preserve peace within doores, espetially if they bee matched to wives of high flying spirits, or difficult to please; And how to put off such servants as they find apt to foster that humor, And how to shake from their tables and stables such as make themselves menyall servants without invitements, and have noe modesty in their abodes; Of which kind I have known the number numerous in this family; Also how to ease expences and save the sale of a manor, when such drones and other excesse had drawn | on a debt that grew clamorous; Also how to spare towards the mariage portion of a daughter or a younger son and the like: And somtime under the colour of pleasure or ease, to retire to an house of less capacity and expence: But ever with this resolution, to hold constantly the first intentions; And not to exceed the determined proportion of yearly spendings: wherein this noble lord would acknowledge, That in some of his Sojournings hee had departed from his first projects, and strayed from those pathes which himself had chalked out to have walked in. 885

5. **Againe**, from the comōn recoveries, fynes, and feoffments of this lord, formerly mentioned, his posterity may understand of what estate they stand seized in fol: 840. 841.

in all their lands and Baronies: and how by operation of law, by reason of those fynes and conveyances, they may bring titles or queſtions pretended againſt any part of their poſſeſſions to a ſpeedy ending and repoſe; which may bee of profitable uſe in their generations to come.

fol: 845.

6. **Againe,** from the obſervation of the ſtory of Queen Elizabeths coming to Berkeley Caſtle and the deſtruction of this lords red deere, before mentioned, his poſterity may the better avoid thoſe Court-traps and toiles wherein this lord Henry by an over haſty expreſſion of his diſcontent for a few deer, had almoſt been intrapped, as his deere were in the Toyle, pitched more truly for him then for them;

fol: 285.

And often to remember the depth of that danger whereinto their valiant Anceſtor the lord Maurice the third did by diſcontent plunge himſelf and his poſterity, had not the favourable hand of heaven miraculouſly redeemed them, As in the lives of himſelf and his heir hath been declared, And to beware thereafter.

[7.] **Againe,** (as my further teſtimony of the regularity of the later part of this lords life,) I tell his poſterity, That for the laſt thirty years or more of his life, ſoe

fol: 838. 839.

exactly were kept the books of his receipts and payments, aſwell forraigne as domeſticall, of what kind ſoever, made either by himſelf, Steward of houſhold, Sollicitor, Receivor, or others, And ſoe orderly caſt up and methodiz'd at his Audit in the end of each year; That before thoſe books were, | after his death, taken

886

away by his Executors, or otherwiſe caſt aſide, It was eaſy for any man but a little acquainted therewith to have taken upon him the accompt of his wholl revenues, certaine or caſuall, raiſed in that time; And ſoe my ſelfe, (though I had nothing to doe therew^{th}) offered to his Executors to have done when they took theſe books into their conſideration, about twenty daies after his death; which they ſoe much approved, that they held them fit preſidents for themſelves and poſterity: But on the other ſide, the firſt part of this lords life hath declared how irregular his firſt houſkeeping and the management of his revenues were; Too many ſervants commanders in his family, few under obedience: his monies paſſing yearly into the hands of many, and iſſued out by more: few were called to accompt, and more unable to have accompted: Of this Aguiſh ſicknes that ſoon ſhaked his eſtate, my ſelf have heard his elder years complaine: I wiſh his grandchild and poſterity may not relapſe, leaſt they bee conſtrained to redeem the like error, with the ſale of much land as this lord was. Fælix quem faciunt aliena pericula cautum; Happy is that ſon that, obſerving his fathers ill footing, faſteneth his ſtepps on a ſurer ground.

8. **Againe,**

8. **Againe**, from the dangerous paſſage of this lords wife and John Bott, formerly menc̃oned, let all the diſcendants of this noble family bee admoniſhed, not to commit ſecrets of ſuch conſequence to unfaithfull ſervants, nor to bee beholding to any living man, (if poſſible they may chuſe,) for their reputation, ſtate, or life; ffor the waies of mans heart are unfordable and paſt finding out.

fol: 846. 847.

9. **Againe**, ffrom the daily practice of this lord Henry, his poſterity hath a vertuous preſident not to let their Anger remaine when the cauſe is removed; And to diſtinguiſh betwixt him that offendeth of infirmity or againſt his will, And him who offendeth malitiouſly or of ſet purpoſe.

10. **Againe**, Let mee note to this lords poſterity that the life of this their Anceſtor was a meere medley, and like a picture wth ſundry faces; from his birth (born a peere) to one and twenty, | none found more happy or hopefull, courted for mariage by many of the greateſt; ffrom 21. to 38. in the 13th of Queen Elizabeths raigne, (what time his brother in law and faſt freind Thomas duke of Norfolk loſt his head,) his alliance and freinds in Court and Country ſoe flowred that adverſity could not bee feared: from thence for 39. years togeather with him, finis unius mali gradus erat futuri, ſoe toſſed in perpetuall ſtormes and law ſuits, That with difficulty in Court and Country hee bore up ſaile; after which time, in the 7th of king James, 4 years before his death, hee entred a quiet harbour; and after thoſe 4. years, peace in the 79th of his age, anchored in thoſe joyes that never ſhall have ending; To which, oh bleſſed God, bring all his diſcendants.

887

11. **Againe**, in reading over the life of this lord, his poſterity cannot but obſerve his ſufferings and loſſes by two indulgently following the wills and Counſells of his mother and firſt wife; Againſt whom I will not (as to him) further ſay then of old hath been ſaid, Non eſt bis in bello peccare, hee that in warre errs twice is without excuſe or pardon; As hee did more then twice; Nor as to them in the application further ſharpen my pen then to tell his poſterity, That when Eve went about to expound the text ſhee miſtooke the text and hurt her huſband: And that Engliſh wives challenge more liberty and enclyne to more ſoveraignty then thoſe of other nations: That female counſells are to bee ſuſpected, as proceeding from an unproper ſphear: Vnicuiq; in ſua arte credentum eſt, nemini extra; what advice can an huntſman give in matters of muſick? And that prodegy of witt whoſe excellencies have conquered both example and imitation, hath told his ſon That wives were ordained to continue the generation of men; To obey, not to rule their affaires: That they are like marchants in a common wealth, the greateſt good or

Sir Walt: Raleigh

the

the worst of evills that can happen to a man ; And to ballence them and their Counsells thereafter.

12. **Againe,** this family may observe how fully the covetous desire of the lady Anne, mother of this lord Henry, labouring to have avoided | the leases of poore tenants for the enriching of her son and enlarging her own livelihood, hath verified the comon proverbe, That covetousnes never brought home clear gaines : ffor, such her covetous intent opened the gap which otherwise had been closed, whereat Queen Elizabeth by the prosecution of Leicesters Earle entred, and laid wast half the ancient vineyard of this lord, the dolefull relation whereof hath taken up a great part of his life ; And that of all infelicities ordained to hurt the estates of great men, none is greater then to bee soe encountred in marriage, as the wife to conceive her self wiser in her husbands affaires then himself or his Counsell.

13. **Againe,** by the passages of Goodman and Nuthall, tending to the extinguishment of this lords memoriall ; A glass is set before the eies of this family, to see how man may plot and purpose, but God alone disposeth as himself pleaseth : And how the Authors of that expurgatory counsell have thereby made that name which they would have rooted out more durable and conspicuous, when their own is forgotten in the place. Of all mens purposes God is the disposer, In whose high Counsell wee see it was ordained that his then dejected family, should againe by weak means stand and rise, notwithstanding the powerfull plots to ruin it ; And those to fall whose stepps seemed to bee rooted in adamant ; And accordingly, let this family acknowledge That foundations of Eternity laid by mortall men in this transitory world, are but like the towers of Babell, either shaken from heaven or made vaine ere the frame is raised to the height, And to turne their waies thereafter.

14. **Againe,** from the two recoveries of Wotton and other manors, unconscionably by packing and practice wrested from this lord, this family may now experimentally see that to bee true which the courses of all times past (duely observed) have verified ; That those who have left but little with honest dealing, God hath blessed the same exceedingly ; whereas those that have left great matters ill gotten insteed of a blessing have left a curse and a snare behind them, punctually found true between the parties to those recoveries | in the persons that pursued them.

15. **Againe,** from the ill requitall of Gerard Try after hee had served the turn of this lord and of the lady Anne his mother and guardian, to their great advantage To have his own land at Binley wrested from him by that greatnes, may warn

servants

servants not to transgresse the bounds of truth in hope of favour or reward, as hee did: And masters not to gaine by wronge, least it fly away before the third generation as that land hath done: And it verifies also what wee read of old, That many love the Treason but hate the Traytor.

16. **Againe**, This noble family may observe, That noe one vertue hath more gloriously comended the life of the lord Thomas the fifth to posterity, then the deafe eare and flow beleife, hee accustomably lent to such persons as presented him with secret accusations against his more eminent servants; Hee wisely considering, that factions were in all families; That malice and envy are oftnest darted against best deservers; And that each accuser hath his private ends covered under his accusations; and therefore that ever memorable lord would never receive complaint till hee had both parties face to face, whereby as hee avoided his own trouble and disquiet, foe hee kept the hearts of his more eminent servants, (whereof greater use was to bee made,) faster tyed to his services; Which wise and just course if this lord Henry had observed from that his grandfathers example, hee had not caused two of his ablest servants to have left him, when hee could not well have spared them; Nor have caused a Steward of houshold who succeeded one of those to have articled with him not to take to beleife any accusaçõn against him till hee were confronted by his accuser; Nor had hee turned off in times of need a most able lawyer and Sollicitor upon a secret informaçõn whispered against them, to have delivered two deeds to his adversaries, when their severall oaths in chancery not only denyed the fact, but the freedom of their hearts from such thoughts: Deeds only mislayed for the time and after found amongst this lords evidences. The speech of the Earle of Dorset, lord Treasurer, in the Starrechamber, about the 4th of King James, was by all present generally applauded, That if accusation became condemnaçõn | without examination, the king would soone have a thin court, and I my self (quoth hee) not left mee one able servant; Adding withall, That hee that judgeth between two before hee hath heard both parties is an unjust judge though hee judge justly. **And** by making a wise use to themselves, to choose with Mary in the Gospel that better part which will sticke by them, and have an honorable memoriall with their posterity.

Cheyney.
Bucknam.
Cresw:

Ch: Yelv:
Als:

890

Luke: 10. 42.

17. **Againe** (that I may not omit any observation tending to the behoofe of this noble family; The life of the lord Thomas the third hath shewed what an excellent servant that lord had all the daies of his life of Thomas Bradston, who a longe while to the losse of his own fortunes supported his masters; And when the errors of his masters youth, (which Bradston could not prevent,) had overthrown them both, Bradston in the time of his masters imprisonment made first his own

Tho: Bradston,
fo:

peace

peace with his masters enemies, And after by his prudence and valour so inwardly twisted himself into their good opinions, That hee set his master on foot againe, and ere longe, wrought the downfall of those that formerly had been the cause of his masters fall and his; and got to boote the hon^ble dignities first of a Banneret and after of a Baron, and an estate answerable for suport of those hon^rs as hath been shewed.

The like excellent servant was Thomas Try, for fourty years in four discents of this family under the lord Maurice the fifth the Marques Berkeleys brother, and under the lord Maurice his son, and under the lord Thomas the fifth his brother and heire, and the lord Thomas his son, by whose spetiall industry a great part of those possessions which the Marques Berkeley had vastly consumed, were againe regained to this family, the principall means it then had to maintaine it self, As in their severall lives hath been related. And for his reward obtained to bee in Comission of the peace as hath been shewed.

The like excellent servant was Thomas Duport, for 35 years under this lord Henry, by whose wise conduct and speciall sollicitation this family was in the time of Queen Mary enriched with the rever-|ter of their Barony of Berkeley; And had by his prudent Counsells further wrought a durable happines in his masters family had not the sic volo of his masters mother, and after of his mistres his masters wife, (woemen too powerfull for the successe of good counsells,) turned his sound advices to his masters losses and dishonor; The greife whereof caused Duport to withdraw from Counsell and service; Hee attained also to bee in comission of the peace, as hath been shewed. **What** other servants of remarkeable meritt this family hath bred, or found usefull, let the pen of others render them their deservings.

Though the rule in husbandry bee true, That the master of a Country family must somtimes carry himself pleasant and courteous to his flocke, and not command them any thing in his chollar, (for boisterous and rough handling will with such vulgar husbandmen prevaile as little as with stiffe necked Jades,) And that if hee speak not somtimes familiarly unto them, laugh and jest somtimes with them, or give them occation thereto, or suffer them somtimes to laugh and bee merry amongst themselves, hee will too often find his works either not done or ill done: Yet Masters in great and honorable familyes attended with servants of better quality and of a more gentile education and imployment, may in their deportment retaine a more awfull greatnes befitting their estates, remembring, That as with ill

bred

bred natures, too much familiarity may breed contempt, foe on the contrary, with the better fort of their houfhold, a chearfull word and countenance begetts a contrary effect; And, doubtles works more ftrongly then double wages; verifyed in thefe three worthies, Bradfton, Try, and Duport, who feverally poffeffing their mafters extraordinary ufage and refpect at home and abroad, thereby doubled their endeavours of doing anfwerable fervices; An able man, is longe in breeding, to gain him by a fair word, is noe coftly purchafe; Soe of able fervants.

I defire the end of this application to bee underftood, rather to continue in this family the memory of thefe three excellent fervants, longe fince in duft, to the raifing up of others like them; than to inftruct the now lord thereof how or in what garbe or pofture to carry himfelf toward | his houfhold fervants, in their different degrees of places and imployments; And to make fuch ufe as beft may [a]dvance his honorable ends and affaires.

18. **Finally**, and for the laft of all the applycations and ufes mentioned in the three volumes of this **Berkeleian** hiftory, drawn from the obfervation of the lives of thefe twenty lords, reflecting upon the piety, vertue, vice, brotherly love or hatred, frugallity, prodigallity, difcontent, adverfity, profperity, pride, humility, affability, induftry, liberty, flattery, anger, impatience, moderation, paffion, goods well or ill gotten, domineering of wives, and weomen, pride in fervants, ingratitude, covetoufnes, valour, cowardice, diligence and negligence in fervants and follicitors, ill education of children, with other like, obferved and applyed by mee in the courfe of the ftory of this ancient and thrice honorable family, as I have for 550. years traced the waies wherein they feverally walked, for the better levelling of the life of the prefent lord George; I conclude for all, and in an humble and lowly manner fay to him, as the fpirit of the moft high by the pen of king Solomon, in the laft of his booke of Ecclefiaftes, counfelled and faid to his eldeft fon, and in him, to all others; Remember (Oh George) thy creator in the daies of this thy youth, fear God and keep his commandments, for this is the wholl duty of man; ffor God will bring every of thy works into Judgment, whether it bee good or whether it bee evill; **And** to put my moft honored lord in mind of this heavenly Counfell, (which if followed will make him happy,) is the greateft requitall I can make to him, his father and mother, grandfather and grandmother, for all the benefits which for many years they have conferred upon mee and mine.

Ecclles: 12. v. 1. 13. 14.

Finis.

APPENDIX

It may be well to append to the Orders cited in the text, certain other Orders for the regulation of the Household given by Jane the second wife of this Lord found at Condover Hall.

AUGUST, 1601.—Orders set down by my lady to be observed by the gentlemen in every respect the which directions shall remain in the gentleman ushers hands to thende that none of them shall for their excuse plead ignorance upon the breach of these appointed orders by forgetting any of them but to cute of [cut off?] that inconvenience I do here appoint that every one of the gentlemen may at any time resort to the gentleman usher and such as can read may here see from time to time what those orders bee whereby they may be the better instructed of their duties and orders appointed to be observed by them.

DIRECTIONS FOR THE GENTLEMEN. } The gentleman usher to see my gentlemen in houshold to live in decent order to be diligent and reverent in their services to my lo: and me to obey all other good orders set down by me in the yeomans book without any breach or contempt of any of them whereby both you shall greatly content my lo: and me with your obedience and well behaviour and tractablenefs and besides be an occasion to procure the meaner sort of my servants in calling to amend their faults by your good examples; and though I do refer you for the most of them to those orders already set down for brevity yet I thought it not good to pass over without directing some orders unto you as the chiefest to be observed.

TO COME EVERY MORNING TO SEE THE DINING CHAMBERS IN GOOD ORDER. } The gentleman usher to come every morning into the dining chamber and withdrawing chamber in the winter season at eight o'clock and in the summer at seven o'clock. If strangers be there then at more early hours and to see that the yeomen of those chambers do keep fires there in the winter and order well and dress up everything in those chambers according to my former directions set down. And if you find any lack in them to see those faults presently amended whereby this place shall be kept orderly to the contentment of my lo: and me, and besides shall be in decent order at all times for the entertaining of strangers, likewise in the summer time to see the chimneys trimmed with green boughs and the windows with herbs and sweet flowers and the chamber strowed with green rushes.

TO ATTEND AT SERVICE TIME. } The gentleman usher all the service days appointed to come up daily with the residue of my gentlemen to hear the service said before my lo: and me, and to come up somewhat before the Yomen and after service he and rest of the gentlemen to remain in the dining chamber and not to go down with the yomen, which is most disorderly; for as the hall is a fit place for the yomen so is the dining room most convenient for the gentlemen to make their most abode in.

FOR WEARING

FOR WEARING THEIR LIVERY COATS FOR A TIME.
} Further when any ftrangers be here, though but one in number, if they be of that calling that they do come into the dining chamber, then my pleafure is that the gentleman ufher and all the reft of gentlemen fhall prefently put on their livery coats for the firft night and all the next day following, unlefs it be funday or holiday, then to put on their cloaks but the next day that is a working day to wear their livery coats then after how long fo ever any ftrangers do tarry unlefs new ftrangers do come before the old be gone, then again to wear their livery coats the firft and the next day after their coming, and all the time after they may with my liking wear their cloaks, fo the former appointed times be obferved; and from henceforth neither my gentleman ufher nor the reft of my gentlemen to depart either with their winter liveries or their fummer liveries till new coats be given them; and I do further appoint that neither my gentleman ufher nor any other of my gentlemen fhall at any time when my lo: or I ride abroad during the time of our being in journey, wear any other upper garment either cloak or other wife, but only his livery coat; and when their liveries be firft given, though no ftrangers be here, yet to wear them two days together unlefs it happen to be one holiday or funday, at what time they do wear their livery coats to keep them on all day without ufing to wear any other garment for that time.

NOT TO COME INTO THE DINING CHAMBER WITH COATS OR CLOKES.
} Further my pleafure is that neither my gentleman ufher nor any other of my gentlemen fhall come into the dining chamber nor fit at play with my lo: and me in his girken or doublett but either in his livery coat or in his cloak, and I do licenfe from hence forth the gentleman ufher and refidue of my gentlemen though no ftrangers be here to come into the dining room at any time when my lord and I am at play there at any kind of game.

TO ATTEND IN THE GREAT CHAMBER
} And when ftrangers be here then my pleafure is that they both after dinner and fupper and at other times, both the gentleman ufher and the reft of my gentlemen fhall keep moft in the dining chamber to make fhow of themfelves both for the honor of my lo: and me and to be ready to do fuch fervice as fhall be commanded them.

MY LA: WALKING ABROAD.
} Further when I fhall walk any way out of the park as into the fields, as more or any of my outward grounds, then would I have the gentleman ufher and the reft of my gentlemen be in a readinefs to wait upon me.

IN THE PARK.
} Further when I do walk in the park then I do licenfe the gentlemen either to walke, bowl, fhoot or ufe any other paftime or a where I walk in this order. If I do walk in the high walk then they may be in the lower walk; if I do walk in the lower walk then they may be in the upper walk. I do not fet down this as an exprefs commandment that I would have them be there only; I do licence them to be there or to be abfent as they fhall think good.

LICENCE TO COME INTO THE GARDEN.
} And at any time when I am in the great garden myfelf, I do for the time of my being there, as well as when no ftrangers be here as when any be here, licence the gentleman ufher and the reft of my gentlemen to come into the garden and there either to bowl or remain there as long time or fhort as they will; or to come in or not to come in as they are difpofed, for I do not fet this down as an exprefs commandment I would have them to be there at fuch times as I walk there, but rather do give them leave without my miflike to come in where they will during the time of my abode there or to be abfent as they fhall think good.

DILIGENT

DILIGENT ATTENDANCE DINNER AND SUPPER	And during the time my lo: and I am at dinner and supper and do sit abroad, my pleasure is that the gentleman usher and the rest of my gentlemen shall with due reverence and great diligence wholly give their attendance to wait upon us, and none for those times to go to rest themselves in other places or to be absent, but to wait diligently and not to go to any bye places to eat meat in corners, nor to take or give away any meat but by the gentleman usher's sufferance and licence, but to give good attendance till they go altogether to take our devercion, and therein All to behave themselves civilly like gentlemen without making any great noise or using any other uncivil orders, to use no playing fence nor disorderly pastimes in the hall which causeth great disorder and gives cause of offence by the great noise that comes by that means.
NOT TO BREAK DAYS HAVING LEAVE TO GO FORTH.	At what time that either the gentleman usher or any other of my gentlemen craves leave either to see their friends or to dispatch earnest business, none of them in any wise but upon great occasion and apparent cause to break the day appointed for their return, and besides not to go unless they do obtain leave of myself.
FOR GREAT PLAY.	Further my pleasure is that neither the gentleman usher nor none of the rest of my gentlemen shall use great play neither at dice, tables, nor cards; for excess of gaming impoverisheth your estate and causeth many disorders and contentions to be amongst fellows; but instead of these games to exercise yourselves in all manner of activity, as bowling, and chiefly exercise of your long bow wherein I take great delight.
ENTERTAINING OF STRANGERS	The gentleman usher to see all strangers well entertained for my lo: honor and mine; every man according to his calling liking and estimation that is to be made of him; to see those that are of credit to be duly served with livery; none to have any in my house under the degree of an esquire of an hundred pounds a year of an inheritance at the least; your office being gentleman usher is not either yet any other of my gentleman to be at the serving of any liveries under the degree of a baron; gentlemens liveries to be served only with yomen, unless it be a knight's son and heir or a gentleman of hundred mark lands of inheritance. An earl's son or baron's son then one gentleman to go with his livery and to place the bread drink and plate upon the cupboard in his chamber.
ENTERTAINMENT IN STRANGERS CHAMBERS	The gentleman usher to give good entertainment to all gentlemen; to see them want nothing in their chambers; to see them have their breakfast in due time or anything else that they lack or their servants that is fit to offer to strangers for their better entertainment and when any gentleman of calling comes to the house he and the rest of my gentlemen to be ready to bring them into the dining chamber; and when they go away the gentleman usher and the rest of my gentlemen to bring them to their horses.
ENDEAVOUR OF GOOD ORDERS	And as for observing of all other good orders, with the eschewing of any breach to the contrary, my pleasure is that the gentleman usher and the residue of my gentlemen should endeavour themselves to the uttermost they may to live orderly, the which good orders though they be at large set down in the yomen's orders at the end of the book, yet I think good to make a brief rehersal of them here.
HOURS FOR DRINKING	The gentleman usher and the rest of my gentlemen to keep due hours for drinking, for the morning at eight o'clock, at night at eight o'clock, and to come to drinking two and two together.

ORDERLY

ORDERLY RIDING ABROAD } When my lo: and I do ride abroad the gentleman usher to see the gentlemen ride afore two and two together orderly without using any undecentness as in loud speech or rude sports one with another.

MODERATE SPEECH IN THE HALL } My pleasure is that when the usher of the hall, hearing great noise at dinner or supper time, shall bid make less noise, no gentleman to seem to scoff or rail at him, but orderly to use moderate speech for the better example of others.

FOR THE DUE OBSERVING OF MY LA: DIRECTIONS } Further my pleasure is that both to contribute my lo: and me to make more services the more acceptable to us who doth so greatly mislike those disorders, and also to give good manners to your fellows of meaner calling, that even as you all tender my favour, the gentleman usher and all the rest of my gentlemen to frame yourselves to the obeying of these reasonable orders set down by my lord and mee.

TO KEEP PRIVATE THE OFFICES } My pleasure is that none of my gentlemen only the gentleman usher excepted, shall come into any of the offices, as Buttry, pantry, cellar, brew house, backhouse, kitchen, scullery, larders, neither yet into the landry or dye house nor in those two last rehearsed nor the gentleman usher to come into them; neither yet he nor any of the rest of my gentlemen to use any carousing in any house to make one another drunk, or to press any stranger to carouse; to frequent no alehouse; not to use great swearing nor any other unhonest kind of life, but to behave themselves orderly and civily like gentlemen.

QUARRELLING } No gentleman to fall out or quarrel one with another but to live lovingly together, without fighting or contention.

FOR BEING NOT A NIGHT OUT } Neither the gentleman usher nor none of the rest of my waiting gentlemen to ly out a nights but to come into their own lodgings, appointed for them by nine o'clock at night.

TENDING AT THE DRESSER } The gentlemen to come at the first call of the usher to the dresser, and there to use themselves decently without loud noise or any rude behaviour and with all duty to endeavour yourselves to obey and observe them without any breach of any of them so near as you can possible, and all you my waiting gentlemen to be obedient to my gentleman usher to do what you shall be commanded by him touching the decent and good ordering of yourselves and doing diligent and dutiful service to my lo: and me; and because you shall well know all these orders are set down by myself, hoping you will the more willingly with obedience frame yourselves and service according to these directions, I have in the end set to my hand and therefore do expect these orders shall be the . .

In the margin of the last page is written:—" found at Cranford, June, 1635." And at the top of the same page an old hand has written:—" Lo: Berkley's orders."

George now Lord Berkeley.

The Life of George the First

Part of the life of George lord Berkeley the firſt of that name, ſtiled in writings Sir George Berkeley knight, lord Berkeley, Mowbray, Segrave, and Breouſe; And may bee called George the traveller, or George the linguiſt.
Contemporary with king James, and king Charles from 1613. till
Part of whoſe life I will deliver under theſe 5 titles; viz!

1.—**In** his abſtracts from his Anceſtors: fol: [895]
2.—**In** his parentage and diſcents. fol: [897]
3.—**In** his birth and education. fol: [899]
4.—**In** his law ſuits ariſen in his minority. fol: [907]
5.—**The** Concluſion of the author. fol: [917]

In this Lord George is compleat the third Septenary number from Harding the Dane, the firſt of his Engliſh race: what men the two former ſeptenary lords, Thomas the ſecond and William the Marques, the beſt and the worſt, were in their generations, their lives have declared.

In this lord George are more quadrately compleat, the odd numbers of threes and Seavens.

Though the bulke whereto this third volume is growne admits noe repetition, yet breifly let the abſtract of this family [bee obſerved, firſt In threes, in numero ternario.

3. **Maurice** the laſt of the firſt three, by his maryage eſtabliſhed this Barony, And ſetled ſo ſure a peace to his family as continues durable to this day. |

6. **Maurice**

896 6. **Maurice** the last of the second three, by his siding in the Barons warrs in the time of king Henry the third, cast himself and his wife into that indigency That if the said king her unckle had not bestowed on her lands in Kent, shee had begged for want of bread, for soe are the words of that Record of the kings guift.

  9. **Thomas** the last of the third three, by his ever memorable industry doubled his revenue; And to his entaile to the heires males are the last eight lords of this lyne b[e]holding for their honor and barony.

  12. **James** the last of the fourth three; his sun set before the rising: hee lived not to see the honor of his Ancestors: born to honor but had it not.

  15. **Maurice** the last of the fifth three; hee had honor by discent, but noe land withall: Insteed of land his brothers malice discended upon him: His suits in lawe were more then the acres of ground left him by his last Ancestor the Marques.

  18. **Thomas** the last of the sixth three; for shortnes of hon^r hee standeth single: his baronage saw but one winter solstice.

  21. **This** lord George, the last of the seaventh three; Hee is the center of threes and seavens, in whom the whole circumference is closed; Lord raise up his spheare in summa ange, in height above his Ancestors.

  Now observe the abstract of this family in Seavens, in numero septenario.

  7. **Thomas** the last of the first seaven, like the active king (Edward the first) in whose daies hee flourished, was a lord compleatly fitted tam Marti quam Mercurio, the greatest scholler, souldier and husband of All his Ancestors. |

897 14. **William** the last of the second seaven, was the most ambitious man that ever lived in his generations; Hee wasted and gave away fower baronyes and half a Dukedome; And left nothing in effect to his heire but a tongue to complaine.

  21. **This** lord **George** the last of the third seaven; speak of him when I am dust and hee at rest; numbers are not the causes of transmutations of families: Lord enoble his character above his Ancestors; I leave him in his minority between hope and fear, And returne to declare him first in his parentage next in his life and actions.

His

His Parentage and discents.

This lord George by Harding his first Ancestor is a Dane of regall parentage. — A Dane.

By Eve wife of Robert the first, and by the wholl difcents of Breoufe and Mowbray, a moft honorable Norman. — A Norman.

By Alice wife of Maurice the firft, and by the wholl lyne of Segrave whereof hee is heire, an Englifh Saxon. — A Saxon.

By Elizabeth mother of James the firft, heire to the ancient families of Reis, Bloet, and Pichard; And by Margaret wife of Thomas the third, (difcended of the Princes of Brittaine and Wales,) And by Anne Morgan wife to his great grandfather Henry lord Hunfdon, is a Brittaine or Welfhman, whereby hee is priveledged to weare a Leeke on S! Davids day the firft of March. — A Welfhman. A Brittaine.

By Ifable wife of Maurice the fecond, and by Ifable wife of James the firft, one of the Coheirs of Thomas de Brotherton eldeft fon of king Edward the firft by Margaret his fecond wife daughter of Phillip le Bel king of ffrance, A ffrenchman, And of the royall bloud of England and ffrance: As Alfo difcending from Edmond fecond | fon to king Henry the third, father of Henry of Monmouth Earle of Lancafter, Leicefter, and Darby, great grandfather of the faid Ifable. — A ffrenchman. Of the roiall bloud. 898

By Margaret wife of Thomas the third, daughter of Roger Mortimer firft Earle of March, fon of Edmond Mortimer lord of Wigmore and of Margaret ffendles his wife daughter of William de ffendles, a Spanniard; Cozen to Queen Elleanor firft wife of king Edward the firft. — A Spanniard. Powell: 316.

By the faid lady Ifable wife to James the firft, difcended from fferdinando Marques of Saluce of the houfe of Saxony in Germany by Alifon his daughter wife to Richard ffitz Alan lord of Clun and Ofwaldeftry; A Germaine. — A Germaine.

By Eve wife of William de Breoufa lord of Brecknock and Gower, ffifth daughter and one of the Coheirs of Ifable daughter and heire of Richard Strongbowe Earle of Penbroke and of Eve his wife daughter and heire of Dermot-mac-murrough fon of Patrick king of Leinfter, (from whom hee in three wayes difcended) An Irifhman; whereby hee is priviledged to weare a red croffe on S! Patricks day the 17!ʰ of March. — An Irifhman. Howe: fol: 152. Vincent: fol: 411. Yorke. fol: Powell. fol: 313.

And

And juſtly by right of diſcent this lord George quartereth theſe twenty coats, very remarkeable in their generations; viz¹, Berkeley, Bloett, Brotherton, Mowbray, Breouſe, Segrave, Chancombe, Bello campo, Longſpey, Albeny, ffitz Allan, Blundevill, Warren, Plantagenet, Mariſhall, Strongbow, Murchas, Mead, Read, and Stanhope; As formerly in theſe relations hath appeared, and how they are come into his bearings.

Grant Lord That in his courſe of age hee may grace this his parentage by his virtues, as his parentage graceth him; And to know That proper virtue joyned with this nobility of birth is enobled with a double honour: **And** now to his life. |

His birth and education.

899   **This** lord George was born at Lowlayton five miles from London, on Wedneſday the 7ᵗʰ of October in the 43ᵗʰ year of Queen Elizabeth, Anno 1601, between the hours of ten and eleaven in the forenoone, And was chriſtened on munday the 26ᵗʰ of the ſame month; his grandfather George lord Hunſdon and Charles Howard Earle of Nottingham being his godfathers, And the lady Jane ſecond wife to his grandfather Henry lord Berkeley, his godmother; And was afterwards created knight of the Bath at the Creation of Charles Prince of Wales, after the death of Prince Henry his elder brother.

It fared with the father and mother of this lord George during their joynt lives, as with younger brethren (though heires to two noble families) who having Anuities for their maintenance, and noe houſes wherein to ſettle themſelves, muſt ſojourn with freinds or hire where they may for money; So conſequently it fell out with this lord, a part of themſelves and the hope of both their poſterities, who (having been nurſed at Envile) moved with them according to their motion, to London, to Claredon, to Newpark, and laſtly to Callowdon, where and at Coventry, till the diſſipaƈõn of his grandfathers family a month after his death, hee remained a ſcholler under Doctor Philemon Holland; And from thence to London with his mother, as hath been ſaid; where between her houſes of Redcroffe ſtreet, Mylend, Durdens, and Cranford, hee continued under the inſtruction and example of Mʳ Henry Aſhwood, his ſober and vertuous tutor, till hee was fitted for Oxford.

Novem: 1613.
Anno: 11. Jac.

In memoriall of whoſe vertue and progreſſe in learning, then but twelve years old and one month, I will borrow leave to tranſmit to poſterity a Lſe of his own writing, which hee from Coventry ſchoole ſent to my ſelf then in London in theſe
words

words; Accepi a te domine Smythe, chronicon Johannis Speedi cum chartis chorographicis in duobus tomis; opus sanè, ut videtur, egregium dignum lectu, jucundumq̨ aspectu; et quod maius est, perlegi epistolam ad me tuam, plenam judicij et gravis consilij, quæ ut inditia veri amoris tui, magni | estimo; Chronicon quidem diligentèr legam, et apud me servabo, cartisque oculos meos pascam; consilium vero tuum, deo volente, sequar; pro utrisq̨ gratias tibi ago, daboq̨ operam posthac, et te redamare, et tibi pro viribus gratiam referre; vale, Coventria. 9 Novembr̃. 1613.

         Tui amantissimus
           Georgius Berkeley.

900

Of whom it may bee truly said, That hee is born generous and capable of vertue; but wisdom is not gotten without paine; folly may bee bought and findeth many Chapmen, but true honor noblenes and wisdom that makes great and happy, are the fruits of wise companions and the counsells of the dead; Hatefull may his memory bee that by his evill company corrupteth these seeds, for honor and reputation in such a one as this young lord is like to prove, is so delicate a thing as a small excesse may blemish it, and acts of indiscretion may ruin it; It is a spirit that goes and returnes not againe.

The 26th of which November in which hee wrote that lre, his grandfather Henry lord Berkeley dyed, as hath in his life been said; And in December following, the lady Elizabeth with this noble gent her son, then lord, came to London, where shee found the grant of the wardship of his body and marriage passed by the said Earle of Northton, both under the seale of the Court of Wards, and of the great seale, And direction given for finding the office after the death of the said lord Henry: which being returned into the petty bagge in Hillary Terme following, the said Earle, whilst hee endeavoured the passing of a lease of the said lord Henries lands, (whereto the king was now, not before, entituled,) dyed the 15th of June following, Anno, 1614. in the 12th year of king James, at Northton house by Charinge crosse; whereby the said lady apprehending the advantage, presently entred into that affaire, as by right of his Ma^{ts} instructions devolved upon her; And the 13th of July following got the lease under seale; And at the same time compounded with the Counsell | of the Court of Wards for the Casualties of Copy-hold ffynes, Advowsons, Copice woods, heryotts, and other perquisites which might arise out of the kings part of her sons lands during his minority, (which were excepted in her said lease,) And obtained a Decree for the better establishment of that agreement; All which by her personall travell were the sooner and better effected.

1. grant 26 ffeb:
10. Jac: regis.
2. grant. 16. Junij
11 Jac:
11. Jac.

Anno. 12. Jac.
1614.

901

Decret̃ in
Cur: Wardo[rum]

This

1613. 1614 11 et 12 Jacobi.

This done, it was the prudent obfervation of this lady That in the five laſt difcents her fons family had not received into it the warmth of any other influence, fave what their Anceſtors left to ſhine upon them, and themſelves by a temperate motion had preſerved and held upon their paternall pole; And thereupon, ſtudious how to enlarge his ſpheare, in ffebruary and March before the ſaid Earle of Northtons death, by the ſpeciall means of the lady Jane the widow of this lords grandfather, a marriage was concluded upon, (wᵗʰ the ſaid Earles conſent,) between this lord and Elizabeth the ſecond daughter and coheire of Sir Michaell Stanhope knight, brother of the ſaid lady Jane, A prudent gent of an honorable diſcent and family; Between whom and this lords mother, the paralell was ſoe equall without giving or taking or opening at either end, That by Indentures dated the thirtieth of March in the 12ᵗʰ of king James in conſideration of the maryage intended between the ſaid parties, hee ſetled upon them a great part of his inheritance in the Counties of Suffolk and Middleſex, then (as hee delivered his pᵗticuler) rented at . 1503ˡⁱ· p Anñ; giving further hope of the faire and uniforme houſe in Sᵗ Johns Street near Clarkenwell, where hee then dwelt, And which two years after hee performed and ſetled upon his ſaid daughter; Neither was the hope unprobable, but that the ſaid Elizabeth might enjoy a coperciners part of the poſſeſſions of Sir Wiłłm Reade of Oſterly knight, whoſe only child (then living) her mother was, which then alſo were eſtimated by him at—3000ˡⁱ· p Anñ: And which upon the death of Sir William, the 11ᵗʰ of Auguſt in the 19ᵗʰ of King James. 1621. came home to that hope.

902 **According** to which agreement, on Thurſday in Eaſter | weeke following, the 13ᵗʰ of Aprill in the 12ᵗʰ of king James, 1614. this lord George maryed her the ſaid Elizabeth in preſence of both their parents in the church of great Sᵗ Bartholomewe in London, He then of the age of thirteen years and ſix months, And ſhee the ſaid Elizabeth of the age of nine years, upon Sᵗ Thomas day the 21ᵗʰ of December then laſt paſt; her elder ſiſter the lady Jane having about one year before at the ſame church been marryed to Henry Viſcount fitʒ Water, ſon and heire apparant to Robert Ratcliffe Earle of Suſſex, with as great a portion of his poſſeſſions ſetled upon her; And having in theſe two honorable families ſetled his poſterity, His next thoughts was reflected upon his own mortallity; And accordingly not longe after, erecting his Tombe at Sudburne in Suffolke where hee intended to bee buried, hee engraved thereupon theſe words, vizᵗ,

Memoria juſtorum in manu dei eſt.

Sir Michaell Stanhope knight in the County of Nottingham left five ſons, Thomas Stanhope knight of the ſame county; Edward Stanhope knight of the County of Yorke

Yorke, and one of the Counfell there eftablifhed; John Stanhope knight, lord Stanhope of Harrington, of the priory Counfell to Queen Elizab.^th and king James, Vice-chamberlaine to them both, and Treaforer to them both; Edward Stanhope knight doctor of the civill lawe; Michaell Stanhope knight, lord of this Manor, who mindfull of his mortality, while hee lived, erected this monument,

Heere refteth in affured hope to rife in Chrift, Sr Michaell Stanhope knight, who ferved at the feet of Queen Elizabeth of moft happy and famous memory in her privy Chamber, twenty years, And of our Soveraigne king James in the fame place the reft of his daies; who maryed Anne daughter to Sir William Reade of Ofterly in the County of Middlefex knight, by whom he had | iffue two daughters; Jane maryed to Henry Vifcount fitz Walter, fon and heire apparant to the Earle of Suffex; And Elizabeth maryed to George lord Berkeley, Mowbray, Segrave, and Breoufe, of Berkeley Caftle in the County of Glouc., this George being the 21.th Baron by difcent.

All honor, glory, praife, and thanks, bee unto thee O glorious Trinity.
Chrift Jefus came into the world to fave finners, whereof I am cheefe.
 I Tim: 1. 15.
Thou haft redeemed mee O lord God of truth.   Pfa: 31. 5.
I defire to be diffolved and to bee with Chrift.   Phil. 1. 23.
Death is to mee advantage.   Phil. 1. 21.
I will take the cup of falvation and call upon the name of the lord.
 Pfal: 116. 13.
He that glorieth, let him glory in the lord.   I Cor. 1. 31.
Faith . hope . charity . on three of the pillers.

This his monument was finifhed two years and more before his death, whereby it may appeare, (if neither his will nor ought elfe were,) what opinion hee held of Mrs Bridget,[1] whom his faid wife (whofe daies longe after lafted not) brought into the world

---

[1] Mrs Bridget Countefs of Defmond whom S.^r M: Stanhope never did own & was brought up in a Cottage, but after his death came in as Heirefs to Sr Michaell Stanhope upon George Lord Berkeleys Hitting his Steward a Box of the Ear, he told him it fhould coft him dear, & carried Mrs Bridget to the Duke of Buckingham who married her to a near relation of his & went to Law with the Ld Berkeley whofe wives fifter fhee was proved.

[2] It was thought S.^r M: Poifoned his wife Imediatly after her lyeing in.

[Thefe notes, from the margin of the Manufcript, are in the handwriting of Lady Elizabeth Germain.—ED. See *Ante* p. 408, *n.*]

world fower years before the erecting of this Tombe; He dyed the 18th of December in the 19th of King James. 1621. his father in Law Sir Willm Read being dead the 11th of August before.

In honour of which lady Elizabeths difcent, I will (out of my mean collections) add, That her faid grandfather Sir Michaell Stanhope, beheaded in the Sixth of king Edward the Sixth, was the fon of Sr Edward Stanhope, fon of Thomas Stanhope, fon of Sr John Stanhope knight, who dyed in 9th of king Henry the 7th, | fon of Richard Stanhope who dyed in the life of his father, fon of Sr Richard Stanhope knight, who dyed in the 14th of king Henry the fixth, fon of John Stanhope Efqr, who dyed in the 46th of king Edward the third, fon of Richard Stanhope knight, fon of Richard Stanhope, who poffeffed ample poffeffions in the North parts of England in the time of king Edward the firft.

In which pedegree I omitt the name and place of Anne Stanhope wife to Edward Seymore Duke of Somerfet, protector of the Realme and of king Edward the fixth; The rather for that in the beft hiftories of thefe prefent daies, fhee is publifhed to bee a woman for many imperfections intollerable, for pride monftrous, exceedingly both fubtill and violent in accomplifhing her ends, for which fhee fpurned over all refpects both of confcience and fhame, &c. And brought to fatall deftinies both her hufband and his brother, and fome of her own kindred. But how defervedly marked with that character, I know not.

The forefaid Henry Earle of Northton in his will (made the day before his death) hath thefe words; I will, That my executors for fuch intereft as I have, fhall affigne over the Wardfhip of the lord Berkeley to Sir Richard Spenfer and Mr Thomas Spenfer his great uncles, To the ufe of the faid lord Berkeley, Hee paying 1500li for the fame to mine executors, being neer about the charge I have been at concerning the faid wardfhip; And of his faid will made his three fervants, John Griffith, William Bynge, and Robert Cole, Executors; who demaund the 1500li of the lady Berkeley and of Sir Michaell Stanhope; And for nonpayment bring againft them a Writ of Ravifhment of ward, upon the Statute of Weftm the fecond: The fute proceedeth, the cafe is drawn, and deliberatly advifed upon with Counfell by the defendants in their own perfons; The writ appeareth to bee miftaken by the Executors, brought by them as Executors to the faid Earle, | whereas they had the fame by the Earles Deed inrolled in Chancery two days before his death, the end and loffe of a years fuite; A new originall was ready to bee purchafed by the Executors; The cafe with the circumftances contained ten poynts, moft of which
were

were doubtfull: propofitions are made for peace, and propounded; the offer imbraced; The agreement was That (befides 300ˡⁱ in hand) 1200ˡⁱ more fhould bee paid at three daies: Security is given, the ravifhment is releafed, the payments are made accordingly, And the 25ᵗʰ of November in the 14ᵗʰ year of king James, a deed is fealed to the faid lady and Sir Michaell Stanhope by John Griffith alone, whereunto the Earles of Suffolk and Worcefter and the lord William Howard, (three of the Earle of Northtons overfeers,) were witneffes; The other two Executors refufing, who were regnum inter fe divifum, at much variance by mutual fuits in Chancery, but to Griffith the lords overfeers adhered. *Carta in caftro de Berkeley.*

Though I covet brevity, and know that truth is not to bee followed too near the heeles, whereby I will omit the ires and anfwers that paffed between this lady and the lords, overfeers to the Earles will, who would have laid the wholl burthen on Sir Michll if thereto her vertuous difpofition would have affented; Yet fhall the Earles gratitude appear to bee fomwhat leffe to this lord George then the merits of his grandmother deferved, (which mine own often imployments between them can witnefs,) adding withall the fugred Ires wᶜʰ hee often wrote to this lady Elizabeth in affurance thereof; And his eftimate of his fifters memory, delivered oft to mee under this valuation, That whilft fhee lived fhee was to him the deareft of all Gods creatures; his ambition only being, (fuch were his words,) to requite her bounties to himfelf in the fweeteft image of her felf: A few lynes of one of which, (written to the faid lady Elizabeth 11. weeks after the death of her hufband,) read in thefe his words, vizᵗ, *dated. 14. ffebr: 1611.*

It is not ftrange to mee (moft noble lady) that you beftow the favour which I find by your token upon your true freind and ally, whom you have already bound by curtefies before this time: But yet I am forry you have fent a token of greater value, then I would willingly receive from a lady that by her vertues deferves rather to command my fortunes: Your life hath been of proofe, your actions moft worthy of refpective imitation, And your kind and tender love to all your late hufbands freinds and Allyes, foe farr above the cuftome and manner of ladies, matched in like degrees, as wee had all great reafon to efteem you as a pretious ornament to that honorable houfe in which you were beftowed, and a comfort to us all that are recordʳˢ of your meritt in the life, and your mindfulnes after the death, of him with whom you lived foe longe with honor. *A jewell of great price.*

2. Touching the care of your hopefull fons education, (worthy lady) though it fhall bee needleffe to repeat what I have written to my brother Berkeley, yet I will add,

add, That fo long as I live, your care your counfell and defires fhall bee regarded as mine own, in any thing that concerns him in any way; And when I dye, my will fhall teftify both what I think of your vertue, and in this cafe what I owe to your affection. During mine own time, I confeffe the height of my ambition is, to expreffe by care of this fweet child in what accompt I held the grandmother, that for her vertues and rare parts, befides her love to my felf, deferves to bee recorded in a gratefull memory; for nothing fhall bee neglected that may tend to the perfection of her fon in all degrees, that both living and dead was moft deare unto mee. Since it is yor La.^{ps} defire that I fhould retaine this token of your favour, I will obey your will, but with this promife, to deferve it to your liking or to fend it back againe with an obligation of thanks. Comand ever as much as any that liveth.

febr. 14. 1611.
      Your affectionate uncle and conftantly
        devoted freind : Northton.

Take alfo a fewe words more drawn from two paragraphs of another lre written by the faid Earle the ffifth of ffebruary, | Anno, 1613. after the death of this lords grandfather, vizt,

Honorable and worthy lady, I fhould blufh to receive foe many favours as I have done from your La.^p at fundry times, if I were not refolved to requite them in the right time, which if I doe not, beleive that I have offended againft you, that are foe near both by allyance and bloud, as to this day I never did to any other by ingratitude. In the mean time refting ready to acknowledge to your La.^p by any fervice and means, the noble favours, befides that conftant and kind affection I have received from your noblenes, I ever reft—Your La.^{ps} affectionate uncle and true freind to ferve you

              Northampton.

This family having obferved what I wrote of the Manor of Bofham in the life of Maurice the fifth, is further to bee informed, That this lady Elizabeth defirous to fee that part of her joynture, in the vacation between the two termes of Eafter and Trinity, a year and an half after it accrued unto her, accompanied with this lord her fon, made thither her firft journey, whom my felf attended: At a Court then holden at the Manor houfe by Nicholas Holborne her fteward, the wednefday in Whitfon week, fhee her felf declared to her tenants then affembled the motives of her journey and of holding that Court, To fee and know them, and to make her fon known amongft them, whofe the inheritance was; Holding it fitting, (for continuance

ance of mutuall right and accord,) That afwell by fight of each of their Coppies as by their further p°fentment, (fith part of their Copihold lands were heriotable, part not, and held by one and the fame copies,) that fuch a diftinction might by their felves now bee made As neither heryot or other fervice might bee hereafter denyed when due, nor her Steward exact that through ignorance which was not juftly payable, with other like words full of fweetnes towards them; Anfwere was made by many, but principally by John Exton an Alderman of the Citie of Chichefter, (many of whofe citizens by reafon of the adjacency of that manor to their Citie are Copyholders,) denying her power | either to call a Court at that time, or that themfelves owed any fervice thereat, with much other matter to that peremptory effect; After time for further deliberation given, till her return from the Ifle of Thorney, the Tenants returned with Counfell, upon a fecond and third meeting, (the former affronts wifely by her diffembled,) promifes were made for fome poore kind of conformity, but in the end after daies againe and againe given by her Steward, till Michaelmas and Hillary Courts following, altogeather unperformed; whereby 908

    Patientia fæpe læfa, vertitur in furorem.
    Patience often wounded, is converted into fury.

Shee in the end of that Hillary Terme in the 14.th of king James, exhibited a bill in Chancery againft the faid John Exton and twenty or more of the cheifeft of thofe Copyholders, wherein nine points were afterwards by two Decrees upon that bill ordered againft them; viz!., The fynes of their Copyhold lands called boordlands declared to bee arbitrable at her will; Old works of villenage (for 120. years laft neglected) reduced to a yearly rent of 74^{li} where nothing formerly was paid. Leafes by them pretended to bee lawfully made for one thoufand years and upwards, reduced to 21, or under, and for a fyne, and by licence; Themfelves declared to bee Copyholders, not freeholders in Ancient demefne in hault tenure, as they mainly infifted upon to have been; And their Indenture of confirmation of their cuftoms made by Henry lord Berkeley in the 7.th year of Queen Elizabeth, (which they for the Canonicalnes thereof called Bofham bible,) declared void, and damned, with other like, as the Decrees doe fhew, And at this inftant themfelves in contempt and likely the next Terme to bee acquainted with the ffleet for their contempts; The fear whereof drives them in much humility to fue for peace in a farre different note from the firft tune of the faid John Exton and others at their firft appearance upon fubpeanaes, then proudly affuring | her La.p That if they were conftrayned to fpend but five fhillings fhee fhould not bee excufed for five hundred pounds: But the cafe did in two years much alter; fhee prevailed above her own expectation, They now avow before her to have fpent—900^{li} in the fuite, willing her La.p foe an end may bee

1.
2.
3.

4.
5.
6.
7.

Triñ. 16. Jac:

Thefe decrees were afterwards vacated by another 909 decree dated 17 Octob. in 18 Jacobi and the tenants reftored to the former claimes and cuftomes, &c.

3 K VOL. II

bee, to propose her own conditions, which not fourteen daies past shee hath done, by their payment of—1960ᴸ to redeem their folly, whereof they accepted ; **This** suite ariseing from so unnecessary a provocation through the peevish refractarynes of proud tenants, hath made them fabula vulgi, a byword to all their neighbors, and president to posterity ; wherein though it pleased her and her brother in lawe Sir Michaell Stanhope, (who much incited this suite,) to leave it wholly unto mee, I can challenge noe more therein then that her good fortune hath brought it and all the like to like successes.

1. **In** the time of which Bosham suite, shee was enforced unto three others in the Court of Wards : The first against John Osborne of Bosham for wrongfully detaining certaine of her demesnes in that Manor as assignee to John Shelly, a bannished recusant, Lessee for his life by the demise of Henry lord Berkeley in the time of Queen Mary ; who lost his terme and shee quietly now enjoys it ; wherein part of the question was whether the lessee or the assignee of his lessee for life should prove the life or death of the tenant for life.

2. **The** second against Richard Byford of Slimbridge for his often infringements of her liberty of Berkeley hundred, the successe of which suite with his punishment more largely followeth.

3. **The** third against Sara Tilladam, who claymed her widows estate in a Copyhold messuage in Bevington in the Manor of Hame, after the death of Thomas Tilladam her husband, according to the custome of that manor ; which was denyed to her, in regard hee being much weakened by longe sicknes and taken in Execution for debt upon a Capias ad satisfaciend, at Berkeley on a Satturday at two in the afternoon, And being that night conveyed to the house of one of the Undersheriffes men in Gloucester, was the next morning there maryed to her ; And that shee being a servant in the house of James Atwood an Inholder in Berkeley (where hee was taken) followed him to Glouc., and soe the next morning by maryage became his wife ; And being within two hours after mariage comitted to the goale, their dyed of his old infirmity within three weeks after, leaving her both maid and widow, as was supposed ; who hereupon claiming her widows estate whilst shee should live sole and chast, was by an Injunction out of the Court of Wards removed out of her possession ; for that by noe reasonable intendment such a bed could have a free bench, neither was fraud and Practice to advantage any Tenant against the true ends of mariage.

Hill. 15. Jac. 1617.

In

In the 18th year of the said king, this lady at her only charges obtained from his Matie a large grant of liberties in the name of this lord her son in all his hundred of Berkeley, and in his burrough and manor of Tetbury, And in his manor and hundred of Portbury; Which liberties were these, viz{t}, A viewe of ffranke pledge and whatsoever thereto belongeth; And all felons goods of what kind soever, whether felons of themselves or otherwise; wayved[1] goods, Estrayes, Treasure trove, Deodands; year, day, and waste; estrepments[2]; goods of fugitives and of convict, Attainted, outlawed, and of wayved persons, before what Judge soever, or in what Court wheresoever such goods shall come to bee forfeited, And all issues and amerciaments lost or forfeited within the said hundred; And all whale fishes, Sturgeons, and all other great and royall ffishes, in whatsoever free fishings within the river of Seavern; And all such faires and marketts as have been accustomed, Togeather with a Court of Pipowders, with all Stalls, pickages, waights, fines, Amerciaments, Tolls, liberties, and free customes, to such faires and markets belonging; And also free Warren in all his demesne lands within the said hundred, and in all other places where his Ancestors have used to have free warren, with divers others the like; **And** in Tetbury, a view of frank pledge within that burrow and manor, and whatsoever thereto belong-|eth, and all marketts and faires there heretofore held and kept, with all Tolls, stalls, pickages, waights, fynes, and amerciaments, to them belonging, or there used; And all waived goods, estrayes and deodands, And all goods of felons, fugitives, felons of themselves, And whatsoever other liberties any of his Ancestors have there had or used, with others more, as by the said grant more at large appeareth. **The** purchase whereof with the successe of the Bosham suite before mentioned, draweth near to her late purchase of the sweet and well seated manor of Cranford in the County of Middlesex, which with the price of—7000{li}, shee hath this present Easter Terme. 1618. in the 16th of king James, purchased in fee simple of the fower Coheires of Sir Robert Aston; having also strengthened her estate therein by a new tres patents from his Matie, Not only preserving her sons possessions during his minority from all diminution with some increase of his rents, but inriching the wholl with more regall liberties then were attained unto by any of his former Ancestors; not speaking of the great advancement which this lord her son wth his posterity is assured to receive by his mariage, obtained by her care and prudence; And this is that charter of liberties wherto I related in the life of the lord Thomas the second under his title of law suits. **Neither** may

Carta. 25. Julij 1616. 14. Jac: in Castro de Berkel: v'e fol: In Berkeley hundred and in Portbury.

In Tetbury. 911

Cranford

fol: [226]

---

[1] Forsaken. [ED.]

[2] Waste made by tenants for life to the prejudice of him in reversion, whether by cutting trees, &c., or by deterioration of the land by continual cropping without manure or other unfair husbandry. [ED.]

may I omit, that in August and September last, 1617. in the 15th of king James, shee was present with this lord her son at all the Courts of his Manors in the Counties of Glouc. and Somersett, and at their severall Leets and Courts of Pleas, perusing the perticular estates of each tenant in each manor, holding by lease or by Copy, comparing all the perticular p.ts of each demise with her own booke to that purpose before hand prepared, noting therein with her own hand, the lives in being, and the rents and other profits reserved upon each estate; wherein shee sate sometimes fowerteen houres without departure from her seate, drawing out those labours at some Manors till near midnight, my self then Steward and attending her in that service: presi-|dents not more rare in a lady of her birth, then noble incitements to her son, present also most of those daies and hours with her.

<blockquote>
Were all wives such, this age would happy bee,
But happier that, of our posterity.
</blockquote>

At which time many complaints being presented unto her touching the daily infringes of the liberty of Berkeley by one Richard Biford of Slimbridge, an atturney at lawe, with the wrongs and oppressions thereby thrown upon his neighbors, shee exhibited a bill in the Court of Wards against him, whereupon after defence by him made, and witnesses examined: hee was heavily censured, fined, and awarded to pay greater costs then his ability at that time might beare; howbeit, by his submission, acknowledgment of his offences in writing, and by appealing to her mercy, hee found greater favor then either his offences deserved, or his guiltines expected, in remission of the heaviest part of the Decree and sentence of the said Court.

From which Charter of liberties in Berkeley hundred, shee in the last year (amongst some others) reaped these fruits in the Manors and lands of other men;

1. One Cullen an Inholder in Dursley by stabbing of himself with his own knife, becoming thereby, felo de se, his goods escheated, which shee had.

2. *A* servant to John Hollister working at his water mill in Wike near Berkeley coveting with a feather in his hand to oyle the coggs, was by their swift motion caught and drawn in by the Arme, and ground almost to peeces, whereby Hollister made composition for the deodand, coggs, wheele, and upper millstone; for quicquid movet ad mortem deodandum est: which the lord of the fee of this mill, a magistrate of Bristoll, armed with a double power of the Charters of that Citie, and with the authority of the generall Eleemoziner to his Ma.tie, would have wrested from her, but could not.

3. The like deodand of wayne and fix oxen happening about | the fame time at Nimpesfeild, a manor of M? John Bridgemans, as it was entring into his gates with wood, when the owner perifhed under the wheele of the wayne. And laftly in this prefent month of May 1618, in the 16th of king James, one Thomas Cafton a tiler in taking down an old farm houfe of Robert Webbs in Cromhall Ligon, the old inheritance of the Dornyes, found hidden between the tiling and feiling over an old oven, fower and thirty peeces of gold of the coine of king Henry the fixth as the infcription fhewed, then of 13^s 4^d, the peece; which hee with others coveting to conceale, A bill was by her exhibited againft fower of them into the Court of Wards, making her title to that treafure trove under the faid Charter of king James; But they feeking peace, found it, And upon receipt of an accompt of the wholl, fhee honorably gave back a part, rewarded fome others, retaining the refidue to her felf. With which compofition, (fith finding of gold is held good fortune,) I end thefe relations, the day this lord George began his firft Journey to Oxford, whither hee came on Thurfday, before Whitfunday the 21th of May in the 16th year of the raigne of king James, Anno, 1618: where in Chrift Church Colledge, I leave him to his booke, under a difcreet tutor, attended with honeft fervants, carefull of his health and honor; himfelf full of ingenuity, quick of apprehenfion, and fweet of nature; of a loving affection towards his wife, almoft three years younger then himfelf, And fhee in a like Sympathy towards him, vertuoufly bred under a prudent father at St John Jherufalem in the parifh of Clarkenwell by London; In fyliall obedience towards his mother, fincerely affecting with brotherly love his vertuous fifter; Thefe feeds promife a fertile increafe; how fruitfull the harveft will prove, God Almighty qui omnia novit et fuaviter difponit, hee only knowes; The living, and not my duft, will tell hereafter when the cropp is inned into the barne; Poffeffed at this time of his ancient caftle of Berkeley, and of more then one thoufand marks of old rents about the fame, which have infeparably accompanied his ancient and honorable | family in all thefe former twenty generations, through the various motions of 550. years: A miracle and bleffing which the God of heaven and earth hath not by the vifible teftimonies of his mercy, beftowed upon any other family of like ranke and honour, in generations never attainted, that the records of this kingdoe declare.

His noble mother I leave at her new purchafe at Cranford,[1] 12 miles from London, amongft her thoufands of books, havinge from the Counfells of thofe dead,

---

[1] Cranford the Country Houfe my Brother James Earl of Berkeley moft delights in to wch he has made large Additions.—*Marginal note in the MS. made by Lady Elizabeth Germain.* [ED.]

dead, brought wisdom and happines to her widdowhood, according to the rithmicall disticke,

> If that thou wilt true counsell have,
> Of dead old men doe thou it crave.

Eccles: ca; 7. v. 27. 28.

And the vertuous lady Theophila his sister with Sr. Robert Coke her husband, at their house near Kingston[1] upon Thames; Of which mother and daughter, I tell their generations to come, That I have found what king Salomon by his own acknowledgment could never find, two good women, And I know (by knowing them from their youths upwards) it lies not in envies power to reprove this passage; And in this I confesse fortunes liberality to my self, That the vertuous memory of these two good ladyes will bee somwhat longer by these my labors continued in the generations to come.

> I'le pray their name and honor n'ere expire,
> But in a melting firmament of fire.

With this addition of comfort to them both, That the one hath a son the other a brother in one person, who having now continued two years in Oxford, is entirely well reported of and beloved throughout the body of that University, and promising for life and learning as hopefully as the University remembreth any of his ranke, in any age before; which in my visits of his Lop. in termly travells that way, I have often, again and againe, heard and observed, and here professe for truth: And that even now ready for travell beyond seas, if forraigne vices corrupt not the excellency of these hopes, or discontent upon returne, hee is likely in ripenes of daies to parrallell, if not outstrip the best of his forefathers, which God grant. Howbeit I may not, in the clasping up hereof, without a staine of ingratitude leave the memory of the said lady Berkeley uncommended to posterity; That when I had to the sixth of king James to the utmost of my endeavors, in behalf of the lord Henry Berkeley, pursued for divers years sundry lawe suits against the lord Viscount Lisle, and gained upon him, as appears in the title of his lawe sutes: His wily agents, not without his privity, observing that the lease I dwelt upon in Nibley, (then the greatest part of my estate,) might bee avoided, secretly contracted for the Revertion, before I had any other inckling, then from a private whispering, that I should shortly either bee taken from those suits, or seeke a new habitation: But getting knowledge of the plot whilst the writings were in drawing, I countermined by my landlady, a powerfull

915

fol:[753] and after.

---

[1] I believe that House near Kingston was Durdens nearer Epsome wch her Husband left in his will to my Grandfather George Earl of Berkeley wch was sold to the Duke of Argyle & by him sold to Ld Guilford. *Marginal note in the MS. made by Lady Elizabeth Germain.* [ED.]

full woman with her husband, And gayning a little upon time, I posted the knowledge thereof to this lady Berkeley, and to her husband, and to the lord Henry his father, desiring their directions what course to stirre in that storme, which must either beat mee from their service, or cast mee lower under hatches, then I hoped ever to have fallen: What I received from the father and son, a part of the ladies ire hereafter telleth, But from the lady her self, I had two such ires in two daies; which remaining as the choicest peeces amongst my evidences, are never to bee forgotten in my generations; In one of which are these words; And I protest unfainedly if you try any other freind you have in England, besides my self, in this buisines, (sith the father and son are noe more sensible,) I will take greater exception to you then ever I meant to have done. The event was, I prevailed by my landlady (the night Crowe) and, to the dishonesty of my landlord her husband, got the purchase my self, being thereto solely and sodainly enabled by the said lady, whereby my footing hath ever since stood the firmer, and my port the quieter, to record the passage to the honor of her memory. |

916 Now have I discharged my self of part of that debt which I owed to this ancient family, To the honor of the now lord George and his vertuous sister, to the memory of their noble grandfather and grandmother, And to his lordships prudent mother, the widowe of my master; And these are those that lived in lumbis Hardingi, that were in the bowells of Hardinge, when, with William Duke of Normandy called the Conqueror, hee first entred England, whereby these wholl relations are but the story of themselves in him, And of him in them: Their Ancestors from him are my circumference, they my center, where all my lynes and labours meete Joyne and end. |

The conclusion of the Author.

917 Sincerely I doe avow before the face of this noble family, That in the volumes of this their story I have dealt clearly without hope or feare; I have not belyed the dust of the dead, nor flattered the face of the living; I have represented things truly, I have not adorned, inlarged, or hyperbolized the matter in a lyne or word; my free genius is at endlesse enmity with such basenes; fflatterers I hold to bee the basest of slaves; I have comended nothing to posterity, but what I have found of record, or taken from venerable manuscripts or the sealed Deeds of men, save that in a fewe of the last yeares I have given beleife in a fewe sallies to the last lord Henry lately dead, And to the eyes and ears of my self, assurances to mee above
exception;

exception; And I know it lies not in the power of envy or malice to reproach mee of falshood or flattery without injustice.

In such places as I seeme to depart from the comon chronicles of the kingdome, in matter, names, dayes, months or years, it is wherein some of them depart from others, and all of them from matter of record, which I have followed as the Authentike Judge of truth, whereof my marginalls are my witnesses, in which kindes I have amended them in many places; Absit jactantia verbo.

Though I know that this and other like noble families have been in divers ages served with many worthy men and minds, yet none have ventured on the history of their lords or masters lives; whereby for ought I have observed, I am the first and alone that hitherto have run this course of a genealogike history of any patrimoniall family.

Then goe my booke, and serve without disgrace,
Till better come, and then see thou give place.

I have taken into hand year after yeare most of the Records in the Tower of London, between the first and last whereof some parts of each of 34 years were spent; And what records and books I have turned over in the offices belonging to the kings bench, Rolls chapple, Chancery, Comon pleas, Exchequer, Treasory, pipe and pell offices, and other places there, let my marginall vouchers, and my books of the lord Berkeleys tenures declare; what remaines to bee further done, (as many eares of the best graines must needs have escaped the reapers hand in so great an harvest,) my wish is, this noble family may send forth another to perfect what my life prooves too short to finish; My travells also and other imployments at home and abroad, whereof each part of my life hath stood in need, have bereft mee of most of that time which otherwise I had given to this history: Also nine other books of mine presented to this family, have been as theeves in stealing much time from this; But why may not my grave expect That this lord George in his maturity of years should, as Cæsar did, write his own Comentaries? And as Octavius the Emperor did, the history of his own life, as Suetonius reports? And as king Cirus is recorded to have transmitted to his sonne the memoriall of his own diurnall actions? And what now remaines of Cæsar soe famous as his Comentaries? And what of Cicero as his books of offices written to his son? which for this lord, or some other branch of this noble family, to performe, would testifie their ability for the present, and perpetuate their memory to posterity; Such a story gaines strength and gets authority

ity by time, And the more antient it waxeth the more excellent is the estimation;
It advanceth their prayses in the Assemblies of their generations, and becomes a living president for future posterities;

   Whereas our Oxford books but only Rules doe give,
   The examples of our fathers teach us how to live.

And let this noble family bee assured that their own true history in their own meridian, erected upon the frame of example and caution, will bee more forcible then a thousand fictions, spending their readings upon impossibillities and views of Castles in the aire. |

Let it not discourage to understand, that I have spent a wholl week togeather in a search, and returned without the gleaning of a note to enlarge a line herein; nor the application of that of the poet,

   Apparent rari nantes in gurgite vasto.

Virgill: Æniad Lib. 1.

The old Atcheivements and actions of private men, appeare but now and then floating in the great gulfe of time.

Industry will double what I have but begun; To the laborious, God is always propitious: And this family can never think their own history, (the story of it self,) too voluminous, which in this prerogative will triumph over all histories; That where others give life and light to the World, this beckens and holds up the finger to this family alone; Others, from others; This family from the Acts and examples of its own Ancestors, ever since time hath left any thing in certainty; whereby they behold their own lyne tryumphing over time, which nothing but eternity hath triumphed over; making those of them that now live, as if they had lived then; and them to represent their dead acts upon the stage of their present view and judgment, As how they flourished, how they stumbled or fell, how vertue and piety made them prosperous, how vice and discontent deformed them; which thereby will bee delivered unto them out of the depth and darknes of the earth: **And**, sith the sons of noble parents are bound by a kind of necessity not to degenerate from the vertue of their Ancestors, let it ever comfort the inlargers of this family to know, That nothing can bee more acceptable to a noble and heroicke family then to read it self; And its self to bee the substance of its own reading; And that their eye cannot bee cast thereon but their Ancestors seem present and represented unto them, And themselves the glasse that represents them to themselves, as in their proper spheare: If they bee vertuous, it will incite them to goe on in nobler undertakings; If otherwise, they will fear the pen, and to avoid reproach with their succeeding
                    generations,

generations, (knowing that books have an immortality above their vices,) will change their courſe, and | not endure to bee held a baſtard branch degenerated from the ſtocke of ſo honorable forefathers; But howſoever the event bee, thou (whoſoever thou art) haſt done the part of an honeſt man, And thy rewarder is in thy boſome. **And** further to incite to ſoe noble an undertaking let this family reſt aſſured, That a maſſe of materialls both legall and hiſtoricall reflecting upon this Berkeleian race, lye hid in manuſcripts and in the records of the kingdome, kept in the Tower of London, Exchequer, Pipe Office, Chapple of the Rolls, in the paper chamber of State affairs at Whitehall, in the Journalls of Parliaments, And in the regiſters of the Biſhops of Worceſter and divers other old Biſhoppricks; And in numberles manuſcripts preſerved in the publick and private libraryes of the Univerſities, Colledges and Halls of Oxford and Cambridge; And alſo in the libraryes and Chapiter houſes of many Cathedrall Churches; And with the old Societies and Companyes of the Citie of London, and other ancient Cities and Burrow townes; And in the private ſtudyes of many excellent men, as Sr. Edward Coke, Sr. Robert Cotton, Sr. John Burrowe, Mr. John Selden, and divers other; Into ſome of which places, though I have but pryed, and others ſcarce ſaluted afar of, yet I confeſſe to have drawn the better half of theſe relations out of ſome of thoſe honorable and ſpatious feilds, where ſtill remaine many fragrant and faire flowers ſweetly reſenting upon the perticuler acts and imployments of this noble family; And my grave ſhall bleſs that foot that walketh after them, And that hand that picks them up and bundles them with theſe.

To conclude, I have now anatomized the filmes and inſides of this noble race, and conſidered of their ſecret walkes for 550. years; And after my 40. years ſweeping of each corner of their habitations, And all my tumblings and toſſings of hiſtoryes and records, printed and manuſcripts, and prying | into the Courts of Judicature, I avow, (my witnes is in heaven,) That I have not at all obſerved ſoe good a race, of twenty diſcents, not any one of them in that length of time, and of times troubles, having been Attainted. **And** it is probable, That it hath been one of the preſervations of this durable family in all their generations, neither to have been often clouded with the frownes of their princes, nor to have ſate too neare to their immoderate favors; but to have had the warmth of the Court in a moderate diſtance, not in too neare nor ſcorching an aſpect or reflexe.

In handling of this Berkeleian hiſtory I have not been able to ſtand upon termes of learning, (though hee writes eloquently that writes honeſtly;) I am too

privy

privy to mine own ignorance; I know well, quàm mihi fit curta fupellex, how my Schoole ftudyes, but fhrubbs and brambles at the beft, have been overlonge difcontinued; And now before the clafping up hereof, fower and thirty years a profeffed plowman, having all that time eaten much of my bread from the labours of mine own hands; And that being but a dwarfe in my beft ftature, I was to creepe upon the fhoulders of taller men for the furniture of this ftory, And with Zacheus to climb other mens trees to fee my wayes the better: And in a word, I willingly with the comicall poet fay That I have herein dealt by way of clofe pilfering; **I only** have had the happines to gather things togeather that were fcattered into many corners of this kingdome, and into fome parts of forraigne nations to bring thofe atcheivements to light that longe had lyen in darknes; And to preferve in one body for the after ages of this family what would have been loft in parts, and could not well have lafted half this age: **This history** thus gathered is now become a portion of the lawfull inheritance and birthright of your noble family; To whom not to prefent it, is a with-holding your right; You not to accept it, how raggedly foever clothed, is to reject a portion of your ancient poffeffions: | for by the providence of the Almighty, the wholl is fallen to your lotts as the right heires and inheritors of them.

An Apoftrophe.

922

Neither in all this hiftory am I otherwife than as your Anceftors Amanuēfis; I write as they did; I am but as the fcribe of their Deeds and fayings; I am not guided by my felf but by their works and words: It refts that you the now lord George propofe to your felf in maturity of years the upright fteps of thofe your Anceftors wherein they honorably walked; than which nothing doth or can more incite you to their vertue and frugallity: You have of them many admirable peeres and couples for your prefidents, excellent examples of eminent vertues; At them to poynt fufficeth; Robert the firft, Thomas the fecond, Thomas the third, Maurice the fifth, Thomas the fifth, &c. their harveft is plentifull and by you to bee Inned; your flefh and bloud is made of theires; Compare you thefe and other your Anceftors paft with your felf prefent, times ancient with moderne, wherein your own genius or noble difpofition will receive beft fattisfaction: They as fathers by preceding had the happines to bee your patterns; you by fucceeding thefe famplers have the advantage of imitating their vertues, and of adding to their honor; The ufuall praife of good kings in the Scriptures phrafe, is That they walked in the waies of their fathers; better prefidents of good fathers you cañot have; The firft fruits being fo holy, the after-lumpe, unlefs you degenerate, cañot be foure: The pomegranate is not more full of kernells then they were in vertuous actions and Almfdeeds;
And

now aged, 16. years 5. months. May. 1618.

And domesticall examples in patronimycall families have with all worthy men ever moved more then forraigne: And as all noble minds doe endeavour to imitate the worthy Deeds of their famous Ancestors, soe do such by all meanes industriate themselves to avoid that which in their predecessors was judged worthy of blame.

Anno. 1618.

923 And finally I doe faithfully tell you my most honoured lord, That towards the later dayes of your noble grand-|father, I related to him upon occation of the composition for Wotton and other Manors, then made with the lord Lisle, many of the most remarkeable passages of these his Ancestors since Harding the Dane; which bee seemed exceedingly to delight in, And willed mee, That I would declare as much to his son Thomas, the better to know his forefathers; And when hee was dead, (wee fallen upon the like subject) that noble lord once or twice in the next two years after, (before himself slept with his forefathers,) willed mee, (And his will thus doubled was to mee more then a treble commandment,) if I lived till the riper years of his grandchild George, (those were his words,) That I would inform him of the same, which I willingly then promised to doe, And have now performed beyond that promise: Howbeit I never Intimated to him, (though I then and divers years before intended it,) my purpose of writing their lives, as now by the favour of God I have done; wch here I end, with this request to you, and to your noble family, (I speak to none other,) That if any of you shall observe any slip of pen, number, marginall, or other small mistake, (which I hope, at the most, are few, if any,) That yee would reforme them favourably, And fairly say, as often I have herein said of others, It was the Scriveners fault, And that no man can depart from the condition of erring: And that men and the works of men are not born perfect and with beards upon their chins; That our best parts are full of errors, And man is the child of dust and father of error: ffigures or notes in my pocket-paper-books cursarily taken in my searches, may bee mistaken, or my clarks erre in often transcribing, both in paper and parchment; And to have reviewed my paynes in both would have exceeded the paynes I reviewed, which the small remains of my withered age, and the monthly affairs of a turmoyled life, would have denyed at my entrance; But if I have erred in matter, (as I hope I have not,) I yet have a

924 happines which some | want, authority for those errors; Witnes the margents of my books.

The God of all mercy and goodnes who hath been gracious to this Family throughout all their generations, shoure down his blessings in greater abundance upon you my hopeful lord, your noble mother, and sister, and your posterities unto the end of all eternity: In honour of whose memories, and as a manifest of my
thankfulnes

thankfulnes to yee and your honorable family, for the education of my youth and the many favours yee have conferred upon mee, And in satisfaction of part of that obligation which I owe by particular duty to each of your vertues, I have undergone these collections, (the labours of my youth and age,) not esteeming with my self any travells or expence therein otherwise valuable then that they have issued from humble endeavours, neither in further degree to bee meritorious then as yee by your benigne acceptance shall value them; towards whom my gray hairs and decaying age shall more glory to bee always found an honest and humble servant, then I shall to comand absolutely in any other calling : With my begging of the All-good, and Allmighty God, That that hand of heaven which happily hath given you three to this family may protect and sheild yee in your goings out and comeings in : And that his mercy may bee evermore nearer unto yee, then yee to any dangers ; The God of goodness perpetuate your happiness and grant you length and prosperity of daies here, peace at the time of your passage out of this world, And an happy resurrection to eternall life ; The which that it may bee let all that read hereon and love your family say, as I pray, Amen, Amen, Amen. |

The request of this History.

925

Read over first, then judge, condemn not thou before,
With judgement just reject, or else imbrace my lore.

Mine author is the first, and last, as I suppose,
That ever did assay, these lives for to disclose.

If ought mistaken bee, and seem to thee unfound,
With pen I pray amend, and not with tongue confound.

H. A. to the Author.

Now with the silke worme thou hast work't thee int' thy Tombe
   As having done thy duty in thy roome,
Thy task is past, And all thy labouring toile is gone,
   And now it rests for them that read hereon.
That when thy paynes for Berkeleis name they see,
Thy love with like, they should requite to thee.
But if malignant bee, the tongue of any groome,
Thy grave tells them, this work doth scorne their doome. |

The same H. A. to the Author.

This firſt of works framed by thy painfull hand,
   A monument of thy deſerts ſhall ſtand,
Which neither time nor malice ſhall deface,
   Outlaſting life, and to thy name a grace.
What forty years both farr and wide hath ſought,
   Thy toilſome foot into this hive hath brought:
In ſpite of thoſe that ſhall thy paines contemne,
   Who Berkeley loves, will honour thee, and them:
ffor why ſtill ſhall this of thy Chronicle bee read,
   It brings back time that's paſt, and gives life to their dead.
And now, what needeth Berkeley more, t'inlarge their name,
   This work itſelf doth Chronicle their living fame.

The same H. A. to the Author thus.

Theſe volumes are a glaſſe to ſee, how thou thy mind haſt bent,
Thy body toyld, thy time beſtow'd, and many a pound haſt ſpent,
In ſleeples nights, in reſtles days, in places farre and neere,
In ſearching this, in finding that, in labors here and there.
Preferring ſtill the Berkeleis good, neglecting ſtill thine own,
And art content that they ſhould reape, the ſeed wch thou haſt ſown.
     And when detraction ſhall forgotten bee,
   This will continue to eternize thee.

The end of the third and laſt volume containing the lives of the ſeaven laſt Anceſtors of the ancient and honorable family of the Berkeleis, including the lord George that now liveth; wherein 127. years are taken up, viz! from the 7th year of king Henry the 7th Anno, 1491, till the 17th year of the raigne of king James, of England, &c. Anno 1618.

Finis.

The record on folio 925 and what is above, except the laſt paragraph, are not in the preſentation copy in Berkeley Caſtle, but that copy contains the following explanations of the Marginal references.— [ED.]

The Authorities breefly quoted in the margents of this hiftory, are **927** thus opened and explayned, viz:

Rot. pip. 3. H. 2. underftand the great pipe roll in the pipe office in the Exchequer of the third year of king Henry the fecond. And fo of yᵉ reft.[1]

Plita in banco Mich. 17. H. 3. rot. 1. underftand the record in the comon place in Michmas Terme in the 17ᵗʰ year of king Henry the third, the firft roll: And fo of the reft.[1]

Fin: in banco. 5. E. 2. underftand, a fyne leavyed in that Court the 5ᵗʰ year of king Edward the fecond: And foe of the reft.[1]

Rot: cart. 7. Johis. nᵒ 80. m. 9. underftand, the Roll in the Tower called the Charter roll in the 7ᵗʰ year of king John, at the 80ᵗʰ number as it is figured, and the ninth fkyn or parchment roll; And foe of the reft.[1]

Plita Affis: coram Abbe de Evefh: 5. H. 3. in banco. underftand the pleas or fuits before the Abbot of Evefham and his fellow Juftices Itinerant, in the fifth year of king Henry the third, in the Court of Comon pleas. And fo of the reft.[1]

Efch: 20. H. 6. nᵒ 30. underftand, an Inquifition or office found after the death of that man, in the 20ᵗʰ yeare of Henry the fixth, the 30ᵗʰ Skyn in that bundle; And foe of others; which if it bee before the firft year of king Richard the third, then it is in the Tower; if after that year, then it is in the Chapple of the Rolls in Chancery Lane.[1]

Aug: cartul: Ideft, A great old book of old Charters and Deeds therein anciently written in Berkeley Caftle.[2]

Rob: de Ricart: Ideft, An ancient parchment manufcript book written in the time of king Edward the fourth, in the Cuftody of yᵉ Townclarke of the Citie of Briftoll for the time being.[3]

By, cart: pat: fin: claus: 4. E. 3. m. 2. nᵒ 3. or Rot. cart., Rot. pat., Rot. fin., Rot. claus:—underftand, the Charter roll, Patent roll, fyne roll, or Roll of the fynes, and

---

[1] All thefe Ancient Records have been collected and are now depofited in the Public Record Office. [ED.]

[2] The Briftol and Gloucefterfhire Archæological Society propofe to print this Manufcript in continuation of SMYTH's Manufcripts. [ED.]

[3] This Volume was Edited by Mifs Lucy Toulmin Smith, and printed for the Camden Society in 1872. [ED.]

and the rolls called clofe rolls, in the Tower or Rolls chapple in thofe years, in the 2ᵗʰ membrana or fkin of p[ch]ment, And yᵉ 3ᵗʰ number, as the fame rolls are marked, And in the 4ᵗʰ year of Edwᵈ the 3ᵈ; And foe of all the like, wherewith each margent almoft hath many: And if it hath | pars. 1. or pars. 2. or pars. 3. Then conceive foe many of that kind of Rolls to bee of that yeare.[1]

Hill: rec: or Hill: fin, or originall: 4. E. 3. rot. 7. in Scc̄io. underftand, the records of Hillary Terme in the 4ᵗʰ year of king Edward the third, the 7ᵗʰ roll, in the Excheqʳ in the office of the lord Treafurers remembrancer, called Ofbornes office; And fo of the roll called the fyne roll, or Rot. finiū and Originalls in the fame place. The like of all others of that kind, whereof very many are in the margents.[1]

Liber feod. milī. in Scc̄io.—Is an ancient book of knights fees in the Excheqʳ wᵗʰ the kings remembrancer, called ffanfhawes office; And fo of lib: rel: to bee a book of Releeves in Ofbornes office aforefaid.[1]

Ad quod damnū. 2. E. 4. nᵒ 112.—underftand, an Inquific̄on taken by the Efcheator upon a Writ called Ad quod damnum, com̄only when lands were to bee alyened in Mortmayne, in the fecond year of king Edward the fecond, and in the 112. Skyn in the bundle. And fo of many of the like.[1]

Pardon, or Rot. pardon. 2. E. 4. m. 5.—underftand the pardon roll of that year, whereby the king granted pardons to his fubjects in that yeare, entred in the 5ᵗʰ membrane or pchment roll, as they ftand numbred in the roll.[1]

Liber M. S.—underftand a manufcript or written booke with that man, or in that place, never printed: And foe of the like.

Ant. Cartæ. B. Are the rolls in the Tower called Antiquæ cartæ, diftinguifhed by the tres of the Alphabet.[1]

Rot. Normañ. Rot. Scotiæ: Rot. vafcoñ: Rot. ffrank: Rot. Romæ: Are called the forren rolls in the Tower, And containe the buifines of yᵉ kings of England in Normandy, Scotland, Gafcoine, and Gwien, ffrance, and in the Court of Rome with the Pope or his Cardinalls.[1]

Plita

---

[1] All thefe Records are now depofited in the Public Record Office. [Ed.]

Ptita coram rege, or in banco regis.—underſtand, the records in the Court called the kings bench, of the year, Terme, and roll there noted: And ſo of other Courts.

Comp: de Ham:, Comp: Rec:, Comp: Gard:, and Carṯ in caſtro de Berkeley, and the like;—Are Accompts of the Reeves of manors, Receiv.ͬ of the lord Berkeley, and of the Wardrobe there, Deeds and the like remaining in Berkeley Caſtle of thoſe years in the Evidence houſe there, wᵗʰ the keys whereof I have been entruſted more then forty years.

The reſt I conceive need no explanaċŏn, by a reader of underſtandinge any whit acquainted with Records. If not let him believe well of that which hee apprehendeth not.

INDEX TO SUBJECTS

Note.—That in this and the following Indices no attempt is made to distinguish the different individuals of the same name, or the different modes of spelling them, and that one reference only is given notwithstanding the name may occur more than once on the same page.

"Acates," explanation of	...398 *n*
Agincourt, Battle of	11
Aid granted to Lord of Manor	333, 373
"Aiell," meaning of	...79 *n*
Altar Plate, Pledged	63
Arms—	
Albiny	426
Bello Campo (Beauchamp)	426
Berkeley, 33, 88 *n*, 94, 146, 213, 239, 240, 255, 426	
Bloett	426
Blundeville	426
Braouse	239, 240, 255, 426
Brotherton, de	146, 213, 240, 255, 426
Chancombe	426
Clare, de	426
Coniers	88
Fitz Alan	426
Longespey	426
Marshal	426
Mead	426
Mowbray	239, 240, 255, 426
Murchas	426
Read	426
Segrave	239, 240, 255, 426
Stanhope	426
Warren	239, 240, 255, 426
Army, Orders to be observed in	197
Array, Commissions of	7
Auconbury M., Customs of	373
Baking, a Manorial custom	342
Baronies, descent of	50, 56
„ lapse through poverty	148, 149
„ by tenure	50
Beauchamp, Earl of Warwick, his contention with James, Lord Berkeley, for possession of the Berkeley Estates	41
Bedford, Barony of	101
Bedford Castle and Manor, tenure by Grand Serjeanty	132
Benevolence granted to Lord of Manor	333
Berkeley, Baronies of Berkeley and Tyes united	2
„ Barony re-created, 207; restitution of the Ancient, 209; Argument for, 210; Restored	275
Berkeley Castle and Lands seized by the Earl of Warwick, 41; Retained by force, 43; Lord Berkeley did fealty for the same, 45; and had seizin	46
Berkeley, consideration of the Barony of	48—56
„ Estates, alienated	118, 119
„ Fair granted at	13
„ Family, their attachment to Gloucestershire	218, 225
Berkeley, Henry I., his extravagance	281
„ Isabel, wife of Maurice V., order of her burial	175—176
Berkeley, Isabella, her letter, 63; Cruelty to her, 71, 81	
„ Lady Jane, her Regulations for the Household	418—421
Berkeley, Lady Katherine, her character, 382; her death, 387; ceremonial of her burial, 388—391; Heralds' Certificates	...391 *n*
Berkeley's Mass	174
Berkeley, Maurice VI., his orders to be observed in the Army, 197; his Will	201
Berkeley, Vicars of	64, 294
„ William Lord Berkeley, created Viscount, 101; Earl of Nottingham, *ib*. Earl Marshall, *ib*., and Great Marshall of England, 102; Marques Berkeley, *ib*. Alienates his Estates	118, 119
Berkeleys of Worcestershire and Herefordshire	83
Board and Lodging, cost of	257
Bosham M., Customs of	373
Bristol, Citizens of	334
Chantries, 17, 84, 106, 134, 203, 215, 249, 361	
"Cheate Loaf," explanation of	...368 *n*

INDEX TO SUBJECTS

Church goods pawned ... 63
Clothing, cost of ... 262
"Coarted," meaning of ... 65 n
Commendations of the Author, by H. A. 445—446
Composition between Lords Berkeley and Lisle 331
"Conuzor," meaning of ... 52 n
Conventicals, Com to enquire into ... 24
Costume ... 284
"Cotquene," explanation of ... 372 n
Courtesy at table ... 381
Coventry, White Friars of ... 377

Deer, malitious destruction of ... 378
" unlawful killing of, 22, 204, 340, 352, 353, 354
Deodand ... 436
Divorced Persons, Argument against marriage of ... 139—141
Documents, Abstraction of by Harvey the Herald, 292—294

Economy, Agricultural ... 5—7, 206, 222, 299
" Household, 195, 282, 284, 285, 286, 287, 418—421
"Eloyned," meaning of ... 59 n
"Estrepment," meaning of ... 435 n

Fairs granted ... 13
Fees of Lawyers ... 282
Flodden Field ... 223
Forfeited lands, the King could not grant them without first having had actual seizin ... 305
France, Wars of ... 8, 10, 24, 81
Franchises, Manorial ... 433—437
Funerals, manner of, 243; Expenses of ... 257

Garter, manner of Election of Knights of, 204, 204 n
Gloucester, Knights of the Shire ... 397
Grand Serjeanty, tenure ... 133
Grays Inn Fields, hunting in ... 281
"Grograin," explanation of ... 391

H. A., his commendations of the Author 445, 446
Harvey, the Herald, his abstraction of Evidences ... 292—294
Household, Regulations of ... 365—367
" Stuff ... 212

Kegworth Advow., Custom as to presentations to 377
Knights Fee, contents of ... 13
Knight Service, tenants who are Minors in wardship of the King not absolved from paying relief for Manors held in Knight Service of other lords ... 350

Lady, an accomplished ... 382
Lawless proceedings ... 69
Lawsuit, the Great Berkeley, termination of, 331, 332
Lisle, Barony of ... 3, 4, 28, 41

Marriage of Divorced persons, Argument against, 139—141
Masses, Cost of ... 243
Misnomer, fatal in law ... 344
Monasteries, Losses by dissolution of, 79, 169, 249, 250
Mowbray, Barony of ... 101, 226
" Elizabeth Duchess of Norfolk, descents from ... 158, 159, 160
Mowbray, Partition of lands of ... 161

Nibley Green, Battle of, 111, 112, 113, 114, 115, 135, 147, 154
Norfolk, Dukedom of ... 101
Nottingham, Earldom of ... 101
Numbers, Mystery of ... 100, 423—424

Orders to be observed in the Army ... 197

Pasture, Common of—special custom ... 348
PEDIGREES—
Arden ... 232, 233
Arthur ... 93
Basset ... 182, 183
Berkeley ... 158, 159, 180—186
" of Beverston ... 239
" " Bradley ... 230
" " Hereford ... 84, 86, 89
" " Stoke Gifford ... 180, 181, 231
Burnell ... 90
Carne ... 185
Codrington ... 94
Coke ... 401
Cooke ... 186
Denis 93, 178, 179, 180, 182, 183, 184, 185, 186
Devereux ... 233
Finch ... 237, 238

INDEX TO SUBJECTS

PEDIGREES—*Continued*—
Foliot	185
Gregory	90
Grey	80
Griffith	85
Howard	158
Huntley	185, 186
Jones	177
Ligon	182, 183, 184, 185
Llewellyn	90
Matthew	230
Mead	172
Mowbray	346
Nevill	160
Norwood	234, 235
Oldisworth	93
Perrot	177
Porter	93, 178, 179
Poyntz	235, 236
Ragland	185
Rowdon	229, 230
Seymour	238, 239
Sheldon	233, 234
Shipward	89
Shirley	403, 404
Smith	85
Stanhope	430, 431
Stanley	159
Throckmorton	181, 230, 231, 232, 234
Trye	91, 92
Willoughby	347
Wingfield	159
Piracy	23
Plague, The	88, 318
Poictiers, battle of	2
"Rash," Explanation of	391 *n*
References, Explanations of	447, 448, 449
Regulations of Household	365—367
Religious Houses of which the Berkeleys were patrons	249
"Rescous," Meaning of	343 *n*

Richard I., his deprivation, 25; his imprisonment, *ib.*	
Ride, Remarkable	381
Riotous Conduct	204, 296, 297, 304
Royal Oak, Knight of	88 *n*
Sacrilege, The Berkeleys not guilty of, in respect to Church Lands	361
Sagacity of a Horse	380
Scotland, Wars in	8, 24
Seals	33, 94, 187, 239, 240, 255
Segrave, Barony of	101, 226, 355
Servants, numbers of	282, 284, 285, 286
"Snoket," Meaning of	176, 176 *n*
Spain, Wars in	7
Sporting	281, 285, 363
Sports and Pastimes	363
Starchamber, Court of—A child 14 years of age might be a defendant in	344
Statute of Northampton	24
,, transferring uses into possession	281
,, de donis conditionalibus	282
,, Scandalus magnatum	303
Summons proclaimed at Church doors	320, 330
Superstition	379
Tetbury, Tolls of, 349; Franchises of	435
Treasure trove	437
Trevisa, John, his works, 22; his death, *ib.*	
Tyes, Barony of, united with Berkeley	2
Wages of Servants	378
Wales, Wars of	9, 10, 11
"Wayved," Meaning of	435 *n*
Wotton, Mayor of	332, 372
Writs of Right, none can bring except tenants in fee	330
Writs of Ravishment de Gard, explained	351 *n*
,, Valore maritagii, explained	339 *n*
,, of Withernam, explained	344 *n*
Wyatt, Rebellion of	279, 280
York and Lancaster Houses, Contentions of	36

INDEX TO NAMES OF PERSONS

Abergavenny, Lord, see *Beauchamp, Nevill*
Abrahall, 186
A-Burrough, 31
Acton, de, 3, 236
Adams 306, 329, 330, 360
Agard, 339
Ailyffe, 377
Albemarle, Duke of, see *Plantagenet*
Alderley, 21
Alſop, 302, 306, 309, 311, 313, 315, 323, 341, 347
Amando, St. de, 14
Anderſon, 309
Andrews, 67, 309, 324
Anjou, Duke of, 314
Anne, Queen, 204 *n*
Ap Adam, 15
Appleton, 234
Appowell, 283
Archard, 373
Archer, 342
Arden, 232, 233, 269, 343
Argyle, Duke of, see *Campbell*
Arnold, 93, 186, 222, 241
Arthur, 13, 93
Arundel, 52, 64, 309
„ E. of, see *Fitz Alan, Howard*
Aſhwood, 426
Aſhton, 341
Aſide, 238
Aſkwith, 201
Aſton, 435
Atfield, 290
Attercliffe, 249
Atwood, 85, 90, 323, 327, 350, 434
Auguſtine's Abbey, Briſtol, Abbot, 242, 309, 310
Axholme, Prior of, 249
Aylworth, 358, 385, 386

Babington, 181
Bacchus, 179
Bacon, 130
Baker, 182, 232
Ball, 186
Banbury, 20
Bangor, Bp. of, 253
Baniſter, 15

Barber, 85
Barker, 343, 375
Barnfeild, 361,
Barty, 93
Barwell, 355
Baſkerville, 181
Baſſet, 182, 183, 185
Bath, Bp. of, 138
 „ Prior of, 201
 „ and Wells, Bp. of, 202
Baugh, 185
Bayly, 85, 345
Baynham, 91, 93, 94, 181, 306
Beamond, 142, 145, 388, 389
Beard, 325
Beauchamp, 11, 15, 28, 29, 30, 41, 42, 43, 44, 45, 46, 47, 48, 49, 51, 52, 57, 58, 59, 61, 66, 71, 73, 74, 117, 132, 133, 143
Beauchamp, Lord, see *Ferrers*
Beaufort, 31, 32, 60, 61, 64, 79
Beconſale, 361
Bedale, 287   [*Nevill*
Bedford, Duke of, see *Plantagenet*,
Bedford, E. of, see *Ruſſell*
Bedle, 169
Beley, 112
Bell, 237, 338
Bendall, 352
Bennet, 237
Benyard, 321, 323
BERKELEY, LORDS OF (*in ſucceſſion*)
 „ ROBERT I., 15, 48, 49, 67, 361, 425, 443
BERKELEY, MAURICE I., 154, 423, 425
BERKELEY, ROBERT, II., 17, 323
 „ THOMAS, I., 100, 246
 „ MAURICE, II., 14, 57, 71, 424, 425
BERKELEY, THOMAS, II., 157, 3 9, 343, 423, 424, 435, 443
BERKELEY, MAURICE III., 181, 184, 203, 231, 293, 412
BERKELEY, THOMAS III., 14, 42, 46, 50, 53, 156, 168, 352, 424, 425, 443
ERKELEY, MAURICE IV., 2, 3, 168
 „ JAMES, the Welſhman, 40, 50, 424

BERKELEY, THOMAS IV., his life, 1—38; his birth and courſe of youth, 2; his huſbandries and hoſpitality, 5; his foreign employments, 7; his recreations and delights, 12; his purchaſes and ſales of lands, 13; his ſuits in law, 16; his alms and devotions, 18; his rewards to ſervants, 20; his miſcellanies, 22; his wife, 27; his iſſue, 28; his ſeals of arms, 33; his death and place of burial, 34; his lands whereof he died ſeized, 34; the application and uſe of his life, 35; a ſhort corollary, 36; ſtyled Thomas the magnificent, 1; 8, 40, 43, 48, 49, 52, 53, 56, 60, 66, 79, 80, 106, 120, 202, 288
BERKELEY, JAMES I., 6, 18, 34, 35; his life, 39–97; his birth and education, 40; his ſuits at law, 41; of the Barony of Berkeley, and of the precedency thereof, 48; his law ſuits, 57; his rewards to ſervants, 76; his miſcellaniæ, 78; his wives, 79; his iſſue, 82; his ſeals of arms, 94; his death and place of burial, 95; the lands whereof he died ſeized, 96; the application and uſe of his life, 96; 100, 102, 103, 104, 105, 119, 125, 138, 154, 161, 164, 173, 174, 178, 207, 246, 347, 425
BERKELEY, WILLIAM LORD, 41, 54, 56, 59, 60, 64, 66, 67, 69, 70, 74, 75, 76, 77, 80, 81, 82, 83, 84, 86, 90, 91, 95, 96; his life, 99—151; his ſoubriquet, 99; his birth and education, 100; his acceſs to honours and offices, 101; his law ſuits, 102; his alienations and ſales of lands, 126; his alms and devotions, 132; his miſcellaniæ or various paſſages, 135; his ſeals of arms, 146; his death and place of burial, 146; the application and uſe of his life, 149; 154, 155, 157, 158, 160, 163, 165, 166, 168, 171,

INDEX TO NAMES OF PERSONS

BERKELEY, WILLIAM LORD—*Continued*—
174, 187, 190, 191, 194, 207, 208, 211, 218, 261, 275, 276, 277, 282, 328, 341, 347, 356, 358, 359, 423, 424

BERKELEY, MAURICE V., 75, 82, 84, 137, 145, 147, 148, 149; his life, 153—192; his birth and education, 154; his suits at law, 154; his wife, 172; his issue, 177; his seals of arms, 187; his death and place of burial, *ib.*; the lands whereof he died seized, *ib.*; the application and use of his life, 190; 203, 231, 247, 275, 277, 283, 328, 347, 358, 416, 424, 432, 443

BERKELEY, MAURICE VI., 49, 81, 89, 155, 161, 162, 165, 166, 171, 177, 178, 189; his life, 193-219; his birth and education, 193; his foreign employments, 196; his creation as Baron, 207; his wife, 210; his seals of arms, 213; his death and place of burial, 213; the lands whereof he died seized, 215; the application and use of his life, 217; 223, 224, 240, 248, 256, 262, 263, 266, 270, 275, 328, 377, 416

BERKELEY, THOMAS V., 56, 147, 160, 166, 168, 171, 177, 178, 186, 194, 201, 210, 217; his life, 222-263; his birth and education, 222; his wives, 227; his issue, 229; his seals of arms, 239, 240; his death and place of burial, 240; his lands whereof he died seized, 245; the application and use of his life, *ib.*; 252, 262, 267, 283, 356, 416, 443

BERKELEY, THOMAS VI., 56, 79, 210, 225, 229, 240; his life, 247-263; his birth and education, 247; his miscellaniæ or various passages, 248; his law suits, 250; his wives, 252; his issue, 254; his seals, 255; his death and place of burial, 256; his lands whereof he died seized, 258; the application and use of his life, 262, 266, 275, 309, 416, 424

BERKELEY, HENRY I., 39, 49, 56, 74, 81, 115, 131, 145, 150, 165, 170, 184, 187, 206, 210, 218, 251, 254, 255, 258, 261, 262; his life, 265-421; his restitu-

BERKELEY, HENRY I.—*Continued*
tion to Berkeley Castle, and to the Barony of Berkeley, 275; his law suits, 288; his sales of lands, 356; his buildings, 362; his recreations and delights, 363; his hospitality, 364; his rewards to servants, 367; his alms and devotions, 368; his miscellanies, &c., 369; his wives, 381; his second wife, 392; his issue, 393; his seales, 404; his death and place of burial, *ib.*; his lands whereof he died seized, 409; the application and use of his life, 410; 426, 427, 433, 434, 438, 439, 444

BERKELEY, GEORGE I., 6, 48, 49, 54, 56, 73, 75, 78, 81, 91, 167, 184, 190, 210, 218, 230, 242, 247, 271, 274, 286, 299, 300, 305, 312, 320, 325, 334, 342, 347, 353, 362, 368, 369, 385, 394; his birth, 396; 404, 405, 406, 407, 410, 417; his life, 423, 424; his parentage and descents, 425; his birth and education, 426; the conclusion of the Author, 439

Berkeley, Charles Earl of, 408 *n*, 438 *n*

Berkeley, James Earl of, 205 *n*, 437 *n*

Berkeley, Alice, 93, 161, 323, 425
" Alienor, 223, 227, 228, 229, 243, 244

Berkeley, Ann, 84, 87, 89, 129, 131, 132, 133, 134, 144, 145, 155, 156, 157, 158, 177, 180, 182, 183, 185, 186, 209, 229, 230, 239, 251, 252, 254, 256, 266, 267, 268, 269, 270, 272, 276, 277, 281, 283, 310, 313, 334, 414, 415

Berkeley, Barbara, 239
" Brice, 230, 267, 268
" Cicely, 223, 228, 229, 231, 240, 248, 250, 251, 256

Berkeley, Dorothy, 89, 182
" Edith, 86, 89
" Edward, 84, 86, 87, 89, 230, 239, 268, 359, 374

Berkeley, Eleanor, 86, 89, 240
" Eliz., 4, 17, 22, 27, 28, 29, 34, 35, 87, 89, 90, 92, 181, 239, 250, 254, 256, 258, 266, 268, 271, 288, 295, 305, 321, 359, 360, 362, 374, 389, 398, 406, 425, 426, 427, 428, 430, 431, 432, 438, 439, 444

Berkeley, Eve, 425
" Fedinando, 393
" Frances, 85, 229, 230, 239, 359, 393, 403
" George, 87, 404
" Giles, 181
" Hellena, 181
" Henry, 87, 89, 184, 239, 399, 407
" Humphry, 86, 89, 212, 214
" Isabella, 63, 71, 74, 77, 81, 82, 83, 84, 89, 90, 91, 93, 95, 100, 115, 120, 126, 127, 134, 147, 149, 154, 159, 172, 173, 174, 175, 177, 201, 203, 425

Berkeley, James, 65, 69, 70, 72, 74, 82, 86, 119, 164, 177, 186, 200, 201, 263, 267

Berkeley, Jane, 89, 132, 133, 142, 394, 418—421

Berkeley, Joan, 4, 74, 75, 81, 82, 83, 85, 86, 89, 102, 112, 118, 142, 144, 229, 235, 236, 237, 239

Berkeley, John, 22, 84, 85, 86, 87, 89, 147, 177, 180, 181, 182, 203, 239, 241, 267, 397

Berkeley, Joyce, 89
" Katherine, 4, 16, 17, 22, 87, 89, 143, 144, 181, 211, 223, 239, 240, 289, 291, 365, 368, 379, 380, 381, 382, 383—391, 392 *n*, 393, 394, 399, 405, 407, 413

Berkeley, Leonard, 87
" Margaret, 4, 18, 19, 22, 27, 28, 29, 84, 86, 87, 89, 90, 181, 239, 425

Berkeley, Margery, 84, 90, 134, 147
" Mary, 86, 87, 89, 144, 178, 181, 182, 201, 239, 250, 251, 252, 393

Berkeley, Maurice, 35, 40, 65, 69, 71, 74, 112, 113, 114, 117, 119, 135, 137, 181, 184, 225, 228, 229, 230, 239, 240, 242, 250, 251, 256, 259, 266, 267, 268, 269, 270, 359

Berkeley, Mirriell, 181, 233, 234, 236, 252
" Nicholas, 3, 14, 86
" Oswald, 86, 231
" Richard, 84, 86, 87, 89, 134, 147, 180, 181, 182, 200, 203, 211, 312, 336, 337, 370

Berkeley, Robert, 87, 88, 88 *n*, 91, 181
" Rowland, 87, 87 *n*, 88, 88 *n*, 89

INDEX TO NAMES OF PERSONS

Berkeley, Sufan, 85, 177, 178
" Theophila, 396, 400, 404, 405, 438, 444
Berkeley, Thomas, fon of Henry, 286, 305, 321, 322, 324, 330, 332, 360, 362, 363, 375, 376, 385, 389, 391, 393, 394, 398, 399, 444
Berkeley, Thomas, 21, 32, 41, 65, 69, 71, 72, 74, 75, 83, 84, 85, 86, 87, 89, 90, 91, 112, 113, 119, 134, 135, 143, 144, 148, 181, 200, 201, 203, 211, 212, 239, 393
Berkeley, William, 61, 74, 86, 87, 88, 88 n, 210, 211, 239
Berry, 93
Bigod, 162, 346
Biford, 77
Bingham, 69, 71, 116
Blanche, Princefs, 26
Blount, 135, 197 n, 230, 235, 256, 374, 375
Birton, 114, 343
Bifhop, 355
Bluet, 164, 425
Bodrugan, 113, 113 n
Boleyn, 32, 257
Boleyn, Q. Anne, 252
Bolton, 292
Bonde, 176
Bone, John, 22, 44
Bott, 379, 380, 413
Boucher, 315
Bourchier, 205
Bourne, 379
Bower, 327, 343
Bowfor, 354
Bowghton, 176
Bowringe, 203
Boyton, 64, 232
Brabazon, 352
Brace, 184
Bracebridge, 235
Bradley, 230
Bradfhawe, 272
Bradfton, 416, 417
Bramwich, 87, 236, 294
Brandon, 144, 146, 157, 197 n, 202, 205
Bray, 130, 164
Breoufe, 158, 425
Brett, 279
Bridgeman, 437
Bridges, 186, 294
Briggs, 401, 406
Bright, 89
Briftol, Black Friars, Pryor of, 242, 244

Briftol, Dean and Chapter of, 310, 313
" Mayor of, 113, 283
" " and Com. of, 14, 44, 70, 283
" Mayor and Conftable of the Staple, 65, 68, 70
Brittaine, 90, 344, 425
Brock, 345
Broke, 241, 249
Brokefby, 93, 370
Bromley, 179
Bromwich, 94
Brook, 200
Brotherton, de, 162, 166, 346, 425
Broughton, 357
Brown, 20, 176, 324, 340, 342
Bruce, 50
Brudnell, 170, 240, 256
Bryers, 92
Bub, 184
Bucke, 185, 241
Buckhurft, 304
" Lord, fee *Sackville*
Buckingham, E. of, fee *Plantagenet*
Buckley, 186
Bucknam, 287, 339
Bullen, 395, 396, 397
Burbage, 272
Burdet, 90, 378, 379
Burghill, 86, 209
Burgoyne, 339, 357
Burnell, 90
Burrow, 359, 442
Burton, 310, 311, 358
" Lazars, Brethren of, 174
Butler, 93, 254, 269, 271
Butteris, 388
Byford, 354, 355, 434, 436
Bynge, 430
Byriat, 353

Cambridge, Earl of, fee *Plantagenet*
Camden, 87, 335
Campbell, 438 n
Cantelo, 141
Canterbury, Archbp. of, 24, 25, 63, 163, 164, 377
Carey, 27, 33, 305, 316, 317, 321, 365, 383, 384, 389, 395, 396, 399, 407, 425, 426
Carne, 185
Carpenter, 139
Carter, 317
Caffey, 25, 135
Cafton, 437
Cafwell, 352
Cater, 172

Cauleigh, 20
Cave, 238, 358
Cecil, 31, 33, 295, 296, 301
Cerney, 354
Chamberlain, 21, 104, 105, 302, 343, 345, 351, 353, 384
Champion, 345
Chaple, 241
Charles, King, 88
" P. of Wales, 426
Charnells, 233
Chedder, 14, 113
Cheney, 339, 357, 365
Chefter, 179, 294, 295, 321
Chichefter, 177
Cholmely, 238
Cholmondeley, 371 n
Chriftopher, 172
Clare, 234, 425
Clarence, Duke of, fee *Plantagenet*
Clark, 344
Clavile, 183
Clement, vij. Pope, 18
Clifford, 72, 91, 230
Clinton, 182
Clough, 329
Clutterbuck, 85, 86, 328, 352
Codrington, 93, 94, 180, 236, 340
Cocke, 282
Cockes, 241
Coke, 32, 55, 56, 210, 301, 304, 309, 318, 333, 365, 400, 401, 402, 405, 406, 407, 438, 442
Cokeine, 178
Cole, 114, 430
Comines, P. de, 253
Compton, 180
Coniers, 88
Conftable, 227
Coneftable, 283
Conway, 239
Cooke, 111 n, 186, 250, 331, 373
Copiner, 20
Copleflon, 178
Corbet, 287
Corbett, 233
Cordell, 283
Cornock, 330
Cornwallis, 33
Cofby, 86
Coffy, 232
Cotton, 179, 317, 388, 442
Courtenay, 29, 205
Cowper, 390, 394, 406
Cox, 287
Craven, 274
Crefwell, 345, 346, 364, 378
Crofts, 323
Cromwell, 205, 248, 309, 353

INDEX TO NAMES OF PERSONS

Crooke, 318
Crosby, 89
Croxton, Abbots of, 249
Cullen, 436
Curnock, 85, 295
Cypress, K. of, 64

Dacres, Lord, see *Fienes*
Dale, 181
Danby, 142
Dansfeild, 346
Danford, 375
Dangerfeild, 329
Danvers, 33, 179, 229, 359
Danyell, 182
Daubeny, 135, 194
Daunt, 117, 296
Davey, 182
Davis, 324, 350, 358
Dawe, 360
Deane, 345
Deighton, 183
De la Hay, 233
De la Warre, 210
Denis, 92, 93, 156, 178, 179, 180, 182, 183, 184, 185, 186, 203, 208, 209, 241, 278, 287, 311, 362, 389, 399
Denton, 318, 319, 320, 324
Derby, 249
    " E. of, see *Stanley*
Despenser, 64
Dethick, 388, 389, 390, 391, 391 n, 392 n
Devereux, 49, 78, 233, 349, 389, 396, 404
Devon, E. of, see *Courtenay*
Digas, 117
Digby, 358
Dilke, 233
Dilkes, 390
Dodderidge, 318
Dormer, 215, 256
Dorney, 182, 183, 437
Dorset, E. and M. of, see *Beaufort, Grey*
Doughtie, 305
Dowle, 179, 268
Downinge, 341
Draycote, 231
Drayner, 92
Drewe, 319
Driver, 352
Dudley, 29, 30, 143, 194, 278, 288, 289, 290, 291, 292, 294, 295, 296, 297, 300, 301, 302, 303, 304, 305, 306, 307, 308, 311, 312, 313, 315, 316, 318, 319, 320, 323, 324, 325, 326, 327,

Dudley—*Continued*—
328, 331, 335, 336, 341, 364, 374, 375, 378, 394
Dunning, 295, 353
Dunstable, 77
Duport, 287, 289, 292, 339, 359, 416, 417
Durham, Bp. of, 228
Dutton, 331, 332, 371, 375, 376
Dyar, 20, 86, 236, 275, 276
Dykes, 114

Ecton, 21
Edward I., King, 14, 50, 51, 132, 157, 236, 425
Edward II., 162, 166, 346, 347
    " III., King, 1, 2, 3, 5, 7, 13, 16, 17, 24, 35, 42, 46, 51, 53, 61, 64, 70, 112, 156, 168, 231, 277, 293, 352, 430
Edward IV., King, 6, 29, 31, 33, 39, 41, 54, 58, 71, 74, 80, 81, 83, 84, 91, 95, 99, 101, 102, 103, 108, 109, 112, 113, 114, 115, 116, 118, 119, 120, 129, 135, 136, 137. 138, 142, 143, 146, 148, 150, 154, 158, 193, 221, 290, 315, 341, 379
Edward V., 99, 119
Edward VI., King, 55, 56, 145, 206, 210, 255, 260, 262, 265, 272, 275, 276, 277, 278, 279, 282, 286, 288, 300, 376, 430
Edwards, 83
Eleanor, Q., 425
Egerton, 304
Elizabeth, Q., 30, 31, 36, 52, 54, 55, 73, 74, 85, 86, 89, 233, 237, 253, 254, 255, 261, 265, 271, 282, 284, 285, 286, 289, 290, 291, 292, 295, 296, 297, 298, 300, 301, 302, 303, 304, 305, 306, 308, 309, 310, 311, 313, 314, 315, 316, 317, 318, 321, 323, 324, 325, 326, 328, 332, 335, 337, 339, 340, 341, 342, 343, 344, 345, 346, 349, 350, 351, 355, 356, 357, 358, 361, 362, 364, 370, 372, 374, 375, 376, 377, 378, 379, 380, 382, 385, 387, 393, 395, 396, 397, 399, 402, 403, 404, 412, 413, 414, 426, 429, 433
Elmer, 185
Elmes, 232, 388
Ely, Bp. of, 272
Essex, Earl of, see *Devereux*
Estcourt, 331, 348, 349, 373, 406, 407

Etherington, 315
Evan, 203
Evans, 180
Exeter, Duke of, see *Holland*
Exeter, E. of, see *Cecil*
Exton, 433

Falkener, 241
Feilding, 233, 376, 389, 390
Fendles, 425
Ferrers, 51, 61, 81, 115, 117, 233
Fewrother, 222
Fienes, 144
Finch, 237, 238
Fisher, 388, 390
Fitz Alan, 159, 160, 162, 425
Fitz Hardinge, 44, 50, 207
Fitz Hugh, 144
Fitz James, 134, 202, 203, 208, 241, 242, 283
Fitz Nicholl, 15
Fitz Walter, Lord, see *Ratcliffe*
Fitz Waryn, 23
Fleetwood, 186
Fleminge, 333
Fleshewer, 68
Flower, 234
Folchard, 401
Foliot, 185
Fortescue, 61, 62, 117, 202, 234
Foster, 92, 186, 321
Fouch, 322, 329
Fourds, 295
Fowler, 86, 272, 353
Francombe, 340
Fransham, 287, 292
Frize, 90
Frogmore, 89
France, Kings of, 64, 224, 425
Fray, 60, 61
Frowick, 161
Fryer, 381
Fyneux, 161

Gaddesden, 375
Gamage, 31
Garlick, 308, 315
Gastrell, 253
Gaunts Hosp., Master of, 201
Gawdy, 377
Gawfell, 346, 347
George, 297
    " I., King, 205 n
Germain, 408 n, 437 n, 438 n
Gerodun, Abbot of, 249
Gerrard, 184, 356
Gilbert, 43
Gifford, 137
Gilman, 327

INDEX TO NAMES OF PERSONS

Glendower, Owen, 9, 10
Gloucester, Archdeacons of, 365
    "   Bishop of, 183, 351
    "   Duke of, see *Plantagenet*
    "   Sheriffs of, 50, 70, 72, 112, 195, 224
Goldesborough, 351
Goldeson, 340, 341
Gonson, 340
Goodman, 324, 325, 330, 414
Goodwyn, 232
Goodyeare, 294
Gorges, 183, 185, 397
Grace dieu, Prior of, 249
Grantham, 310, 313
Green, 294, 314, 349
Gregory, 90, 359
Greisley, 357
Grevill, 49, 77, 170, 171
Grey, 29, 30, 80, 115, 116, 127, 129, 196, 205, 232, 238, 288
Greyndour, 23
Griffin, 231
Griffith, 53, 85, 232, 430, 431
Griffiths, 185
Grococke, 352
Grubb, 375
Guilford, 30
    "   Lord, see *North*
Guife, 93
Gurney, 92
Guy, 84
Gwillim, 179
Gybbon, 236

H. A., 445, 446
Hacket, 298
Hackett, 333, 334
Hale, 295
Hales, 394
Halifax, Lord, see *Montagu*
Hall, 14, 182, 258, 306
Hallam, 296, 298
Halse, 89
Handly, 201
Handlowe, 51
Hannis, 227
Harper, 356, 404
Harding, 295, 303, 444
Hardinge, 36, 76, 78, 79, 100, 423, 425, 439
Harcourt, 241
Harrington, 342
Harris, 37, 75
Harrison, 93, 161
Harsfield, 20, 253
Harvar, 344, 345
Havard, 86
Haverholme, Prior of, 249

Harvey, 292, 293, 294, 346, 351
Hastings, 31, 135, 249, 252, 309
Hatton, 309
Hawford, 377
Hawkins, 241
Haynes, 351
Herbert, 29, 32, 93, 106, 112, 143, 182, 205, 282
Herblinge, 21
Heneage, 237, 241
Henry II., King, 48, 50, 56, 112, 277
Henry III., King, 56, 57, 71, 425
    "   IV., King, 1, 6, 9, 10, 14, 16, 17, 21, 22, 23, 25, 36, 44, 54
Henry V., King, 1, 6, 7, 11, 14, 15, 19, 21, 26, 34, 41, 44, 48, 49, 50, 52, 53, 54, 64, 79, 80, 332, 401
Henry VI., King, 6, 39, 42, 46, 47, 48, 49, 50, 54, 58, 59, 61, 63, 64, 65, 69, 71, 72, 73, 74, 75, 77, 78, 79, 80, 81, 83, 84, 91, 99, 111, 116, 117, 135, 137, 138, 150, 154, 172, 273, 315, 430, 437
Henry VII., King, 29, 71, 86, 90, 99, 102, 114, 116, 125, 129, 130, 131, 134, 135, 136, 144, 145, 146, 150, 156, 160, 161, 162, 165, 166, 167, 169, 171, 172, 190, 194, 206, 207, 208, 210, 211, 222, 227, 228, 247, 261, 275, 276, 277, 282, 315, 347, 430, 446
Henry VIII., King, 30, 49, 52, 79, 81, 84, 85, 87, 89, 90, 91, 92, 162, 169, 173, 174, 194, 195, 196, 197, 197 n, 200, 201, 202, 203, 204, 205, 206, 207, 211, 213, 214, 215, 221, 223, 225, 227, 228, 230, 231, 235, 247, 252, 253, 256, 257, 258, 260, 265, 266, 269, 270, 271, 276, 278, 279, 281, 283, 305, 310, 313, 345, 377, 381
Henry, Prince of Wales, 426
Hereford, Bp. of, 170
Heron, 199, 200
Hewes, 289, 297
Heydon, 164, 316, 317
Heywood, 87, 88
Hiett, 112, 114, 115; see also *Hyet*
Hill, 180, 351
Hilpe, 112, 147, 358
Hobbes, 237 n, 329
Holborne, 432
Holland, 64, 426
Hollister, 356, 436

Holloway, 338
Holt, 78, 104, 105, 107, 109, 110
Hood, 353
Hooker, 392 n
Hopkins, 388, 391
Horsman, 318, 320
Horton, 271, 272, 273
Horwood, 231
Howard, 29, 32, 120, 126, 158, 159, 162, 166, 171, 172, 184, 205, 207, 224, 225, 227, 236, 240, 251, 252, 254, 255, 270, 284, 285, 289, 291, 309, 331, 336, 341, 346, 347, 355, 357, 364, 372, 376, 381, 382, 384, 387, 391, 393, 395, 396, 399, 405, 407, 413, 426, 427, 430, 431, 432
Howell, 117, 183
Huband, 374
Hubart, 168
Hudson, 341
Hues, 86
Hughes, 86, 289, 297, 298, 307
Hungerford, 82, 181, 185, 297
Hunsden, Lord, see *Carey*
Hunt, 350, 375
Huntington, E. of, see *Hastings*
Huntley, 185, 186, 297, 298, 302, 311, 313, 331, 346, 352, 353
Hurd, 12
Hurne, 85, 86
Hussy, 216, 256
Hyet, 294; see also *Hiett*

Ingleby, 222, 228
Inglefeild, 241
Iuyn, 43, 47, 48, 61
Ithel, 77, 286, 287, 351, 377, 378

James, 189
    "   King, 31, 37, 49, 87, 88, 115, 145, 265, 294, 298, 303, 312, 314, 318, 320, 323, 324, 328, 329, 331, 332, 343, 349, 350, 351, 352, 353, 354, 360, 365, 370, 371, 372, 373, 375, 376, 377, 396, 400, 403, 406, 427, 428, 430, 433, 436, 437, 438, 446
James, King of Scotland, 324
Jay, 85
Jermy, 180
Jerningham, 232
Jerrat, 93, 351, 353
Jerusalem, Prior of Hosp. of St. John of, 249
Jevais, 287
Joan, Q. of Sicily, 19

INDEX TO NAMES OF PERSONS

Jobbins, 114, 295, 298, 320, 321
John, King, 50, 112, 277
Johnson, 77, 395
Jones, 177, 342

Katherine of Valois, Q., 63
Kemys, 92, 185, 283
Kenedy, 397
Kimmerly, 296
Kinge, 86, 107, 108
Kingswood, Abbot of, 242, 249
Kirkeby, Prior of, 249
Knevet, 29, 202
Knight, 169, 328
Knightley, 233, 401
Knolles, 22, 30, 32
Knull, 203

Lancaster, Duke of, see *Plantagenet*
Lacon, 71
Lake, 31, 387
Lambert, 317
Lane, 241
Langharne, 177
Langley, 179, 360
Lany, 349
Lapworth, 381, 402
Latimer, 53, 132
  "   Lord, see *Nevill*
Laughan, 380
Laund, Prior of, 249
Lawrence, 86, 362
Lee, 181
Legat, 22
Legge, 114
Leicester, Abbot of, 249
  "   E. of, see *Dudley, Sidney*
Leigh, 357, 389
Lewes, Prior of, 249, 340, 341
Leighton, 233
Lentall, 159
Lewkner, 311
Liare, 170
Ligon, 93, 180, 182, 183, 184, 234, 287, 362, 376, 378, 394, 395, 397, 399
Lisle, de, 2, 3, 4, 17
  "   "   Lord, see *Talbot, Grey, Sidney*
Littleton, 311
Lluen, 201
Lluellin, 90
Logge, 276, 347
London, Bps. of, 46, 47, 185
Longe, 114, 182, 239
Louis, Earl Palatine of the Rhine, 26
  "   XI., K. of France, 253
Lovell, 51, 205
Loveny, 16

Lovericus, 174
Lowe, 403
Lower, 117, 117 n
Lucas, 274
Ludford, 358
Lucy, 69, 186, 234

Machin, 325, 329
Mackworth, 350
Mac Murrough, 425
Maddefon, 237
Mainfton, 354
Mallet, 85, 328
Maltravers, 52
Manners, 31, 32, 301
March, E. of, see *Mortimer*
Margaret, Queen, 58
Markam, 234, 291
Marney, 205
Marrowe, 171, 389
Marten, 179, 360
Martin, 241
Mary, Queen, 30, 52, 55, 86, 169, 210, 229, 253, 255, 265, 273, 274, 275, 276, 277, 278, 279, 280, 281, 284, 286, 288, 289, 290, 293, 300, 341, 361, 373, 376, 381, 404, 416, 434
Maryner, 163
Matthew, 230
Maxey, 186
May, 77
Mayo, 90
Mead, 113, 172, 173, 283
Merbury, 78
Merrick, 239
Merrit, 328
Mill, 76, 145, 236
Millard, 350
Miller, 250
Millet, 93
Mills, 81, 101, 397
Molineux, 236
Monke, 353
Montagu, 204 n
Montague, 197 n, 204 n, 321
  "   Marquis, see *Nevill*
Moore, 5, 7, 15, 21, 89, 137, 232, 235
Morgan, 45, 48, 77, 234, 310, 311, 425
Morris, 230, 319, 329
Mortimer, 7, 8, 425
Mowbray, 53, 80, 106, 118, 119, 120, 131, 132, 133, 138, 141, 142, 143, 146, 158, 159, 160, 161, 162, 171, 255, 341, 346, 355
Mull, 63, 110

Mynne, 87 n, 89
Mynors, 86

Nelme, 85, 243, 340
Nest, 182
Nevill, 32, 33, 60, 111, 132, 137, 138, 142, 148, 160, 166, 277
Newton, 60, 61, 89
Nicholas, 258, 356
Nicholls, 346
Noote, 85
Norman, 86
Norwood, 185, 234, 235
Norfolk, Duke of, see *Brotherton, Howard, Mowbray, Bigod*
North, 438 n,
Northampton, Earl of, see *Howard, Berkeley*
Nottingham, Earl of, see *Howard, Mowbray*
Northumberland, D. of, see *Dudley*
  "   E. of, see *Percy*
Norton, 205
Norwood, 389
Nuce, 238
Nuneaton, Prior of, 249
Nuttall, 325, 374, 414

O'Bryen, 271
Ogle, 52, 53
Ognell, 358
Oldbury, 104, 230
Oldisworth, 93, 296, 297, 302, 303, 329, 360, 375
Oldland, 85
Olive, 351
O'Neale, 370
Organ, 90
Ormond, E. of, see *Butler*
Osborne, 360, 434
Oty, 321, 323
Owen, 177
Oxford, E. of, see *Vere*

Pacy, 283
Paget, 52
Palsgrave, the Prince, 400
Paris, 241
Parmiter, 296, 297, 340
Parry, 289, 374
Paston, 401
Pate, 340
Paul II., Pope, 139
Paunsfoot, 173, 178, 180
Pawlet, 238
Payne, 318, 319, 322, 323, 354, 365
Peers, 232, 344
Peeter, 114
Peito, 377
Pembroke, 136

INDEX TO NAMES OF PERSONS

Pembroke, E. of, see *Plantagenet*
Percy, 25, 32, 33, 64, 160, 309
Perrot, 177, 203
Perry, 360
Persival, 179
Peter, 234, 346, 347, 356
Peter's, St., Abbey, Glouc., Abbot of, 249
Petit, 92, 287
Pettifer, 344
Phelps, 114, 346
Phillip, 77
Philip and Mary, K. and Q., 261, 281, 284
Philip of Spain, 279
Phillips, 177
Phillpot, 268
Pichard, 425
Pigot, 142, 178
Pipard, 2
Plantagenet, 8, 9, 30, 45, 46, 47, 64, 78, 111, 117, 119, 120, 137, 143, 158, 172, 346, 379, 425
Pleadell, 317
Plogenet, 51
Plomer, 21
Plowden, 282
Pole, Cardinal, 274, 275
 " de la, 4, 59
Poole, 15, 290, 300, 331, 336, 337, 360
Popham, 179, 304
Porter, 93, 176, 178, 179, 181, 241, 283, 308, 374
Poyntz, 21, 76, 94, 145, 162, 163, 164, 165, 183, 203, 235, 236, 237, 237 n, 250, 268, 269, 270, 294, 306, 308, 315, 336, 337, 341, 342, 356
Pratt, 184
Price, 177
Printhorpe, 343
Puckering, 338
Pullen, 77
Purefy, 339
Purnell, 114, 169
Pyle, 179, 342
Pynne, 370

Ragland, 185
Rastle, 180
Ratcliffe, 13, 53, 255, 268, 309, 335, 338, 381, 428, 429
Raynesford, 357
Read, 180, 186, 200, 229, 355, 358, 361, 428, 429, 430
Reis, 425
Rice, 103, 177
Rich, 397

Richard I., King, 50, 51, 112, 277
 " II.,   " 1, 4, 5, 7, 9, 12, 13, 17, 18, 22, 23, 24, 25, 27, 36, 69, 73, 80, 103, 116
Richard III., King, 80, 99, 101, 115, 120, 126, 127, 129, 136, 144, 150, 155, 193, 210
Richards, 85
Rig, 20
Rivers, 227
 " Earl of, see *Wydville*
Robert, K., of Scotland, 64
Roberts, 114
Roch, 13
Rochester, Bp. of, 134
Rodborrow, de, 24
Rodney, 235
Roger, 62
Roos, Lord, see *Manners*
Rowdon, 228, 229, 230, 241,
Rowe, 180, 181
Rupert, King of the Romans, 26
Ruffell, 30, 183, 184, 364, 376
Rufwell, 94
Rutland, E. of, see *Manners*
Rynall, 25

Sacheverell, 225, 226, 246
Sackville, 361
Sage, 156
St. John, 36, 40, 178, 38
Saluce, Marquis of, 425
Samborne, 181
Sampson, 135
Sander, 238
Sandes, 197, 197 n, 214, 232
Savacre, 354
Savage, 170, 252, 293, 348, 349, 355, 364, 365, 374, 376
Scarlinge, 359
Scot, 315, 317
Scotland, King of, 64
Scudamore, 179, 181, 186
Sebroke, 44
Segrave, 141, 162, 167, 346
Selden, 442
Selman, 340
Semprigham, Prior of, 249
Sentle, 137
Serjeant, 92
Sever, 228 n
Seymour, 238, 239, 430
Shelden, 233, 234, 342
Shellam, 183
Shelly, 434
Sheppard, 195, 200, 208
Sherington, 45
Shillitoe, 287
Shipman, 93

Shipward, 89, 113, 287, 340, 350
Shirley, 389, 403, 404, 406, 407
Shottesbroke, 21
Shugborough, 233
Sidney, 31, 32, 49, 298, 301, 318, 320, 321, 322, 325, 326, 328, 329, 330, 332, 333, 336, 375
Sileby, Abbot of, 249
Skelton, 135
Skipwith, 92, 357
Skull, 85
Slead, 86
Smallwood, 296, 297
Smith, 85, 114, 183, 231, 298, 331, 339, 355, 360, 371 n, 375, 376, 383, 391 n, 392 n, 398, 427
Snell, 239
Somerfield, 233
Somers, 303
Somerset, 205, 431
 " Duke of, see *Beaufort, Seymour*
Southampton, Mayor of, 44
Speake, 93, 179
Speed, 427
Spenser, 27, 32, 180, 195, 359, 360, 376, 384, 389, 393, 397, 430
Squall, 62
Stafford, 7, 29, 36, 40, 41, 76, 79, 84, 137, 138, 195, 206, 207, 224, 363
Standen, 234
Stanhope, 359, 392, 393, 428, 429, 434
Stanley, 70, 128, 130, 132, 134, 143, 159, 160, 161, 162, 236, 338, 389, 429 n
Stanshawe, 14, 77, 93
Staunton, 145, 360
Stawker, 237
Stephens, 94, 269, 318, 375
Stepneth, 177
Stewart, 400
Stinton, 89
Stonly, Abbot of, 249
Strange, 195, 389
 " Lord, see *Stanley*
Strangwayes, 142, 145
Strickland, 237, 238, 239
Strongbow, see *Clare*
Stuard, 235
Stukeley, 232
Suffolk, Duke of, see *Pole de la, Brandon*
Suffolk, Earl of, see *Howard*
Sulliard, 234
Sussex, Earl of, see *Ratcliffe*
Surrey, Earl of, see *Howard*
Swift, 200

INDEX TO NAMES OF PERSONS

Swynburn, 10
Sydnam, 94, 236
Symes, 238
Symonds, 239, 241

Talbot, 23, 29, 30, 59, 60, 61, 63, 65, 66, 67, 68, 69, 70, 71, 72, 73, 74, 75, 80, 81, 82, 84, 95, 102, 103, 104, 105, 106, 107, 108, 109, 110, 111, 112, 113, 114, 115, 117, 118, 119, 125, 131, 135, 136, 143, 149, 154, 359, 360, 361, 372, 438, 444
Tame, 186, 203
Tamer, 352
Tanfield, 318, 333
Tayer, 358
Teft, 17
Tewe, 65, 68, 69
Tewkefbury, Abbot and Convent of, 168
Thay, 170
Thomas, 302, 327, 388, 391 n
Thorly, 138
Thorpe, 179, 329, 351
Throckmorton, 181, 230, 231, 232, 233, 234, 252, 291, 299, 306, 307, 308, 309, 310, 311, 312, 313, 314, 315, 331, 334, 336, 337, 340, 341
Thynne, 300
Tiler, 135
Tilladam, 434
Tindall, 340
Tirer, 170
Tirrell, 92
Tomfon, 355
Tovy, 269
Townefend, 230, 392, 407
Tracy, 3, 307, 308, 317, 331
Trenton, 234
Trefham, 92
Trevifa, John, 22, 44, 64
Trotman, 227, 230, 231, 279, 294, 297, 307, 324, 327, 328, 329, 340, 360
Trye, 91, 92, 164, 167, 175, 176, 200, 201, 214, 225, 226, 227, 246, 271, 272, 273, 274, 342, 379, 380, 415, 416, 417
Tucker, 87 n, 88 n, 391 n
Tuddington, 308
Tudor, 195
Turner, 359

Turvill, 185
Twifden, 238,
Tyler, 5
Tyrrell, 45

Urban vj., Pope, 18, 19

Valle dei, Abbot of, 249
Varney, 236
Vaughan, 177, 302, 375
Vaux, 231
Vele, 107, 108, 109, 177
Ven, 360
Venables, 63, 77, 164
Vere, 52, 115, 381
Villers, 355, 369
Vincent, 81, 142, 146, 375
Vinton, 403

Wade, 356
Wafery, 233
Wake, 345
Wakeman, 375
Walker, 237
Waller, 315
Walleron, 51, 59
Wallies, 13, 15, 79
Wallin, 183
Walmefley, 326, 335
Walfh, 145, 157, 163, 164, 179, 182
Walter, 237
Walton, 357
Warbeck, Perkin, 207
Warberton, 406
Warre, de la, Lord, fee *Weft*
Warren, 2
Warwick, Earl of, fee *Beauchamp, Dudley*
Wafhborne, 183
Waterton, 20, 84
Watkins, 238
Wayneman, 232
Webb, 238, 239, 317, 437
Wells, 53, 111
Wenlocke, 117
Wentworth, 238
Weft, 53, 54, 55, 138, 141, 354
Weftbury College, Dean of, 242
Weftley, 230
Weftminfter, Abbot of, 105
Weftmorland, Earl of, fee *Nevill*
Wefton, 178, 241
Weyfton, 208, 209
White, 389

Whitgift, 377
Whitinge, 131, 133, 134
Whittach, 86
Wikes, 134, 237, 241
Wild, 89
Wilford, 231
Wilkins, 360
Will, (Black,) 114
William, Duke of Normandy, 439
Williams, 323, 353
Willis, 183, 327
Willoughby, 29, 56, 131, 133, 142, 143, 145, 232, 261, 346, 349, 356
Wilmare, 359
Wiltfhire, Ormond, E. of, fee *Bulleyn*
Winchefter, Bps. of, 48, 100
Wingfield, 159, 160, 205
Winfton, 302, 303
Winter, 20, 182, 186, 317, 331, 334
With, 77
Withrington, 52
Wodburn, 59
Wolfey, 197 n, 202
Wood, 355
Woolcombe, 345
Woodhoufe, 401
Woodward, 227, 274, 321
Worcefter, Bifhops of, 43, 45, 47, 48, 61, 169, 170, 442
Worcefter, E. of, fee *Percy, Somerfet*
    " Sheriffs of, 88
Worfield, 89,
Wotton, Mayor of, 332
    " Rector of, 347
Wray, 309
Wright, 359
Wroth, 321
Wrothefly, 233
Wroughton, 403
Wyatt, 279, 280
Wydville, 111, 142
Wyn, 87 n
Wythers, 134

Yate, 338, 360
Yaxley, 339
Yelverton, 61, 62, 117, 238, 333
York, 146
    " Archb. of, 142
    " Duke of, fee *Plantagenet*
Younge, 232
Yowen, 346

Zouch, 17, 56, 402, 403, 407

INDEX TO NAMES OF PLACES

Abinbury M., 124, 128
Acton, 48, 114, 115, 125
   "   Burnell M., 51
   "   Ilger, 106, 116, 157, 268, 341, 342
   "   Iron, fee "Iron Acton"
Adderley, 63
Alet, 15
Alington M., Suffex, 123
Alkynton M., 12, 15, 16, 20, 21, 34, 73, 77, 78, 84, 96, 106, 119, 125, 129, 143, 145, 157, 206, 224, 261, 275, 288, 291, 295, 298, 299, 330, 347, 374, 375, 409
Allexton M., 309
Allington M., Salop, 124, 128, 166
Almington M., 196, 216, 218, 229, 256, 259, 267, 359
Almondefbury, 84, 179, 203, 249, 259, 294, 356
   "   Advow., 215
Almore M., 124, 128
Alps, The, 399
Alfpath M., 80, 122, 130, 160, 161
Alveston, 89
Andrews St., Baynard's Castle, 13
Antwerp, 234
Appleridge M., 16, 34, 42, 77, 96, 119, 125, 129, 143, 157, 206, 261, 275, 314, 409
Appleridge grounds, 399
Ardeborough, 359
Arden, Forest of, 379
Arlingham, 319
   "   Advow., 129
   "   M., 15, 21, 35, 106, 112, 115, 116, 125, 143, 145, 157, 260, 275, 288, 293, 300, 323, 326, 330, 360, 364, 374, 375, 382
Armere M., 124, 128
Arrow Park, Co. Warwick, 378
Artois, 247
Arundel Castle, 52
Afhborne M., Derby, 122, 188
Afhby Park, 285
Afhelworth, 182
Afhmore gate, 354

Afhton, 173
Afpeley M., 80, 122, 189, 214, 216, 241, 253, 260, 281
Aflwell, 403
Auconbury hermitage, 214
   "   M., Hunts, 122, 189, 200, 214, 216, 228, 240, 259, 292, 360, 373, 382
Augustine's Abbey, Briftol, 201, 228, 241, 243, 249, 310, 361
Aumarle, Duke of, 64
Aufty, 343, 344
Avignon, 18
Awre M., 3, 15, 17
Axholme, Isle of, 249
Aylwefton M., 15

Badlesly Clinton, 358
Badmington, 93
Baies in Horton, 375, 376
Banbury, 113
Baraper, Co. Hants, 364, 376, 394
Barkeway, 285
Barnstaple, Archdeaconry of, 11
Barrow Court, in Tickingham, 282
Barton Hund., 269
Baffet's Court, 343
Bath, 37
Bayefplace, 21
Baynard's Castle, 22
Blandefert M., 52
Bedewall M., 124, 128
Bedford, 217
   "   M., Beds, 121, 127, 132
   "   Co., 118, 121, 127, 130, 178, 357
Bedminster, 173
   "   Hundred, 44
   "   M., 15, 17, 44
Belton M., Co. Lincoln, 121, 127, 130, 160, 161
Benfleet, 234
Bentham, 184
Beoly, 91, 233
Berington, 239
Berkeley, Barony of, 13, 17, 28, 34, 40, 41, 44, 45, 46, 48, 53, 54, 84, 101, 165, 168, 196, 207, 209, 210, 211, 248, 261, 277, 282,

Berkeley, Barony of—*Continued*—
286, 332, 334, 367, 394, 397, 416
Berkeley Borough, 13, 16, 20, 73, 77, 78, 84, 85, 86, 90, 96, 125, 189, 200, 211, 217, 249, 259, 313, 334, 370, 375, 409, 434, 436
Berkeley Castle, 2, 4, 5, 6, 8, 12, 13, 15, 16, 19, 22, 27, 34, 40, 41, 42, 43, 45, 46, 49, 50, 53, 54, 62, 65, 66, 67, 68, 72, 73, 89, 95, 100, 101, 102, 105, 107, 108, 110, 115, 119, 125, 129, 130, 136, 139, 142, 143, 145, 147, 156, 158, 168, 174, 178, 196, 205, 206, 207, 208, 209, 210, 222, 224, 228, 245, 248, 261, 262, 275, 278, 280, 285, 290, 291, 292, 293, 294, 298, 300, 311, 315, 320, 321, 325, 326, 329, 332, 334, 362, 371, 373, 374, 376, 378, 383, 394, 397, 399, 406, 407, 408, 409, 412, 429
Berkeley Chapel, 134
   "   Church, 83, 95, 144, 230, 244, 400
Berkeley Grange, 300
   "   herneffe, M., 15, 21, 34, 42, 44, 46, 49, 50, 53, 54, 73, 83, 119, 129, 143, 157, 162, 206, 207, 208, 209, 210, 261, 275, 277, 351, 374, 409
Berkeley, Honor of, 50, 210, 394, 397
Berkeley Hund., 16, 42, 44, 91, 96, 106, 112, 125, 162, 179, 204, 230, 275, 320, 321, 322, 323, 324, 329, 350, 352, 353, 374, 408, 409, 434, 435, 436
Berkeley's Inn, 22
Berkeley Parish, 309, 375, 399
Berks Co., 21, 34, 232, 234, 403
Berwick, 395
Beverston, 22
Bevington, 346, 352
Bewbufh M. and Park, 189, 217
Binley, 272, 342, 397, 415

INDEX TO NAMES OF PLACES

Binley Bridge, 172, 176
 " Brook, 363
Birdbury M., 231
Bitton M., 196, 215, 218, 228, 240, 251, 256, 259, 269, 275, 344, 374, 382, 397, 409, 410
Blacknonton M., 231
Blakeney, 17
Blediflowe, Hund., 17
Bockhampton, 5, 358
Bointon, 237
Bofham M., Suffex, 123, 166, 167, 168, 194, 200, 201, 217, 241, 311, 347, 354, 373, 382, 410, 432, 433, 434
Bofham and Buckfold M., 189, 217, 260, 292
Bofworth field, 171
Bothall, Barony of, 52
Botulph Bridge, 404
Bouloign, 272, 273
Bourdeaux, 10, 23, 73, 83
Bradgate, 285
Bradley, 14, 20, 267, 319, 359, 374, 376
Bradſton M., 202
Bramfield, 128
Branwood, 224
Brecknock Caſtle, 10
Brember, Barony of, 50
Brene Advow., 17
Breonſe's lands, 357
Bretby, Co. Derby, 122, 188, 200, 201, 216, 241, 253, 260, 359, 382
Bridgewick M., 188
Bridgwater, 17, 238
Brighthelmeſton M., 123, 166
Brind M., 118, 127, 142
Briſtol, 3, 10, 11, 26, 34, 37, 70, 76, 78, 101, 113, 120, 186, 228, 229, 238, 241, 249, 253, 254, 255, 268, 283, 380, 436
Briſtol, Black Friars, 241
 " St. Mary Redcliffe, 283
 " Grey Friars, 65, 70
 " St. Mary Magd., 79, 249
Bradſton, 346
Brittany, 8, 44
Brokenburgh M., 83, 203, 215, 241, 249, 259, 356
Bromefwell, 118
Bromfield M., N. Wales, 124, 127, 158, 169
Bromham M., Beds., 121, 126, 127
Bromley M., Surrey, 189, 217, 260, 357
Bromley in Suffex, 241
Bromyard, 230
Broughtons, 339

Broughtons, lands, 357
Brownſmill, 334
Brommore Priory, 345
Bruton, 184
Brynd M., York, 121
Buckfold M., Suffex, 123, 410
Buckingham Co., 34, 121, 127, 130, 157, 160, 162, 188, 196, 200, 231, 232, 402
Buden M., 5
Burton Lazars Abbey, 249
 "   "   Advow., 216
 "   "   M., 124, 128
Burton-on-Lonefdale, 118, 127, 130, 142, 160, 161, 162
Burton-on-the-Wold, 357
Byland Abbey, 249

Calais, 100, 119, 123, 130, 131, 189, 201, 205, 207, 208, 211, 213, 215, 217, 224, 245, 247, 248, 253, 260, 281, 361
Caldicote M., 289
Caldwell, 357
Callowdon, 84, 91, 118, 171, 176, 184, 225, 226, 227, 253, 254, 272, 273, 284, 285, 292, 293, 310, 325, 331, 337, 343, 349, 354, 355, 362, 363, 365, 368, 370, 378, 379, 382, 384, 386, 387, 388, 394, 395, 399, 401, 403, 406, 426
Callowdon M., 122, 131, 189, 201, 214, 216, 253, 260, 271, 274, 339, 345, 350, 359, 380, 397, 410
Cambridge, 285, 377, 442
 "   Co., 118, 122, 130, 131, 217, 222, 240, 245, 260, 346, 356
Cam Woods, 340
Came M., 17, 20, 34, 42, 48, 57, 58, 60, 62, 74, 75, 96, 119, 125, 129, 143, 145, 155, 157, 206, 210, 211, 261, 275, 288, 294, 300, 301, 303, 308, 315, 316, 317, 318, 326, 330, 332, 374, 375, 409
Came par., 91, 319, 324, 360, 376
Campden, 69, 293, 407
Canonbury M., 361, 362, 409
Canterbury Prov., 11
Cardiganſhire, 178
Carleton Park, als Walling Wells, 132
Carmarthenſhire, 177
Caſſies, 370
Caſtle Bromwich, 233
Caſtle Park, 16

Catherlegh Barony, Ireland, 124, 260, 270
Caughton, Co. Warr. 230
Cernecote M., 47
Cerniwike M., 14
Cerny, ſee *Southcerny*
Charfield, 108
Charleton M., 5, 14, 20
Charnels Hill, 251
 "   Pool, 251, 269
Charters & Murrow M., 228, 240, 260
Chawcombe Abbey, 249
Chedder, 29, 402
Cheeping, 352
Chelfea, 131
Chenies Hoſp., 307, 318
Chepinge lane, 21
Chepſtow, 137, 138
Cheſelhungre, 178, 224, 248
Cheſhire Co., 252
Cheſterford Advow., 166
 "   (Great) M., Effex, 121, 126, 131, 166
Chicheſter, 433
Childewickham, 273
Chilton Foliot M., 5
Cirenceſter, 58, 61, 69, 70, 71, 72, 93, 116, 164, 310, 402
Clapton in Hame, 20, 77, 83
Claredon, 370, 420
Clayton M., Suffex, 123
Cleers, Chace of, Suffex, 123, 166
Clehungre, 91
Cleiton M., 166
Clerkenwell, 428, 437
Clifford, 370
Clinton M., 5
Clowerwall, 93, 94, 181, 306
Clyvedon M., 345
Cobham M., 124, 128
Codnor Caſtle, 402, 403
Cokefield M., Suffex, 123, 166
Colcot M., 5
Coldoverton Advow., 189, 216
 "   M., 118, 122, 126, 188, 200, 211, 216, 240, 249, 253, 259, 281, 344, 360, 382, 397
Collicote M., 5
Combroke, 358
Combe, 342
 "   Abbey, Advow., 216
 "   Glouc., 288, 319, 375, 376
 "   Mon., 171, 249
Compton, 370
Condover Hall, 367 n, 371 n, 398, 418
Cophall, 237
Cornwall Co., 9, 11, 23, 34, 113

463

INDEX TO NAMES OF PLACES

Corrietts, 288, 301, 303, 316, 326, 330, 375
Cotes M., 241, 357
Cothorne M., 158
Cothorpe M., Lincoln, 121, 127
Cotton M., Derby, 122, 188, 200, 216, 241, 253, 260, 357
Cotſwolds, 294
Coventry, 92, 173, 175, 189, 214, 215, 216, 253, 254, 260, 272, 285, 343, 345, 349, 354, 359, 365, 369, 377, 382, 385, 387, 388, 390, 394, 399, 402, 406, 407, 410, 426
Coventry, Friars of, 364
Cowley, 3, 85, 295, 319, 324, 375, 376
Cowley Advow., 16
    " Church, 19
    " M., 17, 34, 42, 44, 48, 57, 58, 60, 61, 65, 66, 69, 70, 74, 102, 125, 129, 143, 145, 157, 168, 206, 261, 275, 332, 374, 409
Cranford, 250, 426, 435, 437, 437 n
Cricklade, 15, 17, 20
    " Advow., 13
Criſton, 17, 48
Crokarſhill, 136
Cromall, 48, 106, 115, 125, 230, 319, 375, 376
Cromhall Ligon, 437
Croxton Abbey Advow., 219, 249
Culverfeild, 77
Culverheys, 224

Daglingworth M., 35, 83, 96, 125, 143, 162, 163, 164, 188, 200, 203, 211, 215, 240, 253, 256, 259, 281, 292, 360, 374, 382, 397
Dalby Chawcombe M., 118, 122, 126, 188, 216, 229, 240, 249, 259, 266, 267, 359, 382
Dartford, in Kent, 257
Dean, Foreſt of, 22, 114, 299, 334
Deerhurſt, 24
Denby, 403
Denge als Dengy M., Eſſex, 121, 130, 160, 188, 200
Derby, 394
    " Co., 122, 130, 188, 200, 216, 241, 245, 253, 260, 268, 339, 357, 359, 367, 382, 402, 425
Derby, Sherifwick of, 101, 126
Devon Co., 9, 11, 15, 34, 118, 178, 283
Dingly, 231

Doddington, 237
Doningworth M., 118, 162
Donyngton M., York, 121, 126, 130, 160, 161, 188
Donver M., 142
Dorkinge, 123, 166
Dorſet Co., 9, 11, 41, 79
Dover, 8
Dovercourt M., Eſſex, 121, 126
Down Amney, 370
Draycote M., 5
Drayton, 11
Dublin, 270
Dunchurch, 357
Dunkerton, 94
Duntiſborne Abbot, 179
Durandſthorpe, 357
Durdens, 426, 438 n
Durham, Biſhoprick of, 88
Dunningworth, ſee Doningworth
Durſley, 20, 83, 86, 90, 106, 296, 319, 375, 376, 430
Dymill M., 124, 128
Dyneſbran Caſtle and M., 128

Eaſtwood Park, 294
Ediſhall M., 35
Egleſecle M., 124, 128, 134
Elmington M., ſee Almington
Elmore, 370
Elſton, 184
Epingham M., 350
Eppeworth M., Co. Lincoln, 121, 127, 130, 160, 162
Eppeworth Priory, 249
Epſom, 438 n
Erlingham, ſee Arlingham
Eſſex Co., 16, 30, 80, 118, 121, 126, 130, 131, 137, 147, 160, 166, 188, 200, 234, 237, 238
Eſtcluſam M., 124, 128
Eſtharleiſey, 228
Eſtpike, 15
Eſtwell M., 352
Eſtwood, 224
Etlowe M., 17
Ewell, 238
Exall, 343
Exeter Archdeaconry, 11
Exholme, Iſle of, 160

Fairford, 186, 307
Farington, 403
Favelore, 5
Fawley, 232
Felond, 173
Fennyſtanton M., Hunts, 122, 166, 168, 189, 214, 216, 228, 240, 248, 259, 292, 360, 382

Fillwood Foreſt, 202
Flekenhoe M., 77, 80, 122, 189, 200, 211, 216, 241, 260, 357, 382
Fluellins Farm, 397
Fountains Abbey, 249
Frampton Cotterell, 238
    " M., 17, 23, 35, 42, 48, 62, 157, 253
Frampton-upon-Severn, 94, 125, 157, 188, 215, 230, 236, 241, 259, 281, 292, 329, 354
France, 64, 81, 82
Fretwell M., 5
Froceſter, 185, 370
Frodſham, 252
Fulham, 5, 27
Funtington M., Suſſex, 123, 189, 200, 217, 241, 260, 292, 382, 410

Gaſgony, 196, 200
Gateborne, 260
Gate Burton M., 158, 357
Genoa, 23
Glouceſter Co., 10, 11, 14, 15, 16, 17, 23, 24, 25, 26, 34, 35, 37, 42, 43, 44, 46, 48, 60, 67, 69, 72, 76, 78, 80, 83, 84, 91, 102, 106, 108, 111, 113, 115, 117, 125, 137, 138, 142, 147, 156, 157, 162, 168, 172, 173, 179, 180, 184, 185, 186, 188, 196, 203, 206, 211, 215, 216, 218, 222, 225, 228, 234, 236, 239, 240, 241, 245, 247, 253, 257, 259, 261, 268, 275, 276, 277, 278, 280, 281, 285, 287, 293, 300, 307, 310, 313, 316, 318, 320, 322, 324, 326, 347, 351, 356, 359, 360, 367, 370, 372, 374, 376, 382, 397, 409, 410, 434, 436
Glouceſter Abbey, 89
    " Caſtle, 71, 103
    " City, 15, 21, 25, 37, 57, 71, 74, 92, 106, 173, 180, 183, 184, 216, 222, 278, 302, 310, 311, 333, 368, 370, 371
Glouceſter, Grey Friars at, 81, 134, 201, 203, 223
Glouceſter, St. Peter's Ch., 112
Goſcote Hund., 122, 126, 157, 188, 216, 240, 248, 253, 259, 272, 281, 382
Goſcote M., 410
Goſeſeild, 238
Goſſington, 351, 375
Gower, 138

INDEX TO NAMES OF PLACES

Grays Inn Fields, 281
Greenhithe, 258
Greenfnorton, 232
Greifley, 357
Gribthorpe M., 118, 121, 127, 142
Groby M., 51, 285
Grofford Advow., 124
Grove Court, 240, 259
Guienne, 196
Guildford, 123, 166
Guyherne and Murrow M., 189, 216, 228, 240, 260

Hackmill, 376
Hadlow, 396, 397
Hambleton, 234
Hame M., 15, 16, 20, 21, 34, 42, 73, 77, 84, 96, 119, 125, 129, 135, 142, 143, 145, 157, 206, 261, 275, 341, 342, 346, 354, 374, 382, 397, 409, 434
Hamering, 282
Hammerfmith, 47
Hampton Court, 197 n
Hannam M., 196, 215, 374, 382, 409, 410
Hants Co., 84, 345, 376, 394
Hardwick, 91
Hareclive Hund., 44, 48
Harefcombe, 236
Harwich M., Effex, 121, 126
Hasfield, 173
Haunce M., Beds., 121, 130
Hawe Park, 300, 329, 374
Hawood Barony, 52
Haxey M., Lincoln, 121, 127, 130, 160, 161, 162
Heme M., 124, 128
Hempton Advow., 215
Henbury, 196, 359
Hereford, 9, 78, 86, 87
    ,, Co., 26, 96, 102, 118, 125, 179, 200, 230
Hereford Deanery, 87
Hertford Co., 88, 122, 130, 206, 234, 262, 275, 282, 316, 318, 324, 339, 357
Hewlington M., 124, 128
Highgate, 281
Highnam, 222
Hill, 14
Hillefly, Chantry at, 106, 125
Hilton M., Hunts, 122, 178, 189, 216, 228, 240, 259, 292, 360, 382
Hinton, 85, 189, 309, 375, 376
    ,, M., Co. Cambridge, 122, 131, 217, 222, 228, 300
Hinton M., Glouc., 16, 21, 34, 42, 48, 57, 58, 60, 62, 74, 75, 78,

Hinton M., Glouc.—Continued—
83, 84, 96, 119, 125, 129, 143, 145, 157, 206, 261, 275, 288, 300, 301, 308, 315, 316, 317, 318, 326, 328, 330, 332, 374, 409
Hinton Woods, 248
Holborn Hill, 380
Holgate M., 51
Holme Lacy, 179
Holt Caftle, 124, 127, 158
Holts, 288, 297, 298, 301, 302, 316, 326, 327, 330, 375
Hordwell M., 5
Horewell M., 5
Horton, 14, 157, 361, 375, 376
Horwood, 21, 106, 115, 125, 157, 376
Hofeley, 118
Houghton, 357
Hounden M., Suffex, 123
Hovingham M., York, 121, 126, 130, 160, 161, 162, 188, 216, 222, 223, 224, 228, 247, 253, 260, 281, 356
Howby, 369
    ,, Advow., 189, 355, 410
Howys M., 188
Howley Kegworth Advow., 216
Hunden M., 166
Huntingford, 108, 295, 297, 319, 376
Hunts Co., 122, 130, 167, 172, 178, 189, 214, 216, 240, 245, 259, 268, 360, 367, 382, 393, 404
Hurdpool, 224
Hurft, 375, 376
    ,, M., 12, 35, 42, 62, 73, 77, 96, 106, 119, 125, 129, 143, 145, 206, 261, 275, 332, 374, 409

Ilford, 123
Inwoods, 91
Ireland, 124, 130, 131, 254, 255, 260, 270, 371
Iron Acton M., 106, 157, 235, 236
Ifcoyd M., 124, 128
Iflington, 281
Itchington, 314
Ivybridge, 314

Katherine's, St., Hofp., Briftol, 17, 249
Kegworth Advow., 189, 377, 410
Keinfham, 344
Keinfhams Bridge, 241
Kellingworth Caftle and M., 374

Kenet M., Co. Cambridge, 122, 131, 217, 261, 346, 356
Kenilworth Park, 285
Keninghall, 376, 381
Kenfington, 130
Kent Co., 231, 232, 234, 238, 257, 258, 280, 396
Kent, Co. Camb., 137, 189
Kentford M., Co. Camb., 122, 189, 217, 261, 356
Kentifh Town, 253, 273, 281
Killpeck, 51
Killruddon, Co. Limerick, 86
Kilvey, 138
Kinge M., 5
Kingfcote, 48, 106, 115, 125, 157, 319, 361, 376
Kingfton, 375
    ,, Co. Notts, 260, 361
    ,, Lifle M., 61
    ,, upon Thames, 438
Kington M., Warr., 122, 206, 261, 275, 358, 382, 385, 386
Kingfwood Abbey, 14, 19, 28
    ,, Co. Warr., 358
    ,, Foreft, 195, 202, 270, 380
Kirkby Malfart M., 118, 121, 127, 130, 142, 160, 161, 162
Kirkby belers, 359
Kirkeby Abbey, 249
Kiflingbury M., 4
Kymer M., Suffex, 123, 166

Lacocke Nunnery, 186
Lampadervar Caftle, 11
Lancafter Co. 111, 425
    ,, Duchy of, 352
Langden Barony, 52
Langdon M., 5
Langley, 294
Lanthony, 178
Lafborough M., 289, 370
Leckhampton, 185, 234, 370
Lee, 260, 357
Leicefter, 78, 294, 339
    ,, Co., 118, 122, 126, 130, 135, 147, 158, 161, 172, 188, 189, 200, 211, 216, 225, 231, 232, 240, 241, 245, 249, 253, 259, 266, 268, 281, 338, 339, 340, 344, 351, 352, 355, 357, 358, 359, 360, 367, 369, 382, 397, 410, 425
Leicefter Foreft, 285
    ,, Houfe, 309
Leigh M., 158, 241
Leons, Caftle of, 124, 128
    ,, Town of, 124, 128

INDEX TO NAMES OF PLACES

Leverton, 5
Lewes M., 340, 341
　　"　　Barony, 123, 166
　　"　　Borough, 123, 166
Lidney, 317, 334
Limeridge M., 48
　　"　　Wood, 106
Lincoln Co., 111, 118, 121, 127, 130, 134, 158, 160, 228, 237, 241, 245, 260, 357
Linley M., 338
Linton M., Derby, 122, 188, 200, 216, 241, 260, 357
Lippiat, 94
Little Britain, London, 381
London, 22, 27, 29, 34, 45, 47, 57, 62, 63, 80, 87, 88, 101, 102, 104, 120, 127, 130, 131, 137, 142, 172, 175, 206, 222, 225, 227, 233, 237, 237 n, 239, 253, 254, 257, 258, 267, 280, 281, 284, 285, 286, 288, 289, 290, 291, 307, 318, 320, 321, 327, 341, 357, 363, 365, 380, 381, 384, 392, 395, 401, 406, 426, 437, 442
London, St. Augustine's Friary, 132, 133, 134, 144, 146, 163, 164, 173, 174, 187
London, Blackfriars, 321
　　"　　Grays Inn, 281
　　"　　Rolls Chapel, 283
　　"　　Tower of, 57, 58, 62, 280, 281, 284, 293, 381, 440
Longbarrowe, 181
Longebridge Priory, 249
Lollington, 357
Low Countries, see *the Netherlands*
Lowestoff, 8
Lowlayton, 426
Lye M., 24

Madresfield, 183,
Mangotesfield, 179, 196, 225, 227, 241, 242, 243, 269, 270, 284
Mangotesfield Ch., 241, 243, 244
Mangotsfield M., 215, 218, 224, 229, 240, 250, 251, 256, 259, 266, 267, 343, 360, 362, 382
Maningford Brews M., 158, 189, 217, 253, 260, 281, 292
Maningford Brews Advow., 357
Manmead, 224
Marlowe M., Bucks, 121, 130, 157
Marshfield M., 35, 83, 203, 256
Mary le Bon M., 261
Mawvy M., Essex, 121, 126
Maxtock Castle, 233
Meadsplace, 172

Mechinge M., Sussex, 123, 166
Melton Mowbray Abbey, 249
　　"　　M., 118, 122, 126, 188, 196, 200, 205, 211, 216, 226, 240, 249, 253, 259, 340, 341, 342, 344, 358, 382, 409
Mereden M., Co. Warr., 122, 130
Michaelwood, 109, 114, 295, 296, 297, 340, 362.
Michaelwood Chafe, 295, 296, 297, 298, 333, 334, 354
Micheldene, 107
Michelhampton, 48
Middleton M., Co. Sussex, 123, 166
Midlesex Co., 118, 123, 130, 131, 166, 261, 276, 277, 428, 435
Milcote, 370
Milford haven, 10, 23
Minsterworth, 84
Moore close, 323
Morecote, 106
Moreton M., 73, 202
Morton faboy M., 124, 128
Mountforrell M., Leic., 122, 126, 157, 188, 200, 211, 216, 229, 240, 248, 253, 259, 266, 281, 344, 351, 353, 382, 410
Mowbray, 237 n
Myryford Abbey, see *Kingswood*
Mytton, 186

Naples, 399
Nethercote M., 5, 15
Netherlands, the, 235
Newburgh Priory, 249
Newenham Priory, 249
Newleyes, 65, 68, 70, 77, 102, 115, 116, 125, 145, 301, 302, 329, 330, 375
Newmarket, 285
Newnham, 376, 389
Newpark, 12, 14, 299, 300, 334, 340, 351, 382, 426
Newport, 12, 85, 375
Newsam M., 118, 121, 127, 142
Nibley, 106, 114, 116, 135, 157, 169, 288, 295, 297, 319, 320, 323, 343, 360, 375, 376, 399, 438
Nibley Church, 334
　　"　　Green, 84, 111, 114, 135, 143, 147, 148, 154, 359
Nimpsfield M., 437
Noke M., 5
Nomansland, Sussex, 123, 166
Norbony, 5
Norham Castle, 395
Normandy, 46, 66

Norfolk Co., 118, 189, 217, 232, 237, 284, 285, 376
Northampton, 285, 403
　　"　　Co., 24, 34, 231, 232, 233, 238
North pedle M., Co. Worc., 123
Northumberland Co., 52, 238
Norton, 14
Nottingham Co., 260, 355, 357, 361, 428
Nottingham, Sherifwick of, 101, 126
Nuneaton, 370

Oakley Park, 376
Oakleys, 224
Oatlands, 302
Ogle, Barony of, 52, 53
Oldbury, 85
Oldcrosse, Seign., 124, 260, 270
Oldminster, 309
Omers St., in Artois, 247, 248
Ordeston M., 5, 21
Orleans, 399
Orwell, 8
Osbaston M., 124, 128
Ofeleston M., 124, 128
Osterly, 428, 429
Otho, 25
Ouston M., Lincoln, 121, 127, 130, 160, 161, 162
Over, 12
Oulpen, 296, 319
Oxford, 381, 388, 395, 437, 438
　　"　　Ch. Ch. Coll., 169
　　"　　Magdalen Coll., 170
　　"　　University, 87, 441, 442
　　"　　Co., 34, 52, 232

Painswick M., 73, 202
Pagham par., 354
Paris, 399
Parkcourt M., 91
Parkhall, 232
Pay, 10
Peckham, East, 238
Pembroke Co., 177
Pensans M., 5, 23
Pickhill M., 124, 128
Pinchburgh, 234
Pinelsend, 295
Plymouth, 10
Portbury, 93, 106
　　"　　Church, 19, 230
　　"　　Hund., 35, 44, 48, 96, 125, 202, 382, 409, 435
Portbury M., 13, 14, 15, 17, 27, 35, 37, 42, 47, 58, 62, 75, 76, 78, 96, 100, 125, 129, 135, 136, 143, 145, 172, 202, 206, 261,

INDEX TO NAMES OF PLACES

Portbury M.—*Continued*—
275, 277, 345, 382, 397, 405, 406, 409, 435
Portbury, Prior M., 345
Portſhead M., 14, 17, 35, 44, 48, 96, 106, 125, 275, 277, 397, 409
Portſhead in Gordon, 14
Potters green, 345
Preſtwold, 357
Pritwell M., 118, 126
Pucklechurch, 90, 92, 184, 202

Ragge, 224
Raglan M., 35, 40
Reading, 88
Redford, 296
Redwood, 178, 224, 248
Reigate, Surrey, 123, 166
Rengworth M., 203
Repington M., Derby, 122, 188, 200, 216, 241, 260, 359
Rhé, Iſle of, 186, 233
Roceter, 234
Rodlyes, 21
Rome, 399
Rouen, 399
Roſtlaſton M., Derby, 122, 188, 200, 216, 241, 253, 260, 357
Rowcliffe, 228
Rowles Court, 375
Ruabon M., 124, 128
Rutland Co., 234, 350
Ryſinge, Co. Norfk., 284, 285, 376

Sackburne, 88
Sages M., 13, 35, 62, 68, 70, 102, 106, 115, 125, 156, 157, 200, 211, 215, 222, 228, 240, 253, 256, 259, 281, 288, 292, 300, 325, 326, 327, 328, 329, 330, 332, 374, 375, 376, 409
Sainbury, 293, 370
Saintly, 17
Salop Co., 73, 118, 122, 128, 232, 233, 340
Sandwich, 9, 10, 11
Saperton, 370
Sapley For., 360
Sartfield, 214
Scotfield M., Beds., 121
Scothurne, 260, 357
Scotland, 397
Seford M., Suſſex, 123, 166
Saggewicke Park, 172
Segrave, Co. Leic., Advow., 189, 216, 253, 361, 409
Segrave M., Co. Leic., 122, 127, 161, 188, 200, 211, 216, 240, 259, 355, 409

Segrave in Pen M., Bucks, 121, 126, 130, 157, 160, 161, 162, 188, 200, 249, 344
Sellington, 235
Serjeants lands, 354
Seſſewike M., 124, 128
Severn, Riv., 12, 178, 248, 351, 353
Seymors lands, 376
Shankton, 232
Shernecliffe, 106, 116, 157, 375, 376
Sherncote M., 15
Shirborne M., 5, 370, 371
Shobenaſh Park, 328
Shoe-lane, London, 281, 285, 288
Shugborough, 233
Sidnam mead, 344
Sileby M., Leic., 122, 126, 135, 157, 188, 200, 211, 216, 240, 248, 253, 259, 344, 359, 382
Simondſhall, ſee *Symondſhall*
Sinwell, 288, 319, 375, 376
Siſton, 93
Slagham M., Suſſex, 123, 130, 161
Slimbridge Advow., 42, 129, 153, 169, 170
Slimbridge Church, 19, 243
" M., 13, 16, 18, 34, 42, 48, 60, 62, 74, 75, 77, 96, 106, 115, 119, 125, 129, 135, 143, 145, 155, 169, 206, 211, 227, 261, 275, 288, 291, 300, 301, 308, 315, 316, 323, 332, 374, 409
Slimbridge par., 106, 157, 351, 354, 375, 376, 434, 436
Slimbridge Warth, 18, 115, 354
Smethmore, 224, 248
Sodbury, 94, 182
Soffam, 285
Somerſet Co., 9, 13, 14, 15, 16, 17, 34, 35, 37, 42, 48, 58, 60, 72, 75, 78, 94, 96, 100, 102, 125, 130, 137, 147, 172, 173, 179, 181, 184, 206, 261, 275, 276, 277, 278, 282, 345, 367, 372, 402, 405, 409, 436
Sonford M., 124, 128
Southampton, 10, 196
Southcerney M., 14, 47
South croxton, 359
Southmundam M., 354
Southwark, 123, 166
Sowe, 93, 343, 394, 397
Specheley M., 87, 87 n, 88 n
Spridlington M., 228
Stafford Co., 113, 231, 233, 234
Stamford, 88 n
Stancombe, 307, 340, 376
Stanford, 184, 357

Staverton, 118
Steepholmes, 17
Stichell, 359
Stinchcombe, 91, 340, 375, 376
" M., 202
Stivechall, 260
Stodeſdon M., Salop, 122
Stoke, Co. Bucks, 402
" Gifford, 196, 210, 231
Stone, 92, 257, 258, 266, 296
Stowe M., 4
Straddewy M., 35
Stranſham, 364, 376
Sudburne, 428
Suffolk Co., 92, 118, 162, 237, 261, 356, 428
Surrey Co., 118, 123, 130, 137, 161, 166, 189, 236, 238, 260, 277, 357
Suſſex Co., 118, 123, 130, 147, 161, 166, 172, 189, 200, 217, 241, 245, 260, 277, 311, 340, 354, 382, 397, 410
Sutton, 118
" Bonington Advow., 189, 216, 355, 410
Swanſea, 182
Syde, 27
Symondſhall, 319, 375, 376
" Advow., 129
" M., 35, 42, 44, 48, 58, 59, 61, 65, 66, 69, 70, 74, 102, 103, 106, 112, 125, 143, 145, 157, 168, 206, 261, 275, 288, 289, 290, 296, 300, 326, 329, 330, 332, 334, 336, 374, 409

Talgarth M., 35
Tame Park, 232
Tamworth Caſtle, 233
" Par., 260
Taunton, 207 n
Tetbury Bor., 188, 195, 196, 349
" M., 158, 188, 200, 201, 206, 211, 215, 240, 253, 256, 259, 275, 281, 292, 348, 352, 374, 382, 397, 407, 408, 409, 410, 435
Tetcote M., 5
" Tithing, 15
Tetbury, Vicarage of, 169, 335, 410
Tewkeſbury, 180, 310
" Abbey, 169
Thames, Riv., 9, 257
Thèrouenne, 197, 197 n, 224
Thornbury, 148, 154, 172, 188, 193, 206, 215, 221, 222, 228, 241, 259, 268, 358

INDEX TO NAMES OF PLACES

Thornbury M., 138
Thorneton M., 118, 121, 127, 142
Thorny M., Suffex, 123, 189, 200, 217, 241, 260, 292, 382, 410
Thorpe, Co. Notts, 260, 361
Thorpfachville M., 249, 259, 266, 267, 358
Thrifke M., York, 121, 126, 130, 160, 161, 162
Thurlafton M., Co. Warr., 122, 189, 200, 211, 216, 241, 260, 357, 382
Thurmafton, 357
Thurneby M., 241, 248, 259, 357, 358, 359
Thwaites M., fee *Twaytes*
Tickingham, 282
Tintern Abbey, 249
Tockington, 180
   "   Advow., 215
Toddington, 339
Toley, 285
Torre M., 35
Tortworth, 108, 181, 308, 309, 315, 334
Totnes Archdeaconry, 11
Tournay, 197, 197 n, 224
Trevilines, 15
Trewarnake M., 5
Tunbridge, 396, 397
Twaytes M., York, 121, 126, 130, 160, 161, 162, 188
Twichen, 12
Twyford M., Leic., 122, 126, 259
Tyburn, ais Mary le Bon M., 123, 130, 166, 261, 276
Tyes, Barony of, 29
Tykenham M., 15, 173

Uley, 91, 182, 318, 319, 322, 376
Uphill, 17, 48
Uplamborne, 5
Upton Cheney, 238
   "   Farm, by Tetbury, 397
   "   St. Leonards, 3
   "   "   Advow., 16
   "   "   M., 17, 20, 35, 42, 96, 119, 125, 188, 216, 222, 228, 240, 259, 397

Venice, 399
Virginia, 238, 303

Wales, 35, 119, 124, 127, 130, 131, 137
Wales, Marches of, 327, 340, 343, 346
Walton Advow., 14
   "   M., 14, 44
   "   upon Trent, 357

Wanfted, 30
Wanfwell, 85, 179
Ware, 285
Warke, 238
Ware de la, Barony, 53, 55
Warth, The, 65, 68, 70, 77, 115, 116, 125, 145, 227, 301
Warwick Caftle, 49
   "   and M. of, 51
   "   Co., 26, 77, 80, 84, 90, 118, 122, 130, 131, 146, 160, 171, 172, 181, 189, 206, 211, 214, 216, 225, 230, 231, 232, 233, 241, 245, 260, 261, 275, 276, 278, 281, 314, 357, 358, 359, 374, 378, 380, 382, 385, 409, 410
Wedgeworth Park, 285
Welby alias Oleby, 259, 358
Wenden M., 16, 17
Wengrave M., 3, 4
Weftridge Hill, 332
Weftburrow M., Lincoln, 121, 127
Weftbury, 93
Weftmancotes land, 116
Weftminfter, 89, 104, 105, 117, 123, 146, 158
Wefton, 234, 292
   "   Baldock M., Co. Herts, 122, 206, 262, 275, 282, 339, 357
Wefton M., Co. Hunts, 122, 189, 200, 216, 228, 240, 259, 360, 382
Wefton in Gordano, 13, 14, 48
Weftridge Wood, 327
Wetherden, 234
Wetherly M., 200, 241, 249
Wexford Co., 270
Weybridge, 360
Whaddon M., 73, 202
Whelpfplace, 14
Whitbey, 238
Whitchurch, 73
Whitcliffe Park, 20, 107, 299, 340, 351, 352, 353, 362
Whitehall, 280, 302
Wichingford, 183
Wigmore, 232, 425
Wike, 90, 106, 114, 375, 376, 436
   "   M., Wilts, 14, 15, 21, 295
Wiken, 349, 350, 354
Wickwicke, 283
Wilts Co., 14, 15, 17, 34, 84, 158, 179, 189, 217, 245, 260, 281, 307, 357
Wimefwold, 357
Winchefter, 318
Winchington, 232

Windfor, 46
Winefthorp M., 188
Winge M., Bucks, 121, 127, 130, 157, 160, 161, 162, 188, 200, 217
Winterbourne Advow., 215
Wike Dangerfield, 20
Wiffelee, Surrey, 123, 130, 161
Wither, 85
Witherley M., Leic., 121, 126, 188, 216, 249, 259, 358, 382
Wittenden, 24
Wixtowe, 14
Wobfton, 128
Wollaton, 29
Wolfton, 124
Woodchefter, 183
Woodfield, 183
Woodford, 20, 114, 295
Woodmancote, 319
Worcefter City, 87
   "   Church of, 19, 87, 88, 132, 133
Worcefter Co., 26, 87, 88, 88 n, 111, 123, 147, 179, 182, 183, 185, 200, 231, 234, 235
Worth Foreft, Suffex, 123, 166
Wortley, 288, 319, 375, 376
Wortly, Chantry at, 106, 125
Worthy Park, 211, 224, 299, 378
Wotton Advow., 42, 106, 116, 125, 129, 153, 168, 169, 261, 375
Wotton Borough, 34, 40, 106, 112, 115, 116, 117, 145, 288, 295, 296, 306, 307, 318, 319, 320, 372, 375
Wotton Church, 19, 27, 34, 57, 334
   "   Forren, 21, 34, 115, 125, 288, 343, 374, 375, 409
Wotton ufurped Hund., 106, 314, 318, 319, 320, 321, 322, 323, 324, 329, 332, 335, 336, 375
Wotton Liberty, 145
   "   M., 12, 15, 21, 22, 23, 27, 41, 42, 43, 44, 47, 48, 57, 58, 59, 61, 65, 66, 68, 69, 70, 73, 74, 84, 102, 103, 106, 108, 109, 110, 112, 113, 114, 117, 125, 135, 143, 145, 157, 168, 169, 288, 289, 290, 291, 295, 296, 297, 298, 319, 326, 329, 330, 332, 374, 375, 378, 409, 414
Wotton Park, 107, 108
   "   under Edge, 14, 34, 60, 108, 115, 116, 230, 256, 261, 267, 275, 289, 360, 368, 374, 376
Woverfthorpe M., 158
Wraxall, 14, 172, 173

INDEX TO NAMES OF PLACES

Wrexham M., Salop, 124, 128, 158
Wrote M., Lincoln, 121, 130, 160, 161
Wye, Co. Hereford, 230
Wykes, see *Wikes*

Yale M., N. Wales, 124, 127, 128, 158, 212

Yate, 14, 21, 194, 195, 196, 201, 202, 212, 218, 222, 225, 230, 236, 253, 254, 257, 259, 267, 268, 270, 280, 284, 285, 287, 356, 362, 403
York, 64, 223
   ,, Convent of Friars Minors, 223
   ,, Co., 118, 121, 126, 130, 142,

York, Co.—*Continued*—
147, 158, 161, 162, 188, 216, 222, 224, 228, 232, 237, 238, 239, 245, 247, 260, 281, 356, 429

Berkeley Manuscripts

LIST OF SUBSCRIBERS

LARGE PAPER COPIES

No. 1 Guife, Sir William Vernon, Bart., F.L.S., F.G.S., Elmore Court, Gloucefter
,, 2 Bamford, Rev. R., Poulton Vicarage, Fairford
,, 3 Lang, Robert, Efq., Mancombe, Henbury, Briftol
,, 4 Paul, Alfred H., Efq., The Clofe, Tetbury
,, 5 Miles, Cruger, Efq., Pen Pole, Shirehampton
,, 6 Maclean, Sir John, F.S.A., Glafbury Houfe, Clifton, Briftol
,, 7 James, Francis, Efq., Edgeworth Manor, Cirencefter
,, 8 Niblett, J. D. T., Efq., M.A., F.S.A., Haresfield Court, Stonehoufe
,, 9 Lang, Samuel, Efq., Langford Lodge, Pembroke Road, Clifton
,, 10 Kerr, Ruffell J., Efq., The Haie, Newnham
,, 11 Fawn, Mr. James, Queen's Road, Briftol
,, 12 Bruton, H. W., Efq., Bewick Houfe, Wotton
,, 13 Skillicorne, W. Nafh, Efq., 9, Queen's Parade, Cheltenham
,, 14 George, W. E., Efq., Howe Croft, Stoke Bifhop
,, 15 Adlam, William, Efq., F.S.A., Manor Houfe, Chew Magna
,, 16 Doggett, E. G., Efq., 31, Richmond Terrace, Clifton, Briftol
,, 17 Blacker, Rev. B. H., M.A., 26, Meridian Place, Clifton, Briftol
,, 18 Heane, William Crawfhay, Efq., The Lawn, Cinderford
,, 19 Clarke, John A. Graham, Efq., Frocefter, Stonehoufe
,, 20 Arrowfmith, Mr. J. W., 99, White Ladies' Road, Clifton, Briftol
,, 21 Smith, R. Vaffar, Efq., Afhfield, Great Malvern
,, 22 Uren, William, Efq., Crofton Houfe, Clifton Down, Clifton, Briftol
,, 23 Baker, Mr. James, The Mall, Clifton, Briftol
,, 24 Fitzhardinge, Craven Hyde, Efq., Dubbo, N.S. Wales
,, 25 Baker, Arthur, Efq., Henbury Hill Houfe, Briftol
,, 26 Holland, W. H., Efq., Gloucefter
,, 27 Price, William P., Efq., Tibberton Court, Gloucefter
,, 28 Philp, Capt. J. Lamb, Pendoggett, Timfbury, Somerfet
,, 29 Walker, C. B., Efq., Norton Court, near Gloucefter
,, 30 Scrope, Mrs., Bedale, Yorkfhire
,, 31 Blathwayt, Wynter E., Efq., Dyrham, Chippenham
,, 32 Berkeley, Francis, Efq., Woodfide, Ripon

LIST OF SUBSCRIBERS

SMALL PAPER COPIES

Ackers, B. St. John, Esq., Prinknash Park, Painswick
Allen, Rev. William Taprell, M.A., St. Briavels' Vicarage, Coleford
Ames, Reginald, Esq., 2, Albany Terrace, Park Square, East, London, N.W.
Arrowsmith, Mr. J. W., 99, White Ladies' Road, Clifton, Bristol

Baker, Mr. James, The Mall, Clifton, Bristol
Barkly, Sir Henry, 1, Bina Gardens, South Kensington, W.
Bartleet, Rev. S. E., M.A., Brockworth Vicarage, Gloucester
Baynes, C. R., Esq., The Lammas, Minchinhampton
Bazeley, Rev. William, M.A., Matson Rectory, Gloucester
Beach, The Right Hon. Sir Michael Hicks, Bart., M.P., Williamstrip Park, Fairford
Beddoe, John, Esq., M.D., F.R.S., Mortimer House, Clifton, Bristol
Berkeley, Francis, Esq., Woodside, Ripon
Berkeley, Rowland W., Esq., 1, Tokenhouse Buildings, London, E.C.
Bibliotheque Nationale, Paris
Blathwayt, Rev. Wynter T., M.A., Dyrham Rectory, Chippenham
Boevey, A. Crawley-, Esq., East India United Service Club, 14, St. James' Square, London, S.W.
Bourne, Rev. G. Drinkwater, M.A., Weston-sub-Edge, Broadway
Bowly, Christopher, Esq., Siddington House, Cirencester
Bramble, James Roger, Esq., Cleeve House, near Yatton, Somerset
Buckley, Rev. Joseph, M.A., Tormarton Rectory, Chipping Sodbury
Bute, The Most Hon. the Marquis of, Cardiff Castle, Glamorganshire

Caldicott, Rev. J. W., D.D., Shipston-on-Stour Rectory, Worcestershire *(Hon. Sec.)*
Cattell, Thomas William, Esq., Blakeford Cottage, King's Stanley, Stonehouse
Chance, T. H., Esq., *Journal* Office, Gloucester
Cheltenham Library, 5, Royal Crescent, Cheltenham
Clark, George T., Esq., F.S.A., Dowlais House, Dowlais
Clifford, The Hon. and Right Rev. Bishop, Bishop's House, Clifton, Bristol
Clough, R. L., Esq., 13, Bellevue, Clifton, Bristol
Colby, Rev. Frederick Thomas, D.D., F.S.A., Litton Cheney Rectory, Dorset
Collier, Colonel, Stanley Hall, Stonehouse

LIST OF SUBSCRIBERS

Collins, J. C., Esq., M.D., Steanbridge House, Slad, Stroud
Cooke, J. Herbert, Esq., F.S.A., Berkeley
Cooke, W. H., Esq., Q.C., F.S.A., 42, Wimpole Street, London
Cornock, Nicholas, Esq., 5, Harold Street, London, S.E.
Cornwall, Rev. Alan Kingscote, M.A., Ashcroft, Wotton-under-Edge
Cowburn, Major J. Brett, Dennil Hill, near Chepstow
Cox, Alfred, Esq., Thornhayes, Clifton, Bristol
Cripps, Wilfrid J., Esq., F.S.A., Barrister-at-Law, Cirencester
Crossman, George D., Esq., Freizewood, near Bristol

Dancy, Charles H., Esq., 6, Midland Road, Gloucester
Davis, Cecil Tudor, Esq., The Court House, Painswick
Derham, Samuel, Esq., Henleaze Park, Westbury-on-Trym
Derham, Walter, Esq., M.A., F.G.S., Henleaze Park, Westbury-on-Trym

Dorington, J. E., Esq., Lypiatt Park, Stroud
Downing, William, Esq., Springfield House, Olton, near Birmingham
Ducie, The Right Hon. the Earl of, P.C., F.R.S., Tortworth Court, Wotton-under-Edge

Ellacombe, Rev. H. T., M.A., F.S.A., The Rectory, Clyst St. George, Topsham
Evans, J. B., Esq., 6, Douro Villas, Cheltenham

Fawn, Mr. James, Queen's Road, Bristol
Forster, Right Hon. W. E., M.P., Wharfside, Burley-on-Wharfdale, Leeds
Fox, Alderman Francis Frederick, Esq., 72, Pembroke Road, Clifton, Bristol
Fox, Charles Henry, Esq., M.D., The Beeches, Brislington
Fryer, Kedgwin Hoskins, Esq., Maitland House, Gloucester

Gaisford, E. Sands, Esq., 12, Bassett Road, N. Kensington, London
Gaisford, Rev. Thos. Amyas, M.A., Wells Road, Bath
George, W. E., Esq., Howe Croft, Stoke Bishop
George, Mr. William, 26, Park Street, Bristol
Giller, William Thomas, Esq., County of Gloucester Bank, Gloucester
Godwin, J. G., Esq., Chiswick House, London, W.
Gosling, Rev. J. F., M.A., Bream Vicarage, Lydney
Greenfield, Benjamin Wyatt, Esq., 4, Cranbury Terrace, Southampton
Gwinnett, William Henry, Esq., Gordon Cottage, Cheltenham

Hale, C. B., Esq., Claremont House, Gloucester
Hale, Robert B., Esq., Alderley, Wotton-under-Edge
Hall, Rev. J. M., M.A., The Rectory, Harescombe, Stroud
Hallett, T. G. P., Esq., Claverton Lodge, Bath
Havard College, U.S.A.
Havilland, General de, Havilland Hall, Taunton
Hazeldine, Rev. William, The Priory, Tyndall's Park, Clifton, Bristol
Heywood, Samuel, Esq., F.S.A., 161, Stanhope Street, London
Holford, Robert S., Esq., Weston Birt House, Tetbury
Holland, W. H., Esq., Gloucester
Hudd, Alfred E., Esq., 96, Pembroke Road, Clifton, Bristol
Hutchinson, Jas. Hutchinson, Esq., 42, Lancaster Gate, Hyde Park, London

Jacques, Thomas W., Esq., 46, Apsley Road, Clifton, Bristol
James, Rev. John, M.A., Highfield, Lydney
Jenkins, R. Palmer, Esq., Beechley, Chepstow

Kay, Sir Brook, Bart., Stanley Lodge, Battledown, Cheltenham
Keeling, George William, Esq., Lydney
Kerslake, Thomas, Esq., 14, Weston Park, Clifton, Bristol

Lancaster, Thomas, Esq., Bownham House, Stroud
Law, W., Esq., Littleborough, Manchester
Leigh, William, Esq., Woodchester Park, Stonehouse
Lewis, Archibald M., Esq., Upper Byron Place, Bristol
Lindsay, W. A., Esq., M.A., Q.C., 17, Cromwell Road, South Kensington
Lloyd, Capt. Owen, 4, Oxford Parade, Cheltenham
London Library, 12, St. James' Square, London
Lucy, William C., Esq., Brookthorpe, Gloucester

Maclaine, William Osborne, Esq., Kington, Thornbury
Macpherson, J., Esq., Aylesmore House, St. Briavels, Coleford (2 copies)
Margetson, William, Esq., Brightside, Stroud
Metford, Joseph Seymour, Esq., 31, Berkeley Square, Bristol
Middlemore, Rev. T. M. Whithard, Teighmore, Cheltenham
Middleton, John, Esq., Westholme, Cheltenham
Middleton, J. H., Esq., F.S.A., 4 Storeys Gate, St. James' Park, London
Morgan, Sir Walter, Naish House, Nailsea, Somerset

LIST OF SUBSCRIBERS

Morrell, Frederick J., Efq., Broughton Lodge, Banbury
Mullings, John, Efq., Park Street, Cirencefter

Niblett, J. D. T., Efq., M.A., F.S.A., Haresfield Court, Stonehoufe
Noel, Colonel, Clanna Houfe, Alvington, Lydney
Norman, George, Efq., High Street, Cheltenham
Norris, Venerable Archdeacon, D.D., Lower College Green, Briftol

Oakeley, Rev. W. Bagnall, M.A., Newland, Coleford
O'fflahertie, Rev. T. R., Capel Vicarage, Surrey

Palmer, Rev. Fielding, M.A., Eaftcliffe, Chepftow
Perceval, Cecil H. Sp., Efq., Henbury, Briftol
Peter, Thurftan C., Efq., Town Hall, Redruth
Phillimore, W. P. W., Efq., M.A., B.C.L., 6, Quality Court, Chancery Lane, London, W.C.
Phillipps, J. O. Halliwell, Efq., F.R.S., F.S.A., Hollingfbury Copfe, Brighton
Playne, Charles, Efq., Nailfworth
Playne, Arthur T., Efq., Longfords, Minchinhampton
Powell, John Jofeph, Efq., Q.C., Fountain Court Temple, London, E.C.
Prankerd, P. D., Efq., The Knoll, Sneyd Park, Briftol
Pritchett, Charles Pigott, Efq., Holme Lea, Redland Grove, Briftol

Rice, The Hon. Maria Elizabeth, Matfon Houfe, Gloucefter
Riddiford, George Francis, Efq., Barnwood Lodge, Gloucefter
Rogers, R. Rogers Coxwell-, Efq., F.S.A., Dowdefwell Court, Cheltenham
Rolt, Mrs. S., Oakhanger, Berkeley
Royce, Rev. David, M.A., Nether Swell Vicarage, Stow-on-the-Wold

Savory, C. H., Efq., St. John Street, Cirencefter
Scott, Charles, Efq., Berkeley
Scrope, Mrs. Emily, Danby-upon-Yore, Bedale, Yorkfhire
Selwyn, Rev. E. J., M.A., Pluckley Rectory, Afhford, Kent
Sewell, Edward C., Efq., Elmlea, Stratton, Cirencefter
Sherborne, Right Hon. Lord, Sherborne Park (2 copies)
Simpfon, J. J., Efq., Glen Llyn, Ravenfwood Road, Redland, Briftol
Smith, Alfred Edward, Efq., The Hollies, Nailfworth
Smith, R. H. Soden, Efq., M.A., F.S.A., Science and Art Department, South Kenfington Mufeum, London, S.W.

Smith, T. Somerville, Efq , Sittingbourne, Kent
Stanton, Charles Holbrow, Efq , 65, Redcliffe Gardens, London, S.W
Stone, John, Efq , 12, Royal Crefcent, Bath
Stroud, Frederick, Efq , Lewifland, Cheltenham
Swayne, Jofeph Griffiths, Efq , M D., 74, Pembroke Road, Clifton, Briftol
Swayne, S H , Efq , 120, Pembroke Road, Clifton, Briftol

Taylor, John, Efq , Briftol Mufeum and Library, Queen's Road, Briftol
Taynton, Thomas, Efq , Wotton Hill Houfe, Gloucefter
Thomas, William, Efq , 7, Charlotte Street, Queen Square, Briftol
Thorpe, Difney Launder, Efq , M.D , (Cantab ,) Lypiatt Lodge, Cheltenham
Trinder, Edward, Efq , Perrots' Brook, Cirencefter
Tuckett, Francis Fox, Efq , F R G S , Frenchay, Briftol

Waddingham, John, Efq , Guiting Grange, Winchcombe
Wefton, J. D , Efq., Dorfet Houfe, Clifton, Briftol
Wefton, John, Efq., Leflie Court, Barnwood, Gloucefter
Wheeler, A C , Efq , Upton Hill, Gloucefter
Whitwill, Mark, Efq , Redland Houfe, Durdham Park, Briftol
Wickenden, Rev J F , M A , Stoke Bifhop, Briftol
Williams, Rev. Auguftin, Todenham Rectory, Moreton-in-Marfh
Williams, Adin, Efq., Lechlade
Wilton, John P , Efq , 10, College Green, Gloucefter
Wifeman, Rev H J., M A , Clifton College, Clifton, Briftol

CPSIA information can be obtained at www.ICGtesting.com
Printed in the USA
BVOW10s1204190514

353940BV00011B/776/P